HISTORICAL DICTIONARY OF THE PROGRESSIVE ERA, 1890–1920

Historical Dictionary of the Progressive Era, 1890–1920

edited by
John D. Buenker
and
Edward R. Kantowicz

GREENWOOD PRESS
New York • Westport, Connecticut • London

Library of Congress Cataloging-in-Publication Data

Historical dictionary of the Progressive Era, 1890–1920 / edited by
   John D. Buenker and Edward D. Kantowicz.
      p. cm.
     Includes index.
     ISBN 0–313–24309–3 (lib. bdg. : alk. paper)
     1. Progressivism (United States politics)—Dictionaries.
   2. United States—Politics and government—1865–1933—Dictionaries.
   I. Buenker, John D. II. Kantowicz, Edward R.
   E661.H6   1988
   973.91′03′21—dc19   88–10241

British Library Cataloguing in Publication Data is available.

Library of Congress Catalog Card Number: 88–10241
ISBN: 0–313–24309–3

First published in 1988

Greenwood Press, Inc.
88 Post Road West, Westport, Connecticut 06881

Printed in the United States of America

The paper used in this book complies with the
Permanent Paper Standard issued by the National
Information Standards Organization (Z39.48–1984).

10 9 8 7 6 5 4 3 2 1

Contents

Preface

The search for "progressivism," Daniel T. Rodgers observed in 1982, "helped attract more historical talent to the first two decades of the twentieth century than to any other period of modern America." Much of this fascination is directly attributable to the multiplicity of people, organizations, ideas, values, goals, programs, motives, and outcomes which scholars have found to be at work and which have formed the raw nucleus for a seemingly endless round of historical debates. Over the past three decades, historians have interpreted the Progressive Era as a response to a "status revolution" by old elites; a "search for order" by newly emerging elites of technicians, bureaucrats, and managers; a "triumph of conservatism" engineered by big business; a "search for social justice" by altruistic intellectuals, social workers, and ministers; "urban liberalism" practiced by the representatives of the foreign-stock working and lower middle classes; and an "organizational revolution" that transformed the economy, society, and polity, to name but the most frequently cited explanations. Small wonder that various observers have pronounced the current state of Progressive Era historiography "a semantic and conceptual muddle," a "babble of disagreement," and as "curiously elusive."

The present volume makes no pretense of resolving this conflict of interpretations. Its major purpose is to provide scholars and students with a useful reference work that contains the basic factual information concerning the most important people, events, organizations, legislation, and concepts—the raw materials used by historians to inform their interpretations. In addition, it aims to assess briefly each topic's historical importance in the overall scheme of the Progressive Era and to provide readers with a brief bibliography of the most useful works for further study. In evaluating our efforts, the reader is asked to bear in mind that this is a dictionary and not an encyclopedia and also to remember the sometimes conflicting principles of being as comprehensive as possible in our coverage while trying to write meaningful, useful entries. To do both within the space allotted was a formidable task, and we make no claims to universal success. For our purposes, the Progressive Era is defined as a broad-gauged response by Americans from many backgrounds and walks of life to the emergence of the United States as a modern, urban, industrial, multicultural world power between 1890 and 1920. This response permeated nearly every important aspect of American life during the period: literature, art, music, education, religion, popular culture, race and ethnic relations, gender roles, family structure, labor-management interaction, and economic conflict, to name only some of the most obvious. In the private sector, it manifested itself primarily in the proliferation of organizations designed either to advance their members' socioeconomic or professional interests and values or to enable them to minister to the needs and concerns of those most adversely affected by the dislocations of the period. In the public sector, it involved the virtual explosion of "reform" and "progressive" candidates, rhetoric, and legislation at the municipal, state, and national levels of government. Not surprisingly, many of these proved to be mutually incompatible, transitory, or of dubious value; but, taken together, they graphically illustrate the complexity and diversity of the reformist impulse and the elasticity of the term "progressive."

The task of fairly representing the Progressive Era's protean nature within the spatial limitations of a single reference work is clearly a formidable one that inevitably involves a considerable degree of subjective judgment. In an effort to objectify the process as much as possible, the editors began by compiling a list of nearly 2,000 possible entries derived from a survey of the major historical overviews or interpretations of the period. Our chief concern was that the list of entries reflect, as faithfully as possible, the historical literature in the sense that each entry appear in at least several of the standard works. This meant that we concentrated on those people, organizations, events, etc., that were truly national in scope or which had a clear national impact. Because an exclusively national focus seriously distorts the reality of the Progressive Era by neglecting the wealth of significant activity at the municipal and state levels, however, we sought to correct the imbalance by including major entries on the most significant states and cities. We are deeply indebted to Richard Jensen for that commonsense solution to our dilemma. The focus of the entries is also on domestic affairs; foreign policy matters were generally included only if they had a significant domestic connection or impact. To reduce our list of entries down to its final length, we solicited the aid of several of the leading Progressive Era scholars in the country and asked them to rank each entry into the categories of 1) deserves a longer entry (400–500 words), 2) deserves an entry of standard length (200–250 words), and 3) is of marginal value compared to the other entries. We are grateful especially to Richard Jensen, Melvin Holli, Peter Filene, Michael Ebner, Richard L. McCormick, David Thelen, Nicholas Burckel, Robert Wiebe, and Bradley Rice for their perceptive evaluation, hard work, and patience in that endeavor. As the formula goes, they saved us from many errors and distortions, but the blame or credit for the ultimate product of the process rests with its designers.

To write the over 800 entries that comprised our final list, the editors engaged in an extensive and intensive search of the literature to identify the scholars most qualified to write each entry. This often led us to many of the leading scholars in the field, but it also frequently directed us to people of lesser reputation who had written the definitive book, article, or dissertation on a particular person, organization, state, or city. Locating the latter in an economy where earning a Ph.D. does not automatically lead one to an academic career frequently proved a difficult and even impossible task. While our final list of contributors is not the one with which we began, it does include enough of our original choices and a phalanx of outstanding replacements to guarantee the overall quality of the entries.

In keeping with the dictionary format, the entries are listed in alphabetical order. Readers who cannot locate the topic they are seeking should consult the indices at the rear of the volume. Numerous cross-references to related entries are found within the text of each entry and are denoted by an asterisk (*). Each entry is signed by its author and a brief biographical sketch of each contributor appears at the end of the book. As an appendix, a chronology is keyed to many of the *Dictionary* entries. Finally, there are three indices, one of people, a second of books, periodicals, and newspapers, and the other a subject index containing organizations, laws, concepts, states, cities, and other matter.

In addition to the consultants and the contributors, we owe a strong debt of gratitude to several other people. Mary Etta McLane kept track of the entries and contributors, prepared the original chronology, and proofread the entire manuscript before she went off to graduate school for relaxation. Constance Nielson Murphy completed work on the chronology, typed most of the correspondence, and gathered the materials for the biographical sketches of the contributors. Josephine McCool typed and corrected the entire manuscript in her usual efficient and effective manner, and cheered us all up when the project got the best of us.

THE DICTIONARY

A

ABBOTT, EDITH (September 26, 1876–July 28, 1957). Born in Grand Island, Nebraska, into a Quaker-abolitionist family, Edith Abbott and her sister, Grace Abbott,* were well-known social work educators and social reformers. After earning a B.A. degree from the University of Nebraska in 1901, Edith studied at the University of Chicago,* where she was influenced by the economist Thorstein Veblen* and received a Ph.D. in economics. She was also influenced by Beatrice and Sidney Webb's ideas about attacking poverty. During this period, Abbott lived in a settlement house in the East End of London, where she came to understand poverty from firsthand experience. Returning to the United States, Abbott and her sister joined the assemblage of remarkable women who lived at Hull House* in Chicago. Edith and Grace collaborated on numerous projects throughout their careers.

Edith's scholarly bent is shown in the more than one hundred articles and books she authored on the problems of women in industry, correctional facilities, juvenile delinquency and truancy, sometimes collaborating with her sister and with Sophonisba Breckinridge.* She helped create the School of Social Administration at the University of Chicago, where she eventually became dean. Abbott's many writings are noted for their careful study of social problems and for their belief that social reform was possible. (Lela B. Costin, "Edith Abbott," in Barbara Sicherman et al., *Notable American Women: The Modern Period* (1980), 1–3; Lela B. Costin, *Two Sisters for Social Justice: A Biography of Grace and Edith Abbott* (1983); Steven J. Diner, "Scholarship for the Quest for Social Welfare: A Fifty-Year History of the *Social Service Review*," *Social Service Review* 51, no. 1 (March 1977): 1–66.)

John M. Herrick

ABBOTT, GRACE (November 17, 1878–June 19, 1939). Abbott was one of a number of outstanding college-educated women with careers in social work and public service during the Progressive Era. Born in Grand Island, Nebraska, and educated at Grand Island College and the Universities of Nebraska and Chicago, she joined Jane Addams,* Sophonisba Breckinridge,* Julia Lathrop,* and other reformers at Chicago's Hull House* in 1908. Active in the Chicago garment workers strike in 1910, the Illinois woman suffrage campaign of 1913, and the peace movement, she focused mainly on the plight of southern and eastern European immigrants. A cultural pluralist and director of the Chicago Immigrants' Protective League from 1908 to 1921, she won national recognition for her research on immigrants, her advocacy of their interests, and her opposition to restrictionism. Director of the federal Children's Bureau from 1921 to 1934, she later focused on problems of child labor and child health and helped draft the Social Security Act. Committed to democratic values and an activist role for government at all levels, Abbott was a link between Progressive reform and the New Deal and a model for women of her generation entering public life. (Edward T. James, et al., *Notable American Women*, vol. 1 (1971), 2–4; Edith Abbott, "Grace Abbott: A Sister's Memories," *Social Service Review* 13 (September 1939): 351–408; Edith Abbott, "Grace Abbott and Hull House, 1908–1921," Parts 1 and 2, ibid., 24 (September and December 1950): 374–94 and 493–518; Lela B. Costin, *Two Sisters for Social Justice: A Biography of Grace and Edith Abbott* (1983).)

Maxine S. Seller

ABBOTT, LYMAN (December 18, 1835–October 22, 1922). A noted Protestant minister who also edited several religious publications, Abbott was initially trained as a lawyer. He turned to the ministry in 1859 and was posted to the Congregational Church of Terre Haute, Indiana, in 1860. After serving in several other posts, he joined Henry Ward Beecher in 1876 to publish the *Christian Union*. In 1887, he succeeded Beecher as pastor of the Plymouth Church of the Pilgrims in Brooklyn, New York, and remained until 1898, after which he edited another publication dedicated to the principles of the Social Gospel,* the *Outlook*. He was widely in demand as a speaker and as a writer on progressive topics, authoring several books including *Christianity and Social Problems*, published in 1896.

Abbott supported many reform positions, including direct election of senators* and direct primaries,* nationalization of key industries, factory reform, and the breakup of monopolies. He was one of the clergymen most active in supporting the Allied cause in the period prior to American entry into the World War.* He was as much known for his support of evolution as a scientifically valid theory as he was for his views on social and economic matters. (Ira V. Brown, *Lyman Abbott, Christian Evolutionist: A Study in Religious Liberalism* (1953); Thomas W. Ryley, "The Social Gospel Movement during the Period of American Reform, 1880–1910" (Ph.D. diss., New York University, 1965).)

Thomas W. Ryley

ADAMS, BROOKS (June 24, 1848–February 13, 1927). Historian and apologist for American imperialism,* Adams was born in Quincy, Massachusetts, the grandson of President John Quincy Adams and the great-grandson of President

John Adams. He was educated at Harvard, earned a law degree, and served for a time as secretary to his father, the diplomat Charles Francis Adams. A somewhat gloomy writer, like his older brother Henry Adams,* he published *The Law of Civilization and Decay* (1895), which predicted that modern capitalist societies would squander the energy accumulated by earlier generations. In later works, *America's Economic Supremacy* (1900) and *The New Empire* (1902), he encouraged Americans to avoid this fate by centralizing their political and economic institutions and expanding their commerce and political control to Asia, which he saw as a potentially vast source of new human energy. In the 1890s, Adams was part of a small circle of imperialist intellectuals which included Alfred Thayer Mahan,* Theodore Roosevelt,* and Henry Cabot Lodge.* His writings influenced the actions of Republican imperialists during the Spanish-American War* and the Roosevelt presidency. (Thornton Anderson, *Brooks Adams, Constructive Conservative* (1951); Arthur F. Beringause, *Brooks Adams: A Biography* (1955); Walter LaFeber, *The New Empire* (1963).)

Edward R. Kantowicz

ADAMS, HENRY BROOKS (February 16, 1838–March 27, 1918). Historian and man of letters, Adams was born in Boston,* the grandson of President John Quincy Adams and the great-grandson of President John Adams. Educated at Harvard and in Europe, he served as private secretary to his father, Charles Francis Adams, first in Washington, then in London when his father became ambassador to England during the Civil War. Henry taught history at Harvard from 1870 to 1877 and edited the *North American Review.** He moved to Washington in 1877 and published several works of history, culminating in his nine-volume *History of the United States During the Administration of Jefferson and Madison* (1891).

Always a somewhat gloomy individual, weighed down by his illustrious family heritage, Henry became more pessimistic after his wife's suicide in 1885. In *Mont-Saint Michel and Chartres* (1904) he contrasted the spiritual unity of the Middle Ages with the mindless multiplicity of modern times. His fin-de-siècle pessimism was more typical of a European intellectual than an American. Yet his *History of Jefferson and Madison* remains valuable for its wit and insight, and his autobiography, *The Education of Henry Adams* (1907), is a brilliant portrait of late nineteenth-century America and a classic of American letters. (James Truslow Adams, *Henry Adams* (1933); Robert A. Hume, *Runaway Star: An Appreciation of Henry Adams* (1951); Robert Mane, *Henry Adams and the Road to Chartres* (1971).)

Edward R. Kantowicz

ADAMS, SAMUEL HOPKINS (January 26, 1871–November 15, 1958). Born at Dunkirk, New York, the son of a Presbyterian minister, Samuel Hopkins Adams became the most successful muckraker dealing with patent medicines. A graduate of Hamilton College (1891), Adams worked for nine years for the

New York *Sun* before joining *McClure's*.* With the advent of muckraking he wrote on communicable diseases: tuberculosis, typhoid, and yellow fever. After lengthy investigations in 1905 he published "The Great American Fraud" in *Collier's*,* thereby fueling a national campaign for pure food and drug legislation. Adams named 264 medicines, doctors, and companies engaged in fraud. His compelling series exposed nostrums filled with alcohol, opiates, assorted acids, and dyes sold through expensive advertising which promised painless, certain cures for cancer and other diseases. The American Medical Association* circulated one-half million copies of "The Great American Fraud" in a successful bid to rally support for the Pure Food and Drugs Law* in 1906. Adams subsequently published a novel on patent medicine, *The Clarion* (1914). Although interested in public health, he devoted most of his later career to writing successful screenplays, including *The Gorgeous Hussy* (1935) and *It Happened One Night* (1935). He died at Beaufort, South Carolina. (James H. Cassedy, "Muckraking and Medicine: Samuel Hopkins Adams," *American Quarterly* 16 (Spring 1964): 85–99; Stewart H. Holbrook, *The Golden Age of Quackery* (1959); James Harvey Young, *The Toadstool Millionaires: A Social History of Patent Medicine in America before Federal Regulation* (1961).)

Harold Wilson

ADAMSON EIGHT-HOUR ACT. In March of 1916 executives of the four railway brotherhoods demanded that the nation's major railroads establish an eight-hour working day and a system of overtime pay. When negotiations which took place during June and August proved futile, President Woodrow Wilson* held conferences with both sides in an attempt to resolve the dispute, but he also met with failure. In light of management's refusal to budge, the railway brotherhoods issued a call for a strike to start on September 4. Faced with the possibility of a nationwide railroad shutdown, Wilson appeared personally before a joint session of Congress and requested passage of a law instituting an eight-hour day for railway employees plus other provisions. On August 31, 1916, Representative William C. Adamson of Georgia introduced a bill embodying the essence of the president's proposals, and both houses passed the bill, which Wilson signed on September 3, one day before the strike deadline. In 1917, when management challenged the law, the Supreme Court, in *Wilson v. New*,* upheld the constitutionality of the act thereby confirming the power of Congress to pass wage and hour legislation in emergency situations. (Arthur S. Link, *Wilson: Campaigns for Progressivism and Peace, 1916–1917* (1965); John Lombardi, *Labor's Voice in the Cabinet: A History of the Department of Labor from Its Origin to 1921* (1942); Selig Perlman and Phillip Taft, *Labour Movements*, vol. 4 of John R. Commons, ed., *History of Labour in the United States, 1896–1932* (1935); Edwin Clyde Robbins, "The Trainmen's Eight-Hour Day, I, II," *Political Science Quarterly* 31 (1916): 541–57 and 32 (1917): 412–28.

Graham Adams, Jr.

ADDAMS, JANE (September 6, 1860–May 21, 1935). Called "beloved lady," and "the only saint America has produced," Addams was the most widely known American woman in the Progressive period. Born to John Huy Addams and Sarah Weber Addams in Cedarville, Illinois, she was valedictorian at Rockford Female Seminary in 1881, returning to receive its first baccalaureate a year later. Visiting Europe with her close friend, Ellen Gates Starr,* she was introduced to Toynbee Hall in London and returned to the United States to found Hull House* in 1889. As the pioneering effort in U.S. social settlements, Hull House became a model for such activities.

Addams, besides administering Hull House, was particularly active in the cause of labor. She wrote about the extension of democracy through the brotherhood of labor unions and served as a mediator during the Pullman Strike.* As author, she wrote twelve books and hundreds of articles interpreting the life of the immigrant and poor to the American middle-class reading public. Her message about women was mixed: she asked for equal opportunities for service while maintaining traditional "breadgiving" roles. Her life played out a new vision of the professional woman making a profound contribution to society while she defended the family and worked for protective legislation for women and children in the work force.

In 1909, she was elected the first woman president of the National Conference of Charities and Correction.* During her tenure, the study of "the national minimum" was adopted. Defining the social justice agenda for an industrial society, it dealt with housing, food, and clothing, defined the work week, workmen's compensation, and old age pensions. The Progressive party,* under Theodore Roosevelt,* adopted it as a platform in 1912, so Addams seconded his nomination and campaigned all over the United States for him to great popular acclaim. She lost financial support for Hull House because of her partisanship, but not nearly so much as was lost from her pacifist activities as America prepared to enter World War I.* In 1915, she became the first president of the Women's International League for Peace and Freedom (WILPF) and led the group through the early 1920s. Addams and three others met with the heads of state of all the belligerents asking that they submit to arbitration; all but Woodrow Wilson* received them positively. (Mary Ellen Heian Schmider, "Jane Addams' Aesthetic of Social Reform" (Ph.D. diss., University of Minnesota, 1983); Allen F. Davis, *American Heroine: The Life and Legend of Jane Addams* (1973); John C. Farrell, *Beloved Lady: A History of Jane Addams' Ideas on Reform and Peace* (1967); Daniel Levine, *Jane Addams and the Liberal Tradition* (1971).)

Mary Ellen H. Schmider

AGRICULTURE. Modern American farmers often hailed the first decades of the twentieth century as their golden age. From 1900 to 1910, the value of the national harvest soared from $3 billion to $5.5 billion. Prosperity was especially evident in the central Plains states, where the price of wheat rose from sixty-two cents a bushel to ninety-one cents, while the price of corn climbed from thirty-five cents a bushel to fifty-two cents. Such increases could be attributed partly to inflation, but the growing population of the United States increased the demand for agricultural products. However, many in the northern Plains and the tobacco-growing region remained poor or in debt. Thus it is not surprising that even in this era, protest organizations flourished, including North Dakota's Non-partisan League,* Kentucky's "Night Riders," and the south's Farmers' Union.*

The outbreak of World War I* heralded the true renaissance of American agriculture. Suddenly Europe desperately needed food and fiber. When the United States entered the struggle in 1917, even marginal land was given over to crops, and the Food Administration* Act of 1917 set high minimum prices to encourage more growing. In 1918, the price of corn rose to $1.52 a bushel, the price of wheat to $2.05 a bushel. By the end of the war, cotton was selling for nearly twenty-nine cents a pound—a price not seen since Reconstruction. A year later, Europe still clamored for American produce, and the value of cotton climbed to thirty-five cents a pound. With such returns, farmers across the country were able to settle old debts and purchase such luxuries as automobiles, victrolas, and washing machines. Many used their profits to buy more land and country banks eagerly joined the boom by offering easy loans. But as European farms recovered from the war, the demand for American crops fell. In 1920, farm prices plunged by one-third; a year later they were 85 percent lower than in 1919. Thousands of farmers went bankrupt and hundreds of rural banks collapsed, beginning a twenty-year depression in agriculture. (Theodore Saloutos and John D. Hicks, *Agricultural Discontent in the Middle West, 1900–1939* (1951); Harold Underwood Faulkner, *American Economic History* (1960); William C. Mullendore, *History of the United States Food Administration, 1917–1919* (1941).)

Barton C. Shaw

ALABAMA. Indirectly influenced by populism and the political turmoil of the 1890s, progressivism in Alabama was marked by several reform campaigns between 1900 and 1919. During the early 1900s, reformers capitalized on public reaction against corruption in state politics and the Democratic party's rejection of proposals for limited political and social change. After 1901, with disfranchisement* and the adoption of the direct primary, most blacks and many poor whites were barred from voting. However, under the primary system, the traditional political domination of Black Belt planters and Birmingham financiers and industrialists (the "big mules") gradually eroded. These changes allowed reformers to influence Democratic party decisions and forced candidates to be more responsive to the voters.

The first reform campaign occurred in 1906–1908, under the administration of Governor Broxton Bragg Comer. Alabama became the first Southern state to utilize the primary to achieve direct election of U.S. senators,* and enacted railroad controls, business regulation, a general municipal code, and larger appropriations for education. Telephone and telegraph companies were placed under the state railroad commission. After 1908, the debate on liquor control replaced railroad regulation as the cause célèbre. A statewide prohibition* law was approved in 1909, but a referendum failed to add a prohibition amendment to the state constitution.

Under Comer's successor, Governor Emmett O'Neal (1911–1915), municipal legislation was adopted, including a commission government* act, and state officials attacked lynch law. The 1915 legislature, dominated by prohibitionists, adopted several reform measures—tax revision,* corrupt practices,* and a juvenile court.* The legislature also established a public service commission with authority over all public carriers and utilities. Although the Progressive Era in Alabama witnessed the adoption of a number of reform measures at the state level, it was essentially progressivism for white males only. "Business progressivism," characterized by a proliferation of local booster organizations and campaigns for governmental efficiency and promotion of trade, formed the basic pattern of urban "reform." (Sheldon Hackney, *Populism to Progressivism in Alabama* (1969); David A. Harris, "Racists and Reformers: A Study of Progressivism in Alabama, 1896–1911" (Ph.D. diss., University of North Carolina, 1967); Allen W. Jones, "Political Reforms of the Progressive Era," *Alabama Review* 21 (July 1968): 173–94.)

David E. Alsobrook

ALDRICH, NELSON WILMARTH (November 6, 1841–April 16, 1915). Conservative Republican senator from Rhode Island, Nelson Aldrich was the leader of the "Big Four" that dominated the Senate during Theodore Roosevelt's* administration. Born on a farm in Rhode Island, he was educated in public schools, went to work for a wholesale grocery firm, soon becoming a partner and earning substantial wealth. He worked his way up in Rhode Island politics, served in Congress from 1878 to 1881, then was elected to the Senate in 1881 and served for thirty years, controlling Senate business during the McKinley* and Roosevelt administrations. A multimillionaire himself, he gave his daughter in marriage to John D. Rockefeller, Jr., thus symbolizing the partnership of big business and politics within the Republican party.* His authorship of the protectionist Payne-Aldrich Tarriff* of 1909 stimulated a revolt by Insurgent* Republicans and helped split the party. Aldrich retired from the Senate in 1911 rather than face possible defeat. Despite his conservatism, he played a major role in reforming the banking system. After the Panic of 1907,* Congress passed the Aldrich-Vreeland Act,* establishing a National Monetary Commission* with Aldrich as chairman. The Commission recommended the formation of a central bank, to be called the National Reserve Association. This "Aldrich Plan," though much amended by the Democrats, laid the foundation for the Federal Reserve Act* passed in 1913. (Nathaniel W. Stephenson, *Nelson W. Aldrich* (1930); H. Parker Willis, *The Federal Reserve System* (1923); George E. Mowry, *The Era of Theodore Roosevelt and the Birth of Modern America, 1900–1912* (1958).)

Edward R. Kantowicz

ALDRICH-VREELAND ACT. An emergency banking law passed after the panic of 1907,* the Aldrich-Vreeland Act marked a first step toward the establishment of the Federal Reserve System.* Under the banking laws in effect in

1907, the currency lacked elasticity; for it was backed solely by U.S. government bonds, which were often in short supply. The Aldrich-Vreeland emergency currency bill, passed on May 30, 1908, authorized national banks to issue additional currency backed by other securities, for a temporary period of six years. It also created a National Monetary Commission,* chaired by Senator Nelson W. Aldrich,* to study the entire banking system and recommend more permanent reforms. The commission reported on January 17, 1911, and recommended the establishment of a central bank with fifteen branches nationwide. This report, called the Aldrich Plan, formed the basis of the Federal Reserve System established in 1913. (Robert H. Wiebe, *Businessmen and Reform* (1962); O.M.W. Sprague, *History of Crises under the National Banking System* (1910); J. Laurence Laughlin, *The Federal Reserve Act: Its Origins and Problems* (1933).)

Edward R. Kantowicz

ALLEN, HENRY JUSTIN (September 11, 1868–January 17, 1950). After barbering and working as a newsman, Henry Allen, along with Joseph L. Bristow,* purchased the Ottawa (Kansas) *Herald* in 1895 and later the Salina (Kansas) *Daily Republican*. Allen owned several other journals before dissolving his partnership, divesting himself of the other properties, and purchasing the Wichita *Beacon* in 1907. Like most Kansas Progressives, Allen first entered politics in the nineties, opposing populism. He was a minor part of the so-called "Leland Political Machine" in Republican affairs and like many of its members embraced reform by 1909. He was a leader of the "Bull Moose" bolt in 1912, but returned to Republicanism when the Progressive party* failed in 1916. He served in the Red Cross and YMCA during World War I* and while in Europe won the Republican gubernatorial nomination and general election in 1918. His candidacy, managed by prominent Kansas "regulars," represented reconciliation of sorts. Ineffective in promoting progressive reform, Allen did cause the legislature to pass the Kansas Industrial Act of 1920, which created the court of industrial relations, empowered to hear and settle industrial disputes, fix wages, and determine maximum hours of labor. This act was strenuously opposed by labor unions, was largely ineffective, and was ruled unconstitutional by the U.S. Supreme Court in 1923. (*The Autobiography of William Allen White* (1946); Domenico Gagliardo, *The Kansas Industrial Court* (1941); Robert S. La Forte, *Leaders of Reform: Progressive Republicans in Kansas, 1900–1916* (1974).)

Robert S. La Forte

ALTGELD, JOHN PETER (December 30, 1847–March 12, 1902). Altgeld was born in Germany, grew up in Ohio, and served in the Civil War. In 1875 he moved to Chicago, where he practiced law and speculated in real estate in the postfire boom. Elected to the Cook County Bench in 1886, Altgeld was nominated by the Democrats for governor in 1892 and won. Though his gubernatorial term was marked by advances in prison reform and progress toward the elimination of child labor, Altgeld is best remembered as the governor who pardoned the anarchists convicted of the Haymarket bombing of 1886, and as the governor who objected to the use of federal injunctions and troops to defeat the American Railway Union in the Pullman Strike* of 1894. His forthrightness on both these issues lost him popularity and destroyed his political career. Many contemporaries, including the poet Vachel Lindsay (in "The Eagle That Is Forgotten") judged Altgeld to be the precursor of the full-blown and intensive progressive movement that became politically fashionable after 1900. (Harry Barnard, *"Eagle Forgotten": The Life of John Peter Altgeld* (1962); Ray Ginger, *Altgeld's America* (1958).)

Dominic Candeloro

AMERICAN ASSOCIATION FOR LABOR LEGISLATION. Between its inception in 1906 and its disbandment in 1945, the American Association for Labor Legislation (AALL) did more than any other voluntary organization to promote social insurance and industrial safety. While labor leaders participated in the AALL, and some big businessmen helped finance the AALL's activities in the years before World War I,* the association was dominated by liberal academic economists and progressive government administrators. Richard T. Ely,* John R. Commons,* Henry R. Seager, and Henry Farnham were especially active within the AALL in its early years, when it was in the forefront of the movement to prevent occupational diseases (succeeding especially in eliminating the use of phosphorous in the manufacturing of matches) and to obtain workmen's compensation. After 1908 the heart and soul of the AALL was its executive secretary, economist John B. Andrews. Andrews edited the association's journal, the *American Labor Legislation Review*, (1911–1942), which was the country's best source of information about social insurance and protective labor legislation. After the enactment of the initial compensation laws (1910–1915), the AALL turned its attention to health insurance. (Irwin Yellowitz, *Labor and the Progressive Movement in New York State, 1897–1916* (1965); Daniel Nelson, *Unemployment Insurance: The American Experience, 1915–1935* (1969).)

Robert Asher

AMERICAN ASSOCIATION OF UNIVERSITY PROFESSORS. Founded in 1915 by such luminaries as John Dewey* and A. O. Lovejoy, the American Association of University Professors (AAUP) was the first national organization devoted to the collective interests of American professors. Because of disciplinary divisions, the hierarchy of instructional ranks, and professorial gentility, association came late. Clashes with business-oriented trustees and strong-minded administrators led to spectacular firings, and complaints about poor pay appeared regularly in prewar magazines. But professors' emphasis on the disinterested nature of their work and their refusal to act as a trade union caused them to focus attention on issues of academic freedom, tenure, and due process involving faculty peers. Thus job security and social legitimacy were linked. In time, the AAUP won wide acceptance for its principles, but even its mild program seemed too militant for many, and until the 1920s the organization excluded junior faculty. Most telling, AAUP leaders eagerly served the government's war effort rather than defending academics fired for insufficient patriotism, and officially advocated severe restrictions on academic free speech. (Mark Beach, "Professional versus Professorial Control of Higher Education," *Education Record*, 49 (1968); 263–73; Carol S. Gruber, *Mars and Minerva: World War I and the Uses of the Higher Learning in America* (1975); Richard Hofstadter and Walter P. Metzger, *The Development of Academic Freedom in the United States* (1955).)

Frank Stricker

AMERICAN ASSOCIATION OF UNIVERSITY WOMEN. The American Association of University Women (AAUW) was established in 1921, after a merger of the Association of Collegiate Alumnae (ACA), founded in 1882, and the Southern Association of College Women. ACA's goals were to create a network for women college graduates, to assist the intellectual growth of its members, and to help raise the standards of women's education. In one of its first projects, the ACA refuted Edward Clark's argument, published as *Sex and Education* (1873), that higher education hurt women's reproductive capabilities. The organization made a detailed study of college women's health and the impact of physical education on women and, as a result, began organizing for better physical conditions in preparatory schools. The growing number of women college graduates increased ACA membership, and in 1921 led to the creation of the AAUW and the formation of a national network. With a primary goal of improving women's education, the ACA, and later the AAUW, lobbied for expanded access to graduate study for women and helped numerous women attend college by awarding fellowships. In the 1920s, the AAUW joined the Women's Joint Coordinating Committee, lobbying for bills such as the Teachers Salary Bill, the Compulsory Education and School Census Bill, and other educational legislation. (Marion Talbot and Lois K. M. Rosenberry, *History of American Association of University Women* (1931); William O'Neill, *Everyone Was Brave: A History of Feminism in America* (1969).)

Marie Laberge

AMERICAN BAR ASSOCIATION. Organized in 1878 as a self-selecting elite, the American Bar Association (ABA) initially confined its efforts mainly to gathering information and raising issues for future action. Despite a rapid increase in membership after 1900 and growing contacts with state bar associations, the ABA remained aloof from most lawyers, including only 10 percent of them in 1920. The ABA's influence was much greater than its membership, however. In 1908 it adopted a code of ethics copied by many state bars, encouraged uniformity in legal reporting and judicial procedures, and pushed a model insurance bill for Washington, D.C. It also campaigned for uniform state laws, dominating the Conference of Commissioners on Uniform State Laws, but focused on technical subjects such as negotiable instruments, sales, and warehouse receipts, rather than on substantive issues. Its interest in raising bar admission standards and improving legal education had little direct impact in the Progressive Era, although its request in 1913 for an evaluation by the Carnegie Foundation led to a very influential report in 1920. More overtly political were the ABA's campaign against judicial recall* and the public opposition by seven ABA presidents and many members to the Supreme Court nomination of Louis Brandeis.* (Edson R. Sunderland, *History of the American Bar Association and Its Work* (1953); James Willard Hurst, *The Growth of American Law: The Law Makers* (1950); Jerold S. Auerbach, *Unequal Justices: Lawyers and Social Change in Modern America* (1976).)

                                                                    Philip R. VanderMeer

AMERICAN CIVIC ASSOCIATION. The American Civic Association, a creation of J. Horace McFarland, was formed in 1904 out of a merger of the American Park and Outdoor Art Association and McFarland's American League for Civil Improvement. Reflecting McFarland's interest in municipal reform, the association became a force nationally, supporting good government candidates, working to throw out the grafters, and advocating city parks and city beautification. The new association began to campaign for state and national parks as part of the grand concert of interests organized by Gifford Pinchot* to promote the expanding conservation movement,* but soon broke away over the issue of preserving natural beauty, a matter not high on Pinchot's list of priorities. Between 1908 and 1913, the association joined with the Sierra Club and other preservationists in an unsuccessful attempt to prevent San Francisco from turning the Hetch Hetchy Valley, a part of Yosemite Park, into a water reservoir. Failure convinced McFarland that national parks needed a strong defender in the federal government, such as the national forests had in the Forest Service.* The American Civic Association played no small role in mustering the support that made possible the creation of the National Park Service* in 1916. (Alfred Runte, *National Parks: The American Experience* (1979); Roderick Nash, *Wilderness and the American Mind* (1967).)

                                                                    James Penick

AMERICAN CIVIL LIBERTIES UNION. This organization was founded during World War I* to protect the civil rights of war protesters. When President Woodrow Wilson* proposed his national defense preparedness* program in November 1915, a group of social workers, civil reformers, and academics organized the American Union Against Militarism (AUAM) to oppose war measures. Roger Baldwin, a native of Wellesley, Massachusetts, who had worked as a sociologist and a settlement house resident in Saint Louis since 1906, joined the national committee of the AUAM in April 1917 and soon became the dominant figure in the organization. He organized a bureau for conscientious objectors and a civil liberties bureau to defend the rights of socialists, pacifists, and other wartime dissenters who were accused of violating the espionage* and sedition* acts. Baldwin himself was imprisoned for draft resistance. The National Civil Liberties Bureau became a separate organization on October 1, 1917, as the AUAM moved toward support of American participation in the war. On January 20, 1920, after the war's end and Baldwin's release from prison, the Civil Liberties Bureau changed its name to the American Civil Liberties Union (ACLU) in order to dissociate it from unpopular wartime causes. The ACLU was the first national organization dedicated to defending the civil liberties of all citizens and not merely representing the special interests of one group. (Donald O. Johnson, *The Challenge to American Freedoms: World War I and the Rise of the ACLU* (1963); Peggy Lamson, *Roger Baldwin* (1976).)

Edward R. Kantowicz

AMERICAN ECONOMIC ASSOCIATION. This is the organization formed on September 9, 1885, in Saratoga Springs, New York, under the leadership of Richard T. Ely* and a group of scholars, ministers, and social reformers, at a time when economics did not exist as an independent academic discipline. Although religious inspiration and reformist zeal played an important role in the association's life, conflict over whether the organization was to engage in scholarly impartiality or serve as a vehicle for reform ultimately was resolved in favor of the former. The early history of the association was interwoven with public reaction to Ely's work. In addition to initiating the organization and serving as its first secretary and primary promoter, Ely wrote extensively on labor, monopoly, and taxation issues, causing some critics to brand him a socialist. While economists of various schools rallied to Ely's support, the resultant friction changed the character of the organization from social reform to a more strictly scientific and scholarly body. After several years of nonparticipation, Ely was surprisingly elected the association's president in 1900. During his presidency, membership expanded and the association prospered, as a conscious effort was made to enlist business and professional men as well as economists. In 1911, the quarterly *American Economic Review* was the first published and eventually became the most prestigious journal in the field of economics. (A. W. Coats, "The First Two Decades of the American Economic Association," *American Economic Review* 50, no. 4 (September 1960): 555–74; A. W. Coats, "The American Economic Association, 1904–29," *American Economic Review* 54, no. 4 (June 1964): 261–85.)

Leon Applebaum

AMERICAN FEDERATION OF LABOR. The American Federation of Labor (A. F. of L.) was leading national federation of labor unions at the turn of the century. After a disastrous depression in the 1870s seriously weakened the existing labor unions, a number of labor leaders, most notably Adolph Strasser and Samuel Gompers* of the Cigarmakers' Union, looked to the British Trade Unions Congress as a model for reorganizing American labor. Accordingly, they called a convention on November 15, 1881, in Pittsburgh which founded the Federation of Organized Trades and Labor Unions. A subsequent convention on December 8, 1886, in Columbus, Ohio, renamed the organization the American Federation of Labor. Samuel Gompers served as president every year, except one, from the organization's founding until his death in 1924. The A. F. of L. was a federation of national (or international, if they included Canada) unions, with one union per skilled trade. It avoided utopian or socialist schemes to remake society, played a limited role in politics, and concentrated on bread-and-butter issues of wages and working conditions. Its strategy of "business unionism" was aptly summed up in one word by Samuel Gompers—"More." The A. F. of L. grew slowly at first, numbering no more than 300,000 members until nearly the turn of the century. Then between 1898 and 1904 membership increased rapidly to 1,750,000, enrolling roughly one in every fourteen nonagricultural laborers. Due to sharp opposition from management groups, such as the National Association of Manufacturers,* and rivalry from socialist "dual unions," membership growth leveled off for the remainder of the Progressive Era. The A. F. of L. was also hampered by its racial and ethnic exclusiveness; it simply barred Negroes from most unions and did not vigorously recruit recent immigrants. Organization along traditional craft lines also proved a limitation, for many modern industries relied heavily on unskilled labor and thus counted few craft unionists. (Lewis Lorwin, *The American Federation of Labor: History, Politics, and Prospects* (1933); Philip Taft, *The A. F. of L. in the Time of Gompers* (1957); Henry Pelling, *American Labor* (1960).)

Edward R. Kantowicz

AMERICAN FORESTRY ASSOCIATION. Founded originally in 1875, the American Forestry Association became an advocate of a national policy of forest conservation in the 1880s (called American Forestry Congress, 1882–1889). It worked for passage of the Forest Reserve Act of 1891, which led to the establishment of national forests, and the Forest Management Act of 1897, which became the legal foundation for a national forest policy. After 1898 the association fell under the control of Gifford Pinchot,* head of the Department of Agriculture's forestry policies. In 1905, it sponsored the American Forest Congress in Washington, D.C., a gathering of the industries and groups whose support Pinchot had courted. This Congress helped push through the legislation transferring the national forests to the jurisdiction of the forestry bureau. When Pinchot subsequently tried to turn the Association into the main vehicle for championing the conservation movement, many members balked at the pursuit of goals often far removed from forestry matters. After 1909, the Pinchot group lost control of the Association, but it remained a significant forest lobby, achieving an important victory with passage of the Weeks Act in 1911. (Henry Clepper,

"Crusade for Conservation: The Centennial History of the American Forestry Association," *American Forests* 81 (October 1975): 19–113.)

James Penick

AMERICAN HISTORICAL ASSOCIATION. Founded at Saratoga Springs, New York, in 1884 under the auspices of the American Social Science Association, the American Historical Association (AHA) was part of an organizational trend, culminating in the Progressive Era, away from local learned societies, supported by gentlemen intellectuals and antiquarians, and toward national professional organizations controlled by research scholars in search of "knowledge." The purpose of the AHA was to apply professional standards to original work resulting from critical, scientific investigation. The Association served as a national clearinghouse for a variety of decentralized activities in the expanding field of history. Historians developed neither a specialized language nor agreement upon specific diagnostic tools; over the years the AHA was called upon to resolve conflicts arising within the guild over historical theory, subject matter, practice, and definition of the appropriate audience. Amateurs prevailed on the executive council and in the presidency of the organization until the turn of the century when, by means of a series of internal reforms, professional specialists became dominant. In 1895, the organization formed branches for church history and state and local historical societies and, in 1899, a public archives commission was formed. In 1915 the *American Historical Review*, founded as an independent scholarly journal in 1895, became the official publication replacing the earlier *Annual Report*. (John Higham, with Leonard Krieger and Felix Gilbert, *History* (1952); David D. Van Tassel, "From Learned Society to Professional Organization: The American Historical Association, 1884–1900," *American Historical Review* 89 (1984): 929–56; Elizabeth Donnan and Leo F. Stock, eds., *An Historian's World: Selections from the Correspondence of John Franklin Jameson* (1956).)

Burton J. Bledstein

AMERICAN INDIANS. Progressive reforms bypassed American Indians until the 1930s New Deal. The turn of the century marked the lowest point in the Indians' condition at the same time that it marked the culmination of assimilationist pressure for citizenship, Christian education, allotment of tribal lands, and destruction of tribal customs. Among the smallest of minority groups in the nation, American Indians were widely if falsely assumed to be "vanishing," so they were not a major focus of Progressive reformers. Indians were scattered across the nation on 171 reservations, in rural areas, and a small but increasing number in towns and cities. The Indian population rose from 270,000 in 1900 to 323,000 in 1910 and to 336,337 by 1920. Over half of all Indian peoples were citizens in 1905, largely as a result of allotment, intermarriage, and inclusion of Indian territory. That number rose to two-thirds in 1917. In 1905 the Bureau of Indian Affairs opened its first employment placement office to locate off-reservation jobs for 600 Indians that year, finding work for Indian men as railroad gang laborers, seasonal agricultural workers, and "outing" employment for Indian women to work as domestic servants. Arch-assimilationists used a series of measures such as the Burke Act (1906) to increase the pace of allotment and the loss of reservation resources.

Commissioners of Indian affairs in the period took steps to slow forced assimilation in favor of gradualism, shifting education from boarding schools to federal day and public schools, and altering curriculum to prepare Indians vocationally for Christian industrial-agricultural jobs. Some Indian people despaired and abused alcohol; others converted to Christianity and worked in their churches; still others maintained membership in a peyote church or participated in traditional ceremonies. Leaders joined self-improvement and lobbying organizations such as the Society of American Indians (founded 1911). The period saw the growth of American anthropology and the preservation of native arts and crafts; E. S. Curtis doggedly photographed a people he feared were nearing extinction; and George Heye incorporated his Museum of the American Indian in 1916. (James Olson and Raymond Wilson, *Native Americans in the Twentieth Century* (1984); Francis Paul Prucha, *The Great Father*, vol. 2 (1984); Frederick E. Hoxie, *A Final Promise: The Campaign to Assimilate the Indians, 1880–1920* (1984); Hazel Hertzberg, *The Search for an American Indian Identity: Modern Pan-Indian Movements* (1971).)

C. B. Clark

AMERICANIZATION. Americanization represented an organized and official effort to indoctrinate immigrants in the principles of Americanism and the "American way." The early twentieth-century Americanization campaign drew upon a long history of anti-immigrant attitudes in the United States, reflected in mid-nineteenth-century nativism and such organizations as the Immigration Restriction League founded in 1894. In 1907, the North American Civic League for Immigrants* was organized by civic leaders, educators, and social service workers to counter the presumed immigrant peril and promote the assimilation of the newcomers. The Americanization movement became particularly strong during World War I,* when it was widely believed that "hyphenated" Americans posed a threat to the American war effort. The movement intensified still further after the war during the so-called Red Scare* of 1919–1920, when exaggerated fears of immigrant radicalism and "creeping Bolshevism" saturated the mass media and the public consciousness. Cultural diversity was perceived as a challenge to "100 percent Americanism"—a slogan whipped up by Theodore Roosevelt* during the political campaign of 1916.

Americanization programs were based on the idea that immigrants must abandon their old-country heritage and loyalties and be assimilated, homogenized, and made over into Americans as quickly as possible. A wide variety of American institutions, ranging from public schools, settlement houses, and churches to businesses, unions, and political parties, accepted these fundamental assumptions and actively participated in the Americanization effort. Government at every level was deeply involved in Americanization activity during and after the war, but two federal agencies attempted to coordinate the Americanization effort: the Bureau of Naturalization in the Department of Labor,* and the Bureau of Education in the Department of the Interior. Bureaucratic infighting among the two agencies and a low level of federal funding often undermined the effectiveness of these efforts. Working closely with the federal Americanizers was the National Americanization Committee, a private business group connected with the U.S. Chambers of Commerce.* Similarly, by 1921, thirty states, hundreds of cities, and thousands of public school systems had established Americanization programs, ranging from teaching English to foreign-born adults to citizenship training and naturalization programs to "American-style" house-keeping, cooking, and health care for immigrant women. Americanizers also sought to control the immigrant press and organized patriotic rallies. When immigrant communities and the ethnic press resisted Americanization, rampant xenophobia led to the rigorous immigration restriction legislation of 1924 and to a larger movement for cultural conformity in the 1920s. (Edward G. Hartmann, *The Movement to Americanize the Immigrant* (1948); John Higham, *Strangers in the Land: Patterns of American Nativism, 1865–1925* (1955); Gerd A. Korman, *Industrialization, Immigrants, and Americanizers: The View from Milwaukee, 1866–1921* (1967); John McClymer, "The Federal Government and the Americanization Movement, 1915–24," *Prologue* 10 (1978): 23–41.)

Raymond A. Mohl

AMERICAN MAGAZINE, THE. In 1904, Ellery Sedgwick, the editor of *Leslie's Monthly Magazine*, asked, "What's in a name?" "Everything," he concluded. *Leslie's* meant "wish-wash and failure," and the thirty-six-year-old periodical was renamed the *American Magazine*. The contents of *Leslie's* and the *American* were a mix of public affairs articles and fiction like their competitors, *Cosmopolitan* and *McClure's*, but Sedgwick refused to join their muckraking crusades. In May 1906, the month after Theodore Roosevelt's* condemnation of muckrakers, Sedgwick's editorial, "The Man with the Muckrake," excoriated the new journalists. Within four months, however, the *American Magazine* was bought by John S. Phillips, who brought with him *McClure's* leading contributors Ida M. Tarbell,* Lincoln Steffens,* Ray Stannard Baker,* William Allen White,* and Peter Finley Dunne,* (Mr. Dooley). This star-studded staff, "pledging past success as security for the future," won financial backing from John B. Wannamaker, Edward Filene,* Charles R. Crane,* and Tom Johnson.* White described the *American*'s mission as carrying "the torch of an evolutionary revolution to the world." It was "an organ of propaganda wrapped in the tinfoil of a literary quality which at least reflected the temper of the times." In the next years Steffens reported on political corruption in San Francisco and the West, Tarbell wrote on the tariff, and Baker on the black experience. Jane Addams's* *Twenty Years at Hull House* and Robert La Follette's* *Autobiography* were serialized. Yet the high point of the *American*'s muckraking was short-lived. Steffens left the staff in 1908 and White soon after. Baker, under the pseudonym David Grayson, began his series "Adventures in Contentment." In 1915, the Phillips Publishing Company sold the magazine to the Crowell Company, publishers of *Woman's Home Companion*. The *American Magazine* reached a circulation of 2,300,000 in the 1920s with an emphasis on success and human interest stories. (Frank L. Mott, *A History of American Magazines, 1865–1885*, vol. 3 (1938); Ellery Sedgwick, *The Happy Profession* (1946); Ray Stannard Baker, *American Chronicle: The Autobiography of Ray Stannard Baker* (1945); C. C. Regier, *The Era of the Muckrakers* (1932).)

Dorothy M. Brown

AMERICAN MEDICAL ASSOCIATION. The opening of the twentieth century marked the emergence of the American Medical Association (AMA) as a prominent professional organization. Founded in 1846 to advance medical education, the AMA had struggled through more than a half century of public obscurity and political ineffectiveness before a reorganization in 1901 set it on an influential course. With a membership growth from about 8,000 in 1900 to over 70,000 in 1910, it assumed a principal role in some of the reform movements of the Progressive Era, including activities of special concern to the medical profession and other matters in which the public also had a direct interest. Among the former was the Association's crusade for the advancement of medical education, which drove out many inferior medical schools and was substantially responsible for reducing the total number of schools from 166 in 1904 to 95 eleven years later and cutting the total enrollment by half. It secured more effective medical practice laws and improved vital statistics legislation. The AMA took leadership in other movements in which the public had a great direct interest. It fought for the enactment and improvement of state and federal pure food and drugs legislation,* led the fight against medical quackery, and sought passage of many measures strengthening boards of health. (Morris Fishbein, ed., *A History of the American Medical Association* (1947); James Harvey Young, *The Medical Messiahs* (1967); James G. Burrow, *AMA: Voice of American Medicine* (1963); James G. Burrow, *Organized Medicine in the Progressive Era: The Move toward Monopoly* (1977).)

James G. Burrow

AMERICAN POLITICAL SCIENCE ASSOCIATION. Founded in 1903 with 214 members, the American Political Science Association (APSA) in its early years encouraged efforts to establish distinct undergraduate and graduate departments of political science, urged the professionalization of standards for admission to the ranks of university and college teachers, and advocated the development and dissemination of specialized political research. Efforts by the first political scientists to define the specifically "scientific" quality of their work sparked much discussion but few definitive conclusions. But such prominent

APSA presidents as Frank Goodnow,* James Bryce,* A. Lawrence Lowell,* and Woodrow Wilson* did achieve near unanimity in their appeals for the kinds of studies that had relevance for the reform of state institutions and public life.

Studying the "real life" of legislatures, bureaucracies, political parties, and elections was thought to be essential to the task of secularizing and modernizing American political thought and practice, removing both from the influence of nineteenth-century ethnic, religious, and rural attachments. Closely linked to the more conservative strains of northeastern and midwestern progressivism, the APSA promoted links between academic study and the training of expert and nonpartisan civil servants and public officials. Early political scientists also sought to awaken public opinion to the task of constructing and supporting positive and efficient government. Before World War I,* such efforts were largely concentrated at the local and state levels, captured in the formation of numerous legislative reference bureaus, expert government commissions, and graduate schools of public affairs. (Bernard Crick, *The American Science of Politics* (1959); Albert Somit and Joseph Tanenhaus, *The Development of American Political Science* (1967); Raymond Seidelman, *Disenchanted Realists: Political Science and the American Crisis* (1985).)

Raymond Seidelman

AMERICAN PSYCHOLOGICAL ASSOCIATION. Founded in 1892, the American Psychological Association (APA) is the major professional association for psychologists in the United States. It publishes the *American Psychologist* and numerous other journals. The Association held its first annual meeting in Philadelphia in 1892 and chose as its first president G. Stanley Hall,* who had established the first experimental psychology laboratory in the United States. The founding of the APA was part of a trend in the late nineteenth century whereby each of the social and behavioral sciences established a separate professional identity. Under the influence of Wilhelm Wundt at Leipzig, American psychologists such as Hall and J. McKeen Cattell* broke away from philosophy and established psychology as a laboratory-based, experimental science. The stated purpose of the APA—"to advance psychology as a science and as a means of promoting human welfare"—typifies the twin impulses behind all the emerging social and behavioral disciplines, a passion for reform and a worship of science. (American Psychological Association, *Biographical Directory* (1970); A. A. Roback, *History of American Psychology* (1952).)

Edward R. Kantowicz

AMERICAN SOCIETY FOR MUNICIPAL IMPROVEMENTS (later American Society of Municipal Engineers). This group was organized in 1894 by George H. Frost, publisher of *Engineering News*, and M. J. Murphy, street commissioner of Saint Louis, Missouri. Its first meeting in Buffalo, New York, was attended by more than sixty representatives of sixteen different cities, including mayors, councilmen, administrative officers, heads of bureaus, and municipal engineers. The society's purpose was to concentrate on the physical improvement of cities in the "most skillful, thorough and economical manner." Standing committees included Street Paving, Electric Lighting, Sewerage and Sanitation, Water-works and Water Supply, Taxation and Assessments, City Government and Legislation, and Disposition of Garbage and Street Cleaning. In 1897, the society refused to become part of the newly formed League of American Municipalities, a group that attracted away many of its mayor and councilmen members. (*Proceedings of the American Society for Municipal Improvements* (1897–1917); N. P. Lewis, "The Work and Aims of the American Society of Municipal Improvements," in *Proceedings of the Seventh Annual Meeting of the National Municipal League, 1901* (1901); A. Prescott Folwell, "The American Society of Municipal Improvements," *Annals of the American Academy of Political and Social Science* 25 (1905): 364–66.)

Marilyn Thornton Williams

AMERICAN SOCIETY OF EQUITY. James A. Everitt, an Indiana farm editor, founded the American Society of Equity (ASE) in 1902. Everitt believed that farmers should emulate businesses in their seeming ability to set prices, and unions in theirs to set wages. He dismissed any sentimental notions about farming being a special way of life. It was an economic enterprise and farmers could only earn an adequate return if they scientifically set a price on their commodities and refused to sell until that level was reached. In 1903, Everitt advised farmers to hold wheat off the market until it reached a dollar a bushel. He took credit when the price surpassed that level even though other factors had intervened. By 1905 ASE members began to reject Everitt's leadership and his one-track method. Wisconsin farmers collaborated with unions to establish cooperative stores. Dakota wheat growers campaigned for a huge producers' cooperative. Kentucky tobacco raisers formed a sellers' pool to break the international buyers' monopoly. The group also constituted themselves as the Night Riders, who frequently resorted to violence. After national schisms in 1907 and 1910 in addition to the disagreements over goals, the membership of the ASE declined. It exemplified one of the main characteristics of the Progressive Era—professional organization—but it never achieved the number of members adequate to set prices. (Robert H. Bahmer, "The American Society of Equity," *Agricultural History* 14 (1940): 33–63; Theodore P. Saloutos and John D. Hicks, *Agricultural Discontent in the Middle West, 1900–1939* (1951); Lowell K. Dyson, *Farmers' Organizations* (1986), 24–30, 78–81, 102–4, 122–23.)

Lowell K. Dyson

AMERICAN SOCIOLOGICAL SOCIETY. With the formation of this society in 1906, American sociology was the last of the "modern" social sciences to organize professionally, joining history (1884), economics (1885), and political science (1905). Although courses in sociology first appeared in American universities in the 1870s, its practitioners initially coexisted with reformers and social science amateurs in the American Social Science Association (1865–1909). During the 1890s, the discipline took more definite shape with the founding of graduate departments at Columbia under Franklin Giddings and at Chicago under Albion Small.* Small also served as first editor of the *American Journal of Sociology* (founded 1896), a University of Chicago* publication that became the unofficial organ of the society.

In its choice of presidents, the society honored the founders of the discipline: Lester Ward* (1906–1907), author of *Dynamic Sociology* (1883); William Graham Sumner* (1908–1909), whose *Folkways* (1906) had just appeared; and Giddings (1910–1911) and Small (1912–1913). Their successors included two of the more original theorists of the Progressive Era, Edward A. Ross* (1914) and Charles Horton Cooley* (1918), authors respectively of *Social Control* (1901) and *Human Nature and the Social Order* (1902). Although early programs reflected the reformist interests of many members, the variety of these theoretical perspectives mirrored the complexity of progressivism itself. Beginning with an attack on "Christian sociology" in the late 1890s, the society strove steadily to become more "professional" and "scientific," a movement that reached high tide after 1920. (Roscoe Hinkle, *Founding Theory of American Sociology 1881–1915* (1980); Howard Odum, *American Sociology* (1951); Anthony D. Oberschall, "The Institutionalization of American Sociology," in *The Establishment of Empirical Sociology* (1972).)

Robert C. Bannister

ANDERSON, SHERWOOD (September 13, 1876–March 8, 1941). Anderson was born in Camden, Ohio, worked in advertising in Chicago, and served as president of United Factories Company in Illyria, Ohio, from 1907 to 1912. A nervous breakdown brought on by business and personal pressures caused him to return to Chicago to recuperate, at the time that the "Chicago Renaissance" was underway in that city. Contact with important magazines, editors, and writers ultimately led to his third and best-known novel, *Winesburg, Ohio*, in which Anderson deals with the effects on midwest America of the Industrial Revolution, "the beginning of the most materialistic age in the history of the world . . . when the will to power would replace the will to serve and beauty would be well-nigh forgotten in the terrible headlong rush of mankind toward the acquiring of possessions." In *Winesburg*, Anderson blames industrialism for bringing into the world the neurotic character of our time, thus implicitly recognizing the influence of Freudian psychology. Besides advancing the development of psychological fiction, Anderson was instrumental in creating the new twentieth-century style whose simplified vocabulary and sentence structure shows the seminal influence of Gertrude Stein and that later was given further development by Ernest Hemingway. Anderson helped to popularize the use of the interior monologue and stream-of-consciousness techniques invented by James Joyce. (Walter B. Rideout, "Sherwood Anderson," in Jackson R. Bryer, ed., *Sixteen Modern American Authors* (1973), 3–28; David D. Anderson, *Sherwood Anderson: An Introduction and Interpretation* (1967).)

Philip Gerber

ANTHRACITE COAL STRIKE OF 1902. On May 12, over 140,000 mine workers struck a powerful combination of coal operators, railroad barons, and eastern bankers in a struggle which lasted until October 23. This confrontation grew out of an organizing drive begun in 1899 by the United Mine Workers of America* (UMWA) and its young president, John Mitchell.* Strike in 1900 had resulted in the coal operators conceding a modest wage increase rather than engaging in a prolonged struggle during a presidential election year. In 1902, however, the mine workers walked out after the operators had refused to discuss their demands with UMWA representatives. The mine workers wanted an eight-hour day, a 20 percent wage increase, coal paid for by weight, and, most importantly, recognition of the UMWA.

Although the strike began in May, it did not attract widespread attention until early fall when newspapers predicted a resultant fuel shortage. After much be-hind-the-scenes maneuvering involving Mitchell, national politicians (Senator Mark Hanna),* financiers (J. P. Morgan),* and cabinet members (Secretary of War Elihu Root),* public pressure convinced President Theodore Roosevelt* to intervene and force the operators and mine workers to accept arbitration by a specially appointed presidential commission. On March 21, 1903, the Anthracite Coal Strike Commission awarded contract miners a 10 percent wage increase, gave day workers a reduction in hours from ten to nine, allowed the employment of check-weighmen, and established a joint mine worker–operator Board of Conciliation. The commission refused to grant union recognition to the UMWA. The strike and accompanying settlement propelled Mitchell into the national limelight. President Roosevelt reaped handsome political dividends since his even-handed actions underscored his Square Deal* for capital and labor. For the mine workers, the failure to achieve union recognition meant continued operator authoritarianism. (Robert Cornell, *The Anthracite Coal Strike of 1902* (1957); Victor Greene, *The Slavic Community on Strike* (1968); Joseph Gowaskie, "John Mitchell and the Anthracite Mine Workers: Leadership Conservatism and Rank-and-File Militancy," *Labor History* 27 (Winter 1985–86): 54–83.)

Joseph Gowaskie

ANTI-CATHOLICISM. By 1900, America's volatile anti-Catholic tradition was checked temporarily by the prosperity and cosmopolitanism of the early Progressive Era. But the tradition resurfaced in 1910, ebbed during World War I,* then erupted in the turbulent twenties. Anti-Catholic ferment was marked by rumors of Catholic plots to establish papal tyranny, the tirades of such ambitious politicians as Georgia populist Tom Watson,* such magazines as the *Menace* (fl. 1911) and the emergence of the Ku Klux Klan. The phobias of Anglo-Saxon Protestants stimulated by foreign immigration, the frustrations of Progressive reformers, the anti-German hostilities and superpatriotic conformity generated by the war, all found release in anti-Catholic crusades. These years, according to John Higham, marked the historic transition of anti-Catholicism from city to countryside, where it helped to express the deepening conflict between rural Protestant fundamentalism and an urban culture, subject to alien forces, especially an immigrant Catholicism dominated by foreign loyalties. (John Higham, *Strangers in the Land: Patterns of American Nativism, 1860–1925* (1955); Kenneth T. Jackson, *The Ku Klux Klan in the City, 1915–1930* (1967); Edward Cuddy, "The Irish Question and the Revival of Anti-Catholicism," *Catholic Historical Review* 67 (April 1981): 136–55.)

Edward Cuddy

ANTI-IMPERIALIST LEAGUE. In Boston on June 15, 1898, opponents of territorial expansion held a public meeting to protest the "adoption of an imperial policy by the United States." An outcome of the meeting was the formation of a committee of correspondence to advance the anti-imperialist cause. The committee's activities helped foster the founding of the Anti-Imperialist League on November 19, 1898. In October 1899, the league became the New England branch of the American Anti-Imperialist League, a national organization with headquarters in Chicago. League members represented a broad spectrum of religious and political persuasions. Distinguished statesmen, named honorary vice presidents, helped give the organization national stature. In advocating anti-imperialism, the league's members conducted meetings, circulated petitions, issued publications, and supported political candidates. They argued that territorial expansion, especially acquisition of the Philippine Islands, was imperialistic because it violated the democratic principle that the right to govern is derived from the consent of those to be governed. League members also argued that imperialism was unconstitutional, immoral, and impractical. The anti-imperialists were concerned that concentrating on overseas expansion and administering a colonial system would distract Americans from dealing with domestic reforms. League activities reached a high point in 1899 and 1900, dropping off following the reelection of William McKinley* in 1900. (Robert L. Beisner, *Twelve against Empire: The Anti-Imperialists 1898–1900 (1968); Berkeley E. Tompkins, Anti-Imperialism in the United States: The Great Debate, 1890– 1920* (1970); Fred Harvey Harrington, "The Anti-Imperialist Movement in the United States, 1898–1900," *Mississippi Valley Historical Review* 22 (1935): 211–30; Maria Lanzar-Carpio, "The Anti-Imperialist League," *Philippini Social Science Review* 3 (1930): 7–41.)

James A. Zimmerman

ANTI-SALOON LEAGUE. This national pressure group organized the movement for prohibition* of alcoholic beverages. Founded by Rev. H. H. Russell in Oberlin, Ohio, in 1895, the Anti-Saloon League (ASL) united local Protestant congregations throughout the country into a grassroots organization. The league focused its publicity on the threat of the saloon to home and family, and shrewdly adopted a pragmatic, step-by-step strategy, starting with local option laws that permitted municipalities and countries to vote themselves dry, then moving on to lobby for statewide prohibition. By 1916, twenty-three states, mostly in the West and South, were legally dry; and the Webb-Kenyon Act,* passed by Congress in 1913, banned interstate shipment of liquor from wet states to dry ones. Wayne B. Wheeler, an Oberlin lawyer, worked his way up in the league to the positions of general counsel and legislative superintendent, and he directed the final campaign for national prohibition, beginning in 1913. Wheeler raised over $ 2 million a year, mostly in donations of less than $ 100 each, which the league spent to elect dry congressmen. He helped draft the Prohibition amendment to the Constitution which Congress passed in 1917, and he wrote most of the Volstead Act, which put Prohibition into effect in 1920. The Anti-Saloon League is usually considered the most successful example of a one-issue lobby, and "Wheelerism" became a synonym for the hard sell. (Peter H. Odegard, *Pressure Politics: The Story of the Anti-Saloon League* (1928); Norman H. Clark, *Deliver Us from Evil: An Interpretation of American Prohibition* (1976); Perry R. Duis, *The Saloon* (1983).)

Edward R. Kantowicz

ANTITRUST LEGISLATION. Business people in the same line of trade, as Adam Smith remarked in *The Wealth of Nations* (1776), seldom meet together without conspiring with one another to raise the price of their product or service. In the late nineteenth century, the Industrial Revolution vastly increased both the benefits and the fixed costs of doing business. The income from giant new transportation and manufacturing enterprises surpassed any other cash flow in economic history, but these same industries also required unprecedented investments for the construction and operation of railroads, pipelines, refineries, and factories. Overall, the urge felt by business managers to protect profits from the new industries while simultaneously serving their fixed costs pushed the tendency to combine to a new plateau. The result throughout the industrialized world was an increased reliance on cartels, pools, and other combines as ways to hedge the problem of overcapacity and declining prices.

What made the American experience different was the nation's historic prejudice against all forms of monopoly. The perceived need for powerful political action as a counterweight to the "trusts" (the contemporary generic term for all pools, monopolies, and cartels) led to an outburst of legislation: in the 1880s, numerous state antitrust laws; in 1890, the Sherman Antitrust Act;* in 1914, the Federal Trade Commission Act* and the Clayton Antitrust Act,* which was designed to strengthen and clarify the Sherman law of 1890. Because the terms "monopoly," "monopolization," "fair competition," and "restraint of trade" have ambiguous meanings, the administration of the antitrust laws, which contain these terms in their texts, posed difficult problems for judges and prosecutors. Only twenty-two cases were brought by the Department of Justice during the fifteen years after 1890, but at the high tide of the Progressive Era, "trustbusting" became a national preoccupation. From 1906 to 1915, the government prosecuted 130 companies, winning victories in such important suits as *Standard Oil** and *U.S. v. American Tobacco** (both in 1911).

Over the long history of antitrust cases, the record shows that about six out of seven prosecutions have come not against big businesses but against small firms, either individually or in combination; that the government has won more than 80 percent of its cases; that overt price-fixing has become rare; and that American companies have experienced powerful incentives to innovate organizationally as a means of avoiding illegal cartelization. In this way, antitrust legislation promoted tight horizontal and vertical integration, and therefore bigness. This was an unintended but sometimes therapeutic effect that helped American companies become the world's most efficient economic organizations during several decades after passage of the Sherman Act—but not for the reasons its Progressive Era proponents would have imagined. (A. D. Neale, *The Antitrust Laws of the U.S.A.* (1970); Richard A. Posner, *Antitrust: Cases, Economic Notes, and Other Materials* (1974); William Letwin, *Law and Economic Policy in America* (1965).)

Thomas K. McCraw

ANTIUNIONISM. Antiunion sentiment among employers at the beginning of the twentieth century was widespread, but prosperity and a new pragmatism among some businessmen temporarily brought a more conciliatory spirit to the relations between labor and capital. The bitter class conflict and cyclical economic instability of the late nineteenth century had persuaded corporate leaders in some of the nation's largest mass-production industries to seek a truce with labor. The Erdman Act of 1898, a direct outgrowth of the massive Pullman boycott,* established a framework for labor peace in the strife-torn railroad industry by prohibiting railroads from discriminating against union members and outlawing the use of the yellow-dog contract* and blacklist. The National Civic Federation* (NCF), founded in 1900, initially encouraged its employer members to adopt a conciliatory posture toward "responsible" unions and to welcome trade agreements with labor. Samuel Gompers,* president of the American Federation of Labor,* and John Mitchell,* president of the United Mine Workers of America,* were invited to represent labor in the NCF's "industrial department."* This "era of good feeling" occurred in the context of widespread and successful organizing between 1897 and 1904 by unions affiliated with the A. F. of L.

As unions became more assertive and successful, underlying employer opposition surfaced in a variety of forms. Citizens Industrial Alliances in many smaller industrial towns had begun "open-shop" campaigns as early as 1901. Spreading rapidly across the country, this open-shop campaign was officially endorsed by the National Association of Manufacturers *(NAM) in 1903. Even the NCF began to back away from conciliation after 1904. One of its leading figures, Judge Elbert Gary,* president of the U.S. Steel Corporation, declared in 1909 that his firm was officially an open-shop employer. Union growth stalled after 1904 in the face of increasingly belligerent employer opposition.The fight by employers to limit union organizing was successfully carried on in the courts, where injunctions prohibiting union boycott and strike activities were routinely secured. A series of federal court decisions defined the labor boycott as a conspiracy in restraint of trade and made unions and their leaders liable for damages under the Sherman Antitrust Act.* (See *Loewe v. Lawlor** and *Buck's Stove and Range Case.**) The NAM and the American Anti-Boycott Association carried on a propaganda campaign against the ''labor trust,'' while traditional strike-breaking tactics limited union growth in the mass-production industries. Defensive-minded craft unions evidenced little interest in organizing the unskilled. Spectacular but short-lived victories by immigrant strikers with the assistance of the Industrial Workers of the World* (IWW) in places like McKees Rocks, Paterson,* and Lawrence* did little to break this antiunion tide. (Clarence E. Bonnett, *A History of Employers' Associations in the United States* (1956); James Weinstein, *The Corporate Ideal in the Liberal State* (1968); Marguerite Green, *The National Civic Federation and the American Labor Movement; 1900–1925* (1956).)

Shelton Stromquist

ARBITRATION. Despite numerous attempts, Progressive Era reformers were never able to solve the dilemma of maintaining voluntary arbitration during national industrial emergencies. The Erdman Act (1898), which provided for voluntary arbitration in rail disputes, was invoked twenty-six times between 1906 and 1913. The Newland Act (1913) settled fifty-eight rail disputes voluntarily between 1913 and 1917. After 1913, the new Department of Labor* provided its services as arbitrator. Between 1903 and 1916 the National Civic Federation* offered its Industrial Department as the foremost arbitrator of disputes. Numerous state agencies aided in settling disputes during the nineteenth century, especially in the garment and coal industries. By 1916, Herbert Croly,* John R. Commons,* and Louis Brandeis* influenced President Woodrow Wilson* to think of using compulsory arbitration in national emergency industrial situations. Strenuously objecting, organized labor pressured Wilson to continue voluntary arbitration in the Adamson Act* (1916). World War I* forced Wilson to face compulsory arbitration under the wartime industrial acts, but in 1920, voluntary arbitration returned, especially with the Esch-Cummins Act.* (John R. Commons, *Industrial Goodwill* (1919); Arthur S. Link, *Woodrow Wilson and the Progressive Era, 1910–1917* (1954); Philip S. Foner, *History of the Labor Movement*, vol. 5; *The AFL in the Progressive Era, 1910–1915* (1980).)

Frank Grubbs

ARENA, THE. This reform magazine was published in Boston* by Benjamin Orange Flower* from December 1889 to August 1909. Flower was an idealistic young journalist when he arrived in Boston in 1885 and began publishing the

American Spectator. He merged this journal with another magazine in 1889, renaming it the *Arena*. He took the title from a passage by the German poet Heinrich Heine: "We do not take possession of our ideas, but are possessed by them. They master us and force us into the arena, where, like gladiators, we must fight for them." Flower gathered a group of lively writers, each of whom specialized in a particular subject, e.g., Minot J. Savage on religion, Frank Parsons on economics, and Hamlin Garland* on literature. The *Arena* sounded an alarm that America was in crisis, a crisis which might lead to revolution unless reforms were forthcoming. Accordingly, the magazine proposed radical but nonsocialist reforms. The *Arena* has been called the "first successful muckraking magazine in America," but it was more serious, more intellectual, and less sensational than most publications of the muckraking* genre. (Arthur Mann, *Yankee Reformers in the Urban Age* (1954); Howard F. Cline, "Benjamin Orange Flower and *The Arena*, 1889–1909," *Journalism Quarterly* 17 (June 1940): 139–50.

Edward R. Kantowicz

THE ARMORY SHOW, was probably the most influential and important art exhibition ever held, and certainly it was the largest ever organized by a group of artists. It was officially known as the International Exhibition of Modern Art and was originally organized by the infant Association of American Painters and Sculptors as a showcase for their own work. It was originally scheduled to show only at the 69th Regiment Armory in New York City, but was eventually also viewed at the Art Institute of Chicago and at Copley Hall in Boston. The exhibit ran from February 17 to March 15 (1913) in New York, March 24 to April 15 in Chicago, and April 28 to May 18 in Boston and was seen by almost three hundred thousand people. The exhibition (as shown in New York) consisted of about 1,300 paintings and prints, drawings and sculptures, of which about one-third were foreign.

The aim of the organizers had been to promote the work of contemporary American artists and it was a clear reaction against the direction and dictates of the National Academy of Design (NAD), although most of the "Ash Can"* followers of Robert Henri,* who organized the exhibition, were members of the NAD. Although the work of Americans outnumbered that of the historical and contemporary European artists by two to one, it was the impact of the work of Henri Matisse, Pablo Picasso, Odilon Redon, Marcel Duchamp, and Francis Picabia that captured both the artistic and public spotlight. Conservatives among the artists and the public were shocked and offended, while those open to the messages of the new art had their eyes opened and changed artistic and collecting directions. Academic art was put on the defensive, and the American world was changed forever. (Milton W. Brown, *The Story of the Armory Show* (1963); Munson-Williams-Proctor Institute, *The Armory Show—50th Anniversary Exhibition* (1963).)

David M. Sokol

ATLANTA. Between 1900 and 1920, Atlanta more than doubled its population (89,872 to 200,616) and its municipal boundaries. With rail connections to every remote corner of the South and to major northern cities, Atlanta became one of the nation's leading shipping and commercial centers. Often called "the metropolis of the South, and "a branch of New York," Atlanta was known for its energetic white "commercial-civic elite" who were devoted to the "New South Creed." The city's emerging black middle class, tied closely to Atlanta University, pursued an aggressive, if segregated, brand of "business progressivism." Yet, life for Atlanta's blacks was anything but "progressive," as evidenced by the bloody race riot of 1906 and the squalor of segregated housing in the southwest portion of the city.

Atlanta's municipal and political affairs often were overshadowed by actions of the state government, which made many of the crucial decisions affecting the city. In contrast to other cities of the era, Atlanta never experienced a concerted campaign for home rule.* Civic and congressional leaders often were more visible in municipal politics than were mayors and councilmen. The struggle over city school reform in 1914–1918 dissolved into a contest between the forces of U.S. Senator Hoke Smith* and Clark Howell, editor of the *Constitution*, two Democratic factions which represented the interests of both the city and the state. Atlanta also lacked an entrenched political machine that would-be reformers could attack. Except for the occasional appearance of loosely organized political pressure groups, no major reform organizations were influential in the city's development during this period. (Thomas M. Deaton, "Atlanta during the Progressive Era" (Ph.D. diss., University of Georgia, 1969); Eugene J. Watts, *The Social Bases of City Politics: Atlanta, 1865–1903* (1978); Wayne J. Urban, "Progressive Education in the Urban South: The Reform of Atlanta Schools, 1914–1918," in Michael H. Ebner and Eugene M. Tobin, eds., *The Age of Urban Reform: New Perspectives on the Progressive Era* (1977).)

David E. Alsobrook

ATLANTIC MONTHLY, THE. Founded in 1857 the *Atlantic Monthly* became the quintessential library-table magazine, literary as well as reform-minded. Its early editors, James Russell Lowell and James T. Fields, infused the magazine with a decidedly New England flavor. The editorship of William Dean Howells* (1881–1890) broadened the geographical background of contributors to include writers beyond the boundaries of New England, and particularly of Harvard University. As editor, Walter Hines Page* introduced a more vigorous style, and Bliss Perry (editor, 1899–1909) reaffirmed the magazine's tradition of genteel political reform. In Ellery Sedgwick's term as editor from 1909 to 1924, the small, elite circulation was enlarged as the *Atlantic* addressed more of the social and political issues of the day. Sedgwick had previously worked for S. S. McClure* and learned the commercial as well as ethical value of social concerns from the muckrakers. Throughout the Progressive Era, the *Atlantic's* title page carried its self-description: "A Magazine of Literature, Science, Art, and Politics." (Frank Luther Mott, *A History of American Magazines, 1850–1865* (1957, 1968); Bliss Perry, *And Gladly Teach* (1935); Ellery Sedgwick, *The Happy Profession* (1946).)

Salme H. Steinberg

AUSTRALIAN BALLOT. The term "Australian ballot" refers to the electoral use of the secret ballot, pioneered in Australian parliamentary elections and adopted by most American states by the late 1890s. Prior to the adoption of the Australian ballot, American elections were conducted by party ballot. Each political party printed ballots, listing only its own candidates, and distributed them to its followers, who deposited them at a polling place on election day. Though many elections were legally required to be secret, the distinctive appearance of each party's ballots made true secrecy impossible. The Australian ballot was first used in the United States at the 1888 municipal election in Louisville, Kentucky. That same year Massachusetts adopted it for all elections. American practice differs somewhat from the Australian, for the ballot is much longer, including elections for many offices, and party designations are usually included; but it retains the essentials of secrecy and public sponsorship. It was adopted so rapidly because it struck directly at the control of politics by party machines. (Spencer D. Albright, *The American Ballot* (1942); Elden C. Evans, *A History of the Australian Ballot in the U.S.* (1917); L. E. Fredman, *The Australian Ballot* (1968).)

Edward R. Kantowicz

B

BAILEY, LIBERTY HYDE (March 15, 1858–December 25, 1954). A country life philosopher, reform publicist, and horticulturist, Bailey taught horticulture at Michigan Agricultural College (1885–1888) and at Cornell University (1888–1903). From 1903 to 1913, he was dean of the New York State College of Agriculture at Cornell. While at Cornell, he pioneered farm extension work, nature study, and the inclusion of agricultural economics, rural sociology, and home economics in the curriculum of agricultural colleges. Bailey's views on education and his educational reform proposals, especially that education should involve experience and that schools should be community social centers, were very similar to the ideas John Dewey* was developing independently at the time. In 1908, Bailey served as chairman of President Roosevelt's Commission on Country Life* which became the important galvanizing event of the Country Life Movement.* He was also an ardent conservationist and a prolific writer who had a great impact on rural reform through his many books and articles. Among his influential books were *The Country-Life Movement* (1911) and *The Holy Earth* (1915). (Andrew D. Rodgers III, *Liberty Hyde Bailey* (1949); Phillip Dorf, *Liberty Hyde Bailey* (1956); George H. M. Lawrence, "Liberty Hyde Bailey, 1858–1954: An Appreciation," *Baileya* 3 (1955): 27-40; William L. Bowers, "Liberty Hyde Bailey's Philosophy of Country Life," *Baileya* 18 (1972): 145–59.)

                                                                    William L. Bowers

BAILEY V. DREXEL FURNITURE COMPANY, 259 U.S. 20 (1922). In 1922, this Supreme Court decision held the child labor tax unconstitutional. After *Hammer v. Dagenhart,** Congress imposed a 10 percent excise tax on the profits of any mine which employed children under fourteen, and any factory employing adolescents fourteen to sixteen years old for more than eight hours a day, six days a week, or between 7:00 P.M. and 6:00 A.M. Chief Justice William Howard Taft* delivered the majority opinion that the provisions of the act showed that Congress intended the law to regulate conditions of labor, not to raise revenue. Therefore, the principles in this case were indistinguishable from *Hammer v. Dagenhart*. Congress had no authority to use the tax power to "coerce" the people of a state "to act as Congress wishes them to act" in a matter which was "completely the business of the state government." The decision left the proponents of child labor reform with no recourse but to enter a long, exhausting, and fruitless effort to secure a constitutional amendment. (Stephen B. Wood, *Constitutional Politics in the Progressive Era: Child Labor and the Law* (1968); Robert W. McAhren, "Making the Nation Safe for Childhood: A History of the Movement for Federal Regulation of Child Labor, 1900–1938" (Ph.D. diss., University of Texas–Austin (1967).)

Robert W. McAhren

BAKER, NEWTON D. (December 3, 1871–December 25, 1936). He served as assistant to Postmaster General Woodrow L. Wilson from 1894 to 1897, and after practicing law in Martinsburg, he moved to Cleveland, Ohio. Baker became a legal adviser to the social reform Mayor Tom L. Johnson* in 1901, his law director until 1903, and city solicitor until 1912. He was the chief legal adviser to Johnson throughout his four-term struggle for municipal reforms. In 1911, Baker successfully campaigned for mayor on a Johnsonian platform of three-cent streetcar fares and a three-cent electricity rate. Baker was a leading advocate of home rule,* and under his leadership Cleveland secured a progressive charter. As mayor from 1912 to 1915, he secured his campaign promises and declined to run for a third term. In 1916 he became Secretary of War under President Woodrow Wilson,* and in 1921 he returned to his Cleveland law firm. He was mentioned as a possible candidate for the 1932 presidential nomination. (C. H. Cramer, *Newton D. Baker* (1961); Hoyt L. Warner, *Progressivism in Ohio, 1897–1917* (1964); Thomas F. Campbell, *Daniel E. Morgan: The Good Citizen in Politics 1877–1949* (1966).)

Thomas F. Campbell

BAKER, RAY STANNARD (April 17, 1870–July 12, 1946). Born in Lansing, Michigan, and educated at Michigan State, Baker began a career in journalism at the *Chicago News-Record* in the 1890s. From 1898 to 1906 he was a staff member at *McClure's*, where he helped pioneer the hard-hitting, fact-filled literature of exposure that President Theodore Roosevelt* soon branded "muckraking." In 1906, Baker with his associates Ida Tarbell* and Lincoln Steffens* left *McClure's* to found the *American Magazine*.* Meanwhile, using the pseudonym "David Grayson," he published the first of nine volumes of *Adventures in Contentment* (1907–1942) that eventually sold more than two million copies. Although sometimes criticized for reporting facts without conclusions, Baker during the *McClure's* years worked indirectly in support of Roosevelt's programs, notably the Hepburn railroad bill. While David Grayson and the *American Mag-*

azine celebrated the happier aspects of the American scene, Baker wrote a pathbreaking account of race relations in *Following the Color Line* (1908), and for a time flirted with socialism. In 1912, however, he supported Woodrow Wilson,* and devoted the remainder of his life to Wilsonian principles. (Ray Stannard Baker, *Native American* (1941); Ray Stannard Baker, *American Chronicle: The Autobiography of Ray Stannard Baker* (1945); Robert C. Bannister, *Ray Stannard Baker* (1966); John E. Semonche, *Ray Stannard Baker* (1969).)

Robert C. Bannister

BALCH, EMILY GREENE (January 8, 1867–January 9, 1961). Balch was a member of the first class to graduate from Bryn Mawr College. After graduate study at Harvard, the University of Chicago, and the University of Berlin, in 1896 she joined the faculty of Wellesley College, where she taught courses on immigration, socialism, and the labor movement. These reflected her background as a founder of Denison House, a social settlement, and her previous publications on juvenile delinquency and poor relief. Her best-known work is *Our Slavic Fellow Citizens* (1910), which is the classic study of Slavic immigration. While at Wellesley, Balch was among the founders of the National Women's Trade Union League* and campaigned for minimum wage legislation. In 1915, she was among the delegates from the International Congress of Women that tried to bring about mediation to end World War I.* In 1918, her social change and pacifist activities cost her her job with Wellesley College. (Mercedes M. Randall, *Improper Bostonian: Emily Greene Balch* (1964); Mercedes M. Randall, ed., *Beyond Nationalism: The Social Thought of Emily Greene Balch* (1972).)

Judith Ann Trolander

BALLINGER-PINCHOT CONTROVERSY. This 1910 controversy, one of the reasons for the rift between President William Howard Taft* and his predecessor, Theodore Roovevelt,* contributed to the split in the Republican party* in 1912, making possible the election of Democrat Woodrow Wilson.* Charges of malfeasance against Secretary of the Interior Richard A. Ballinger, though levied by a disgruntled employee, were sponsored by (and drafted in) the Forest Service,* an agency in the Department of Agriculture. When Chief Forester Gifford Pinchot* defied a presidential order to remain silent and publicly defended the role of his bureau in airing the charges, he was sacked by Taft. In the joint congressional investigation that ensued, Pinchot lost on the issues before a subcommittee voting along straight party lines, but proved more adept than Ballinger in making his case before the court of public opinion. The real issue was perpetuation of Pinchot's influence and control over federal resource policies. Under Roosevelt, he had functioned as a virtual secretary of conservation, minister-without-portfolio in a shadow cabinet. His attempt to continue in this role was blocked at every turn by Ballinger. The result was Pinchot's bid to discredit

Ballinger with Taft, and that failing, with the general public. (James Penick, *Progressive Politics and Conservation: The Ballinger-Pinchot Affair* (1968).)

James Penick

BALTIMORE. The Progressive Era in this city began in 1895 with a Republican defeating the mayoral candidate of the Democratic political boss, Issac Freeman Rasin. In its early stages, progressivism was characterized by journalistic muckraking and good government advocacy. In city and state politics, Baltimore reformers worked for honesty, efficiency, and economy. They wrote new city and school board charters; appointed professional public health officials, engineers, and school superintendents; introduced civil service reform; established a municipal research bureau; supported utility regulation; and began city planning. Major concerns of Baltimore progressives were child welfare and public health. The passage and enforcement of laws to limit child labor; require school attendance; inspect tenements, dairies, slaughterhouses, bakeries, and restaurants—along with the provision of playgrounds, kindergartens, public baths, and tuberculosis sanitoria—contributed to declining mortality rates. Baltimore's character and location as a border city resulted in three attempts to disfranchise black voters. All failed, in part because of a coalition of black and white Republicans, reform Democrats, and ethnic voters also fearful of being excluded. Still, Jim Crow laws were passed and progressive reforms were rarely enforced in the ghetto. (James B. Crooks, *Politics and Progress: The Rise of Urban Progressivism in Baltimore, 1895–1911* (1968); Sherry H. Olson, *Baltimore: The Building of an American City* (1980); and James B. Crooks, "Maryland Progressivism," in Richard Walsh and William Lloyd Fox, eds., *Maryland; A History, 1632–1974* (1974).)

James B. Crooks

BANK DEPOSITORS GUARANTY LAWS. These acts represent an ideological connection between progressivism, populism, and the New Deal. They also demonstrate the nationalization of reform in modern America. The idea of state-insured bank deposits first received significant support from Populists, but although many legislatures considered such programs, only Kansas,* Nebraska,* Oklahoma,* Mississippi,* North Dakota,* South Dakota,* Texas,* and Washington* enacted them during the Progressive Era. Oklahoma passed the first depositors guaranty law in 1907, while North Dakota and Washington were the last to act in 1917. Specific features of each plan varied, and because the Taft* administration would not allow national banks to participate, most national bankers opposed the law, as did most large banks and banks in states that permitted branch banking. As a result of these laws, small state banks proliferated and increased the amount of deposits they held during the Progressive Era, fulfilling the intention of the programs' most zealous supporters. All of the systems failed in the Troubled Twenties, but they provided precedents for the Federal Depositors Insurance Corporation, which Congress created in 1933. (Thomas Bruce Robb,

The Guaranty of Bank Deposits (1921); Eugene Nelson White, *The Regulation and Reform of the American Banking System, 1900–1929* (1983); Robert S. La Forte, "The Bank Depositors Guaranty Law of Kansas, 1909," in Burton J. Williams, ed., *Essays on Kansas History in Memoriam George L. Anderson, Jayhawker Historian* (1977).)

Robert S. La Forte

BANKHEAD, JOHN HOLLIS, SR. (September 13, 1842–March 1, 1920). Like Hoke Smith* of Georgia,* Park Trammell of Florida,* and Oscar W. Underwood* of Alabama,* John Hollis Bankhead, Sr., was among a host of southern "Progressives" who helped institute a variety of changes in the South during the early twentieth century. In 1886, when Bankhead was first elected to Congress from Alabama's Sixth Congressional District, populist causes were very appealing to many members of his rural constituency. Bankhead, however, often found statutory reforms less attractive than more indirect methods. He believed, for example, that the best way to harness the railroad monopoly was through competition and sponsored several bills that called for the canalization of harbors and rivers. Bankhead was one of the first congressmen to become active in the national good roads movement.* In 1898, he helped organize the North Alabama Good Roads Association, and ten years later, when he first ran for the U.S. Senate, his platform included a plank calling for federal subsidy of road building. His efforts at road reform led directly to passage of the Federal Aid Road Act of 1916* and to the more comprehensive Federal Highway Act of 1921.* (Margaret S. Koster, "The Congressional Career of John Hollis Bankhead" (M.A. thesis, University of Alabama, 1931).)

Howard L. Preston

BARUCH, BERNARD MANNES (August 19, 1871–June 20, 1965). Baruch was a Wall Street speculator, chairman of the War Industries Board* during World War I,* and a self-styled "elder statesman." Born in Camden, South Carolina, of German-Jewish parents, he moved to New York with his family and graduated from City College of New York in 1889. He worked at a wholesale firm for a time, but in 1891 he took a job with a stockbroker and soon showed an uncanny instinct for making money in the market. At age thirty-one he estimated he had gained $ 100,000 for each year of his life.

A supporter of Woodrow Wilson,* he served on various committees as a dollar-a-year man during World War I. On March 4, 1918, Wilson appointed him chairman of the War Industries Board (WIB). As a Wall Streeter, Baruch was familiar with industrialists but was not one of them himself. This gave him the right mix of knowledge and perspective to carry out his difficult task of coordinating war production without much legal enforcement authority. His success at the WIB marked the high point of his career. Thereafter, he promoted himself as an elder statesman, advising presidents from Franklin Roosevelt* to Lyndon Johnson, and frequently setting up his "office" on a park bench in

Lafayette Square, opposite the White House. (Bernard Baruch, *Baruch: My Own Story* (1957); Jordan A. Schwarz, *The Speculator: Bernard Baruch in Washington, 1917–1965* (1981); Robert D. Cuff, *The War Industries Board: Business–Government Relations During World War I* (1973).)

Edward R. Kantowicz

BEARD, CHARLES AUSTIN (November 27, 1874–September 1, 1948). Charles Austin Beard was a historian, political scientist, public administration consultant, and publicist. From 1898 through 1902, Beard lived in England, studying English constitutional and political history at Oxford University and joining in the establishment of a school for workers called Ruskin Hall. Returning to the United States in 1902, Beard took up graduate study at Columbia University, earning a master of arts in 1903 and a doctorate in 1904. That same year, Beard was appointed lecturer in the history department at Columbia under James Harvey Robinson,* with whom he became a collaborator on a successful textbook. With Robinson, Beard became identified as an exponent of the New History,* linking historical research to the social sciences and making it an element of reform. Leaving the Department of History for the Department of Public Law at Columbia in 1907, Beard gained national prominence and a measure of controversy for his 1913 *An Economic Interpretation of the Constitution of the United States* and his 1915 *Economic Origins of Jeffersonian Democracy.* He resigned from Columbia in 1917 in protest over the dismissal of three faculty members who opposed American participation in World War I.* From 1917 to 1922, Beard directed the Training School for Public Service of the New York City Bureau of Municipal Research. He joined in establishing the New School for Social Research in 1919. (Ellen Nore, *Charles A. Beard: An Intellectual Biography* (1983); Richard Hofstadter, *The Progressive Historians: Turner, Beard, Parrington* (1968); Howard K. Beale, ed., *Charles A. Beard: An Appraisal* (1954); Bernard C. Borning, *The Political and Social Thought of Charles A. Beard* (1962).)

Morey D. Rothberg

BEHRMAN, MARTIN (October 14, 1864–January 12, 1926). Behrman, a leader in New Orleans' Fifteenth Ward, was a founding member of the Choctaw Club of Louisiana. In 1898, he was a delegate to the state constitutional convention that disfranchised blacks. In 1900, he was reappointed assessor, and in 1904, he became state auditor, but subsequently was elected mayor of New Orleans as the regular Democratic candidate. Behrman won reelection in 1908, 1912, and 1916. His administration was noted for efficiency and economy, control of the police department, aid to streets and education, and the establishment of the Public Belt Railroad.

Although a supporter of labor early in his administration, Behrman cultivated business interests in later years and sought compromises with reformers. In 1912, he advocated the creation of a commission council. His administration, nonetheless, was characterized by machine politics, toleration of gambling and prostitution, and loose enforcement of liquor laws. In 1917, Behrman resisted the closing of Storyville, a legalized vice district. (John R. Kemp, ed., *Martin Behrman of New Orleans: Memoirs of a City Boss* (1977); George M. Reynolds, *Machine Politics in New Orleans, 1897–1926* (1936); Harold Zink, *City Bosses in the United States* (1931).)

Edward F. Haas

BELLAMY, EDWARD (March 26, 1850–May 22, 1898). Bellamy was born near Chicopee Falls, Massachusetts, and after working as a newspaper writer in the 1870s, he turned to fiction, writing four novels between 1878 and 1884. His novels and a philosophical piece, "The Religion of Solidarity" (1874), reflected an idealistic concern for an ethical and communal solution to social problems. In 1888, Bellamy published *Looking Backward*, a utopian novel that contrasted the socioeconomic inequality, poverty, and miseries of the late nineteenth century with the social harmony and well-being of an imaginary cooperative Christian commonwealth in the year 2000. *Looking Backward* was an immediate success, selling hundreds of thousands of copies. With Henry George's* *Progress and Poverty*, it was the most significant book in awakening the American social conscience in the years preceding the Progressive Era. The "Nationalist" social philosophy of *Looking Backward* stimulated the rise of Bellamy Nationalist Clubs in the early 1890s, which sought to transform American society from competitive individualism to a cooperative form of welfare socialism. Bellamy wrote a sequel, *Equality*, in 1897. (Sylvia E. Bowman, *The Year 2000: A Critical Biography of Edward Bellamy* (1979); Arthur E. Morgan, *Edward Bellamy* (1974); John L. Thomas, *Alternative America: Henry George, Edward Bellamy, Henry Demarest Lloyd and the Adversary Tradition* (1983).)

Peter J. Frederick

BEMIS, EDWARD W. (April 7, 1860–September 25, 1930). Bemis pioneered in university extension education in several midwestern cities before joining the faculty of Vanderbilt University in 1889. By the 1890s, he was a prolific writer on contemporary social issues and a founding member of the American Economic Association.* His "radical" views led to his dismissal from subsequent appointments at the University of Chicago* and Kansas State Agricultural College.

In 1901, reform Mayor Tom L. Johnson* invited Bemis to Cleveland to be the superintendent of the city's waterworks. Bemis developed an inadequate system into one that was admired nationally for its technical improvements and efficiency, which were reflected in a sharp drop in deaths from typhoid. His program of compulsory installation of water meters lowered consumer costs. In Mayor Johnson's battles for lower streetcar fares and utility rate decreases, Bemis appeared as an expert witness before courts and legislative bodies. His extensive writings on Cleveland's municipal reforms gave national publicity to Johnson's administration. Following Johnson's defeat in 1909, Bemis joined the New York administration of Mayor William J. Gaynor, but his exposure of waste and inefficiency resulted in his dismissal. Bemis continued to battle for efficiency and lower utility charges as a consulting engineer until his death. (Daniel M. Holgren, "Edward Webster Bemis and Municipal Reform" (Ph.D. diss., Case-Western Reserve University, 1963); Tom L. Johnson, *My Story* (1911); Lincoln Steffens, "Ohio: A Tale of Two Cities," *McClure's Magazine* 25 (July 1905): 293–311.)

                                                                    Thomas F. Campbell

BERGER, VICTOR LOUIS (February 28, 1860–August 7, 1929). Born in Nieder-Rehbach, Austria, Berger immigrated to the United States in 1878 and settled in Milwaukee, Wisconsin. By 1897 he had become the editor of the Wisconsin *Vorwärts* and was immersed in socialist politics. Berger's lifelong journalistic career as editor of the *Social Democratic Herald* (1900–1913) and the socialist Milwaukee *Leader* (1911–1929) was tangential to his political activities. He was a founder of the Social Democracy of America in 1897, the Social Democratic party in 1898, and the Socialist party in 1901. As socialism's leading revisionist, he advocated reforms through electoral politics in order to promote a collectivist society. He opposed orthodox Marxists who, in turn, called him an opportunist. In Milwaukee, he dominated the local Social Democratic party which was a major force in municipal politics for over thirty years. In 1910, Berger became the first socialist to be elected to the U.S. Congress. He cooperated with reformers while inserting a class perspective into congressional debates. In World War I,* his newspapers lost their second-class mailing privileges, and he was indicted under the Espionage Act* for his dissenting policies. After his conviction, Congress twice excluded him, but the Supreme Court overthrew his conviction and he served three more terms. (Victor L. Berger, *Broadsides* (1912); Sally M. Miller, *Victor Berger and the Promise of Constructive Socialism, 1910–1920* (1973); Edward John Muzik, "Victor L. Berger, A Biography" (Ph.D. diss., Northwestern University, 1960).)

                                                                    Sally M. Miller

BEVERIDGE, ALBERT JEREMIAH (October 6, 1862–April 27, 1927). A Progressive Republican* senator from Indiana,* Beveridge was best known as an advocate of American imperialism.* Long noted as a political orator, he delivered a speech entitled "The March of the Flag" on September 16, 1898, which made him famous and earned him an appointment to the U.S. Senate in 1899. Beveridge's jingoistic speech exalted American conquests during the Spanish-American War* and urged President William McKinley* to retain possession of the Philippine Islands.

During his two terms in the Senate (1899–1911), he drafted the Meat Inspection Act,* passed in 1906; opposed child labor; favored a tariff commission;* and continued to support American expansion and a strong navy. He was defeated in 1911 because of his opposition to President Taft* and the Payne-Aldrich

Tariff,* and he bolted the Republican party for the Progressive* ticket in 1912. Turning then to history, he published the ponderous *Life of John Marshall* in four volumes from 1916 to 1919. (George E. Mowry, *Theodore Roosevelt and the Progressive Movement* (1946); Claude G. Bowers, *Beveridge and the Progressive Era* (1932); John Braeman, *Albert J. Beveridge: American Nationalist* (1971).)

                                                                   Edward R. Kantowicz

BIRTH CONTROL . Large numbers of Americans limited their fertility during the nineteenth century through contraception, induced abortion, and sexual abstinence. Social leaders viewed the decline of fertility among native-born white women as a sign of social decay, however, and both state and federal laws were passed to suppress abortion and contraceptive practice. Between 1915 and 1925 a number of voluntary associations with such names as the American Birth Control League, the Voluntary Parenthood League, and the Committee on Maternal Health were created by middle-class social activists who organized to remove the legal and social taboos on contraception. Birth control advocates included civil libertarians concerned with the right of individuals to manage their sexuality, those who hoped that the ability to separate sex from procreation would promote stable families by strengthening erotic bonds between spouses and relieving economic pressures, and eugenicists alarmed by differential birthrates between classes and ethnic groups and hoping to "democratize" the restrictive habits already practiced by the Protestant middle classes.

Despite the association of birth control in the public imagination with feminism, sexual immorality, and antinatalism, a number of court decisions resulting from defiance of the legal prohibitions on contraception established the right of physicians to give contraceptive advice. The birth control movement made it easier for highly motivated women to pursue their self-interest; but its various organizations probably never enlisted more than 50,000 members, and their efforts had little impact on the differential fertility rates that concerned eugenicists. The movement's greatest accomplishments were the examples of feminist activism associated with Margaret Sanger* and the birth control clinics that she promoted. (James Reed, *The Birth Control Movement and American Society* (1984) and "Public Policy on Human Reproduction and the Historian," *Journal of Social History* 18 (March 1985): 383–97.)

                                                                         James Reed

BIRTH OF A NATION. D. W. Griffith's* controversial film, released on February 8, 1915, reflected the antiblack racial attitudes which were prevalent among white Americans during the Progressive Era. Based on Thomas Dixon's* racist novel and play *The Clansman*, the script depicted Reconstruction as a time of tragedy for white Southerners and used negative racial stereotypes to impute the responsibility to black Americans. The film's theme was that the American nation was born at the end of Reconstruction when the two warring white nations, the

Union and the Confederacy, with the Ku Klux Klan playing a major role, ended the attempt by blacks to gain equality and united to preserve white supremacy.

The NAACP* waged a long campaign to have the film banned, but this effort succeeded only in having about 500 feet of the most objectionable portions deleted. The *Birth of a Nation* had long and profitable runs before enthusiastic audiences in most major cities, partly because of the work of press agents but also because the film represented a significant advancement in the art of film making. (Thomas Cripps, *Slow Fade to Black: The Negro in American Film, 1900–1942* (1977); Daniel J. Leab, *From Sambo to Superspade: The Black Experience in Motion Pictures* (1975).)

Arvarh E. Strickland

BLACK AMERICANS. The problems faced by black Americans were not among the main concerns of Progressive reformers, but this largest of American minority groups did not go untouched by the ferment of this period. During the closing years of the nineteenth century, the southern states began disfranchising their black voters, and by 1910, black Americans had been effectively disfranchised by constitutional or other means in all of the southern states. In the wake of disfranchisement, the walls of segregation and caste were raised higher and higher by both law and custom. Between 1900 and 1911, laws requiring separation of the races in transportation facilities were passed in ten southern states. By 1910, custom in Atlanta* dictated that whites and blacks use separate elevators, and in 1915, the state of Oklahoma* passed a law requiring separate telephone booths. Several cities passed residential segregation ordinances, and in 1913, a movement began in North Carolina* to segregate farmlands. As politics closed as an avenue of racial advancement, many black leaders counseled turning to economic development as the best way to advance the race. Booker T. Washington* became the main articulator of this strain of black thought. Others, however, did not abandon the struggle for political and civil rights. W. E. B. Du Bois* came to represent this protest tradition in black thought.

The Progressive reformers helped to foster a climate of opinion that gave rise to interracial organizational efforts to better the conditions of black Americans. The National Association for the Advancement of Colored People* and the National Urban League* resulted from these efforts. One of the most significant developments in black American life during the Progressive Era, however, was the Great Migration, the movement of approximately 400,000 black people from the South into northern cities during World War I.* In 1900, 87.7 percent of the black population lived in the South, but by 1920, as a result of the Great Migration, this percentage had dropped to 85.2 percent. (John Hope Franklin, *From Slavery to Freedom: A History of Negro Americans* (1980); August Meier, *Negro Thought in America, 1880–1915: Racial Ideologies in the Age of Booker T. Washington* (1963).)

Arvarh E. Strickland

BLATCH, HARRIOT STANTON (January 20, 1856–November 20, 1940). Daughter of the famed feminist Elizabeth Cady Stanton and abolitionist Henry Stanton, Harriot Stanton Blatch facilitated reconciliation of the American and

National Woman Suffrage Associations in 1890 by recording the former's accomplishments in the multivolume *History of Woman Suffrage*. Her twenty years in England after she married British businessman William Henry Blatch in 1882 brought exposure to the Pankhursts and to socialist views she would later adopt. Blatch plunged into suffrage work anew on her return by launching the Equality League of Self-Supporting Women (later the Women's Political Union) in New York in 1907. The league organized thousands of factory women, pressured legislators, shattered precedent by holding open-air meetings and the first suffrage parades (1910), and inspired similar efforts in other states. Unable to work with Carrie Chapman Catt,* Blatch merged with Alice Paul's* Congressional Union and helped shape its political strategy. Blatch ardently supported American involvement in World War I,* served as head of the Food Administration's* Speakers' Bureau and a director of the Woman's Land Army, and supported the League of Nations.* (Harriot Stanton Blatch, with Alma Lutz, *Challenging Years* (1940); Inez Haynes Irwin, *The Story of the Woman's Party* (1921).)

Sidney Bland

BOAS, FRANZ (July 9, 1858–December 21, 1942). Boas was born at Minden, Westphalia, Germany. He made his first expedition to study the Eskimos of Baffinland in 1883–1884 and, for the next sixteen years, served in various positions in ethnographic and anthropological museums from Berlin to Chicago and New York and lectured on anthropology at Clark University in 1888. By 1892, he was chief assistant at the World Columbian Exposition; two years later he was curator at the Field Museum in Chicago. Joining the staff of the American Museum of Natural History in 1896, he became a lecturer at Columbia University, where he was a major force in the creation of the modern social science of anthropology.

A professor by 1899, Boas taught several generations of future and famous anthropologists including Margaret Mead, participated in the Jesup North Pacific Expedition which explored relationships between the North American aborigines and the Asian tribes, and published his three-volume work, the *Handbook of American Indians*. Boas inaugurated a reorientation of the discipline away from armchair theory and toward careful records of fact and scholarly monographs, ushered in an accent on empirical history, contributed to the development of functionalism, and discredited unilinear evolutionism with its easy assumption of the innate superiority of Western society. *The Primitive Mind* (1911) was a well-written attack on racism and evolutionism in anthropology. He also published *Primitive Act* (1927), *Anthropology and Modern Life* (1928), and *General Anthropology* (1938). Two years later he collected a selection of his significant articles as *Race, Language and Culture*. His scholarly activities ranged from a study of head-form for the Immigration Commission (1911) to lectures on primitive art to editing the *Journal of American Folk-Lore* (1908–1925) and founding the *International Journal of American Linguistics*. (George W. Stocking, Jr., ed., *The Shaping of American Anthropology 1883–1911: A Franz Boas Reader* (1974); Melville J. Herskovits, *Franz Boas: The Science of Man in the*

Making (1953); Leslie A. White, "The Ethnography and Ethnology of Franz Boas," *Bulletin of the Texas Memorial Museum* no. 6 (April 1963).)

Donald K. Pickens

BOK, EDWARD WILLIAM (October 9, 1863–January 9, 1930). Born in Helder, the Netherlands, Bok migrated to Brooklyn, New York, with his family at the age of seven. He was employed by Henry Ward Beecher and later headed the advertising department for the publisher Charles Scribner. At the age of twenty-five, Bok became the highest-paid editor in the United States when Cyrus H. K. Curtis appointed him to edit the *Ladies' Home Journal** in 1889. He married the boss's daughter, Mary Louise Curtis, in 1896.

Bok introduced many advertising innovations that assisted both advertiser and consumer. As he gained the trust of reader and advertiser, he also introduced the *Journal* audience to reform activities that were characteristic of progressivism and middle-class interests and concerns in the areas of consumer protection, the environment, and educational innovation. Although ambivalent about women's role in society, Bok gave space to proponents of woman suffrage. He befriended U.S. presidents and published such popular writers as William D. Howells,* Mark Twain, and Rudyard Kipling. His editorial and advertising innovations became standard in the magazine field. Bok left the *Journal* in 1919, and published a Pulitzer Prize–winning autobiography in 1920. (Salme Harju Steinberg, *Reformer in the Marketplace: Edward W. Bok and "The Ladies' Home Journal"* (1979); Edward W. Bok, *The Americanization of Edward Bok* (1920).)

Salme H. Steinberg

BONAPARTE, CHARLES JOSEPH (June 9, 1851–June 21, 1921). A paternal descendant of Napoleon Bonaparte, Bonaparte allied himself with state and local reform politics, and helped found the Baltimore Reform League, which brought him into contact with Civil Service Commissioner Theodore Roosevelt.* Bonaparte was a colorful personality who manifested an attractive independent streak. Roosevelt appointed him secretary of the navy in 1905, in part because of Bonaparte's intense patriotism, in part because Roosevelt knew Bonaparte shared his big navy, big battleship proclivities. In December 1906, Bonaparte became U.S. attorney general, a position in which he developed a national reputation as a trust-buster by bringing twenty antitrust suits. He especially won fame for work on the case dissolving the American Tobacco Company.* In March 1909, he returned to private practice in Baltimore, where he helped found the National Municipal League* and later served as its president. He also supported Roosevelt in his presidential bid in the election of 1912* and worked to unify the Republican party for the subsequent election of 1916.* (J. B. Bishop, *Charles Joseph Bonaparte: His Life and Public Services* (1922); E. F. Goldman, *Charles J. Bonaparte, Patrician Reformer: His Earlier Career* (1943); George

E. Mowry, *The Era of Theodore Roosevelt and the Birth of Modern America, 1900–1912* (1958).)

Wayne A. Wiegand

BORAH, WILLIAM E. (June 29, 1865–January 19, 1940). One of the Senate's great orators, "the Lion of Idaho" held office from 1906 until his death in 1940. Uncomfortable with the emerging urban and organizational character of American life, he was ambivalent about the role of government. He favored it as an enforcer of antitrust laws and protector of the "general interest," especially against big business, yet he worried about bureaucracy and threats to individual initiative and localism. Reforms that he especially supported included the federal income tax,* popular election of senators,* direct primaries,* prohibition,* and laws to protect workers.

Although his capacity to capture attention was great, his maverick qualities and tendency to place rhetoric ahead of action limited his effectiveness as a leader. His isolationist approach to world affairs was a complex mixture of nationalism and anti-imperialism. A supporter of American expansionism at the turn of the century, he increasingly warned that big business was responsible for interventionist policies aimed at protecting economic interests abroad. To Borah, America had to be "a great moral force, disentangled." He regretted his vote for America's entry into World War I,* and he opposed the League of Nations* as a dreaded entangling alliance and a prop for corrupt European empires. (Claudius O. Johnson, *Borah of Idaho* (1936); Marian C. McKenna, *Borah* (1961); LeRoy Ashby, *The Spearless Leader: Senator Borah and the Progressive Movement in the 1920's* (1971).)

LeRoy Ashby

BOSTON. By 1890 Boston had grown, through a series of annexations, to an area of thirty-nine square miles and a population of 560,892. The city counted 748,060 inhabitants in 1920, but its economy had been stagnant for some time and had begun to decline as textile mills from the surrounding area moved south. Still, Bostonians considered their city the "Hub of the Universe," a center of culture, learning, and traditional American values. The Puritan tradition of service to the community, however, had grown more defensive, as the founding of the Immigration Restriction League by a group of young Boston Brahmins in 1894 signified. A deep division between old-stock Yankees and Catholic Irish-Americans* dominated Boston life and politics. The Irish, who had arrived unwelcomed at the time of the potato famine in 1848, had begun to enter the middle class; but memories of "No Irish Need Apply" signs on Yankee factories and shops still rankled. The Yankees, for their part, feared the growing power and influence of the Catholic Church and labor unions.*

Contrary to popular myth, the Irish did not step off the boats and go directly to city hall. Not until 1884 did Hugh O'Brien become the first Irish mayor of Boston. For the next decade and a half, an alliance of rising Irish politicians and a handful of old-stock Yankee Democrats controlled city politics, with mayors such as Nathan Matthews* and Josiah Quincy fronting for the Irish. This tenuous coalition fell apart at the turn of the century, and a group of Irish Democratic ward bosses, such as Martin Lomasney* and John F. "Honey Fitz" Fitzgerald,* vied for power. Former mayor Nathan Matthews led the Good Government Association in revising the city charter in 1909 to reduce the influence of the ward bosses; but in the first election under the new charter in 1910, Fitzgerald defeated a blue-ribbon Yankee candidate. In 1914, James Michael Curley* won the first of several terms as mayor in his long and colorful career. The period ended with the bitter and divisive Boston Police Strike* of September 1919, which pitted the largely Irish police force against a Yankee governor and police commissioner. (Barbara M. Solomon, *Ancestors and Immigrants* (1956); Ronald P. Formisano and Constance K. Burns, *Boston 1700–1980: The Evolution of Urban Politics* (1984); John Koren, *Boston 1822–1922: The Story of Its Government* (1923); Howard Mumford Jones and Bessie Zaban Jones, *The Many Voices of Boston* (1975).)

Edward R. Kantowicz

BOSTON POLICE STRIKE. A labor walkout in September 1919, the Boston police strike was one of a series of spectacular strikes which followed World War I* and contributed to the Red Scare.* Underpaid and finding it hard to cope with rising postwar prices, the Boston police joined the American Federation of Labor* in the summer of 1919. Police Commissioner Edwin Upton Curtis declared this union affiliation illegal, and on September 8, 1919, he suspended nineteen officers for union membership. Commissioner Curtis rebuffed the advice of Mayor Andrew Peters and refused to compromise, so the police walked off the job on September 9. Violence and looting broke out, two people were killed, and Massachusetts Governor Calvin Coolidge called out the State Guard to keep order. Samuel Gompers,* president of the A. F. of L., called for arbitration of the strike, but Commissioner Curtis refused and began to recruit an entirely new police force. When Gompers asked Governor Coolidge to force arbitration, he declined, stating: "There is no right to strike against the public safety by anybody, anywhere, anytime." This strike illustrated the deep division between New England Yankees and the Boston Irish,* who made up most of the police force. It also showed the rabid fear of unions and radicalism which followed World War I. Cooligde's response to Gompers earned him a national reputation and resulted in his election as vice president in 1920. (Francis Russell, *A City in Terror: 1919, The Boston Police Strike* (1975); Frederick Lewis Allen, *Only Yesterday* (1931); William Allen White, *A Puritan in Babylon* (1938).)

Edward R. Kantowicz

BOURBONISM refers to the politics of the dominant Democrats of the post-Reconstruction South. Many of the leaders who overthrew Republican power were ultraconservative "Bourbons" in their glorification of the Confederacy, their emphasis upon white supremacy themes, and their willingness to do whatever was necessary to defeat opponents. Since white voters were in fact divided on various issues, control of black votes was essential to the preservation of conservative regimes; thus the planter-bosses of the Black Belts were important elements in Bourbon coalitions. Yet a number of prominent Bourbons were entrepreneurs based in the cities of the New South. Notably, Georgia's "Triumvirate" of Joseph E. Brown, Alfred H. Colquitt, and John B. Gordon virtually monopolized the high offices of the state from 1872 to 1890, at the same time engaging in railroad and other speculations. Bourbons believed in minimalist government, though some state administrations supported higher education and care of the handicapped. Bourbons bitterly opposed the demands of the Farmer's Alliance and People's Party (1880s–1890s). (C. Vann Woodward, *Origins of the New South, 1877–1913* (1951); Allen J. Going, *Bourbon Democracy in Alabama, 1874–1890* (1951); Jonathan Wiener, *Social Origins of the New South: Alabama, 1860–1885* (1978).)

Paul M. Pruitt, Jr.

BOURNE, JONATHAN, JR. (February 23, 1855–September 1, 1940). Bourne, born in Bedford, Massachusetts, arrived in Portland, Oregon, in May 1878. In addition to a law practice and business and real estate ventures, he became increasingly involved in state and national Republican politics. With his father's death in 1889, he inherited a considerable fortune, much of which he invested in silver and gold mines causing him to become a Bryan silverite in 1896. Elected to the Oregon House of Representatives that year, he organized a coalition of Republican, Democratic, and Populist legislators to block the reelection of Senator John Mitchell,* a gold Republican, resulting in the famous "Holdup" legislature of 1897. Beginning in 1902, he supported William S. U'Ren* in the passage of a series of democratic reforms known as the "Oregon System." In 1907, by means of one of these reforms, he became the first member of the U.S. Senate to be elected by popular vote. In 1911, he was a cofounder and first president of the National Progressive Republican League.* He was defeated for reelection to the Senate in 1912, but remained in Washington, D.C., as a Republican maverick. (Jonathan Bourne, "Popular versus Delegated Government," *Congressional Record*, 45, pt. 6, 61st Cong., 2d sess. (1910), 5823–30; Jonathan Bourne, "Oregon's Struggle for Purity in Politics," *Independent* 68 (June 23, 1910): 1374–78; Jonathan H. Pike, Jr., "Jonathan Bourne, Progressive" (Ph.D. diss., University of Oregon, 1957).)

Thomas C. McClintock

BOURNE, RANDOLPH (May 30, 1886–December 22, 1918). Randolph Bourne used his lyrical gifts to transcend a crippled body and become spokesman for rebellious youth of the Progressive Era. His undergraduate essays, *Youth and Life* (1913), vividly illustrated the spirit and dilemma of that rebellion. On the one hand, following his mentor, John Dewey,* Bourne advocated a socialized

state that would offer opportunity for each person to lead an "experimental life."
On the other hand, inspired by Walt Whitman and William James,* Bourne
placed individual will and expressiveness beyond the reach of any collective
authority. His "Transnational America" (1916) advocated a federation of distinct
immigrant cultures, while decrying the prevalent melting pot attempt to reduce
ethnic strains to a facsimile of the Anglo-Saxon. That same year, Bourne attacked
the Gary Plan* of education in the *New Republic*.*

Bourne's perplexity over the strain between creative impulse and organized
society climaxed in World War I.* Dismayed that Dewey and kindred reformers
could view that bloody conflict as an opportunity for Progressive expertise,
Bourne charged in "War and the Intellectuals" and "Twilight of Idols" that
pragmatism had proven worthless in time of crisis because it lacked values and
could merely adjust to dominant forces. Bourne died soon after the war's end.
His posthumous autobiographical fragment, "The History of a Literary Radical"
(1919), succeeded, however, in making him a prophet for postwar intellectuals
by advocating a "new criticism" that would seek the regeneration of culture
under the lead of artists within the American tradition. (Randolph Bourne, *War
and the Intellectuals*, ed. Carl Resek (1964); Edward Abrahams, *The Lyrical
Left: Randolph Bourne, Alfred Stieglitz, and the Origins of Cultural Radicalism
in America* (1986); Bruce Clayton, *Forgotten Prophet: The Life of Randolph
Bourne* (1984); Sherman Paul, *Randolph Bourne* (1966).)

                                                                    R. Alan Lawson

BOY SCOUTS OF AMERICA. General Robert Baden-Powell introduced
scouting's main features in Britain in 1908. The Boy Scouts of America (BSA)
was incorporated in 1910 and reorganized in 1911 under Chief Scout Executive
James E. West. The executive board consisted primarily of businessmen, some
with ties to Theodore Roosevelt.* West tried to make the BSA businesslike,
with centralized registration of scoutmasters and boys, a standardized program,
and salaried local scout executives. Claiming to solve adolescent problems, the
BSA limited enrollment to boys aged twelve through eighteen until the late
1920s, when Cub Scout experiments began. The BSA brought organized camping
to masses of boys nationwide for the first time. Scout leaders promised to teach
character and citizenship; a congressional charter in 1916, uniforms resembling
the army's, and highly publicized sales of World War I* bonds identified the
BSA with American patriotism. Protestant churches sponsored half the troops
in the 1910s. Despite rapid turnover in membership, the BSA claimed 391,000
boys by 1921—disproportionately middle-class but many from prosperous working-class families. The 33,000 scoutmasters were almost all white-collar employees, small businessmen, or professionals. (Jeffrey P. Hantover, "The Boy
Scouts and the Validation of Masculinity," *Journal of Social Issues* 34, no. 1
(1978): 184–95; David I. Macleod, *Building Character in the American Boy:*

The Boy Scouts, YMCA, and Their Forerunners, 1870–1920, (1983); Robert W. Peterson, *The Boy Scouts: An American Adventure* (1984).)

David I. Macleod

BRANDEIS, LOUIS DEMBITZ (November 13, 1856–October 5, 1941). Although not a holder of public office until his appointment to the Supreme Court in 1916, Brandeis was one of the most effective contributors to the reform efforts of the progressive years. After his mastery of law and the underlying facts combined with skillful advocacy had made him a wealthy man by his mid-thirties, he devoted himself to public service work, for which he often took no fees and quickly earned the title of "People's Attorney." Brandeis cared deeply and brought a moral fervor to his causes, whether exposing the abuses of the insurance industry and devising a plan for savings bank life insurance, or arguing causes for consumers, minority stockholders, or striking laborers.

To convince others, no matter what the forum, he amassed facts and statistics behind the position he defended. For instance, the so-called Brandeis brief was a response to the Supreme Court's claim in *Lochner v. New York** that the New York regulation of the hours bakers could work was unreasonable. So, in arguing the case for Oregon's limitation of the workday for women (see *Muller v. Oregon*),* Brandeis overwhelmed the justices with social and economic data, historical experience, and expert opinion, relegating legal precedents to less than two of the hundred pages. Drawing upon the findings of the Pujo Committee,* he exposed the control that investment bankers had over American industry in a series of magazine articles, published as *Other People's Money, and How the Bankers Use It* in 1914.

The advocate's visibility as a challenger of vested interests led his critics to label him a "radical." His ideas on the desirability of encouraging competition drew him to Woodrow Wilson,* and even before election the candidate tapped Brandeis's experience and knowledge in filling out the dimensions of the New Freedom* program. Although the advocate's alleged "radicalism" prevented his selection for the cabinet, Brandeis continued to advise President Wilson and played a significant role in the formation of the Federal Trade Commission* in 1914. To capture new support from progressives who had voted for Theodore Roosevelt* in 1912, Wilson nominated Brandeis to the Supreme Court, which brought vigorous protest from those who regarded him as a radical. Brandeis was accused of violating the ethics of his profession, although he personally felt that anti-Semitism animated the opposition. Although continuing his advocacy on the Court, Brandeis eventually won over his old adversary, William Howard Taft,* who headed the Court from 1921 to 1930. (Alfred T. Mason, *Brandeis: A Free Man's Life* (1946); Melvin I. Urofsky, *Louis D. Brandeis and the Progressive Tradition* (1981).)

John E. Semonche

BRECKINRIDGE, MADELINE MCDOWELL (May 20, 1872–November 25, 1920). Madeline McDowell was the great-granddaughter of Henry Clay. Her career as a progressive began in 1899 when she led the Gleaners of Christ Church

Episcopal in establishing a social settlement school in Beattyville, Kentucky. The following year she helped found the Associated Charities, which administered "scientific" charity by the casework method, and the Lexington Civic League, which initiated programs for city parks and playgrounds, public kindergartens, and manual training in the city's schools. Through the Civic League, she also worked for compulsory education* and child labor laws,* a juvenile court system,* and a "model" school in Irishtown, the poorest section of the city. She was extremely active in the movement to eradicate tuberculosis and participated in the Kentucky Federation of Women's Clubs campaign for improvements in the state's education system. Always using her husband's newspaper to advocate reforms, from 1905 to 1908 she edited a woman's page in the Sunday *Herald*. Contacts made through her sister-in-law, Sophonisba P. Breckinridge,* enabled her to bring many Chicago progressives to Lexington to speak. She directed lobbying efforts in 1908, 1910, and 1912 for passage of an act granting women the right to vote in school elections. Thereafter, she devoted most of her time to the cause of woman suffrage,* serving as president of the Kentucky Equal Rights Association from 1912 to 1915, and again in 1920 when Kentucky ratified the Nineteenth Amendment. (Melba Porter Hay, "Madeline McDowell Breckinridge: Kentucky Suffragist and Progressive Reformer" (Ph. D. diss., University of Kentucky, 1980); James C. Klotter, *The Breckinridges of Kentucky: Two Centuries of Leadership* (1986).)

Melba Porter Hay

BRECKINRIDGE, SOPHONISBA P. (April 1, 1866–July 30, 1948). After a short career as a high school teacher of mathematics, she attended the University of Chicago,* where she earned a Ph.D. in economics and political science in 1902. A short time later, she became one of the first women to receive a juris doctor degree from the University of Chicago, and the first woman to pass the bar exam in Kentucky. In 1906, she was asked to join the faculty of the Chicago School of Civics and Philanthropy, eventually becoming its dean. Under Breckinridge's leadership, the school, in 1920, became part of the University of Chicago, and was renamed the School of Social Service Administration.

It was from this position as a senior faculty member at the University of Chicago that Breckinridge became one of the most influential people in the development of social work as a profession and in the advancement of public welfare policy. During the Progressive Era, Breckinridge was a leading figure in the development of the juvenile court system* and the Mother's Pensions Movement.* She published numerous influential scholarly articles on these and related topics such as housing problems, and she wrote a number of books including *The Delinquent Child and the Home, The Family and the State*, and *Truancy and Non-Attendance in the Chicago Schools* (co-authored with Edith Abbott). Two themes were dominant in her published work and her many lectures: the state had an important role to play in the humanization of urban industrializing

America, and social workers needed a professional journal, the *Social Service Review*, published through the School of Social Service

Until 1920, she was a part-time resident of Jane Addams's* Hull House.* She was also active in the National Women's Trade Union League,* helping organize the Chicago garment trade strikes of 1910 and 1911. Breckinridge helped to organize and became the first secretary of Chicago's Immigrant Protective League.* She was active in the National American Woman Suffrage Association,* the Urban League,* and the National Association for the Advancement of Colored People.* (James C. Klotter, *The Breckinridges of Kentucky: Two Centuries of Leadership* (1986); Allen F. Davis, *Spearheads for Reform: The Social Settlements and the Progressive Movement, 1890–1914* (1967).)

Anthony Travis

BRISBANE, ARTHUR (December 12, 1864–December 25, 1936). A well-known journalist during the late nineteenth and early twentieth centuries, Brisbane was the son of Albert Brisbane, one of America's earliest advocates of utopian socialism. The younger Brisbane began his career as a journalist under Charles A. Dana of the New York *Sun*, eventually rising to the position of editor. In 1890, he abandoned Dana to work for Joseph Pulitzer* and the New York *World*, and seven years later he shifted his allegiance once again, this time to William Randolph Hearst.* As an editor for Hearst's New York *Tribune*, Brisbane became one of the nation's leading practitioners of yellow journalism. He developed such techniques as the large type headline, use of simple English, and a sensationalist approach.

Although Brisbane was regarded in some quarters as a reform editor, his primary goal was sales; therefore, he took whatever side of an issue he thought would make the best copy. He attacked all the progressive presidents while supporting the conservatives of the 1920s. Arthur Brisbane's syndicated column, "Today," became one of the most widely read and influential columns in the country, and his value to the Hearst empire was reflected in his salary, which rose to $250,000 per year. Brisbane's patriotism came under question, but the Hearst papers tended to be pro-German between 1914 and 1917. When America became directly involved, he shifted his editorial position and was able to clear himself. (Ray Vanderburg, "The Paradox That Was Arthur Brisbane," *Journalism Quarterly* 47 (1970): 281–86; Oliver Carlson, *Brisbane: A Candid Biography* (1937); Willard G. Bleyer, *Main Currents in the History of American Journalism* (1927).)

Kenneth E. Hendrickson

BRISTOW, JOSEPH LITTLE (July 22, 1861–July 14, 1944). As owner of the Salinas (Kansas) *Evening Journal*, Bristow became a leading member of the so-called Leland Political Machine during the 1890s and served as private secretary to Governor Edmund N. Morrill. An ardent supporter of William Mc-

Kinley,* he was appointed fourth assistant postmaster general in 1897. His investigations of the Cuban postal system reduced corruption during the American occupation, but when he uncovered dishonesty in the U.S. system, Theodore Roosevelt* forced him to resign in 1905.

He lost a bid for the U.S. Senate in 1906, but won the office in 1909 as a result of Kansas's first nonbinding primary. A leader of the state's progressive Republican faction, he became a prominent member of the Senate insurgency, developing close ties to Robert M. La Follette.* Bristow was best known for his opposition to William Howard Taft.* He helped lead the fights against the Mann-Elkins Act* and the Payne-Aldrich Tariff.* He authored the Seventeenth Amendment to the U.S. Constitution and introduced a woman suffrage* amendment that failed. After supporting La Follette's presidential effort which faltered in 1912, he reluctantly endorsed Roosevelt. He refused to join the Progressive party because he thought it futile. Without Progressive support in 1914, he lost the Republican nomination to Charles Curtis. Bristow served several years as a member of the Kansas public utilities commission before resigning to seek election once more to the Senate. He was overwhelmingly defeated in the primary of 1918 by Arthur Capper,* and moved to Fairfax County, Virginia, where he became a wealthy land developer. (A. Bower Sageser, *Joseph L. Bristow: Kansas Progressive* (1968); Kenneth W. Hechler, *Insurgency: Personalities and Politics of the Taft Era* (1940); Robert S. La Forte, *Leaders of Reform* (1974).)

Robert S. La Forte

BROOKS, VAN WYCK (February 16, 1886–May 2, 1963). Brooks was born in Plainfield, New Jersey, and educated in the public schools. Following his graduation from Harvard in 1907, he went to England and worked as a journalist for a year and a half during which time he published his first book, *The Wine of the Puritans*. Returning to New York, he was an editorial assistant to Walter H. Page* on the *World's Work.* In 1911 he went to Carmel where he was married, and from 1911 to 1913 he was an instructor in English at Stanford. In 1913 he again went to England, and it was there that he produced *America's Coming of Age*, perhaps the most important work of literary criticism of the Progressive Era, in 1915. In this book he provides his distinction between "Highbrow" and "Lowbrow," and demonstrates how American literature had embraced the "thin moral earnestness of the highbrow," a realm where real life was essentially rejected. This thesis received its most complete form in *The Ordeal of Mark Twain* in 1920. When the war began he returned to a position with the Century Company in New York and later served as associate editor of *The Seven Arts*. His *The Flowering of New England* received a Pulitzer Prize in 1937. (James Hoopes, *Van Wyck Brooks: In Search of American Culture* (1977);

Raymond Nelson, *Van Wyck Brooks: A Writer's Life* (1981); William Wasserstrom, ed., *Van Wyck Brooks: The Critic and His Critics* (1979).)

Robert W. Schneider

BROWNSVILLE AFFAIR. On August 3, 1906, a dozen black soldiers from the 25th U.S. Infantry, angered by racial harassment and discrimination, shot up the town of Brownsville, Texas. None of the men in the three black companies based at Brownsville would identify the guilty parties, so on November 5 President Theodore Roosevelt* dishonorably discharged all 160 men. Roosevelt had previously been considered a friend of the black race due to his highly publicized breakfast with Booker T. Washington* at the White House, but this affair outraged black sentiment. It also damaged relations between the president and Congress, for in January 1907 Senators Ben Tillman and Joseph Foraker* proposed a congressional investigation. Senator Foraker planned to run for president in 1908. As Republican candidates relied heavily on black patronage workers in southern states to secure nomination at the national convention, Foraker hoped his investigation would break Roosevelt's hold over the "black and tan" southern machines. The investigation, however, was postponed indefinitely and never held, Foraker's candidacy aborted, and the Brownsville affair faded away; but it may have hurt Roosevelt when he ran again in 1912 and found he had lost the black vote. (Emma Lou Thornbrough, "The Brownsville Episode and the Negro Vote," *Mississippi Valley Historical Review* 44 (1957): 469–93; James A. Tinsley, "Roosevelt, Foraker, and the Brownsville Affair," *Journal of Negro History* 41 (1956): 43–65; Ann J. Lane, *The Brownsville Affair* (1971).)

Edward R. Kantowicz

BRUERE, HENRY (January 15, 1882–February 17, 1958). A civic reformer in New York, the founder of the Bureau of Municipal Research,* Henry Bruere was born in Saint Charles, Missouri, and educated at Cornell and the University of Chicago. Pursuing social work and further education in Boston and Chicago, he finally settled on the field of municipal administration and moved to New York in 1905. He convinced Andrew Carnegie,* John D. Rockefeller,* and E. H. Harriman* to finance a Bureau of City Betterment, later renamed the Bureau of Municipal Research. Bruere's studies of Tammany Hall* payroll padding so irritated Tammany stalwarts that they called his agency the "Bureau of Besmirch." Bruere served as city chamberlain in the reform administration of Mayor John Purroy Mitchel* from 1914 to 1916. He shocked New Yorkers by resigning from office and recommending that his post be abolished. He devoted the rest of his life to business and financial affairs, serving as president of the Bowery Savings Bank from 1931 to 1952. He represented the wing of urban reform known as business progressivism, which believed in businesslike efficiency as the antidote to machine rule. (*New York Times* Obituary, February 19,

1958; Henry Bruere, *New City Government* (1912); Edwin R. Lewinson, *John Purroy Mitchel: The Boy Mayor of New York* (1965).)

Edward R. Kantowicz

BRYAN, WILLIAM JENNINGS (March 18, 1860–July 26, 1925). Born in Salem, Illinois, young Bryan obtained his ideas about democracy and religion from his parents. After graduating from Illinois College, Jacksonville, Illinois, he obtained a law degree from what is now Northwestern University. Unhappy in the law in Jacksonville, he moved to Lincoln, Nebraska, in 1890, and found the agricultural situation there extremely aggravated. He began his political career with demands for tariff and anti-monopoly reform.

Elected to Congress in 1890 and 1892, he first demanded tariff reform and then free silver at a ratio of sixteen to one because the latter would enable debtors to repay with inflated currency debts incurred during a period of rapid deflation. Prior to the Democratic national convention of 1896, Bryan spoke about a plethora of progressive issues but concentrated upon banking and currency reform, saying that political democracy could not exist without economic democracy. His preconvention politicking, plus his "Cross of Gold" speech, won him the Democratic nomination and he also obtained that of all other anti-McKinley parties. Arrayed against him were all the conservative forces of the press and of the business world, which condoned bribery and coercion in order to win votes for McKinley. Except for playing up the antitrust and anti-imperialism issues in 1900, Bryan ran essentially on his 1896 platform and was again defeated. In 1904 he permitted conservative Democrats to have their (disastrous) inning, but in 1908 he was renominated and defeated for the third time. For a generation thereafter he remained, through his voice and his personal newspaper, the *Commoner*, the liberal leader of the Democracy, a star on the Chautauqua Circuit, and a sponsor of conservative religion and prohibition.

In 1912 Bryan dropped his mantle upon Woodrow Wilson,* who made him his secretary of state. During his twenty-two months in that post, Bryan wrote thirty conciliation treaties and was the only cabinet member to be truly neutral with respect to the Great War. Meanwhile, on strategic gounds he made the Caribbean an American lake and the Central American states client nations. Bryan was a potent force in the passage of the Sixteenth through Twentieth Amendments to the Constitution and also in the passage of the New Freedom* legislation on tariff, banking and currency, and antimonopoly reform. Increasingly, however, he campaigned for a literal interpretation of the Bible and laws prohibiting the teaching of the theory of evolution as an established fact, culminating in the "monkey trial" at Dayton, Tennessee, in 1925. (Robert W. Cherny, *A Righteous Cause: The Life of William Jennings Bryan* (1985); Paolo

E. Coletta, *William Jennings Bryan*, 3 vols. (1964–1969); Louis W. Koenig, *Bryan: A Political Biography of William Jennings Bryan* (1971).)

Paolo E. Coletta

BRYCE, JAMES (May 10, 1838–January 22, 1922). (Viscount Bryce of Dechmont). Born in Belfast, Ireland, Bryce was enabled by family wealth to travel widely in the British Isles and on the Continent. His formal education began at Glasgow University in 1854, and in 1857, he entered Trinity College, Oxford. His outstanding academic record and family connections won him a seat in Parliament. Three visits to the United States (1870, 1881, and 1883) resulted in his widely acclaimed *American Commonwealth* (1888). The work reflected on the political issues and organizations of the 1880s but did not explore the basic reasons for the success of American political machines. Although he was sympathetic to the plight of black Americans, he did not challenge the status quo. Because his writing about America revealed his admiration for the nation, he was very popular in the United States. Theodore Roosevelt admired Bryce's work, and when Bryce was appointed British ambassador to the United States, the two became good friends. In 1889 he married Marion Ashton. (Herbert A. L. Fisher, *James Bryce* (1927); Edmund S. Ions, *James Bryce and American Democracy: 1870–1922* (1970).)

David J. Maurer

BUCK'S STOVE AND RANGE COMPANY CASE (*Buck v. Beach*, 206 U.S. 392 (1907)). This case strengthened the common-law principle that boycotts conducted by organized labor constituted criminal conspiracy, and it subordinated the constitutional principles of free speech where such conspiracy was shown to have existed. The contest, played out in the courts between 1907 and 1914, pitted Samuel Gompers* and the leaders of the American Federation of Labor* against J. W. Van Cleave, president of Buck's Stove and Range Company of Saint Louis and, between 1906 and 1909, president of the stridently antiunion National Association of Manufacturers.*

The origins of this case lay in a labor dispute between the Metal Polishers Union and the Buck's Stove and Range Company in 1906. Union members, demanding a nine-hour day, ceased working longer hours. When union leaders were fired, members of the union struck the firm. When the firm's name appeared on the "We Don't Patronize" list of the American Federation of Labor, the strike itself was quickly overshadowed by a legal battle over the boycott instituted by the A. F. of L. in support of the striking metal polishers. The company filed a complaint in the Supreme Court of the District of Columbia on August 19, 1907, and on December 18 the court issued a temporary injunction prohibiting local union officers and the leaders of the A. F. of L. from carrying out the boycott. That injunction was made permanent on March 23, 1908. In December 1908 A. F. of L. officers Samuel Gompers, John Mitchell,* and Frank Morrison were declared in contempt of court for continuing activities on behalf of the boycott.

In subsequent rulings the Court of Appeals sustained the injunction, while narrowing its scope, and rejected the defendants' First Amendment defense by holding that rights of free speech and free press did not apply in cases of criminal conspiracy. The death of Van Cleave in 1909 and changes in the firm's management brought a termination of the dispute between the Buck's Stove Company and the union and dismissal of the case on the issue of the injunction. The question of the criminal contempt of the A. F. of L. leaders for violating the injunction remained. Gompers, Morrison, and Mitchell faced prison sentences and fines for their speeches and publications in defiance of the injunction. Finally, in 1914, the Supreme Court dismissed the contempt cases on the grounds that the statute of limitations had been exceeded. (Leo Wolman, *The Boycott in American Trade Unions* (1916); Charles O. Gregory, *Labor and the Law* (1949); Barry F. Helfand, "Labor and the Courts: The Common-Law Doctrine of Criminal Conspiracy and Its Application in the Buck's Stove Case," *Labor History* 18, no. 1 (1977): 91–114.)

Shelton Stromquist

BUNTING V. OREGON (243 U.S. 426 (1917)). By a five-to-three decision, the Supreme Court in this case upheld Oregon's right to establish a ten-hour workday for all persons in the state's mills and manufacturing establishments and to allow up to three hours of overtime labor at the rate of one and one-half times the normal hourly wage. The ruling virtually overruled the infamous *Lochner** decision of 1905 in which the Court, by a five-to-four count and utilizing the liberty of contract doctrine, pronounced New York's attempt to regulate the workday for bakers an unreasonable exercise of the state's police power. Substituting its judgment for that of the state legislature, the Court provoked a storm of opposition from those critics who felt that government interference was necessary to redress clear imbalances in the bargaining relationship between employers and employees. In 1917, responding to the type of factual brief that Louis D. Brandeis* had made famous in his earlier successful defense of Oregon's law regulating the hours women could work (see *Muller v. Oregon*), the Court rejected the notion that it should inspect the reasonableness or wisdom of the law. Instead, Justice Joseph McKenna, for the majority, found considerable constitutional room for the state's police power to operate. However, the conclusion that *Bunting* had overruled *Lochner* was premature, for the 1920s Court would find new life in the old decision. (Alexander M. Bickel and Beno Schmidt, Jr., *Oliver Wendell Holmes Devise History of the Supreme Court of the United States*, vol. 9; *The Judiciary and Responsible Government, 1910–21* (1984), 592–604; Harlan B. Phillips, *Felix Frankfurter Reminisces* (1960), 94–103.)

John E. Semonche

BUREAU OF CORPORATIONS. The Bureau of Corporations was established as a division of the Department of Commerce and Labor* in 1903, on a recommendation of the U.S. Industrial Commission. The purpose of the bureau was to investigate corporations and publish those findings which the president had approved. These reports could then be used to develop legislation or to restrain illegal practices by threat of publication. There were no specific guidelines for the bureau's operations nor instructions as to what business practices it could study or how it might enforce the Sherman Antitrust Act.

Originally, the lack of specifics gained support from small and middle-sized businessmen who saw the bureau as a means of limiting competition with big trusts and monopolies, but the first chairman, James R. Garfield,* thought that the bureau should investigate illegal competition and oversee the formation of combinations, thus preventing as many illegal activities as possible. The bureau investigated the use of public timber lands and conducted an inventory of the nation's water capacity. It also came under public and congressional pressure to investigate the enforcement of the Sherman Antitrust Act, but lacked legal power to initiate judicial proceedings. The bureau very much reflected the economic philosophy of Theodore Roosevelt,* who preferred regulation of trusts to their breakup. Roosevelt saw the commission's task as one "which should neither excuse nor tolerate monopoly, but prevent it when possible and uproot it when discovered," and he believed it should apply to large and small corporations alike. (James Weinstein, *The Corporate Idea in the Liberal State: 1900–1918* (1968); Arthur M. Johnson, "Theodore Roosevelt and the Bureau of Corporations," *Mississippi Valley Historical Review* 45 (1959): 571–90; Robert H. Wiebe, *Businessmen and Reform* (1962).)

Albert Erlebacher

BUREAU OF MUNICIPAL RESEARCH, THE. The Bureau of Municipal Research (BMR) was incorporated in New York City in 1907, succeeding the Bureau of City Betterment created by the Citizens Union* in 1905. Although largely financed by the wealthy civil reformer R. Fulton Cutting and industrialists Andrew Carnegie* and John D. Rockefeller,* the BMR was the brainchild of reform-minded professionals William H. Allen, Frederick A. Cleveland, and Henry Bruere.* These progressives sought to shift the focus of reform away from changing the governing personalities to helping city officials administer more effectively and efficiently. The BMR and its staff of experts worked with municipal officeholders to evaluate city needs and services; apply standardized budgeting, accounting, and other business and scientific management procedures to public administration; professionalize governmental personnel; and increase executive authority. In addition, the BMR aided in the organization of research bureaus in cities across the nation; produced a literature of public administration, including the magazine *Municipal Research*; opened the Training School for Public Service in 1911; helped in the establishment of the New York Municipal Reference Library in 1913; and inspired universities to develop graduate programs in public administration. In 1921, the training school and BMR were reorganized as the National Institute of Public Administration. (Norman N. Gill, *Municipal Research Bureaus* (1944);

Jane S. Dahlberg, *The New York Bureau of Municipal Research* (1966); Martin J. Schiesl, *The Politics of Efficiency: Municipal Administration and Reform in America, 1880–1920* (1977).)

Augustus Cerillo, Jr.

BURLESON, ALBERT SIDNEY (June 7, 1863–November 24, 1937). Born in San Marcos, Texas, Burleson came from a prominent family. (His grandfather had been vice president of the Texas Republic in the 1840s.) From 1899 to 1923, Burleson served in Congress, where he was known as an able legislator, fierce Democratic party loyalist, and zealous guardian of the interests of the cotton growers of his district. An early supporter of Woodrow Wilson,* he directed the Speakers' Bureau during the campaign of 1912. As postmaster general throughout Wilson's two terms in office, Burleson adroitly manipulated patronage to assure the president's control over established Democratic organizations. He promoted efficiency and innovation in postal operations, expanding the postal savings system, rural mail service, and parcel post system; he also established an extensive government-owned and -operated urban postal truck service and a pioneering coast-to-coast air mail service. He argued—unsuccessfully—for government ownership of the telephone and telegraph systems. Burleson came under attack for his unsympathetic attitude toward organized labor and blacks and for his heavy-handed operation of the wartime censorship system. He was an opponent of the Ku Klux Klan and supporter of Al Smith* during the 1920s. (*Dictionary of American Biography*, vol. 22; Lewis L. Gould, *Progressives and Prohibitionists: Texas Democrats in the Wilson Era* (1973); William M. Leary, *Aerial Pioneers: The U.S. Air Mail Service, 1918–1927* (1985).)

William M. Leary

BURNHAM, DANIEL HUDSON (September 4, 1846–June 1, 1912). Architect, city planner, leading advocate of the City Beautiful* movement, Burnham began work in 1891 as chief of construction for the World's Columbian Exposition of 1893. Burnham organized the work of numerous architects into a harmonious whole, with most of the buildings at the fairgrounds designed in a monumental, neoclassic style. Following the success of the World's Fair, Burnham applied the principles of symmetry, monumentality, and classical harmony to city planning. He served as chairman of the Senate Park Committee which restored the L'Enfant Plan for Washington, D.C., in 1901. He prepared plans for San Francisco* and for Manila in the Philippines, then in 1909 he unveiled his most ambitious work, the Plan of Chicago. Though Burnham's plan for broad boulevards, sweeping vistas, and harmonious classical architecture was only partially realized, it has influenced the development of Chicago ever since. Burnham's famous dictum, "Make no little plans," epitomized the spirit of Chicago. (Daniel H. Burnham and Edward H. Bennett, *Plan of Chicago* (1909);

Charles Moore and Daniel H. Burnham, *Architect, Planner of Cities* (1921); Thomas S. Hines, *Burnham of Chicago*(1974).)

Edward R. Kantowicz

BURNS, LUCY (July 28, 1879–December 22, 1966). Born in Brooklyn, New York, Burns was educated locally at the Packer (Collegiate) Institute and at Vassar College. She pursued graduate work for several years at Yale (1902–1903) and the universities of Bonn and Berlin (1906–1909). While at Oxford in 1909, she met the Pankhursts and was soon working full-time with the English suffrage militants. Burns served as a salaried organizer in Scotland from 1910 to 1912; she earned a medal of valor following several arrests and prison hunger strikes. Burns returned to the United States and, with Alice Paul* (the two met in England), became head of the congressional committee of the National American Woman Suffrage Association.* In 1914 they broke with the conservative suffrage group to form a rival national organization, the Congressional Union (after 1917 the National Woman's Party*), to work solely for a federal amendment. Burns's tasks for the Woman's party included spearheading early lobby efforts, organizing western women against the Democratic party in 1914 and 1916, and editing its newspaper, the *Suffragist* (1915–1916). She headed the well-publicized demonstrations against President Woodrow Wilson* during World War I* and was frequently jailed. After ratification of the Nineteenth Amendment, Burns retired to Brooklyn to pursue family and church activities. (Inez Haynes Irwin, *The Story of the Woman's Party* (1921); Doris Stevens, *Jailed for Freedom* (1920); Sidney R. Bland, " 'Never Quite as Committed as We'd Like': The Suffrage Militancy of Lucy Burns," *Journal of Long Island History* 17, no. 2 (Summer/Fall 1981): 4–23.)

Sidney Bland

BUTLER, NICHOLAS MURRAY (April 21, 1862–December 7, 1947). Educated at Columbia University and the University of Berlin, Butler founded the New York College for the Training of Teachers, which, in 1891, affiliated with Columbia University as Teachers College. He founded the *Educational Review* in 1891 and served as its editor until 1919. He was also influential in the National Education Association* from the 1880s until 1910 and was a founder of the College Entrance Examination Board in 1900. He led the good government reform group that centralized the administration of the New York city schools in the 1890s. He became president of Columbia University in 1901 and served in that position for over twenty years. During his tenure as president, Columbia grew and prospered as a university, but Butler was also involved in the dismissal of James McKeen Cattell* because of his opposition to American participation in World War I.* In addition to his educational duties, Butler was active in Republican party politics at the state and national levels, was an intimate of Theodore Roosevelt,* a close adviser to William Howard Taft* and to Warren G. Harding,* and an avid writer on political affairs and on international relations.

(N. M. Butler, *Across the Busy Years*, 2 vols. (1939); Richard Whittemore, *Nicholas Murray Butler and Public Education* (1970); Albert Marrin, *Nicholas Murray Butler* (1976).)

Wayne J. Urban

C

CALIFORNIA. California joined the ranks of the progressive states in 1910 with the election of Hiram Johnson* as its governor. Johnson, an attorney from San Francisco* who had aided in prosecuting the Ruef machine, campaigned on an antirailroad, anticorruption platform and had secured the support of a number of urban middle-class reform groups such as the Lincoln-Roosevelt League.* The 1911 legislature secured the passage of over three hundred measures ranging from the establishment of enforceable regulatory laws for railroads and utilities to the passage of the initiative,* referendum,* and recall* plus a strengthened direct primary bill,* a minimum wage law, and an eight-hour day measure for women. Woman suffrage,* civil service,* a pure food and drug law, and tax reform* were added to the list of accomplishments. Theodore Roosevelt* described the 1911 California legislative session as "the most comprehensive program of constructive legislation ever passed at a single session of any American legislature." In 1912 Governor Johnson became Roosevelt's vice presidential candidate on the Progressive party ticket. The original thrust of the California progressives had been aimed at the Southern Pacific Railroad and at what they considered to be special public utilities interest groups. With the passage of the Public Utilities Act in 1911 and its implementation in 1912, California reformers expanded their reform program to include a broad range of social and labor reforms such as a workmen's compensation* law. The reelection of Johnson as governor in 1914 indicated the shifting of support in the progressive movement from southern California rural and business groups to urban ethnic and labor groups, especially in the northern part of the state.

In 1916, Johnson was elected to the U.S. Senate, and he reluctantly turned over the governorship to his successor, Lieutenant Governor William D. Stephens, but California's brand of progressive reform remained very much alive. During Stephens's tenure as governor, new regulatory agencies were created; innovative highway, irrigation, and conservation programs were developed; and new policies in governmental management, taxation, budgeting, and accounting were adopted. In their search for a more democratic and more efficient system of government, the progressives had, through their direct democracy reforms, shattered the traditional political alliances and parties. (George E. Mowry, *The California Progressives* (1951); Spencer C. Olin, Jr., *California Politics, 1846–1920: The Emerging Corporate State* (1981); Spencer C. Olin, Jr., *California's Prodigal Sons: Hiram Johnson and the Progressives, 1911–1917* (1968); Jackson K. Putnam, *Modern California Politics*, 2d ed. (1984); Michael P. Rogin and John L. Shover, *Political Change in California: Critical Elections and Social Movement, 1890–1966* (1970).)

Jack D. Elenbaas

CANADIAN RECIPROCITY refers to a free-trade treaty negotiated between Canada and the United States in 1911 but never ratified by Canada. Trade between the United States and Canada was highly complementary, with Canada exporting farm produce in exchange for U.S. manufactured goods; an earlier reciprocity treaty had been in effect from 1855 to 1866. In January 1911, Secretary of State Philander C. Knox* negotiated a treaty which removed tariffs from most agricultural goods and a long list of manufactures. President William Howard Taft* called a special session of Congress in April 1911 and, over the opposition of Republican Insurgents* from farm states in the West, secured ratification. Progressives denounced Taft for favoring businessmen over farmers. This widened the Insurgent/Conservative split in the Republican party and made Taft's reelection in 1912 virtually impossible.

Ironically, all the president's efforts proved fruitless, for Canada refused to ratify the treaty. Reciprocity proved an even more emotional issue in Canada than in the United States, for free trade over the border aroused Canadians' fears of eventual absorption and annexation by their giant American neighbor. Outraged Canadian nationalism stymied the reciprocity treaty and defeated the Liberal party government of Sir Wilfred Laurier, which had proposed it. (L. Ethan Ellis, *Reciprocity, 1911* (1939); George E. Mowry, *Theodore Roosevelt and the Progressive Movement* (1946); Henry F. Pringle, *The Life and Times of William Howard Taft* (1939).)

Edward R. Kantowicz

CANNON, JOSEPH GURNEY (May 7, 1836–November 12, 1926). Cannon was the longtime Republican Speaker of the House whose archconservatism and tyrannical control of the House became a lightning rod for congressional Insurgents.* He was first elected to Congress from Illinois in 1872, defeated in 1890, then reelected in 1892. He became Speaker of the House in 1901 and strongly opposed most progressive legislation, using the Speaker's formidable power to appoint all members of committees, including the Rules Committee. During the administration of William Howard Taft,* a coalition of Democrats and Insurgent Republicans opposed ''Cannonism.'' In March 1910, they voted new rules for the House which broke the Speaker's power over the Rules Committee. Cannon remained as Speaker until the end of the session when the Democrats captured control of the House, then was defeated in his Illinois district in 1912. He returned to the House, but not to the Speakership, in 1914, finally retiring in 1923. The revolt against Cannonism marked a crucial step in the growth of Republican Insurgency, leading to the formation of the Progressive party.* (William R. Gwinn, *Uncle Joe Cannon* (1957); Kenneth W. Hechler, *Insurgency: Personalities and Politics of the Taft Era* (1940); John D. Baker, "The Character of the Congressional Revolution of 1910," *Journal of American History* 60 (1973):679-91.)

                                                                Edward R. Kantowicz

CAPPER, ARTHUR (July 14, 1865–December 19, 1951). Born in Garnett, Kansas, Arthur Capper ended his formal education upon graduation from high school. He purchased his first newspaper in 1893 and, ultimately, controlled at least twenty-seven publications, the best known being the widely read farm journal *Capper's Weekly* and the Topeka *Daily Capital*. He also owned radio stations in Topeka and Kansas City, Kansas. A steadfast Republican, he became increasingly involved in politics during the Progressive Era. His first and only electoral defeat was in 1912 when he lost the governor's race by twenty-nine votes to the Democrat George Hodge. Two years later he reversed the results and was reelected in 1916.

Capper was the first native-born Kansan to serve the state as governor and U.S. Senator. He overwhelmed William R. Stubbs and Joseph L. Bristow,* two former progressive friends, in the Republican primary in 1918 and easily defeated the Democrat William H. Thompson. As governor, he selectively supported what remained of the progressive agenda, while compromising with resurgent regulars who controlled the party. Thus, he favored the woman suffrage amendment and prohibition, but opposed expansion of the initiative* and referendum* law. A mild-mannered, shy person, Capper was a masterful campaigner, the most popular man in the state's political history, and in general a true reflection of his constituents' dreams and aspirations. (Homer E. Socolofsky, *Arthur Capper: Publisher, Politician, Philanthropist* (1962); Homer E. Socolofsky, "The Capper Farm Press," University Microfilms (1954); Robert S. La Forte, *Leaders of Reform* (1974).)

                                                                Robert S. La Forte

CARNEGIE, ANDREW (November 25, 1835–August 11, 1919). Born in Dunfermline, Scotland, the son of a hand-weaver, Carnegie migrated to Allegheny, Pennsylvania, in 1848. He worked as a bobbin boy, telegraph messenger and operator, private secretary, railroad executive, bond salesman and investor, and built a fortune on the basis of "insider" information. From 1873 on, he applied cost-accounting management techniques, a mania for efficient organization, and a determination to finance growth and expansion from internal profits to the steel business; entered a partnership with Henry Clay Frick, the "Coke King," in 1882; and, by the late 1880s was the leading American steel producer. In 1892, by being out of the country, he avoided some of the opprobrium from the violence of the strike in his Homestead plant.

In the 1880s, he began a career as an author and lecturer, developing his ideas about "The Gospel of Wealth" (first published in 1886) and the responsibilities of the very rich in a democratic society. In 1901, he sold all his steel holdings to the newly formed United States Steel Corporation (for nearly $400 million), and, until his death, devoted himself to the continuing exposition of progressive views on the responsibilities of wealth, and to philanthropic interests including the Carnegie Endowment for Peace, massive educational programs, and the Carnegie libraries. (Joseph F. Wall, *Andrew Carnegie* (1970); Harold C. Livesay, *Andrew Carnegie and the Rise of Big Business* (1975); Andrew Carnegie, *Triumphant Democracy* (1886), *The Gospel of Wealth and Other Timely Essays* (1901), and *Problems of To-Day; Wealth, Labor, Socialism* (1909).)

James Oliver Robertson

CARVER, GEORGE WASHINGTON (1864(?)–January 5, 1943). Born in Diamond, Missouri, near the close of the Civil War, Carver was the son of a slave owned by Moses and Susan Carver. Orphaned in infancy, he was raised by his former owners. He entered Simpson College in 1890, and after a year there, transferred to Iowa State University, where he earned both bachelor's and master's degrees. Upon graduation in 1896, he accepted Booker T. Washington's job offer at Tuskegee Institute in Alabama. There he headed the agricultural department and established an agricultural experiment station. Remaining there until his death, Carver engaged in research and extension work in the mainstream, and sometimes in the forefront, of the scientific agriculture movement at the turn of the century. Plagued by low funding, he sought inexpensive solutions to the plight of poor farmers. He became interested in peanuts as a high protein substitute for meat, was adopted as a publicist for the peanut industry in the 1920s, and became known as the "peanut man." His fame as a "creative chemist" obscured his earlier, important work, and he became a symbol for a myriad of causes, including black advancement and segregation. (Linda O. McMurry, *George Washington Carver: Scientist and Symbol* (1981); Rackham Holt, *George Washington Carver: An American Biography* (1943).)

Linda O. McMurry

CATHER, WILLA S. (December 7, 1873–April 24, 1947). Born in Virginia, Cather moved to Nebraska at the age of ten, settling with her parents and family near Red Cloud. Cather attended the University of Nebraska from 1890 to 1895, learning her craft and writing numerous articles for local newspapers. She became a schoolteacher, then editor of *McClure's Magazine* (1906–1912), just following its "muckraking" period. In 1912, she published her first novel, *Alexander's Bridge*, and from that time devoted herself to full-time writing. Three important novels established her position as a major author: *O Pioneers!* (1913), *The Song of the Lark* (1915), and *My Antonia* (1918). The first and the third of these, in particular, along with a host of short stories, depict the plight of the farmer on the Nebraska "Divide" during the 1880s and 1890s. Cather was an admirer of William Jennings Bryan* and was emotionally in tune with the Populist movement. In 1923, her novel *One of Ours* was awarded the Pulitzer Prize. Among other accomplishments, Cather is remembered as one of the most important stylists in American literature. (Bernice Slote, "Willa Cather," in Jackson R. Bryer, ed., *Sixteen Modern American Authors* (1973), 29–73; David Stouck, *Willa Cather's Imagination* (1975).)

Philip Gerber

CATT, CARRIE CLINTON LANE CHAPMAN (January 9, 1859–March 9, 1947). Catt was born in Ripon, Wisconsin, grew up in Iowa, and graduated from Iowa State College in 1880. After the death of her first husband, Leo Chapman, a newspaperman, she became a lecturer for the Iowa suffrage society and the temperance movement in 1886. She was remarried in 1890 to George W. Catt, a civil engineer, who warmly supported her reform activities. His death in 1905 left her financially independent. Catt was present in 1890 at the founding of the National American Woman Suffrage Association* (NAWSA) and rapidly ascended to positions of leadership, succeeding Susan B. Anthony as president in 1900. Forced by personal problems to resign in 1904, she dropped out of the national movement for a decade, devoting herself to New York suffrage work and to the International Woman Suffrage Alliance. When she was again elected president of the NAWSA in 1915, her organizational genius and political acumen became essential ingredients in the passage of the Nineteenth Amendment. She was instrumental in founding the League of Women Voters* and played a prominent role in the interwar world peace movement. (William L. O'Neill, *Everyone Was Brave: The Rise and Fall of Feminism in America* (1969); Edward T. James, et al., eds., *Notable American Women*, vol. 1 (1971); Mary Gray Peck, *Carrie Chapman Catt* (1944).)

Paul E. Fuller

CATTELL, JAMES MCKEEN (May 25, 1860–January 20, 1944). Pioneer American psychologist, editor of science magazines, and academic reformer, Cattell was born at Easton, Pennsylvania, and graduated from Lafayette College in 1880. He studied philosophy and the new science of psychology with Wilhelm Wundt in Germany, earning a doctorate from Leipzig in 1886. He took the first American professorship in psychology, at the University of Pennsylvania in 1889. Moving to Columbia University in 1891, he conducted pioneering experiments in the measurement of perception and learning. He was a founder of the American Psychological Association* in 1892 and served as the association's president in 1895. He purchased *Science* magazine in 1894, then gradually bought up and edited other scientific publications. After 1900 he worked to reform university government by giving greater influence to faculty members. To this end he founded the American Association of University Professors* in 1915. His reform activities brought him into conflict with Columbia's president, Nicholas Murray Butler,* who finally dismissed him from the faculty in 1917. Columbia historian Charles A. Beard* resigned in protest and the case became a cause célèbre for academic freedom. (*Dictionary of American Biography*, supplement 3; Michael M. Sokol, "The Unpublished Autobiography of James McKeen Cattell," *American Psychologist* 26 (July 1971): 626–35; Michael M. Sokol, "The Education and Psychological Career of James McKeen Cattell, 1860–1902" (Ph.D. diss. Case Western Reserve University, 1972).)

Edward R. Kantowicz

CENTURY MAGAZINE, THE. Founded in 1870 as *Scribner's Monthly*, a "first-class magazine," *Century Magazine*, was renamed in 1881 following the death of its editor, Dr. Josiah Gilbert Holland, and a falling out with Scribner's publishing house. From the beginning it competed ably with *Harper's* and *Atlantic*. Its Civil War battle series created the "greatest interest ever felt in any series of articles," while its talented staff of artists made *Century* the most elegant and richly illustrated American magazine. *Century* featured serial biographies of Lincoln, Napoleon, Luther, and Saint Francis, novels by Jack London,* William Dean Howells,* and John Hay, and short fiction, particularly scoring a hit with Frank Stockton's "The Lady or the Tiger?"

The editorial rooms of the *Century* were a "rallying point of good causes," such as tenement house reform, forest conservation, the Australian ballot,* international arbitration, and copyright legislation. It achieved its highest circulation of 200,000 in the 1880s but, through advertising and the Century Company publishing house, continued profitably through the first decades of the twentieth century, attracting attention because, as one of its readers observed, "it was always breaking out in new spots." In 1913, newspaperman Robert Sterling Yard became editor, asserting, "It is time we looked this question of the present squarely in the eye." Theodore Roosevelt* wrote on the Progressive party* and Edward A. Ross* contributed his series, "The Old World in the New." (Frank L. Mott, *A History of American Magazines, 1865–1885*, vol. 3 (1938); Robert Underwood Johnson, *Remembered Yesterdays* (1923); Algernon Tassin, *The Magazine in America* (1916).)

Dorothy M. Brown

CHANDLER, WILLIAM E. (December 28, 1835–November 30, 1917). The self-styled "first progressive" began his political career in 1856 and remained a loyal Republican through six decades, rising from state to national prominence in elective and appointive positions: state legislator, Secretary of the Navy, secretary of the Republican National Committee, U.S. Senator. Convinced that public office was a trust and that corporate influence on politics violated democratic principles, this self-made man fought for regulation of corporations, especially public utilities. During the 1880s and 1890s, his persistent criticism of railroad domination of New Hampshire politics resulted in his defeat for reelection to the Senate in 1901. In 1906, however, Chandler had yet another opportunity to work for reform. When Winston Churchill* led the progressive charge, Chandler both served as adviser to Churchill and wrote the reform platform. Although his maverick-like personality invariably resulted in conflict with other reformers, he repeatedly involved himself in reform efforts for the last ten years of his life. In 1910 he supported Robert Bass's successful attempt to become the first progressive Republican governor east of the Mississippi. Then, in 1912, Chandler backed William Howard Taft* and unsuccessfully warned Bass not to bolt the Republican party in support of Theodore Roosevelt,* a division Chandler foresaw as wrecking reformism in the GOP. Before he died, he saw the Roosevelt people return to Republican ranks. (Thomas R. Agan, "The New Hampshire Progressive Movement" (Ph.D. diss., State University of New York at Albany, 1975); Leon Burr Richardson, *William E. Chandler: Republican* (1940).)

Thomas Agan

CHARITY ORGANIZATION SOCIETIES. Charity Organization Societies were organizations of scientific philanthropy intended to make almsgiving more efficient and to ensure that only the "deserving poor" received relief. The Charity Organization Society (COS) originated in London, England, in 1869; the first American COS was founded in Buffalo, New York, in 1877. Ninety-two American societies appeared in the next decade and a half. Most of these societies did not grant relief to the poor but rather served as clearinghouses of information and bureaus of investigation for numerous private charity agencies. "Friendly visitors," the great majority of them women, tried to discern whether relief applicants were truly needy, and they also counseled the poor to make the best use of relief funds. Gradually, professional social workers replaced these volunteer visitors. Josephine Shaw Lowell, founder of the New York COS, believed that improving the character of the poor was more important than relieving their need. Irish-Catholic poet John Boyle O'Reilly castigated this condescending attitude, calling it "the organized charity, scrimped and iced, in the name of a cautious, statistical Christ." The charity organization societies marked an important step in the professionalization of social work and the development of the casework method. (Robert Bremner, *From the Depths: The Discovery of Poverty in the United States* (1956), and *American Philanthropy* (1960); Roy Lubove, *The Profesional Altruist* (1965); Frank Dekker Watson, *The Charity Organization Movement in the U.S.* (1922).)

Edward R. Kantowicz

CHAUTAUQUA. The Chautauqua movement provided adult education for the rural masses in an outdoor, camp-meeting setting. In August 1874, Methodist minister John Heyl Vincent organized a two-week training course for Sunday

school teachers at Lake Chautauqua in southwestern New York State. In succeeding summers, these sessions of serious, moralistic lectures in a pleasant
summer resort atmosphere grew longer and became exceedingly popular. Independent Chautauquas sprang up at over 200 sites, especially in the rural
Midwest, combining the fervor of a revival meeting, the excitement of a circus,
and the earnest respectability of a lyceum lecture. Starting in 1904, tent or circuit
Chautauquas began traveling from town to town, with many noted speakers.
William Jennings Bryan* delivered his favorite lecture, "The Prince of Peace,"
hundreds of times over thirty years. In the jubilee year of 1924, nearly thirty
million people (one-third of the U.S. population) attended a Chautauqua lecture
in one of 12,000 towns. Radio and the automobile, however, eroded the lecture
circuit's appeal by making other forms of information and amusement accessible.
The last tent Chautauqua folded in 1932. In their heyday, these cultural revival
meetings brought evangelism, education, and exercise to millions of rural and
small-town Americans. (Victoria Case and Robert Ormond Case, *We Called It
Culture* (1948); Joseph E. Gould, *The Chautauqua Movement* (1961); Paul W.
Glad, *The Trumpet Soundeth: William Jennings Bryan and His Democracy,
1896–1912* (1960).)

Edward R. Kantowicz

CHICAGO. Chicago was a major focal point during the Progressive Era. As
the fastest growing urban center in the United States in the late nineteenth century,
Chicago was confronted with all the economic, political, and social problems
created by modernization. The capital of the heartland, Chicago boasted the
world's largest stockyards as well as the agricultural commodities exchange.
The building of skyscrapers was pioneered in Chicago by such architects as Louis
Sullivan.* Daniel Burnham's* plan for Chicago illustrates the progressive desire
to rationalize the environment. Many of the major events of the period occurred
in Chicago. It had been the scene of the Pullman strike* in 1894, and as the rail
center of the nation, Chicago played host to nearly all the national political
conventions of the era. William Jennings Bryan's* "Cross of Gold" speech and
the founding of Theodore Roosevelt's* Progressive party* also occurred in Chicago. Reform literature such as Upton Sinclair's* *The Jungle* and Theodore
Dreiser's* *Sister Carrie* were set in Chicago. Chicago was home to Jane Addams,* who founded the profession of social work in the United States, and
from whose base, Hull House,* emerged a steady stream of reformers and reform
ideas on the full range of topics from street sanitation to world peace. A mul-
tiethnic city, Chicago claimed a population that was largely foreign-born and
the children of the foreign-born. Heavy concentrations of Germans, Poles, Italians, and Jews characterized the pre–World War I population. The wartime
shortage of labor brought in a large influx of southern blacks and race conflict
that resulted in a major riot in 1919. (Harold Mayer and Richard Wade, *Chicago:*

Growth of a Metropolis (1969); Irving Cutler, *Chicago: Metropolis of Mid-Continent* (1982); Perry Duis, *Chicago: Creating New Traditions* (1976).)

Dominic Candeloro

CHICAGO COMMONS was a social settlement house founded in 1894 by Graham Taylor.* Taylor arrived in Chicago in 1892 to teach Christian sociology at Chicago Theological Seminary. Desiring a "laboratory" for his students and impressed by Hull House,* he moved his wife and four children into an old house in the northwestern sector of the city and named it Chicago Commons. Within five years there were twenty-five residents sponsoring a kindergarten, day nursery, clubs, classes, and a civic forum. Taylor and Raymond Robins* worked closely with the Seventeenth Ward branch of the Municipal Voters' League. In 1901 Chicago Commons moved into its own five-story brick building on West Grand Avenue, complete with gymnasium and auditorium. Taylor's son, Graham Romeyn Taylor, helped edit a monthly magazine about the settlement house movement, the *Commons*. Irish, German, and Scandinavian neighbors of the 1890s gave way to Poles, Italians, and other southeast European immigrants in the early twentieth century. (Graham Taylor, *Pioneering on Social Frontiers* (1930); Graham Taylor, *Chicago Commons through Forty Years* (1936); Louise C. Wade, *Graham Taylor: Pioneer for Social Justice, 1851–1938* (1964); Allen F. Davis, *Spearheads for Reform: The Social Settlements and the Progressive Movement, 1890–1914* (1967).)

Louise C. Wade

CHICAGO SCHOOL OF SOCIOLOGY. The first sociology department in an American university began in 1892 as one of the original departments established at the University of Chicago* by its founding president William Rainey Harper. Albion Small,* the first department head, wanted to develop a field of sociology which would discover the laws of society and apply them to the solution of social problems. Small himself was primarily a theorist, but under his leadership a wide variety of intellectual approaches and styles of research flourished. One of Small's best-known faculty members was Charles R. Henderson, a Baptist minister who became an expert in charities, prisons, and employment and a leader in a wide variety of reform movements. W. I. Thomas,* another early member of the department, is best known for his monumental work *The Polish Peasant in Europe and America* and for his studies of immigration within the framework of social disorganization. Thomas brought Robert E. Park to the department in the mid-1910s, and Park continued work on immigration, and also on race, the urban press, and other aspects of urban sociology. The key intellectual figures associated with the "Chicago school" in addition to Park and Thomas were Louis Wirth, Ernest W. Burgess, and philosopher George Herbert Mead.* Among the key works associated with Chicago are Park and Burgess's text, *Introduction to the Science of Sociology*, a series of monographs on the city of Chicago developed as dissertations by doctoral students, including *The*

Gold Coast and the Slum, The Gang, The Ghetto, The Taxi Dance Hall, The Negro Family in Chicago, and Wirth's seminal essay, "Urbanism as a Way of Life." (Robert E. L. Faris, *Chicago Sociology, 1820–1832* (1967); Steven J. Diner, "Department and Discipline: The Department of Sociology at the University of Chicago, 1892–1920," *Minerva* 13 (1975): 514–53.)

                                                                                      Steven J. Diner

CHILD LABOR LEGISLATION. During the Progressive Era no object was more central than the crusade to abolish child labor and to ensure the healthy development and effective education of dependent and exploited children. This campaign soon became national in scope, with the National Child Labor Committee,* founded in 1904, taking the lead in securing legislation to end the worst conditions of child employment. Although children had always worked in America, the rapid and largely unrestricted industrialization of the nation following the Civil War began to produce new and disastrous conditions. Large numbers of children working outside the home were deprived of previously existing constraints on exploitation, danger, and abuse.

It was not until the turn of the century, however, when reform agitation attracted significant attention to these conditions, that a powerful social impulse developed to eliminate abuses by remedial legislation. The more progressive states, particularly in the northeast, led in this crusade, restricting hours of labor, excluding children from dangerous occupations, and attempting to ameliorate conditions generally. In time, these restrictions on employment were buttressed with complementary child welfare legislation such as compulsory school attendance laws. The central thrust of the movement was to achieve uniform regulatory standards throughout the country. But American federalism thwarted this effort, imposing barriers to reform legislation and rendering enforcement difficult. To overcome this twofold resistance, child labor reformers shifted their efforts to congressional action in 1913.

In Woodrow Wilson's* first term, congressional leaders increasingly came to believe that federal legislation under the commerce power met constitutional requirements. The Supreme Court's legitimization of federal police powers served to remove the remaining reservations, and public concern to secure the rights of childhood became irresistible, dictating the establishment and enforcement of uniform national protective standards. Congress responded in 1916, enacting the Keating-Owen Law, which extended to goods intended for interstate commerce, barring hazardous labor for children under sixteen, and establishing the eight-hour day and other protective standards for children between fourteen and sixteen, but the Supreme Court struck down this legislation in *Hammer v. Dagenhart*,* asserting that Congress had exceeded its regulatory authority and invaded jurisdiction reserved to the states. Congress almost immediately reestablished the identical regulatory standards, using the federal taxing power as its nexus and instituting a confiscatory 10 percent tax to exact employer compliance. The southern textile manufacturers again contrived a suit to invalidate the tax, condemning the mechanism as an improper use of congressional authority in (*Bailey v. Drexel Furniture Company*).* Child labor reformers, twice stymied, succeeded in persuading Congress to propose an abortive constitutional amendment in 1924. (Grace Abbott, "Federal Regulation of Child Labor, 1906–1938," *Social Service Review* 13, no. 3 (September 1939): 409–30; Thomas G. Karis, "Congressional Behavior at Constitutional Frontiers, from 1906, the Beveridge Child Labor Bill, to 1938, the Fair Labor Standards Act" (Ph.D. diss., Columbia University, 1951); Stephen B. Wood, *Constitutional Politics in the Progressive Era: Child Labor and the Law* (1968).)

Stephen B. Wood

CHILDREN'S BUREAU, UNITED STATES. Established in April 1912, the U.S. Children's Bureau was a major outgrowth of progressive child-saving.* An idea of Lillian Wald* and Florence Kelley,* it drew its inspiration and much of its leadership from the settlement house movement, from social feminists* who hoped to extend the influence of the home into the government, and from the era's faith in scientific knowledge as a means to solve social problems. It represented the first declaration of federal responsibility for the welfare of the nation's children, a governmental role that Theodore Roosevelt's* calling of the 1909 White House Conference on Dependent Children had suggested. Housed in the Department of Commerce and Labor* (and after 1913 in the newly formed Department of Labor),* the bureau's charge was purely educational. Its mission was to gather and dispense information regarding "all matters pertaining to the welfare of children and child life." The bureau's strongest advocates saw this as a wedge for a broadened concept of social welfare: to protect children, it was essential to help the family and the larger society as well. Julia Lathrop,* the first woman to head a federal agency, served astutely as the bureau chief from 1912 to 1921, ensuring its role as an avenue of mobility and influence for emerging career women. (Louis J. Covotsos, "Child Welfare and Social Progress: A History of the United States Children's Bureau, 1912–1935" (Ph.D. diss., University of Chicago, 1976); Nancy P. Weiss, "Save the Children: A History of the United States Children's Bureau, 1912–1918" (Ph.D. diss., University of California–Los Angeles, 1974); Jacqueline K. Parker and Edward M. Carpenter, "Julia Lathrop and the Children's Bureau: The Emergence of an Institution," *Social Service Review* 55 (March 1981): 60–77.)

Leroy Ashby

CHILDS, RICHARD S. (May 24, 1882–September 26, 1978). The founder of the "council-manager" form of municipal government, Richard Childs was born in Manchester, Connecticut, in 1882. After graduating from Yale in 1904, he became a moderately successful businessman, serving most notably as general manager of the Bon Ami Company from 1911 to 1920. His lifetime interest in municipal reform developed early. Seeking to eliminate the long ballot—the "politician's ballot," as he called it—he formed the National Short Ballot Organization in 1909.

After this "short ballot"* campaign achieved considerable success, Childs moved toward support of what he first called the "commission-manager" plan. He opposed the new "commission" form of municipal government* as too complicated for citizens to assure the election of effective administrators. He believed the "strong-mayor" form represented a perversion of democracy. He thus espoused the structural reform* of a nonpartisan elected "commission" or "council" with an appointed professional "manager" to administer municipal government. This "council-manager" system became an article of faith with progressive municipal reformers. For the rest of his long life, Childs remained an uncompromising champion of this form of local government, opposing even those who advocated that the mayor, under the council-manager system, assume the role of political leadership in council. Although active in a number of civic organizations, Childs became most closely identified with the National Municipal League,* serving in various capacities over the years, and his influence with this organization caused it to be the leading force in introducing the council-manager plan into many cities. (John Porter East, *Council-Manager Government: The Political Thought of Its Founder, Richard S. Childs (1965).*)

William A. Baughin

CHILD-SAVING. More than any previous generation, progressive reformers focused on the welfare of children. They established child labor laws,* juvenile courts,* junior republics,* new institutions and strategies for dealing with dependent and delinquent youths, the playground movement,* the 1909 White House Conference on Dependent Children; the U.S. Children's Bureau,* numerous youth-oriented organizations ranging from scouting to the Big Brothers and Big Sisters, and myriad reforms in education, health, and hygiene. Competing motives and strategies marked this "gospel of child-saving," as Denver's Ben Lindsey* described it. Compassion for the plight of neglected, endangered, and exploited children vied with fears of delinquency and disorder. Reforms were thus often double-edged, mixing benevolence and control. While some child-savers stressed hereditarian influences on children, most were strong environmentalists who believed that healthy, safe conditions bred responsible, civic-minded adults. Often concerned with salvaging the reputedly endangered American family, they ironically enlarged the interventionist role of agencies outside the home. Child-saving was initially voluntaristic, and suffused with religious and rural sentiments, but it increasingly became the domain of government and of trained professionals concerned with bureaucratic structures and scientific methods—standardization, efficiency,* and classification. (Susan Tiffin, *In Whose Best Interest? Child Welfare Reform in the Progressive Era* (1982); Leroy Ashby, *Saving the Waifs: Reformers and Dependent Children, 1890–1917* (1984); Ronald Cohen, "Child-Saving and Progressivism, 1885–1915," in Joseph M. Hawes and N. Ray Hiner, eds., *American Childhood: A Research Guide and Historical Handbook* (1985).)

LeRoy Ashby

CHURCHILL, WINSTON (November 10, 1871–March 12, 1947). Winston Churchill had already achieved national recognition as a writer when he won election to the New Hampshire legislature in 1904. His legislative experience convinced him that the railroad enjoyed significant political power, a view developed in his 1906 novel *Coniston*. The book portrayed corrupt political power, catapulted Churchill into the political limelight, served as a kind of progressive political platform, and led to Churchill's unsuccessful attempt that year to win the Republican gubernatorial nomination under the Lincoln Republican Club banner. Churchill hoped, in his words, "to make out of New Hampshire a model commonwealth," restoring political power to the common man. Labeled a carpetbagger because he had not been born in the state, he had the support of only five of seventy-five weekly newspapers, but he finished a strong second in his bid for the nomination. Despite Churchill's own defeat, Progressives were elected to the legislature, and a progressive platform was adopted by the Republican party. Churchill remained active in politics for another six years, working for William Howard Taft* in 1908 and on behalf of the progressive Robert Bass's successful gubernatorial bid in 1910. In 1912 he and Bass led the nascent Progressive party, with the novelist making another unsuccessful bid for the governorship. After 1912, Churchill dropped from politics. (Thomas R. Agan, "The New Hampshire Progressive Movement" (Ph.D. diss., State University of New York at Albany, 1975); Richard Hofstadter and Beatrice Hofstadter, "Winston Churchill: A Study in the Popular Novel," *American Quarterly* 2 (Spring 1950): 12–28.)

Thomas R. Agan

CINCINNATI. Political activity in Cincinnati during the Progressive Era involved principally local struggles against the deeply entrenched Republican organization headed by celebrated "boss" George B. Cox. After the turn of the century, an increasing number of "silk-stocking" Progressive reformers waged sporadic warfare on Cox. Democrat John Dempsey won the mayoralty briefly in 1907, but the first serious challenge to Cox's power came with the surprise victory of young reformer Henry T. Hunt in 1911. Supporters of Hunt's administration soon divided, however, over the question of municipal ownership of utilities,* and Cox was able to recapture the city in 1913. The ailing boss retired in 1914, and leadership of the Cox organization fell to his chief lieutenant, Rudolph K. "Rud" Hynicka. Although a shrewd political strategist, Hynicka faced an increasingly serious financial crisis between 1914 and 1923, while his business interests in New York caused him to neglect organization.

In 1923, Progressive Republican Murray Seasongood,* a wealthy attorney, led a campaign to defeat an extra tax levy submitted by Hynicka's supporters.

Disaffected elements in the city rallied behind Seasongood, and in 1924, in what has been aptly called a "late bloom of Progressivism," Seasongood and ally Henry Bentley led a coalition of "urban gentry" Progressive Republicans, middle-class Democrats, and Robert La Follette* supporters in a successful campaign to amend the city charter to bring the council-manager form of government to the Ohio city. (Zane L. Miller, *Boss Cox's Cincinnati: Urban Politics in the Progressive Era* (1968); William A. Baughin, *Murray Seasongood and Cincinnati Reform in the 1920s* (forthcoming, 1988).)

William A. Baughin

CITIZENS UNION. In 1896 the City Club, a leading New York reform organization, called for an independent citizens' movement for the municipal elections of the following year. Anticipating the creation of Greater New York—the consolidation of Manhattan, Brooklyn, and parts of Queens in 1898—reformers hoped to deprive Tammany Hall* of access to the impending increased opportunities for patronage and plunder. The Citizens Union resulted. Calling for honest, nonpartisan municipal government, as well as for the divorce of municipal from state and national politics, the new organization also demanded stronger civil service laws,* more parks and recreational facilities in poorer areas, the eight-hour day for city employees, and improved public transportation, schools, and health conditions. Some members further wanted public ownership of utilities.

Former Brooklyn president Seth Low* became the Citizens Union candidate for mayor in 1897 but lost to Tammany Hall candidate Robert Van Wyck largely because the reform group refused to ally with Republicans. Four years later it did accept a fusion ticket, and Low won the mayoralty race, only to lose again as a fusion candidate in 1903. The Citizens Union, divided by the question of fusion, transformed itself from a political party into a public interest group. In its efforts to improve local government and educate voters, it undertook a variety of activities that included assessing the qualifications of political candidates, undertaking taxpayers' suits, and preparing miscellaneous reports on municipal matters. (Gerald Kurland, *Seth Low: The Reformer in an Urban and Industrial Age* (1971); Gerald Kurland, "The Amateur in Politics: The Citizens Union and the Greater New York Mayoral Campaign of 1897," *New-York Historical Society Quarterly* 53 (October 1969): 352–84; Wallace S. Sayre, *Governing New York City* (1960).)

Robert Muccigrosso

CITY BEAUTIFUL. This multifaceted, elite-initiated movement to upgrade the physical appearance of towns and cities began in the 1890s, flourished throughout the nation from 1902 to about 1909, and waned thereafter. Commentators differ sharply over its origins, nature, and significance, with some dating it from the Chicago World's Fair of 1893, which served as the model for Chicago architect Daniel H. Burnham's* city plans for San Francisco* (1905) and Chicago* (1909). Historians who have investigated the City Beautiful see it more as a complex cultural movement expressive of urban progressivism than as a purely architectural and planning movement. They date it from 1897–1901 when the "City Beautiful" phrase came into use and when the major organizations promoting piecemeal beautification first found common cause.

When Charles Mulford Robinson published *The Improvement of Towns and Cities* in 1901, the movement found its "bible." A virtual beautifier's manual, it reflected the diverse currents of American aesthetic culture then converging: municipal or civic art, village and civic improvement outdoor art, gardenesque beauty, historic and scenic preservation, environmental sanitation, and outdoor advertising regulation. Local "improvement" organizations, numbering 2,426 by one 1905 estimate and often led by women, typically promoted small-scale, workable projects and, only occasionally, spectacular civic centers and grand city plans. The City Beautiful movement is significant for giving environmental expression to the enlarged conception of the public interest that permeated urban progressivism, for giving rise to city planning, and for popularizing norms of urban beauty and public amenity that still influence us. (Jon A. Peterson, "The City Beautiful Movement: Forgotten Origins and Lost Meanings," *Journal of Urban History* 2 (1976): 415–34; Richard Guy Wilson, "The Great Civilization" and "Architecture, Landscape, and City Planning," *The American Renaissance, 1876–1917* (Brooklyn Museum Staff, 1979): 9–109; William H. Wilson, "The Ideology, Aesthetics, and Politics of the City Beautiful Movement," in Anthony Sutcliffe, ed., *The Rise of Modern Urban Planning, 1800–1914* (1980): 165–98.)

Jon A. Peterson

CITY MANAGER PLAN OF MUNICIPAL GOVERNMENT (also called council-manager). Under the city manager plan the legislative power of the city is in a small council usually, though not always, elected at large. One of the council members serves as mayor, designated by the council or by the voters, but the chief executive officer is the city manager, who is hired by the council and serves at its pleasure. Although the exact duties vary by city, the manager is usually responsible for proposing a budget, appointing and removing city administrators, and generally supervising municipal operations.

Credit for pioneering the manager plan is shared by several different individuals and communities. Sumter, South Carolina, and Staunton, Virginia, both had managers by 1913, the year that Dayton, Ohio, became the first city of significant size to adopt the plan. Richard S. Childs,* executive secretary of the Short Ballot* Organization, is often called the "father of the city manager plan," and his organization, nominally chaired by Woodrow Wilson,* vigorously promoted the idea. In Dayton and elsewhere, the business community pushed for a change, making an analogy between city manager organization and the structure of a corporation, with the council analogous to the board of directors and the voters analogous to the stockholders. In 1919, the National Municipal League* included the council-manager plan in its influential model city charter. By 1920, about 150 cities had city managers, and three years later the number had reached 270.

Early managers were often municipal engineers, businessmen, or lawyers, but the profession was organized into the City Managers' Association in 1914, and academic training in public administration became the typical route. In their early evolution, manager plans were often seen as modifications of the Galveston–Des Moines commission system,* because they frequently called for a small body elected at large (with few, if any, other municipal officials elected), non-partisanship, merit appointment, and direct democracy. But the manager plan rejected the method of assigning each commissioner charge of a specific department. The plan was most popular in small to medium-sized cities, especially outside the Northeast. (Richard J. Stillman II, *The Rise of the City Manager: A Public Professional in Local Government* (1974); John Porter East, *Council-Manager Government: The Political Thought of Its Founder, Richard S. Childs* (1965); Harold A. Stone et al., *City Manager Government in the United States* (1940).)

Bradley R. Rice

CITY PLANNING. The emergence of city planning as a novel field of public endeavor was a major achievement of urban progressivism. By 1917, a city plan typically addressed an existing city's street layout and traffic circulation; its railroad station and freight facilities; its public building placement, especially its civic center; its park system, including parkways, playgrounds and waterfronts; and its zoning and subdivision rules. Undergirding the new field was the comprehensive city planning ideal: the belief that all major elements of a city's framework, public and private, should be developed as an interconnected whole, preferably through a general plan devised by one or more experts. In 1893, the Chicago World's Fair emboldened big-city architects to promote large-scale civic design schemes. In 1902, the McMillan Commission (U.S. Senate Park Commission) issued a spectacular plan for Washington, D.C. Of unprecedented scale and complexity for an existing city, it integrated as never before various architectual, park system, sanitary, and transportation elements and gave compelling expression to the impulse of many reformers to address the city as a whole. The City Beautiful movement,* just then cresting, popularized comprehensive city planning as the key lesson of the McMillan Plan.

From 1904 to 1909, almost forty private organizations and public authorities took heed, hiring experts to devise general plans. By 1909, Chicago architect Daniel H. Burnham* and City Beautiful apologist Charles Mulford Robinson had become the premier makers of City Beautiful plans. Landscape architects had also entered the new field, notably Frederick Law Olmsted,* Jr., and John Nolen. In 1909, Benjamin C. Marsh,* a spokesman for New York City social progressives, summoned the first National Conference on City Planning and challenged the movement to heed social welfare issues, especially population decongestion. By 1910, Olmsted had asserted leadership over the conference, seeking to cultivate city planning as a body of practical knowledge more geared to managing the stresses of urban growth (e.g., traffic) than achieving the City Beautiful* or ending congestion. By 1917, when the American City Planning Institute was founded as a quasi-professional organization, city planning had developed into an enduring field of expertise, backed by state enabling acts, planning commissions, annual conferences, and an extensive literature. (Christine M. Boyer, *Dreaming the Rational City: The Myth of American City Planning* (1983); Jon A. Peterson, "The Nation's First Comprehensive City Plan: A Political Analysis of the McMillan Plan for Washington, D.C., 1900–1902," *Journal of the American Planning Association* 51 (1985): 134–50; Mel Scott, *American City Planning since 1890* (1969); Anthony Sutcliffe, *Toward the Planned City: Germany, Britain, the United States, and France, 1780–1914* (1981).)

Jon A. Peterson

CIVIL SERVICE REFORM. The civil service reform campaign attempted to remove government employees from political influence and introduce a merit system of employment. The growing size and complexity of government gradually outmoded the patronage system, so reformers championed a merit system of competitive examinations to choose candidates for appointment and promotion and sought to forbid dismissal for political reasons. George William Curtis, the editor of *Harper's Weekly*, led the reform movement, serving as president of the National Civil Service Reform League from its founding in 1881 to his death in 1892. The assassination of President James A. Garfield by a disappointed office seeker, Charles Guiteau, created public sentiment for reform.

Senator George Hunt Pendleton, a Democrat from Ohio, introduced a bill which created a Civil Service Commission to supervise competitive examinations for all government positions on a classified list. The president was authorized to expand the number of classified positions at his discretion. When the Republicans lost the congressional elections in 1882, the lame-duck Congress, still controlled by Republicans, passed the Pendleton Act in order to appear virtuous for the next election and at the same time to protect Republican officeholders from dismissal. The Civil Service Act became law on January 16, 1883. Over the next few decades, presidents expanded civil service coverage, usually just before leaving office in order to prevent their successors from firing officeholders. In 1883, fewer than 15,000 jobs were classified under civil service; by 1897, over 86,000, nearly half of all federal employees, were covered. When Theodore Roosevelt* left office in 1909, over two-thirds of federal employees enjoyed civil service protection.

After passage of the Pendleton Act, civil service reformers attacked the patronage of local bosses in big-city political machines.* Throughout the Progressive Era, civil service reform functioned as the lowest common denominator among reformers, who agreed that an honest, nonpolitical, efficient corps of government employees was a necessary precondition for further reforms in the public interest. (Carl R. Fish, *The Civil Service and the Patronage* (1920); Ari Hoogenboom, *Outlawing the Spoils* (1961); Gordon Milne, *George William Curtis and the Genteel Tradition* (1956).)

Edward R. Kantowicz

CLARK, JAMES B. "CHAMP" (March 7, 1850–March 4, 1921). In 1876, Clark moved from his native Kentucky to Pike County, Missouri, and began his career in Democratic politics as city and county attorney. After a single term in the Missouri legislature, he won election to the U.S. House of Representatives in 1892. Except for two years from 1895 to 1896, he served continuously in the House until his death. Clark advocated the free coinage of silver, tariff reform, a federal income tax,* and various direct democracy measures. Democrats and insurgent Republicans elected him Speaker of the House in 1911, thus ending the autocratic power wielded by Speaker Joseph Cannon.* Clark's reputation as an orator and reformer boosted his chances for winning the Democratic presidential nomination in 1912, but he could not transform the majority vote accorded him on thirteen ballots to the then necessary two-thirds vote. He served President Woodrow Wilson* loyally with the notable exceptions of opposing the war resolution of 1917 and conscription. (Champ Clark, *My Quarter Century of American Politics* (1920); Geoffrey F. Morrison, "A Political Biography of Champ Clark" (Ph.D. diss., St. Louis University, 1972).)

Franklin D. Mitchell

CLARK, JOHN BATES (January 26, 1847–March 21, 1938). Clark taught economics at Carleton College (1877–1881), Smith College (1881–1892), Amherst College (1892–1895), and Columbia University (1895–1923). Along with several other economists trained in Germany, Clark in his early career challenged the extreme laissez-faire views of the prevailing classical economists. In his first book, *The Philosophy of Wealth* (1886), he insisted that economic decisions should consider ethical issues and rejected static in favor of dynamic principles. At the theoretical level, Clark contributed to the marginal utility theory of value and argued that goods might contain a "bundle" of values rather than a single value. In the first decade of the twentieth century he gave special attention to the trust issue, arguing for a regulatory approach. Clark also served on a committee to study the New York Stock Exchange in 1911. A longtime member of the American Peace Society, Clark served as head of the Division of Economics and History of the Carnegie Endowment for International Peace from 1910 to 1923. (Joseph Dorfman, *The Economic Mind in American Civilization*, vol. 3 (1959); John R. Everett, *Religion in Economics: A Study of John Bates Clark, Richard T. Ely, Simon N. Patten* (1946); J. H. Hollander, ed., *Economic Essays Contributed in Honor of John Bates Clark* (1927).)

Benjamin G. Rader

CLAY, LAURA (February 9, 1849–June 29, 1941). An important woman's rights leader and the best-known early Southern suffragist, Laura Clay organized the Kentucky Equal Rights Association in 1888 and served as its president until

1912, leading the women of the state to a number of victories in educational, property, voting, and co-guardianship rights. A member of the National American Woman Suffrage Association* (NAWSA) from its inception in 1890, she chaired the Southern Committee, which was charged with organizing the South, and served as an officer and member of the executive board from 1896 to 1911, while lecturing nationwide. In the final months of the suffrage struggle, Clay became controversial when her states' rights convictions caused her to withdraw from NAWSA and support state rather than federal enfranchisement. A founder of the Democratic Women's Club of Kentucky, she remained active in politics and women's rights until her death. (Paul E. Fuller, *Laura Clay and the Woman's Rights Movement* (1975); Aileen S. Kraditor, *The Ideas of the Woman Suffrage Movement, 1890–1920* (1965); Melba Porter Hay, "Madeleine McDowell Breckinridge: Kentucky Suffragist and Progressive Reformer" (Ph.D. diss., University of Kentucky, 1980).)

Paul E. Fuller

CLAYTON ANTITRUST ACT. Named after Congressman Henry Del Clayton, the Clayton Antitrust Act was passed in October 1914, during the administration of Woodrow Wilson.* In the quarter century since the enactment of the Sherman Antitrust Act, it had become clear that judicial interpretation of the 1890 statute had weakened its strict prohibitions against monopolization. In the presidential campaign of 1912, both Wilson and Theodore Roosevelt* had advocated strengthening the hand of the federal government against private monopolies.

In remedying some of the defects in the Sherman Act, Sec. 7 of the Clayton Act forbade the acquisition by one company of stock in competing firms, while Sec. 2 disallowed price discrimination designed to stifle competition. Furthermore, the law declared illegal interlocking directorates (Sec. 8) and made corporate officers responsible as individuals for antitrust violations. One of the most significant sections of the 1914 law recognized the right of organized labor to bargain collectively and to strike, in contradistinction to judicial practice which treated unions as combinations in restraint of trade under the terms of the earlier Sherman Act. Samuel Gompers,* longtime head of the American Federation of Labor,* hailed this proviso as labor's "magna carta," but subsequent court interpretation diluted the protective clause. Enforcement of the Clayton Act's various provisions was the responsibility of the Department of Justice's antitrust division, although in recent years the Federal Trade Commission* has overseen Sec. 2 of the statute.

The government's aim was to have the courts declare offensive practices illegal and forbid the respondent from continuing such practices thereafter. One of the provisions of the Clayton Act permitted private suits for triple damages caused by anything prohibited in the antitrust law. Private injunctive actions were also permitted. The major provisions of the original Clayton law were designed to deal with practices that *could* lead to adverse competitive results, and this illegality was demonstrated when an act or practice led to a lessening in actual competition. (Earl W. Kintner and Mark R. Joelson, *An International Antitrust Primer* (1974); Richard A. Posner, *Antitrust Law* (1976); Hans B. Thorelli, *The Federal Antitrust Policy* (1955).)

                                                                    John Quentin Feller

CLEVELAND. In 1900 Cleveland was the seventh largest city in the United States with a population of 381,768, which increased to over 800,000 by 1920. Its growth was made possible by transportation of coal and iron ore to a commercially strategic location. Although it escaped the widespread corruption that characterized many rapidly growing cities, it was ill-prepared to meet its civic responsibilities. Its streets were largely unpaved, its water supply was a breeding place for disease, and most of its newly arrived immigrants lived in wretched housing.

While structural reforms* were introduced in the 1890s and the seeds of the reform movement were planted by young middle-class, largely Republican, college-graduate reformers, who established the Municipal Association in 1896, significant progressive reform awaited the election of mayoral entrepreneurs, Tom L. Johnson* in 1901 and his disciple Newton D. Baker* in 1912. Johnson fought the railroad interests, the streetcar companies, and the entrenched political forces of a Republican party dominated by Mark Hanna.* He educated the public on the unfairness of the existing property tax system, fought to break the monopolies of private utility companies, and won the affection of urban immigrants. When conservative state governments opposed his efforts, he campaigned for home rule.* His administration housed elderly people and juvenile offenders in attractive, humanely run buildings. The city's police force was professionalized and humanized. Hundreds of shacks were eliminated to develop a group of civic buildings and public malls. Parks, municipal baths, and recreational facilities were built. The end of the era saw the creation of an extensive metropolitan park system.

Johnson stimulated both Democratic and Republican reformers and gave impetus to the creation of a myriad of civic and cultural organizations, such as Karamu settlement house, the Consumers League, the Cleveland Foundation, the Community Chest, the Welfare Federation, and the Cleveland Museum of Art. Newton D. Baker believed the city should be as noted for its culture as for its Municipal Light Plant. Nevertheless, a 27 percent socialist vote in 1917 reflected the limitations of progressive reforms. In 1915 the election of a Republican party regular over Peter Witt, a disciple of Johnson, signaled the end of a unique period in Cleveland history. (Tom L. Johnson, *My Story* (1911); Eugene C. Murdock, "Buckeye Liberal: A Biography of Tom L. Johnson" (Ph.D. diss., Columbia University, 1951); Hoyt L. Warner, *Progressivism in*

Ohio 1897–1917 (1964); Thomas F. Campbell, *Daniel E. Morgan: The Good Citizen in Politics 1877–1949* (1966).)

Thomas F. Campbell

COAL MINING SAFETY LEGISLATION. The Avondale mine fire of September 1869, in which 108 mine workers lost their lives near Wilkes Barre, Pennsylvania, led most coal-producing states to pass safety laws, especially emphasizing the ventilation of dust and gases and providing for mine inspection systems. Much of this legislation was poorly drafted and weakly enforced and did not address the single most recurrent cause of mine deaths—the fall of rock or coal from the roof or face. Between 1890 and 1910, hundreds of miners died each year in mining accidents. The United Mine Workers of America* lobbied for certification laws requiring an apprenticeship period for the inexperienced miner. A series of mine accidents in December 1907 in which 702 men were killed (361 miners died in a single accident at Monongah, West Virginia) stunned the public. Since safety legislation varied widely from state to state and tough legislation raised the cost of production, the search turned to defining industry-wide standards. The necessary cooperation among operators, miners, and legislators from competing states proved impossible to secure, and the movement died after a promising start. Support coalesced for the creation of a federal bureau which would conduct scientific investigations, then educate and advise the industry about mine safety, but coal operators fiercely opposed an agency with investigatory and regulatory powers. In 1910, Congress established the Bureau of Mines, which focused on instructing miners and operators in the proper techniques and equipment of mine rescue and first aid. Lacking investigatory powers and regulatory authority, the bureau was unable to transcend the divisions between miners, operators, technicians, and bureaucrats. (William Graebner, "The Coal-Mine Operator and Safety: A Study of Business Reform in the Progressive Period," *Labor History* 14 (Fall 1973): 483–505; William Graebner *Coal Mining Safety in the Progressive Period* (1976); Keith Dix, *Work Relations in the Coal Industry: The Hand-Loading Era, 1880–1930* (1978).)

Joseph M. Gowaskie

COBB, TYRUS RAYMOND "TY" (December 18, 1886–July 17, 1961). Cobb grew up in Royston, Georgia, and left home at seventeen to play professional baseball. In August 1905, just as he was about to join the Detroit Tigers, his father died from gunshots fired by his mother. Although Amanda Cobb was subsequently acquitted of a manslaughter charge, Cobb remained determined to vindicate the family name and his father's reluctant consent for him to become a ballplayer. Sensitive, distrustful, and humorless, he reacted violently against the hazing he received and became an outsider and a loner. Cobb's volatile disposition and fierce drive to excel, rather than great natural athletic ability, account for his phenomenal success from 1907, when he first led the American League in batting, until he retired from the game in 1928.

A master of the place-hitting, base-stealing style of play that characterized the "dead-ball" era up to 1920, Cobb won twelve batting titles in thirteen seasons, topped .400 three times and set records for career base hits and season and career stolen bases that endured for decades. As a player he sparked the Tigers to league championships in 1907–1909. During his years as player-manager, 1921–1926, Detroit finished as high as second only once. Cobb spent his last two seasons with the Philadelphia Athletics, retiring with an insurmountable lifetime batting average of .367. A chronic critic of the homerun-oriented style of baseball ascendant after 1920, Cobb died still convinced that baseball's best years had been his own best as a player. (Charles C. Alexander, *Ty Cobb* (1984); Ty Cobb, with Al Stump, *My Life in Baseball: The True Record* (1961); John McCallum, *Ty Cobb* (1975); Lawrence Ritter, *The Glory of Their Times* (1965).)

Charles C. Alexander

COLBY, BAINBRIDGE (December 22, 1869–April 11, 1950). Born in Saint Louis and educated at Williams College and Columbia University, Colby entered law practice in New York City, served in the New York State Assembly (1901–1902), and in 1912 was among the leaders of those who followed Theodore Roosevelt* out of the Republican convention to form the Progressive Party. Woodrow Wilson* named him a member of the wartime Shipping Board (1917–1919) and, in March 1920, secretary of state. He led an abortive move in the 1920 Democratic convention to nominate Wilson for a third term. Of distinguished appearance, he was considered a brilliant orator, and his speech in the 1920 Democratic convention countering the platform proposals of William Jennings Bryan* was called the best of the convention. He favored nonrecognition of Russia's Communist government, curbing Japan's expansion, and less armed intervention in Latin America. In 1921 he and Wilson formed a law partnership. In 1933 he supported Franklin D. Roosevelt,* but in 1934 he helped form the anti-Roosevelt American Liberty League. (Bainbridge Colby, *The Close of Woodrow Wilson's Administration and the Final Years* (1930); Daniel M. Smith, *Aftermath of War: Bainbridge Colby and Wilsonian Diplomacy, 1920–21* (1970).)

Wesley M. Bagby

COLLECTIVE BARGAINING. Collective bargaining eventually appealed to many reformers as democracy in action, but others never overcame their preference for individually negotiated contracts. Collective bargaining was often referred to as the Trade Agreement. In 1901 the National Civic Federation,* with its foremost emphasis on industrial conciliation, led the effort for collective bargaining, supported by John R. Commons.* By 1906, the National Child Labor Committee,* American Association for Labor Legislation,* and the National Consumers League* were supporting collective bargaining. Edward A.

Filene* and Louis D. Brandeis* negotiated the first needles trades collective-bargaining agreement, called the "Protocol of Peace," in 1910. Numerous collective-bargaining agreements were supported by various state agencies. In his presidential campaign of 1912, Woodrow Wilson* was converted to voluntary collective bargaining by Brandeis, thus drawing the practice into the mainstream. World War I* created the greatest number of collective-bargaining agreements under wartime labor-industrial laws. The Industrial Conferences* (1919) heard organized labor call for collective bargaining, but employers supported only voluntary efforts. Wartime collective-bargaining laws were abandoned in 1920, and not until the National Labor Relations Act of 1935 did compulsory bargaining with unions come about. (Lewis L. Lorwin, *The American Federation of Labor: History, Politics, and Prospects* (1933); Marc Karson, *American Labor Unions and Politics, 1900–1918* (1958); Bruno Ramirez, *When Workers Fight: The Politics of Industrial Relations in the Progressive Era, 1898–1916* (1978).)

Frank Grubbs

COLLIER'S MAGAZINE. *Collier's* was launched in 1888 as *Once a Week*, a literary magazine. It adopted a new format in 1898: profuse pictures and illustrations, short articles on public affairs, and numerous editorials. In 1903 when Norman Hapgood became editor, circulation was 300,000, but it rose to 600,000 by 1912. *Collier's* rarely joined the ranks of the muckraking journals, but in 1905, it published Samuel Hopkins Adams's* *The Great American Fraud*, a series on patent medicines. (The magazine's rejection of Upon Sinclair's* *The Jungle* was later fictionalized in that author's *The Brass Check*.) Hapgood's editorials supported the essential progressive agenda on income taxes, child labor, and women's rights, while an article signed by Louis Glavis in 1909 inaugurated the struggle of the Progressives against Interior Secretary Richard A. Ballinger's conservation policy.* Through weekly columns from Washington, Mark Sullivan,* who became editor in 1914, supported insurgent assaults on Speaker Joseph G. Cannon* and Senator Nelson W. Aldrich.* A supporter of Theodore Roosevelt* in 1912, the magazine later criticized Woodrow Wilson's* policies. Will Irwin's series *The American Newspapers*, muckraking the press for succumbing to yellow and commercial journalism, appeared in 1911. (Norman Hapgood, *The Changing Years: Reminiscences of Norman Hapgood* (1930); Mark Sullivan, *The Education of an American* (1938); *New York Times*, April 24, 1909, and November 9, 1918.)

Harold S. Wilson

COLORADO. First settled in the Pikes Peak gold rush of 1859, Colorado became a territory in 1861 and was admitted to statehood in 1876. Its population numbered 413,249 in 1890 and grew to 939,629 by 1920. Mining remained important throughout the period, but by 1910 irrigated farming had surpassed it as the state's leading industry. Tourism developed as well, with the federal government designating Mesa Verde National Park in 1906 and Rocky Mountain

National Park in 1915. Corporations, such as John D. Rockefeller's* Colorado Fuel and Iron Company, George J. Gould's railroads, and the Guggenheim smelting interests, dominated the state and sparked bloody labor warfare. Gold miners struck at Cripple Creek in 1894, silver miners at Leadville in 1897, and coal miners at Trinidad in 1903 and in 1913. A generation of industrial warfare culminated in the Ludlow Massacre* of 1914, leading to federal intervention and some improvements in wages and conditions.

Colorado miners and laborers elected Populist* Davis H. Waite governor in 1892, and the entire Populist ticket carried the state that year. After the turn of the century, middle-class voters in Denver* supported progressive reforms championed by Edward P. Costigan,* George Creel,* and Judge Ben Lindsey.* Democrat John F. Shafroth won two terms as a Progressive governor (1908–1912) with the strong support of Thomas Patterson's *Rocky Mountain News*. The state capital of Denver developed rapidly as a regional metropolis for Colorado and surrounding states, and the choice of Denver as the site of the Democratic national convention in 1908 ratified the city and state's established status. (Carl Abbott, *Colorado: A History of the Centennial State* (1976); George S. McGovern and Leonard F. Guttridge, *The Great Coalfield War* (1972); James E. Wright, *The Politics of Populism: Dissent in Colorado* (1974); Fred Greenbaum, *Fighting Progressive: A Biography of Edward P. Costigan* (1971); Charles Larsen, *The Good Fight: Life and Times of Ben B. Lindsey* (1972).)

Edward R. Kantowicz

COMMISSION FORM OF GOVERNMENT. A structural reform* intended to improve the efficiency of city government by vesting both executive and legislative power in a single governmental body, the city commission. This reform was first developed in Galveston, Texas, in 1900 when a hurricane devastated that city. Finding the traditional mayor-council form of government too cumbersome for the task of rebuilding, a citizens' group placed all governmental power in a temporary, five-man commission. Since this form of government proved satisfactory, Galveston adopted it permanently; and by 1917, 500 cities in the United States had done likewise.

Advocates of commission government likened the city to a business corporation; the voters were municipal stockholders who voted for city commissioners to act as a board of directors maximizing the stockholders' interests in a businesslike, efficient, frugal manner. Though the commission form proved useful in dealing with straightforward business and engineering matters, it was ill-suited to deal with complex human conflicts between racial and ethnic groups in large, diverse cities. As a result, commission government has survived only in small or medium-sized cities with homogenous populations. (Ernest S. Bradford, *Com-*

mission Government (1911); Clinton R. Woodruff, *City Government by Commission* (1911); Charles R. Adrian, *Governing Urban America* (1961).)

Edward R. Kantowicz

COMMISSION ON COUNTRY LIFE. This was the commission appointed by President Theodore Roosevelt* in 1908 to investigate the rural situation. Chaired by Liberty Hyde Bailey,* dean of the New York College of Agriculture at Cornell, the commission consisted of Kenyon L. Butterfield, president of the Massachusetts College of Agriculture; Gifford Pinchot,* chief forester in the Department of Agriculture; Walter Hines Page* editor of *World's Work*; Henry C. Wallace,* editor of *Wallace's Farmer*; Charles S. Barrett, president of the Farmers' Union;* and William A. Beard, editor of *Great West* magazine. Between August 1908 and January 1909, the commission gathered data on rural conditions by examining more than 100,000 responses to questions sent to over 500,000 rural residents, carrying on personal inquiries, conducting public discussions in twenty-nine states, and studying results forwarded from some of the thousands of meetings held by country people across the land.

The commission issued a report in January 1909 which recommended that a national program of extension services for farmers be established, agricultural surveys be conducted nationwide, and an agency to guide a national campaign for rural improvement be created. Congress resented Roosevelt's appointment of the commission without its approval and refused to appropriate money to publish and disseminate the report, but it was issued in limited quantity as Senate Document 705, 60th Congress, 2d session, 1909. The life of the commission ended when both Congress and President William Howard Taft* failed to support it. (Clayton S. Ellsworth, "Theodore Roosevelt's Country Life Commission," *Agricultural History* 34 (1960): 155–72; William L. Bowers, *The Country Life Movement in America, 1900–1920* (1974); Donald Jerome Tweton, "The Attitudes and Policies of the Theodore Roosevelt Administration toward Agriculture" (Ph.D. diss., University of Oklahoma, 1964).)

William L. Bowers

COMMISSION ON INDUSTRIAL RELATIONS. The U.S. Commission on Industrial Relations was created in the midst of a wave of industrial conflict, epitomized by the bombing of the *Los Angeles Times* headquarters on October 1, 1910. Pressured by reformers, liberal businessmen, and religious leaders, President William Howard Taft* asked Congress in early February 1912 to create a commission "to discover the underlying causes of dissatisfaction in the industrial situation." Although the legislation creating the commission passed with broad support, Taft's generally conservative appointees were not approved before he left office. Woodrow Wilson's* nominations to the commission, like Taft's, included representatives of labor, management, and the public, led by chairman

Frank P. Walsh,* a Kansas City attorney with close ties to social justice Progressives and strong sympathies with the labor movement.

For two years, the commission held hearings and gathered testimony on labor relations and the struggle, as Walsh described it, between "industrial feudalism" and "industrial freedom." The most dramatic moments in the commission's work came during its investigation of the "civil war" in Colorado between coal miners and the Colorado Fuel and Iron Company during 1913–1914, when Walsh confronted John D. Rockefeller,* Jr., directly. The commission's final report revealed the deep divisions that erupted in its ranks. Walsh and the labor members of the commission advocated economic democracy with the federal government as guarantor of economic equity and industrial peace, while John R. Commons* argued for administrative regulation and a federally guaranteed system of "collective bargaining" through voluntary commissions representing labor and capital. None of the commission's major proposals were directly implemented, but they codified a labor reform agenda that helped to define the federal government's war labor program. (Graham Adams, Jr., *Age of Industrial Violence, 1910–1915: The Activities and Findings of the United States Commission on Industrial Relations* (1966); James Weinstein, "The Federal Government as Social Investigator: The Commission on Industrial Relations," in *The Corporate Ideal in the Liberal State* (1968).)

Shelton Stromquist

COMMISSION ON INTERRACIAL COOPERATION. Organized in Atlanta on April 9, 1919, by black and white Southerners fearing postwar violence, the commission brought community leaders of both races together to ease tensions. It was founded by Will W. Alexander, a former Methodist pastor and YMCA social worker who drew the urban middle-class into local, county, and state interracial committees. Financed largely by white philanthropy and comprised mostly of educated whites who embraced Booker T. Washington's* theories, the commission accepted accommodation, gradualism, and segregation. Yet it was eager to curb lynchings. Also unlike the Progressives, commissioners opposed discrimination and worked more directly with blacks, correcting racial affronts and organizing training sessions, college courses, and Race Relations Sunday. The commission, always a potpourri of racial opinion and never truly interracial, disbanded in 1943. (Edward Flud Burrows, "The Commission on Interracial Cooperation, 1919–1944: A Case Study in the History of Interracial Movement in the South" (Ph.D. diss., University of Wisconsin, 1955); Wilma Dykeman and James Stokley, *Seeds of Southern Change: The Life of Will Alexander* (1962); Morton Sosna, *In Search of the Silent South: Southern Liberals and the Race Issue* (1977).)

Dominic J. Capeci, Jr.

COMMITTEE ON PUBLIC INFORMATION. The committee was a propaganda agency established by the Woodrow Wilson* administration to mobilize public opinion during World War I.* The secretaries of war, navy, and state proposed the formation of an official government information agency immediately after the United States entered the war in April 1917. Wilson established the Committee on Public Information (CPI), not as a censorship bureau but as a publicity agency; and he appointed George Creel,* an experienced, muckraking* journalist, its director. Creel organized an army of "Four-Minute Men" who delivered brief patriotic speeches across the country. The CPI distributed 75 million pamphlets and issued 6,000 press releases. It organized Americanization* classes for immigrants, closely monitored the foreign-language press for unpatriotic sentiments, and helped the American Federation of Labor* fight socialists in labor unions.

Though Creel's committee used persuasion, rather than coercion, its all-pervasive propaganda created a hate-filled atmosphere and a mood of intolerance which encouraged vigilantism. Throughout the war, overzealous patriots harassed immigrants, campaigned to stamp out German place-names, and looked for radicals everywhere. The wartime hysteria created by Creel's committee led directly to the postwar Red Scare.* (George Creel, *How We Advertised America* (1920); James R. Mock and Cedric Larson, *Words That Won the War* (1939); David M. Kennedy, *Over Here: The First World War and American Society* (1980).)

Edward R. Kantowicz

COMMONS, JOHN R. (October 13, 1862–May 11, 1945). Sociologist, economist, and labor historian, Commons earned his doctorate at Johns Hopkins University under the tutelage of Richard T. Ely* and, after several academic appointments, settled permanently at the University of Wisconsin in 1902. His early writings demonstrate his effort to unite Christian ideals with the new social sciences. He wrote many essays for the *Kingdom* magazine, assembled several more in his book *Social Reform and the Church* (1894), and helped form the American Institute for Christian Sociology.

From his involvement with the Ohio Anti-Saloon League, through his support of the national Prohibition party, and in his early sociological writings, Commons espoused temperance legislation. But by the time of his Wisconsin years, his scholarship had become less moralistic and more empirical. He involved himself actively in the Progressive administrations of Governors Robert La Follette* and Francis E. McGovern.* He drafted the Civil Service Law, the Public Utility Act, and the Industrial Commission Law, benchmarks of Wisconsin's national reputation in the Progressive Era. Commons's liberalism reflected strongly the often strenuous ethnocentrism of the Progressive movement, and his *Races and Immigrants in America* (1907) argued in a naturalistic vein that democratic institutions derive from the racial qualities of the Anglo-Saxons. (Lafayette G. Harder, *John R. Commons and His Assault on Laissez-Faire* (1962); John R. Commons, *Myself: The Autobiography of John R. Commons* (1963); J. David

Hoeveler, Jr., "The University and the Social Gospel: The Intellectual Origins of the 'Wisconsin Idea,' " *Wisconsin Magazine of History* 59 (Summer 1976): 282–98.)

J. David Hoeveler, Jr.

CONNECTICUT. The achievements of the Progressive Era in Connecticut were severely limited by the basic conservativism of middle-class reformers and by the control exercised by the Republican organization headed by J. Henry Rorabock. Coming from a rival background and having become president of the Connecticut Light and Power Company, Rorabock personified the coalition of rural Yankees and manufacturing and financial concerns, over which he presided as chairman and treasurer of the Republican state central committee. So powerful was his control over party machinery and state government that he was easily able to ward off interval challenges mounted by both urban politicians with immigrant, working-class constituencies and by good government reformers. When the latter bolted to the Progressive party in 1912, Rorabock lost the governorship to Democrat Simeon Baldwin, but maintained tight control over the legislature thanks to malapportionment.

The major challenge to the Rorabock Republicans came from urban Democrats, mostly Irish-American from New Haven, Hartford, Bridgeport, and other industrial centers, who headed a "party of the outs, the immigrants, the Catholics, and the poor." The Democrats pressed unsuccessfully for reapportionment and for other democratization measures, but they did unite with urban Republicans to ratify both the Seventeenth and Nineteenth amendments. Their efforts to pass a myriad of labor and welfare measures were usually similarly frustrated, but they did enact workmen's compensation* in 1913. They also forced the Rorabock Republicans to accept a watered-down Public Utilities Commission and to fend off statewide prohibition. Otherwise, Rorabock control of the state remained secure until the 1930s. (John D. Buenker, "Progressivism in Connecticut: The Thrust of the Urban New Stock Democrats," *Connecticut Historical Society Bulletin*, 35 (1970): 97–109; Duane Lockard, *New England State Politics* (1959); Herbert Janick, "The Mind of the Connecticut Progressive," *Mid America* 52 (1970): 83–101.)

John D. Buenker

CONSCIENTIOUS OBJECTORS. During World War I,* the Selective Service Act* offered restricted exemption, from combat only, for drafted members of the traditionally recognized pacifist faiths. From the outset, however, a number of liberals, particularly those organized in the Fellowship of Reconciliation and the American Union Against Militarism's National Civil Liberties Bureau, the predecessor of the American Civil Liberties Union* (ACLU), lobbied for official recognition of other religious and secular conscientious objectors to war. Among the leaders of this movement were Oswald Garrison Villard,* Crystal Eastman,* and Roger Baldwin. As a result of 64,700 claims, local draft boards recognized

56,800 men as conscientious objectors; 20,873 of those passed the physical and other examinations and were inducted into the wartime army. Secretary of War Newton D. Baker* encouraged training camp commanders to segregate these men from other draftees, and the resulting sense of isolation and rejection caused nearly 80 percent to change their minds and rejoin their outfits. However, nearly 4,000 continued to refuse to train for combat.

Although Baker had directed commanders to treat conscientious objectors with tact and consideration, some of these dissenters were beaten with sticks, sprayed with cold water, jabbed with bayonets, and starved on bread and water in solitary confinement. At least two died and one committed suicide as a result. Ninety-nine percent of the 4,000 conscientious objectors were religious objectors, and 1,300 of them ultimately agreed to serve in the Medical Corps or other non-combatant branches of the army. The other 2,700 "absolutists" refused to comply with any military order or cooperate with the military in any manner. By the end of the war, some 1,300 of these had been furloughed for civilian work in agriculture or industry; 940 remained segregated in the training camps; and 450 absolutists, many of them socialist political objectors to the war, were court-martialed for disobedience and incarcerated in military prisons. (H. C. Peterson and Gilbert C. Fite, *Opponents of War, 1917–1918* (1957); Charles Chatfield, *For Peace and Justice: Pacifism in America, 1914–1941* (1971); John W. Chambers II, *To Raise an Army: The Draft Comes to Modern America* (1987).)

John Whiteclay Chambers II

CONSERVATION. Conservation embraced the multifaceted concerns for which the word *environmental* is descriptive today. It has been claimed by science, economics, sociology, and philosophy with equal justice but has always belonged to politics first. Two political themes were predominant in the Progressive Era, the one utilitarian, the other aesthetic (or "preservationist"). The utilitarian theme was represented by Gifford Pinchot's* Forest Service,* which advocated the multipurpose use of the forest reserves. An astute bureaucratic politician, Pinchot used this doctrine to win the support of the numerous industries and interest groups interested in exploiting the reserves for profit under a judiciously exercised system of government regulation that eliminated wasteful competition and conflict. The massive public relations campaign he organized at the end of Theodore Roosevelt's* second term, Gifford called the Conservation Movement. Not much came of this crusade immediately, but it did transform conservation into a word heavily laden with political meaning. The aesthetic branch was a part of Pinchot's great concert of interests, but split off after the Hetch Hetchy controversy in 1913. This involved the question of whether a part of Yosemite National Park should be used as a water reservoir for San Francisco, which Pinchot supported, or whether it should be preserved for its natural beauty, as advocated by John Muir,* a beloved professional nature lover well-known to readers of mass-circulation magazines. The Hetch Hetchy Valley became a reservoir, and the controversy split the conservation forces.

When the National Park Service* was established in 1916, the aesthetic branch acquired a federal bureau to rival the utilitarian Forest Service. The first director, Stephen Mather, was as adept as Pinchot at arming his agency with the strong support of friendly industries and interest groups, such as major railroads and automobile clubs, whose managers understood the commercial benefits awaiting those who helped service the recreation needs of a rapidly growing urban middle class. (Samuel P. Hays, *Conservation and the Gospel of Efficiency: The Progressive Conservation Movement, 1890–1920* (1959); James Penick, "The Progressives and the Environment," in Lewis L. Gould, ed., *The Progressive Era* (1974).)

James Penick

CONSUMER CONSCIOUSNESS. Consumer consciousness was an important ingredient in movements to regulate business and in housewives' increasing focus on consumption over home production. Consumerism involved boycotts led by the National Consumers' League* for better products and improved working conditions and product-testing by the Housewives League and the emerging profession of home economics. Stirred by muckrakers, it was a potent, if unorganized and evanescent, force behind legislation and regulatory action controlling insurance rates, tariff levels, and tax legislation. It was an aspect of the meat and rent boycotts led by women in New York City's working-class districts. Often, apparently consumer-oriented legislation, especially on the federal level, was supported by business in an effort to stabilize and rationalize an industry.

Some consumer organizations cooperated with business and advertisers and focused their efforts on educating the consumer. Economists recognized the importance of consumption demand as a factor in economic growth, but they and others worried for the survival of thrift, restraint, and even the family. Novelists and other writers often blamed women's extravagance and conspicuous consumption for the high cost of living. But, by 1920, long-term increases in incomes, new economic ideas, and the growing sophistication of advertisers had helped to complete America's adaptation to the virtues of spending. (John E. Hollitz, "The Challenge of Abundance: Reactions to the Development of a Consumer Economy, 1890–1920" (Ph.D. diss., University of Wisconsin–Madison, 1981); Paula E. Hyman, "Immigrant Women and Consumer Protest: The New York City Kosher Meat Boycott of 1902," *American Jewish History* 70 (1980): 91–105; David P. Thelen, *The New Citizenship: Origins of Progressivism in Wisconsin, 1885–1900* (1972).)

Frank Stricker

COOKE, MORRIS LLEWELLYN (May 11, 1872–March 5, 1960). Morris Cooke was born in Carlisle, Pennsylvania, and graduated from Lehigh University in mechanical engineering. He became one of Frederick W. Taylor's* early disciples and endeavored to give Scientific Management* a wide social application. One of his first efforts (1910) for the Carnegie Foundation for the Advancement of Teaching was a controversial application of Taylor's ideas to university education in which he recommended, among other things, the standardization of lectures.

Far more influential was Cooke's work for the reform administration of Mayor Rudolph Blankenburg in Philadelphia (1912–1916) in which Cooke, as director of public works, set up a model department and extended his notions of planning to the entire administrative apparatus of the city government. Responding to sympathetic criticism of reformers like Louis D. Brandeis,* Cooke tried to bring democratic notions into what in its essential axioms seemed to be a nondemocratic system of management. In government, Cooke urged a partnership of the expert and the citizen; in the factory, he recommended "maximum decentralization that is consistent with strong and able and far-sighted central control." Cooke became a leading proponent of cooperation between the Taylorites and the trade unions. During World War I,* he brought his organizational skills to the Shipping Board, which for the duration of the war nationalized and directed the American merchant fleet. (Jean Christie, "Morris Llewellyn Cooke, Progressive Engineer" (Ph.D. diss., Columbia University, 1963); Samuel Haber, *Efficiency and Uplift: Scientific Management in the Progressive Era, 1890–1920* (1964); Milton J. Nadworny, *Scientific Management and the Unions, 1900–1932* (1958).)

Samuel Haber

COOLEY, CHARLES HORTON (August 17, 1864–May 7, 1929). Cooley received his Ph.D. in 1894 from the University of Michigan in his hometown with a dissertation entitled "The Theory of Transportation," a pioneer work in human ecology. He remained the rest of his life at Michigan, where his conservative social background and position allowed him to explore the potential "radicalism" of the new discipline of sociology. His main concern was the development of the concept of self. Rejecting the early influence of Herbert Spencer,* Cooley was greatly affected by William James's* writings with considerable intellectual debts to James Mark Baldwin and G. Stanley Hall.* He published *Human Nature and the Social Order* in 1902, *Social Organization* in 1909, and *Social Process* in 1918. After his death, a collection of his essays was published as *Sociological Theory and Social Research*. Cooley was not a dynamic speaker, but his ideas appealed to graduate students and the larger audience of progressives.

In formulating his concept of self, Cooley stressed the psychic importance of the primary group. The self came into being from interaction with significant others and from self-examination, or introspection. Cooley's concepts came from his observation of his own children and his reading of progressive literature. He observed that society and the individual were two aspects of the same basic reality, with the mind, the individual, society, and the self all social in origin and function. The irony was that his speculative and "armchair" approach to society was later validated by empirical studies, and his concepts provided the theoretical basis for much of social engineering. (Edward C. Jandy, *Charles*

Horton Cooley, His Life and Thought (1969); Marshall Cohen, *Charles Horton Cooley and the Social Self in American Thought* (1982); Mary E. Healy, *Society and Social Change in the Writings of St. Thomas, Ward, Sumner and Cooley* (1972).)

Donald K. Pickens

COOLING-OFF TREATIES. As a pacifist, William Jennings Bryan* accepted the portfolio of secretary of state from President Woodrow Wilson,* contingent upon the president-elect's approval of Bryan's objective of negotiating arbitration treaties with other countries. These treaties would provide that the parties in a diplomatic dispute agree to a six-month to one-year cooling-off period while negotiations proceeded, without resorting to armed force or increased armaments. At Wilson's suggestion, Bryan presented his proposal to the Senate Committee on Foreign Relations and explained his idea to the Washington diplomatic corps. To win public support, he gave a stirring and persuasive address on May 13, 1913.

During the next seventeen months, Bryan negotiated some thirty bilateral agreements to run for five years with automatic renewal unless abrogated. Parties agreed to submit all irresolvable disputes to a permanent commission. Although twenty treaties were eventually ratified, none was ever employed as a means to settle differences. Bryan regarded the treaties as his greatest achievement as secretary of state and his efforts paved the way for the peace movement in the 1920s and Pact of Paris of 1928. (Arthur S. Link, *Wilson: The New Freedom* (1956); R. W. Leopold, *The Growth of American Foreign Policy* (1962); M. E. Curti, "Bryan and World Peace," *Smith College Studies in History*, 16 (April-July 1931): 113–262; Paolo E. Coletta, *William Jennings Bryan*, 3 vols. (1964–1969).)

C. David Tompkins

COOPERATIVE MOVEMENT. The origin of the modern cooperative movement is usually traced to a plan implemented by twenty-eight weavers working in the mills of Rochdale, England, in 1844. From there the movement spread throughout the Western world during the nineteenth and twentieth centuries. Like the prototype, consumer cooperative societies are usually formed by people who live in the same community or who have similar interests. Most often they involve retail stores, but can be any form of business. Members buy into the business through the purchase of shares much as if they were investing in a corporation. They buy goods at the lowest possible prices, and at the end of the year or accounting period, dividends are distributed to the shareholders on a pro rata basis.

In America the origins of the cooperative movement are also to be found in the 1840s when four producers' cooperatives were established by foundry workers. In the producers' cooperative, the primary objective was the manufacture and distribution of goods without the interference of capitalist or middleman, but otherwise the principles were the same. The peak of the cooperative movement in America came in the 1880s when the Knights of Labor established over 200 producers' and consumer societies. During the Progressive Era, there were 230 cooperative societies founded in the United States. These were primarily retail stores, but also included marketing, and gasoline and oil associations. Opponents of the cooperative movement have always insisted upon branding it as a form of socialism, while socialists themselves and advocates of cooperation usually deny this link. In fact, cooperation contains elements of both capitalism and socialism, and the dispute has never been resolved. (J. E. Johnson, J. V. Garland, and C. E. Phillips, *Consumer Cooperatives* (1937); Robert Jackall and Henry M. Levin, *Workers' Cooperatives in America* (1984).)

Kenneth E. Hendrickson, Jr.

CORPORATION EXCISE TAX ACT. In effect from 1909 to 1913, the act levied an excise tax of one percent on the privilege of doing business as a corporation as measured by a company's net income after its costs of doing business had been deducted. It required that all corporations netting over $5,000 a year file reports on their organization and operations, a feature which its chief advocates, President William Howard Taft* and Attorney General George W. Wickersham,* regarded as a necessary prerequisite to federal licensing and regulation of corporations. The tax was proposed by Taft along with a proposed income tax amendment to the Constitution, as a substitute for the income tax section that Republican Insurgents* attempted to append to the Payne-Aldrich Tariff.* As such it was opposed by the Insurgents as a ruse and by the Stalwarts and corporations as an invasion of privacy and an unreasonable levy. Nelson W. Aldrich* frankly admitted that he only accepted the corporation excise tax to defect the income tax, while Robert M. La Follette* and the Insurgents generally voted for it as the only course available. Sixteen different corporations instituted suits against the operation of the tax which also inspired a Conference of Industrial and Commercial Organizations and Representatives of Corporations in Chicago. In 1911, the Supreme Court, in the case of *Flint v. Stone Tracy Company,* upheld the validity of the tax as an excise rather than an income levy. The tax was eventually incorporated into the income tax section of the Underwood-Simmons Tariff* of 1913. (John D. Buenker, *The Income Tax and the Progressive Era* (1985).)

John D. Buenker

CORRUPT PRACTICES LAWS are federal and state laws regulating the use of money in election campaigns. Bribery, intimidation, and fraud have always been illegal in common law, but beginning in 1890 more sophisticated measures were passed to regulate, limit, and publicize campaign contributions and election expenditures. Using the English Corrupt-Practices Act of 1883 as a model, New York State passed the first law regulating campaign contributions in 1890, followed by a more effective Massachusetts law in 1892. The fund-raising activities of Mark Hanna* as Republican national chairman and the insurance company* investigations in New York in 1905 led to the passage, on January 26, 1907, of a federal law banning all campaign contributions by corporations. A federal publicity law was passed in 1910 requiring the publication of campaign contributions by special-interest committees. By 1925, when the federal Corrupt Practices Act consolidated the previous election laws, nearly all the states had passed similar acts, limiting contributions and requiring publication of expenditures. (Earl R. Sikes, *State and Federal Corrupt-Practices Legislation* (1928); Helen M. Rocca, *Corrupt Practices Legislation* (1928); 75th Congress, 1st sess. Committee on the Judiciary. Senate Document No. 11, *Corrupt Practices at Elections* (1937).)

Edward R. Kantowicz

CORTELYOU, GEORGE B. (July 26, 1862–October 23, 1940). Born in New York, Cortelyou became Grover Cleveland's stenographer in 1895 and, five years later, William McKinley* appointed him secretary to the president. Theodore Roosevelt* retained him in that position until 1903, when he appointed Cortelyou as secretary of the newly created Department of Commerce and Labor.* Most of his administrative attention was consumed with organizing the department. After running Roosevelt's campaign in 1904 and successfully turning back accusations that he had used his cabinet position to press major corporations for campaign contributions, Cortelyou was appointed postmaster general, a position he held until 1907 when he became Roosevelt's secretary of the treasury. Here he played a central role in the federal government's efforts to address the financial panic* of October 1907. In 1909 he became president of the New York Consolidated Gas Company, where he harnessed the managerial efficiency skills he had honed in Washington to expand the company's service area from Manhattan to all of metropolitan New York. (George E. Mowry, *The Era of Theodore Roosevelt and the Birth of Modern America, 1900–1912* (1958); Willard B. Gatewood, Jr., *Theodore Roosevelt and the Art of Controversy: Episodes of the White House Years* (1970); Horace S. Merrill and Marion G. Merrill, *The Republican Command, 1897–1913* (1971).)

Wayne A. Wiegand

COSMOPOLITAN MAGAZINE. After a faltering start, *Cosmopolitan Magazine* was bought in 1889 by John Brisben Walker, who built the circulation from 16,000 to 400,000. He sliced the twenty-five cent price to ten cents to better compete with rivals *Munsey's* and *McClure's* and attracted ninety-two pages of advertising. The flamboyant Walker offered to purchase Cuba's independence from Spain for $100 million, while Stephen Crane* covered the Boer War. The fiction of Mark Twain, Jack London,* H. G. Wells, and Edith Wharton was matched by rich illustrations contributed by Charles Dana Gibson, Harold Pyle, and Frederic Remington. Special series included great industries of America, great passions of history, and educational reforms. Walker's most ambitious scheme was founding Cosmopolitan University, a free correspondence school.

Walker sold *Cosmopolitan* for $400,000 to William Randolph Hearst* in 1905, and it provided an outlet for socialist and radical writers. "The Treason of the Senate," by David Graham Phillips,* raised circulation 450,000 in 1906. In the next year, *Cosmopolitan* followed with Edwin Markham* writing on child labor, Richard Berry on black peonage in the South, and Charles Edward Russell's* study of bosses. By 1912, *Cosmopolitan* turned increasingly to fiction and success stories, becoming the best-selling magazine in the world. (Frank L. Mott, *A History of American Magazines, 1885–1905* vol. 4 (1957); Louis Filler, *Crusaders for American Liberalism* (1939); W. A. Swanberg, *Citizen Hearst: A Biography of William Randolph Hearst* (1961).)

Dorothy M. Brown

COSTIGAN, EDWARD PRESENTISS (July 1, 1874–January 17, 1939). Denver* lawyer and reformer, liberal U.S. Senator, Edward Prentiss Costigan was born in Virginia* but moved to Colorado* with his family in 1877. He was educated in public schools, at the preparatory school of Notre Dame University in Indiana,* and at Harvard. He began law practice in Denver in 1900 and joined numerous civic reform associations. He earned notoriety by defending the striking coal miners accused of murder in the 1914 Ludlow Massacre.* Originally a Republican, he bolted to the Progressive party* in 1912, running unsuccessfully for governor twice. In 1916 he supported Democrat Woodrow Wilson* for reelection as president, and Wilson appointed him a member of the newly formed Tariff Commission* in 1917. Costigan's career ran the full gamut of progressive reform, from local politics to labor disputes to the New Deal in Washington. (Colin B. Goodykoontz, *Papers of Edward P. Costigan Relating to the Progressive Movement in Colorado, 1902–1917* (1941); Colin B. Goodykoontz, "Edward P. Costigan and the Tariff Commission, 1917–1928," *Pacific Historical Review* 16 (1947) 410–19; Fred Greenbaum, *Fighting Progressive: A Biography of Edward P. Costigan* (1971).)

Edward R. Kantowicz

COST OF LIVING (COL). After falling 33 percent from the Civil War to 1900, consumer prices jumped 20 percent between 1900 and 1914. Middle-class writers exaggerated the effects of inflation on their class because it symbolized anxieties about large-scale organizations such as unions and trusts and jeopardized traditions of thrift and simple living. Progressive humanitarianism, social science empiricism, and the regulation of the poor led to pioneering studies of working-class households. The cost of an "adequate" living for a worker's family was set at $600–$900, and a third to a half of working-class families fell below this. Few studied the middle class; estimates of adequate income levels ranged from $1,000 to $3,000. Budget estimates reflected hierarchical assumptions about class needs, as inflation in food prices (40 percent, 1900–1914) most hurt the poor who spent a larger portion of their budget on basics.

During World War I,* consumer prices surged 100 percent. With American intervention, government agencies supervised labor relations and—to hold labor to its no-strike pledge—enunciated the principles that wages should keep up with inflation and that every worker deserved a living wage. But it was largely because of the demand for industrial labor rather than government paternalism that blue-collar and farm laborers increased their real earnings while white-collar workers lost to inflation. (Daniel Horowitz, *The Morality of Spending: Attitudes toward the Consumer Society in America, 1875–1940* (1985); Albert Rees, *Real Wages in Manufacturing, 1890–1914* (1961); Frank Stricker, "The Wages of Inflation: Worker's Earnings in the World War One Era," *Mid-America*, 63 (1981); 93–105.)

Frank Stricker

COTTON FUTURES ACT. First enacted by Congress August 18, 1914, this act was designed to control the purchase of cotton futures contracts by taxing such contracts unless they conformed to certain regulations governing the sale. These specifications were to be drawn up in contract form by the secretary of agriculture. Buying and selling contracts for cotton to be delivered at a future date had begun in the South before the Civil War. Following the war, however, the practice led to widespread speculation in cotton prices as traders often sold cotton they did not have and resold cotton contracts numerous times.

Farmers charged the speculators with manipulating the price of cotton and in the late nineteenth century supported legislation in Congress to prevent such speculation. The opposition of businessmen and the doubtful constitutionality of such a measure stymied efforts to regulate cotton marketing until 1914, when the Democrats controlled Congress. Spurred on by increasingly powerful farm organizations, the cotton crisis caused by the outbreak of World War I,* and the leadership of Southern members of Congress, the first Cotton Futures Act was passed that year. Declared unconstitutional in a federal district court because it was a tax bill which had not originated in the House, it was altered to meet the court's objections and attached to the Agricultural Appropriation Act for 1917, and reenacted August 11, 1916. (Cedric B. Cowing, *Populists, Plungers, and Progressives: A Social History of Stock and Commodity Speculation, 1890–1936* (1965); Theodore Saloutos, *Farmers Movements in the South, 1865–1933* (1960); James E. Boyle, *Cotton and the New Orleans Exchange: A Century of Commercial Evolution* (1934).)

Wayne E. Fuller

COUGHLIN, JOHN JOSEPH (August 15, 1860–November 8, 1938). Born in Chicago,* Coughlin was the epitome of the ward political boss. He was first elected to the Chicago City Council in 1892 and served in that body until his death. For nearly half a century, Coughlin and his cohort Michael "Hinky Dink"

Kenna ruled the First Ward which included the Chicago Loop as well as the bordello district to the south. Coughlin grew up poor and worked at a variety of jobs, including running a bathhouse, which gave him the name "Bathhouse John."

A sometimes comic figure, Coughlin dressed in garish fashion and pretended to write a mawkish kind of poetry. He represented the worst side of urban politics, collecting tribute from the gamblers, prostitutes, and saloon keepers in the First Ward. Yet he was instrumental, under the leadership of Mayor Carter Harrison II,* in defeating the traction magnate Charles Tyson Yerkes* in his effort to control the Chicago street railways. The influence of Coughlin waned after the advent of Prohibition in the 1920s, which brought the intrusion of the Capone mob into local politics along with the coming to office of Republican William Hale (Big Bill) Thompson as mayor. Coughlin liked to live in high fashion, but his later years were lived out in poverty and bitterness as his political influence declined. Some efforts have been made to make him out as a Robin Hood figure, but in general, any vote he cast for reform was carefully calculated to be to his advantage. (Lloyd Wendt and Herman Kogan, *Bosses of Lusty Chicago: The Story of Bathhouse John and Hinky Dink* (1943).)

Donald F. Tingley

COUNCIL OF NATIONAL DEFENSE. The council was the parent agency for most of the boards and bureaus that directed the United States' economic efforts in World War I.* In part, its genesis lay in the initiatives of the scientists and engineers of the Navy's industrial preparedness Committee (1915), but in equal measure, it was the product of the Army War College's study of economic mobilization and its emphasis on the need for a board to oversee the process. In the National Defense Act of 1916, Congress accepted the need for some centralized economic planning, and by a rider to the Army Appropriations Act of August 29, 1916, it established the council to consist of the secretaries of war, navy, interior, agriculture, commerce, and labor. The council was assisted by an advisory commission that established more than 150 industry subcommittees covering the industrial spectrum to supply it with information and handle price agreements and contract awards.

In the summer of 1917, in response to charges of inefficiency and conflict of interest, the council replaced the General Munitions Board with the War Industries Board,* and dissolved the industry subcommittees. Most of these were reestablished as private War Service Committees. As the War Industries Board increased its direction of the war effort, the council focused its attention on the issues of postwar reconversion and civilian morale. (Robert Cuff, *War Industries Board: Business-Government Relations during World War I* (1973); Daniel R. Beaver, *Newton D. Baker and the American War Effort, 1917–1919* (1966);

William J. Breen, *Uncle Sam at Home: Civilian Mobilization, Wartime Federalism, and the Council of National Defense, 1917–1919* (1984).)

Robert David Ward

COUNTRY LIFE MOVEMENT. Ostensibly an effort to improve rural living, the Country Life movement was a complex and ambiguous concern for individualism, social-mindedness, nostalgia for the past, morality, national integration based on science and efficiency, and distrust of materialism and special privilege. Its support came mainly from the professional agricultural leadership, those in the rural school and church, and urban groups with a variety of motives. The leaders, like those of most progressive movements, were relatively young, middle-class, urban (although of rural antecedents), Protestant, and well-educated.

The movement sought to improve country life by encouraging organization, scientific control, and planning while preserving traditional rural ideals. It received support from President Theodore Roosevelt* in 1908 when he appointed the Commission on Country Life,* which investigated rural conditions, summarized deficiencies, and recommended improvements. The commission's work signaled the flowering of rural reform activity. The same analysis had been made earlier, but it was not until the Progressive Era that the many diverse reform impulses became an identifiable movement. Within it, however, were two distinct approaches to rural betterment—one aimed at social amelioration and the other at making farmers into efficient businessmen. In spite of their common work for a variety of rural changes, the two elements could not harmonize their differences and in 1919–1920, they split into the American Country Life Association and the Farm Bureau Federation. (William L. Bowers, *The Country Life Movement in America, 1900–1920* (1974); Liberty Hyde Bailey, *The Country-Life Movement* (1911); David Dambom, *The Resisted Revolution* (1979); Robert Merwin Swanson, "The American Country Life Movement, 1900–1940" (Ph.D. diss., University of Minnesota, 1972).)

William L. Bowers

COX, JAMES M. (March 31, 1870–July 15, 1957). After teaching school briefly in his late teens, Cox worked for papers in Middletown and Cincinnati before becoming secretary to an Ohio congressman in 1894. In 1898, he returned to Ohio and bought the Dayton *Daily News*, the first of numerous acquisitions that would create a chain of newspapers and radio and television stations in Ohio, Florida, and Georgia. He won election twice, in 1908 and 1910, in Ohio's Third Congressional District and participated actively in House struggles against the Payne-Aldrich Tariff* and Speaker Joseph G. Cannon's* powers.

Elected governor in 1912 and reelected in 1916 and 1918, Cox presided over the flowering of progressive reform in Ohio, as causes long nurtured in Ohio's cities won statewide approval. Achievements for which Cox deserves at least partial credit include compulsory workmen's compensation,* reorganization of the schools, public utilities and banking regulation, home rule* for the cities, a child labor law, an industrial-relations commission, and important administrative reforms. Nominated by the Democrats for the presidency on the forty-fourth ballot in 1920, he loyally but futilely campaigned for Wilson's League of Nation.* (James E. Cebula, *James Cox: Journalist and Politician* (1985); James M. Cox, *Journey through My Years* (1946); Landon H. Warner, *Progressivism in Ohio, 1897–1917* (1946).)

Jacob H. Dorn

CRANE, CHARLES RICHARD (August 7, 1858–February 15, 1939). This Chicago-based civic reformer was a highly successful businessman and a noted internationalist. Taking a round-the-world cruise as a young man, the Chicago-born Crane showed a facility for languages and developed a lifelong interest in the countries of the Middle East and the Orient. He became vice president of the Crane Company in 1894 and president in 1912, selling his interest in the company to a brother in 1914. An active participant in local reform politics, he served as president of the Municipal Voters' League, a citizens' body dedicated to the election of honest aldermen, from 1900 to 1905.

Crane contributed heavily to Woodrow Wilson's* election campaign in 1912, served as a member of the diplomatic mission, headed by Elihu Root,* which traveled to Russia after the revolution in 1917, and studied the question of Turkish mandates for the Allied Powers at the Versailles Conference after World War I.* He served briefly as ambassador to China in 1920, managing postwar famine relief in that vast country. At a time of great international turmoil, he proved useful to the Wilson administration because of his many international contacts. (*New York Times* Obituary, February 16, 1939; *National Cyclopedia of American Biography*, vol. 30 (1943); *Dictionary of American Biography*, Supplement 2.)

Edward R. Kantowicz

CRANE, STEPHEN (November 1, 1871–June 5, 1900). Crane, orphaned in 1890, went to New York City to pursue a career as novelist and poet. During this period he found time for several one-sided love affairs, all with ladies older, more experienced, and considerably higher on the social scale than he. Living and learning in the Bowery, he wrote the great realistic novel *Maggie: A Girl of the Streets*, which he was forced to publish privately because no established publisher would touch it. Both Hamlin Garland* and William Dean Howells* were impressed by it, however, and Crane's brief career was launched. *The Red Badge of Courage*, the quintessential novel of a young man entering combat for the first time, followed, and Crane was established as a unique talent. The result of his new reputation was that Crane found employment as a war correspondent whose activity centered in Greece and Cuba.

It is ironic that, while he was interested in the realistic portrayal of life in his own day, his only real income stemmed from his extraordinary skill in depicting the lives of everyday soldiers in war. In the process of these activities his health was ruined, and he contracted the tuberculosis which led to his early death. His brilliant adventures into poetry were ignored. In New York the "Crane Myth" developed and he was accused of drug use, or alcoholism, and general depravity by the New York Police Department. Crane died at the age of twenty-eight, having produced twelve brief but intense volumes of prose and verse, and having carved for himself a definite niche in the history of American letters. (Daniel G. Hoffman, *The Poetry of Stephen Crane* (1957); Robert W. Schneider, *Five Novelists of the Progressive Era* (1965).)

Robert W. Schneider

CRAWFORD, COE I. (January 14, 1858–April 25, 1944). Cory Isaac Crawford, better known as "Coe I.," was born into a poor Allamakee County, Iowa, farm family but managed to graduate from the University of Iowa Law School in 1882. After a stint as a schoolteacher and an unsuccessful attempt at practicing law, Crawford left the Hawkeye State, attracted by the "Great Dakota Boom." Selecting the raw prairie community of Pierre (after 1889, South Dakota), he quickly established a thriving law practice and became involved in politics. Possessing oratorical skills and political sense, he rose from Hughes County District Attorney to South Dakota Attorney General between 1886 and 1892.

While serving as legal counsel for the Chicago & North Western Railway, Crawford became disenchanted with his employer's political involvement and found Alfred B. Kittredge, the state's Republican party "boss," and his "machine" totally disgusting. In 1903, Crawford resigned his lucrative position with Chicago & North Western and broke with GOP stalwarts, helping to organize the state's insurgents. Elected governor in 1906, he oversaw enactment of a variety of uplift measures, including curbs on legislative lobbying, free textbooks for public school students, and valuation of railroad property. As his biographer concludes, "[Crawford] had achieved such an overwhelming victory in 1906 and was such a strong executive that he accomplished in two years what Governors La Follette [Wisconsin] and Cummins [Iowa] did in their respective states in six."

Elected to the U.S. Senate in 1908, Crawford continued to embrace the spirit of progressivism, although he voted for the Payne-Aldrich Tariff* in 1909. He soon redeemed himself by regularly siding with Republican insurgents led by Robert M. La Follette,* but the bitter split within the GOP that occurred in 1912, coupled with Crawford's failure to turn out the reform vote, led to his defeat in the 1914 Republican primary. (Calvin Perry Armin, "Coe I. Crawford and the Progressive Movement in South Dakota," *South Dakota Historical Collections* 32 (1964): 26–330; Herbert S. Schell, *History of South Dakota* (1961).)

H. Roger Grant

CREEL, GEORGE (December 1, 1876–October 2, 1953). Muckraking* journalist, director of the Committee on Public Information* during World War I,* Creel founded the *Kansas City Independent* in 1899. He crusaded unsuccessfully for ten years against the Pendergast political machine in Kansas City, then in

1909 he moved to Denver,* writing first for the *Denver Post* and later for the *Rocky Mountain News*. In 1914 he published an exposé of child labor, entitled *Children of Bondage*, written with Judge Benjamin Lindsey* and poet Edwin Markham.* President Woodrow Wilson* named him to head the Committee on Public Information in April 1917, and he directed this agency's war propaganda so vigorously that it became popularly known as the Creel Committee. Creel organized an army of "Four-Minute Men" who delivered brief patriotic speeches across the country. Their efforts proved so successful that they unwittingly fanned the flames of intolerance for dissent and contributed to a mood of wartime hysteria. After the war, Creel retired from journalism to write popular histories. (George Creel, *How We Advertised America* (1920), and *Rebel at Large* (1947); James R. Mock and Cedric Larson, *Words That Won the War* (1939).)

Edward R. Kantowicz

CRISIS, THE. The official organ of the National Association for the Advancement of Colored People (NAACP),* the *Crisis* first appeared in November 1910. W. E. B. Du Bois,* the only black officer of the new association and the editor of the *Crisis* from its inception until 1934, considered the magazine his "soul-child," a creation independent of and equal to the parent organization. This messianic attitude occasioned countless squabbles about editorial policy between Du Bois and white NAACP officials and ultimately led to his resignation from the organization. Nevertheless, Du Bois's *Crisis* magnificently adhered to the general aim of the NAACP by eloquently condemning race prejudice and espousing equal rights. It assailed lynching,* disfranchisement,* forced segregation, and unequal education. To the consternation of those in NAACP headquarters and many others, the *Crisis* also pilloried Booker T. Washington,* the black press, and white religion and advocated economic reform, black solidarity, and Pan-Africanism.

Using a flamboyant style often characterized by vituperation and bitter sarcasm, the *Crisis* thrived. Its circulation, 80 percent of which was black, reached more than 100,000 a month in 1919. By the 1920s, the *Crisis* had helped forge a new measure of black unity and pride and shape an Afro-American intelligentsia tied to the liberal agenda of the well-rooted NAACP. (Charles Flint Kellogg, *NAACP: A History of the National Association for the Advancement of Colored People, 1909–1920* (1967); Elliott M. Rudwick, *W. E. B. Du Bois: Propagandist of the Negro Protest* (1968); W. E. B. Du Bois, *Dusk of Dawn: An Essay toward an Autobiography of a Race Concept* (1940).)

David W. Southern

CROLY, HERBERT (January 23, 1869–May 17, 1930). Croly is the man Walter Lippmann* called "the first important political philosopher who appeared in America in the twentieth century." In 1886, Croly began a much-interrupted, fourteen-year career as a Harvard undergraduate. He left Cambridge without a degree in 1899, and from 1900 to 1906 he edited the *Architectural Record* in

New York. Croly burst onto the national scene with the publication of his masterwork, *The Promise of American Life* (1909). That book, which diagnosed the ills of American society, analyzed their causes, and advocated a vigorous program of nationalized social reform, exerted a major influence on the Progressive movement—particularly upon that wing of it led by ex-president Theodore Roosevelt,* who read Croly's book and incorporated some of its ideas. Croly also wrote a second, less influential book of political commentary, *Progressive Democracy* (1914), and biographies of Mark Hanna* (1912) and Willard Straight* (1924). He founded and edited until his death the *New Republic*,* an illustrious journal of progressive political opinion and cultural observations. His own writing was sometimes labored and difficult; his personality was often withdrawn and reclusive. (David W. Levy, *Herbert Croly of "The New Republic": The Life and Thought of an American Progressive* (1985); Charles Forcey, *The Crossroads of Liberalism: Croly, Weyl, Lippmann and the Progressive Era, 1900–1925* (1961); Dorothy Elmhirst et al., "Herbert Croly," *New Republic* 63 (July 16, 1930): 243–71.)

David W. Levy

CUMMINS, ALBERT BAIRD (February 15, 1850–July 30, 1926). A native of Pennsylvania, Cummins migrated to northeast Iowa, tried Chicago, studied law, and married. Returning to Des Moines, Iowa, he won a farm organization's lawsuit against a barbed wire manufacturer. A staunch Republican, he opposed the party majority on prohibition* without success, but revealed the individualism which became his trademark. Rebuffed by the Old Guard on two tries for the Senate, he became leader of a well-defined progressive faction of his party, won three terms as governor (1902–1908), and put through a complete progressive program. Finally elected to the Senate in 1909, he joined the Insurgents* and became a great force in senatorial battles, but lost on the high-tariff Payne-Aldrich bill.* He voted for Theodore Roosevelt* in 1912 but would not change parties. A severe critic of President Woodrow Wilson,* he loyally supported the war effort. Three years as president pro tempore of the Senate and passage of the Esch-Cummins Transportation Act* in 1920 enhanced his prestige. (Ralph Mills Sayre, "Albert Baird Cummins and the Progressive Movement in Iowa" (Ph.D. diss., Columbia University, 1958); Thomas Richard Ross, *Jonathan Prentiss Dolliver: A Study in Political Integrity and Independence* (1958); Leland L. Sage, *William Boyd Allison: A Study in Practical Politics* (1956).)

Leland L. Sage

CURLEY, JAMES MICHAEL (November 20, 1874–November 12, 1958). Four-time Democratic mayor of Boston,* the most notorious political boss* in Boston's history, James Michael Curley was born in Boston to Irish immigrants. He attended public school through the eighth grade then took a variety of jobs as a factory worker or a teamster. He was elected to the Common Council in 1900, to Congress in 1911, and to his first term as mayor in 1913, building a lucrative insurance business on the side. Curley rotated in and out of office for the next forty years, winning the mayoralty again in 1921, 1929, and 1945, and a single term as governor of Massachusetts in 1935, but losing many elections as well.

Boston politics was heavily factionalized, with no citywide political machine like New York's Tammany Hall,* so Curley survived in this jungle with a highly personal blend of jobs, favors, and blarney. Yet the fundamental secret to his success was the deep-rooted hatred of the working-class Irish* for the well-heeled Boston Brahmins. Curley played on the sympathies and resentments of his constituents and proved most potent politically when he seemed to be down and out. In 1945, for example, though seventy years old, sick, and facing a trial for contract fraud, he won the mayoral election and served part of his term in federal prison. A classic example of the boss as lovable rogue, Curley has been fictionalized by James Carroll in *Mortal Friends* and by Edwin O'Connor in *The Last Hurrah*. (James M. Curley, *I'd Do It Again* (1957); Edward J. Donnelly, *That Man Curley* (1947); Alfred Steinberg, *The Bosses* (1972).)

Edward R Kantowicz

D

DANIELS, JOSEPHUS (May 18, 1862–January 15, 1948). "Don't get pessimistic. Optimism is the only thing worthwhile," Daniels said to a friend in 1916 in a way that typified his doughty spirit. Born in tobacco country in Wilson, North Carolina,* Daniels rose from modest circumstances to become the premier North Carolina editor, to serve as Woodrow Wilson's* secretary of the navy (with young Franklin Delano Roosevelt* as assistant), and capped his long career as ambassador to Mexico during the New Deal. A staunch Methodist and temperance man, Daniels developed the Raleigh *News and Observer* into a force for North Carolina progressivism, stressing economic development through industrialization, diversification, and improved education, including the founding and improvement of North Carolina State University (then North Carolina Agricultural and Military). Like most southern Progressives, Daniels was deeply prejudiced against blacks, assisting in their disfranchisement and supporting only "separate and unequal" schools. On the other hand, he resisted extreme negrophobic violence and used the *News and Observer* to campaign for a degree of racial tolerance in an era of extremism. In Wilson's cabinet, Daniels demonstrated political growth, supporting a modern-style ethnic politics in the Northeast and an actively pro-labor policy in the "Preparedness Campaign"* of naval building. With progressivism's demise, Daniels remained important as a journalist. (David E. Cronon, ed., *The Cabinet Diaries of Josephus Daniels*, (1963); Joseph L. Morrison, *Josephus Daniels, the Small-d Democrat* (1966); Joseph L. Morrison, ed., *Josephus Daniels Says* (1962).)

John H. Roper

DARROW, CLARENCE S. (April 18, 1857–March 13, 1938). Born in Kinsman, Ohio, Darrow was educated at Allegheny College and spent one year at the University of Michigan Law School. He was married twice and had one son, Paul, by his first wife, Jessie Ohl. He was admitted to the Ohio bar in 1878, and in 1888, he became a junior partner in the Chicago law firm of John Peter Altgeld.* There he began his career as a famous trial lawyer—only one of the fifty people he defended against first degree murder charges was executed. He served as counsel for organized labor, including Eugene Debs,* the socialist leader charged with conspiracy in the Pullman Strike* of 1894; ''Big Bill'' Haywood* of the Industrial Workers of the World,* who were charged as accessories to the murder of the governor of Idaho in 1907; and the McNamara brothers, who were accused of bombing the *Los Angeles Times* building and killing twenty people in 1910. Using psychiatric evidence, he defended Nathan Leopold and Richard Loeb in the murder of Robert Franks (1924). In the trial of John T. Scopes for teaching evolution (1925) in Dayton, Tennessee, Darrow ruthlessly cross-examined William Jennings Bryan,* who defended bibical fundamentalism. Abandoning his usual support for the less fortunate, he was defense attorney for Lt. Thomas Massie in the kidnapping and murder trial (1932) in Honolulu, resulting in a light sentence for his client. In 1927 he retired from regular practice to devote his time to writing and lecturing. He died in Chicago on March 13, 1938. His publications include *A Persian Pearl* (1899), *The Story of My Life* (1932), *Farmington* (1905), and *Crime; Its Cause and Treatment* (1925). (Arthur Weinberg, ed., *Attorney for the Demand* (1959); Charles Y. Harrison, *Clarence Darrow* (1931); Irving Stone, *Clarence Darrow for the Defense* (1941).)

John R. Aiken

DAVIS, RICHARD HARDING (April 18, 1864–April 11, 1916). Born in Philadelphia,* Davis grew up in a literary household and became a reporter for the *Philadelphia Record* in 1886, after dabbling in sports and campus journalism at Lehigh and Johns Hopkins universities. Despite his dandified airs, he was a tough and resourceful investigator, with a colorful style and a genuine sympathy for the underdog. After his removal to New York in 1889, he became internationally famous as a travel writer and war correspondent. A confirmed social Darwinist,* Davis espoused the ''strenuous life'' advocated by his friend Theodore Roosevelt,* and celebrated the Spanish-American War* as a romantic adventure that evoked the finest qualities of Anglo-Saxon manhood. His popular fiction and plays, including *Ranson's Folly* (1902) and *The White Mice* (1909), often featured genteel heroes and heroines who lived by a strict moral code and championed individual rights without ever questioning the legitimacy of the emerging corporate state. Such idealistic plots appealed strongly to a new middle class of college graduates and university-trained professionals. Davis's first marriage to Chicago socialite Cecil Clark ended in divorce in 1910. On July 8, 1912, he married actress Bessie McCoy (Elizabeth G. McEvoy), by whom he had a daughter. He died suddenly at his home in Mount Kisco, New York. (Charles B. Davis, ed., *Adventures and Letters of Richard Harding Davis* (1917); Fairfax

Downey, *Richard Harding Davis: His Day* (1933); Larzer Ziff, *The American 1890s: Life and Times of a Lost Generation* (1966).)

Maxwell H. Bloomfield

DEBS, EUGENE VICTOR (November 5, 1855–October 20, 1926). Born in Terre Haute, Indiana, Debs attended school until age fifteen, and then worked for the local railroad, organizing a lodge of the Brotherhood of Locomotive Firemen. An officer and editor of the brotherhood, he served as city clerk and one term as a Democrat in the Indiana legislature. In 1885 he married Katherine Metzel. By then established as a labor leader, Debs opposed structuring unions by craft and founded an industrial union, the American Railway Union, and, much later, the Industrial Workers of the World.* In 1894, Debs's leadership of a strike against the Pullman* Car Company resulted in his brief imprisonment for violation of an injunction, during which he converted to socialism.

Adding class consciousness to his values of egalitarianism, republicanism, and democracy, the charismatic and humane Debs ran for president five times and epitomized the Socialist Party of America* to the public. He aligned with the party's leftists but eschewed ideological factionalism and, instead, held himself above the fray. Debs's World War I* dissent saw him imprisoned in Atlanta Penitentiary under the Espionage Act,* while he won almost one million ballots for president in 1920. His sentence was commuted, and he tried unsuccessfully to unify the socialist movement until his death in Chicago. (Eugene V. Debs, *Writings and Speeches of Eugene V. Debs*, (1948); Ray Ginger, *The Bending Cross: A Biography of Eugene Victor Debs* (1949); Nick Salvatore, *Eugene V. Debs: Citizen and Socialist* (1982).)

Sally M. Miller

DE LEON, DANIEL (December 14, 1852–May 11, 1914). Leader of the Socialist Labor Party,* Daniel De Leon was one of the most uncompromising and doctrinally rigid socialists in America. Born on the Dutch West Indian island of Curaçao to Jewish parents, he was educated in Germany and the Netherlands, moved to New York in 1874, and earned a law degree from Columbia University in 1878. He joined the Knights of Labor in 1888 and the Socialist Labor party in 1890, swiftly assuming a dominant position as the party's national lecturer and the editor of the party newspaper, the *People*. Finding both the Knights of Labor and the American Federation of Labor* insufficiently dedicated to class struggle, he founded the Socialist Trade and Labor Alliance in 1895, giving rise to charges of "dual unionism," that is, dividing the ranks of labor.

De Leon's uncompromising Marxist ideology led many moderate socialists to split from him and start the Socialist Party of America* in 1901. De Leon helped organize the Industrial Workers of the World* in 1905, but he eventually split from them as well. He died in New York in 1914. De Leon's doctrinally pure interpretations of Marx endeared him to no less a socialist than Lenin, but in America his rigidity tended to retard the acceptance of socialist ideas and to cause numerous factional disputes. (Arnold Petersen, *Daniel De Leon: Social Architect* (1941); Carl Reeve, *The Life and Times of Daniel De Leon* (1972).)

Edward R. Kantowicz

DELL, FLOYD (June 28, 1887–July 23, 1969). Born in Barry, Illinois, Dell was educated in the school of Quincy. He married Margery Curry in 1909 in Chicago, but they were divorced in 1913. He subsequently married B. Marie Gage in New York, and they had one son. Dell early espoused atheism and a rudimentary socialism, read widely, began to write, and got his first job as a journalist. In 1908 Dell moved to Chicago, a center of literary and radical activity. Living briefly in Graham Taylor's* settlement house, Chicago Commons,* Dell met more radicals, got a job as a reporter on the *Evening Post*, and became the literary editor.

In 1913, Dell moved to New York, living in Greenwich Village where, as in Chicago, he became a part of both the literary and the radical crowd. He met Margaret Sanger,* John "Jack" Reed,* Dorothy Day, and, most importantly, Max Eastman,* publisher of the radical magazine the *Masses** and its successor the *Liberator*. Dell became the editor of the latter and for a decade was prominent in radical circles. Near the end of World War I,* Dell and Eastman were indicted under the Espionage Act* for opposing the war. Charged with encouraging conscientious objectors, and defended by Morris Hillquit* and Dudley Field Malone, socialist lawyers, both Dell and Eastman were acquitted.

During the 1920s and after, Dell devoted himself to writing. He published plays, biography, and commentary but was most noted as a novelist. Beginning with *Moon Calf* (1920) his novels dealt with the disillusionment of the postwar generation. Sinclair Lewis liked to refer to Dell as a "faun on the barricades." (Floyd Dell, *Homecoming: An Autobiography* (1933).)

Donald F. Tingley

DEMOCRATIC PARTY. The Democratic party fell upon hard times during the Civil War since most Southern secessionists were Democrats and Northern Democrats were suspected of disloyalty. For decades after the war, Republicans would "wave the bloody shirt" at Democratic candidates, branding the Democrats the party of rebellion. Despite this handicap, the Democratic party made a remarkable recovery at the end of Reconstruction. In the four presidential elections between 1880 and 1892, Democrats won two and Republicans won two. Both houses of Congress were closely divided throughout this period.

The Democrats relied heavily on their base in the Solid South. The states of the former Confederacy disfranchised most blacks, and white Southerners voted in one-party unanimity for Democrats. Elsewhere in the country, party loyalty followed ethnocultural* lines. Pietist, evangelical Protestants, mainly of Anglo-Saxon origin, voted Republican, whereas Catholics and ritualistic Protestants, such as German Lutherans, voted Democratic. Pietist Republicans favored a morally activist government, which had abolished slavery and wanted to prohibit alcohol; immigrant Catholic Democrats wanted government to leave them alone and not disturb their foreign customs and habits. The Democratic party, in short, was the party of outsiders—former secessionists in the South, Catholic immigrants in the North.

After 1892 the outsider Democrats became a decided minority party as well. The second administration of Grover Cleveland (1893–1897) bore the blame for the sharp depression of the 1890s.* Then, when William Jennings Bryan,* a spokesman for evangelical Protestant America, captured the Democratic nomination in 1896, he muddied the formerly clear ethnocultural lines between the two parties. Republican William McKinley* preached prosperity and toned down the moralistic appeals, thus drawing away many Democratic voters. After Bryan's defeat by McKinley in 1896, the Democrats remained the minority party until the depression of the 1930s.

Woodrow Wilson* was the only Democrat elected president during the forty-year period, and his election in 1912 was due to a division among the Republicans. Bryan remained the party's titular leader until 1912, running unsuccessfully for president in 1900 and 1908. The choice of Judge Alton B. Parker,* a lackluster conservative, as candidate in 1904 proved even more disastrous. The organization of the party was dominated by the Solid South and by Northern political bosses such as Tammany Hall's* Charles F. Murphy,* Indiana's Thomas Taggart,* and Illinois's Roger Sullivan.* Wilson's two terms as president (1913–1921) resulted in much progressive legislation and the entrance of America into World War I.* The party lapsed back into minority status, however, in the 1920s, until Franklin Roosevelt* molded all the outsiders in America into a winning and long-lasting coalition. (Edward R. Kantowicz, "Politics," in Stephan Thernstrom, ed., *Harvard Encyclopedia of American Ethnic Groups* (1980); Eugene H. Roseboom, *A Short History of Presidential Elections* (1957); Dewey W. Grantham, *The Democratic South* (1963); Richard J. Jensen, *The Winning of the Midwest: Social and Political Conflict, 1888–1896* (1971); J. Rogers Hollingsworth, *The Whirligig of Politics: The Democracy of Cleveland and Bryan* (1964); Paul W. Glad, *The Trumpet Soundeth: William Jennings Bryan and His Democracy, 1896–1912* (1960); Arthur S. Link, *Woodrow Wilson and the Progressive Era* (1954).)

Edward R. Kantowicz

DENVER. First settled in the Colorado gold rush of 1859, Denver became the territorial capital in 1868 and state capital in 1876, and grew rapidly as a supply center for mining camps along the Front Range of the Rocky Mountains. Though counting only 106,713 inhabitants in 1890, Denver was the largest city for 500 miles in any direction. Annexations in 1902 brought the city's area to 59 square miles, and its population grew to 256,000 by 1920. Its percentage of foreign-born residents, 18 percent in 1900, was among the lowest in the nation. The city was home to ambitious social climbers, such as the "Unsinkable" Molly Brown, and dedicated social reformers, such as Judge Ben B. Lindsey,* who established a juvenile court in 1907. City utility companies, in league with the state's railroad and mining corporations, controlled Denver politics at the turn of the century. Democrat Robert W. Speer made an alliance with the utility magnates in 1903, promising to protect their interests if they would support civic improvements and increased spending for the poor. The city and county governments were consolidated in 1904, and Speer was elected mayor.

From 1904 to 1912, Speer launched a City Beautiful* movement, building roads, bridges, parks, and an elegant neoclassic civic center. He held the allegiance of the working class with a liberal attitude on liquor and generous welfare spending. He secured the Democratic National Convention for the city in 1908. Though branded a boss, Speer was in fact a master broker who got things done. Thomas Patterson's *Rocky Mountain News* and Republican reformers, such as Edward P. Costigan,* opposed Speer; and in 1912 they elected Henry Arnold mayor on an antitax platform. Arnold's office was replaced by a city commission* in 1913, but this proved so unsatisfactory that the mayor-council form of government was reestablished in 1916, and Robert Speer was reelected, serving until his death in 1918. Boom town, state capital, regional marketing and manufacturing center, Denver became the metropolis for nearly half a continent. (Constance McLaughlin Green, "Cities of the Great Plains: Denver and Wichita," in *American Cities in the Growth of the Nation* (1957); Lyle W. Dorsett, *The Queen City: A History of Denver* (1977); Carl Abbott, *Colorado: A History of the Centennial State* (1976).)

Edward R. Kantowicz

DEPARTMENT OF COMMERCE AND LABOR. The Department of Commerce and Labor was created by an act of Congress on February 14, 1903. Its purpose was "to foster, promote, and develop the foreign and domestic commerce, the mining, manufacturing, shipping and fishery industries, the labor interests, and transportation facilities, and the insurance business in the United States." Its secretary was to be a member of the cabinet. The long-term cause of the new department was an attempt by the federal government to become more involved in the issue of trusts and monopolies. The short-term impetus for the bill came from the Anthracite Coal Strike of 1902* and President Theodore Roosevelt's* role in settling the strike. While many groups in the country had been calling for legislation to outlaw all trusts and monopolies, the president wanted legislation that would permit the executive to regulate the conduct of trusts rather than clear cut prohibition. Thus the president insisted that a Bureau of Corporations* with power to investigate the activities of trusts be a part of the new department. Some members of the big-business community supported the bureau as a potential ally. If they could receive advance approval of their expansion projects, they would avoid possible prosecution. In the long run the Department of Commerce became a promoter of business interests both at home and abroad. It subsumed many existing bureaus, such as the Patent Office and Census Bureau, and it added many functions to promote foreign trade. (*New*

York Times, November 16, 1902 through February 15, 1903; Lewis L. Gould, *Reform and Regulation: American Politics, 1900–1916* (1978); Robert H. Wiebe, "Business Disunity and the Progressive Movement, 1901–1914," *Mississippi Valley Historical Review* 44 no. 4 (1958): 664–85.)

Albert Erlebacher

DEPARTMENT OF LABOR. Leaders of both the Knights of Labor and the American Federation of Labor* long agitated for "a voice in the President's Cabinet." In 1884 a Bureau of Labor was established in the Interior Department, under the direction of Massachusetts statistician Carroll D. Wright.* It was renamed the Bureau of Labor Statistics in 1888, reflecting its major activity, and was made an independent agency, but without cabinet status. In 1903 Theodore Roosevelt* merged it into a new cabinet-level Department of Commerce and Labor.*

Union leaders objected to this linking of capital and labor in a single agency, so on March 4, 1913, a Democratic Congress created a separate Department of Labor. President Woodrow Wilson* appointed Pennsylvania Congressman William B. Wilson,* a former secretary of the United Mine Workers* and the chairman of the House Labor Committee which framed the Labor Department bill, as first secretary of labor. The new department encompassed the Immigration and Naturalization Service, the Bureau of Labor Statistics, a Children's Bureau,* a Women's Bureau, an Employment Service, and a Mediation and Conciliation Service. Secretary Wilson, who served throughout President Wilson's two terms, took a special interest in the mediation of labor disputes and provided a strong voice for labor in the cabinet. (John Lombardi, *Labor's Voice in the Cabinet: A History of the Department of Labor from Its Origins to 1921* (1942); James Leiby, *Carroll Wright and Labor Reform* (1960); Roger Babson, *William B. Wilson and the Department of Labor* (1919).)

Edward R. Kantowicz

DEPRESSION OF THE 1890s. The failure of the National Cordage Company on May 4, 1893, inaugurated the panic that initiated the depression of the nineties. The banking community, already jittery over the reduction of the U.S. Treasury's gold reserve below $100 million in April and the bankruptcy of the Philadelphia and Reading Railroad in February, began to call loans, while western and southern banks withdrew their deposits from the New York banks. A currency famine soon followed. The business community worried about its ability to secure payment for goods and services and, lacking currency to pay their workers, decided to shut down their businesses. The railroad, the great engine of American prosperity since the depression of the seventies, was overbuilt and highly leveraged by the 1890s, and as a result, declining rail traffic forced a significant number of railroads into bankruptcy. By the year's end, 500 banks and over 16,000 businesses failed.

The combination of factors noted above created massive unemployment that widened and deepened the country's economic distress. By December, Samuel Gompers,* president of the American Federation of Labor,* estimated unemployment at three million, while *Bradstreet's*, the business publication, concluded that one million were unemployed. Modern scholars estimate that unemployment was probably 2,500,000. No one counted the millions who were underemployed because of a shortened work week or substantial cuts in wages. The situation for farmers was desperate: the price of wheat fell to $.491 per bushel in 1894 with a similar decline in cotton prices.

The response of the Cleveland administration to the depression was to urge the repeal of the Sherman Silver Purchase Act of 1890 and to revise downward the McKinley Tariff Act of 1890. The administration assumed the repeal of the Silver Act would restore the confidence of the business community and that tariff reform would reduce prices at home and spur export of American raw materials, foodstuffs, and manufactured goods. Repeal of silver did not attack the underlying causes of the depression, and the Wilson-Gorman Tariff Act of 1894 was a mockery of the word "reform" because only wool and lumber were added to the free-of-duty list. The administration turned its back on plans to stimulate recovery by a public works program, but many cities and some states provided a measure of relief by that method. Private charity attempted to provide some aid, but the suffering of millions of Americans, urban and rural, continued until late 1897 when the economy began to improve slowly. (Harold U. Faulkner, *Politics, Reform and Expansion, 1890–1900* (1959); Gerald T. White, *The United States and the Problem of Recovery after 1893* (1982); Samuel Rezneck, *Business Depressions and Financial Panics* (1968).)

David J. Maurer

DETROIT. Detroit during the Progressive Era underwent one of the most profound economic and industrial transformations of any large U.S. city. The city's political life changed less because a powerful model for urban reform had already been laid down a decade earlier by Detroit Mayor Hazen S. Pingree* (1890–97), who also was governor of Michigan (1897–1901). Reform mayors William B. Thompson (1907–1908, 1911–1912) and James Couzens (1919–1922) consciously emulated Pingree and used his name and memory to rally public support for their programs. The city government was reformed with a new charter in 1918 that abolished partisan elections and the ward system of representation and brought in at-large elections with a downsized council of nine and more appointive offices. The tax base was also broadened, and improved safety and health were provided for by ordinances. All of this occurred during one of the most profound economic transformations Detroit was ever to experience.

In 1900 Detroit was a medium-sized city of 285,000 and ranked thirteenth in population, with a mixed manufacturing-service base which included railroad freight-car shops, metal craft industries, marine engineering, and a large consumer product manufacturing sector. The largest single industry, the railroad freight car shops, employed about 7,000 men, less than 12 percent of manufacturing employees. A dramatic change occurred by 1920 when an overwhelming 45 percent of the city's 308,000 industrial employees were in automobile and automobile accessory manufacturing, and the city's population had skyrocketed to nearly one million, fourth in the nation. (Melvin G. Holli, *Detroit* (1975), and "Urban Reform in the Progressive Era," in Lewis L. Gould, ed., *The Progressive Era*, (1974); Jack D. Elenbaas, "Detroit and the Progressive Era: A Study of Urban Reform, 1900–1914" (Ph.D. diss., Wayne State University, 1968).)

Melvin G. Holli

DEVINE, EDWARD THOMAS (May 6, 1867–February 27, 1948). Social worker and editor of the major social work journal, Devine was born on a farm in Iowa;* he was educated at Methodist schools and taught both grammar school and high school in his home state. He earned a Ph.D. in economics at the University of Pennsylvania in 1893, then served as general secretary of the New York Charity Organization Society* from 1896 to 1918. He founded a summer school of philanthropy in 1898, which later became the Columbia University School of Social Work. In 1897 he founded and edited a social work magazine, *Charities*, which became the official organ of the National Conference on Charities and Correction* (later named the National Conference on Social Work). In 1905 it merged with the Chicago Commons* journal and was renamed *Charities and the Commons*. Retitled the *Survey** in 1909, it became the leading journal of social activism and social research. Devine remained chief editor until 1912, then was associate editor until 1921. Thereafter he held a number of posts as professor, writer, and administrator for various social work agencies. An able synthesizer and publicist of social work principles, he greatly advanced the professionalization of social work. (*New York Times* Obituary, February 28, 1948; Edward T. Devine, *When Social Work Was Young* (1939); Clarke A. Chambers, *Paul U. Kellogg and The Survey: Voices for Social Welfare and Social Justice* (1971).)

Edward R. Kantowicz

DEWEY, JOHN (October 20, 1859–June 1, 1952). Born and raised in Burlington, Vermont, Dewey was educated at the University of Vermont and took his Ph.D. at Johns Hopkins University in 1884. His distinguished academic career began at the University of Michigan, continued at the University of Chicago* in 1894, and concluded at Columbia University, 1904–1930, with nine additional years as emeritus philosopher in residence. Prior to his death, Dewey published over 40 books and 750 articles which helped to make him the most influential thinker of the Progressive Era. The half-century-long direct impact of his ideas is evident in such diverse fields as sociology, art, psychology, religion, political science, education, law, and philosophy.

Dewey's personal involvement in progressivism is illustrated by his role in the founding of such organizations as the National Association for the Advancement of Colored People,* the American Association of University Professors,* the American Federation of Teachers, the American Civil Liberties Union,* and the People's Lobby and by his work in the settlement house movement in Chicago* (Hull House* with Jane Addams)* and New York City (Henry Street Settlement* with Lillian Wald).* His belief in and shaping of progressive thought can be seen in continuous contributions to the *New Republic** and his identification with liberal causes such as women's rights, industrial and professional unions, children's rights, immigrants' welfare, the Trotsky Commission, the Sacco-Vanzetti case, and such educational alternatives as the New School for Social Research and the Brookwood Labor College.

Progressives were able to justify much of their social-political program with Dewey's instrumentalist thinking, defined by historian Merle Curti as an "attempt to adapt the scientist's technique of hypothesis, checked through experiment and experience, to the problems of society." In *Ethics*, Dewey provides the following statement which epitomizes the goals of progressivism: "A just social order promotes in all its members habits of criticizing its attained goods and habits of projecting schemes of new goods. It does not aim at intellectual and moral subordination. Every form of social life contains survivals of the past which need to be reorganized . . . Not order, but orderly progress, represents the social idea." (Jo Ann Boydston, ed., *Guide to the Works of John Dewey* (1970); Merle Curti, *The Social Ideas of American Educators* (1935); George Dykhuizen, *The Life and Mind of John Dewey* (1973).)

Chris Eisele

DEWEY, MELVIL (December 10, 1851–December 26, 1931). Born in Adams Center, New York, and graduated from Amherst (1874), Dewey helped form the American public library movement (1876–1920) as founder (1876) and early leader of the American Library Association (twice serving as its president), founder and director of the world's first library school (Columbia College, 1886), and creator of the Dewey Decimal Classification (1876). In 1888, he became New York State librarian and secretary to the board of regents of the University of the State of New York. As state librarian (1888–1905) he introduced innovations like traveling libraries and library services to the handicapped. As secretary (1888–1899) he pressed for improvements in the certification and verification of New York's professional programs.

Dewey was an early advocate of universal use of the metric system, simplified spelling, and managerial efficiency. In 1905, under pressure from New York Jews, he resigned as state librarian to devote full time to the Lake Placid Club, which he had started in 1894 and from which Jews were excluded. Dewey introduced winter sports to America at the club, and expanded it into a major recreation facility for upstate New York. (Grosvenor Dawe, *Melvil Dewey: Seer, Doer, Inspirer* (1932); Sarah K. Vann, *Melvil Dewey: His Enduring Presence in Librarianship* (1978); Gordon Stevenson and Judith Kramer-Greene, eds., *Melvil Dewey: The Man and the Classification* (1983).)

Wayne A. Wiegand

DEWITT, BENJAMIN PARKE (September 21, 1889–June 1, 1965). Born in New York City, he received his B.A. (1909) and M.A. (1912) from New York University and LL.B. from New York Law School (1913). He taught at New York University as a lecturer in English (1910–1913) and subsequently as a lecturer in government. In 1914 he was an unsuccessful candidate for the New York Assembly on the Progressive party* ticket. Most of his life, however, was spent as a practicing attorney. In 1915 he published his pioneering work on progressivism as it was manifested in the Democratic,* Republican,* Progressive, Socialist,* and Prohibition* parties. The emphasis of his work was his observation that the desire of the reformer is to remove self-interest from government, to bend the structure to respond to the majority, and to alleviate social and economic distress. (Benjamin P. DeWitt, *The Progressive Movement* (1968).)

David J. Maurer

DINGLEY TARIFF. A high tariff measure introduced by Republican Representative Nelson Dingley of Maine, the Dingley Tariff was passed by Congress in 1897. Tariff policy had long separated the two major political parties, with Republicans* believing in a high protective tariff and Democrats* favoring tariff reductions. Republican William McKinley* had sponsored a high tariff act in 1890, while still in Congress, but a Democratic administration had made some downward revisions in the Wilson-Gorman Act of 1894. When McKinley became president in 1897, he called a special session of Congress to restore tariff protection to American industry. The Dingley Act, which passed Congress on July 24, 1897, raised rates to an average of 52%. Throughout the Progressive Era, tariff policy remained highly partisan and divisive. Democrats and many Republican Insurgents* used the term "Dingleyism" as a synonym for plutocratic, standpat conservatism. (E. N. Dingley, *Nelson Dingley* (1902); Frank W. Taussig, *The Tariff History of the United States* (1931); Harold U. Faulkner, *Politics, Reform, and Expansion: 1890–1900* (1959).)

Edward R. Kantowicz

DIRECT ELECTION OF U.S. SENATORS. This change in electoral procedure was accomplished by the Seventeenth Amendment to the Constitution, adopted by Congress in 1912 and ratified in 1913. Although the Constitution provided for election of U.S. Senators by state legislatures, amendments to shift to direct popular election were inaugurated in the lower house as early as 1828. State Constitutions prescribed a uniform procedure under which each legislative house first voted separately by roll call and, in case of disagreement, met daily in joint session until one candidate received a clear majority. In 1868, President

Andrew Johnson issued a special message advocating election of senators by popular vote. Agrarian radicals, urban Socialists, and moderate middle-class reformers increasingly portrayed the Senate as filed with corrupt state bosses, retired millionaires, and venal-minded corporation lawyers who represented the will of vested "interests" and blocked or undermined legislation sought by "the people." Journalistic exposés and occasional congressional investigations demonstrated that a number of important senators had received major financial assistance from giant corporations and that others were products of corrupt state political machines. Under public pressure, the House adopted constitutional amendments providing for popular election of senators in 1893, 1894, 1898, 1900, and 1902 (the last by a nearly unanimous vote), but each time the Senate, whose members regarded it as a threat to their political security, either ignored or voted down the proposed change.

Meanwhile, a number of states, mostly in the West, began to adopt primary laws which allowed voters to express their preference for U.S. Senators, which state legislators were pledged to ratify automatically. Nebraska adopted such a primary in 1875 and Nevada in 1899; by 1912, twenty-nine states in essence directly elected their senators. A scandal in 1911 over revelations of wholesale bribery in the Illinois Assembly in the election of William Lorimer* provided a majority for the long-sought reform. The Senate refused to seat Lorimer, and following the retirement of ten senators who had opposed the amendment, the upper chamber adopted the Seventeenth Amendment by five votes over a two-thirds majority in June 1911. It received ratification by three-fourths of the state legislatures and went into effect on May 31, 1913. The achievement of popular election helped to alter significantly the composition of the Senate. There were fewer political bosses and retired millionaires and a greater turnover of senators during the following decades. However, popular election also enormously increased the cost of winning an election. (George H. Haynes, *The Election of Senators* (1912); George H. Haynes, *The Senate of the United States: Its History and Practice* (1938); Linsay Rogers, *The American Senate* (1926); Richard F. Fenno, Jr., *The United States Senate: A Bicameral Perspective* (1982).)

John Whiteclay Chambers II

DISFRANCHISEMENT. Beginning in Georgia and Mississippi in the 1870s, and spreading across the region in succeeding decades, voter disfranchisement created a one-party, overwhelmingly Democratic South. Violence intimidated Mississippi blacks long before the passage of the constitutional disfranchisement of 1890. A cumulative poll tax effectively barred poor black Georgia voters in 1872. Other states passed restrictive laws in the 1880s. Florida copied South Carolina's scheme in which voters had to put separate ballots correctly into eight boxes, each representing a different political office, or be disqualified. South Carolina also used discretionary voter registration to disfranchise black voters. Tennessee introduced the secret ballot, or Australian ballot,* as an electoral reform which put a premium on voter literacy in a region where black illiteracy ranged from 39 to 61 percent.

By the 1890s, six states had eliminated three-quarters or more of their black voters, while two more maintained them, but in the Democratic column. The constitutional conventions and amendments to complete the disfranchisement of blacks took place between 1890 and 1910 in eight states. Only Alabama put the issue to the voters; the other states avoided ratification by simply proclaiming disfranchisement. Voter restrictions reduced black participation from more than 50 percent in nine Southern states in the 1880s to less than 10 percent in all but two Southern states by 1910. The poll tax enacted in every ex-Confederate state by 1904 discouraged poor people, both black and white, from voting, as did literacy tests. As a result, white voter registration and election tallies declined substantially across the region. During these same years, a number of Northern states also introduced literacy tests and the Australian ballot as "reforms" to eliminate illiterate foreign voters.

In the South, disfranchisement was identified with progressive reform, but leading advocates were highly partisan. Except for Mississippi, most efforts to limit the franchise followed the challenge of opposition parties to Democratic rule. The effect of disfranchisement created not only a one-party South that lasted for more than half a century, but it resulted in the increasing governmental services of the Progressive Era and beyond being largely limited to middle-class whites, a "reactionary revolution." (J. Morgan Kousser, *The Shaping of Southern Politics: Suffrage Restriction and the Establishment of the One-Party South, 1880–1910* (1974); C. Vann Woodward, *Origins of the New South, 1877–1913* (1951); William Alexander Mabry, "The Disfranchisement of the Negro in the South" (Ph.D. diss., Duke University, 1933).)

James B. Crooks

DISTRIBUTION OF WEALTH AND INCOME. Distribution data is poor, but certainly wealth ownership was highly concentrated. G. K. Holmes estimated that in 1890 the richest 9 percent of the families owned 71 percent of all wealth, and 4,047 millionaires had 20 percent. Wealth concentration probably increased slightly from 1890 to 1914, lessened during World War I,* and intensified in the twenties. For incomes we lack systematic government surveys before the thirties, and mountains of pay data have received little comprehensive analysis. Stanley Lebergott estimates that half of all families had annual incomes under $700 and fewer than one in ten families had a middle-class income of $1,200 or more. Ethnic and occupational maldistribution was sharp. Of nonfarm families, 89.2 percent of nonwhites and 34.3 percent of whites had less than $700 a year. In 1904, railroad executives earned $2,803, full professors $2,000 and instructors $ 800; small-town schoolteachers earned only $446 and farm laborers $290. On the whole, income gaps probably widened in the Progressive Era; the poverty rate among manufacturing workers was roughly the same in 1890 and

1914 and showed a sharp increase from 38.63 percent to 43.89 percent between 1900 and 1909. During World War I,* incomes became more equal as unskilled and farm laborers' wages surpassed the 100 percent rate of inflation, and most white-collar and artisan groups lost purchasing power. (Jeffrey G. Williamson and Peter H. Lindert, *American Inequality: A Macroeconomic History* (1980); Stanley Lebergott, *The American Economy: Income, Wealth, and Want* (1976); Peter R. Shergold, "Wage Differentials Based on Skill in the United States, 1899–1914: A Case Study," *Labor History* 18 (1977): 485–508; G. K. Holmes, "The Concentration of Wealth," *Political Science Quarterly* 81 (1893): 589–600.

Frank Stricker

DIVORCE. One of the most disturbing social issues of this era was divorce. Contemporaries referred to a "divorce crisis," observing not only an increase in the number of divorces but also a near doubling in the ratio of divorces to existing marriages. While some commentators blamed women's liberation and others pointed to immorality, all agreed that divorce was dangerous because it threatened the stability of the family, which was the basis of civilization. Discussion was most intense from 1904 to 1912 and included various proposals for restrictive, uniform legislation. Some, like Theodore Roosevelt,* favored a constitutional amendment and federal control. More supported state enactment of model divorce laws, proposed by the National Conference of Commissioners on Uniform State Laws and by the National Divorce Congress, which met in 1906 with delegates from nearly every state. Although few states adopted the uniform law, many passed restrictive legislation. The provisions included a longer residency requirement, a waiting period before remarriage, public defense for an absent party, less judicial discretionary power, and fewer grounds. Divorce was also blamed on inadequate marriage laws, and many states raised the age of consent, required public notice and medical tests, and prohibited the marriage of certain persons. (William L. O'Neill, *Divorce in the Progressive Era* (1967); Elaine Tyler May, *Great Expectations: Marriage and Divorce in Post-Victorian America* (1980); Nelson M. Blake, *The Road to Reno* (1962).)

Philip R. VanderMeer

DIXON, JOSEPH M. (July 31, 1867–May 22, 1934). Born of Quaker parents in Snow Camp, North Carolina, Dixon was educated at Earlham and Guilford colleges. He moved to Missoula, Montana, in 1891 to study law and practice law and politics. After serving as county attorney and state legislator, Dixon became Montana's lone congressman in 1903 and a senator in 1907. Dixon's independence of the national Republican leadership was noticeable by 1910, and he also alienated the Amalgamated Copper Mining Company and Montana Power, both ruthless forces in state politics.

A devout Rooseveltian, Dixon was one of the few holders of a major office to leave his party. He managed both the preconvention and the Progressive party* campaigns in 1912. These duties compelled him to make his unsuccessful bid for reelection in absentia. With his political career apparently ended, Dixon published and edited the *Missoulian* until 1917. He survived a six-man Republican gubernatorial primary in 1920, and was elected in November when "The Company" felt compelled to support him against the misnamed "Bolshevik Burt" Wheeler.* In 1924, however, "The Company" marshaled its forces to successfully punish Dixon for his Rooseveltian behavior and measures. Failing in a bid for a senatorial seat in 1928, Dixon ended his political career as Hoover's assistant secretary of the interior. (Oscar Davis King, *Released for Publication* (1925); Shirley Jean DeForth, "The Montana Press and Governor Joseph M. Dixon, 1920–1922" (M.A. thesis, University of Montana, 1959); Jules A. Karlin, *Joseph M. Dixon of Montana*, 2 vols. (1974).)

Jules A. Karlin

DIXON, THOMAS (January 11, 1864–April 3, 1946). Born in Shelby, North Carolina, Dixon graduated from Wake Forest College in 1883 with an M.A. and went on a scholarship to Johns Hopkins University, where he became friends with his fellow student Woodrow Wilson.* Restless, he left for an initial try at the stage, returning to North Carolina where he was elected to the state legislature in 1884, received an LL.B from Greensboro Law School in 1886, and left politics for the Baptist ministry. From 1886 to 1899, he preached with controversial eloquence and passion in Raleigh, Boston, and New York City. His speaking ability brought him success in politics and the pulpit, on the stage and the lecture tour.

In 1899, he left the ministry and began writing historical novels. He was to write twenty-two novels, nine stage plays, and six screen scripts, and to produce five movies. After seeing a production of *Uncle Tom's Cabin*, he wrote the "true story" of the South, *The Leopard's Spots* (1903), and continued his emotional explanation in many of his subsequent novels. His Ku Klux Klan story, *The Clansman* (1905), was the basis of D. W. Griffith's* epic movie *The Birth of a Nation.** In his writing, Dixon rejected slavery, biracialism, the Klan of the 1920s, which his book helped revive, and the dangers of capitalist greed, socialism and communism, the "new woman," and the New Deal. (Raymond A. Cook, *Thomas Dixon* (1974); *Dictionary of American Biography*, Supplement 4.)

David Chalmers

DODD, WILLIAM EDWARD (October 21, 1869–February 9, 1940). Born near Clayton, North Carolina, Dodd graduated from Virginia Polytechnic Institute in 1895 and went to Leipzig in 1897 where he completed his doctoral dissertation, *Thomas Jeffersons Ruckkehr zur Politik, 1796* (1899). Among the first specialists in Southern history, Dodd began teaching at Randolph-Macon in 1900, and after 1908 spent the remainder of his academic career at the University of Chicago.* In 1934 he was elected to the presidency of the American Historical Association.* Dodd's publications were numerous, though not of enduring interest to scholars in the field, for instance, *Jefferson Davis* (1907), *Expansion and Conflict* (1915), *The Cotton Kingdom: A Chronicle of the Old South* (1919), *Lincoln or Lee* (1928). Dodd's style was succinct but literary; his manner was described by admiring students as gracious and quaint in the Jeffersonian tradition of high public thinking and simple but comfortable living.

A Jeffersonian ideologue and publicist, Dodd viewed both antebellum Southern aristocracy and late nineteenth-century industrial monopoly as forms of feudalism, obstructing the historical formation of middle-class economic democracy. He drew a straight historical line from Jefferson to Lincoln to Woodrow Wilson,* for whom Dodd penned popular partisan defenses as well as co-edited the public papers. An academic man of affairs, Dodd ended his career in a controversial tour as the American ambassador to Nazi Germany. *Dictionary of American Biography*, vol. 22; Wendell Holmes Stephenson, *The South Lives in History: Southern Historians and Their Legacy* (1955).)

Burton J. Bledstein

DOLLAR DIPLOMACY. Although used generically to apply to any American effort to influence international affairs with American economic strength, dollar diplomacy is most specifically associated with the foreign policy of President William Howard Taft,* who believed that ''substituting dollars for bullets'' served American strategic, economic, and humanitarian interests. Advocated by Secretary of State Philander C. Knox,* a former corporate lawyer, the policy was most actively pursued in relations with China and the Caribbean. The American government urged American bankers to join French, German, and British bankers in Chinese railroad financing. The foreign bankers and Chinese authorities also had to be convinced of the wisdom of American involvement. Similar effort to join or replace Japanese and Russian interests in a Manchurian railroad were repelled. Taft also endeavored to stabilize or install friendly Caribbean government and keep out European influence by providing government loans and supporting American corporate investments. Responding to criticism of American economic imperialism, President Woodrow Wilson* launched his administration by denouncing dollar diplomacy as practiced in both China and Latin America. (Scott Nearing and Joseph Freeman, *Dollar Diplomacy: A Study in American Imperialism* (1925); Dana G. Munro, *Intervention and Dollar Diplomacy in the Caribbean, 1900–1921* (1964); Walter V. Scholes and Marie V. Scholes, *The Foreign Policies of the Taft Administration* (1970).)

Martin I. Elzy

DOLLIVER, JONATHAN PRENTISS (February 6, 1858–October 15, 1910). An Insurgent Republican senator from Iowa, Dolliver was born in Kingwood, Virginia, educated at West Virginia University, and practiced law in Fort Dodge, Iowa, from 1878 to 1888. Elected to Congress in the latter year, he served six terms before being appointed to the U.S. Senate upon the death of John H. Gear. Elected in 1903 and 1907, he served until his own death. Prior to 1909, Dolliver generally sided with Republican regulars, following the lead of senior Iowa Senator William B. Allison in supporting imperialism, the gold standard, and unregulated business activity. But the rise of the "Iowa Idea" promoted by Governor, later Senator, Albert B. Cummins* and the arrival in the Senate of Robert M. La Follette* and other midwestern Insurgents* pushed Dolliver to the left. During the critical 1909 session of Congress, he joined the Insurgents in pushing for stringent railroad regulation, a federal income tax, and postal savings banks, and in backing Gifford Pinchot* when he was fired by President William Howard Taft.* Most notably, he lent his considerable oratorical skills and his expertise to Insurgent efforts to lower the Payne-Aldrich Tariff.* He is perhaps best remembered for his observation that "President Taft is an amiable man completely surrounded by men who know exactly what they want." (Thomas Richard Ross, *Jonathan Prentiss Dolliver: A Study in Political Integrity and Independence* (1958).)

John D. Buenker

DORR, RHETA CHILDE (November 2, 1866–August 8, 1948). Born in Omaha, Nebraska, Dorr attended the University of Nebraska and in 1890 moved to New York City. A suffragist since age twelve, Dorr became a prominent investigative journalist and writer on feminist and women's issues after securing in 1902 a position on the New York *Evening Post*. Under the auspices of the General Federation of Women's Clubs,* Dorr gathered a coalition of women reformers that campaigned successfully for the first major investigation of the conditions of working women conducted by the U.S. Bureau of Labor. While traveling in Europe in 1906, Dorr renewed her commitment to woman suffrage, and in 1914 became the first editor of the *Suffragist*, published by the Congressional Union for Woman Suffrage, forerunner of the National Woman's Party.* Dorr's most notable book, *What Eight Million Women Want* (1910), presented her views on woman suffrage, the condition of wage-earning women, and various facets of the women's movement. Briefly a member of the Socialist party,* Dorr servered her radical and many reform ties following the Russian Revolution, the subject of *Inside the Russian Revolution* (1917). Dorr died in New Britain, Pennsylvania. (Rheta Childe Dorr, *A Woman of Fifty* (1924); Ishbel Ross, *Ladies of the Press* (1936); Louis Filler, *Crusaders for American Liberalism* (1939).)

Mari Jo Buhle

DRIER, MARY ELIZABETH (September 26, 1875–August 15, 1963). Born in Brooklyn, New York, of German immigrant parents, the sister of Margaret Dreier Robins,* Dreier began a career as a settlement house worker in 1899. Four years later, she joined the National Women's Trade Union League,* serving as president of its New York chapter from 1906 to 1914. Arrested during a 1909 shirtmakers strike that led to the "uprising of the Twenty Thousand," she was appointed to the New York State Factory Investigating Commission* after the tragic Triangle Shirtwaist fire that took 146 workers' lives in 1911. Fellow member Alfred E. Smith* later called her the "soul" of the commission. Turning her attention to woman suffrage,* Dreier chaired the New York City Suffrage party and headed the industrial section of the party's state organization. A delegate to the Progressive party* convention in 1912, she supported Charles Evans Hughes* in 1916, voted for Robert M. La Follette in 1924, and endorsed Franklin D. Roosevelt and the New Deal in the 1930s. (Leon Stein, *The Triangle Fire* (1962); J. Joseph Huthmacher, *Senator Robert F. Wagner and the Rise of Urban Liberalism* (1968); Nancy Schrom Dye, *As Equals and as Sisters: Feminism, the Labor Movement, and the Women's Trade Union League of New York* (1980).)

John D. Buenker

DREISER, THEODORE (August 27, 1871–December 28, 1945). The twelfth child of an indigent German Catholic immigrant, Theodore Dreiser was the first important American writer whose family was not English or Scotch-Irish. Raised in almost unrelieved poverty, Dreiser left home at fifteen to go to Chicago and work at odd jobs until a former teacher provided him with the money to attend college for a year. His break came when his Chicago newspaper editor recognized his abilities and got him a job on the Saint Louis *Globe Democrat*. He left there in 1894 to work his way toward New York. It was on this journey that he read Herbert Spencer* and Thomas Henry Huxley, a discovery that he said blew him "intellectually to bits," and gave form and meaning to the brutality of life which the young reporter had himself witnessed.

After a successful stint as a magazine editor, he turned to writing short stories and then to the publication of the controversial *Sister Carrie*. An unsuccessful marriage led to a temporary breakdown, after which he did physical labor until he was able to write again. Following success editing magazines in which his own writings would never have been allowed to appear, he found considerable fame with the publication of *Jennie Gerhardt*. His most sensual novel *The "Genius"* was already underway, but publishers were much more interested in his projected study of Charles T. Yerkes,* which became *The Titan* and *The Financier*. Dreiser's chief problems during the remainder of the Progressive years revolved around the conflict he stirred up with the watchdogs of American morals. The chief battle concerned publication of *The "Genius"* and involved the continuing support of Dreiser's close friend, H. L. Mencken. It was in 1925 that Dreiser produced his most famous work, *An American Tragedy*, in which he argued that the real criminal was not the individual that he portrayed, but the deprived environment in which he was raised. (Robert W. Schneider, *Five Novelists of the Progressive Era* (1965); F. O. Matthiessen, *Theodore Dreiser* (1951); Ronald Lingeman, *Theodore Dreiser: At the Gates of the City, 1871–1907* (1986).)

Robert W. Schneider

DU BOIS, WILLIAM EDWARD BURGHARDT (February 23, 1868–August 27, 1963). Born in Great Barrington, Massachusetts, W. E. B. Du Bois bore French Huguenot, Dutch, and African ancestry. A precocious youth, he earned baccalaureates from Fisk University and Harvard University, studied at the University of Berlin, and received a doctorate from Harvard in 1895. He became a faculty member of Wilberforce College, the University of Pennsylvania and, from 1897 to 1910, Atlanta University.

Du Bois espoused the "Talented Tenth" concept of educated, black leadership, seemingly paradoxical theories of racial solidarity and full integration, and belief in solving racial discord through social science research. Like Booker T. Washington,* he advocated black self-help and economic development, but he opposed the Tuskegeean's emphasis on industrial education, abdication of civil and political rights, and willingness to accommodate white racism. As the position of Afro-Americans deteriorated, Du Bois openly criticized Washington in *The Souls of Black Folk* (1903). He headed the mostly northern-bred, college-educated black "radicals" who challenged Washington through the Niagara Movement (1905). Their neo-abolitionist effort failed in the face of financial limitations, internal squabbles, Washington's maneuvers, and white racism. Yet it helped lay the basis for the National Association for the Advancement of Colored People.* In 1909, Du Bois and the radicals drew support from a handful of northern progressives and socialists horrified by the 1908 race riot in Springfield, Illinois.

Du Bois became editor of the *Crisis** and, upon Washington's death in 1915, the most influential black spokesperson until the emergence of Marcus Garvey in the 1920s. Still he alienated many blacks by shelving racial grievances during World War I,* and he never trusted his progressive allies. Like them, he believed in pragmatism and organization as the means to guarantee Afro-Americans equal opportunity and first-class citizenship; unlike most of them and despite his own elitism, he stressed the group, promoted Pan-Africanism, examined socialism, and challenged white supremacy. His greatest influence occurred during the Progressive Era as protester and propagandist for black manhood. (Francis L. Broderick, *W. E. B. Du Bois: A Study in Minority Group Leadership* (1960); W. E. B. Du Bois, *The Autobiography of W. E. B. Du Bois: A Soliloquy on Viewing My Life from the Last Decade of Its First Century* (1968).)

Dominic J. Capeci, Jr.

DUKE, JAMES BUCHANAN (December 23, 1856–October 10, 1925). Born near Durham, North Carolina, Duke received intermittent education, but his primary education and evident skill lay in the family's business—first farming, then hand manufacture and "drumming" of tobacco products, and later under his direction mass production and mass advertising of cigarettes. At the age of twenty-eight, "Buck" opened a branch factory in New York City which was furnishing half the country's total production of cigarettes within five years. After a "tobacco war" among the five principal manufacturers, Duke emerged as president of the American Tobacco Company, which became a multinational corporation within a decade. Through numerous combinations, both foreign and domestic, Duke interests controlled the manufacture of a variety of tobacco products before the U.S. Supreme Court ordered the dissolution of the trust as a combination in restraint of trade in 1911. As textile interests expanded, the search for economical water power led the Dukes into the hydroelectric field with the founding of the Southern, later Duke, Power Company in 1905. Ardently Republican and sympathetic to the downtrodden, Duke gave to numerous causes and established the Duke Endowment and Duke University. (Duke Family Papers, University Archives, Duke University; Robert F. Durden, *The Dukes of Durham* (1975); Earl W. Porter, *Trinity and Duke, 1892–1924* (1964).)

William E. King

DUNNE, EDWARD F. (October 12, 1853–May 24, 1937). Born in Waterville, Connecticut, Dunne was educated at Trinity College, Dublin, and the Union College of Law. After practicing law in Chicago from 1877 to 1892, he was appointed a Cook County circuit judge, and won reelection in 1897 and 1903. Advocating municipal ownership of the traction system, he was elected mayor of Chicago on April 4, 1905. Although he failed to achieve municipal ownership, Dunne compiled a progressive record in education, labor relations, and utilities regulation. He also served as vice president of the National Civic Federation* and president of the League of American Municipalities in 1906. Narrowly defeated for reelection as mayor in 1907, Dunne was elected governor of Illinois in 1912. The Dunne administration (1913–1917) distinguished itself in its concern for labor, welfare, regulatory, and penal reform and enactment of limited woman suffrage, but failed to create a tax commission, adopt direct legislation, build a deep waterway, control electoral practices, or obtain home rule* for Chicago. In 1916, Dunne was defeated by Frank O. Lowden* and devoted the rest of his life to law, Democratic politics, and Irish-American causes. In 1919, he led a delegation for Irish independence to the Versailles Conference. (William L. Sullivan, comp., *Dunne: Judge, Mayor, Governor* (1916); Richard E. Becker, "Edward Dunne: Reform Mayor of Chicago, 1905–07" (Ph.D. diss., University of Chicago, 1971); John D. Buenker, "Edward F. Dunne: The Urban New Stock Democrat as Progressive," *Mid-America* 50 (1968): 3–21.)

John D. Buenker

DUNNE, FINLEY PETER (July 10, 1867–April 24, 1936). Born in Chicago and educated in public schools, Dunne went to work as a reporter in 1884, then worked for six different papers over the next few years. In 1893 he began a series of Irish dialect stories for the *Chicago Evening Post*, featuring saloon keeper Martin Dooley of the Archey Road, who commented on local politics and other issues of the day. Through the voice of Dooley, his faithful listener Hennessey, and the other characters who trooped through Dooley's saloon, Dunne re-created the life of ordinary working-class immigrants in the neighborhood of Bridgeport on Chicago's South Side. Beginning with *Mr. Dooley in Peace and in War* (1898), collections of the Dooley stories appeared regularly in book form. Dunne moved to New York in 1900 and wrote both Dooley stories

and standard journalism for *Collier's*.* He joined with Lincoln Steffens* and
other muckrakers* in 1906 to establish the *American Magazine*,* but he returned
to *Collier's* in 1915 and retired in the mid-1920s. Dunne's Dooley stories continued a Chicago tradition of hard-hitting political journalism and expanded the
horizons of vernacular, direct humor. (Elmer Ellis, *Mr. Dooley's America* (1941);
Barbara C. Schaaf, *Mr. Dooley's Chicago* (1977); Charles Fanning, *Finley Peter
Dunne and Mr. Dooley: The Chicago Years* (1978).)

Edward R. Kantowicz

E

EASTMAN, CRYSTAL (June 25, 1881–July 8, 1928). Born in Marlborough, Massachusetts, Eastman graduated from Vassar College in 1903, received a master's degree in sociology from Columbia University and a law degree from New York University Law School. She joined Paul Kellogg* on the Pittsburgh Survey,* where she investigated industrial accidents. As secretary to the New York State Employer's Liability Commission, Eastman drafted New York's first workmen's compensation* law, later used as model legislation. An active suffragist, she served as campaign manager for the Wisconsin Political Equality League in the unsuccessful 1912 suffrage campaign. In 1913, she helped found the Congressional Union and served as its representative to the International Woman Suffrage Alliance in Budapest. At this time, Eastman became active in the international women's peace movement, and in 1914 organized the New York branch of the Woman's Peace Party* and later cofounded the National Woman's Peace Party and the American Union Against Militarism (AUAM). With U.S. entry into the war, Eastman, Roger Baldwin, and Norman Thomas organized a committee within the AUAM, the Civil Liberties Bureau, to help defend conscientious objectors. In 1917, she became managing editor of the radical journal *Liberator*. Throughout her life, she supported herself by writing about feminism and socialism for various journals. (Barbara Sicherman et al., *Notable American Women: The Modern Period*; Blanche Wiesen Cook, *Crystal Eastman on Women and Revolution* (1971).)

Marie Laberge

EASTMAN, MAX (January 4, 1883–March 25, 1969). Eastman was a prominent publicist, critic, and editor whose career took him from origins of clerical piety to fervent radicalism and ultimately to far-right conservatism. Educated at Williams College and Columbia University, he came to New York City in 1907 and soon secured a place for himself among rebellious Greenwich Village intellectuals. He became active in the woman's rights movement, linking this cause to political democracy and socialism. In 1912 he assumed the editorship of the *Masses*,* a magazine of political and cultural radicalism that boldly challenged conventional beliefs. A person of considerable energy and spirit, Eastman was able to gain the support of talented colleagues and contributors.

As an opponent of American involvement in World War I,* Eastman was indicted under the repressive Espionage Act* although two trials failed to produce a conviction. Initially sympathetic to the new Soviet regime, Eastman in 1921 traveled to Russia, where he was greatly impressed with Trotsky and formed a close friendship with the Russian leader. Shortly after Lenin's death, Eastman wrote a book, *Since Lenin's Death*, that justified Trotsky's position. Eastman later emerged as a leading critic of Soviet society, a rigid, doctrinaire anticommunist, and a supporter of Senator Joseph R. McCarthy in the 1950s. (Milton Cantor, *Max Eastman* (1970); William L. O'Neil, *The Last Romantic: A Life of Max Eastman* (1978); Max Eastman, *Love and Revolution: My Journey through an Epoch* (1964).)

Herbert Shapiro

EDDY, MARY BAKER (July 16, 1821–December 3, 1910). Born near Concord, New Hampshire, she received most of her education at home because of frail health. In 1862, she met Phineas P. Quimby, a mind healer, who influenced her life and thought but whose ideas she significantly modified. In 1866, while confined to bed, she read the biblical account of Jesus' healing a paralytic (Matthew 9:2–8) and claimed a miraculous healing which gave her a mission in life. She published *Science and Health* (1875), the major statement of her beliefs, and founded and pastored the first Church of Christ, Scientist (1879), which appealed predominantly to urban middle- and upper-class women in the United States. She organized the Massachusetts Metaphysical College for the training of practitioners (1881) and founded the monthly *Christian Science Journal* (1883), the weekly *Sentinel* (1898), and the daily *Monitor* (1908). Mrs. Eddy discovered an enormously successful way to integrate mental health with religion. She projected an equal feminine nature and image for God and encouraged equality of the sexes, although she played no important role in the women's rights movement. She offered a religion in the patriarchal nineteenth century in which a woman could play a leading role. (Robert Peel, *Mary Baker Eddy*, 3 vols. (1966–1977); Edward T. James, et al., *Notable American Women*, vol. 1 (1971); Dr. Julius Silberger, Jr., ''Mary Baker Eddy,'' *American Heritage* 31 (December 1980): 56–64.)

Paul C. Witt

EDUCATION, ADULT. The quickening pace of economic and social life in the late nineteenth century, sparked by massive industrialization* and immigration, stimulated an interest among reformers, schoolmen, and others in offering a variety of evening programs for adults. Centered in settlement houses,

YMCAs,* businesses, and particularly public schools, classes were offered in a variety of academic, vocational, and recreational areas. Urban public schools often became night social centers—a concept pioneered in Rochester, New York, and copied in other cities such as Gary, Indiana—offering a large array of academic, industrial, and commercial courses, public speakers, films, recreational facilities, and public meetings. Americanization* of the immigrants was particularly popular in large cities among public officials, reaching a frenzy during and after World War I,* with an emphasis on English and citizenship. Although many participated, attendance was spotty. Long working days left little time for night schooling, and many were suspicious of the programs, such as immigrant women offended by the homemaking classes offered in the schools and settlement houses. In some cities, attendance continued to grow; the night enrollment exceeded the day enrollment in the Gary schools by the early 1920s. Purely voluntary, adult education offered native and immigrant alike the opportunity to learn skills, go swimming, hear a lecture, and meet others within a supervised environment. (Edward J. Ward, *The Social Center* (1913); William J. Reese, *Power and the Promise of School Reform: Grass Roots Movements during the Progressive Era* (1986); John F. McClymer, "The Americanization Movement and the Education of the Foreign-Born Adult, 1914–25," in Bernard J. Weiss, ed., *American Education and the European Immigrant: 1840–1940* (1982), 96–116.)

Ronald D. Cohen

EDUCATION, COMPULSORY. Most (thirty-one) states had passed compulsory attendance legislation by 1900. The last state to do so was Mississippi in 1918. After 1900, most states passed amendments that made the legislation enforceable, especially passage of effective child labor legislation, but the effect of legislation on school attendance rates was relatively marginal and confined to the poor and chronically truant. The decline in the demand for youth labor, and widespread occupational and status aspirations, were far more important in promoting universal education.

The justification of more effective compulsory attendance legislation relied on the doctrine of *parens patriae* and claims that the survival of republican institutions, the protection of property, and the prevention of crime and pauperism necessitated it particularly in light of urbanization, immigration, and social conflict. Opponents claimed that compulsory education usurped the rights of parents and violated the pluralist principles of American life.

In Illinois and Wisconsin in 1889, the state legislatures attempted to require public and private schools to teach the English language, but opposition from ethnic and religious groups forced repeal of the laws. In *Pierce v. Society of Sisters* (1925) the U.S. Supreme Court ruled that the state of Oregon lacked the authority to compel all children to attend public schools. It did, however, recognize the right of the state, in the interests of "good citizenship," to require "inspect, supervise and examine" private schools, although it left ambiguous the right of the state to compel attendance per se at any school, public or private. (Forest C. Ensign, *Compulsory School Attendance and Child Labor* (1921); Belvedere Press, *Oregon School Cases* (1925); Richard J. Jensen, *The Winning of the Midwest: Social and Political Conflict, 1888–96* (1971); David J. Hogan, *Class and Reform: School and Society in Chicago, 1880–1930* (1985).)

David Hogan

EDUCATION, INDUSTRIAL. Industrial education began as part of the broader vocational education movement in the late nineteenth century. With the decline of union apprenticeship programs and the rise of massive industrialization, both capital and labor recognized the need for job training programs. Courses were offered in public and private day and night schools, industries, YMCAs,* and other agencies. Part of the Booker T. Washington* program at Tuskegee Institute in Alabama and other black schools in the South was industrially oriented. While promoters emphasized meeting the needs and interests of students, particularly blacks and recent immigrants, they were also concerned about increasing industrial efficiency through producing trained, docile workers, male and female.

Trade classes were usually found in comprehensive secondary schools, such as the Froebel school in the steel town of Gary, Indiana, which offered forge, foundry, and sheet metal classes. There were also separate facilities, such as New York's Vocational School for Boys, and in some cities, such as Fitchburg, Massachusetts, classes were held in various factories. Private vocational bureaus were early established to place students in jobs, but they were replaced after 1910 by vocational guidance counselors in the secondary schools who would reconcile the needs of industry and the interests of students. Industrial education was flourishing at various levels by World War I,* but its effectiveness was questioned, as most workers still learned on the job. (Robert L. Church and Michael W. Sedlak, *Education in the United States: An Interpretative History* (1976); Paul Violas, *The Training of the Urban Working Class: A History of Twentieth Century American Education* (1978); Harvey Kantor and David B. Tyack, eds., *Work, Youth, and Schooling: Historical Perspectives on Vocationalism in American Education* (1982).)

Ronald D. Cohen

EDUCATION, PROGRESSIVE. Too heteronomous in ideology, personnel, and support to constitute a unitary reform ''movement,'' ''progressive education'' is primarily useful as an omnibus term to incorporate widely disparate reform activities between the late 1880s and the mid-1920s: passage of effective compulsory education* and child labor legislation;* the rapid expansion of secondary education; the introduction of junior high schools, ability grouping, intelligence testing, vocational guidance, and kindergartens; the creation of juvenile courts* and reformatories; the Americanization* of immigrant children; the centralization and bureaucratization of school governance; the professionalization of school administration and the unionization of teachers; curricula reform, es-

pecially manual training, vocational education,* the "education for life" recommendations of the National Education Association's* "Cardinal Principles"
(1918), John Dewey's* Laboratory School, W. H. Kilpatrick's "project
method"; the extension of elementary and vocational education to some southern
blacks; the triumph of developmentalist and behaviorist perspectives in educational psychology; and child-centered pedagogies.

Three competing but sometimes overlapping ideological perspectives developed: a "social efficiency" wing that worked to integrate public education into
the labor market as a hierarchically governed social sorting institution, a utili-
tarian-democratic perspective that stressed the "adjustment" of schools to new
social and educational conditions and problems, and a "child-centered" wing
that focused on introducing pedagogical and curricula innovations that aroused
the "curiosity" and served the "interests" of children. In 1919 activists formed
the Progressive Education Association. (John Dewey, *Democracy and Education*
(1916); Lawrence A. Cremin, *The Transformation of the School: Progressivism
in American Education, 1877–1957* (1961); Raymond E. Callahan, *Education
and the Cult of Efficiency* (1962); David B. Tyack, *The One Best System: A
History of American Urban Education* (1974); David J. Hogan, *Class and Reform: School and Society in Chicago, 1880–1930* (1985).)

David Hogan

EDUCATION, TEACHER. Teacher training was in a state of considerable
ferment in the years between 1890 and 1930. The nation's public school system
grew rapidly in this period, and demand for new teachers was acute, particularly
in the cities. There was wide variation in the educational requirements for teaching from one part of the country to another. A survey of American teachers
conducted in 1910, focusing particularly on rural teachers, found that nearly
two-thirds of them had not received any training beyond the high school level.
The vast majority of such poorly educated teachers were employed in elementary
schools; high school teachers were generally required to have some college-level
training. Young men and women could be prepared to teach in a high school or
academy, in a normal school, or at a college or university. In time, the role of
high school in teacher education was eclipsed by that of the normal schools,
which started their evolution into state teachers colleges in this period. The
commitment of the colleges and universities to teacher education grew as well,
particularly as larger numbers of their graduates found employment in the rapidly
expanding high schools.

At the same time, there was considerable variation in the methods used to
educate teachers. The traditional approach, which probably exerted its greatest
influence in the normal schools, was to combine a smattering of academic subjects
with courses in pedagogical principles, history and/or philosophy of education,
and some practice teaching. Innovative teacher education curricula were developed by Francis Parker at the Cook County Normal School and John Dewey*
at the University of Chicago* who stressed academic preparation for teachers

and the importance of psychology as a way of comprehending the learning process. Dewey's essay "The Relation of Theory to Practice in Education" (in the *Third Yearbook of the National Society for the Scientific Study of Education*, Bloomington, Illinois, 1904) is a classic Progressive statement on teacher education, and continues to exert considerable influence today. (Merle L. Borrowman, *Teacher Education in America: A Documentary History* (1965); Merle L. Borrowman, *The Liberal and the Technical in Teacher Education: A Historical Survey of American Thought* (1956); Walter S. Monroe, *Teaching-Learning Theory and Teacher Education, 1890–1950* (1952).)

John Rury

EDUCATION, VOCATIONAL. Manual training was introduced into American public schooling in the 1870s. The movement had various influences: Calvin Woodward's connection of the "cultured mind" and the "skillful hand" in Saint Louis, the adoption of neo-Pestalozzian teaching methods that emphasized learning by doing, and the English reformers John Ruskin and William Morris. By the turn of the century, John Dewey's* connection of hand and mind gave the movement, now widespread, a sure footing. With the rise of industrial capitalism and the rapid increase of school populations, the movement became more vocational in the public schools as well as in the numerous private trade schools. Businessmen, led by the National Association of Manufacturers,* supported vocational programs in order to acquire reliable, trained workers. The American Federation of Labor* backed them after 1907 in order to have some influence, although insisting on incorporating trade training in comprehensive high schools. The Smith-Hughes Act* in 1917 provided federal funds for trade and industrial, home economics, and agriculture courses in public secondary schools. Much more popular, however, were the commercial and business subjects, with the boys preferring the latter, and an increasing number of girls enrolling in typing, stenography, and bookkeeping. (Harvey Kantor and David Tyack, eds., *Work, Youth, and Schooling: Historical Perspectives on Vocationalism in American Education* (1982); Marvin Lazerson and W. Norton Grub, eds., *American Education and Vocationalism: A Documentary History, 1870–1970* (1974); Marvin Lazerson, *Origins of the Urban School: Public Education in Massachusetts, 1870–1915* (1971).)

Ronald D. Cohen

EFFICIENCY. The Progressive Era gave rise to an efficiency craze (1910–1916), an outpouring of ideas and emotion in which a gospel of efficiency was preached without embarrassment to businessmen, workers, reformers, politicians, administrators, housewives, teachers, and even preachers. This secular great awakening was set off by Louis D. Brandeis's* extraordinary argument before the Interstate Commerce Commission* in the Eastern Rate Case* (1910–1911) claiming that the railroads, by adopting new and more efficient management techniques, could cut costs and raise wages without a rate increase. He not only persuaded the commission but stirred the enthusiasm of a broad public. Men as disparate as William Jennings Bryan* and Walter Lippmann* discoursed avidly on efficiency. In the optimistic years before U.S. entry into World War I,* *efficient* and *good* came closer to meaning the same thing than in any other period of American history.

There were at least four principal ways in which the word *efficiency* was used in this era. First of all, it described a personal attribute. An efficient person was an effective person, and that characterization brought with it a long shadow of latent associations and predispositions; a turning toward hard work and away from feeling, toward discipline and away from sympathy, toward masculinity and away from feminity. Second, the word signified the energy output-input ratio of a machine. The concept of mechanical efficiency developed out of the application of the laws of thermodynamics to the technology of the steam engine, and it became a central idea for engineering. Commercial efficiency, the output-input ratio of dollars, was a third meaning, and one which even engineers, who were concerned with the relation of material means to ends, could not ignore. Finally, efficiency signified a relationship between men. It meant social harmony and the leadership of the "competent." Progressives often called this social efficiency.

At the center of the efficiency craze was Frederick W. Taylor's* *Scientific Management*,* which embodied all four meanings of efficiency. The concept had an intrinsic appeal to reformers who were trying to create a program of reform without an appeal to conscience, who called the experts in the name of democracy and asked for the elevation of the college-bred to positions of influence in the interest of social harmony. Such reformers usually favored the city manager movement,* the short ballot,* the executive budget, and bureaus of municipal research. These reformers often talked of social control, national guidance, and the end of laissez-faire. They rejected the disorder of the uncontrolled market but usually wished to preserve middle-class independence through the expanding realm of professionalism.* Efficiency, in general, provided a standpoint from which those who had declared their allegiance to democracy could resist the leveling tendencies of the principle of equality. (Samuel Haber, *Efficiency and Uplift: Scientific Management in the Progressive Era, 1890–1920* (1964); Martin J. Schiesl, *The Politics of Efficiency: Municipal Administration and Reform in America, 1880–1920* (1977); Raymond Moley, *The State Movement for Efficiency and Economy* (1918).)

Samuel Haber

ELECTION, AT-LARGE. In a traditional mayor-council form of city government, each member of the city council was elected from a specific ward, or district, of the city. This mode of election maximized local accountability of the aldermen and ensured representation for geographically concentrated social, ethnic, or economic groups. It also, however, tended to produce a fragmented, decentralized government made up of quarreling, narrowly focused, special-interest representatives. Around the turn of the century, many progressives attempted to reform the structure of city government by reducing the size of city councils and mandating that all aldermen be elected at large. In theory, this system would favor candidates with a broad vision of the public interest who cared about the city as a whole. In practice, though, it diluted the representation of minority groups and resulted in the election of wealthier professionals and businessmen to city government. This innovation was often adopted along with other structural reforms,* such as the city manager* plan or a commission form of government.* (Samuel P. Hays, "The Politics of Reform in Municipal Government in the Progressive Era," *Pacific Northwest Quarterly* 55 (1964); 157–69; Samuel P. Hays, "The Changing Political Structure of the City in Industrial America," *Journal of Urban History* 1 (1974): 6–38; Charles R. Adrian, *Governing Urban America* (1961).)

Edward R. Kantowicz

ELECTION, NONPARTISAN. Nonpartisan elections are those in which candidates run simply as individuals, with no party identification listed on the ballot. The National Municipal League* advocated nonpartisanship, and other structural reforms,* for city elections as a means of destroying political machines* and bosses. In the reformers' eyes, city government consisted largely of housekeeping functions; so political parties, which dealt with national issues, had no place. "There is no Democratic or Republican way to pave a street," the reformers intoned. Nonpartisanship, in tandem with at-large elections* where the candidates ran citywide rather than from a particular ward, also enabled the election of a "better" class of individuals. Well-known business and professional men, with ready access to news media, stood a better chance of election than working-class machine candidates.

In 1909, Boston became the first large city to adopt nonpartisan elections. In some cases, such as Chicago, aldermanic ballots were technically nonpartisan, but the party machine remained strong behind the scenes. In many others, local civic parties replaced the Democrats and Republicans. Overall, nonpartisanship was one of several reforms which gradually shifted power in cities from working-class machines to professional managers. (Edward C. Banfield and James Q. Wilson, *City Politics* (1963); Martin J. Schiesl, *The Politics of Efficiency: Municipal Administration and Reform in America, 1880–1920* (1977); Eugene C. Lee, *The Politics of Nonpartisanship* (1960).)

Edward R. Kantowicz

ELECTION OF 1896. The election of 1896 cleared the political stage for the Progressive Era by resolving the main political issues of the nineteenth century and by installing in power for forty years a party committed to rapid industrialization. The severe depression of 1893–1897* destroyed the Democratic party's* claim to be the best manager of an industrial economy. It also validated the claim of Ohio Republican William McKinley* that unless the GOP controlled economic policy, America would suffer poverty, economic backwardness, and a general failure to attain the opportunities that were within the grasp of an enterprising people.

After the Republican landslide of 1894, the Democratic cause seemed hopeless. McKinley was the greatest campaigner of the era, but the Democrats found his equal in the young Nebraska orator William Jennings Bryan.* The election aroused more interest than any in American history, with over 90 percent voter turnout in many states. Bryan, backed by both Democrats and Populists in the South and West, repudiated Grover Cleveland as a failure and as a puppet of the exploiters; rejected banks, railroads, factories, cities, and economic modernization* as false sources of wealth; and appealed to the people who "really" produced the wealth, the yeomen farmers and laborers. His "Free Silver" policy would flood the nation with cheap money, thereby destroying the wicked bankers. Do that, the Republicans warned the voters, and the bankers would indeed be hurt, but you will be back in poverty and your children will be poor as well. Reject Bryanism/Populism/anarchism, endorse the gold standard and the high tariff, and prosperity would be available to all.

The Republican countercrusade blunted Bryan's appeal, especially in the Northeast, Midwest, and Pacific Coast. Germans were especially attracted by the Republican message and repelled by Bryan's. To secure their votes, however, McKinley had to promise pluralism—the moralistic crusades his party had often supported, such as prohibition,* would no longer be Republican policy. No coercion was necessary, and none was used to achieve McKinley's sweeping landslide in the heartland and most of the border. Factory workers, clerks, businessmen, professionals, and commercial farmers voted more heavily Republican than usual. The large German vote, previously Democratic, now favored McKinley. Unskilled laborers, Irish and Slavic Catholics, and noncommercial farmers in the heartland, plus wheat and cotton farmers, voted for Bryan. Prosperity and pluralism were irresistible in 1896. Most voters became strongly and permanently committed to McKinleyism, guaranteeing that politics for the next generation would operate under the broad consensus that his•smashing victory had established. (Stanley Jones, *The Presidential Election of 1896* (1964); Richard J. Jensen, *The Winning of the Midwest: Social and Political Conflict, 1888–1896* (1971).)

Richard Jensen

ELECTION OF 1900. The presidential election of 1900 was a rematch of 1896, pitting Republican President William McKinley* against Democrat William Jennings Bryan.* McKinley's acceptance of Theodore Roosevelt* as a running mate was a far more portentous decision than anyone realized. The Republican platform praised the accomplishments of the McKinley administration, especially the Dingley Tariff* and the preservation of the gold standard as guarantors of prosperity. It also praised it for giving a "new birth of freedom" to the people of Cuba, Puerto Rico, and the Philippines. The Democrats responded positively to efforts to make the election a referendum on imperialism, but spread their fire on free silver, tariff reduction, antitrust legislation, and relief for laborers and farmers. The presidential field also included candidates of the People's* (both fusionists and middle-of-the-road nominees), Silver Republican, Prohibition, Social Democrat, and Socialist Labor parties.

McKinley received 51.67 percent of the popular vote to 45.51 percent for Bryan; the electoral votes were distributed 292–158. The Great Commoner carried only the Solid South plus the silver states of Colorado, Idaho, Montana, Nevada, and Missouri. The House of Representatives contained 198 Republicans, 153 Democrats, and 5 Populists of various hues. The Senate eventually ended up with 56 Republicans and 34 Democrats, once the state legislatures completed the process. Of the 27 gubernatorial races, the Republicans captured 21, while the Democrats won outright only in Kentucky, Maryland, Missouri, and Montana, and in fusion with the Populists in Colorado and Idaho. (Robert L. Beisner, *Twelve against Empire: The Anti-Imperialists, 1898–1900* (1968); Kirk H. Porter and Donald B. Johnson, *National Party Platforms, 1840–1968* (1970); Paolo E. Coletta, *William Jennings Bryan*, 3 vols. (1964–1969).)

John D. Buenker

ELECTION OF 1904. The Republicans nominated Theodore Roosevelt* for reelection and drafted a platform that was essentially a paean to his first administration's accomplishments in both domestic and foreign affairs. In an effort to woo Republican conservatives from the "radical" Roosevelt, the Democrats replaced two-time loser William Jennings Bryan* with the more safe and sane Alton B. Parker.* Parker was also expected to have greater appeal to northern, urban Democrats who had cut Bryan in 1896 and 1900. The Democratic platform emphasized tariff revision, civil service reform,* conservation,* the direct election of senators,* and Canadian Reciprocity.* The Peoples,* Prohibition, Socialist,* and Socialist Labor* parties also ran presidential candidates.

The election was a Roosevelt landslide as he garnered 57.4 percent of the popular vote to Parker's 37.6 percent; the electoral vote split 336 to 140. Socialist candidate Eugene V. Debs* managed about 3 percent in his first try for the presidency. Without Bryan's free silver appeal, Parker carried only the Solid South and Maryland. The GOP also realized big gains in the House of Representatives, increasing a 207–178 edge to a 250–136 one. The eventual margin in the Senate was 57–33 Republican. The Republicans also captured twenty-two of the twenty-nine governorships being contested; only Kentucky, Maryland, Massachusetts, Minnesota, Montana, Missouri, and Tennessee elected Democratic chief executives (George E. Mowry, *The Era of Theodore Roosevelt and the Birth of Modern America, 1900–1912* (1958); John Morton Blum, *The Re-*

publican Roosevelt (1954); Kirk H. Porter and Donald B. Johnson, *National Party Platforms, 1840–1968* (1970).)

John D. Buenker

ELECTION OF 1908. The Republicans nominated Secretary of War William Howard Taft,* handpicked successor to President Theodore Roosevelt.* The platform lavishly praised Roosevelt and his predecessor William McKinley* for insuring domestic prosperity and international power. In response to popular concerns that a high level of tariffs caused inflation, the Republican platform promised "revision of the tariff by special session of Congress immediately following inauguration of the next president." It also called for a federal banking system, intensification of "trust-busting" efforts, and relief for farmers, workers, and Negroes. The Democrats called for tariff revision, a federal income tax, the direct election of senators, postal savings banks,* and control of Asian immigration. In return for the endorsement of the American Federation of Labor,* William Jennings Bryan,* running for a third time, pledged the curtailment of antiunion injunctions. The campaign also featured Independence party candidate William Randolph Hearst* and Socialist Eugene V. Debs,* as well as Populist,* Prohibition, and Socialist Labor* party hopefuls.

Taft captured 51.57 percent of the popular vote to 43.05 percent for Bryan; the electoral vote divided 321–162 as Bryan added Colorado, Nebraska, Nevada, and Oklahoma to the Democratic Solid South. Debs received 2.8 percent and Eugene W. Chafin, the Prohibition candidate, 1.7 percent. Although suffering a loss of three congressional seats, the GOP still controlled the House of Representatives 219–172 and the Senate 60–32. The Republicans also won nineteen of the twenty-seven gubernatorial races, although the Democrats, in a portent of things to come, captured such traditionally Republican states as Indiana, Ohio, and North Dakota. (George E. Mowry, *The Era of Theodore Roosevelt and the Birth of Modern America, 1900–1912* (1958); Henry F. Pringle, *The Life and Times of William Howard Taft* (1939); Paolo E. Coletta, *The Presidency of William Howard Taft* (1973).)

John D. Buenker

ELECTION OF 1910. This was one of the most significant off-year elections in U.S. history, one which gave the Democrats control of Congress as well as of such critical states as New York, New Jersey, and Massachusetts. So sweeping was the Democratic victory in the northeastern United States that the *New York Times* hailed it a "political revolution" and opined that "from Eastport to the Indiana border, broken only by a corner of New Hampshire and Pennsylvania's Erie frontage, stretches a broad belt of Democratic territory." Democratic gains were generally attributed to the popular association of a high protective tariff with an increase in the high cost of living and with the promotion of trusts. The Republicans lost nearly one-quarter of their congressional seats in New England

and the Middle Atlantic states; the Democrats gained twelve seats in New York, eight in Ohio, five in Illinois, and four each in Pennsylvania, Missouri, New Jersey, and West Virginia. All told, the Democrats gained fifty-nine seats and controlled the house by a decisive 228–162 advantage. In the Senate, the Republican margin slipped to 51–41. Although the Republicans captured sixteen of the twenty-six gubernatorial races, party regulars in several states were ousted by such progressives as Hiram Johnson* in California, Francis E. McGovern* in Wisconsin, and Robert P. Bass in New Hampshire. In Oregon and Minnesota, progressive Republicans defeated Democratic opponents. Democratic governors were inaugurated in ten states, including New York, New Jersey (Woodrow Wilson*), Massachusetts, Maine, Kentucky, and Colorado. This combination of insurgent Republicans and resurgent Democrats helped make the 1911 sessions of several state legislatures extremely productive of reform legislation. (Samuel P. Hays, *The Response to Industrialism, 1885–1914* (1957); John D. Baker, "The Character of the Congressional Revolution of 1910," *Journal of American History* 60 (1973): 679–91; George E. Mowry, "Theodore Roosevelt and the Election of 1910," *Mississippi Valley Historical Review* 25 (1939): 523–34.)

John D. Buenker

ELECTION OF 1912. The 1912 election was significant because of the nature of the public debate and the popular mandate for reform evident from the election results. In the Republican Party,* an insurgent progressive movement, particularly strong in the agrarian regions of the Middle and Far West by 1910, challenged the conservative eastern leadership of the GOP President William Howard Taft,* who had alienated progressives through his support for the Old Guard and a high tariff and irritated his Wall Street constituency through his vigorous use of the antitrust laws. Taft so angered his predecessor, Theodore Roosevelt,* by his suit against U.S. Steel that the former president decided to challenge him for the nomination, splitting the Republican vote. He won the delegations in the dozen states with direct primaries. But Taft used patronage and other powers to garner the majority of convention delegates. In control at the GOP convention in Chicago,* Taft's champions ruled against Roosevelt in the majority of contested state delegations. Roosevelt bolted the GOP, assured of financial support by publisher Frank A. Munsey* and financier George W. Perkins,* and called for a convention of the Progressive party* in Chicago on August 5, 1912.

Although the majority of party professionals stayed with the GOP, a host of largely middle-class reformers met at Chicago and nominated Roosevelt on the Progressive ticket, virtually guaranteeing victory for the Democrats who had been gaining strength in the North and West beyond their base in the solidly Democratic South. They had won control of the House of Representatives in the 1910 election and had produced several politically attractive candidates including the new Speaker of the House James Beauchamp "Champ" Clark* of Missouri and Governor Woodrow Wilson* of New Jersey. At the Democratic convention in Baltimore, Clark obtained a majority (556) of the delegates on the tenth ballot, but the party's requirement of a two-thirds majority enabled anti-Clark forces to block his nomination. Emphasizing Wilson's national prominence, progressivism, and electability, his campaign managers eventually won the support of William Jennings Bryan* and a number of urban party bosses, winning on the forty-sixth ballot.

The election of 1912 offered American voters a wide range of choices. Taft emphasized conservative constitutionalism. Eugene V. Debs* called for a socialist democracy in which the workers would own the means of production. Roosevelt's "New Nationalism" offered a bold and comprehensive vision of a liberal, urban, corporate society in which a strong central government would regulate and protect every interest, including large corporations, unions, consumers, and the poor. Wilson, under the guidance of crusading Boston lawyer Louis D. Brandeis,* expanded traditional Democratic themes of states' rights and limited government into a concept he called the "New Freedom," which emphasized tariff reduction and the use of antitrust laws to undermine monopoly and restore economic competition and opportunity.

Even though Wilson won only 42 percent of the popular vote, he greatly exceeded that of Roosevelt's 27 percent and Taft's 23 percent. Roosevelt ran strongest in the fastest growing northern cities and progressive western states. Taft drew upon rural and suburban Republican support particularly in the Northeast and Middle West. Wilson gained the bulk of his support in the agrarian South and West but was able to add Massachusetts, New York, New Jersey, and Ohio. Debs won 6 percent of the popular vote, mostly in former Populist, sharecropping areas of Oklahoma; in urban, ethnic working-class districts; and in Milwaukee and New York City. Taft carried only Vermont and Utah (8 votes), while Roosevelt won 11 of California's votes and all of Pennsylvania, Michigan, Minnesota, South Dakota, and Washington (a total of 88). Wilson received 435 electoral votes and the Democrats won control of both houses of Congress. (John Allen Gable, *The Bull Moose Years: Theodore Roosevelt and the Progressive Party* (1978); Arthur S. Link and Richard L. McCormick, *Progressivism* (1983); George E. Mowry, "Election of 1912," in Arthur M. Schlesinger, Jr., ed., *The Coming to Power: Critical Presidential Elections in American History* (1972); Lewis L. Gould, *Reform and Regulation: American Politics from Roosevelt to Wilson*, 2d ed. (1986).)

John Whiteclay Chambers II

ELECTION OF 1914. Although Democratic Party* maintained its control of Congress, the election of 1914 was an exceptionally important congressional, state, and local election for the continued existence of the Progressive Party,* formed around Theodore Roosevelt* in 1912. Many Progressive party members and leaders between 1912 and 1914 worked to establish the local roots—organizations, volunteers networks, officeholders, and patronage—seen as essential to a national party. Roosevelt's support of such efforts was not enthusiastic, as he had come to view the party primarily as a vehicle for his own reelection to the presidency. The national party organization lost important financial and media backing with the defection of wealthy publisher Frank Munsey* in 1913, and George W. Perkins,* Roosevelt's choice for national executive chairman of the party, did not provide the financial support local organizations needed. Party leadership had been split since the 1912 campaign over the role of Perkins (a partner in the J. P. Morgan bank and a wealthy advocate of "progressive" big-business leadership in public affairs), whom Roosevelt considered necessary as financial backer and efficient manager. Many other leaders distrusted Perkins and wished to create a permanent party independent of Roosevelt.

Despite strenuous local campaigns and organizational efforts in 1914, Progressive candidates for local, state, and congressional offices lost. The total popular Progressive vote fell below two million (as compared to about six million for each of the major parties); only one of the fourteen Progressive congressmen elected in 1912 was reelected. Such eminent Progressive leaders as national committee chairman Joseph Dixon* of Montana and James R. Garfield* of Ohio were defeated for the Senate. The election marked the collapse of all organized effort to make the Progressive party a national, lasting major party. The Republican Party,* from which many Progressives had moved in 1912, made significant gains toward reestablishing its majority position in national politics, and many of its leading figures who had suffered defeat in 1912 were reelected to Congress and local offices in 1914. (George E. Mowry, *Theodore Roosevelt and the Progressive Movement* (1946); Amos R. E. Pinchot, *History of the Progressive Party, 1912–1916*, Helen M. Hooker, ed. (1958).)

James Oliver Robertson

ELECTION OF 1916. President Woodrow Wilson* was reelected by a sparse twenty-three electoral votes over Republican candidate Charles E. Hughes.* Wilson's reelection was an uphill battle since the Republican party,* split in 1912, was mending by 1916. Democratic strategists touted the slogan "He Kept Us Out of War," as well as Wilson's progressive record on labor, agriculture, and industrial regulation. Though threatened by the desertion of business interests, the Wilsonian emphasis on peace and progressivism curbed a threatened defection of Irish voters alienated by his "pro-British" diplomacy and forged a winning coalition of southern and western states, farmers, small businessmen, workers, reformers, and Republican progressives. The elections of 1912* and 1916 may have contributed to a long-range party transformation. While the Old Guard tightened its grip over the Republican party after the 1912 split, Wilson's progressivism, accentuated by the 1916 campaign, helped transform the Democrats from a conservative party into a vehicle for modern liberalism. This trend, eclipsed in the 1920s, would surface in the New Deal coalition, although some historians claim that Wilsonian policies actually preempted radical reforms while creating a political economy controlled by corporate interests. (Edward Cuddy, "Irish-Americans and the 1916 Election: An Episode in Immigrant Adjustment,"*American Quarterly* 21 (Summer 1969): 228–248; Arthur S. Link, *Wil-*

son: *Campaigns for Progressivism and Peace, 1916–1917* (1965); S. D. Lovell, *The Presidential Election of 1916* (1980).)

Edward Cuddy

ELECTION OF 1918. This was a fiercely contested election just before the Armistice brought World War I* to an end. Issues of loyalty and support of the war effort were paramount, used by both parties to gain support. A flu epidemic killed a half-million Americans while the campaign was going on. Within the Democratic Party,* support for President Woodrow Wilson* and his war administration was crucial. Wilson made every effort to gain reelection of congressional supporters and personally directed campaigns against important figures who opposed his leadership or his war policies. Within the Republican Party,* the issues were reunification of the party, control of its organization and program, and reestablishing the "normal" Republican control of national politics. The campaign centered around questions of Wilson's management of the war, politically and domestically as well as militarily and diplomatically. Democratic efforts to equate opposition to Wilson and his administration with disloyalty to the nation in war may have aroused resentment and helped defeat Democrats.

Voters concerned with progressive issues were still an important part of the electorate and influenced the calculations of major party leaders. The Progressive Party* organization had disappeared—many leaders and supporters had rejoined the Republicans in 1916, and remnants of the national committee had amalgamated with the Prohibition Party in 1917. For many voters, particularly progressives, prohibition* was as important an issue in 1918 as the war. The Nonpartisan League,* which widely appealed to progressives in the upper West, was a vital factor in the 1918 election. The Republicans achieved only a slim majority of 2 in the Senate but controlled the House 237 to 193. The election was a personal defeat for Wilson, and it presaged the great political battle over the Versailles treaty that followed. (Seward W. Livermore, *Politics Is Adjourned: Woodrow Wilson and the War Congress, 1916–1918* (1966); David Burner, *The Politics of Provincialism: The Democratic Party in Transition, 1918–1932* (1968); James Oliver Robertson, *No Third Choice: Progressives in Republican Politics, 1916–1921* (1938).)

James Oliver Robertson

ELECTION OF 1920. Progressive reform had taken a back seat to the war, and the 1920 election would reveal whether the return of peace would bring its resumption. Wilsonian Democrats, paralyzed by the sick Woodrow Wilson's* refusal to withdraw as a candidate, lost control of the party to northern bosses who nominated James M. Cox* for the presidency, but gave them Franklin D. Roosevelt* as his running mate. The Republican Party* also moved to the right, choosing party regular Warren G. Harding* for the presidency, and a second conservative, Calvin Coolidge, for the vice presidency. Starting far behind in the polls, Cox strove to overcome Harding's lead by sounding progressive themes. When the response proved disappointing, he emphasized membership in the League of Nations.* But Harding so obscured this issue as to get the support of both leading advocates and leading opponents of the League, as well as most other groups in the electorate. Harding's victory was of landslide proportions—16,143,407 to Cox's 9,141,750, 404 to 127 electoral votes—and his party's majority in the Senate rose to 22 and in the House to 172. (Wesley M. Bagby, *Road to Normalcy: The Presidential Campaign and Election of 1920* (1962); Robert K. Murray, *The Harding Era: Warren G. Harding and His Administration* (1969); James M. Cox, *Journey through My Years* (1946).)

Wesley M. Bagby

ELIOT, CHARLES W. (March 20, 1834–August 22, 1926). Born in Boston, Massachusetts, Eliot attended the Boston Latin Grammar School and Harvard College, from which he graduated in 1853. He served on the Harvard faculty for nine years, in mathematics and chemistry. He left Harvard for two years of study in Europe, where he studied the operation of the schools, as well as the sciences. He took a position as professor of chemistry at the Massachusetts Institute of Technology, and in 1896, he was appointed the president of Harvard College, a position he held until 1909. As president, he presided over the transformation of that institution from a largely undergraduate college to a comprehensive university. His most famous accomplishment was the introduction of the elective system in place of the almost completely prescribed curriculum of undergraduate studies.

Upon retirement from Harvard, he continued to write and speak out on the educational issues of the day. In addition to his impact on higher education, Eliot studied and wrote on the problems of popular education in the lower schools. He was instrumental in the report of the Committee of Ten of the National Education Association,* which dealt with the relations between the colleges and the high schools, and defended its recommendations against criticism from notable educators such as G. Stanley Hall.* (Hugh Hawkins, *Between Harvard and America: The Educational Leadership of Charles W. Eliot* (1972); Henry James, *Charles W. Eliot, President of Harvard University*, 2 vols. (1930); Edward A. Krug, ed., *Charles W. Eliot on Popular Education* (1961).)

Wayne J. Urban

ELKINS, STEPHEN BENTON (September 26, 1841–January 4, 1911). Wealthy mine and railroad owner, Republican senator from West Virginia, sponsor of two major railroad laws, Elkins was born in Ohio; he moved to Missouri with his family, graduated from the University of Missouri in 1860, then enlisted in the Union Army. He passed the bar in 1864 and moved to New Mexico Territory to practice law. While serving in a variety of political posts, including territorial delegate to Congress from 1873 to 1877, he became wealthy as a landowner and mine operator. He moved to his own company town of Elkins, West Virginia, in 1890, served as secretary of war under President Benjamin

Harrison from 1891 to 1893, then was elected to the Senate in 1895, serving until his death.

As chairman of the Senate Committee on Interstate Commerce after 1899, he introduced the Elkins Anti-Rebating Act* of 1903, which forbade railroads to offer rebates to favored shippers. In 1910, he helped formulate the Mann-Elkins Act,* which strengthened the power of the Interstate Commerce Commission to regulate railroad rates. Though progressives viewed Elkins as a classic example of a man who exploited public office for private gain, he was flexible enough to cooperate with progressives in fashioning reform legislation. (Oscar D. Lambert, *Stephen Benton Elkins* (1955); Gabriel Kolko, *Railroads and Regulation* (1965); Albro Martin, *Enterprise Denied: Origins of the Decline of American Railroads, 1897–1917* (1971).)

                                                                        Edward R. Kantowicz

ELKINS ACT. This act was needed because railroad officials were constantly pressured to extend rebates and lower rates to large shippers, particularly at points where there was competition from other railroads. The shippers were in effect playing one railroad off against another. As a result, a significant portion of railroad traffic was being carried at rates far below published tariffs. This act, supported by the railroads, passed Congress in 1903 without opposition.

The act had four important provisions. First, it made railroad corporations as well as their employees liable for violations of the law. Second, provisions of the act made it unlawful to receive or solicit concessions. A third part of the act made a misdemeanor any departure from the published rate, and a fourth provision made changes in the penalties for violations of the law and authorized the courts to enjoin railroads from continuing unlawful departures from published rates. (Philip D. Locklin, *Economics of Transportation* (1966); Roy J. Sampson and Martin T. Farris, *Domestic Transportation—Practice, Theory, and Policy* (1979); I. L. Sharfman, *The Interstate Commerce Commission*, vol. 1 (1931).)

                                                                        Curtis Richards

ELY, RICHARD T. (April 13, 1854–October 4, 1943). Ely was born in Ripley, New York, an area still influenced by strong evangelical Protestantism. His father, a strict Sabbatarian, instilled a strong religious outlook in his son, but Ely never underwent the expected conversion experience. Nonetheless, though influenced later by Darwinism, Ely saw his academic work as an extension of Christian ideals. He studied at Johns Hopkins University and in Germany, where he internalized a strong critique of the prevailing laissez-faire ideology of academic economics in the United States.

Ely was the primary founder of the American Economic Association* in 1885, which announced the goals of the ''New Economics'': the more effective role of the state as a vehicle of human progress, greater use of historical and empirical studies in economics, and amelioration of the conflict between labor and capital through the involvement of the state, church, and other agencies. At the same time, Ely urged that these goals all reflect the genuine spirit of Christianity. Ely was a pioneer of the Social Gospel* movement, and his *The Social Aspects of Christianity* (1889) became an influential contribution to its literature.

Ely achieved his greatest influence after 1892 when he headed the School of Economics, Political Science, and History at the University of Wisconsin.* Despite controversy, and with vindication by the university's regents in an important academic freedom case, Ely involved many professors from the school in the legislative and bureaucratic operations of the state government, thus providing the close affiliation of university and state that became a hallmark of the "Wisconsin Idea." (Benjamin G. Rader, *The Academic Mind and Reform: The Influence of Richard T. Ely in American Life* (1966); Richard T. Ely, *Ground under Our Feet: An Autobiography* (1938); Arthur J. Vidich and Stanford Lyman, eds., "Secular Evangelism at the University of Wisconsin," in *American Sociology: Worldly Rejections of Religion and Their Directions* (1985).)

J. David Hoeveler, Jr.

EMPLOYERS' LIABILITY. In the 1840s and 1850s, the emergence of mechanized transportation (steamboats and railroads) and mechanized factory production led to an increasing number of industrial accidents. Workers who attributed their injuries to the negligence of employers began to sue their employers for lost pay and medical expenses. But judges developed law doctrines (the defenses of assumption of risk, contributory negligence, and the fellow-servant rule) that prevented most damage suits from going to trial before a jury. The judges who developed and applied these doctrines believed that capital accumulation in newly emerging, economically vulnerable industries would be facilitated by a common law that reduced the financial risks of doing business. Judges steeped in the ideology of "rugged individualism" believed that if injured workers could expect damages, they would not be as careful as they would be if they were completely responsible for their financial losses.

As unions grew in the years after the Civil War, city and state labor federations were formed to lobby for labor legislation. From the 1870s onward, labor unions took the initiative in proposing employers' liability laws that weakened the judge-made common-law defenses. Railroad workers were especially successful in obtaining strong employers' liability laws, capitalizing on the hostility of people of all classes toward railroads. During the first decade of the twentieth century, judges in state courts, aware that industrial development had advanced beyond its early, high-risk stage, began to give more weight to protecting the welfare of injured workers and inclined more to the view that accident prevention would be promoted by making employers liable for their negligence. In 1910 drastic employers' liability laws, applying to most industrial occupations, were passed by the Ohio, Oregon and New York legislatures. These laws and the threat of similar statutes in other states accelerated the acceptance of workmen's compensation* laws that were intended to reduce tort litigation, awarding injured workers financial relief for economic losses—irrespective of the negligence of employees or employers. (William L. Prosser, *Handbook of the Law of Torts* (1941); Robert Asher, "Failure and Fulfillment: Agitation for Employers' Liability Legislation and the Origins of Workmen's Compensation in New York State, 1876–1910," *Labor History* 24 (Spring 1983): 198–222.)

Robert Asher

ENVIRONMENTALISM. In the intellectual or ideological history of progressivism, environmentalism was a large, all-inclusive concept, covering various philosophic aspects or schools of thought. For example, the "discovery of society" was a synonym for environmentalism because in the nature-nurture argument within the Darwinian legacy, many progressives stressed the nurture or environmental side of the formula. In reacting against assumed Darwinist determinism, scholars such as Albion Small,* George Herbert Mead,* and Lester Frank Ward* substituted social and geographical variables for racial assumptions. They argued that such a substitution meant a stronger empirically based sociology which in time would be further developed by statistical analysis. At the same time, William I. Thomas,* by using this "discovery of society" concept, advanced the study of personality and culture. Many scholars discounted the biological factor in human society, and Lamarckian theories of inheritance placing emphasis on environmental factors became the essential scientific model for American social science. These theories allowed a positivistic social science and antiformalism in the Progressive Era to reject the nineteenth-century legacy of romantic individualism and moral absolutes.

Drawing on John Locke's argument that men learn through experience, progressive reformers and social scientists attempted to create a "conditioned virtue" for a proper environment. Simply stated, men became what they have experienced in society; hence education and proper family life were major progressive social concerns in the reconstruction of American urban and industrial life. The final element in progressive environmentalism was the development of the sociology of knowledge expressed in two modes, social-technological and critical-emancipatory. In both forms, knowledge, either to run the society or to critique the philosophy of the social order, came from the world of human endeavor. All of these elements in environmentalism contributed to the rise of William James's* pragmatism* and John Dewey's* instrumentalism* in reforming progressivism and to the larger shape of later twentieth-century intellectual history. (Ellsworth R. Fuhrman, *The Sociology of Knowledge in America, 1883–1915* (1980); Anthony Leeds, "Darwin and 'Darwinian' Evolutionism in the Study of Society and Culture, "in Thomas Glick, ed., *The Comparative Reception of Darwinism* (1974); George W. Stocking, Jr., "Lamarckianism in American Social Science: 1800–1915, "*Journal of the History of Ideas* 23 (April-

June 1962): 293–356 Hamilton Cravens, *The Triumph of Evolution; American Scientists and the Heredity-Environment Controversy, 1900–1914* (1978).)

Donald K. Pickens

ESCH-CUMMINS ACT (THE TRANSPORTATION ACT OF 1920). This act was passed by Congress at the time of transition between wartime operation of the railroads by the federal government and the return of the railroads to private ownership. The underlying philosophy of regulation prior to World War I* was to force railroads to compete with each other and, where no competition existed, to substitute controls by the Interstate Commerce Commission. Several defects became apparent, among them lack of control of rail capitalization, rail service to customers, and absence of procedures to settle labor disputes. Excessive and often wasteful competition was encouraged, and severe restrictions were placed on the abilities of railroads to set rates at a level high enough to encourage capital investment in the railroad industry. This act, for the first time, recognized the need of the railroads to earn a fair rate of return if well managed. The act also addressed the weak-strong railroad problem, the issue of minimum rates, new construction restrictions, merger and financial regulations, intrastate rates, regulation of railroad abandonments, and procedures to handle rail labor disputes. For the most part the constructive policies of the act were helpful to the railroad industry during the decade of the 1920s. (Philip D. Locklin, *Economics of Transportation* (1966); I. L. Sharfman, *The Interstate Commerce Commission*, vol. 1 (1931); Roy J. Sampson and Martin T. Farris, *Domestic Transportation— Practice, Theory, and Policy* (1979).

Curtis Richards

ESPIONAGE (SEDITION) ACT. The Espionage and Sedition Acts were laws curtailing freedom of speech and dissent during World War I.* Representative Edwin Webb of North Carolina and Senator Charles Culberson of Texas introduced the Espionage Act on April 2, 1917, immediately after President Woodrow Wilson* called for a declaration of war. Passed on June 5, the act provided $10,000 fines and prison terms up to twenty years for the obstruction of military operations or military recruitment and $5,000 fines and five-year prison terms for sending treasonous material through the mail. Attorney General Thomas Gregory and Postmaster General Albert Sidney Burleson* enforced this law vigorously, imprisoning many socialists and other antiwar agitators and virtually clearing the mails of socialist publications. On May 16, 1918, amendments were added to the Espionage Act which prohibited "any disloyal, profane, scurrilous, or abusive language about the form of government of the United States, or the Constitution of the United States, or the flag of the United States, or the uniform of the Army or Navy." This very broad attack on free speech came to be known as the Sedition Act. The Supreme Court upheld the Espionage Act as amended in three cases decided after the war, but the statute expired in 1921. (David M.

Kennedy, *Over Here: The First World War and American Society* (1980); William Preston, *Aliens and Dissenters* (1963); Harry N. Scheiber, *The Wilson Administration and Civil Liberties* (1960).)

Edward R. Kantowicz

ETHNOCULTURAL CONFLICT. The sources of immigration to America shifted sharply in the 1890s. For nearly a century, the British, Irish,* Germans,* and Scandinavians* from northwestern Europe had predominated in the immigration stream, but after 1893, they were outnumbered by Italians,* Poles,* and other immigrants from southern and eastern Europe. These "new immigrants"* poured through Ellis Island at the rate of over a million per year after the turn of the century, congregating primarily in the big cities of the Northeast and the Midwest. The new immigrants were predominantly Catholic and Jewish in religion, and their languages sounded strange to Anglo-Saxon ears. As Woodrow Wilson* wrote in his *History of the American People*: "Now there came multitudes of men of the lowest class from the south of Italy and men of the meaner sort out of Hungary and Poland, men out of the ranks where there was neither skill nor energy nor initiative of quick intelligence. . . . "

Three Boston Brahmins founded the Immigration Restriction League in 1894 to agitate for a curb on the entry of new immigrants. Pseudoscientific racial theories, which divided the white race into resourceful Nordics, stolid Alpines, and mercurial Mediterraneans, buttressed their arguments for immigration restriction.* Though several presidents vetoed restrictive laws, a literacy test for immigrants finally became law in 1917, and a full battery of discriminatory national origins quotas went into effect in the 1920s. In the largest American cities, immigrants and their children comprised nearly 80 percent of the populace in the early decades of this century. Hostilities between natives and foreigners, and between different kinds of foreigners, occasionally broke out into violence. Youth gangs from separate nationalities fought under railroad viaducts; workers on strike attacked scab laborers from other immigrant groups imported by the employers. During a 1915 refinery workers' strike in Bayonne, New Jersey, Polish strikers sacked three Jewish-owned stores and an Irish saloon but did not touch any Polish-owned businesses.

The very separateness of ethnic groups, however, kept such violence to a minimum. Each immigrant group staked out its own turf in American cities, built a complex of ethnic businesses and cultural institutions, and kept away from others. Old-stock Americans and more assimilated immigrants fled to the suburbs and rarely encountered the newcomers. The American myth of social mobility further damped down conflict. Immigrants came to America primarily to work and to better themselves, and they gained just enough monetary rewards to assure them that their children might get ahead economically even if they didn't. Finally, the American political system accommodated ethnic conflict and transformed it into political rivalry. (John Higham, *Strangers in the Land: Pat-*

terns of American Nativism, 1860–1925 (1955); Maldwyn Jones, *American Immigration* (1960).)

Edward R. Kantowicz

ETHNOCULTURAL POLITICS. An interpretation of American voting behavior first applied by Lee Benson, ethnocultural politics received its fullest elaboration in detailed studies of midwestern politics in the 1890s by Richard Jensen and Paul Kleppner. According to this interpretation, American voters, at least during the nineteenth century, divided along ethnic and religious lines as a response to such cultural issues as nativism, prohibition,* Sunday blue laws, and English-language use in parochial schools. Generally, pietistic groups, oriented toward enforcing proper behavior by legislative action, joined the Republican Party*—including most Yankee-descended churches, Methodists (both native-born and immigrants), Dutch Reformed, and pietistic elements among Scandinavian immigrants. On the other hand, immigrants and the native-born from churches espousing a more liturgical-ritualistic approach to religious life favored the Democratic Party* with its laissez-faire attitude toward personal behavior. Thus Irish,* German,* Polish,* and other Catholic immigrants moved overwhelmingly into the Democratic party along with most German Lutherans, many Scandinavians* favoring the high state church Lutheran synods, and some native-stock ritualistic Protestant church members such as Episcopalians. This pattern was broken in the political realignment of the 1890s when the Republicans, led by William McKinley* and Mark Hanna,* decided to downplay cultural issues and to stress the broader economic issue of tariff protection. At the same time, Democrats turned to William Jennings Bryan,* whose moralistic, revivalistic rhetoric offended traditional ritualistic Democrats.

While a number of studies have pursued this area of analysis, especially concentrating on the 1890s and earlier, much less work has been done on the electoral sources of progressive-conservative divisions in the early twentieth century. Progressive concerns of regulating big business and ameliorating the most serious problems caused by industrialism and urbanization* do not fall easily into the pietistic/ritualistic-liturgical dichotomy. On the other hand, the moralistic rhetorical stance of such progressive leaders as Robert La Follette* and Woodrow Wilson* might be expected to attract and repel voters according to their religious orientation. An extended study of Wisconsin* voting behavior, while largely ignoring the religious-cultural dimension, found significant differences in the manner in which ethnic groups responded to the Wisconsin progressive movement, led by La Follette. New Englanders tended toward the conservative, old-guard Republican side of the political spectrum; Scandinavian voters, traditionally Republican, turned to La Follette in large numbers. Most Catholic ethnic groups stayed solidly Democratic, voting for Woodrow Wilson in 1912, despite his moralistic stance. Theodore Roosevelt's* third-party effort made its heaviest inroads among Polish and Swedish voters, coming from opposite ends of the ethnic spectrum. Beginning with the 1916 election, issues generated by Democratic-led involvement in World War I* aligned Wisconsin voting even more along ethnic lines. (Richard J. Jensen, *The Winning of the Midwest: Social and Political Conflict, 1888–1896* (1971); Paul Kleppner, *Cross of Culture; A Social Analysis of Midwestern Politics, 1850–1900* (1971); David L. Brye, *Wisconsin Voting Patterns in the Twentieth Century, 1900–1950* (1979).)

David L. Brye

EUGENICS. An Englishman, Sir Francis Galton (1822–1911), created the modern eugenics movement. He believed that culturally desirable physical and mental qualities were unevenly distributed in the population but could be scientifically identified and encouraged to multiply. Using a Darwinian rhetoric in analyzing a society that revealed innate racial (and hence class) superiority and inferiority, Galton thought state intervention could prevent racial deterioration and encourage human biological improvement. This creed appealed to some progressives, including Theodore Roosevelt.* The result was a eugenic element in a wide range of reforms including birth control,* sterilization, psychology, and anthropology. Socially improved Americans must reject egalitarian social assumptions and sentimental charitable social policies. Accordingly, Americans could not ignore the Darwinian biological reality of struggle and natural selection. Their program consisted of restrictive immigration laws, stronger state sterilization legislation, and increased scientific investigation into innate racial differences. Eugenics has lost much of its philosophical, political, and scientific appeal, but echoes are present in the current debates over the racial basis of intelligence and aspects of human sociobiology and genetic engineering. (Mark H. Haller, *Eugenics: Hereditarian Attitudes in American Thought* (1963); Donald K. Pickens, *Eugenics and the Progressives* (1968); Daniel J. Kevles, *In the Name of Eugenics: Genetics and the Uses of Human Heredity* (1960).)

Donald K. Pickens

EVERYBODY'S MAGAZINE. *Everybody's* was established in 1896 by John Wannamaker, the Philadelphia merchant. With more emphasis upon romantic fiction than political reform, the magazine achieved a circulation of 150,000. In May 1903, Erman J. Ridgway and John A. Thayer, veteran journalists from *Munsey's* and the *Delineator* respectively, assumed control with the intent of making a "cheery" magazine rather than engaging in an "epileptic fit of virtue." The magazine claimed a circulation of 250,000 by July 1904, when it became a muckraking journal.

The publication of Thomas W. Lawson's* "Frenzied Finance—The Story of Amalgamated" added 60,000 new subscribers in one month. Lawson (1853–1925), a former president of Bay State Gas and assorted copper companies, charged that worthless copper stocks were being unloaded upon the public at par value by Standard Oil insiders. He described his own market manipulations, pools, stock waterings, political payoffs, and techniques of consolidation. His well-written articles broke public confidence in Amalgamated Copper, and some charged that he profited from this development. But *Everybody's* circulation rose to 735,000, and the government soon initiated antitrust action against Standard Oil.* *Everybody's* subsequently enlarged its scope with Charles E. Russell's* "The Greatest Trust in the World," an analysis of the beef trust. Jack London,* Dorothy Canfield, and O. Henry supplied the magazine with fiction. *Everybody's* was discontinued in January 1930. (*Everybody's Magazine*; *New York Times*, February 8–11, 1925; Frank Luther Mott, *A History of American Magazines, 1865–1905* (1957).)

Harold S. Wilson

EXPERTISE, the knowledge of experts, was prized by those progressives who looked for a more effective instrument of reform than the traditional appeal to conscience. Comptroller Herman Metz of New York City epitomized the reformer's notion of expertise in the declaration: "The practical man knows *how*. The scientific man knows *why*. The expert knows *how* and *why*." Expertise was both scientific and practical, and reformers might use it to guide and restrain the marketplace and the ballot box. To the extent that expertise was scientific, it seemed to promise immunity from partisan and even class bias; to the extent that it was practical, it might be employed to further human betterment. This new-fashioned idea rested upon the old-fashioned optimistic assumption that somehow morality was written into the workings of the universe.

Many reformers endorsed Scientific Management* and regulatory commissions as a means of bringing disinterested expertise into the economy; they favored the city manager,* the short ballot,* the executive budget, the bureaus of municipal research—and more generally the separation of administration from politics—as a means of bringing such expertise into government. Expertise was particularly attractive to the college-bred reformers in that it promised a new and important role for trained intelligence in both government and the economy. The prewar writings of Herbert Croly* and Walter Lippmann* provided the most comprehensive justifications for expertise, arguing that the increased scale and complexity of social and economic life made technical issues all-important and expertise indispensable. (Henry F. May, *The End of American Innocence: A Study of the First Years of Our Own Time, 1912–1917* (1959); Samuel Haber, *Efficiency and Uplift: Scientific Management in the Progressive Era, 1890–1920* (1964); Donald T. Critchlow, *The Brookings Institution, 1916–1952: Expertise and the Public Interest in a Democratic Society* (1985).)

Samuel Haber

F

FAGAN, MARK M. (September 29, 1869–July 16, 1955). Born in Jersey City, New Jersey, the son of Irish immigrant parents, Fagan became one of the nation's outstanding progressive mayors. He began his public career in 1896 as a Republican member of the Hudson County (New Jersey) Board of Chosen Freeholders. Though defeated for reelection and a subsequent try for the state senate, Fagan used his popularity among Jersey City's working-class voters to become the youngest mayor in his city's history. During his three terms in office (1902–1908), he joined with city corporation counsel George L. Record* in the fight for equal taxation of railroad property and the regulation and franchise limitation of "public" utilities. Fagan championed an advanced program of social welfare that included public baths and playgrounds, free milk and medical care, evening concerts in the parks, public kindergarten care, and the city's first juvenile court. Following his defeat for a fourth term in 1907, in part due to the opposition of the Catholic church over his failure to enforce Sunday saloon-closing laws, Fagan remained active in public affairs. He was an unsuccessful candidate of the progressive "New Idea" forces for mayor (1909) and county sheriff (1911) and a member of the county tax commission (1910–1913). In 1913 Fagan was chosen Jersey City's first mayor under the commission plan of government* and he worked to improve municipal poor relief, purify the city's milk and water supply, and provide a seat for every child in the public schools. Defeated by a ticket led by Frank Hague* in 1917, Fagan retired from public life. (Ransom E. Noble, Jr., *New Jersey Progressivism before Wilson* (1946); Eugene M. Tobin, "The Progressive as Politician: Jersey City, 1896–1907," *New Jersey History* 91 (1973): 5–23; Eugene M. Tobin, " 'Engines of Salvation' or 'Smoking Black Devils': Jersey City Reformers and the Railroads 1902–1908," in Michael H.

Ebner and Eugene M. Tobin, eds., *The Age of Urban Reform: New Perspectives on the Progressive Era* (1977), 142–55.)

Eugene M. Tobin

FAIRBANKS, CHARLES W. (May 11, 1852–June 4, 1918). The twenty-sixth vice president was born in rural Ohio, graduated from Ohio Wesleyan University in 1872, read law, and passed the bar in 1874. As a railroad lawyer and director in Indiana, Fairbanks acquired a considerable fortune, and in the late 1880s, he turned his attention to politics. A highly effective political manager, Fairbanks won control of the party by 1894, aligned himself with William McKinley,* and was elected to the U.S. Senate in 1897. Focusing on patronage and espousing conservative positions on high tariffs and big business, his friendship with the president brought national attention, but McKinley's assassination weakened Fairbanks's power and prospects.

President Theodore Roosevelt* supported Indiana's other senator, Albert Beveridge,* and won the 1904 presidential nomination. Fairbanks was selected for vice president to provide geographical and ideological balance. As vice president, Fairbanks worked with conservative GOP leaders in Congress, but his chances for the 1908 nomination disappeared when Roosevelt picked William Howard Taft.* Returning to Indiana, he disliked political developments and sat out the 1912 campaign. In 1916 he again balanced the Republican ticket, running for vice president, and lost. (Herbert J. Rissler, "Charles Warren Fairbanks: Conservative Hoosier" (Ph.D. diss., Indiana University, 1961); James H. Madison, "Charles Warren Fairbanks and Indiana Republicanism," in Ralph Gray, ed., *Gentlemen from Indiana: National Party Candidates, 1836–1940* (1977); John Braeman, *Albert Beveridge: American Nationalist* (1971).)

Philip R. VanderMeer

FARMERS' UNION. In 1902, hard-pressed farmers in Rains County, Texas, created the Farmers' Educational and Cooperative Union. Largely the brainchild of Newton Gresham, a former member of the Farmers' Alliance, the new organization proved to be immensely popular. By 1905, it was well established in the lower South, and to reflect its growing ambitions, it changed its name to the National Farmers' Union. A year later the order elected Charles Barrett of Georgia as president. Under Barrett's guidance the organization grew to several million members and spread to the upper South and to the West.

In many respects the Farmers' Union resembled the Farmers' Alliance of the late nineteenth century. It sponsored cooperative stores, gins, and warehouses and kept lawyers, bankers, and merchants from its ranks. Its members were generally landowners rather than tenants. In 1904, 1906, and 1907, the organization tried to drive up cotton prices by urging growers to plow under, store, or destroy a portion of their crop. Such schemes only encouraged farmers to plant more cotton. In 1909 membership in the South began to decline, and within a decade, the order was all but dead in that region. The Farmers' Union, however, was more successful in the wheat belt, where it continued to flourish throughout the Progressive period. (Theodore Saloutos and John D. Hicks, *Agricultural Discontent in the Middle West, 1900–1939* (1951); Carl C. Taylor, *The Farmers' Movement, 1620–1920* (1953); John A. Crampton, *The National Farmers' Union: Ideology of a Pressure Group* (1965).)

Barton C. Shaw

FEDERAL AID ROAD ACT OF 1916, THE. Not until 1916 did Congress deliberately address the overwhelming problem of inadequate, poorly maintained public roads in the United States. Since the Constitution only authorized post road construction, the long-standing policy was to leave highway building to the discretion of state and local governments. Instead of constructing roads during the nineteenth century, Congress subsidized private companies that built a vast railroad network. By the dawn of the automobile age, therefore, there was no national system of roads, and existing state and local roads were miserably inadequate to meet the needs of the twentieth century. In 1916, responding to pressure not only from reform-oriented good roads advocates but also from such special interest groups as the American Automobile Association and the American Automobile Dealers Association, Congress passed the first law which recognized that good roads were important to the national welfare. The Federal Aid Road Act of 1916 made $75 million of matching funds available to all forty-eight states over a period of five years. Among its provisions, the new law required states to establish highway departments before they could receive any of the allocated money. (Charles L. Dearing, *American Highway Policy* (1949); T. H. MacDonald, "History of the Development of Road Building in the United States," *Transactions of the American Society of Civil Engineers* 92 (1928): 1181–206.)

Howard L. Preston

FEDERAL COUNCIL OF CHURCHES OF CHRIST IN AMERICA, THE. This council was created in 1908 as a medium through which the principle of the Social Gospel* might be expressed. It was the culmination of efforts covering several years to develop a body which might argue from the standpoint of the Protestant faiths those ideas and precepts which would apply the authority of Christ as the basis for the solution of human problems. The original constituent members were some thirty separate Protestant groups. The first step was to develop a credo for the organization which would state the need to resolve human problems within a Christian matrix. The credo and the specific suggestions were not binding on member churches, but its statements carried considerable weight as it was considered as the voice for those clergymen associated with agitation for social and economic reform during the Progressive Era. It was strongly pro-labor and developed close ties to the union movement. It was an ardent supporter of Prohibition* and was associated with the Peace Movement* in the days before World War I,* although for the most part its members supported the government after the declaration of war. In 1923, to counter bigotry, it set up a Commission on Goodwill between Christians and Jews which later evolved into the National Council of Christians and Jews. (Ronald C. White and Charles Howard Hopkins, *The Social Gospel: Religion and Reform in Changing America* (1976); Paul A. Carter, *The Decline and Revival of the Social Gospel: Social and Political Liberalism in American Protestant Churches, 1920–1940* (1956); Robert T. Handy, ed., *The Social Gospel in America, 1870–1920* (1966).)

Thomas W. Ryley

FEDERAL FARM LOAN ACT. One of the most vexing problems that faced farmers in the early years of the twentieth century was the high cost of mortgage loans. In an attempt to provide relief, Congress passed the Federal Farm Loan Act in July 1916. Largely the work of Senator Henry F. Hollis of New Hampshire and Congressman Asbury Francis Lever of South Carolina, this legislation called for the creation of the Federal Farm Loan Board, which would supervise the activities of twelve district farm loan banks. These banks were authorized to offer long-term agricultural loans at an interest rate of no more than 5 percent with farm land as security. To take advantage of this service, the farmer was required to join a national farm loan association. Although progressives generally favored the bill, President Woodrow Wilson* had earlier denounced a similar proposal as class legislation. But with the presidential election of 1916 just a few months away, Wilson signed the measure into law. (Arthur S. Link, *Wilson: Confusion and Crisis, 1915–1916* (1964); George B. Tindall, *The Emergence of the New South, 1913–1945* (1967).)

Barton C. Shaw

FEDERAL RESERVE ACT. Also known as the Glass-Owen Act of 1913, this measure was the first comprehensive attempt to reorganize the national banking system after the Civil War. During the 1912 presidential campaign, Democrats charged that Senator Nelson W. Aldrich's* plan for a central bank and a "National Reserve Association" would perpetuate Wall Street's domination of U.S. financial affairs. Progressive Democrats, led by William Jennings Bryan,* argued that sole authority over banking and currency belonged to the federal government. Conservative Democrats, championed by Congressman Carter Glass,* advocated creation of a decentralized reserve system, owned and controlled by private bankers, but completely dissociated from Wall Street. As chairman of the House Committee on Banking and Currency, Glass drafted a bill for a system with as many as twenty regional reserve banks under private control.

President Woodrow Wilson,* after tentatively accepting this proposal, asked Glass to include in his bill a measure for a central government board with minority representation for bankers. Progressives reacted angrily to Glass's original bill, and Senator Robert L. Owen* of Oklahoma, chairman of the Senate Committee on Banking and Currency, submitted an alternative banking plan providing for government control. Meanwhile, Secretary of the Treasury William Gibbs

McAdoo* urged that the new banking system be established as an adjunct of the Treasury Department. Louis D. Brandeis* agreed with the progressives' assertion that the government should control all banking and currency matters and convinced Wilson that private bankers should be denied representation on the proposed Federal Reserve Board. The ensuing congressional debate lasted for six months. Agrarian representatives forced the inclusion of an amendment for the discounting of short-term agricultural paper but continued to oppose the Glass bill because it authorized private control of reserve banks. Bankers denounced the bill as socialistic. Nevertheless, the bill passed the House on September 18, the Senate on December 19, and Wilson signed it on December 23, 1913.

The Federal Reserve Act provided for twelve districts, each with a Federal Reserve bank. Every national bank had to join the system and contribute 6 percent of its capital to the Federal Reserve bank. State banks and trust companies also could join the system. Federal Reserve banks were empowered to issue Federal Reserve notes to member banks. These notes were funded by commercial and agricultural paper and a 40 percent gold reserve. This act also established a Federal Reserve Board of Governors in Washington, D.C., composed of the secretary of the treasury, the comptroller of the currency, and six other members appointed by the president. The act provided for a more flexible currency which would be responsive to business demands. In the event of economic crises, the banking reserves of a region or of the entire nation could be mobilized. Largely because of progressives' political pressure, the final act offered benefits to farmers and businessmen and permitted a degree of public regulation. However, Senate amendments deprived the board of authority over Federal Reserve banks' discount rates and added a bankers' advisory commission to the board. (Arthur S. Link, *Woodrow Wilson and the Progressive Era, 1910–1917* (1963); Gabriel Kolko, *The Triumph of Conservatism: A Reinterpretation of American History, 1900–1916* (1963); H. Parker Willis, *The Federal Reserve System* (1923).)

David E. Alsobrook

FEDERAL TRADE COMMISSION. An independent regulatory agency, the Federal Trade Commission (FTC) was created by a congressional act of the same name on September 26, 1914. It consists of five commissioners, of whom no more than three may be members of the same political party, appointed by the president to serve seven-year terms, subject to the approval of the Senate. The chief executive designates one of the five to serve as chairman. This agency replaced the Bureau of Corporations* established in 1903 as part of the original Department of Commerce and Labor.* The FTC possesses broad investigatory powers and may require both special and annual reports from businesses. Under Section 5 of the 1914 statute, it may issue cease and desist orders. Complaints brought against businesses may be handled in several ways including formal proceedings before trial judges and consent settlement procedures negotiated between the FTC's staff and the offending party. The commission also conducts trade practice conferences, issues trade rules and publishes guides, and renders advisory opinions. Frequently used among the commission's arsenal of informal techniques is administrative treatment. Congress has vested the FTC with broad authority to ascertain unfair business practices. Although it works in conjunction with a number of federal agencies, the FTC enjoys a special relationship with the antitrust division of the Department of Justice with which it exchanges information, since both are charged with the enforcement of the Clayton Act* of 1914. (Earl W. Kintner, *An Antitrust Primer* (1973); Richard A. Posner, *Antitrust Law* (1976).)

John Quentin Feller

FEMINISM. Feminism is the advocacy of women's emancipation in all areas of life, including full economic, political, and social equality with men. Feminism is also the organized activities on behalf of women's rights. During the Progressive Era, the term had only recently come into usage and its exact definition seems to have been vague. There were, however, two recognizable strands of feminism, one which emphasized women's different and special nurturing abilities and the other which emphasized women's equality with men.

The Progressive Era saw an increaase in women's organized activities, divided into roughly three groups: suffragists, "social feminists,"* and radicals. Suffragists were interested in the vote as a means of redressing the political inequalities of women. These included women active in the National American Suffrage Association* and the more militant National Woman's Party.* "Social feminists" were reformers particularly interested in issues concerning women, children, and the home. They actively supported a number of issues, such as protective labor laws, pure food and drug acts, and maternal and infant mortality. These organizations included the General Federation of Women's Clubs,* the National Consumer's League,* the National Women's Trade Union League,* settlement house workers, and the women's trade union movement. The third category, radical women, included a wide range of activists from Socialist party* members to militant feminists active in the National Women's Party and other radical organizations, to sex radicals, such as Emma Goldman* and Margaret Sanger,* who advocated legal birth control and sexual freedom. Concerned with challenging sexual relations, as well as changing social institutions, these radical women were active in a variety of organizations.

Black women's activism expanded during this period, focusing on social reforms, antilynching legislation, and woman suffrage.* Excluded from most white women's organizations, black women formed their own organizations, such as the National Association of Colored Women, to create opportunities and improve the lives of black women and children in such areas as health care. By the 1910s, an overwhelming commitment to woman suffrage brought these diverse women together into a mass women's movement, which included a variety of tactics and encouraged political diversity. (Mari Jo Buhle, *Women and American Socialism, 1870–1920* (1983); Paula Giddings, *When and Where I Enter:*

The Impact of Black Women on Race and Sex in America (1984); William O'Neill, *Everyone Was Brave: A History of Feminism in America* (1969).)

Marie Laberge

FILENE, EDWARD ALBERT (September 3, 1860–September 26, 1937). Born in Salem, Massachusetts, Filene was the second of five children of German-Jewish immigrant parents. His father was a small retail merchant who moved his operation to Boston in 1881. Young Filene proved to be a talented merchant and developed William Filene's Sons into a Boston landmark. Filene served as its president until 1928, when he was removed by his family and associates for controversial policies. Filene was an early progressive reformer in Boston, working with Louis Brandeis* to regulate the Boston Elevated Railway Company and create the Public Franchise League. Turning to governmental corruption, he supported the Good Government Association and brought Lincoln Steffens* to Boston to muckrake the city. He joined with James J. Storrow to found the reformist City Club and, with Steffens, to found Boston 1915, a movement of civic uplift.

After the failure of Boston reform, Filene turned to national and international activities. He remained a progressive, optimistic about the improvement of society through cooperation, the scientific application of knowledge, and government activism. To these ends, he founded and endowed the Twentieth Century Fund, a research and policy-setting organization. He encouraged cooperation among businessmen for civic betterment, sponsoring the Chamber of Commerce movement in Boston, then nationally and internationally. He also sponsored the credit union movement, advocated unemployment and health benefits, and wrote and lectured widely on the social benefits of mass distribution. (E. A. Filene, *Speaking of Change: Collected Speeches and Articles* (1939); Gerald W. Johnson, *Liberal's Progress* (1948); Mary LaDame, *The Filene Store* (1930).)

Constance Burns

FINNISH-AMERICANS. Finnish immigrants (361,000 emigrated to the United States between 1866 and 1930) were remarkably active in progressive-radical causes: the labor movement, the left-wing press, and consumer cooperatives. The Finnish Socialist Federation, organized in 1906, affiliated with the national party and flourished in prewar years (13,846 members in 1913). Two ruptures decimated its strength: thirty-eight midwest locals were lost to the Industrial Workers of the World,* in 1914, while nearly all central and western regions fell to pro-Communist elements in 1920. Ideological newspapers took part in the campaigns: Fitchburg (Massachusetts) *Raivaaja* (1905–   ); Superior (Wisconsin) *Tyomies-Eteenpain* (1903–   ) and *Tyovaen Osuustoiminitalehti* (1930–1965); Duluth (Minnesota) *Industrialisti* (1915–1976); and Astoria (Oregon) *Toveri* (1907–1931). The co-op movement was nurtured in a Socialist environment. By 1916, Finns across the country were operating some seventy stores, many in rural areas. Regional wholesales emerged, notably, the Central

Cooperative Wholesale in Superior, Wisconsin, started in 1917, which served thirty-one member outlets by 1920. (John I. Kolehmainen, *Sow the Golden Seed* (1955, 1979); Michael Karni et al., *For the Common Good* (1977).)

John I. Kolehmainen

FISHER, IRVING (February 27, 1867–April 29, 1947). Born in Saugerties, New York, Fisher was educated at Yale University, receiving his A.B. in 1888 and his Ph.D. in 1891. Fisher spent his entire academic career at Yale University where he taught mathematics from 1892 to 1895. From 1892 until 1935, when he became a professor emeritus, Fisher was a member of the faculty of political economy. Fisher's contributions to economics and statistics were manifold. He was a skilled mathematical economist at a time when most economists lacked such skills and was the founding president of the Econometrics Society.

Fisher's writings on monetary theory and policy and index numbers have earned special acclaim. In his classical quantity-theory-of-money equation $MV + M'V' = PQ$, Fisher made the purchasing power of money (or its reciprical, the general price level P) completely determined by the stock of money in circulation M, its velocity of circulation V, the volume of bank accounts M', their velocity of circulation V', and the total quantity of transactions Q. Fisher advocated "100 percent money"; that is, all bank deposits should be backed by 100 percent reserves, rather than fractional reserves, to control the business cycle. Fisher made important contributions to the theory of interest and capital. He saw clearly that the higher the rate of inflation the higher the interest rate. Fisher investigated the meaning and determination of income, wealth, and the capital stock. Fisher's reputation was tarnished somewhat by his prediction, made not long before the stock market crash of 1929, that the United States had reached a permanent plateau of prosperity. (Irving Norton Fisher, *A Bibliography of the Writings of Irving Fisher* (1961); Irving Norton Fisher, *My Father, Irving Fisher* (1956).)

Leon Applebaum

FISHER, WALTER L. (July 4, 1862–November 9, 1935). Born in Wheeling, West Virginia, Fisher graduated from Hanover College in 1883. He was admitted to the Illinois bar in 1888, and for a brief time served as special assessment attorney for Chicago. In 1899 he became actively involved with Chicago's Municipal Voters' League (MVL), a group of progressive reformers dedicated to eradicating political corruption. Fisher so distinguished himself as MVL secretary that he was elected president in 1906; from this platform he helped solve the city's sticky and perpetually controversial transit problem. In 1903 he served as first president of the City Club of Chicago, which sponsored several studies and assisted in investigation of a variety of city departments. He became president of the Conservation League of America in 1908, vice president of the National Conservation Association* in 1910, and succeeded Richard A. Ballinger as William Howard Taft's* secretary of the interior in 1911. While in Washington he concentrated on extending the government's conservation program and addressing Alaska's unique problems. He returned to Chicago in 1913 to resume his law practice and participate in urban reform politics, particularly in the area of mass transit. (Alan B. Gould, " 'Troubled Portfolio' to Constructive Conservation: Secretary of the Interior Walter L. Fisher, 1911–1913," *Forest History* 16 (1973): 4–12; Alan B. Gould, "Walter L. Fisher: Profile of an Urban Reformer, 1880–1910," *Mid-America* 57 (1975): 157–72.)

Wayne A. Wiegand

FITZGERALD, JOHN FRANCIS (February 11, 1863–October 2, 1950). Born in Boston of Irish immigrant parents, Fitzgerald attended Boston Latin School and Harvard Medical School, dropping out when his father died. After a brief stint in the insurance and investment business, he plunged into a political career. On September 18, 1889, he married Mary Josephine Hannon, a union that lasted sixty-one years and produced six children, including Rose, the mother of President John Fitzgerald Kennedy and U.S. Senators Robert F. and Edward M. Kennedy. Elected to the city council in 1892 and to the state senate the following year, "Honey Fitz" served in Congress from 1895 to 1901, opposing the immigration literacy test of 1897, supporting civil rights legislation for blacks, and attacking the "meat trust" for providing embalmed beef to Spanish-American War soldiers.

Retiring from Congress, he published a weekly newspaper that brought him sufficient income to pursue his political career. Elected mayor in 1905 over the opposition of the Good Government Association, Fitzgerald backed organized labor and expanded urban services to the poor, but tolerated vice, circumvented civil service regulations, and built a citywide political machine through patronage and the awarding of contracts. When the Good Government Association secured adoption of a reform charter, Fitzgerald was reelected by a narrow margin. Challenged by fellow Democratic ward boss James Michael Curley* in 1914, Fitzgerald withdrew and backed an unsuccessful Good Government Association candidate. Two years later, he lost an election for the U.S. Senate to Republican Henry Cabot Lodge.* Although never again elected to office, Fitzgerald lost races for Congress (1918) and governor (1922 and 1930). (John Henry Cutfer, *"Honey Fitz": Three Steps to the White House: The Life and Times of John F. "Honey Fitz" Fitzgerald* (1962); J. Joseph Huthmacher, *Massachusetts People and Politics* (1959).)

John D. Buenker

FLINT V. STONE TRACY COMPANY (220 U.S. 107) (1911). The Supreme Court decision in *Flint V. Stone Tracy Company*, rendered on March 13, 1911, upheld the constitutionality of the corporation excise tax* of 1909. The decision resulted from a consideration of eleven cases first argued in Vermont, New York, Massachusetts, Illinois, Minnesota, or Ohio and involving corporations involved in real estate, insurance, public utilities, banking, multigraphics, mining, and the taxicab business. In a unanimous decision, the Court accepted the government's defense of the corporation excise tax without reservation, rejecting each of the thirty-two contentions of the plaintiffs which ranged from the argument that the Senate had no right to initiate revenue bills to the assertion that being required to file a tax return constituted unreasonable search and seizure. On the main question, the Court ruled that the tax was not a direct one, within the meaning of the Constitution, but rather "an excise upon the particular privilege of doing business in a corporate capacity" and, as such, could be measured by the entire income of the parties affected, even though part of that income was derived from tax-exempt property. Referring to the case of *Pollock v. Farmers Loan and Trust Company*,* the Court insisted that the difference between the current tax and the 1894 income tax "is not merely nominal but rests upon substantial differences between the mere ownership of property and the actual doing of business in a certain way." (Sidney Ratner, *A Political and Social History of Federal Taxation* (1942); Randolph E. Paul, *Taxation in the United States* (1954); John D. Buenker, *The Income Tax and the Progressive Era* (1985).)

John D. Buenker

FLORIDA. The seeds of Florida's Progressive movement were sown during the 1880s and 1890s. Between 1880 and 1901, the state granted over eleven million acres of land to railroads and land companies. Railroad magnates Henry B. Plant and Henry M. Flagler were closely associated with Bourbon Democrats who controlled the state legislature. Most Floridians supported railroad and land development and were reluctant to inhibit the efforts of investors and corporate leaders. However, an anticorporation spirit, especially regarding railroads, emerged in the 1880s. Populists and reform Democrats frequently criticized the legislature's preferential treatment of railroads, combining to enact a railroad commission in 1897. As in neighboring states, Florida's progressivism was marked by limited social and political reform programs and concerted efforts to legislate public morality.

Because of the state's sparse, largely rural population, Florida progressives failed to organize energetic reform coalitions, and interest groups did elect several influential governors. Governor William Sherman Jennings (1901–1904), an Illinois native and a cousin of William Jennings Bryan,* successfully recovered substantial amounts of public land claimed by railroads and laid the foundation for a progressive political organization. During the U.S. Senate primary of 1903, progressive Democrats aggressively attacked corporate abuses in Florida. Governor Napoleon Bonaparte Broward (1904–1908) launched the Everglades drainage project and sponsored educational reforms, child labor laws, regulation of public utilities, and pure food legislation. His philosophy dominated the administrations of his successors, Albert W. Gilchrist and Park Trammell (1908–1916). Under Gilchrist, Florida's first farmers' cooperative act was adopted, and a juvenile court system was created. Trammell championed measures to regulate primary elections,* strengthen the state railroad commission, eradicate corrupt practices, and encourage conservation. He established a state tax commission, a highway department, and a bureau of vital statistics. In 1916 Sidney J. Catts, a Baptist minister and insurance salesman, won the governorship as an independent, drawing considerable political support from rural north Florida with his anti-Catholic and prohibitionist appeals. His reform accomplishments included abolition of convict leasing, compulsory school attendance, increased aid to dependent children, and creation of an insane asylum for whites. (David R. Colburn and Richard K. Scher, *Florida's Gubernatorial Politics in the Twentieth Century* (1980); Samuel Proctor, *Napoleon Bonaparte Broward: Florida's Fighting Democrat* (1950); Wayne Flynt, *Cracker Messiah: Governor Sidney J. Catts of Florida* (1977).)

David E. Alsobrook

FLOWER, BENJAMIN O. (October 19, 1858–December 24, 1918). Reform editor and author, Flower was born in Albion, Illinois, and educated at the University of Kentucky and Transylvania University Bible School. Choosing journalism over the ministry as a career, Flower edited some short-lived journals in the 1880s before moving to Boston in 1889. It was there that he made his reputation as editor of the *Arena*, the most intellectually respectable reform publication of the early Progressive Era. Flower left the *Arena* in 1896 to publish the *New Times* and the *Coming Age* in Chicago before returning to lead the *Arena* again from 1900 to 1909.

Flower's many journals and several books were marked by a strong literary style in the service of such causes as the initiative,* referendum* and recall,* municipal reform, government ownership of public utilities, universal suffrage and women's rights, compulsory arbitration of labor disputes, and the abolition of child labor, saloons, and prostitution. In the last years of his life, Flower's writing focused less on these mainstream progressive causes than on such issues as psychic phenomena, Christian Science, the dangers of public medicine, and his irrational fear of the Catholic "menace" to the nation. (Howard F. Cline, "Benjamin Orange Flower and *The Arena*, 1889–1909," *Journalism Quarterly* 17 (June 1940): 139–50; Roy P. Fairfield, "Benjamin Orange Flower: Father of the Muckrakers," *American Literature* 22 (1950): 272–82; Peter J. Frederick, *Knights of the Golden Rule: The Intellectual as Christian Social Reformer in the 1890s* (1976).)

Peter J. Frederick

FOLK, JOSEPH W. (October 26, 1869–May 28, 1923). Folk was born and grew up in the small western Tennessee town of Brownsville, graduated from Vanderbilt University Law School in 1890 and, in 1893, joined the law firm of his mother's brother in Saint Louis. A Democrat, he was elected circuit attorney of the city in 1900. A year later, he won indictments of and convicted one "Colonel" Ed Butler, the "boss" of Saint Louis, an ostensible Democrat, and a number of "his" city councilmen of accepting bribes and other malfeasances.

Folk became famous overnight, thanks in no small part to the sensationalized "Tweed Days in St. Louis," an article by Claude Wetmore and Lincoln Steffens* in the then nationally circulated *McClure's Magazine*.

In 1904, campaigning for "honesty in government," Folk won the Missouri governorship. Vigorous and courageous, the young governor enjoyed the support of a generally friendly legislature. His program was the post-Populist middle-class reformism of his time: expansion of pure food legislation; an increase in law enforcement personnel; extension of the statute of limitations on bribery charges; legislation to curb gambling, including horse racing; fixing railroad freight and passenger rates as well as curbing railroad lobbyists; mandating an eight-hour day for mine workers; prohibiting industrial employment of boys under fourteen; requiring compulsory school attendance; and altogether setting a tone of law enforcement, including ousting corrupt public officials. Excluded from a second successive term by law, Folk set his eyes upon securing the Democratic presidential nomination in 1912, but had to settle for a second-level federal post under President Woodrow Wilson.* After winning some fame as the Interstate Commerce Commission prosecutor of the New Haven case, he resigned and returned to Missouri for a run for the Senate in 1918, but was decisively defeated. (Louis G. Geiger, *Joseph W. Folk of Missouri* (1953); Claude Wetmore and Lincoln Steffens, "Tweed Days in St. Louis," *McClure's Magazine* 19 (October 1902): 577–86; Louis Filler, *Crusaders for American Liberalism* (1939).)

Louis G. Geiger

FOLKS, HOMER (February 18, 1867–February 13, 1963). Deeply affected by his parents' religious values and passionately devoted to a life of practical service to others, Folks rejected the ruling social Darwinistic* premises of extreme individualism in the late nineteenth century and became a leading figure in the development of modern conceptions of social service and the practice of social work. Educated at Albion College and Harvard University, he began his influential career in child welfare activities and rapidly advanced to national prominence as a leader in practical efforts to improve public health, welfare, and security. For more than fifty years (1892–1947), he served as secretary of the New York State Charities Aid Society and used this pivotal position to play a leading role in the crusade for social justice.

An idealistic and inspiring leader endowed with superabundant energy and instinctively given to action, Folks acquired exceptional political skills, becoming particularly adept at articulating emerging reform ideas and galvanizing public support for them. His greatest contribution to the American reform tradition probably can be found in the practical understanding of the course of reform he inculcated. Social workers, he argued, must seek to alter societal conditions fundamentally, not merely respond to the consequence of social dependence, and service functions inevitably should become integrated into governmental structures, displacing the pioneering efforts of private charity agencies. (Homer

Folks, "The Reminiscences of Homer Folks," Oral History Project (Columbia University, 1949); Walter I. Trattner, *Homer Folks, Pioneer in Social Welfare* (1968); Savel Zimand, "Homer Folks: A Biographical Sketch," in Homer Folks, *Public Health and Welfare: The Citizen's Responsibility—Selected Papers of Homer Folks*, Savel Zimand, ed. (1958).)

Stephen B. Wood

FOOD ADMINISTRATION. An agency designed to conserve, encourage, and control food production during World War I,* the Food Administration was established under the authority of the Food and Fuel Control Act of August 10, 1917. The law was bitterly contested in Congress because it granted unprecedented powers to the president and provided for control over wheat and other grains, but not over cotton. Nevertheless, under the direction of Asbury Lever, chairman of the House Agricultural Committee, the bill passed Congress largely in its original form. To administer the law, President Woodrow Wilson* appointed Herbert Hoover* head of the Food Administration.

Working through county extension agents and others, Hoover established over 3,000 county and district food administration centers by November 1918, through which much of his work was carried on. Rationing of sugar was done at the local level, and to encourage production, Wilson established the price of wheat slightly above the $2 a bushel minimum called for in the law. Working mostly through middlemen, Hoover maintained high prices for beef and struck a balance between the price of corn and hogs to encourage hog production. Primarily, however, food control was accomplished through voluntary cooperation. Publicity given to such voluntary projects as meatless-wheatless days and victory gardens helped save food and encourage production. (Gary Dean Best, *The Politics of American Individualism: Herbert Hoover in Transition, 1918–1921* (1975); William C. Mullendore, *History of the United States Food Administration, 1917–1919* (1941); David Burner, *Herbert Hoover: A Public Life* (1978).)

Wayne E. Fuller

FORAKER, JOSEPH BENSON (July 5, 1846–May 10, 1917). Conservative Republican senator from Ohio, Joseph Foraker was born on a farm in Highland County, Ohio; he enlisted in the Union Army and served with General William T. Sherman on his "March to the Sea." After the war he graduated from Cornell University in 1869, was admitted to the Ohio bar the same year, and settled in Cincinnati. He worked his way up in Ohio politics, served two terms as governor from 1885 to 1889, then was elected senator in 1896 and reelected in 1902. He opposed most of President Theodore Roosevelt's* reform legislation, but he backed the president for renomination in 1904 against his rival boss from Ohio, Senator Mark Hanna.*

When Roosevelt discharged three companies of Negro soldiers after a racial incident in Brownsville,* Texas, in 1906, Foraker demanded a congressional investigation. He planned to run for president in 1908, but a revelation in the

Hearst* papers that he had been on the payroll of Standard Oil throughout his terms as senator ended both his presidential ambitions and his political career. Foraker is a good example of the archconservatives Roosevelt opposed within the Republican party.* (Joseph B. Foraker, *Notes of a Busy Life* (1916); Herbert B. Croly, *Marcus Alonzo Hanna: His Life and Work* (1912); George E. Mowry, *The Era of Theodore Roosevelt* (1958).)

Edward R. Kantowicz

FORD, HENRY (July 30, 1863–April 7, 1947). Born near Dearborn, Michigan, Ford died in the same city. Raised on a farm with little formal education, Ford was a natural mechanic who by 1896 had personally designed and built an automobile. He subsequently formed and reformed automotive companies culminating in the 1903 organization of the Ford Motor Company. Ford adopted two concepts that were to assure success, the moving mass-production assembly line and a marketing goal to manufacture an inexpensive automobile accessible to most families. Fame came with his 1914 introduction of the eight-hour day with a five-dollar daily minimum wage. This popular innovation and his apparent struggle against an auto trust (the Association of Licensed Automobile Manufacturers) made him one of the most popular businessmen in progressive America.

Ford opposed American entry into World War I* and in 1915 financed a Peace Ship expedition to Europe. As soon as war was declared, however, he devoted his company's resources to the war effort. In 1918 he was an unsuccessful senatorial candidate in Michigan. During the last three decades of Ford's life, he suffered a considerable decline in popularity as he vigorously opposed labor unions, financed an anti-Semitic newspaper, and lost market share to more innovative auto companies. (Henry Ford and Samuel Crowther, *My Life and Work* (1922); Allan Nevins and Frank Ernest Hill, *Ford*, 3 vols. (1954–1963); David L. Lewis, *The Public Image of Henry Ford* (1976).)

Martin I. Elzy

FORD, HENRY JONES (August 25, 1851–August 29, 1925). Born in Baltimore, Maryland, Ford graduated from Baltimore City College in 1868 and received an LL.D. from the University of Maryland in 1918. During the last several decades of the nineteenth century, he was a journalist with the *Baltimore Sun* and several Pittsburgh newspapers. In 1906–1907, Ford was a lecturer at Johns Hopkins University and then, at the invitation of Woodrow Wilson,* he joined the faculty at Princeton University as professor of politics. Wilson was impressed with Ford's most important work, *The Rise and Growth of American Politics*, published in 1898. Ford's thesis was that an increase in presidential authority was inevitable. He also explored the two distinct functions of the presidency: the ceremonial, as head of state, and the presidential, as head of government. Because the double role is beyond endurance of any man, Ford believed that the president would create a bureaucracy that would take on a life of its own and maintain the presidency as its raison d'être. In 1912, Governor

Wilson appointed Ford to the New Jersey commission on banking and insurance, and in 1920, President Wilson appointed him to the Interstate Commerce Commission. In addition, he served as president of the American Political Science Association* in 1918–1919. ("Henry Jones Ford," *The National Cyclopedia of American Biography*, vol. 21, 14; *Dictionary of American Biography*, vol. 6, 1.

David J. Maurer

FOREST SERVICE, U.S. The Division of Forestry, a small research agency created in the Department of Agriculture in 1881, became the Bureau of Forestry in 1901 under the management-oriented leadership of Gifford Pinchot,* and the Forest Service in 1905 after the transfer of the national forests from the Department of the Interior to the Department of Agriculture gave him something to manage. Pinchot looked upon trees as a crop to be harvested as long as annual cutting never exceeded annual growth, but his training in European forestry methods had taught him to think of a forest as an entity capable of supporting industries other than merely timber cutting.

Under Pinchot's adroit leadership, the national forests were steadily augmented until they totaled nearly 195 million acres in 1909. Congressional appropriations kept pace with this expansion, and a well-trained force of rangers managed a program that included, besides timber cutting, regulated stock grazing, mining, and hydroelectric power development under permits defining the terms and conditions of use. The Forest Service was the moving force behind the Conservation* movement during the presidency of Theodore Roosevelt,* but differences over goals within the movement and creation of the National Park Service* (1916) soon gave voice to rival views and rival bids for leadership. (Samuel P. Hays, *Conservation and the Gospel of Efficiency: The Progressive Conservation Movement, 1890–1920* (1959).)

James Penick

FORUM, THE. Established in June 1886 by Isaac L. Rice, a railroad lawyer and entrepreneur, this monthly magazine appealed to the serious reader by offering an informed analysis of significant contemporary problems. Prominent experts often debated the merits of new movements in American politics, society, and the arts. During the Progressive period, the *Forum* presented divergent and insightful perspectives on a host of reform issues, from socialism to eugenics. While never a muckraking* journal, it did explore such controversial subjects as prostitution and the white-slave trade, which more conservative publications ignored.

Editor Frederick Taber Cooper, a literary critic, added fiction and poetry to the magazine's contents in 1908, launching a trend that reached fulfillment under his successor, Mitchell Kennerley (1910–1916). Besides serializing new works by John Galsworthy, H. G. Wells, and other leading British novelists, Kennerley patronized a younger generation of talented American short story writers and poets, including Vachel Lindsay, Edna St. Vincent Millay, Joseph Hergesheimer, and Floyd Dell.* By 1916, the *Forum* had achieved an enviable reputation in belles lettres, and served as an important bridge between the Progressive Era and the Jazz Age. In later decades it underwent many changes of format and nomenclature before it was finally absorbed by *Current History* in February 1950. (Maxwell H. Bloomfield, *Alarms and Diversions: The American Mind through American Magazines, 1900–1914* (1967); Frank L. Mott, *A History of American Magazines, 1885–1905* (1957).)

Maxwell H. Bloomfield

FOUNDATIONS. Foundations are commonly defined as nongovernmental, nonprofit organizations, endowed with significant capital funds, run by their own officers, and established with broadly defined purposes to serve the general welfare. They tend to grant money to other bodies rather than administer permanent programs themselves. Until the 1940s, most were endowed by individuals rather than corporations. Andrew Carnegie's* essay "The Gospel of Wealth" (1889) furnished an ideology for large-scale philanthropy as justifying great aggregations of wealth, though he still contemplated direct personal giving.

The Peabody Education Fund, founded in 1867 to improve southern schools, formed an institutional prototype; but the first huge foundation was the General Education Board (GEB), founded in 1902 by John D. Rockefeller.* The GEB worked to improve southern public schooling, enlarge college endowments, and upgrade medical education. It multiplied its influence by encouraging governmental units to take over some of its programs and by often demanding that its grants be matched by other donors. The Carnegie Foundation for the Advancement of Teaching (1905) began pensions for professors and issued Abraham Flexner's 1910 report which spurred a drastic overhaul of medical education. The smaller but influential Russell Sage Foundation (1907) sponsored pioneering social surveys and other research basic to the professionalization of social work and social research. The Carnegie Corporation (1911) at first supported mainly its founder's pet projects. The giant Rockefeller Foundation (1913) concentrated on public health, medical research, and medical education in the United States and abroad. Other early foundations included the Cleveland Foundation (1914, the first community foundation, funded by many individuals and serving local needs), the Julius Rosenwald Fund (1917, building schools for southern blacks), the Laura Spelman Rockefeller Memorial (1918), the Commonwealth Fund (1918), and the Twentieth Century Fund (1919).

Foundations shifted philanthropy from individual, localized, palliative charity towards large-scale projects intended to find causes of and cures for medical and social problems, reflecting contemporary enthusiasm for science, professionalism, and efficiency. Claiming disinterested expertise, foundation-sponsored professionals initiated projects to improve education, public health, and social welfare and to impose social control, intervening in matters where local elites or the U.S. government was unable or unwilling to act. Repeated failures to win the Rockefeller Foundation a congressional charter and investigation of the foundation in 1915 by the Commission on Industrial Relations spurred denunciations of foundations as menacing extensions of monied power, but Congress failed to act. Recent critics have charged the early foundations with reinforcing existing forms of hegemony and strengthening cultural imperialism. (Robert F. Arnove, ed., *Philanthropy and Cultural Imperialism: The Foundations at Home and Abroad* (1980); Barry D. Karl and Stanley N. Katz, "The American Private Philanthropic Foundation and the Public Sphere, 1890–1930," *Minerva* 19 (1981): 236–70; Harold M. Keele and Joseph C. Kiger, eds., *Foundations* (1984).)

David I. Macleod

FRANK, LEO MAX. In 1913 Leo Max Frank, an Atlanta factory superintendent, was tried for the murder of one of his employees, Mary Phagan. Frank was a prominent Jew, and Phagan was a thirteen-year-old Gentile. The evidence suggested that the killer was Jim Conley, a black man who also worked for Frank. Nevertheless, the state was swept by a storm of anti-Semitism. Frank was found guilty and sentenced to death. But the governor of Georgia, John M. Slayton, was troubled by the questionable evidence. At length he commuted Frank's sentence to life in prison. Mobs attacked the governor's mansion, and on the evening of August 16, 1915, armed men broke into the prison holding Frank and kidnapped him. The next morning they lynched Frank near Marietta, Georgia.

Most students of the case have consistently argued that Frank was innocent. In 1982 Alonzo Mann, an eighty-three-year-old Virginian, told a reporter that, on the day of the murder, he saw Jim Conley carrying away Mary Phagan's body. A lie detector test confirmed that Mann was telling the truth. Two years later, the Georgia board of pardons granted Frank a posthumous pardon. (Leonard Dinnerstein, *The Leo Frank Case* (1968); Frank Ritter, Jerry Thompson, and Robert Sherborne, "An Innocent Man Was Lynched," Nashville *Tennessean*, March 7, 1982; *New York Times*, March 12, 1986.)

Barton C. Shaw

FREUND, ERNST (January 30, 1864–October 20, 1932). Born in New York City but educated in Germany, Freund returned to the United States and practiced law before he earned his Ph.D. in political science from Columbia in 1897. From 1894 to his death, he was a prominent scholar and respected teacher at the University of Chicago.* His continuing interest in the social sciences made him a founder of the first graduate school of social service in the country and president of the American Political Science Association* in 1915. While his fellow legal scholars were attracted to common-law adjudication, Freund embarked upon pioneer studies of legislation and administration. *The Police Power*, published in 1904, was a pathbreaking study of the regulatory authority of the states. Although sensitive to constitutional limitations, he realized that the very nature of the power required restraints on liberty and property, and he was a critic of the doctrine of liberty of contract that the Supreme Court at times invoked to strike down state regulatory power. His *Standards of American Legislation*, published in 1917, concentrated on illuminating the sound principles of legislation and remained both instructive and in print long after his death. But Freund was no detached scholar; he drafted model state laws on subjects of social legislation, served as a consultant to governmental bodies, and worked over twenty-five years with the Immigrants' Protective League.* (Oscar Kraines, *The World and Ideas of Ernst Freund: The Search for General Principles of Legislation and Administrative Law* (1974); Francis A. Allen, Preface to *Standards of American Legislation by Ernst Freund,* 2d ed. (1965).)

John E. Semonche

FRICK, HENRY CLAY (December 19, 1849–December 2, 1919). Born in West Overton, Pennsylvania, to a poor farmer, Frick received very little formal education and worked from an early age at a variety of menial jobs. However, his maternal grandfather was a wealthy distillery owner, and by the end of the 1860s, Frick was working for the distillery as a bookkeeper. During the 1870s, Frick built a personal wealth of over $1 million by purchasing Pennsylvania coal land and building and operating coke-ovens, recognizing the value of coke to the growing steel industry.

Early in the 1880s, Frick became an associate of Andrew Carnegie* and, by the end of the decade, became chairman of Carnegie Steel Company. His greatest notoriety came with the 1892 Homestead strike, during which he was shot and stabbed by an anarchist. Frick fiercely represented his company's interests, using first privately hired Pinkerton guards and then the Pennsylvania National Guard to break the strike. At the turn of the century, Frick split with Carnegie and associated with J. P. Morgan* in the organization of United States Steel Corporation.* For the remaining two decades of his life, Frick served as a director of United States Steel and other major companies. (Arundel Cotter, *Authentic History of United States Steel Corporation* (1916); B. C. Forebes, *Men Who Are Making America* (1917); George Harvey, *Henry Clay Frick* (1928).)

Martin I. Elzy

FUEL ADMINISTRATION. Established by the wartime Food and Fuel Control Act (the Lever Act) of August 10, 1917, the Fuel Administration was charged with increasing the production, restricting the nonessential use, and regulating the price of coal and oil. Before the War Labor Board* was created in April 1918, the Fuel Administration also set labor policies for the coal fields, prohibiting union efforts for the closed shop while blocking company attempts to fire union members. President Woodrow Wilson* named Harry A. Garfield, president of Williams College, as fuel administrator on August 23, 1917.

Fuel conservation efforts centered around public campaigns for "gasless Sundays" and "heatless Mondays." The administration set coal prices at a level to bring marginal mines into production, and the major problems of fuel management became those of transportation and distribution. In the hope of greater efficiency, the "natural" pattern of coal distribution was interrupted, and coal shipments to consumers were made on a zone or district basis. The bitterly cold winter of 1917–1918 intensified the problems, and great suffering was caused by the appalling confusion in railroad management that disrupted deliveries to homes and factories. On January 17, 1918, Garfield announced that all "dispensable" factories east of the Mississippi would be closed for four days to allow the railroads to unsnarl the congestion, causing critics to underscore their demands for a "war cabinet" or a congressional oversight committee. The argument led instead to the passage of the Overman Act on May 20, 1918, and a sweeping victory for presidential authority in economic matters.

When coal shortages and war demands increased the importance of petroleum products, the Fuel Administration established an Oil Division, and still later added natural gas to its list of regulated fuels. The agency was formally disbanded on June 30, 1919. (Harry A. Garfield, *Final Report of the United States Fuel Administration, 1917–1919* (1921); James P. Johnson, "The Wilsonians as War Managers: Coal and the 1917–18 Winter Crisis," *Prologue* 9 (1977): 193–208; David M. Kennedy, *Over Here: The First World War and American Society* (1980); Harold J. Tobin and Percy W. Bidwell, *Mobilizing Civilian America* (1940).)

Robert David Ward

FUNDAMENTALISM. This Protestant movement arose out of the emotional debate over Darwinism in the 1870s and reached its zenith in the mid-1920s. Fundamentalists regarded modern science as a threat to the "faith of their fathers" and insisted upon a literal interpretation of the Bible. Largely rural people, they were shocked by the new morality of the modern city and staunchly supported Prohibition,* movie censorship, and various blue laws. Although fundamentalism in much of the country simply involved a zealous commitment to conservative theology, it included a significant evangelical movement, particularly in the South and West. Evangelists such as Billy Sunday toured the nation, attracting large, enthusiastic revival crowds. By the early 1920s, fundamentalists had gained considerable political strength and public support for antievolution laws in schools.

The chief opponents of fundamentalists were the modernists*—urban, middle-class men and women who sought to reconcile religion with modern science and the realities of secular society. Modernist clerics such as Lyman Abbott* asserted that science and religion were complementary sources of divine truth and that the Bible should be interpreted for its spirit. The Social Gospelists* of the late nineteenth century eagerly embraced the modernist creed. The great clash between modernists and fundamentalists came in the debate between Clarence Darrow* and William Jennings Bryan* at the famous Scopes "Monkey Trial" of 1925. (Norman Furniss, *The Fundamentalist Controversy* (1954); George M. Marsden, *Fundamentalism and American Culture: The Shaping of Twentieth-*

Century Evangelicalism, 1870–1925 (1980); Ferenc M. Szasz, *The Divided Mind of Protestant America, 1880–1920* (1982).)

David E. Alsobrook

FURUSETH, ANDREW (March 12, 1854–January 22, 1938). Longtime president of the International Seamen's Union, Furuseth was the guiding light behind the La Follette Seamen's Act* of 1915 which "emancipated" sailors. Born Anders Andreassen in a village in Norway, he later took the name Furuseth from the cottage in which he was born. Going to sea at age nineteen, he arrived on the West Coast of the United States in 1880, quit active seamanship in 1891, and devoted the rest of his life to union activities.

Beginning in 1894, Furuseth spent twenty years of his life working to end the "enslavement" of sailors, who were bound by maritime law to remain with their ships for the duration of their contracts and could be imprisoned for desertion. He acted as legislative agent in Washington for the seafarers' unions and became president of the International Seamen's Union in 1908. He convinced Senator Robert M. La Follette* of the justice of his cause, and La Follette's Seamen's Act was passed by the House in 1913, by the Senate in 1914, and finally was signed by President Woodrow Wilson* on March 4, 1915. The law provided safety standards for American merchant vessels and permitted sailors to leave their ships before the expiration of their contracts. The reciprocal provisions of the law permitting the same rights to foreign sailors required the abrogation of numerous maritime treaties. Furuseth remained union president until his death. (Hyman Weintraub, *Andrew Furuseth: Emancipator of the Seamen* (1959); Belle Case and Fola La Follette, *Robert M. La Follette, 1855–1925*, 2 vols. (1953); Jerold S. Auerbach, "Progressives at Sea," *Labor History* 2 (1961): 344–60.)

Edward R. Kantowicz

G

GARDEN CITY MOVEMENT. This is the name given to a movement dedicated to the creation of an ideal suburbia, small self-sufficient cities surrounded by a greenbelt of forest and farms. This concept was developed by the Englishman Ebenezer Howard in his 1898 book, *Tomorrow, a Peaceful Path to Real Reform*, distributed in later editions as *Garden Cities of Tomorrow*. Howard's ideas included the ownership of the land by the community, the need for interior green space, small neighborhoods with local schools and community service, super-blocks with cul-de-sac streets, separation of pedestrian and bicycle traffic from automotive vehicles, and the dedication of major spatial elements to recreational use.

The Garden City Movement was taken up in the United States by Henry Wright, a landscape architect, and Clarence S. Stein, a designer. Both had worked on the federal government's project for providing housing for war industry workers, from 1916 to 1918, and both were founders of the Regional Planning Association of America. Their first major projects were Sunnyside, in Queens, New York (1924–1928); Chatham Village, in Pittsburgh, Pennsylvania (1929); and Radburn, New Jersey (1928). The largest and last of these, Radburn, was compromised by the depression, and it was only with the advent of the New Deal and the satellite cities of Greendale, Wisconsin; Greenhills, Ohio; and Greenbelt, Maryland, that fully developed Garden Cities were realized. (John Burchard and Albert Bush-Brown, *The Architecture of America: A Social and Cultural History* (1966); Arthur C. Comey and Max S. Wehrly, *Planned Communities* (1939); Ebenezer Howard, *Garden Cities of Tomorrow* (1946).)

David M. Sokol

GARFIELD, JAMES RUDOLPH (October 17, 1865–March 24, 1950). Garfield was born in Hiram, Ohio, the son of a congressman who would later become twentieth president of the United States. After studies at Williams College and

Columbia University, Garfield entered legal practice in Cleveland. He became involved in politics as a good-government Republican, winning two terms in the Ohio senate starting in 1895. Garfield was appointed to the U.S. Civil Service Commission in 1902, and the next year moved to the Department of Commerce and Labor* as commissioner of corporations. His industrial investigations and administrative skills attracted the attention of President Theodore Roosevelt,* who named him secretary of the interior in 1907. Garfield's two-year tenure in this office was notable for his reorganization of the department and for his support of the conservation activities of chief forester Gifford Pinchot.* The subsequent Ballinger-Pinchot* controversy was among the factors prompting Garfield to join Roosevelt in the new Progressive party in 1912. However, his own overwhelming defeat as Progressive candidate for Ohio governor in 1914, coupled with the general decline of the party, led him back to orthodox Republicanism. (Jack M. Thompson, "James R. Garfield: The Career of a Rooseveltian Progressive, 1895–1916" (Ph.D. diss., University of South Carolina, 1958); Jack M. Thompson, "James R. Garfield: The Making of a Progressive," *Ohio History* 74 (1965): 79–89; James Penick, Jr., *Progressive Politics and Conservation: The Ballinger–Pinchot Affair* (1968).)

John R. Schmidt

GARLAND, HAMLIN (September 14, 1860–March 4, 1940). Garland was born in a log cabin near the village of West Salem in Wisconsin. When he was nine, his family moved to Iowa, and he spent his youth on a "Middle Border" farm until he left to attend Cedar Valley Seminary in Osage, Iowa. In 1883 he held down a claim on a farm in MacPherson County, North Dakota. The following year he sold this and went to Boston, where he intended to prepare himself to teach American literature. His famous collection of short stories (*Main-Travelled Roads*, 1887) and his first novel (*A Spoil of Office*, 1893) were written in Boston before he moved back to West Salem in 1893. In 1899, he married the sister of sculptor Lorado Taft and moved to Chicago in 1907. Following a move to New York City in 1915, he published his most famous novel, *A Son of the Middle Border* (1917). The sequel, *Daughter of the Middle Border* (1922), won him the Pulitzer Prize. Together, these two books won him an appointment as one of the directors of the American Academy of Arts and Letters. It is generally agreed that Garland wrote moving, honest stories that remain some of the best regional fiction in the history of American literature. (Joseph B. McCullough, *Hamlin Garland* (1978); Donald Pizer, *Hamlin Garland's Early Work and Career* (1960); Robert Mane, *Hamlin Garland: L'homme et l'oeuvre* (1968).)

Robert W. Schneider

GARNER, JOHN NANCE (November 22, 1868–November 7, 1967). Garner resided and practiced law in Uvalde, Texas. A committed Democrat, Garner served in the legislature and in 1902 was advanced to a seat in Congress. In

Washington, "Cactus Jack" was a persistent advocate of the income tax.* In 1913 he worked to add a large-income surtax to the provisions of the Underwood-Simmons Act.* Later he opposed the "trickle-down" tax cuts of the Harding administration. Chosen Speaker of the House in 1931, Garner proposed significant federal aid to public works projects and to the needy. Backed by William Randolph Hearst* in the presidential primaries of 1932, he secured about one hundred delegates, which he released to Franklin D. Roosevelt* in exchange for the vice presidential nomination. Garner worked closely with FDR during the first New Deal, but after the 1936 election he was alienated by the administration's labor policies and by Roosevelt's court-packing plan. Garner was the presidential hope of conservative Democrats in 1940, but was unable to prevent FDR's nomination to a third term. (Bascom N. Timmons, *Garner of Texas: A Personal History* (1948); George B. Tindall, *The Emergence of the New South, 1913–1945* (1967); David C. Roller and Robert W. Twyaman, eds., *The Encyclopedia of Southern History* (1979).)

Paul M. Pruitt, Jr.

GARY, ELBERT HENRY (October 8, 1846–August 15, 1927). Born near Wheaton, Illinois, Gary became a prominent lawyer and politician in his hometown. Legal prominence and political acumen led to work as corporate counsel and seats on corporate boards. In 1898, he cooperated with J. P. Morgan* in the creation of the Federal Steel Company, which he served as president. In 1901 Gary and Morgan collaborated to create the United States Steel Corporation,* which Gary ruled in various capacities until his death in New York City. Gary's effort to avoid antitrust dissolution of United States Steel was rewarded in 1920 when the Supreme Court ruled that the corporation was not an illegal monopoly.

Nonetheless, Gary favored cooperation rather than unbridled competition among corporations in the same industry, as was exemplified by his "Gary dinners" at which steel executives discussed common problems and by his creation of the American Iron and Steel Institute, a forerunner of the trade associations* of the 1920s. Although Gary provided workers with improved benefits, he was among the most prominent leaders of the open-shop movement. His refusal to meet worker demands led to the bitter 1919 steel strike, which hobbled unions in the steel industry until their resurgence in the 1930s. (Ida M. Tarbell, *The Life of Elbert H. Gary* (1925); U.S. Steel Corporation, *Elbert Henry Gary: A Memorial* (1927); Arundel Cotter, *The Gary I Knew* (1928).)

Martin I. Elzy

GARY PLAN. The most widely imitated plan for progressive education, crafted in Gary, Indiana, by Superintendent of Schools William A. Wirt beginning in 1907. In the new industrial city, founded by U. S. Steel Corporation in 1906, Wirt established an innovative school program based on both administrative efficiency and enriched learning environments. In the Gary schools, Wirt supplemented the traditional academic subjects with art, music, dancing, dramatics, industrial arts, and physical education, as well as with special facilities such as science laboratories, workshops, libraries, gymnasiums, swimming pools, and auditoriums—all very rare for schools of the time. Underlying these enrichment programs was the idea that children learned by participating—an educational philosophy drawn from John Dewey,* with whom Wirt had studied at the University of Chicago.*

By dividing the students into "platoons," moving them about from classrooms to special facilities, and carefully scheduling the use of all school facilities throughout the day, the Gary Plan also seemed superefficient. Because of this appeal, the Gary Plan was adopted elsewhere in the Progressive Era, notably in New York City where reform mayor John P. Mitchel* hired Wirt in 1913 to implement the plan. This effort failed, as school reform got caught up in city politics and actually led to a week of widespread school rioting in 1917 and the subsequent electoral defeat of Mayor Mitchel. There was a resurgence of interest in the Gary Plan in the 1920s, when the U.S. Office of Education promoted the idea under the name of the "platoon school" or "work-study-play school" plan. By 1930, more than 200 cities had adopted the plan to various degrees. (Randolph S. Bourne, *The Gary Schools* (1916); Abraham Flexner and Frank P. Bachman, *The Gary Schools: A General Account* (1918); Roscoe D. Case, *The Platoon School in America* (1931); Ronald D. Cohen and Raymond A. Mohl, *The Paradox of Progressive Education: The Gary Plan and Urban Schooling* (1979).)

Raymond A. Mohl

GAYNOR, WILLIAM J. (February 2, 1848–September 12, 1913). Born in the village of Whitesboro in central New York, Gaynor was educated at the Catholic Assumption Academy. He taught at parochial schools from 1864 to 1868, then read law in Utica and was admitted to the bar in 1871. After a short stay in Boston, he moved to Brooklyn in 1873, briefly worked as a journalist, began a successful law practice, and fought against municipal corruption and bossism. In 1893 he was elected a justice of the New York State Supreme Court and was reelected in 1907. His unconventional personality and acid tongue notwithstanding, Judge Gaynor was respected for his efficient and judicious handling of cases and his defense of personal freedom.

Gaynor was elected mayor of New York City in November 1909. Despite his impaired physical and emotional health after he was struck by a would-be assassin's bullet on August 9, 1910, Gaynor provided New Yorkers a mildly progressive administration in the areas of labor, transportation, administrative and fiscal reform, and ethnocultural concerns. He failed, however, to secure a municipally owned transit system, revise the city's charter, eliminate police corruption, defend striking city workers, or support woman suffrage. Rejected by the major parties, Gaynor was nominated for a second term on September 4, 1913, by an independent citizens' committee. He died while on a European cruise. (Mortimer B. Smith, *William Jay Gaynor* (1951); William R. Hochman,

"William J. Gaynor: The Years of Fruition" (Ph.D. diss., Columbia University, 1955); Lately Thomas, *The Mayor Who Mastered New York* (1969).)

Augustus Cerillo, Jr.

GENERAL FEDERATION OF WOMEN'S CLUBS. The General Federation of Women's Clubs, founded in New York City in 1890, united existing women's organizations devoted to literary and cultural study, social interaction, and civic improvement. In an era when women's place was said to be in the home, the organization directed its membership—largely white, leisured, wives of prominent business and professional men in America's cities and towns—on an ambitious program of "Municipal Housekeeping" or urban reform. In fact, its huge membership, generously estimated at one million in 1914 but probably peaking in 1927 at a somewhat lower figure, served as the backbone of Progressive Era reform, its departments articulating problems and instituting solutions in art, civics, civil service reform, conservation, education, household economy, industrial and social conditions, public health, legislation, and literature and library extension. Although the association did not endorse woman suffrage until its 1914 biennial convention, its history is the story of efforts on behalf of women's rights issues such as higher salaries for teachers, the hiring of police matrons, and improved education for children via vocational education, well-equipped classrooms, public libraries, parks, and playgrounds. In 1922 the federation moved to Washington, D.C., where it has remained. (Mrs. Jane Cunningham Croly, *The History of the Woman's Club Movement in America* (1898); Mary I. Wood, *The History of the General Federation of Women's Clubs* (1912); Mildred White Wells, *Unity in Diversity: The History of the General Federation of Women's Clubs* (1953).)

Karen J. Blair

GEORGE, HENRY (September 2, 1839–October 29, 1897). Henry George was born in Philadelphia, but after the end of his formal schooling in 1853, a year at sea, and a short apprenticeship as a printer, he migrated to California where he ultimately became a journalist. In 1879, he completed his major work, *Progress and Poverty*, in which he argued that the root of America's economic problem—increasing want in the face of increasing wealth—lay in the monopoly of land. Rent deprived labor and capital of a fair return. His solution was not to confiscate property but to confiscate rent through taxation. This prescription later came to be called the "single tax."* George's book won him a great deal of attention, although not acceptance, in England, Ireland, and other countries. Academic economists were generally critical.

In 1880, George moved to New York, and in 1886, he ran for mayor of the city as the candidate of a labor coalition. Assailed as a radical, George polled an impressive number of votes but lost to the Tammany Hall* candidate. In 1887, the George forces ousted the socialists from the newly formed United Labor party, and soon thereafter the party collapsed. In his writings George also emphasized free trade and, in later years, municipal ownership of public utilities.* Municipal ownership was a key issue in his second quest for the mayoralty of New York in 1897, but he died a few days before election day. Although he won no major political office, he had a strong influence on such reformers as Tom Johnson,* Brand Whitlock,* Frederic C. Howe,* and Louis Post.* (Charles Albro Barker, *Henry George* (1955); John L. Thomas, *Alternative America: Henry George, Edward Bellamy, Henry Demarest Lloyd and the Adversary Tradition* (1983); Herbert H. Rosenthal, "Sun Yat-sen and Henry George; A Reassessment," *American Studies* (Taipei) 13 (1983): 1–23.)

Herbert H. Rosenthal

GEORGIA. Like many southern states, Georgia enacted a host of progressive measures between 1900 and the early 1920s. A few reforms, including a mild child-labor law,* occurred during the administration of Governor Joseph M. Terrell (1902–1907), but it was Terrell's successor, Hoke Smith* (1907–1909, 1911), who truly led the progressive movement in Georgia. One of Smith's early successes came in 1907 when he helped shepherd a prohibition* bill through the Georgia legislature. A year later Smith encouraged the general assembly to abolish the convict-lease system. He strengthened the railroad commission by appointing a former Populist as its special attorney. Smith also established juvenile courts* and outlawed free railroad passes. In 1911 an antilobbying bill was enacted.

Although Smith's successors were in many respects conservatives, reforms still continued. In 1914, the legislature passed a new child labor law; in 1916, it created a highway commission and endorsed a compulsory education bill; in 1917, it enacted the "bond-dry law"—possibly the nation's strictest prohibition statute. Reformers were also at work on the local level. Some Georgia towns hired more policemen, put up street lamps, built parks, and provided other services. Churches occasionally founded vocational schools, and in 1912, Mary De Bardeleben established a settlement house for blacks in Augusta.

On the surface such activity appears impressive, yet many of these reforms were weak and ineffective. It was not until 1916 that the state hired a factory inspector to make sure the child labor laws were enforced, and loopholes nearly emasculated the compulsory education act. Other proposals, such as the demand for woman suffrage,* were simply too radical for Georgia. Finally, racism profoundly influenced the reform movement. Smith fought for the disfranchisement* of blacks, and in 1908, the legislature established a voter literacy test. This, in addition to the poll tax, virtually ended black involvement in state politics. (Dewey W. Grantham, Jr., *Hoke Smith and the Politics of the New South* (1958); Alton DuMar Jones, "Progressivism in Georgia, 1898–1918"

(Ph.D. diss., Emory University, 1963); John Dittmer, *Black Georgia in the Progressive Era, 1900–1920* (1977).)

Barton C. Shaw

GERMAN-AMERICANS. The Progressive Era coincided with a period of decline of German-Americans as an element in the population. Their numbers peaked at 2.75 million in the census of 1890, just after the last great wave of German migration; by 1920, the German-born numbered about 1.66 million. Yet German-Americans continued to wield influence in society and politics because of their long-established institutions, their concentration in areas like the Northeast and Midwest, and the continued identification of many second- and third-generation immigrants with the group.

German-Americans were a diverse group with many internal conflicts arising from differences of class, religion, and geographical origin. Their elaborate institutional network also encouraged fragmentation. In 1901, Germans achieved a national organization by founding the National German-American Alliance; this, however, was an "umbrella" organization of German societies to which many individual German-Americans felt little attachment. German political loyalties were likewise usually divided. The issues which potentially could arouse and unite them were cultural ones like prohibition, enforcement of Sunday laws, and the use of the German language in the schools. Germans were wary of progressivism if its "reforms" seemed to include temperance and immigration restriction, or to reflect presumptions of Anglo-Saxon cultural superiority. Feminism also clashed with German cultural traditions. Despite these misgivings, German-Americans might support specific progressive measures in matters like corporation regulation, labor rights, and social welfare. In Wisconsin,* for example, Germans were not prominent among the elements bearing Robert La Follette* to power in state politics; yet the mild socialism which advocated municipal reforms in Milwaukee during the same period rested principally on German support.

World War I* overshadowed all other issues for German-America after 1914. The National German-American Alliance, which had mostly occupied itself with fighting prohibition before 1914, undertook to defend the German position in the European conflict. The political objective of most German-Americans was to maintain American neutrality and thereby avoid the dilemma of conflicting loyalties. The U.S. declaration of war in 1917 exposed German-Americans to attack for their previous sympathies. Many newspapers, institutions, and other symbols of German ethnicity did not survive the wartime onslaught of public hostility. The election of 1920* saw Germans joining strongly in the reaction against Woodrow Wilson* and the Treaty of Versailles. The war experience drove many German-Americans toward conservatism and made of them a strong supporting element in the isolationism of the interwar period. (Frederick C. Luebke, *Bonds of Loyalty: German-Americans and World War I* (1974); Clifton

J. Child, *The German-Americans in Politics, 1914–1917* (1939); Kathleen Con-
zen, "Germans," in Stephan Thernstrom, ed., *Harvard Encyclopedia of American Ethnic Groups* (1980), 405–25.)

James M. Bergquist

GIBBONS, JAMES (CARDINAL) (July 23, 1834–March 24, 1921). Catholic
archbishop of Baltimore from 1877 to 1921, the second American named to the
College of Cardinals, Gibbons was the de facto leader of American Catholicism
in the late nineteenth and early twentieth century. Born in Baltimore in 1834,
James Gibbons moved to Ireland with his family at age four, but he returned to
the United States for his clerical training and was ordained in 1860. Named a
bishop in 1868, he was the youngest prelate in attendance at the First Vatican
Council. He was appointed archbishop of Baltimore in 1877, presided over the
Third Plenary Council of Baltimore in 1884, and was raised to the College of
Cardinals in 1886. Gibbons led the Americanist wing of the Catholic Church in
the United States, those priests and bishops who wholeheartedly accepted political democracy and church-state separation and wished to adapt the Roman
church to American customs. He encouraged the rapid assimilation of immigrants
and tried to foster American Catholic scholarship by founding the Catholic
University of America in Washington, D.C.

Gibbons was not a political or social liberal, and he usually exercised his
leadership by a prudent use of behind-the-scenes influence, what he called "masterful inactivity." In 1887, however, he spoke out forcefully against a Vatican
plan to condemn the Knights of Labor. Gibbons's defense of the workingman's
right to organize trade unions and bargain collectively with employers prevented
a Vatican intervention which might have proven disastrous. Following Gibbons's
lead, American bishops, however conservative on other matters, consistently
championed the rights of non-Socialist labor unions, thus preventing the alien-
ation of the workingclass from the church which occurred in Europe. (John Tracy
Ellis, *The Life of James Cardinal Gibbons* (1952); Robert D. Cross, *The Emergence of Liberal Catholicism in America* (1967); Edmund Roohan, "American
Catholics and the Social Question, 1868–1900" (Ph.d. diss., Yale, 1952).)

Edward R. Kantowicz

GILMAN, CHARLOTTE ANNA PERKINS STETSON (July 3, 1860–Au-
gust 17, 1935). Born in Hartford, Connecticut, and mainly self-educated, Gilman
attended briefly the Rhode Island School of Design in Providence, where she
spent her childhood. In 1884 she married Charles Walter Stetson, gave birth to
a daughter the following year, and separated in 1888. By the time she secured
a divorce in 1894, Gilman had established herself as a successful writer and
lecturer. She wrote several important volumes on the material basis of sex
relations, including the feminist classic *Women and Economics* (1898), *The Home*
(1903), and *Man-Made World* (1911). In addition she produced her own monthly
magazine, the *Forerunner* (1909–1916).

Throughout this period, Gilman was the most prominent lecturer and leading intellectual of the women's movement. She appeared frequently at meetings of the National American Woman Suffrage Association* and, in 1913, addressed the International Suffrage Convention in Budapest. In 1915, she became a founding member of the Woman's Peace Party.* She married George Houghton Gilman in 1900. Dying of breast cancer, Gilman took her own life in Pasadena, California. (Charlotte Perkins Gilman, *The Living of Charlotte Perkins Gilman* (1935, 1963); Mary A. Hill, *Charlotte Perkins Gilman: The Making of a Radical Feminist, 1860–1898* (1980); Carol Ruth Berkin, "Private Woman, Public Woman: The Contradictions of Charlotte Perkins Gilman," in Carol Ruth Berkin and Mary Beth Norton, eds., *Women in America: A History* (1979).)

Mari Jo Buhle

GLADDEN, WASHINGTON (February 11, 1836–July 2, 1918). Born in Pottsgrove, Pennsylvania, and reared on a farm near Owego, New York, Gladden studied at Williams College (B.A., 1859) and Union Theological Seminary. Entering the Congregational ministry, he served parishes in New York and Massachusetts and was an editor of the influential *Independent* before moving in 1883 to the First Congregational Church of Columbus, Ohio, where he spent the remainder of his life. One of the earliest proponents of both liberal theology and the Social Gospel,* he was widely known for accepting evolution and critical biblical scholarship and for interest in the welfare of industrial workers. In Columbus, he supported virtually every progressive reform, including all the proposals made by the Ohio Constitutional Convention of 1912, served a term on the city council (1900–1902), and founded a settlement house. His support for labor led him to advocate strong unions, help to arbitrate strikes, and interpret tolerantly radical labor groups and socialists.

A Republican since the party's formation, Gladden supported the Progressive* candidacy of Theodore Roosevelt* in 1912 and the Democratic Woodrow Wilson* in 1916. He strenuously opposed entry into World War I* until 1917, when Wilson's democratic war aims and hope that the war would serve progressive social ideals persuaded him to support intervention. (Jacob H. Dorn, *Washington Gladden: Prophet of the Social Gospel* (1967); Robert T. Handy, ed., *The Social Gospel in America, 1870–1920* (1966); Washington Gladden, *Recollections* (1909).)

Jacob H. Dorn

GLASS, CARTER (January 4, 1858–May 28, 1946). After several years' service as a journeyman printer on rural Virginia newspapers, Glass returned to his hometown and assumed the editorship of the Lynchburg *Daily News*. In 1888 he bought the paper and later combined it with the *Daily Advance*. As an editor he gained regional and national attention through his advocacy of conservative Democratic policies; however, in the early 1890s he espoused free silver and antimachine political reforms.

Elected to the Virginia legislature in 1898, Glass played an influential role in the state constitutional convention of 1901, where he sponsored the poll tax and literacy test to disfranchise* blacks. After the convention, he was appointed to fill a vacancy in the Sixth Congressional District. In 1902 Glass won this seat on his own, holding it until 1918. At the 1912 Democratic National Convention, despite concerted opposition from Senator Thomas S. Martin, he delivered the entire Virginia delegation to Woodrow Wilson.* Glass exerted minimal influence in Congress until 1913, when, as chairman of the Committee on Banking and Currency, he drafted and sponsored the Federal Reserve Act* (Glass-Owen Act). He served as Wilson's secretary of the treasury (1918–1920) and then resigned to fill Martin's Senate seat, which he held until his death. A self-styled "Jeffersonian Democrat," he tirelessly advocated states' rights and restrictions on federal authority, strict interpretation of the U.S. Constitution, and racial segregation. He was the principal author of the 1933 Glass-Steagall Act, which created the Federal Deposit Insurance Corporation. (Carter Glass, *An Adventure in Constructive Finance* (1927); Harry E. Poindexter, "From Copy Desk to Congress: The Pre-Congressional Career of Carter Glass" (Ph.D. diss., University of Virginia, 1966); Raymond H. Pulley, *Old Virginia Restored: An Interpretation of the Progressive Impulse, 1870–1930* (1968).)

David E. Alsobrook

GOLDMAN, EMMA (June 27, 1869–May 14, 1940). Born in Kovno, Russia (Kaunus in modern Lithuania), Goldman emigrated to the United States in December 1885 and settled in Rochester, New York. By 1889, she had espoused anarchism and moved to New York City where she became associated with the emigré Russian revolutionist Alexander Berkman and with Johann Most, editor of the anarchist paper *Die Freiheit*. During the next several decades, she took part in strikes, waged numerous fights for free speech, raised funds for the Industrial Workers of the World,* published the anarchist magazine *Mother Earth* (1906–1917), and toured the country lecturing on subjects ranging from Ibsen to birth control to the evils of patriotism. Her commitment to anarchism prompted her to oppose demands for state social welfare programs on the grounds that such programs would only increase the power of government. She also actively urged people not to vote or hold any positions in government. In 1919, after spending twenty months in prison for opposing the draft during World War I, Goldman was deported to Russia where she remained until the end of 1921. Denied reentry into the United States, she remained active as a lecturer and writer in exile, mainly in England, Canada, France, and Spain. A staunch defender of the Catalonian revolutionists during the Spanish Civil War, Goldman died in Canada. (Richard Drinnon, *Rebel in Paradise: A Biography of Emma*

Goldman (1961); Emma Goldman, *Living My Life* (1931); Alice Wexler, *Emma Goldman: An Intimate Life* (1984).)

Frederick C. Giffin

GOLDMARK, JOSEPHINE CLARA (October 13, 1877–December 15, 1950). Social reformer and researcher, Goldmark was born in Brooklyn to a prominent family of Austrian Jewish* background; she was educated at private schools, then graduated from Bryn Mawr College in 1898. She became the lifelong collaborator of Florence Kelley* as research and publications director for the National Consumers' League.* She gathered social data and did most of the research for her brother-in-law, Louis D. Brandeis,* when he argued the landmark Supreme Court case of *Muller v. Oregon* (1908),* upholding a state law which limited the hours of working women. She served on the New York State Factory Investigating Commission* after the disastrous Triangle shirtwaist factory fire and conducted numerous other studies of working conditions. Late in her life, she wrote a biography of Florence Kelley which was published posthumously. Always overshadowed by more famous associates, such as Kelley, Brandeis, Eleanor Roosevelt, and Frances Perkins,* she was a tireless behind-the-scenes worker for social reform. (*New York Times* Obituary, December 16, 1950; Edward T. James et al., *Notable American Women*, vol. 2 (1971); Walter Trattner, ed., *Biographical Dictionary of Social Welfare in America* (1986).)

Edward R. Kantowicz

GOMPERS, SAMUEL (January 27, 1850–December 13, 1924). First president of the American Federation of Labor,* Gompers was the dominant labor leader in America for nearly forty years. Born in London, England, to a Dutch-Jewish family, he quit school at age ten to work as a cigarmaker, then emigrated to New York with his family in 1864 and continued to practice his trade. In 1877 he reorganized the Cigarmakers' Union, and in 1881 he joined with other craft unionists to found the "Federation of Organized Trade and Labor Unions," modeled after the British Trade Unions Congress. This umbrella organization for national and international craft unions was renamed the American Federation of Labor in 1886, and Gompers served as its president every year, except one, until his death.

Though familiar with Marx's writings and personally acquainted with many socialist immigrants, Gompers did not espouse the socialist* cause. Instead, he advocated "pure and simple unionism" or "business unionism." Each craft or trade would organize one national union; it would use the threat of strikes to bargain collectively for higher wages and better working conditions; and it would not interfere with management's prerogatives or attempt to remake society. Gompers's philosophy was summed up in one word—"More." He worked for more wages, more leisure, more liberty for the worker, a bigger slice of the pie for labor. (Samuel Gompers, *Seventy Years of Life and Labor* (1925); Bernard Mandell, *Samuel Gompers: A Biography* (1963); Philip Taft, *The A. F. of L. in the Time of Gompers* (1957).)

Edward R. Kantowicz

GOODNOW, FRANK J. (January 18, 1859–November 15, 1939). Born in Brooklyn, Goodnow graduated from Amherst College in 1879 and Columbia Law School in 1881. From 1883 to 1911, he was a member of the Columbia School of Political Science. In 1903, he was elected the first president of the American Political Science Association.* In 1911, he was appointed by President William Howard Taft* to a Commission on Economy and Efficiency. In 1913, he became legal adviser to the Chinese government, and from 1914 to 1929, he served as president of Johns Hopkins University in Baltimore, where he lived for the remainder of his life.

Goodnow is best remembered for his solution to the problem of how to make government in the explosively growing cities of the Progressive Era efficient— able to meet the new physical and technological challenges—and at the same time truly representative. In *Politics and Administration* (1900) he articulated a theory separating the formulation of policy from its administration that was accepted without question for a generation and was the basis of textbooks for forty years. While not a muckraker, Goodnow was a reformer and was closely related to other Progressive figures in that his approach was opportunistic and evolutionary in spirit, featured collecting data and presenting it to the public, and focused on pragmatic institutional changes. (Lurton W. Blassingame, "Frank J. Goodnow: Progressive Urban Reformer," *North Dakota Quarterly* 40 (1972): 22-30; Lurton W. Blassingame, "Frank J. Goodnow and the American City" (Ph.D. diss., New York University, 1968); Austin Ranney, "The Political Philosophy of Frank J. Goodnow," *Southern Social Science Quarterly* 20 (1950): 268–76.)

Lurton W. Blassingame

GOOD ROADS MOVEMENT. The movement to reform governmental commitment to the construction and maintenance of public roads in the United States grew from the fertile soil of late nineteenth-century American populism. Farmers equated poor roads with expensive hauling costs, low farm values, inaccessible markets, high railroad freight rates, and rural isolation. Most farmers, however, were unwilling to pay additional taxes to have better roads and left the politics of road reform to another group directly affected by poor roads. Bicyclists, who liked to tour outside urban areas, organized themselves into an effective lobby and, in 1892, persuaded Congress to fund the establishment of a national highway commission and, in 1893, the Office of Road Inquiry. These agencies had little impact on improving the nation's public roadways, and by 1910, good roads proponents could point to only a few localities where road improvements were a priority.

Widespread automobile ownership during the second decade of the twentieth century called greater attention to poor roads, and to the dismay of farmers, the focus of the good roads movement shifted from an emphasis on the improvement of farm-to-market roads to the construction of interstate tourist highways. By 1915, the good roads movement was primarily in the hands of businessmen, land developers, and highway boosters, who saw automobile tourism as a means of achieving financial objectives. (Wayne Fuller, "Good Roads and Rural Free Delivery of Mail," *Mississippi Valley Historical Review* 42 (June 1955): 67–83; Harry W. McKown, Jr., "Roads and Reform: The Good Roads Movement in North Carolina, 1885–1921" (M.A. thesis, University of North Carolina, 1972); Philip P. Mason, *The League of American Wheelmen and the Good Roads Movement, 1880–1905* (1958).)

Howard L. Preston

GORDON, KATE M. (July 14, 1861–August 24, 1932). Born in New Orleans, Gordon was the daughter of a schoolmaster father and a socially prominent mother. She became active in the suffrage movement during the 1890s and was one of the women who asked the constitutional convention of 1898 to enfranchise females. In 1901 she became corresponding secretary of the National American Woman Suffrage Association,* an office which she filled until 1909. From 1904 to 1913, she was president of the Louisiana State Suffrage Association. In November 1913, she organized the Southern Woman Suffrage Conference and served as its president until it disbanded in 1917.

Though a dedicated suffragist, Gordon did not favor the enfranchisement of women through a federal amendment. She thought that the states should control the electorate within their borders, and when the Susan B. Anthony Amendment was submitted in June 1919, she opposed its ratification. Gordon advocated juvenile courts,* humane treatment for animals, higher standards for nurses, and the admission of women medical students by Tulane University. She was instrumental in establishing the New Orleans Anti-Tuberculosis Hospital in 1926, and in February 1931, she became superintendent of the Milen Home for Feebleminded Girls. (Kenneth R. Johnson, "Kate Gordon and the Woman Suffrage Movement in the South," *Journal of Southern History* 38 (1972): 365–92; B. H. Gilley, "Kate Gordon and Louisiana Woman Suffrage," *Louisiana History* 24 (1983): 289–306; Elizabeth Cady Stanton et al., eds., *History of Woman Suffrage*, vol. 4 (1902): 678–88, vol. 5 (1922): 671–73, vol. 6 (1922): 216–26; *New York Times* Obituary, August 25, 1932.)

A. Elizabeth Taylor

GORE, THOMAS P. (October 10, 1870–March 16, 1949). Born near Embry, Mississippi, Gore was educated at Cumberland University in Lebanon, Tennessee, graduating in 1892. On December 27, 1900, he married Nina Kay. As the result of two separate childhood accidents, he was totally blind by the time he was twenty years old. After participating in Mississippi and Texas Alliance and

Populist politics, Gore was elected one of Oklahoma's Democratic senators when it became a state in 1907. He generally favored progressive legislation during the Roosevelt,* Taft,* and Wilson* administrations. As chairman of the Senate Agriculture and Forestry Committee, he helped pass bills associated with the New Freedom* legislation and with World War I.* Also, he had interest in legislation relating to oil and Indians. During the early years of World War I, he was coauthor of the Gore-McLemore resolutions designed to protect American neutrality by warning American citizens not to travel on belligerent ships. After he opposed the United States' joining the League of Nations,* he was defeated for reelection in 1920. Gore died in Washington, D.C. (Monroe Lee Billington, *Thomas P. Gore: The Blind Senator from Oklahoma* (1967).)

Monroe Billington

GRANT, MADISON (November 18, 1865–May 30, 1937). Madison Grant was born in New York City to a distinguished upper-class family. He received his bachelor's degree from Yale in 1887 and then took a law degree at Columbia University in 1890. A bachelor all of his life, Grant had patrician instincts befitting his upbringing. He was concerned with the natural world and the environment, and expressed those concerns through official positions in such groups as the New York Zoological Society, the American Museum of Natural History, and the Save the Redwoods League.

But Grant's interests were not confined to preserving the natural world; he also became one of the most articulate spokesmen for upper-class, Anglo-Saxon culture in the United States. An avid genealogist and charter member of the Society of Colonial Wars, Grant believed fervently in the prevailing doctrines of Anglo or Nordic superiority—that the explanation of American success in the world was a racial or ethnic one. Grant was active in the Eugenics Research Association and the Immigration Restriction League,* and feared that American institutions would be destroyed by the influx of "new immigrants"* in the late nineteenth and early twentieth centuries.

Grant's point of view gained national attention in 1916 when he wrote *The Passing of the Great Race*. Arguing that Nordic institutions were the political, economic, and military genius of the world, Grant said that Nordic mixture with Jews, East Europeans, and South Europeans would dilute American culture and send the United States into a decline from which it would never recover. Couched in the language of science, *The Passing of the Great Race* played an important role in the immigration restriction legislation which reached fruition in the National Origins Act of 1924. (*Who Was Who in America* (1943), I:477; *New York Times*, May 31, 1937; Madison Grant, *The Passing of the Great Race* (1916); John Higham, *Strangers in the Land: Patterns of American Nativism, 1860–1925* (1963).)

James S. Olson

GRIFFITH, D. W. (January 22, 1875–July 23, 1948). Born near Crestwood, Kentucky, Griffith was the product of a failing Southern family still doting on antebellum glories. After a decade as an actor and struggling writer, he moved to New York, where he received work as an actor and a scenario writer for different movie companies, establishing himself with the Biograph studio from 1908 to 1913. During that time, Griffith was the studio's principal director and production supervisor, gaining a reputation as a maker of films which, while very popular with audiences, frequently relied on socially conscious themes such as the evils of business speculation.

Griffith's abilities for using inherently cinematic techniques like crosscutting and the close-up as part of a coherent film *language* were exemplified in *The Birth of a Nation** (1915) which, despite its glorification of the Ku Klux Klan, was hailed as the clearest expression of the uplifting potential of moving pictures. Griffith's next film, *Intolerance* (1916), detailed man's inhumanity to man, but its labyrinthine structure and ill-timed pacifism confused audiences. Griffith's work took a more melodramatic turn in the war years and in the decade that followed, but his sentimental Victorianism gradually lost favor with moviegoers. (Richard Schickel, *D. W. Griffith* (1984); Karl Brown, *Adventures with D. W. Griffith* (1973); D. W. Griffith, *The Man Who Invented Hollywood: The Autobiography of D. W. Griffith* (1972).)

                                                                              Chris Foran

H

HADLEY, HERBERT S. (February 20, 1872–December 1, 1927). Hadley was born in Olathe, Kansas, graduated from the University of Kansas and Northwestern University Law School, and practiced law in Kansas City until his appointment as first assistant city counselor in 1898. Two years later he was elected prosecuting attorney of Jackson County, but was defeated for reelection. He won election as state attorney general on the Republican ticket, serving from 1905 to 1909, and established a reform record, prosecuting major businesses, including Standard Oil, International Harvester, railroads, and insurance companies.

   Aided by his own progressive record and a split within the Democratic party,* Hadley won election as the first Republican governor in over thirty years, serving from 1909 to 1913. As governor, Hadley faced a Democratically controlled legislature that blocked many administration bills, including ones granting certain cities authority to establish a commission form of government,* creating a statewide public utilities commission, taxing corporations' capital stock, taxing inheritances, and creating a state board of control. He did succeed with laws limiting the hours women could work per day and preventing passenger rate discrimination on railroads. At the national Republican convention of 1912 he was a leading progressive supporter of Theodore Roosevelt.* Although frequently in poor health, Hadley remained active after leaving office, serving for a time as special counsel to the Interstate Commerce Commission, law professor at the University of Colorado, then finally as chancellor of Washington University in Saint Louis. (Lloyd Edson Worner, ''The Public Career of Herbert Spencer Hadley'' (Ph.D. diss., University of Missouri, 1946); Harlan Hahn, ''Republican Party Convention of 1912 and the Role of Herbert S. Hadley in National Politics,'' *Missouri Historical Review* 59 (1965): 407-23; Hazel Tutt Long, ''Attorney General Herbert S. Hadley *Versus* the Standard Oil Trust," *Missouri Historical Review* 35 (1941): 171–87.)

Nicholas C. Burckel

HAGUE, FRANK (January 17, 1876–January 1, 1956). Born in Jersey City, New Jersey, Hague left school at age fourteen and worked at various odd jobs for the next decade. His political career began with his election as second-ward constable in 1896. A party loyalist, he served as county committeeman, deputy sheriff, and state house sergeant-at-arms. In 1908, Hague was chosen as second ward leader by the local Democratic boss, and appointed city hall custodian by the new mayor. Their falling out involved Hague in desperate battles for political survival, during which he supported James Smith, Jr., for U.S. Senate and opposed Woodrow Wilson's* nomination for the presidency.

By late 1912, with only a handhold on power in his second ward, Hague changed tactics and outwardly embraced progressive reform. Over the next four years he attacked railroad and utility abuses, prostitution, narcotics, and other bêtes noires of progressivism. Reversing his earlier opposition, he supported the introduction of commission government* in Jersey City and won election to the first commission. He modernized the police and fire departments and, in 1917, won election as mayor, a post he held until 1947 with only one serious challenge. His control of city and county made him the dominant force in New Jersey, maker of governors and Democratic national vice-chairmen. (Richard Connors, *A Cycle of Power* (1971); Mark S. Foster, "Frank Hague of Jersey City: 'The Boss' as Reformer," *New Jersey History* 86 (1968): 106–17; Dayton McKean, *The Boss: The Hague Machine in Action* (1940).)

Joseph F. Mahoney

HALEY, MARGARET (November 15, 1861–January 5, 1939). Haley was a Chicago teacher of Irish ancestry who emerged from her teaching experience in the Chicago stockyards district to become the president of the Chicago Teachers' Federation (which began as a mostly female union in 1897). As a progressive, Haley espoused the idea that the key to equitable treatment for all in the school system lay in the reform both of the tax laws and the corrupt political system. She backed the election of Edward F. Dunne* as mayor in 1905 and supported his attempts at municipal ownership of the transit system and reform of the tax base for the school system. Haley fought for woman suffrage, the professionalization and unionization of teaching, and the reform of the National Education Association.* (Mary T. Herrick, *The Chicago Schools: A Social and Political History* (1971); Robert L. Reid, ed., *Battleground: The Autobiography of Margaret Haley* (1982).)

Dominic Candeloro

HALL, G. STANLEY (February 1, 1844–April 24, 1924). Born in Ashfield, Massachusetts, Hall was educated at Williams College (B.A. 1867, M.A. 1870) and Union Theological Seminary and took a Ph.D. at Harvard (1878, the first doctorate in psychology in the United States), with postdoctoral study in Germany. His important academic posts were at Johns Hopkins in experimental psychology from 1881 to 1888 and as president of Clark University, where from 1889 to 1919 he provided strong impetus for the concept of the modern research university. Hall wrote over 300 articles and a dozen books, and gave hundreds of speeches primarily related to the empirical study of human behavior with a strong emphasis on natural and developmental (genetic) psychology and the need to organize society accordingly.

Hall's most important contribution to the Progressive Era was establishing an agenda for psychological research which had a profound impact on the way Americans thought about children, adolescence, and education. Hall's specific contributions can be seen in three areas: (1) He was the originator of the organized, "scientific" study of children in the United States. Through his work, the concept of the child was radically altered in ways that gave very strong support to the progressive education movement. (2) Hall produced the first important study of adolescence, essentially creating the concept, in his 1904 book, *Adolescence: Its Psychology and Its Relation to Physiology, Anthropology, Sociology, Sex, Crime, Religion, and Education*. The book was praised for its pathmaking discussions of human sexuality. (3) Through lectures, publications and a major conference (1909) bringing Freud, Jung, Brill, and other psychologists and psychiatrists together, Hall introduced European psychiatry to the United States. (Dorothy Ross, *G. Stanley Hall: The Psychologist as Prophet* (1972); Charles E. Strickland and Charles Burgess, *Health, Growth and Heredity: G. Stanley Hall on Natural Education* (1965); Merle Curti, *The Social Ideas of American Educators* (1935).)

Chris Eisele

HAMILTON, ALICE (February 27, 1869–September 22, 1970). Born in New York City, Alice Hamilton was raised in Fort Wayne, Indiana, in a comfortable home, where she was taught that she should follow her high aspirations. After attending Miss Porter's School in Farmington, Connecticut, Hamilton decided on a career in medicine, since she saw it as the only profession in which women would be independent and useful, and received her M.D. degree in 1893 from the University of Michigan. After further studies in Europe and the United States, she accepted a position as professor of pathology at the Women's Medical School of Northwestern University in 1897. She became a resident at Hull House,* where she worked closely with the social reformers Jane Addams,* Florence Kelley,* and Julia Lathrop.*

Hamilton combined her interests in social reform with her scientific abilities. She investigated a typhoid epidemic in the Hull House neighborhood and fought against cocaine trafficking. She made important contributions to industrial medicine, serving on the Illinois Commission on Occupational Diseases and in 1910 becoming supervisor of the Illinois survey of industrial toxins which examined the extent of lead poisoning in industry. She later became an investigator for

the United States Bureau of Labor. Active in the women's peace movement*
during World War I,* she became Harvard's first woman professor when she
accepted a position as assistant professor of industrial medicine. Hamilton remained active as an author and consultant on industrial medicine, serving as
president of the National Consumers' League* from 1944 to 1949. (Alice Hamilton, *Exploring the Dangerous Trades* (1943); Wilma Ruth Slaight, "Alice
Hamilton: First Lady of Industrial Medicine" (Ph.D. diss., Case Western Reserve University, 1974); Barbara Sicherman, *Alice Hamilton: A Life in Letters*
(1984).)

John M. Herrick

HAMMER V. DAGENHART (247 U.S. 251) (1918). In this 1918 decision,
the Supreme Court held the Keating-Owen* child labor act unconstitutional.
Delivering the majority opinion for the Court, Justice William R. Day declared
that Congress was not regulating commerce at all; its aim was to affect conditions
of labor. Because manufacture was a process distinct from commerce, he said,
Congress had no jurisdiction over the conditions of labor in factories and mines;
that was a power reserved to the states. That part of the act limiting adolescents
between fourteen and sixteen to an eight-hour day and six-day week was a
regulation of working conditions, and conservatives had long opposed both state
and federal child labor laws,* fearing a precedent for government supervision
of adult as well as children's working conditions. In 1941 the Supreme Court
reversed *Hammer v. Dagenhart*. Writing for the majority, Justice Harlan Stone
declared the decision a "departure" from the traditional interpretation of the
commerce clause. (Stephen B. Wood, *Constitutional Politics in the Progressive
Era: Child Labor and the Law* (1968); Robert W. McAhren, "Making the Nation
Safe for Childhood: A History of the Movement for Federal Regulation of Child
Labor, 1900–1938" (Ph.D. diss., University of Texas–Austin, 1967).)

Robert W. McAhren

HANNA, MARCUS ALONZO (September 24, 1837–February 15, 1904).
Hanna was born in New Lisbon, Ohio, and after a brief flirtation with college,
he entered the family grocery firm in Cleveland. His 1864 marriage to Charlotte
Augusta Rhodes brought Hanna into his father-in-law's coal and iron business;
eventually, he moved into such other fields as banking and street railways. He
also became involved in local Republican politics in both contributory and managerial roles, most notably in the cause of Congressman William McKinley.*
Hanna helped elect McKinley to two terms as governor of Ohio, and in 1896
masterminded his protégé's successful bid for the presidency.

Because of his corporate connections, his centralized direction of Republican
campaigns, and his imagined domination of the new president, Hanna became
a favorite subject of political cartoonists. He was himself elected to the U.S.
Senate in 1897. There he continued to advance the conservative, high-tariff, pro-
business agenda. Though McKinley's death removed his close friend from the

White House, Hanna continued to wield considerable influence. He played a major part in the settlement of the 1902 coal strike, an action which also illustrates his conciliatory, "practical" approach to labor relations. By 1904, certain conservative elements within the Republican party* were advancing the senator as an alternative to President Theodore Roosevelt.* Hanna made no public declaration either way. At the height of the speculation, he suffered a short illness and died. (Herbert Croly, *Marcus Alonzo Hanna: His Life and Work* (1912); Thomas Beer, *Hanna* (1929); Clarence Ames Stern, *Resurgent Republicanism: The Handiwork of Hanna* (1963).)

John R. Schmidt

HARD, WILLIAM (September 15, 1878–January 30, 1962). Hard was a prominent journalist of the muckraking* era whose career began with involvement in Chicago's settlement house movement and concluded with a position as editor of the *Reader's Digest*. After he attended Northwestern University, his first journalistic assignment was as editorial writer for the *Chicago Tribune*, and from 1903 on, he wrote magazine articles on such questions as the grievances of stockyards workers and unsafe industrial conditions. He became a featured writer on *Everybody's Magazine*,* and in the period from 1908 to 1914, he wrote several series for *Everybody's* and the *Delineator* on issues pertaining to the status of women in modern society. In the postmuckraking era, Hard's career continued with work for the *Metropolitan* and the *New Republic*,* where for three years he was a regular contributor. In 1920, he wrote *Raymond Robin's Own Story*, an account of the efforts by this leading Chicago reformer to impel American policy toward a stable, cooperative relationship with newly established Soviet Russia. Moving in the late 1920s to broadcast journalism, Hard emerged as a conservative defender of the established order. (Materials relating to Hard are available at the University of Wyoming's Archive of Contemporary History and at the Seeley G. Mudd Manuscript Library at Princeton. His books include *Raymond Robin's Own Story* (1920), *Who's Hoover* (1928), and collections of his magazine articles: *Injured in the Course of Duty* (1910), *The Women of Tomorrow* (1912), and *How the English Take the War* (1917).)

Herbert Shapiro

HARDING, WARREN GAMALIEL (November 2, 1865–August 2, 1923). An amiable man of moderate ability and less judgment, Harding was elected the twenty-ninth president of the United States in 1920. Born in rural Morrow County, Ohio, he moved with his family to Marion, the county seat, in 1882. There Harding briefly studied law but soon turned to journalism. Working as a reporter on the weekly *Democratic Mirror*, he became co-owner of the struggling weekly *Marion Star* within a year. He transformed the *Star* into a successful daily, and he grew in community importance and in political influence. Elected to the state senate in 1898, in 1903 he became lieutenant governor on the

Republican ticket headed by Myron T. Herrick.* Rather than seek reelection he returned to his newspaper enterprise after the two-year term.

A party regular, Harding served as a sacrificial lamb in the 1910 gubernatorial campaign against incumbent Democrat Judson Harmon.* Because of his reputation as an orator, Harding was chosen to place the name of President William Howard Taft* in nomination at the 1912 Republican National Convention. Two years later Harding entered and won the Republican party* primary for the U.S. Senate and easily won the general election. Continuing his party regularity, Harding served six years in the Senate without distinction. He opposed the confirmation of Louis D. Brandeis* for the Supreme Court, supported a protectionist tariff policy, opposed high taxes on business, and supported entrance into World War I.* During the postwar years he voted for the Eighteenth and Nineteenth amendments to the U.S. Constitution, but as a member of the foreign relations committee he faithfully endorsed Senator Henry Cabot Lodge's* amendments to the Versailles treaty.

The choice for the 1920 Republican presidential nomination of a small group of leading Republican senators, Harding was nominated after the convention deadlocked. He overwhelmingly defeated James M. Cox,* the Democratic party* candidate, as voters registered their discontent with President Woodrow Wilson,* the Democrats, and post–World War I conditions. Harding avoided specific policy recommendations and finessed his position on the League of Nations* question. (Robert K. Murray, *The Harding Era; Warren G. Harding and His Administration* (1969); Francis Russell, *The Shadow of Blooming Grove: Warren G. Harding in His Times* (1968); *Dictionary of American Biography*, vol. 4.)

James E. Cebula

HARLAN, JOHN MARSHALL (June 1, 1833–October 14, 1911). Nurtured in the southern Whig tradition and reared in the slavocracy of border state Kentucky, Harlan was forced to choose between the Union and the Confederacy. His choice, largely determined by loyalty to the nation and its enduring values, quickened his equilibrium convictions and transformed his antebellum attitudes about race. As a rising Republican politician, he championed "the great principle of the equality of citizens before the law" and fervently sought to protect "the civil rights, common to all citizens" against governmental aggression. Once named to the Supreme Court by President Hayes, Harlan evolved a distinctive constitutional philosophy, reaching his own conclusions with little regard for intellectual fashion or his brethrens' predictable interpretations.

During nearly thirty-four years of service (1877–1911), Harlan became known as a staunch defender of democracy and human dignity, the strength of his convictions often leading him to dissent forcefully from the illiberal opinions of laissez-faire majorities, especially resisting their persistent judicial activism in defense of property. In cases adjudicating governmental powers, he took his lead from his namesake, John Marshall, who held a broad construction of congressional authority, typically voting to sustain pioneering progressive regulatory enactments. But Harlan's reputation rests primarily upon his powerful defense, notably while dissenting in *Plessy v. Ferguson*,* of the constitutional rights of freedmen and upon his conviction, also articulated in a series of dissents, that the Fourteenth Amendment incorporated the Bill of Rights against the states. (Mary C. A. Porter, "John Marshall Harlan and the Laissez Faire Court, 1877–1910" (Ph.D. diss., University of Chicago, 1971); Symposium, "John Marshall Harlan, 1833–1911," *Kentucky Law Journal* vol. 46, no. 321 (1958): 321–475; Alan Westin, "John Marshall Harlan and the Constitutional Rights of Negroes," *Yale Law Journal* vol. 66, no. 637 (1957):637–710.)

Stephen B. Wood

HARMON, JUDSON (February 3, 1846–February 22, 1927). The forty-fifth governor of Ohio, Harmon was born in Newtown, Ohio, and died in Cincinnati. He attended Denison University and the Cincinnati Law School. Several stints of public service alternated with periods in which he practiced law in Cincinnati. As Grover Cleveland's attorney general from 1895 to 1897, he directed antitrust suits against the Trans-Missouri Freight Association and the Addystone Pipe and Steel Company, and in 1905, as a special commissioner for the Justice Department, he investigated charges of rebating by the Atchison, Topeka and Santa Fe Railroad.

A conservative Democrat, Harmon became mildly reformist in the Progressive Era, preferring good-government reforms to social-welfare measures. He won the governorship in 1908 and was reelected by a large margin over Warren G. Harding* in 1910. He helped secure Ohio's ratification of the Sixteenth Amendment, corrupt practices legislation,* an optional workmen's compensation act,* and a measure for direct election of senators.* Initially a strong contender for the Democratic presidential nomination in 1912, he was unacceptable to the Bryanite wing of the party, which damned him as Wall Street's candidate. Narrowly winning Ohio's primary, he came in a weak third on the first ballot at the national convention and resolutely retired from politics. (James C. Burke, "The Public Career of Judson Harmon" (Ph.D. diss., Ohio State University, 1969); James C. Burke, "Judson Harmon: The Dilemma of a Constructive Conservative," *Cincinnati Historical Society Bulletin* 31 (Spring 1973); 28–47; Landon H. Warner, *Progressivism in Ohio, 1897–1917* (1964).)

Jacob H. Dorn

HARPER, IDA A. HUSTED (February 18, 1851–March 14, 1931). A notable publicist in the woman's rights movement, she was born in Fairfield, Indiana. After public school and a year at Indiana University, she was named principal of the high school in Peru, Indiana, in 1869. Interested in writing since high school, Harper began a lifelong career of writing on subjects of interest to women with articles and a column in local newspapers in the 1890s. During the next decade, her combination of journalistic skills and advocacy of woman suffrage brought her to the attention of Susan B. Anthony, who selected Harper to handle press relations for the California suffrage campaign of 1896. While living with Anthony in Rochester, New York, Harper wrote the *Life and Work of Susan B. Anthony* and collaborated with her on the fourth volume of the *History of Woman Suffrage*. In 1916 Carrie Chapman Catt* chose Harper to head the publicity department of the National American Woman Suffrage Association* during its successful campaign for passage of the Nineteenth Amendment. The capstone of her suffrage work and her lasting monument was her compilation and writing of the final two volumes of the *History of Woman Suffrage*, published in 1922. (Edward T. James, et al., eds., *Notable American Women*, vol. 2 (1971); Alma Lutz, *Susan B. Anthony* (1959).)

Paul E. Fuller

HARRIMAN, EDWARD HENRY (February 25, 1848–September 9, 1909). Harriman was born in Hempstead, New York, left school at fourteen to work on Wall Street, and had purchased a seat on the New York Stock Exchange by the age of twenty-two. In 1881, he began his long career in railroad management, most prominently with the Illinois Central and the Union Pacific. For the next three decades, Harriman was among the most important figures in one of the most important industries in the rapidly developing American economy. At the dawn of the twentieth century, a railroad ownership battle between Harriman and James J. Hill led to the compromise formation of the Great Northern Securities Company, which was dissolved in 1904 by the Supreme Court. Harriman lost the subsequent battle for control, but from his Union Pacific base began purchasing stock in other railroad companies, an effort investigated by the Interstate Commerce Commission during 1906 and 1907. Harriman's association with an industry often criticized by farmers and industrialists, his unrepentant securities manipulation, and his aloof manner combined to assure that he was regarded by the public as the stereotypical greedy, heartless businessman against whom progressive America was rebelling. (George Kennan, *E. H. Harriman: A Biography*, 2 vols. (1922); Hamilton J. Eckenrode and Pocahontas Wight Edmunds, *E. H. Harriman: The Little Giant of Wall Street* (1933); Lloyd J. Mercer, *E. H. Harriman: Master Railroader* (1985).)

Martin I. Elzy

HARRISON, CARTER HENRY II (April 23, 1860–December 26, 1953). Together, Harrison and his father served ten times as mayor of Chicago* and dominated Chicago politics for almost four decades. Young Carter's early political career saw him benefit from his family advantages. He received an outstanding education in both American and German schools, married a wealthy southern Catholic socialite, and pushed his advantage as the city's first home-born mayor. Harrison parlayed his background with a solid and practical no-nonsense approach to politics and human behavior and became the master of the politics of balance.

During the early Progressive Era, Harrison fought gas and transit "robber barons" as hard as any other reform-minded mayor in the country. As mayor from 1897 to 1905, he cooperated with the Municipal Voters League in cleaning up the city council, before declining to run for reelection in the face of popular demand for municipal ownership of the traction utility. At the same time Harrison, like his father, allied himself with political rogues who advocated "personal liberty"; he believed vice should be regulated and segregated rather than allowed to run wide open throughout the city. This balancing act often required Harrison to attend a charitable fund-raiser with his wife early in the evening then go off with the boys to have a drink with his most famous political allies, Michael "Hinky Dink" Kenna and John "Bathhouse John" Coughlin.* Ironically, his efforts to suppress public vice during his fifth term (1911–1915) led to his political demise and the election of William Hale Thompson. (Carter H. Harrison, *Stormy Years: The Autobiograhy of Carter H. Harrison* (1935); Edward Kantowicz, "Carter H. Harrison II: The Politics of Balance," in Paul M. Green and Melvin G. Holli, eds., *The Mayors: The Chicago Political Tradition* (1987).)

Paul Michael Green

HARVEY, GEORGE BRINTON MCCLENNAN (February 16, 1864–August 20, 1928). Born in Peacham, Vermont, Harvey became a journalist and served as managing editor of *New York World*, 1891–1893. He built a successful career in the electric railway industry in the United States and in Havana, Cuba. He purchased *Harper's Weekly** and the *North American Review** in 1899. His editorial success with the *North American Review* was not matched at *Harper's Weekly*, and he sold the *Weekly* in 1912, although he served as president of Harper and Brothers from 1900 to 1915. Harvey was a self-styled president maker. His early boostering campaign for Woodrow Wilson* for president failed because of Harvey's close connections with J. P. Morgan* and his apparent eagerness to defeat the progressive reform faction within the Democratic party.* Although he stirred up the anti-Wilson campaign, he failed in his designs in 1912. He villified Theodore Roosevelt* in 1912, but praised him in 1916. Harvey also supported the candidacy of Charles Evans Hughes* in the election of 1916.* From his Chicago hotel suite in 1920, Republican cronies nominated Warren G. Harding.* (Arthur S. Link, *Wilson: The Road to the White House* (1947); Willis F. Johnson, *George Harvey* (1929); James Playsted Wood, *Magazines in the United States: Their Social and Economic Influence* (1949).)

Salme H. Steinberg

HAYWOOD, WILLIAM DUDLEY (February 4, 1869–May 18, 1928). Born in Salt Lake City, Utah, Haywood first gained prominence as a labor leader when he became secretary-treasurer of the Western Federation of Miners. Unlike the American Federation of Labor* (AFL), Haywood believed in industrial rather than craft unions, in economic rather than political action, and in organization of the unskilled as well as of the skilled. In 1905, he chaired the convention which created the Industrial Workers of the World* (IWW) in opposition to AFL. In 1906 Haywood, along with two others, was charged with the assassination of former Idaho governor Frank R. Steunenberg, but defense attorney Clarence Darrow* won him an acquittal. Haywood played a leading role in major strikes at Lawrence,* Massachusetts, and at Paterson,* New Jersey; in 1914 he assumed the post of secretary-treasurer of IWW.

After the United States entered World War I,* the federal government successfully prosecuted Haywood and a number of other IWW leaders for conspiracy to sabotage the war effort and related charges. Haywood skipped bail pending an appeal and fled to the Soviet Union. Although at first treated as a revolutionary hero, he found himself increasingly ignored by the communist leadership. Haywood died in Moscow. (Peter Carlson, *Roughneck: The Life and Times of Big Bill Haywood* (1983); Joseph R. Conlin, *Big Bill Haywood and the Radical Union Movement* (1969); William D. Haywood, *Bill Haywood's Book: The Autobiography of Big Bill Haywood* (1929).)

Graham Adams, Jr.

HEALTH INSURANCE LEGISLATION. Significant agitation for compulsory health insurance legislation came late in the Progressive Era. It arose after a number of voluntary health insurance schemes had demonstrated their inadequacies and in the wake of the early victories won by advocates of workmen's compensation* laws who looked upon health insurance as the "next step" in social reform. Compulsory health insurance advocates proposed this insurance to provide economic protection against the incidence of sickness just as workmen's compensation insurance provided economic protection from industrial hazards.

The American Association for Labor Legislation* (AALL) led the movement, gaining support from many public health officials, some consumer and labor groups, and some doctors. Drafting a bill for adoption by state legislatures providing health insurance for many industrial workers with annual incomes of $1,200 or less, the AALL got support for its measure from legislative committees and committees of medical societies in several states. Entrance of the United States into World War I* sent the movement into a decline from which it never recovered. Doctors enjoying greater prosperity and disturbed by the advance of contract practice and abuses in workmen's compensation schemes lost interest in compulsory health insurance, which the American Medical Association* officially rejected in 1920. (Roy Lubove, *The Struggle for Social Security, 1900–1935* (1968); Ronald L. Numbers, *Almost Persuaded: American Physicians and Compulsory Health Insurance, 1912–1920* (1978); James G. Burrow, *Organized Medicine in the Progressive Era: The Move toward Monopoly* (1977).)

James G. Burrow

HEARST, WILLIAM RANDOLPH (April 29, 1863–August 14, 1951). Born into wealth in San Francisco, Hearst assumed control of the San Franciso *Examiner* in 1886, where his editorials supported the local labor party and assaulted the powerful Southern Pacific Railroad. In 1895 Hearst purchased the New York *Journal*, where he imitated the sensationalism of Joseph Pulitzer* with accounts of scandal and sex, and profuse illustrations. In catering to the new immigrant and laboring population he developed a Sunday supplement, including the "Yellow Kid" cartoon, sports, lovelorn advice, and personal interest stories. In 1897 Hearst hired socialist Arthur Brisbane* as editor. Together they played an especially prominent role in the advent of the Spanish-American War.* Following the war Hearst devoted much energy to the new social reform movement and heightened his attacks on trusts.

In 1900, Hearst founded the Chicago *American* as a party organ, the third of over twenty newspapers he came to control. Because of generous contributions to William Jennings Bryan's* campaign, he became the national president of an association of Democratic clubs. Hearst enjoyed a considerable political career which included two terms in Congress (1902–1906), a candidacy for the presidency which gained him 200 delegates at the 1904 Democratic convention, a New York mayoralty race in 1905 in which Tammany* fraud deprived him of certain victory, and a gubernatorial bid in New York in 1906 lost by fewer than 60,000 votes. After 1912, Hearst supported Woodrow Wilson* but disapproved of his foreign policy. His publishing empire acquired thirteen magazines. (Roy Everett Littlefield, *William Randolph Hearst: His Role in American Progressivism* (1980); John Tebbel, *The Life and Good Times of William Randolph Hearst* (1952); W. A. Swanberg, *Citizen Hearst: A Biography of William Randolph Hearst* (1961).)

Harold S. Wilson

HENDRICK, BURTON JESSE (December 8, 1871–March 23, 1949). Born in New Haven, Connecticut, Hendrick graduated from Yale (B.A. 1895, M.A. 1897). After editorial posts on the New Haven *Morning News* and the New York *Evening Post*, he was an associate editor of *McClure's Magazine** (1905–1913) and of *World's Work** (1913–1927). As *McClure's* urban corruption specialist during the muckrake era, he wrote on the slum landlords such as the Astors and Trinity Church, the Wall Street manipulation of life insurance company funds ("The Story of Life Insurance"), and the exploitation of municipal utilities ("Great American Fortunes and Their Making"). As a historian and biographer, he won Pulitzer Prizes in 1920, 1922, and 1928 for *The Victory at Sea*, with Admiral William Sims, *The Life and Letters of Walter Hines Page*, and *The Training of an American*. He also wrote on Andrew Carnegie,* the Lees of Virginia, and on Union and Confederate leadership during the Civil War. He died in New York City. (David Chalmers, *The Social and Political Ideas of the Muckrakers* (1964).)

David M. Chalmers

HENEY, FRANCIS JOSEPH (March 17, 1858–October 31, 1937). Born in Lima, New York, Heney grew up in San Francisco, California, where he joined the bar in 1884 following a limited education and experience as a miner and teacher. Moving to Arizona in 1886, he was appointed territorial attorney general for 1893–1894. He returned to San Francisco the next year, where he quickly established a successful legal practice. His appointment in 1903 as prosecutor of Oregon timber land grant frauds established his reputation as a reformer. He uncovered a conspiracy involving the U.S. Attorney for Oregon as well as the sitting U.S. Senator, John H. Mitchell. In 1906 Heney began the prosecution of San Francisco municipal graft. He soon alienated many businessmen by his abusive manner and exposure of corporate bribery. Despite obtaining over 300 indictments, he won only four convictions, three of them later overturned.

Heney was soundly defeated for San Francisco attorney general in 1909 and was overlooked as a candidate for reform governor the next year. He headed the 1912 California delegation to the Republican and Bull Moose conventions, but in 1914 lost his bid to become U.S. Senator as a Progressive. He rejoined the Democrats in 1916 as a Woodrow Wilson* elector but failed to win the party's gubernatorial nomination two years later. In 1931 he was appointed superior court judge for Los Angeles and continued to serve until his death in Santa Monica. (Walton Bean, *Boss Ruef's San Francisco: The Story of the Union Labor Party, Big Business, and the Graft Prosecution* (1952); John Messing, "Public Lands, Politics, and Progressives: The Oregon Land Fraud Trials, 1903–1910," *Pacific Historical Review* 35 (1966): 35–66; Helene Hooker Brewer, "A Man and Two Books," *Pacific Historical Review* 32 (1963): 22–34.)

Robert E. Hennings

HENRI, ROBERT (June 24, 1865–July 12, 1929). Robert Henri (pronounced "Hen-rye") was born Robert Henry Cozad in Cincinnati. Living first in Cozaddale, Ohio, and then Cozad, Nebraska, towns his father founded, Robert and his parents changed their names when he was seventeen, after his father shot and killed a man. In 1886 Henri enrolled at the Pennsylvania Academy in Philadelphia, and two years later at the Académie Julian in Paris. Returning to Philadelphia in 1891, he began teaching at the School of Design for Women, at the same time attracting a coterie of newspaper artists which included John Sloan.* In 1898 Henri married Linda Craige (died 1905), one of his pupils.

Settling in New York in 1900, Henri became renowned as a teacher, influencing an entire generation with his credo to work with great emotion and speed in depicting the everyday life of the city. Because of this emphasis, his followers became known as the Ash Can School and the New York Realists. By the early 1900s Henri's own style had undergone a transformation, from an early predilection for impressionist scenes to full-length portraits employing the dark palette of Édouard Manet, Diego Velasquez, and Frans Hals.

Although elected an academician by the National Academy of Design, Henri became the acknowledged leader of the Independent Movement which toppled the Academy from its role as tastemaker of the day. He organized the landmark exhibit of "The Eight" in 1908 and the 1910 Exhibition of Independent Artists, which led to the 1913 Armory Show.* (Robert Henri, *The Art Spirit* (1923);

William Innes Homer, *Robert Henri and His Circle* (1969); Bennard B. Perlman, *The Immortal Eight* (1962); Bennard B. Perlman, *Robert Henri: Painter* (exhibition catalogue, 1984).)

Bennard B. Perlman

HENRY STREET SETTLEMENT. In 1893 two nurses, Lillian Wald* and Mary Brewster, established Henry Street Settlement on New York's Lower East Side. In addition to the usual social settlement program of clubs and classes plus work for social reform, the two women began a unique visiting nurse service for the poor. Head Lillian Wald financed the settlement with philanthropists' money and by attracting well-to-do individuals who donated their services, either as actual residents in the settlement house or as volunteers.

Henry Street documented the plights of dispossessed tenants, the unemployed, child laborers, and working women. The settlement's demonstration project of seeking out tuberculosis patients and helping them with proper hygiene was taken over by the city's department of health in 1905. Henry Street also established one of the first playgrounds in 1895 and campaigned successfully for the creation of more public parks. To convince the local government of the value of public school nurses, Henry Street paid the salaries of nurses in a model program. The settlement also demonstrated the value of kindergartens, adult education,* and special classes for retarded children. Although Wald's pacifism and her support for the Progressive party* and organized labor generated controversy, the settlement continued to expand. (Lillian Wald, *The House on Henry Street* (1915); Allen F. Davis, *Spearheads for Reform: The Social Settlements and the Progressive Movement, 1890–1914* (1967); Beatrice Siegel, *Lillian Wald of Henry Street* (1983).)

Judith Ann Trolander

HEPBURN ACT. A 1906 law granting the Interstate Commerce Commission (ICC) power to regulate railroad rates, the Hepburn Act was the major reform legislation of President Theodore Roosevelt's* administration. Opposition had been building for many years against discriminatory railroad rates that favored large shippers and certain sections of the country, and the Elkins Act* of 1903 had failed to curb the most flagrant abuses. So in 1906 Congressman William P. Hepburn introduced the president's rate regulation bill, and it passed the House with only seven dissenting votes. Senator Nelson W. Aldrich,* however, led conservative opposition in the Senate, amending the bill to allow broad judicial review of all rate decisions. Roosevelt shrewdly compromised and left the scope of court review vague.

The Hepburn Act authorized the ICC to set aside a railroad rate, upon complaint of a shipper, and prescribe a reasonable maximum rate, subject to court review. The act further prescribed a uniform system of bookkeeping for the railroads and authorized the commission to inspect their books. Though its regulatory procedure was cumbersome, the Hepburn Act proved to be a landmark in the

government control of industry. Later strengthened by the Mann-Elkins Act*
and the Transportation Act of 1920 (see Esch-Cummins Act), it laid the ground-
work for thorough regulation of the transportation industry. (John Morton Blum,
The Republican Roosevelt (1954); Gabriel Kolko, *Railroads and Regulation*
(1965); Albro Martin, *Enterprise Denied: Origins of the Decline of American
Railroads, 1897–1917* (1971).)

                                                                    Edward R. Kantowicz

HERRICK, MYRON TIMOTHY (October 9, 1854–March 31, 1929). Born
in Huntington, Ohio, Herrick was educated at Ohio Wesleyan University. He
was admitted to the bar in Cleveland in 1877 but spent most of his business
career in banking and financial management, organizing several companies,
including Quaker Oats. By the 1880s he emerged as a force in Ohio politics. A
close friend of Mark Hanna,* Herrick played an influential role in the election
of William McKinley* in 1896 but declined offers of two government posts—
secretary of the treasury and ambassador to Italy. In 1903 he was elected governor
of Ohio on a conservative platform that supported the gold standard and opposed
the taxation theories of Tom L. Johnson* and the Ohio progressives.

Defeated for reelection, Herrick gained national fame as ambassador to France
following the outbreak of World War I.* Appointed by William H. Taft* in
February 1912, Herrick remained in Paris because the Woodrow Wilson* administration had difficulty naming a successor. As ambassador, Herrick handled the
interests of several belligerent nations in France and organized the American
Relief Clearing House for the distribution of aid, a field in which he continued
to work after his return to the United States in December 1914. He ran unsuccessfully as the Republican nominee for senator from Ohio in 1916. In 1921
Warren G. Harding* reappointed him ambassador to France, a post he held until
his death in Paris. (Bentley T. Mott, *Myron T. Herrick, Friend of France: An
Autobiographical Biography* (1930); *Dictionary of American Biography*, vol. 8).

                                                                    Robert C. Hilderbrand

HERRON, GEORGE D. (January 21, 1862–October 9, 1925). Born in Mon-
tezuma, Indiana, Herron entered the Congregational ministry in 1883 with no
formal education beyond the preparatory department of Ripon College. He had
a meteoric career in reform circles in the 1890s. From a chair in applied Christianity endowed for him at Iowa (Grinnell) College in 1893, he charismatically
led the "Kingdom Movement," voicing the social discontent of the Midwest
and appealing to followers of Edward Bellamy,* Populists, and Social Gospelers.* Increasingly strident criticism of existing institutions and marital difficulties, however, alienated him from the churches. He resigned his professorship
in 1899 and was deposed from the ministry in 1901, following his divorce and
remarriage to the daughter of his benefactress.

Herron's radicalism led him into the Socialist party,* and he played a brief
but significant role in the "unity convention" of 1901 and in founding the Rand

School of Social Sciences in New York. After 1901 he developed an extensive acquaintance with European statesmen, intellectuals, and writers from a villa near Florence, Italy. His advocacy of intervention in World War I* earned him the confidence of the Wilson* administration, for which he performed varied diplomatic services related to the peace settlement. (Robert T. Handy, "George D. Herron and the Social Gospel in American Protestantism, 1890–1901" (Ph.D. diss., University of Chicago Divinity School, 1949); Mitchell P. Briggs, *George D. Herron and the European Settlement* (1932); Robert M. Crunden, *Ministers of Reform: The Progressives' Achievement in American Civilization, 1889–1920* (1982).)

Jacob H. Dorn

HILLQUIT, MORRIS (August 1, 1869–October 7, 1933). Born in Riga, Latvia, Hillquit was educated at the gymnasium and the New York University Law School, receiving his law degree in 1893. Hillquit joined the Socialist Labor party* at the age of eighteen. In 1899 the party split, with Daniel De Leon* leading one faction representing a pure socialist movement, and Hillquit, who believed in a broad basis for socialism and in working with the established labor movement, heading the other. Both factions sought to use the name Socialist Labor party, and after a long legal battle the De Leon faction was awarded the title.

In 1901, Hillquit, together with Eugene V. Debs* and Victor L. Berger,* established the Socialist party of America.* Hillquit engaged in many historic confrontations in which he took the middle road between the conservative tradition of Samuel Gompers* and the doctrinaire socialism of De Leon. Early in his career, Hillquit was active in organizing garment workers in New York City and, from 1913 until his death, was general counsel of the International Ladies' Garment Workers Union.* While he had a number of corporations as clients, Hillquit's legal career was closely associated with his lifelong efforts in the cause of socialism.

Hillquit led the Socialist party in its opposition to American participation in World War 1,* on the grounds that it was the result of international economic rivalries and would hurt labor and hinder the advancement of international socialism. Under his leadership, the American Socialist party broke with the Russian Communists after they had attempted to involve the American movement in their doctrine of violent revolution. Hillquit was an unsuccessful candidate for Congress on five occasions and for mayor of New York City on three occasions. (Norma Fain Pratt, *A Political History of an American Jewish Socialist* (1979); Morris Hillquit, *Loose Leaves from a Busy Life* (1934).)

Leon Applebaum

HITCHCOCK, GILBERT (September 18, 1859–February 2, 1934). Hitchcock was born in Omaha, educated in Germany and at the University of Michigan. In 1888, he founded the *Omaha World Herald*, which became a voice for progressivism in Nebraska. For a time, the *Herald* employed William Jennings Bryan* as editor. Later, Hitchcock broke with Bryan, and the two headed rival factions of the state Democratic party. Running as a Democrat-Fusionist, he was elected to the House in 1902, where he was noted as a critic of the administration in the Ballinger-Pinchot dispute.*

Hitchcock went to the Senate in 1910, following a generally progressive course, although he opposed the Federal Reserve Act* and woman suffrage. He was a critic of administration foreign policy between 1914 and 1917, sponsoring a resolution to bar the shipment of munitions to belligerents, although he ultimately shifted and introduced the war resolution. He became chairman of the Foreign Relations Committee in 1918 and, later, acting minority leader. He had the responsibility for guiding the Versailles treaty through the Senate, which ultimately refused to ratify. He was defeated for reelection in 1922 and returned to his role as publisher of the *World Herald*. (*Dictionary of American Biography*, Supp. 1; Robert Foster Patterson, "Gilbert M. Hitchcock: A Story of Two Careers" (Ph.D. diss., University of Colorado, 1940).)

Thomas W. Ryley

HOLMES, OLIVER WENDELL, JR. (March 8, 1841–March 6, 1935). Born in Boston, son of the poet, Holmes was educated at Harvard, (A.B., 1861, LL.D., 1866). He served in the Union Army in the Civil War, rising to the rank of lieutenant colonel and being wounded three times. He was admitted to the bar in 1867 and practiced in Boston. He taught law at Harvard, becoming a professor there in 1882. Holmes was associate justice of the Massachusetts Supreme Court (1882–1899), chief justice (1899–1902), and associate justice of the U.S. Supreme Court (1902–1932).

Holmes took a liberal interpretation of the Constitution. In *Swift v. U.S.** (1905) his "current of commerce" led to a wider interpretation of the commerce clause of the Constitution. Dissenting in *Lochner v. New York** (1905), he attacked economic Darwinism, saying that "the 14th Amendment does not enact Herbert Spencer's *Social Statics*." During the Red Scare* and Palmer Raids of 1918–1919, he defended free speech; in *Abrams v. U.S.* (1919) he opposed the Sedition Act* of 1918. But he also argued, in *Schenck v. U.S.* (1919), that free speech is limited if it would "create a clear and present danger." In *Hammer v. Dagenhart** (1918), dealing with child labor, and in *Adkins v. Children's Hospital* (1923), concerning women's wages, he argued that the Constitution did not prevent reasonable legislation regulating hours and wages. (Felix Frankfurter, "Hours of Labor and Realism in Constitutional Law," *Harvard Law Review* 29 (February 1916): 353–73; Felix Frankfurter, *Mr. Justice Holmes and the Supreme Court* (1938, 1961); Oliver Wendell Holmes, *The Common Law* (1881).)

John R. Aiken

HOME RULE is the legal power for cities to amend their charters, raise taxes, and administer their governments independent of state control. Constitutionally, cities are creatures of the state government which incorporated them and, theoretically, could abolish them. In practice, states have traditionally mistrusted city governments and kept them on a short leash, with low tax and debt limits and numerous other restrictions. Frequently, important city officials, such as police commissioners, have been appointed by the governor of the state; and state legislatures occasionally pass "ripper" bills which remove city officials from office. Such interference with local government has been especially marked when a large city is controlled by Democrats and the state legislature by Republicans.

Reformers demanded amendments to state constitutions to grant home rule, or governmental autonomy, for cities. Missouri was the first state to comply, in 1875, and eventually more than half the states followed suit. Over two-thirds of cities with more than 200,000 inhabitants currently enjoy home rule. This reform has not proven as effective as hoped, however, for states usually retain some broad limits on city actions; and, in addition, acts of city governments are often challenged in the courts. (Walter T. Arndt, *The Emancipation of the American City* (1917); Charles R. Adrian, *Governing Urban America* (1961); Edward C. Banfield and James Q. Wilson, *City Politics* (1963).)

Edward R. Kantowicz

HOOVER, HERBERT CLARK (August 10, 1874–October 20, 1964). Born in West Branch, Iowa, Hoover graduated from Stanford University in 1895. His work as a mining engineer took him to Australia in 1897; two years later, he became chief engineer for the Chinese bureau of mines, supervising mineral explorations throughout the Celestial Kingdom. By 1907 he had earned an international reputation as an executive engineer and, residing in California, was engaged as a consultant for the administration of mining and railway operations in several areas of the world. In Europe in 1914, lobbying for the Pan-Pacific International Exposition, Hoover helped in the repatriation of Americans stranded by the World War.* This experience, and his reputation as an international administrator, led to his organization of the American Commission for Relief in Belgium, which supplied food and other necessities of life to those living in the war zone. Virtually governmental in its scope and responsibilities, the commission spent over a billion dollars during the war.

After U.S. entry into the war, Hoover was named food administrator in the Woodrow Wilson* administration. Besides controlling speculation and the distribution of foodstuffs, he promoted voluntary efforts to expand production and restrict consumption. After the Armistice, Hoover organized the American Relief Administration to sell and distribute surplus American foodstuffs in Europe. He planned and administered relief for the Soviet Union during the famine of 1921–1923. As an advocate of the League of Nations* he worked for the ratification of the Versailles treaty. Hoover served as secretary of commerce in the Harding* and Coolidge administrations, and was elected president in 1928. (Herbert C. Hoover, *Memoirs of Herbert Hoover*, 3 vols. (1951–1953); Joan Hoff Wilson,

Herbert Hoover, Forgotten Progressive (1975); George H. Nash, *The Life of Herbert Hoover* (1983).)

Robert C. Hilderbrand

HOURS OF SERVICE ACT. This was the second in a series of laws passed by Congress dealing with railroad safety. Federal powers for safety are grounded in the commerce clause of the Constitution, but the objective of these laws was to protect employees, passengers, and property rather than to achieve economic regulation of the railroads. The first safety law, the Safety Appliance Act of 1893, required railroads engaged in interstate commerce to equip their cars with automatic couplers and continuous brakes. The Hours of Service Act, passed in 1907, attempted to reduce accidents resulting from human error caused by overwork, rather than by equipment failure. Accident information gathered by the Interstate Commerce Commission indicated that overwork by employees was an important contributing cause of railroad accidents. The act made it unlawful for railroads to require or permit employees engaged in the movement of trains to remain on duty for a period longer than sixteen consecutive hours, and after continuous service for sixteen hours, to go on duty again until at least ten consecutive hours had elapsed. All state regulations governing hours of employees were superseded by this act. (I. L. Sharfman, *The Interstate Commerce Commission*, vol. 1 (1931).)

Curtis Richards

HOUSE, EDWARD MANDELL (July 26, 1858–March 28, 1938). House was a Texas landowner and banker. He entered politics in the 1890s as a behind-the-scenes backer of Democrats, notably governors James S. Hogg and Charles A. Culberson; his organizing talents helped defeat People's party candidates. After the turn of the century he was influenced by progressivism and took an interest in international affairs. In 1911 he published (anonymously) a novel, *Philip Dru, Administrator*, whose hero is part of a movement to restructure the U.S. government. House worked for Woodrow Wilson's* presidential candidacy and became Wilson's close friend and adviser. With the outbreak of World War 1,* House conducted negotiations aimed at achieving peace on the basis of *status quo ante bellum*; he was in general accord with the pro-Allied stance of the administration. Wilson consulted with House over the Fourteen Points, but their friendship cooled during the tense Paris conference. After the war House published essays and memoirs, and kept up his international contacts. (Charles Seymour, *The Intimate Papers of Colonel House*, 4 vols. (1926–1928); *The Dictionary of American Biography*, vol. 9; Arthur S. Link, *Woodrow Wilson and the Progressive Era, 1910–1917* (1951); C. Vann Woodward, *Origins of the New South, 1877–1913* (1951).)

Paul M. Pruitt, Jr.

HOUSING REFORM. The movement for housing reform centered in New York City,* where high density created a housing problem unique to that city. Hundreds of thousands of New Yorkers lived in the notorious dumbbell tenements built between 1879 and 1900. Shaped like a dumbbell, lined up side by side on narrow 25' × 100' lots with only narrow air shafts between them, these five-story walkup tenements created a dark, airless, unhealthful environment for the immigrant poor. Early reformers appealed to the philanthropic instincts of the wealthy, entreating them to build model tenements and manage them in an enlightened fashion. Alfred T. White in Brooklyn and the City and Suburban Homes Association in New York constructed some decent housing on the model of "philanthropy plus five percent," but there were never enough enlightened landlords or model tenements.

After Jacob Riis* exposed the tenement house problem to public view in his 1890 book, *How the Other Half Lives*, state and private housing commissions recommended restrictive laws to regulate the building of tenements. Lawrence Veiller,* who headed the Charity Organization Society's* Tenement House Committee, led the fight for stricter laws. He organized a tenement exhibition in February 1900, which graphically depicted conditions of squalor and overcrowding. Largely due to Veiller's efforts, New York passed a stringent new Tenement House Law in 1901 which banned all further construction of dumbbell tenements, mandated adequate space between buildings, required a separate water closet in each apartment, and laid down strict fireproofing standards.

Though other cities did not have dumbbell tenements, they all had dilapidated and unhealthful housing for the poor. Many cities, therefore, imitated New York's restrictive housing code and regulated the construction of new housing after 1900. Veiller founded the National Housing Association in 1910 to disseminate the principles of restrictive legislation and a model tenement house law nationwide. Though Veiller's regulatory laws prevented bad housing from being built, they did nothing to provide good housing. No public housing was built in the Progressive Era, except for some limited experiments during World War I.* (Robert W. DeForest and Lawrence T. Veiller, eds., *The Tenement House Problem* (1903); Roy Lubove, *The Progressives and the Slums: Tenement House Reform in New York City, 1890–1917* (1962); Robert H. Bremner, *From the Depths* (1972).)

Edward R. Kantowicz

HOUSTON, DAVID FRANKLIN (February 17, 1866–September 2, 1940). Born in North Carolina and educated at the College of South Carolina, Houston worked as a school superintendent before leaving for Harvard to study economics and political science. After three years he accepted a position at the University of Texas, serving there as professor and dean, as president of Texas A & M University (1902–1905), and as president of the University of Texas (1905–1908). From 1908 to 1911 he served as chancellor of Washington University, Saint Louis, Missouri. Houston concluded his academic career in 1912, when Texas businessman-politician Edward M. House* arranged for his appointment as secretary of agriculture. A conservative economist, Houston worked to delay passage of a system of federally backed rural loans. Yet he expanded his de-

partment's activities and expertly administered various programs of federal assistance to the states. Houston was secretary of the treasury in 1920–1921; his
anti-inflation policies were blamed for sharply declining crop prices. From the
close of the Wilson* administration until his death, Houston engaged in business.
(David F. Houston, *Eight Years with Wilson's Cabinet*, 2 vols. (1926); Arthur
S. Link, *Woodrow Wilson and the Progressive Era, 1910–1917* (1954); *The
Dictionary of American Biography*, vol. 11.)

Paul M. Pruitt, Jr.

HOWE, FREDERIC C. (November 21, 1867–August 3, 1940). Born in Mead-
ville, Pennsylvania, Howe was educated at Allegheny College, Johns Hopkins
University, the University of Halle (Germany), the University of Maryland Law
School, and New York Law School. When Howe came to Cleveland in 1892,
he lived in a settlement house, practiced law, and was a founding member of
the Municipal Association. Although elected to the city council in 1901 as a
Republican, he was attracted to Mayor Tom Johnson's* personality and philosophy and soon became a part of his inner circle. Defeated for reelection in 1903,
he switched parties and ran successfully for the Ohio Senate. Howe exposed
corruption in the state treasurer's office and earned a reputation as an effective
crusader for progressive reforms, including constitutional changes which were
eventually achieved under Governor James M. Cox* (1912–1916). In 1909 he
was elected to the Board of Assessors and applied precepts of single tax theory*
to make land evaluations more equitable for low-income homeowners. Howe
moved to New York in 1910 to write on cities and publicize the work of Tom
Johnson. He served as commissioner of immigration from 1914 to 1919, but
resigned over the repressive policies of the Wilson* administration. He served
as consumer counsel for the Agricultural Adjustment Administration from 1933
to 1935, and was the author of ten books. (Frederic C. Howe, *Confessions of
a Reformer* (1974); Tom L. Johnson, *My Story* (1911); Hoyt L. Warner, *Progressivism in Ohio 1897–1917* (1964).)

Thomas F. Campbell

HOWELLS, WILLIAM DEAN (March 1, 1837–May 11, 1920). Born in a
small Ohio town, Howells received most of his education from working with
his father in his print shop. Actual and imagined illnesses, along with his intellectual interests, set Howells apart from his contemporaries and turned him
against small-town life. His campaign biography of Abraham Lincoln allowed
him to escape a distasteful environment and led to his appointment as consul in
Venice, where he remained during the Civil War. When he returned to America
he was given a position with E. L. Godkin and the *Nation* and, in 1866, he
joined the *Atlantic*,* becoming editor of that journal in 1871. During these years
he accepted many socioeconomic articles for publication in The *Atlantic*, but he
remained essentially conservative.

In the 1880s, however, his attitudes began to change. His move from Boston to New York, the "civic murder" of the Chicago anarchists following the Haymarket affair, the death of his daughter, and the invalidism of his wife all occurred within a short period. He developed a strong social consciousness and lost the buoyant spirit of his earlier years. In 1886, he took over "The Editor's Study" for *Harper's** and used that column to expound his theories on realism in literature and to encourage many younger writers. After a short stint as editor of *Cosmopolitan** he returned to *Harper's* to conduct the "Easy Chair" column in the years after 1900. During the 1880s and 1890s, Howells produced several highly successful novels condemning the acquisitive society of which he found himself a part, along with two utopian novels that depicted what society might be like under a better system. (Edwin H. Cady, *William Dean Howells, Dean of American Letters*, 2 vols. (1956–1958); Robert W. Schneider, *Five Novelists of the Progressive Era* (1965); John W. Crowley, *The Black Heart's Truth: The Early Years of W. D. Howells* (1985).)

Robert W. Schneider

HUGHES, CHARLES EVANS (April 11, 1862—August 27, 1948). Born in Glens Falls, New York, Hughes was educated at Madison (now Colgate) and Brown universities and the Columbia University Law School. From 1884 to 1906, he practiced law in New York City,* with a brief interruption in the early 1890s when he served as professor of law at Cornell University. As chief counsel, in 1905–1906, for two joint committees of the New York legislature—the first to investigate the gas utilities in New York City, the second to investigate the insurance industry—Hughes won immediate fame. With President Theodore Roosevelt's* help, he received the Republican nomination for governor in 1906. Elected that year and reelected in 1908, he gave New York State efficient and progressive government. He continuously fought the conservative leadership of his own party as well as the Tammany* Democrats.

He advocated an ambitious program that emphasized political-governmental reforms, corporation regulation, and social-labor reforms. Among the measures passed in these years were the Moreland Act (1907), which strenghtened the governor's control of the executive branch of government; the Public Service Commissions Act (1907), which established two independent regulatory bodies, one for New York City and the other for the upstate; and the Workmen's Compensation Act* (1910), which adopted the principle of automatic compensation payments for workers injured in certain hazardous industries. Hughes also sponsored legislation regulating the insurance and banking industries and waged a two-year battle for a direct primary. He was unsuccessful in the direct nominations fight, but in 1913, the Democrats enacted a law much like the one he had championed.

Disgusted with the myopic attitude of New York's entrenched leaders and still interested in the law, Hughes, in 1910, accepted President William Howard Taft's* offer to become an associate justice of the U.S. Supreme Court. He remained on the court until 1916, when he resigned after he received the Republican presidential nomination. He lost in a close election to President Woodrow Wilson.* Hughes continued to distinguish himself in the public service as U.S. secretary of state (1921–1925) and chief justice of the United States (1930–1941). (Merlo J. Pusey, *Charles Evans Hughes* (1951); Dexter Perkins, *Charles Evans Hughes and American Democratic Statesmanship* (1956); Robert F. Wesser, *Charles Evans Hughes: Politics and Reform in New York, 1905–1910* (1967).)

                                                                        Robert F. Wesser

HULL, CORDELL (October 2, 1871–July 23, 1955). Born in a log cabin in the Cumberland Mountains of Tennessee, the son of a lumberman who had lost an eye in the Civil War and then murdered the man he thought responsible for the handicap, Hull grew up a bookish boy who, despite, or perhaps because of, a slight speech impediment, sought recognition in public debate and politics, becoming a member of the state legislature at twenty-one. After little more than a decade as an attorney and then state judge, the serious bachelor won a seat in Congress in 1906. Hull came to Congress with an obsession to restore the income tax* which he believed the eastern establishment had wrongfully defeated. His teenage idol, Congressman Benton McMillin of Tennessee, had pushed through an income tax in 1894, and then the Supreme Court, in the five-to-four Pollock decision,* struck down the tax as part of a conservative backlash.

Hull identified himself as a William Jennings Bryan* Democrat committed to restoring the income tax. He agitated the question in Congress for six years, won a seat on the Ways and Means Committee in 1910, and finally achieved victory after ratification of the Sixteenth Amendment and passage of the Underwood-Simmons Tariff* in 1913, for which he drafted the income tax section. As the progressive tax specialist in Congress, Hull also pushed the inheritance tax to take revenue from the fortunes of the rich, passing an estate tax in 1916. His progressive taxing policies were intellectually linked with free trade; during the twenties he worked in Congress against increased protectionism within the Democratic party.* Hull joined Franklin Roosevelt's* administration as secretary of state, serving from 1933 to 1944, for which his free trade and United Nations efforts received the Nobel Peace Prize in 1945. (Cordell Hull, *The Memoirs of Cordell Hull* (1948); John D. Buenker, *The Income Tax and the Progressive Era* (1985).)

                                                                        David M. Tucker

HULL HOUSE. The name symbolizes the social settlement movement. A mansion built by Charles J. Hull in 1856 on Halsted Street in Chicago,* it was acquired by Jane Addams* and her associate, Ellen Gates Starr,* and opened on September 18, 1889, as an experiment in neighborliness on the model of Toynbee Hall in London. At its height, the settlement, administered by Addams, numbered thirteen buildings providing playgrounds, preschool, kindergarten, theatre, music lessons, a woman's club, workingmen's debating society, book bindery, library, shops for handicrafts, coffee house, labor museum, evening school for the twenty-six ethnic groups which crowded Chicago's Nineteenth Ward, and the Jane Club, an apartment building for single working women. It was the civic center whose activities helped bring immigrants into the mainstream of American life. As home to the seventy-five people who worked there, it provided an alternative family for professional women and an "ethical bohemia" for university students who interned in the city.

Through Hull House, social reform in Chicago and beyond was grounded in a place, but it was even more potent as an idea. It was the center from which Addams, Starr, Florence Kelley,* Julia Lathrop,* Edith and Grace Abbott,* Robert Hunter,* Alice Hamilton,* Alzina Parsons Stevens, and others worked out the social reform agenda of the Progressive Era. Activities in education; labor; legislation in ward, city, and nation for the protection of women and children, the retarded and mentally ill; and the eradication of poverty were among their concerns. Hull House embodied democracy in action, mixing the educated with the immigrant poor in friendship and concerted action to solve the problems of city living. (Jane Addams, *Twenty Years at Hull House* (1910); Allen F. Davis, *Spearheads for Reform: The Social Settlements and the Progressive Movement, 1890–1914* (1967); Robert A. Woods and Albert J. Kennedy, *The Settlement Horizon: A National Estimate* (1922).)

Mary Ellen H. Schmider

HUNTER, ROBERT (April 10, 1874–May 15, 1942). Social worker and "millionaire Socialist" born in Terre Haute, Indiana, he was educated in public schools and graduated from Indiana University in 1896. Pursuing a career in social work, he served as organizing secretary of Chicago's Board of Charities from 1896 to 1902, living at Hull House* much of this time. He moved to New York* in 1902 and became head resident of University Settlement* for a year. Inheriting wealth from his father, he married an even greater fortune in Caroline Phelps Stokes; and after 1903, he held no regular job. In 1904 he published *Poverty*, the first statistical study of the poor. He joined the Socialist party* in 1905, serving frequently as a candidate, and sitting for a time on the national executive committee. He broke with the party in 1914, moved with his family to California in 1918, and became progressively more conservative. Though Hunter was a minor figure in reform and socialist circles, his book *Poverty* remains a classic document on social conditions at the turn of the century. (*Dictionary of American Biography*, supplement 3; Peter d'A. Jones, Introduction to the 1965 paperback edition of *Poverty*; David A. Shannon, *The Socialist Party of America* (1955).)

Edward R. Kantowicz

I

ICKES, HAROLD LECLAIR (March 15, 1874–February 3, 1952). Born in Blair County, Pennsylvania, Ickes had a long career as an urban reformer in Chicago. He was educated at the University of Chicago,* where he earned his A.B. in 1897 and his J.D. in 1907, Ickes's energies were always in politics and usually with losing causes and candidates. He learned his political skills from association with Chicago's social settlement community as well as from some of the city's most powerful machine bosses. Ickes was a tireless supporter of municipal ownership of Chicago's transportation system and mobilized effective citizen campaigns against Charles T. Yerkes* and, later, Samuel Insull.* As a young journalist for several independent city newspapers, Ickes developed a keen analytic eye and an acid pen. He utilized these in behalf of mayoral candidates John M. Harlan* and Charles Merriam* and against incumbents Carter Harrison II* and William "Big Bill" Thompson. In 1912 he eagerly joined the Progressive party* and, as a convention delegate and later as a member of the national executive committee, became part of Theodore Roosevelt's* inner circle. A friend of Gifford* and Amos Pinchot,* Ickes opposed the rule of George Perkins* and, after 1916, played a leading role in keeping the progressive remnant together. He organized progressives for James Cox* in 1920 and managed Hiram Johnson's* presidential bid in 1924. (Harold L. Ickes, *Autobiography of a Curmudgeon* (1943); Linda J. Lear, *Harold L. Ickes, The Aggressive Progressive* (1981); Robert E. Hennings, "Harold Ickes and Hiram Johnson in the Presidential Primary of 1924," in Donald F. Tingley, ed., *Essays in Illinois History* (1968); Graham White and John Maze, *Harold Ickes of the New Deal* (1985).)

Linda J. Lear

ILLINOIS. Having been admitted to statehood in 1818, Illinois achieved solid growth throughout the nineteenth century, reaching a population of 4,821,550 in 1899. By that year, the census showed that more than half of the population lived in urban centers. Chicago,* with a population of 1,698,575, was by far the largest city, but Peoria, Quincy, Springfield, Rockford, East Saint Louis, Joliet, Bloomington, Elgin, Decatur, and Danville were substantial cities, most of which were in the northern half of the state. Urbanization had come with industrialization.* The manufactured products of Illinois reached an astounding value of $1.25 million in 1899. Illinois ranked high in the nation in meat packing, foundry and machine shop products, steel, distilling, and agricultural implements. Culturally, Illinois reached the zenith of its influence. A great symphony, the Art Institute, and the opera complemented Chicago's reputation as a literary center featuring *Poetry Magazine* the *Little Review*, and the *Dial*. The University of Chicago,* Northwestern, and the University of Illinois all flourished, and lesser colleges were in every part of the state.

Despite all of these gains, industrialization and urbanization brought many evils: slums, poor working conditions, low pay, long hours, political corruption, and rapid concentration of business. In this situation, the wealth of the state tended to be concentrated in the hands of a few, and the situation of the laboring class grew more desperate. Three major race riots in twenty years testified to the poor condition of black citizens. Settlement houses, such as Jane Addams's* Hull House* and Graham Taylor's* Chicago Commons* aimed at aiding the neighborhoods in the ghettos. There were social surveys of various cities, and the Senate Vice Committee investigated prostitution. Workingmen created labor unions. Reform groups such as the Municipal Voters League in Chicago focused on municipal corruption. Muckrakers such as Lincoln Steffens* and William T. Stead* studied problems in Chicago. More radical approaches were born in Chicago: Industrial Workers of the World,* the Communist party, and the Communist Labor party. Governors Charles Deneen, Edward F. Dunne,* and Frank Lowden* were a cut above the average of Illinois governors in honesty and reform. Nonetheless, Illinois attracted a well-deserved reputation as a state loaded with political corruption. William Lorimer,* Republican boss from Chicago, was elected to the U.S. Senate, but was denied his seat because he had bribed a substantial portion of the Illinois General Assembly. (Donald F. Tingley, *The Structuring of a State: The History of Illinois, 1899–1928* (1980).)

Donald F. Tingley

IMMIGRANTS' PROTECTIVE LEAGUE. In 1908 a Chicago Women's Trade Union League committee to assist immigrant women extended its services to all immigrants and became the independent Immigrants' Protective League (IPL). Funded by private philanthropy, the IPL was supported by reformers from Hull House,* the Chicago Commons,* the Chicago School of Civics and Philanthropy, and the Chicago Women's Trade Union League, including Jane Addams,* Sophonisba P. Breckinridge,* Julia Lathrop,* Mary E. McDowell,* Agnes Nestor, and Margaret Dreier Robins.*

The IPL helped immigrants locate friends, family, and jobs; protected them from unscrupulous cabdrivers, employment bureaus, and banks; provided emergency relief; and served as their advocate in the courts and the government bureaucracies. It was less successful, however, in persuading state and federal governments to assume these responsibilities. After the immigration restriction* of 1924, the IPL increasingly provided legal and technical rather than social services. (Robert L. Buroker, "From Voluntary Association to Welfare State: The Illinois Immigrants' Protective League 1908–1926," *Journal of American History* 58 (December 1971): 643–60; Henry B. Leonard, "Immigrants' Service League," in Peter Romanofsky, ed., *Encyclopedia of American Institutions*, vol. 2: Social Service Organizations (1978); Lela B. Costin, *Two Sisters for Social Justice: A Biography of Grace and Edith Abbott* (1983).)

Maxine S. Seller

IMMIGRATION COMMISSION. A federal government investigating commission, appointed in 1907, the Immigration Commission reported its findings in a massive forty-two-volume report in 1910. When congressional advocates of immigration restriction* attempted to pass a literacy test for immigrants in 1906, Speaker of the House Joseph Cannon* and President Theodore Roosevelt* stalled action on the controversial matter by appointing a study commission. The nine-member commission was composed of three senators, three representatives, and three experts chosen by the president, with Senator William P. Dillingham, Republican senator from Vermont, as chairman.

The commission experts gathered and published vast quantities of data on the literacy, education, and employment of immigrants, but the report was marred by an assumption that the "new immigrants"* from Southern and Eastern Europe were fundamentally inferior to the old Anglo-Saxon and Teutonic immigrants. The commission found evidence that new immigrants were less educated and had accomplished less in America, but it failed to take into account the crucial factor of duration of settlement. As a result, the Immigration Commission seemed to provide "scientific" backing for advocates of immigration restriction, and it served as the intellectual rationale of the national origins quota acts passed in the 1920s. (61st Congress, 2d Session, *Reports of the Immigration Commission* (1911); Oscar Handlin, *Race and Nationality in American Life* (1957); Maldwyn Jones, *American Immigration* (1960).)

Edward R. Kantowicz

IMMIGRATION RESTRICTION. A dramatic change in the nation's previously open immigration policy began in 1882 with the exclusion of most Chinese and culminated in 1924 with the sharp limitation of South and East Europeans. Despite restrictionists' claims to the contrary, the "new" Asian and South and East European immigrants entering Progressive Era America in unprecedented numbers were similar to earlier immigrants in motivation, skills, and adjustment. The closing of the frontier, periodic depressions, and the growing concentrations of wealth and class antagonisms of industrialization, however, undermined the national confidence.

While restriction can be viewed as "progressive" social engineering, its advocates also included conservatives and cut across class lines. Labor saw immigrants as tools of the corporations, breaking strikes and replacing American workers at "coolie" wages. Middle-class reformers sought immigration restriction as a solution to crime, disease, political corruption, and radicalism, while nostalgic patricians hoped it would restore the tranquility of an earlier era. Anti-Catholicism and anti-Semitism contributed to restrictionism, but were less important than pseudoscientific claims that "new" immigrants were undermining the nation's vigor and polluting its genetic pool.

In 1882, Congress barred the Chinese. In 1885, all contract laborers were barred and, subsequently, sick persons, polygamists, anarchists, and those likely to become a public charge. Japanese immigration was curtailed by a "gentlemen's agreement" in 1907–1908. Legislation limiting European immigration was blocked for decades, however, by a coalition including businessmen who wanted cheap labor, politicians who wanted ethnic votes, ethnic lobbies, cultural pluralists, and humanitarians. A literacy test, vetoed in 1896, 1913, and 1915, became law in 1917 with little effect on the flow of "undesirables." Strengthened by the chauvinistic legacy of World War I* and the Red Scare,* restrictionists were victorious in the early 1920s. The Johnson Act of 1921 introduced nationality quotas and the Reed-Johnson Act of 1924 limited the annual number of entrants of each admissible nationality to 2 percent of its representation in the 1890 census, guaranteeing small quotas for South and East Europeans. (William S. Bernard, "Immigration: History of U.S. Policy," in Stephan Thernstrom, ed., *Harvard Encyclopedia of American Ethnic Groups* (1980); John Higham, *Strangers in the Land* (1963); Roy Garis, *Immigration Restriction* (1928); Maxine S. Seller, *To Seek America* (1977); Maxine S. Seller "Historical Perspectives on American Immigration Policy" in Richard R. Hofstetter, ed., *U.S. Immigration Policy* (1984).)

Maxine S. Seller

IMPERIALISM. In the late nineteenth century, the industrialized nations of Europe raced to acquire overseas colonies and markets in Africa, Asia, and Latin America. The United States joined this imperialist race rather tardily, at the time of the Spanish-American War* of 1898, when it annexed Hawaii and acquired Puerto Rico, the Philippines, and Guam as the spoils of war. Thereafter, the United States acquired no new colonies, but it did remain active in the worldwide struggle for power and wealth. The fundamental causes of imperialist expansion were economic. Maturing industrial economies required vast quantities of raw materials, so nations struggled to acquire resource-rich colonies, strategic ports, and naval coaling stations to keep raw materials flowing into their factories. At the same time, modern industries produced more consumer goods than most nation's domestic economies could absorb; therefore, the big powers constantly looked for new markets overseas. The dream of putting cotton shirts on the backs of 800 million Chinese drew many textile manufacturers to imperialist adventures.

Big-power politics and strategy supported the economic arguments for imperialism. As the nations of Europe acquired colonies and influence worldwide, U.S. leaders realized they might be left isolated if they did not participate. Furthermore, Captain Alfred Thayer Mahan,* an influential writer and lecturer, stressed the importance of sea power in deciding the fate of nations. Mahan's writings led to a rebuilding of the U.S. Navy in the 1880s and 1890s, culminating in the Great White Fleet which President Theodore Roosevelt* sent around the world in 1907. Intellectuals provided a host of rationalizations for imperialism.

Social Gospel* minister Josiah Strong* charged Americans with a duty to spread the Protestant religion and American democracy. The American people were peculiarly susceptible to this "spreading of democracy" appeal, for they had long believed they had a mission and a destiny as keepers of the democratic flame. A rising tide of Anglo-Saxon racism further strengthened the feeling that Americans were obliged to spread their "superior" way of life to less fortunate peoples. Buoyed by such sentiments, the United States annexed the Philippines, fought a savage war to pacify Filipino rebels, and entered the twentieth century with a small empire but large ambitions to play an important role on the world stage. (Ernest R. May, *Imperial Democracy* (1961); Ernest R. May, *American Imperialism: A Speculative Essay* (1968); Walter LaFeber, *The New Empire* (1963); Richard W. Leopold, "The Emergence of America as a World Power: Some Second Thoughts," in John Braeman, ed., *Change and Continuity in Twentieth Century America* (1964); Howard K. Beale, *Theodore Roosevelt and the Rise of America to World Power* (1956); David H. Burton, *Theodore Roosevelt: Confident Imperialist* (1964).)

Edward R. Kantowicz

INCOME TAX, FEDERAL. This system of taxation was inaugurated in 1913, based upon the power granted to Congress by the Sixteenth Amendment. The new tax was designed to generate sufficient revenue to permit downward tariff revision and to meet the fiscal needs of an expanding federal government, to shift the bulk of the tax burden onto the principal holders of the nation's financial and industrial assets, and to redress the sectional economic balance on behalf of the South and West against the industrial Northeast. Western and southern spokesmen consistently advocated enactment of the tax, joined increasingly by economists and tax experts, social reformers, organized labor, socialists, and several mass-circulation newspapers.

The 1908 Democratic platform called for a constitutional amendment to circumvent the 1895 *Pollock* decision,* and Republican presidential candidate William Howard Taft* opined publicly that a tax could be drafted in such a manner as to satisfy the Court. When the regular Republican leadership asked for presidential aid to prevent the inclusion of the tax into the Payne-Aldrich Tariff bill* by a Democrat-Insurgent* coalition, Taft proposed to substitute a corporation excise tax* and a resolution calling for an income tax amendment to the Constitution. The struggle for ratification took place between September 1909 and February 1913, with every state except Virginia, Florida, Utah, Rhode Island, Connecticut, and Pennsylvania eventually giving its assent. The critical margin of victory came through a political upheaval in the 1910 and 1912 elections that elevated Democrats into unexpected control of the legislatures of New York, New Jersey, Massachusetts, Illinois, Ohio, Maine, and Indiana. Ratification was staunchly opposed by regular Republicans, conservative southern Democrats, and prominent industrialists and financiers.

Urged by Woodrow Wilson,* the majority Democrats moved swiftly to add an income tax section to the Underwood-Simmons Tariff,* which the president signed on October 3, 1913. The income tax section provided for a levy of 1 percent on incomes of over $3,000 for single persons and of over $4,000 for married couples, thereby exempting an estimated 96 percent of income receivers. There was also an "additional" tax graduated from 1 percent on income over $20,000 to 6 percent on that over $500,000 and a 1 percent tax on corporate income. (John D. Buenker, *The Income Tax and the Progressive Era* (1985); Sidney Ratner, *A Political and Social History of Federal Taxation* (1942); Randolph E. Paul, *Taxation in the United States* (1954).)

John D. Buenker

INCOME TAX, STATE. Between 1911 and 1919 a number of states completely abandoned the traditional principle of benefit taxation and moved, by enactment of state income taxes, to the principle of ability to pay. Major forces behind these changes—begun in Wisconsin,* New York,* Massachusetts,* and Missouri*—were organized business interests, academicians, and administrators; but most potent in each of these states was the National Tax Association.* Wisconsin claimed the initial demonstration of the efficiency of such income taxation, but New York State, though its income tax was passed in 1919, actually predated Wisconsin's efforts through a gradual statutory process begun in 1903.

Unprecedented authority was granted in each state to tax commissioners: appointment of assessors responsible to the commissions, and power to demand information from individuals and corporations for enforcement. Such measures pleased urban populations, without frightening either corporations or individuals with exorbitant rates. In light of rising state indebtedness and rising popular expectations, especially for tax justice and improved public services, and despite divisions within reformer's ranks, a severe blow was dealt to the inflexibilities, inequities, and inadequate revenues previously derived chiefly from general property taxes. (E. R. A. Seligman, *The Income Tax: A Study of the History, Theory and Practice of Income Taxation at Home and Abroad* (1911); Clifton K. Yearley,

The Money Machines (1970); Richard A. Musgrave, The Theory of Public Finance (1959).)

Clifton K. Yearley and Kerrie L. MacPherson

INDEPENDENT, THE. Henry C. Bowen founded the Independent in 1848 as an organ of reform. The journal never abandoned its original espousal of racial justice and evangelical theology. In the post–Civil War period Henry Ward Beecher served as a general editor and Washington Gladden* edited the religious columns. At the height of the Progressive period, the weekly was under the guidance of William Hayes Ward, who joined the staff in 1868.

Not in the main a muckraking magazine, the Independent was filled with poetry and fiction, as well as articles on religion, foreign travel, and industrial problems. But the weekly excelled in exposing the "Southern problem." The issue of March 17, 1904, contained articles on "The Race Problem," the "Experiences of the Race Problem," and "The Southern Race Problem." Disfranchisement,* segregation, peonage, and lynching* produced a constant flow of material, much of it written by blacks. A significant contribution in 1904 was "The New Slavery in the South," an exposé of the convict lease system by a South Carolina Negro. Other kindred subjects were treated, such as profiles of black reform leaders Frederick Douglass and Fannie B. Williams, Jewish assimilation, and the "Yellow Peril." The magazine suffered financial difficulties and merged with the Outlook* in 1928. (Theodore Peterson, Magazines in the Twentieth Century (1956).)

Harold S. Wilson

INDIANA. Indiana experienced but did not lead in the major social, economic, and political changes of this era. Indiana ranked ninth in population and manufacturing, but its economy remained diversified, and it ranked only eighteenth in urbanization. The state was politically important primarily because its strongly partisan and competitive politics produced able politicians: vice president Thomas Marshall* and Charles Fairbanks,* several nationally prominent U.S. senators, and two national party chairmen. Progressive state laws dealt with various health and welfare issues as well as child labor,* factory and railroad safety, employers' liability, and workmen's compensation.* Business reforms included railroad and public utilities commissions,* and regulation of banks* and insurance companies.* Though numerous, these laws often lagged behind those of other states, and their coverage and powers were too often incomplete. Political reforms included such anticorruption laws as voter registration, residency, and penalties for vote buying, but not democratizing reforms like the referendum* or initiative* Finally, controversial moral issues remained at the center of politics and were reflected in major debates and laws concerning pornography, prostitution, divorce, the sale of cigarettes, and, most importantly, the control of liquor. (Clifton J. Phillips, Indiana in Transition: The Emergence of an Industrial Common-

wealth, 1880–1920 (1968); Phillip VanderMeer, *The Hoosier Politician: Officeholding and Political Culture in Indiana, 1896–1920* (1985); Leslie Ward Carson, "The Life of J. Frank Hanly: Log Cabin to Governor" (M.A. thesis, University of Illinois, 1928).)

Phillip R. VanderMeer

INDUSTRIAL CONFERENCES. In September 1919, Woodrow Wilson* called for a conference to confront the problems plaguing labor and management. The president demonstrated the progressive ideal of voluntary cooperation between labor, management, and government. The conference opened in Washington, D.C., October 6, with fifty delegates representing the public, organized labor, and employers. The labor group was skeptical of Wilson's motives. Since all three groups had to agree on the passage of resolutions, the conference bogged down over collective bargaining. On October 14, Samuel Gompers* introduced a resolution for collective bargaining in the ongoing United States Steel strike, but Judge Elbert H. Gary,* of U.S. Steel called for voluntary collective bargaining only. When Wilson asked for a compromise, Gompers introduced a resolution that called for union organizing in all industry. The resolution was blocked by the employer group, and the conference failed. On December 1, the public group met with Secretary of Labor William B. Wilson,* and Gompers proclaimed that public hearings were useless in labor disputes. The conference endorsed collective bargaining on a voluntary basis only. (Philip Taft, *The A.F. of L. in the Time of Gompers* (1957); Samuel Gompers, *Seventy Years of Life and Labor* (1925); John Lombardi, *Labor's Voice in the Cabinet: A History of the Department of Labor from Its Origin to 1921* (1942).)

Frank Grubbs

INDUSTRIAL DEMOCRACY. The term *industrial democracy* had a number of meanings from a description of the operation of democracy within labor unions as used by Beatrice and Sidney Webb to a description of the nature of industrial relations. American socialists used the term to mean the elimination of private ownership of the means of production, while Samuel Gompers* stated, "The old political democracy is the father of this new industrial democracy; the trade union is the potential new industrial democracy." During World War I,* the term was used to cover various programs for joint industrial relations to avoid labor disputes that might inhibit the American war effort. Many of these wartime plans provided employee representation schemes based on the concept of collective bargaining with unions.

The end of the war saw many employers turn against unions, and during the 1920s, many employee representation plans became company unions controlled by employers and devices to prevent the establishment of legitimate trade unions. At this time, the term *industrial democracy* referred to a particular type of plan under which the organization of the company union was patterned after the federal government with a house composed of employee representatives, a senate composed of supervisory representatives, and a cabinet with veto power composed of representatives of top management. Whether companies used this type of plan, employee representation plans, work councils, or shop committees, the basic purpose was to prevent legitimate union organization. (Beatrice and Sidney Webb, *Industrial Democracy* (1920); John R. Commons, *Industrial Government* (1921).)

Leon Applebaum

INDUSTRIAL WORKERS OF THE WORLD. In June of 1905 a convention of union leaders, socialists, and radicals founded the Industrial Workers of the World (IWW/Wobblies). The delegates, who wished to overthrow capitalism and to replace it with a worker-dominated cooperative commonwealth, denounced the capitalist craft unionism of the American Federation of Labor* and endorsed industrial unionism. IWW soon found itself rent with dissension. Members of the Socialist party* and the Western Federation of Miners bolted the union. The remaining membership split into two camps: those who emphasized direct economic action and those who placed a greater stress on political activism. Direct-action Wobblies established their headquarters in Chicago* and emerged as the dominant force.

On the West Coast, IWW achieved early success in fights for its right to free speech. Its greatest victory came when it won the 1912 mill workers strike in Lawrence, Massachusetts.* IWW then suffered defeats in Paterson, New Jersey,* Akron, and Detroit. The union also led organization drives among agricultral laborers on the Great Plains and among West Coast lumber workers. In 1918, Department of Justice prosecutions sent almost the entire leadership of IWW to jail. By 1924, further external assaults plus more internal divisions all but destroyed the union. (Paul F. Brissenden, *The I.W.W.: A Study of American Syndicalism*(1919); Melvyn Dubofsky, *We Shall Be All: A History of the Industrial Workers of the World* (1969); Philip S. Foner, *History of the Labor Movement in the United States*, vol. 4: *The Industrial Workers of the World, 1905–1917* (1965); John S. Gambs *The Decline of the I.W.W.* (1932).)

Graham Adams, Jr.

INITIATIVE. The initiative is a governmental mechanism permitting a percentage of registered voters to demand that a policy proposal be submitted to the people for ratification. Along with the referendum* and the recall,* the initiative was one of the direct democracy reforms borrowed from Switzerland and widely adopted by states and local governments in the Progressive Era. Reformers wished to break the control of corrupt political machines* over the government by appealing directly to the people. In reply to pessimists, who claimed democracy had failed, they asserted that "the cure for democracy is more democracy."

South Dakota* was the first state to adopt the initiative as an ordinary agency of government, authorizing it in the state constitution in 1898. Approximately twenty other states adopted it shortly thereafter. Though the initiative has not been used as often as the referendum, it has functioned occasionally as an important means of protest, especially in California* and Oregon.* Recently, a 1978 tax revolt in California resulted in the adoption of Proposition 13, a state-wide initiative demanding a drastic cut in property taxes. (William B. Munro, *The Initiative, Referendum and Recall* (1912); V. O. Key and Winston W. Crouch, *The Initiative and the Referendum in California* (1939); Patrick B. McGuigan, *The Politics of Direct Democracy in the 1980s* (1985).)

Edward R. Kantowicz

INSTITUTIONAL ECONOMICS refers to an approach to economics that emphasized the role of institutions rather than the static laws of the marketplace that were central to classical economics. The origins of institutional economics can be found in the German historical school, the ideas of Karl Marx, and in the evolutionary sciences. Institutionalists shared many presuppositions with the sociological jurisprudence* of Roscoe Pound,* the pragmatism of William James* and John Dewey,* and the New History* of Charles A. Beard* and James Harvey Robinson.*

Thorstein Veblen* was by far the most original and inspirational thinker identified with the institutional school. Veblen defined institutions broadly as habits of thought (sometimes manifested in such legal devices as private property) that had accrued by cultural evolution. Institutions, along with inherited instincts and intelligence, determined human behavior. Of the three, Veblen gave little weight to the creative role of intelligence. Other economists of an institutional bent examined specific aspects of economic life, ranging from the business cycle to governing labor relations. Frequently progressives seized upon the ideas of the institutional economists to recommend changes in existing institutions. (Joseph Dorfman, *The Economic Mind in American Civilization*, vol. 3 (1959); W. H. Hamilton, "The Institutional Approach to Economic Theory," *American Economic Review* (1919): Supp., 280–90 and 309–24.)

Benjamin G. Rader

INSTRUMENTALISM. Instrumentalism is one of several terms (pragmatism, experimentalism) used to describe a philosophy whose development is generally credited to John Dewey.* More accurately described as a metatheory rather than a fully developed philosophy, instrumentalism primarily concerns questions about the nature of inquiry, i.e., concerns about how problems are solved. Dewey, a leading progressive thinker, developed instrumentalism as a way of explaining how man solves, or should solve, problems. Philosopher Brand Blanshard provides two general illustrations of the use of Deweyan, instrumentalist thinking in traditional philosophy: (1) logic becomes a study of the processes by which doubts are satisfactorily removed rather than the study of self-evident and changeless principles; (2) ethics is the study of how to solve problems in which values are involved, not the study of principles which make an act right

(164, 165). Ideas become "instruments" with which change can be accomplished.

Progressive reformers were able to use instrumentalist thinking to justify discarding the "old" in favor of the "new," with additional benefit of having the "new" always subject to change. Continuous progress becomes possible because—as the *Dictionary of Philosophy* puts it—with instrumentalism "ideas are used to control . . . and create possibilities for human experience . . . Thinking is to be judged according to its success in helping an organism adjust and thus survive socially and environmentally." (Brand Blanshard, *Reasons and Goodness* (1961); John Dewey, "The Public and Its Problems," *The Middle Works*, vol. 2 (1984); Morton White, *The Origin of Dewey's Instrumentalism* (1943).)

Chris Eisele

INSULL, SAMUEL (November 11, 1859–July 16, 1938). A Chicago* electrical utilities magnate, Insull was born in London, England. He left school at age fourteen, started work as an office boy and stenographer, then served as secretary to Thomas Edison's London agent. In 1881 he emigrated to America to serve Edison himself as private secretary, soon managing the business end of the inventor's many enterprises. In 1889 he became vice president of the Edison General Electric Company, but he resigned in 1892 to take over the Chicago branch of the Edison Company and try out his own ideas on electrical distribution.

He vigorously promoted the use of central generating stations for large districts of the city and soon mastered both the technical and financial details of power distribution. After 1898 he concentrated on the expansion of electrical use by heavy advertising and the lowering of rates. In the 1920s, he devised numerous holding companies to finance the expansion of his power network into the suburban region of northern Illinois. Though his operating companies remained sound and efficient, the paper pyramid of holding companies collapsed in the Great Depression. Insull was tried for fraud and embezzlement in 1934 but acquitted. (Forrest McDonald, *Insull* (1962); Thomas P. Hughes, *Networks of Power* (1983); Harold L. Platt, "Samuel Insull and the Electric City," *Chicago History* 15 (1986): 97–108.)

Edward R. Kantowicz

INSURANCE COMPANIES, REGULATION OF. Public regulation of insurance was spearheaded by Massachusetts and New York, which sought to control corporate practices, particularly in banking and insurance, early in the nineteenth century. But the overall nature of reform changed dramatically with rapid expansion of the life- and fire-insurance fields following the Civil War. The former alienated countless policyholders with their frequent reluctance or refusal to meet their contractual obligations; the latter commonly charged what consumers considered to be unreasonable rates. Abusive marketing practices likewise infuriated owners of both life and fire policies who clearly had no use for "lightning" agents who rebated and "twisted" policies. Policyholders nationally sought thoroughgoing reforms; the more conservative and better-managed companies joined consumer-oriented politicians to end such marketing abuses as rebating and "twisting" and fly-by-night and insolvent firms.

In the life insurance sector, more fundamental changes came in the wake of the New York State Armstrong Committee probe of the life giants in 1905. The committee, expertly guided by its legal counsel, Charles Evans Hughes,* recommended to the legislature tough regulatory proposals that became public law. These measures included liberalization of policy provisions, an end to high-paying corporate nepotism, and "mutualization" of many firms. Wisconsin not only conducted its own careful investigation but launched a program of public life insurance in October 1913. In the fire insurance field two principal types of corrective measures were sought: antitrust laws designed to force rate competition, and after 1909, state-made rates where charges would be determined "scientifically" by insurance departments or rating commissions. The goals of both approaches were identical: to provide consumers with equitable charges. So successful were state reformers that some company executives crusaded for federal supervision after 1905. Fortunately for policyholders, the Supreme Court had ruled in the 1869 case of *Paul v. Virginia* that Congress lacked power to regulate the industry because an insurance policy was a contract of indemnity, not a transaction in commerce, and hence immune from federal regulation. (Harry Chase Brearley, *The History of the National Board of Fire Underwriters* (1916); H. Roger Grant, *Insurance Reform: Consumer Action in the Progressive Era* (1979); Morton Keller, *The Life Insurance Enterprise, 1885–1910* (1963).)

H. Roger Grant

INSURGENTS. This is a term used to describe members of the U.S. Congress in the Taft* and Wilson* administrations who rebelled against Republican party* leadership. The Insurgents, mostly from western states, revolted in the first Congress of the Taft administration in 1909 when a handful of them refused to vote for the reelection of Joseph G. Cannon* as Speaker of the House of Representatives. The House Insurgents led by George Norris* of Nebraska then joined with most Democrats to adopt reforms in the rules of the House designed to reduce the power of the Speaker and democratize House rules. In the U.S. Senate in the same Congress, a small band of senators broke with the Republican majority over the Payne-Aldrich Tariff.* The House bill satisfied the desires of the Insurgents to reduce tariff duties on eastern manufactured products, but in the Senate Finance Committee chaired by Senator Nelson W. Aldrich,* tariff rates were substantially increased. Maintaining that Aldrich's bill betrayed promises made by President Taft in 1908 to lower tariff duties, the Senate Insurgents led by Robert M. La Follette* of Wisconsin mounted an aggressive but unsuccessful attack on Aldrich's revisions. President Taft signed the Payne-Aldrich bill and declared it to be "the best tariff act" ever passed.

The Ballinger-Pinchot controversy* in 1910 contributed to the increasingly bitter and emotional intraparty conflict. Gifford Pinchot,* Theodore Roosevelt's personal friend and adviser, charged that Taft's Secretary of the Interior Richard A. Ballinger had betrayed Roosevelt's conservation policies. Taft defended Ballinger and fired Pinchot, but most Republican Insurgents backed Pinchot and accepted the view that Taft himself was disloyal to Roosevelt's policies. In the Republican primary election in 1910, Taft attempted to defeat several of the most objectionable Insurgents, and in the election of 1912, most of the Insurgents opposed Taft's renomination. Many supported Roosevelt, but few followed him into the Progressive party.* The Insurgents' role in the events which by 1910 had divided the Republican party was a significant one which helped make possible the election of Woodrow Wilson* and a Democratic majority in Congress in 1912. (Kenneth W. Heckler, *Insurgency: Personalities and Politics of the Taft Era* (1940); James Holt, *Congressional Insurgents and the Party System, 1909–1916* (1967); George E. Mowry, *The Era of Theodore Roosevelt, 1900–1912* (1958).)

Howard W. Allen

INTERNATIONAL LADIES' GARMENT WORKERS UNION. Organized in 1900, the union's members came mostly from the great number of Jewish and Italian immigrants who entered the United States in the late nineteenth and early twentieth centuries. Factional political battles, low income, and a lack of discipline all contributed to the failure of earlier organizational efforts. The United Hebrew Trades, established by a group of needle trades unions, was instrumental in spreading the doctrine of unionism among immigrant Jewish workers and also served as a forum in which such issues as socialism were debated. A group of eleven delegates representing seven locals in four cities with a combined membership of 2,000 organized the International Ladies' Garment Workers Union which received a charter from the American Federation of Labor.*

A turning point came in 1909 and 1910 when the International was involved in two major strikes in New York City. The first involved 20,000 shirtwaist makers, 80 percent of whom were young women. While the strike did not result in total victory for the union, it showed that women workers wanted organization and were willing to fight to improve their circumstances. The second strike involved between 50,000 and 60,000 cloakmakers and was resolved with the aid of Louis Brandeis,* when the union and the employers' association signed an agreement which became known as the "Protocol of Peace." In addition to improving wages, hours and conditions of employment, the Protocol provided a Board of Sanitary Control, a tripartite board of arbitration to settle all major differences, and a committee on grievances to settle minor matters. While the Protocol ran into difficulties, it was a vital step toward civilizing a low-wage competitive industry and led to reforms that plagued the industry. (Lewis Levine, *The Women's Garment Workers* (1924); Benjamin Stolberg, *Taylor's Progress* (1944).)

                                                                    Leon Applebaum

IOWA. In Iowa the Republican party* from Civil War days on had only nominal opposition from the Democrats, but was often torn by factionalism. The open division into conservative and progressive factions owes much to the politics of 1897–1900. Leslie M. Shaw, congenitally conservative, opposed moderate Matt Parrott and liberal Abraham B. Funk for the Republican nomination for governor, with Shaw the winner. Two years later the Old Guard was so determined to block liberal Albert B. Cummins* from the Senate that they put up a "dead man," John H. Gear, who won but died within six weeks. Jonathan P. Dolliver* was put in as a compromise, and the frustrated Cummins had to be content with the governor's office a year later.

    Aided by a group of talented lieutenants, mostly editors and lawyers, Cummins put through a much needed reform program: regulation of railroad finances; abolition of the free pass and the two-cent fare; reform of the insurance industry; pure food and drug laws; a single board of regents for the three major state schools; biennial elections; the direct primary; and many lesser reforms. Conservatives fought back with some success, and the split continued into the 1920s. (Thomas Richard Ross, *Jonathan Prentiss Dolliver: A Study in Political Integrity and Independence* (1958); Leland L. Sage, *A History of Iowa* (1974); William L. Bowers, "The Fruits of Progressivism," *Iowa Journal of History* 57 (January 1959): 34–60.)

                                                                    Leland L. Sage

IRISH-AMERICANS. The 1910 census recorded 4,504,360 people of Irish birth or parentage—the second largest immigrant group in the United States. Their considerable influence was enhanced by a strong ethnic identity, forged from an ardent devotion to Ireland, Catholicism, and the Democratic party* and reinforced by widespread anti-Catholic prejudice in American society. Though heavily concentrated in the working class, a significant minority, by 1900, was moving into the upper classes through careers in business and the professions. Irish power was most formidable in three areas—religion, labor, and politics— where they often functioned as brokers between the newer immigrant groups and the larger society. No other ethnic group was so closely identified with Catholicism. The church, in leadership, style, and moral outlook, had been powerfully shaped by its large Irish presence. From 1886 to 1921, the church was guided through several controversies by the astute James Cardinal Gibbons* of Baltimore.

    A major force in the labor movement, the Irish constituted the largest nationality group, as both members and leaders, in the American Federation of Labor.* Generally conservative in outlook, they focused on bread-and-butter issues and resisted the growth of socialism in labor unions. Father John A. Ryan* emerged as the foremost scholar relating Catholic doctrine to labor issues. Thanks to their political skills and strategic concentration in big cities, the Irish controlled many of the urban political machines by the turn of the century. Though notoriously corrupt, the Irish machines did much to integrate the immigrants into American society, while providing jobs, social services, and a ladder of mobility for the urban poor. Numerous Irishmen, like Edward F. Dunne* (Illinois) and Al Smith* (New York), became distinguished reform leaders.

American politics during the Wilson* years was complicated by Ireland's increasingly violent struggle against British rule. During America's neutrality period (1914–1917), activists campaigned feverishly for Irish freedom while opposing American support for the British war effort. In 1917–1918, they supported the American war effort, claiming that Wilson's "war to make the world safe for democracy" committed America to Irish freedom. Bitterly disillusioned after the war, they played an important role in the defeat of the Treaty of Versailles. (Joseph Edward Cuddy, *Irish-America and National Isolationism, 1914–1920* (1976); William V. Shannon, *The American Irish* (1966); Lawrence J. McCaffrey, *The Irish Diaspora in America* (1976).)

Edward Cuddy

ITALIAN-AMERICANS. An average of over 200,000 Italians migrated to the United States annually between 1900 and 1914. Except for the colonies in northern California and in New Orleans, Italian-Americans were concentrated in the large cities of the North were mostly male in the early years, and took unskilled jobs in construction and factory work. Most immigrants originally had intentions of returning to (usually southern) Italy, and a good many did repatriate. Chain-migration patterns resulted in the growth of Little Italies (often organized by town of origin). Viewed alternately as objects of charity, as dangerous radicals, and as villainous mafiosi, the group's family-based value system served it well in creating viable ethnic enclaves. Italian Catholic parishes, often led by Scalabrini fathers, and mutual benefit societies were other key institutions that reinforced group survival. Few political figures aside from Fiorello La Guardia emerged in this era. The reform-minded pseudosociology of Madison Grant* and *The Dillingham Commission Report* led progressives to advocate immigrant restriction laws,* and antiethnic measures such as Prohibition* negatively impacted this group. (Luciano Iorizzo and Salvatore Mondello, *The Italian Americans* (1980); Lydio Tomasi, ed., *The Italians in America: The Progressive View, 1891–1914* (1978); *Proceedings of the American Italian Historical Association*, vols. 1–17 (1970–present).)

Dominic Candeloro

IVES, CHARLES E. (October 20, 1874–May 19, 1954). Born in Danbury, Connecticut, Ives received his early musical training from his father, a bandmaster and musical jack-of-all-trades. He studied with the composer Horatio W.

Parker at Yale and, after graduating in 1898, went into the life insurance business in New York City, where he achieved success as an agency manager for the Mutual Life Insurance Company of New York, retiring in 1930. During the Progressive Era, he composed extensively but privately in his spare time while living the life of a genteel businessman, isolated from the musical world. In many of his compositions, Ives used literary and philosophical "programs," often of an "American" nature, and quoted American tunes, while the path-breaking technical experiments of these eclectic works frequently predated the comparable modernism of Europeans such as Arnold Schoenberg and Igor Stravinsky.

In the decade from 1907 to 1917 Ives produced his most significant large-scale works, such as the orchestral compositions *The Fourth of July* and *Three Places in New England*, the *Fourth Symphony*, and the *Second Piano Sonata* (*Concord, Mass., 1840–60*). Still little known musically when he stopped composing in the 1920s, Ives subsequently received performances and recognition through the efforts of other musicians. Since his death in New York City, he has come to be generally acknowledged as America's preeminent composer of art music. (Frank R. Rossiter, *Charles Ives and His America* (1975); Charles E. Ives, *Memos*, ed. John Kirkpatrick (1972); Vivian Perlis, *Charles Ives Remembered: An Oral History* (1974).)

Frank Rossiter

J

JAMES, HENRY (April 15, 1843–February 28, 1916). The most important American prose stylist at the turn of the century, Henry, like his brother William,* was born in New York, and was given an eclectic and cosmopolitan education by his father, a man of leisure with strong philosophical and theological ideas. Henry attended Harvard Law School and also studied painting, but he dedicated his life to writing fiction. Strongly attracted to Europe, where he had lived for some time with his family, he moved there permanently in 1875, settling in London in 1876 and becoming a British subject.

James's fiction was realistic but refined, marked by complexity of characterization and psychological subtlety. He explored the international triangle between Paris, London, and New York better than any previous writer. In such works as *The American* (1877), *Daisy Miller* (1879), *Portrait of a Lady* (1881), and *The Ambassadors* (1903), he portrayed the sharp contrasts between American and European society. Though resented in his own time for his expatriation, and ridiculed as a ''paleface,'' in the word of critic Leslie Fiedler, for his supposedly bloodless and sexless novels of manners, James remains a major figure in American literature. His international novels and his own life story reflect the growing closeness between England and America which proved so vital when World War 1* broke out. (F. W. Dupee, *Henry James* (1951); F. O. Matthiessen, *Henry James, The Major Phase* (1944); Leon Edel, *Henry James, A Life* (1985).)

Edward R. Kantowicz

JAMES, WILLIAM (January 11, 1842–August 26, 1910). William James developed his ideas out of neurotic anxiety and a career ambivalently divided between science as the key to modern knowledge and a personal attraction to art and metaphysics. His early years on the Harvard faculty as a scientist culminated in his magnum opus, *The Principles of Psychology* (1890). With the aim of exploring beyond the laboratory, James then became a professor of philosophy in 1897, concentrating on issues of religious faith and ethics for the rest of his life.

James focused his thought, which he interchangeably called "pragmatism" and "radical empiricism," on the concept of a stream of consciousness. Emotional desire, he contended, governed thought; and emotion, in turn, flowed from physiological disturbance. James fixed upon the will both as the means of determining what action would result from the stream of consciousness and as the shaper of personality. From that view of life as a reciprocal process, human existence emerged as the sum of experiences arising from encounters between will and environment; and the meaning of a particular experience was seen to vary according to each person's assessment of the consequences.

Jame's conviction that the meaning of thought and action resides in their consequences served to mediate the tension—which he shared with his large professional and lay audience—between religious faith, individual freedom, and social duty. In *The Will to Believe* (1896) James argued both for freedom and religious loyalty by contending that one is entitled to hold as true whatever beliefs will satisfy one's needs, providing those beliefs do not conflict with empirical evidence or harm others. Social duty came to the fore in *The Moral Philosopher and the Moral Life* (1891) and *What Makes a Life Significant?* (1896), where James insisted that life is a test of character requiring one to perceive and respond sympathetically to the plight of others. Accordingly, James was moved to issue protests of permanent value against militarism, lynching, vivisection, the "Ph.D. Octopus," and other manifestations of cruelty and regimentation. (Frederick H. Burkhardt et al., eds., *Essays in Philosophy: The Works of William James* (1978); Gay Wilson Allen, *William James* (1967); Ralph Barton Perry, *The Thought and Character of William James* (1935); Howard M. Feinstein, *Becoming William James* (1984); Gerald E. Myers, *William James: His Life and Thought* (1986).)

R. Alan Lawson

JAMESON, JOHN FRANKLIN (September 19, 1859–September 28, 1937). Born in Somerville, Massachusetts, and graduating from Amherst in 1879, Jameson received the first doctorate in history from Johns Hopkins University in 1882, where he taught until 1888, then at Brown (1888–1900) and the University of Chicago* (1901–1905). In 1895 he helped found the *American Historical Review* and became its first managing editor, a position which he held until 1928. Disclaiming the title "historian," Jameson published little in the field, most notably the lectures *The American Revolution Considered as a Social Movement* (1926).

His career was dedicated to the institutionalization of professional standards for historical research, documentation, and writing—to the making of factual "bricks" (as he phrased it) necessary to building historical interpretations. In 1895–1896 he helped create and became chairman of the Association of the Historical Manuscripts Commission. In 1905 he became director of the Bureau of Historical Research of the Carnegie Institution. Jameson actively campaigned to preserve government records, efforts which led to the establishment of the National Archives and the National Historical Publication Commission. He participated in the founding of the American Council of Learned Societies (1919) and its sponsorship of the publication of the *Dictionary of American Biography* (1927–1936). In 1927, Jameson was named both chief of the manuscripts division at the Library of Congress and the first holder of its chair of American history. (Elizabeth Donnan and Leo F. Stock, eds., *An Historian's World: Selections from the Correspondence of John Franklin Jameson* (1956); Victor Gondos, Jr., *J. Franklin Jameson and the Birth of the National Archives, 1906–1926* (1981); Morey D. Rothberg, "Servant to History: A Study of John Franklin Jameson, 1859–1937" (Ph.D. diss., Brown University, 1982).)

Burton J. Bledstein

JEWISH-AMERICANS. There were about 250,000 Jews in the United States in 1880, mostly well-established German Jews; but in the next forty years, a wave of immigration from the Russian Empire swelled the numbers of Jewish-Americans to over 4 million. German Jews were relatively prosperous, they spoke German or English, and they practiced a Reformed Jewish religion. Their co-religionists from Russia, however, arrived in America impoverished, they practiced a strict Orthodox Jewish ritual, and they spoke Yiddish, an amalgam of Hebrew, German, and Polish.

Since 1791 Jews in the Russian Empire had been restricted to an area called the Pale of Settlement, comprising most of present-day Poland, the Ukraine, and Lithuania. Jews were required to live within the Pale but were forbidden to own land; so they clustered in small country towns, or shtetls, and worked as craftsmen or shopkeepers. The assassination of Tsar Alexander II in 1881 led to numerous pogroms, or massacres, as Russian authorities chose the Jews as scapegoats. The migration of Jews from Russia to the United States showed several distinctive features. Religious persecution was the prime motive for emigration, and most emigrants intended to settle permanently in America. Because of their background in the old country, Jewish immigrants had a higher proportion of skilled workers than other groups, and most were literate. They concentrated more heavily in cities than any other immigrant group. Indeed, the majority of Russian Jews settled in one city, New York, whose commerce and light industry provided jobs which they found congenial. Many started in business by selling from pushcarts and later opened shops of their own. Others found work as tailors or cutters in the garment industry. Whole families laboring in sweatshops developed an unusual workers' solidarity and became strong union advocates. New York Jews eventually experienced substantial upward mobility in business and the professions.

Jewish voters showed a diverse pattern in Progressive Era politics. Established German Jews often voted Republican, but the mass of Russian Jews voted for Tammany* Democrats, like most working-class immigrants. Republican Presi-

dent Theodore Roosevelt* neatly bridged this gap by appointing Oscar Straus,*
a German Jew with Democratic leanings, as his secretary of commerce and labor
in 1906. A substantial minority of Jewish workers backed the Socialist party,*
electing Meyer London* as congressman from the Lower East Side in 1914.
Many Jews who dropped away from the orthodox practice of their religion in
America found a secular, humanitarian substitute in the socialist movement.
(Nathan Glazer, *American Judaism* (1957); Moses Rischin, *The Promised City:
New York Jews, 1870–1914* (1962); Irving Howe, *World of Our Fathers* (1976).)

Edward R. Kantowicz

JOHNSON, ARTHUR JOHN "JACK" (March 31, 1878–June 10, 1946).
Born in Galveston, Texas, Jack Johnson grew up in the midst of the poverty
and racial subjugation that were the common lot of black people in the southern
states. As a teenager, Johnson gave up working on the Galveston wharves for
professional boxing. For a decade he traveled back and forth across the United
States, fighting anybody—white or black—where a purse could be got up. A
masterful boxer with a strong punch, Johnson had beaten virtually every heavyweight of note by 1907. By humiliating white opponents, loudly proclaiming
his own abilities, and insisting on treatment as a racial equal, he infuriated much
of the white sporting public.

Late in 1908, in Australia, Johnson hammered heavyweight king Tommy
Burns into submission and became the first black heavyweight champion. From
the white press came the call for a "white hope" to take back the title from the
black champion. A year-and-a-half later, in his most famous title defense, Johnson easily disposed of ex-champion Jim Jeffries at Reno, Nevada. The outcome
produced flare-ups of racial violence in towns and cities throughout America.
Subsequently, the U.S. Justice Department, taking advantage of Johnson's notorious fondness for white women, charged him with violating the Mann Act*
in transporting his paramours across state lines.

Following his conviction in 1913, Johnson fled to Europe to escape imprisonment. Unable to obtain profitable matches abroad, he finally agreed to defend
his title in Havana against the giant Jess Willard. In July 1915, Willard's twenty-
sixth-round knockout of the overage and out-of-shape Johnson prompted rejoicing
throughout white America. In 1920 Johnson returned home to serve a year in
federal prison. For the remainder of his life, he made a modest living by boxing
exhibitions, refereeing matches, and managing other boxers. (Randy Roberts,
Papa Jack: Jack Johnson and the Era of White Hopes (1983); Finis Farr, *Black
Champion: The Life and Times of Jack Johnson* (1965); Al-Tony Gilmore, *Bad
Nigger! The National Impact of Jack Johnson* (1975).)

Charles C. Alexander

JOHNSON, HIRAM WARREN (September 3, 1866–August 6, 1945). Hiram
Johnson was born in Sacramento, California, graduated from the city's public
schools, entered the University of California in 1884, and withdrew two years

later. Admitted to the bar in 1888, he practiced law with his father and his older brother. Johnson was active in local politics, participating in the management of his father's campaigns for the U.S. Congress, but publicly broke with the elder Johnson in 1901 to support a reform ticket in the Sacramento mayoralty contest. In 1906, assuming a central role in the prosecution of the San Francisco graft trials, he was catapulted into public prominence. A spokesman for the Lincoln-Roosevelt League,* he was that organization's choice for governor in 1910.

Denouncing the political control exercised by the Southern Pacific Railroad, Johnson stumped the state, winning the Republican primary and the general election. He was reelected in 1914. As governor, Johnson forcefully championed a progressive agenda which included political reform, railroad and utility regulation, and measures to protect labor. When, in 1912, Theodore Roosevelt* failed to secure the Republican presidential nomination, Johnson urged the formation of the Progressive party* and became Roosevelt's running mate. In 1916, Johnson was elected to the U.S. Senate, where he remained until his death. In 1920 and 1924, he unsuccessfully sought the Republican presidential nomination. As senator, Johnson was best known as a spokesman for isolation, opposing American entry into the League of Nations,* but he also supported liberal domestic causes. (Spencer C. Olin, Jr., *California's Prodigal Sons: Hiram Johnson and the Progressives, 1911–1917* (1968); H. Brett Melendy and Benjamin F. Gilbert, *Governors of California* (1965); Robert E. Burke, ed., *The Diary and Letters of Hiram Johnson*, 7 vols. (1983).)

Richard C. Lower

JOHNSON, TOM L. (July 18, 1854–April 10, 1911). Born in Blue Springs, Kentucky, the son of a cotton planter, Johnson had two years of grade school before beginning as an office boy with a streetcar company. Johnson became an owner of streetcar companies until the 1890s, when he bought steel mills. After being attracted to the ideas of Henry George,* he served two terms as a Democratic congressman in the 1890s, was elected mayor of Cleveland* on a social reform platform in 1901, and served four terms before his defeat in 1909. He was defeated for governor in 1903, but his platform of progressive legislation and home rule* was largely adopted after his death.

Johnson's mayoralty was distinguished by acquisition of a municipal light plant to serve as a ''yardstick,'' reform of the tax system, lower streetcar fares, and social reforms which improved the quality of life for working-class citizens. By means of tent meetings, he educated Cleveland citizens on the issues of the day and brought the immigrant masses into the mainstream of American politics. Johnson gathered around him a remarkable group of progressives and stimulated both Republican and Democratic reformers, leaving behind a city that was neither content nor corrupt. (Tom L. Johnson, *My Story* (1911); see also the introduction by Melvin G. Holli in the 1970 University of Washington Press reprint of *My Story*; Carl Lorenz, *Tom L. Johnson* (1911); Hoyt L. Warner, *Progressivism in*

Ohio: 1897–1917 (1964); Eugene Murdock, "Buckeye Liberal: A Biography of Tom L. Johnson" (Ph.D. diss., Columbia University, 1951).)

Thomas F. Campbell

JONES, SAMUEL M. "GOLDEN RULE" (August 3, 1846–July 23, 1904). Born in Wales, Jones grew up in Collinsville, New York, after his parents emigrated in 1849 or 1850. With little formal education, he worked in a sawmill, on steamers, and, after 1865, in Pennsylvania's oil fields. He eventually went into business and invented an improved sucker-rod for deep drilling that made him wealthy. Awakened to social issues after moving to Toledo in 1892, Jones applied the Golden Rule to his Acme Sucker-Rod Company by offering generous wages, hours, and benefits, not using piecework or child labor, and supporting trade unions. In 1897, he won the Republican mayoral nomination by surprise and then the election. Though the party rejected him, he won again as an independent in 1899, 1901, and 1903. In 1899 he ran for governor as an independent but lost.

More interested in social and economic reforms that touched workers' daily lives than in antivice crusades or structural changes in government, he expanded and humanized Toledo's public services to make the city, like his factory, reflect the Golden Rule. Mystical and idealistic, an admirer of Leo Tolstoy and Giuseppe Mazzini, he envisioned an altruistic coming "Cooperative Commonwealth." His success in Toledo brought him into reformist and Christian socialist circles across the country. After he died in office, Brand Whitlock* continued his reforms. (H. Landon Warner, *Progressivism in Ohio, 1897–1917* (1964); Peter J. Frederick, *Knights of the Golden Rule: The Intellectual as Christian Social Reformer in the 1890s* (1976); Harvey S. Ford, "The Life and Times of Golden Rule Jones" (Ph.D. diss., University of Michigan, 1953).)

Jacob H. Dorn

JONES, WESLEY L. (October 9, 1863–November 19, 1932). Born in Bethany, Illinois, Jones graduated from Southern Illinois College, read law, and was admitted to the Illinois bar in 1885. He moved to North Yakima, Washington, in 1889, established a law practice, and was elected to the House of Representatives as a Republican in 1898. He was consistently returned to the House until elected to the Senate in 1908, where he served until his defeat in 1932. Jones's pragmatic, compromising approach to the political issues of his day enabled him to survive the conflicts that split the Republican party.* Describing himself as a "progressive conservative," Jones avoided public controversy or identification with either the insurgent or the regular wing of the party. He remained loyal to his party but supported such moderate measures of federal regulation as antitrust legislation, the La Follette Seamen's Act,* and child labor legislation.* His perceptions of his constituents' desires usually coincided with his own principles: tariff protection, immigration restriction, state control of conservation policies that would emphasize development, and reclamation projects. He was willing to relax his attachment to the principle of private property in order to secure the Alaska railroad, the Merchant Marine Act of 1920, and federal hydroelectric projects because of the contribution these would make to the economic development of his state. (William Stuart Forth, "Wesley L. Jones, A Political Biography" (Ph.D. diss., University of Washington, 1962).)

Robert D. Saltvig

JORDAN, DAVID STARR (January 19, 1851–September 19, 1931). Born in Gainesville, New York, Jordan attended district schools and the Gainesville Female Seminary and was a part of the first graduating class of Cornell University, where he concentrated in botany and, in 1872, graduated with a master of science degree. In the summer of 1873, he studied with the noted European scientist Louis Agassiz, and his scientific interests turned toward marine biology and ichthyology. Jordan was the author of several hundred books and papers on various fish species. He held a variety of teaching positions before becoming professor of zoology at Indiana University in 1879.

In 1885, he was chosen to be the president of Indiana, a post he held until 1891, when he became the inaugural president of Stanford University. He held that position until 1913. As a president, he emulated the reform ideas of Andrew D. White, president of Cornell while Jordan was a student there. Under Jordan, Indiana and Stanford flourished, although the careful oversight of Mrs. Leland Stanford at the latter institution was a burden. In addition to scientific and administrative accomplishments, Jordan published several works on social problems. He was an avowed hereditarian in human as well as scientific affairs, and a fervent advocate of world peace, even during World War I.* (Edward McNall Burns, *David Starr Jordan: Prophet of Freedom* (1953); Thomas D. Clark, *Indiana University, Midwestern Pioneer,* vol. 1: *The Early Years* (1970); Orrin L. Elliott, *Stanford University: The First Twenty Five Years* (1937).)

Wayne J. Urban

JUDGES, ELECTION OF. Within American culture there have been two often contradictory attitudes toward the judiciary: that it be fair, impartial, and independent and that it be accountable to the public. Until the Jacksonian era, state judges were generally chosen by the legislature and/or by the governor. More than half the states continue such an appointive process in the 1980s. However, beginning in the 1830s, a movement for popular election of judges gained strength; every new state entering the Union between 1846 and 1912 provided for election of state judges. Pragmatic, moderate lawyers in the major political parties sought to open judicial appointment beyond the patronage of party cliques in the statehouse and to increase public support of the judiciary and judical review as a counterweight to legislative power.

In the second half of the nineteenth century, however, in response to fears of machine politics and a new emphasis on professionalism* and expertise,* dissatisfaction increased with popular, partisan election of state judges. In the years between 1880 and 1920, revisions were made in the nominating process, the ballot form, and the scheduling of judicial and other elections, in an attempt to limit the role of political parties in promoting democratic accountability and to emphasize instead the need for an independent, professional, and nonpartisan judiciary.

The changes in the machinery of judicial elections achieved by the urban elites dominant in the American Bar Association* in conjunction with progressive political reformers increased the role of the professional bar in the judicial selection process. Unlike its vigorous opposition to measures for the recall* of unpopular judges, the bar generally accepted popular election of the state judiciary. The use of the secret* and nonpartisan* ballot and the direct primary* also reduced the previous influence of party leaders, as did scheduling of judicial selection separate from major elections. Studies of the impact of those reforms have suggested that incumbent elected judges who wished to remain on the bench almost invariably won renomination and reelection. (Russell D. Niles, "The Popular Election of Judges in Historical Perspective," *Record of the Association of the Bar of the City of New York* 21 (1966):523–38; Jack Ladinsky and Allan Silver, "Popular Democracy and Judicial Independence," *Wisconsin Law Review* (Winter 1967): 128–69; Kermit L. Hall, "Progressive Reform and the Decline of Democratic Accountability," *American Bar Foundation Research Journal* (Spring 1984) :345–70.)

                                                        John Whiteclay Chambers II

JUNIOR REPUBLICS. Among the most original and imaginative of the "child-saving"* schemes, junior republics (JRs) epitomized the Progressive Era's emphasis on democratic principles and good citizenship. In their purest form, the republics were miniature states in which the youngsters governed themselves, electing leaders, establishing their own laws and courts, and running their local economy on scrip. As scaled-down versions of the "Big Republic," these experiments in self-government were supposed to dissolve class barriers and teach the responsibilities of citizenship. William R. "Daddy" George established the first and most famous of the JRs, Freeville, in upstate New York in the 1890s, but there were others, including the Ford Republic outside Detroit and Allendale Farm in Illinois—all residential locations for dependent and delinquent youths.

The self-governing approach also influenced numerous nonresidential youth organizations, ranging from newsboys' associations to student government in high schools. Although the nature of the republics (e.g., the amount of self-rule) varied widely, they dramatized progressive efforts to relate institutions to perceived social needs, and to reshape the environment through education that stressed actual experiences. By around 1914, the more democratic experiments had faded, giving way to increasingly ritualistic gestures of self-government. (Jack M. Holl, *Juvenile Reform in the Progressive Era: William R. George and the Junior Republic Movement* (1971); Leroy Ashby, *Saving the Waifs: Reformers and Dependent Children, 1890–1917* (1984); Steven L. Schlossman and

Ronald D. Cohen, "The Music Man in Gary: Willis Brown and Child-Saving in the Progressive Era," *Societas* 7 (Winter 1977): 1–17.)

LeRoy Ashby

JUVENILE COURTS. Also called Children's Courts, juvenile courts are tribunals which have original jurisdiction over delinquent and neglected children. Under this system, the child is considered a ward of the court, and the state, through the court, is acting in its role as *parens patriae*. While courts vary widely in structure and procedures, they share a common underlying philosophy, an informal and personalized approach to the children and an objective to rehabilitate, not punish, the delinquent. Wards of the court vary in age, ranging from sixteen to twenty-one, with the majority of states classifying juvenile as under eighteen. The movement to grant children special help had precedents in the nineteenth century with the juvenile reformatories which began in New York in 1825 followed soon by Boston (1826) and Pennsylvania (1828) and the foster home movement, especially the Children's Aid Society (1853).

The first American juvenile court was established in Chicago* in 1899. Ten years later twenty states had similar courts in operation. The Denver court, headed by the "Kid's Judge," Benjamin Barr Lindsey* served as the preferred model in part because it had the advantage of revising the Chicago model and in part because of its charismatic leader. Critics have charged that juvenile courts are too often plagued with problems of inadequate funding and public support. The result is that the best officials are badly overworked and underpaid and cannot possibly handle each case with the sufficient individual care. Not enough people with excellent training, benevolent attitudes, or all-consuming interest are employed as judges or probation officers. Too often these courts lack access to adequate medical, psychiatric, and counseling services. (Ellen Ryerson, *The Best-Laid Plans: America's Juvenile Court Experiment* (1978).)

D'Ann Campbell

K

KALLEN, HORACE MEYER (August 11, 1882–February 12, 1974). A rabbi's son, Kallen was born in Berenstadt, Silesia, and taken to the United States in 1887. He studied and taught philosophy at Harvard University with William James,* George Santayana, and Josiah Royce,* taught at Clark University and the University of Wisconsin,* and was a founder of the New School for Social Research in New York city in 1919, where he taught until his retirement in 1970. Author of almost 40 books and over 400 articles, he applied pragmatic philosophy to education, religion, society, and the arts. A humanist and civil libertarian, he was active in education and labor reform, Zionism, and minority rights. He is best known for his theory of cultural pluralism, introduced in the *Nation* * in 1915 and elaborated in *Culture and Democracy in the United States* in 1924. Responding to clamor for restriction of immigration and assimilation of "hyphenated" Americans (intensified by World War I* and the "Red Scare"),* Kallen affirmed the value of unity through diversity, arguing that the maintenance of ethnic group identity confirmed the American democratic tradition and enriched American culture. (Horace M. Kallen, *Culture and Democracy in the United States* (1924, 1970); Horace M. Kallen, *What I Believe and Why—Maybe: Essays for the Modern World*, ed. Alfred J. Marrow, (1971); William M. Newman, *American Pluralism: A Study of Minority Groups and Social Theory* (1973).)

Maxine S. Seller

KANSAS. The Progressive movement began in Kansas as a consequence of antirailroad sentiment in 1906 that caused the formation of the "Square Deal" clubs. Its ideological roots were to be found in the agrarian reform tradition of the late nineteenth century, not only in the views of the People's party, but in the platforms of the Labor Reform, Prohibition, and Greenback parties as well. Equally significant as its cause was a half-century of Republican factionalism.

The boss-buster movement of 1899–1900 was but one phase of continuous intraparty rivalry. The "boss" who was "busted," Cyrus Leland, Jr., was more reform-oriented than the boss busters. Many of progressivism's leaders—William Allen White,* Joseph Little Bristow,* Henry Justin Allen,* Victor Murdock*— were aligned with Leland during the 1890s. Out of power, these factionalists no doubt saw reform as a vehicle of political rejuvenation, although it would be wrong to assume their commitment was purely opportunistic. They were much influenced by Theodore Roosevelt* and Robert M. La Follette,* two men whose careers also present historians with the problem of disentangling altruistic motives from opportunistic acts.

The Progressive faction captured control of the Republican party* and Kansas government as a result of the first statewide primary* in 1908. Governor Walter Roscoe Stubbs,* elected in 1908, was responsible for causing most of the Progressive agenda to be enacted. He and his supporters created a public utilities commission, passed a corrupt practices* act and antilobbying legislation, and enacted sundry pieces of election, education, health, and human welfare laws. They were the second state legislature to enact a bank depositors guaranty program* and the first ever to create a "Blue Sky" commission to regulate stock and bond sales. In Congress, the Kansans were prominent in the Republican insurgency. Representative Victor Murdock was a leader in the Cannon* rules fight, and Congressman Edmond H. Madison spoke for them in the Ballinger-Pinchot affair.* Bristow helped in the unsuccessful struggles against the Payne-Aldrich Tariff* and the Mann-Elkins Act* and authored the Seventeenth Amendment to the U.S. Constitution. Several factors contributed to the Progressive Republicans' decline, including the creation of the Progressive party,* World War I,* and the inability of the Progressives to create new, moderate reform ideas. (Robert S. La Forte, *Leaders of Reform: Progressive Republicans in Kansas, 1900–1916* (1974); A. Bower Sageser, *Joseph L. Bristow: Kansas Progressive* (1968); Homer E. Socolofsky, *Arthur Capper: Publisher, Politician, Philanthropist* (1962).)

Robert S. La Forte

KEATING-OWEN ACT. On September 1, 1916, President Woodrow Wilson* signed this act which used the commerce clause to regulate the conditions of labor of persons fourteen to sixteen years old and forbade the interstate shipment of products of mines and factories employing children under fourteen. The National Child Labor Committee* (NCLC) originally rejected federal legislation but later came reluctantly to accept the necessity and was instrumental in securing passage of the law. Wilson had earlier declared that federal child labor legislation was an "obviously absurd" extravagance, but Alexander J. McKelway* of the NCLC urged Wilson to move to the left in order to capture the Progressive party* constituency. The approach of the 1916 campaign found Wilson paying a surprise visit to a Senate anteroom where he demanded that the Democratic leaders put the child labor bill on the list of "must" legislation. With its emphasis upon national solutions, the Keating-Owen Act represented the most advanced form of progressivism. (Stephen B. Wood, *Constitutional Politics in the Progressive Era: Child Labor and the Law* (1968); Robert W. McAhren, "Making the Nation Safe for Childhood: A History of the Movement for Federal Regulation of Child Labor, 1900–1938" (Ph.D. diss., University of Texas–Austin, 1967); Elizabeth H. Davidson, *Child Labor Legislation in the Southern Textile States* (1939).)

Robert W. McAhren

KELLER v. U.S. (213 U.S. 138). This 1909 Supreme Court case invalidated a congressional attempt to curtail the importation of prostitutes into the United States and subsequently contributed to the growth of public sentiment and legislation against the so-called white-slave trade. In an attempt to assist the Bureau of Immigration in restricting international traffic in prostitutes, Congress, in 1907, passed a law making it a federal crime to harbor an alien woman for immoral purposes for any period within three years after she had arrived in the United States. However, the Supreme Court, by a 6–3 decision in the *Keller* case, ruled against the government and held the law unconstitutional. In the majority opinion, Justice David J. Brewer declared that Congress had unlawfully invaded the police power of the states in its attempt at what the Court considered the local regulation of prostitution.

As a result of this invalidation, immigration officials proved largely ineffective in controlling the international traffic in prostitutes and, as the Bureau of Immigration informed President William Howard Taft* in 1909, absolutely powerless to intervene in the increasing traffic across state lines within the United States. A series of articles in *McClure's* magazine and in a number of newspapers in 1909 contributed to widespread public outcry against the white-slave trade, leading Representative James R. Mann* to introduce a bill which prohibited the transportation of women for immoral purposes in interstate or foreign commerce. Although some denounced the bill as a deceptive use of the interstate commerce clause in order to give the national government unprecedented police powers, public enthusiasm for the bill was so great that Congress readily adopted it. (Alfred H. Kelly and Winfred A. Harbison, *The American Constitution: Its Origins and Development* (1983).)

John Whiteclay Chambers II

KELLEY, FLORENCE (September 12, 1859–February 17, 1932). Social settlement* resident, advocate of protective legislation for working women and children, Kelley was born in Philadelphia,* the daughter of industrialist William D. "Pig Iron" Kelley. She was educated privately, then graduated from Cornell University in 1882. She studied in Europe and married Lazare Wischnewetzky in 1884. She had three children, but she divorced her husband in 1891 and resumed her maiden name. Taking up residence at Hull House* in Chicago* in 1891, she conducted a study of sweatshop conditions which led to the passage of the Illinois Factory and Workshop Inspection Act of 1893. Governor John Peter Altgeld* appointed her the first state factory inspector; she served from 1893 to 1897.

In 1898 she moved to New York,* taking up residence at Henry Street Settlement* and becoming secretary of the National Consumers' League.* As the guiding force of the Consumers' League from 1898 to 1932, she advocated laws banning child labor,* setting maximum hours for working women, and prescribing minimum wages for all workers. In 1921 she successfully lobbied for the Sheppard-Towner Maternity and Infant Protection Act.* Kelley spent much of her last decade opposing the Equal Rights Amendment advocated by the National Woman's party,* for it would have overturned the network of state protective laws for women which were her legacy. (Josephine Goldmark, *Impatient Crusader* (1953); Dorothy Rose Blumberg and Florence Kelley, *The Making of a Social Pioneer* (1966); Allen F. Davis, *Spearheads for Reform: The Social Settlements and the Progressive Movement, 1890–1914* (1967).)

                                                                                                   Edward R. Kantowicz

KELLOGG, PAUL U. (September 30, 1879–November 1, 1958). Born in Kalamazoo, Michigan, Kellogg began his long journalistic career as editor of his high school paper. Upon graduation, he became a reporter for the Kalamazoo *Daily Telegraph*, rising to city editor by 1898. In 1901, he moved to New York City and enrolled as a special student at Columbia University. The following year he became the assistant editor of *Charities*,* the organ of the New York Charity Organization Society.* In 1905, when *Charities* merged with the *Commons*, he became managing editor. Two years later he was chosen to direct the Pittsburgh Survey,* the first systematic investigation of the new urban, industrial, and polyglot America. In 1912, Kellogg became editor in chief of the newly renamed *Survey* magazine, a post he held until it finally ceased publication in 1952. Under Kellogg's editorial leadership, the *Survey* became noted for its thorough, and accurate, reporting of social conditions and for its advocacy of a wide array of reforms ranging from child and women's labor legislation to the arbitration of labor disputes to suffrage for women.

During World War I* Kellogg served with the American Red Cross in Europe. He also was a founding member of the Foreign Policy Association, the American Red Cross, and the American Civil Liberties Union.* During the 1920s, the *Survey* became a strong advocate of black civil rights, while Kellogg became a strong New Dealer in the 1930s and served on the advisory commission that recommended social security legislation. (Clarke A. Chambers, *Paul U. Kellogg and "The Survey": Voices for Social Welfare and Social Change* (1971); John F. McClymer, *War and Welfare: Social Engineering in America, 1890–1925* (1980).)

                                                                                                   John F. McClymer

KELLOR, FRANCES (October 20, 1873–January 4, 1952). A social reformer, author, and arbitration specialist, Kellor was born in Columbus, Ohio, received an LL.B. degree from Cornell Law School in 1897, and studied sociology at the University of Chicago.* She investigated the problems of black migrants and immigrants in northern cities and sought government action to improve urban life. She became nationally known for her work with government and industry on the Americanization* of immigrants. She began this work as secretary of the New York State Immigration Commission in 1908 and continued it until after World War I* with the Committee for Immigrants in America and into the 1920s with the Inter-Racial Council and the Association of Foreign Language Newspapers. Valuing national unity, industrial efficiency, and social control, and fearing the influence of radical ideologies, she defined Americanization as assimilation to the language and ideology of middle-class English America. Founder and executive of the American Arbitration Association from 1926 to 1952, she devoted her later years to the pursuit of industrial and international peace through arbitration. (Barbara Sicherman et al., eds., *Notable American Women: The Modern Period* (1980), 393–95; William Joseph Maxwell, "Frances Kellor in the Progressive Era: A Case Study of the Professionalization of Reform" (Ph.D. diss., Teachers College, Columbia University, 1968); Edward George Hartman, *The Movement to Americanize the Immigrant* (1948).)

Maxine S. Seller

KENT, WILLIAM (March 24, 1864–March 13, 1928). Born in Chicago* to wealthy parents, Kent spent his youth in Marin County, California. He was educated in private schools and graduated from Yale University in 1887. After college, Kent returned to Chicago where he engaged in real estate and the livestock business. He was one of the founders of the Municipal Voters League, a reform group which aimed at removal of the grafters from the Chicago City Council. These "gray wolves," as the league called them, were heavily entrenched grafters such as John Powers, John Coughlin,* and Michael Kenna. The efforts of the league were only modestly successful but, with their support, Kent was elected to the city council for a single term, 1895–1897. In 1907, Kent moved to California, where he was elected to the U.S. Congress for three terms, serving from 1911 to 1917. Despite generally liberal and reformist views, Kent was never accepted into the inner circle of California progressives because Hiram Johnson* disliked him. In 1916, Kent headed the Woodrow Wilson* Independent League. President Wilson appointed him to the U.S. Tariff Commission in 1917 and he served until 1920. (Robert L. Woodbury, *William Kent: Progressive Gadfly, 1864–1928* (1967).)

Donald F. Tingley

KENTUCKY. Progressive issues became important in Kentucky briefly during the gubernatorial campaign of 1899 when Democrat William Goebel challenged the established leadership of the party and campaigned for railroad regulation, directing much of his rhetoric against the state's largest line, the Louisville and Nashville Railroad. Within days of being declared the winner in a controversial vote of the Democratically controlled legislature, Goebel was assassinated. With his death, progressive reform died as a statewide issue until 1911. In that year, former Democratic governor James B. McCreary ran on a progressive platform and succeeded, during two legislative sessions, in passing several reforms, including a direct primary,* workmen's compensation,* regulation of insurance companies,* a uniform system of accounting, and establishment of an Illiteracy Commission.

A. D. Stanley, six-term congressman from the tobacco-growing district, followed McCreary after having already established a progressive record in Congress where he led antitrust investigations against the American Tobacco Company* and United States Steel.* As governor he worked with the legislature to enact antilobby, antitrust, and antirailroad pass laws, a corrupt practices act,* public utilities and tax commissions, and a revised tax structure. Additional progressive reform foundered, however, on the divisive issue of Prohibition* and the election in 1919 of Republican Edwin Morrow. (James C. Klotter, *William Goebel: The Politics of Wrath* (1977); Nicholas C. Burckel, "From Beckham to McCreary: The Progressive Record of Kentucky Governors," *Register of the Kentucky Historical Society* 76 (1978): 285–306; Nicholas C. Burckel, "A. O. Stanley and Progressive Reform, 1902–1919," *Register of the Kentucky Historical Society* 79 (1981): 136–61.)

                                                                        Nicholas C. Burckel

KERN-McGILLICUDDY ACT. This 1916 law created a workmen's compensation* system for federal employees. It was part of a multifaceted national campaign to protect workers against industrial accidents, which, by 1900, resulted in 35,000 deaths and half a million injuries annually. Although revising the common-law definition of an employer's liability provided some relief, compensation still required litigation, and the awards were unpredictable. Thus, after 1909, reform efforts focused on developing accident insurance with inclusive coverage, which would provide adequate and predictable compensation. By 1911, twenty-three states had organized commissions to study the subject and, by 1915, thirty-five states had enacted workmen's compensation laws. Demands for action by the federal government rose from its authority over interstate commerce and federal employees—who were only partially and inadequately covered. Furthermore, given the uneven quality of state laws, reformers wanted a federal law as a model for state action. Democrats endorsed a system for federal employees in 1912, but by 1916, they had taken no action. Then, following the party's convention and pressure by President Woodrow Wilson,* the measure was passed. Drafted by the American Association for Labor Legislation,* it included all federal employees in an equitable workmen's compensation system. (Arthor S. Link, *Wilson: Campaigns for Progressivism and Peace, 1916–1917*

(1965); U.S. Bureau of Labor Statistics, *Bulletin 203: Workmen's Compensation Laws of the United States and Foreign Countries* (1971).)

Philip R. VanderMeer

KINGSBURY, JOHN ADAMS (August 30, 1876–August 3, 1956). Health is as much everyone's birthright as education, according to this social worker/educator whose life centered on the public health movement. Born in Horton, Kansas, he attended Washington State College and the University of Washington and graduated from Teachers College, Columbia University, with a B.S. degree in 1908. As assistant secretary of the State Charities Aid Association of New York, he organized the 1910 Conference of Mayors of New York State. He worked for the New York Association for Improving the Condition of the Poor and served as Commissioner of Public Charities of New York City. After the Triangle Factory fire, he served on the New York Commission on Safety with Frances Perkins.* Although they were close friends, she occasionally found him too fanatical on institutional reform related to the care of young children. He helped revise New York State health laws as a member of Governor William Sulzer's* Public Health Commission. As a pioneer in the public health movement, he numbered among the "Heroes of Health" of the period. (George Martin, *Madam Secretary: Frances Perkins* (1976).)

Lillian H. Mohr

KNOX, PHILANDER C. (May 6, 1853–October 12, 1921). A rich conservative Pennsylvania lawyer, Knox served as attorney general under William McKinley* and Theodore Roosevelt* (1901–1904), then one term as U.S. senator. President William H. Taft* relied heavily upon Knox's advice when the latter served as secretary of state. Knox quickly reorganized the State Department along the now familiar politico-geographical desks, supported the Monroe Doctrine and the open door policy,* and eschewed territorial aggrandizement, but on occasion he called for the temporary use of military force, as in Nicaragua, to support American interests. On the other hand, he endorsed Taft's demand for the establishment of a genuine judicial tribunal for the adjudication of differences among nations and for tariff reciprocity with Canada.*

When Knox tried to obtain political and economic stability abroad, he gained ill will even though he substituted dollars for bullets in a policy known as "dollar diplomacy."* In Central America, he attempted to make the countries client states with private loans—insured by American control over customs collections. He also tried to force American capital into China. He thereby angered Central America, various European countries, and Russia and Japan as well. (Paolo E. Coletta, *The Presidency of William Howard Taft* (1973); George E. Mowry, *The Era of Theodore Roosevelt, 1900–1912* (1958); Walter V. Scholes and Marie V. Scholes, *The Foreign Policies of the Taft Administration* (1970).)

Paolo E. Coletta

L

LABOR LEGISLATION, STATE. The negative impact of industrialization upon American workers, and the increasingly bitter conflict between capital and labor, led some progressives to call for a broad-based set of reforms through continuous intervention by government. They argued that only law could insure social justice,* and that only social justice could prevent the growth of radicalism. Labor leaders supported regulation of the working conditions of women and children, the establishment of safe and healthy workplaces, the prohibition of labor at home and, after some indecision, a workmen's compensation* system. However, many labor leaders opposed state intervention generally for fear that the politically divided workers would be unable to prevent the use of government by powerful employers to repress both workers and their unions. This fear prevented full cooperation between progressives and the labor movement on reforms that concerned the wages and hours of male workers or the establishment of health or unemployment insurance.

Constitutional limitations on the power of the federal government placed the campaigns for labor legislation into the states. Here the combined progressive and labor forces were able to enlist the support of some powerful urban politicians, such as Al Smith* and Robert Wagner,* who realized the value of supporting legislation which so clearly represented the interests of their constituents. Although business leaders generally opposed labor legislation, they ultimately played a crucial role in the legislative process. In some cases, including workmen's compensation, business leaders offered support once the bill had been reshaped to take their views into account.

The most significant areas of state labor legislation were the regulation of child labor,* the limitation of hours of work for women, the establishment of factory health and safety codes, and the creation of state-operated programs for workmen's compensation. Since the legislation varied among the states, there was a constant problem with enforcement as business in the more highly regulated states sought to avoid the higher costs created by such legislation. This body of state labor legislation was important not only in itself but in its acceptance of state intervention in the economy on behalf of some workers. (John D. Buenker, *Urban Liberalism and Progressive Reform* (1973); John R. Commons et al., *History of Labour in the United States*, vol. 3 (1935); Irwin Yellowitz, *Labor and the Progressive Movement in New York State, 1897–1916* (1965).)

Irwin Yellowitz

LABOR UNIONS. Organizations of working men and women experienced gains in membership and legal status during the Progressive Era. They also faced the opposition of business on the right, challenges from socialists on the left, and an ambivalent attitude by middle-class progressives. The American Federation of Labor,* founded in 1886 and ably led by Samuel Gompers,* dominated organized labor. Its membership had increased rapidly from about 300,000 in 1898 to 1,750,000 by 1904. The A. F. of L. organized workers into national unions along traditional craft lines and concentrated on bread-and-butter issues, attempting to improve wages and working conditions by collective bargaining.* After 1904 the National Association of Manufacturers* mounted a sharp anti-union campaign which slowed membership growth of the A. F. of L. In 1908 the Supreme Court ruled, in the Danbury Hatters Case (*see* Loewe v. Lawlor), that labor boycotts violated the Sherman Antitrust Act. Similarly, many employers obtained court injunctions banning strikes on the grounds that they constituted an "unreasonable restraint of trade." The A. F. of L. also faced a challenge from the Industrial Workers of the World,* founded in 1905, which attempted to organize unskilled miners, lumbermen, and factory workers into one big union.

Middle-class progressives sympathized with working men and women who struggled to improve their wages, and working and living conditions, but they viewed labor unions as "special interest groups." Accordingly, many progressives supported labor causes through such organizations as the National Women's Trade Union League,* but their relations with the unions remained uneasy and often condescending. Faced with all these challenges, the A. F. of L. became more active politically, endorsing Democratic presidential candidates in 1908 and 1912. Woodrow Wilson* became the first president to pay serious attention to labor leaders. His administration created a cabinet-level Department of Labor* and passed the Clayton Act* of 1914, which exempted unions from the antitrust laws; the La Follette Seamen's Act* of 1915, which regulated working conditions for sailors; and the Adamson Act* of 1916, mandating the eight-hour day for railroad workers. Many of labor's legal gains were later nullified by the court, and union membership again declined in the 1920s. (John R. Commons, *History of Labour in the United States*; Henry Pelling, *American Labor* (1960); Philip Taft, *The A. F. of L. in the Time of Gompers* (1957); Melvyn Dubofsky, *We Shall Be All: A History of the Industrial Workers of the World* (1969); Marc Karson, *American Labor Unions and Politics, 1900–1918* (1958); William M.

Dick, *Labor and Socialism in America* (1972); Irwin Yellowitz, *Labor and the Progressive Movement in New York State, 1897–1916* (1965).)

Edward R. Kantowicz

LADIES' HOME JOURNAL, THE. By the 1890s, continuing immigration, urbanization, and industrialization built a national market. The advertising industry, therefore, began a major growth phase, and its chief vehicle was the mass general-interest magazine which it viewed as a product to be marketed. The *Ladies' Home Journal,* founded in 1883, was the successful pioneer in the mass magazine field and the first U.S. magazine with a million subscribers (fall 1903). The publisher, Cyrus Curtis, and the editor, Edward W. Bok,* used strategies that gauged the expectations of two sets of audiences, readers and advertisers. Middle-class readers, men and women, wanted to be informed, entertained, and given practical information and were receptive to suggestions for political and social reforms.

Throughout the Progressive Era, Curtis and Bok were pacesetters for mass journalism and periodical advertising. Their success set the standard for advertising copywriting, design, and art; they innovated in the new field of marketing research and reliability in the analysis of circulation data. The *Journal* offices performed functions that later were the province of advertising agencies, and its strong financial base enabled the magazine to take a measure of risk in reform activism, such as the pure food and drug agitation and the sex education campaigns. (Salme Harju Steinberg, *Reformer in the Marketplace: Edward W. Bok and ''The Ladies' Home Journal''* (1979); Frank Luther Mott, *A History of American Magazines* (1957, 1968); Edward William Bok, *Twice Thirty* (1925).)

Salme H. Steinberg

LA FOLLETTE, ROBERT MARION, SR. (June 14, 1855–June 18, 1925). The future Wisconsin governor, U.S. senator, and political leader, was born in Dane County, Wisconsin, and grew up there on a farm. He attended the University of Wisconsin (1875–1879), where he edited the campus paper and gained local fame when he won the Interstate Oratorical contest. He studied law and was admitted to the bar in 1880, the same year he won election as district attorney. In 1884 he entered Congress, serving three terms as a regular Republican. Defeated in 1890, he returned to Wisconsin* and entered state politics, an insurgent against the stalwart Republican establishment. In 1900, he was elected governor and at once pushed a reform program featuring direct primary elections,* corporate tax reform, a railroad commission, a tax commission, a civil service commission, and a conservation commission. He also promoted the growth of the university and made wide use of specialists from the campus on state boards and commissions.

Elected to the U.S. Senate in 1905, he soon became the leader of a group of progressive senators who prodded successive presidents toward a more liberal reform program. He advocated and was in part responsible for a revitalized

Interstate Commerce Commission, employers' liability* laws, federal income tax,* direct election of senators,* conservation measures, and the La Follette Seamen's Act.* In 1909 he established *La Follette's Magazine*,* which spread his views on important topics nationwide. In 1912 La Follette sought the Republican presidential nomination against incumbent William Howard Taft.* He failed to win the nomination, but contributed to the split in the Republican party* led by Theodore Roosevelt* and the election of Democrat Woodrow Wilson.*

During the Wilson administration he stood for strict neutrality, an arms embargo, and restrictions on foreign credit, and opposed the declaration of war in 1917. Wilson supporters denounced him as an isolationist and even a pro-German sympathizer. A Senate committee investigated his conduct, many friends turned against him, and the Wisconsin legislature denounced his actions. In general, he supported the war effort but favored a pay-as-you-go fiscal policy and an excess profits tax. At war's end he took a leading role in defeating the Versailles treaty which, he predicted, would soon lead to a second war. He also opposed the Esch-Cummins Transportation Act,* which returned the nation's railroads to private control. In 1924 La Follette ran for president on an Independent and Progressive ticket, polling nearly five million votes but carrying only Wisconsin. (Robert S. Maxwell, *La Follette and the Rise of the Progressives in Wisconsin* (1957); Robert S. Maxwell, ed., *La Follette* (1969); Belle Case and Fola La Follette, *Robert M. La Follette, 1855–1925*, 2 vols. (1953); David P. Thelen, *Robert M. La Follette and the Insurgent Spirit* (1976).)

                                                                 Robert S. Maxwell

LA FOLLETTE SEAMEN'S ACT. The La Follette Seamen's Act was passed during the ''New Freedom''* period of Woodrow Wilson's* administration to safeguard sailors' rights and upgrade maritime safety. Andrew Furuseth,* president of the International Seamen's Union, campaigned for years to secure for American sailors the same rights enjoyed as a matter of course by workers in other industries. In 1910 Furuseth found a powerful friend in Senator Robert M. La Follette* of Wisconsin, who agreed to sponsor Furuseth's bill in Congress and work for its passage. The *Titanic* disaster of 1912 on which, inquiry disclosed, there were only some sixteen lifeboats, caused a great public outcry and heightened concern for safety at sea. With the support of President Wilson and Secretary of Labor William B. Wilson,* the bill finally passed both houses and became law March 4, 1915. Over the years since its passage, the La Follette Seamen's Act has been less significant than its sponsors believed because of general flight of shipping from the American flag. (Belle Case and Fola La Follette, *Robert M. La Follette, 1855–1925*, 2 vols. (1953); Hyman Weintraub, *Andrew Furuseth: Emancipator of the Seamen* (1959); Silas Blake Axtell, comp., *A Symposium on Andrew Furuseth* (1949).)

                                                                 Robert S. Maxwell

LA FOLLETTE'S MAGAZINE. Founded in 1909 by Robert M. La Follette, Sr.,* as *La Follette's Weekly Magazine*, the journal was published as *La Follette's Magazine* from 1914 to 1929, when it adapted its present title, the *Progressive*.

From the beginning, the magazine was largely the personal expression of its publisher, who wrote many of its editorials, selected most of its articles, and contributed its "roll call" feature which detailed the votes of congressmen on critical issues. Many of his speeches were also reprinted in its pages. Reflecting La Follette's own self-image, the magazine proclaimed itself the tribune of the people against "special privilege," especially against the "giant industrial organization." Much of the original investment was provided by Charles R. Crane,* while advertising by small business in Wisconsin and Illinois helped keep the venture afloat. Even so, it was constantly in financial difficulty and was frequently saved by contributions from well-to-do supporters and by La Follette's speaking fees.

Beginning with a circulation of 3,000 in 1900, it peaked at 50,000 in 1912, the year La Follette made his first run for the presidency. Even so, the magnetism of La Follette's personality and reputation attracted contributions from most of the leading muckrakers* and from progressive political figures around the nation. The magazine suffered greatly from La Follette's opposition to World War I* but recovered during the 1920s and achieved the status of a liberal bible by the 1930s as the *Progressive*. (John A. Ziegler, "The Progressive's Views on Foreign Affairs, 1909–1941: A Case Study of Liberal Economic Isolationism" (Ph.D. diss., Syracuse University, 1970); William A. Hesseltine, "Forty Years the Country's Conscience," *Progressive* 13 (December 1949): 7–10; Russel Blaine Nye, "Fifty Years," *Progressive* 230 (January 1959): 7–11.)

John D. Buenker

LANDIS, KENESAW MOUNTAIN (November 20, 1866–November 25, 1944). Born in Milville, Ohio, Landis was named after the Civil War battle in which his doctor father was wounded. A semipro baseball player, newspaperman, and court stenographer, after graduating from Chicago's Union College School of Law in 1891, he served as secretary to President Grover Cleveland's secretary of state. Afterward, as a Republican lawyer in Chicago, he was appointed judge of the Northern Illinois Federal District by Theodore Roosevelt* in 1905. In 1907, in a typically dramatic move, he fined Standard Oil of Indiana $29,240,000 for railroad rebating, but as often happened, he was reversed on appeal. During World War I* he presided over Industrial Workers of the World* and socialist sedition trials with a much applauded prosecutorial zeal. His resulting reputation for hard-fisted probity appealed to the baseball club owners after the scandal over the "fixing" of the 1919 World Series. They offered him autocratic power as baseball commissioner, which he accepted, later resigning his federal judgeship in 1922 under pressure over his dual responsibilities. For twenty-four years he ruled players and owners with a dictatorial hand, particularly concerned with protecting baseball from gambling ties. (J. G. Taylor Spink, *Judge Landis and*

Twenty Years of Baseball (1947); David Q. Voigt, *American Baseball: From the Commissioners to Continental Expansion* (1970); *Current Biography* (1944).)

David Chalmers

LANE, FRANKLIN K. (July 15, 1864–May 18, 1921). Born on Prince Edward Island, Canada, Lane grew up in the San Francisco Bay area. After working as a reporter for several years, he studied at the University of California in Berkeley and at the Hastings Law School and was admitted to the bar in 1888. For the next several years, Lane pursued a journalistic career, including almost four years as owner and editor of the *Tacoma Daily News*. In 1898, while practicing law in San Francisco, Lane won the first of three elections as city attorney.

Four years later, running as a "TR Democrat," he lost a close race for governor but won national attention. Roosevelt appointed Lane to the Interstate Commerce Commission in 1906 where he served with distinction until 1913, when Woodrow Wilson* named him secretary of the interior. Lane, who favored development of natural resources under federal control, helped to channel the conservation movement into legislation: the Alaskan Coal-Leasing Act (1914), the National Park Service Act (1916), and the General Leasing Act (1920). He was an early and ardent supporter of U.S. participation in World War I* and in the League of Nations.* (Anne Wintermute Lane and Louise Herrick Wall, eds., *The Letters of Franklin K. Lane* (1922); Leonard J. Bates, *The Origins of Teapot Dome: Progressives, Parties, and Petroleum, 1909–1921* (1963); Keith W. Olson, *Biography of a Progressive: Franklin K. Lane, 1864–1921* (1979).)

Keith W. Olson

LANSING, ROBERT (October 17, 1864–October 30, 1928). Born in Watertown, New York, Lansing graduated from Amherst College and then read law in his father's office. In 1889, he was admitted to the bar and became his father's junior partner. Between 1892 and 1914, Lansing frequently served as agent or counsel of the United States before international arbitration tribunals. Lansing also helped to establish the American Society of International Law (1906) and the *American Journal of International Law* (1907), for which he served as an editor until his death.

In April 1914, he became counselor for the Department of State, and when William Jennings Bryan* resigned in June 1915, President Woodrow Wilson* named Lansing secretary of state. He agreed with the president's neutrality and subsequent World War I* policies, but served in the shadow of Wilson and his closest adviser, Colonel Edward M. House.* At the Paris peace conference, Lansing's legalistic approach clashed with Wilson's idealistic attitude, and he lost the president's confidence. In February 1920, Wilson demanded Lansing's resignation, ostensibly because he had called cabinet meetings during Wilson's illness. Lansing wrote three books about his secretaryship and practiced international law in Washington until his death. (Julius W. Pratt, "Robert Lansing, Secretary of State," in S. F. Bemis, ed., *American Secretaries of State and*

Their Diplomacy (1929); Robert Lansing, *The War Memoirs of Robert Lansing* (1935); Daniel Smith, *Robert Lansing and American Neutrality* (1958).)

Keith W. Olson

LATHROP, JULIA CLIFFORD (June 29, 1858–April 15, 1932). A lawyer's daughter, Lathrop was born in Rockford, Illinois. She attended Rockford Seminary, where her mother had been valedictorian of the first graduating class, and Vassar College, which she later served as trustee. Strong family ties, laced with Lincoln republicanism, suffragism, and sensitivity to human rights, prepared her for Hull House* in the 1890s. She helped launch Jane Addams's* first book, bringing the "pure milk of the word" to the public. Lathrop and Florence Kelley* then conducted one of the first urban social surveys, *Hull House Maps and Papers.*

Lathrop became an expert in the care and treatment of the mentally ill as Governor John Peter Altgeld's* appointee to the Illinois State Board of Charities. Her investigations in the field and abroad, and her use of the National Conference of Charities and Corrections* and the *Journal of the American Medical Association* as forums, established her national reputation. In Chicago, she worked to create the first juvenile court,* establish a diagnostic clinic, secure mothers' pensions* administered through the court, and launch a school of social work.

After a world trip, her report on the Philippine school system, her administrative abilities, and Attorney General George W. Wickersham's* scrutiny of her lack of radical taint led to President William Howard Taft's* appointing her to head the U.S. Children's Bureau. Lathrop's decade as chief is marked by empirical investigations, preventive health campaigns, and the passage of the Sheppard-Towner Act* of 1921. Noted for her political acuity, subtle wit, and modesty, Lathrop was later named counselor to the national League of Women Voters* and child welfare assessor for the League of Nations.* She died in the midst of a campaign to promote her successor, Grace Abbott,* to the cabinet to protect the health and welfare mission of the Children's Bureau. (Jane Addams, *My Friend, Julia Lathrop* (1935); Edward T. James, et al., *Notable American Women*, vol. 2 (1971); Walter Trattner, ed., *Biographical Dictionary of Social Welfare in America* (1986); Jacqueline K. Parker and Edward M. Carpenter, "Julia Lathrop and the Children's Bureau: The Emergence of an Institution," *Social Service Review* 55 (March 1981): 60–77.)

Jacqueline K. Parker

LAUCK, W(ILLIAM) JETT (August 2, 1879–June 14, 1949). Born in Keyser, West Virginia, Lauck received an A.B. degree from Washington and Lee University in 1903 and studied economics at the University of Chicago* (1903–1906) before becoming associate professor of economics and political science at Washington and Lee (1905–1908). In 1908, he married Eleanor Moore Dunlap, with whom he later had three children, and began a long Washington–based career. He was director of industrial investigation for the U.S. Immigration

Commission* (1907–1910); chief examiner of the U.S. Tariff Board (1910–1911); secretary of the Southeastern States of the National Citizens League for the Promotion of a Sound Banking System (1911–1912); managing expert and statistician for the U.S. Commission on Industrial Relations (1913–1915); and secretary of the national War Labor Board* (1918–1919).

He regularly represented labor in arbitrations and served on special commissions. Lauck supported federal action to secure "industrial democracy"* and a living wage for the American worker. After World War I,* he became the economic adviser of John L. Lewis and Democratic politicians, and helped to draft the National Industrial Recovery Act. He wrote numerous articles and government reports, six books, and volumes 4–18 of the report of the U.S. Immigration Commission, in which he advocated restriction. (Graham Adams, Jr., *Age of Industrial Violence, 1910–1915: The Activities and Findings of the United States Commission on Industrial Relations* (1966); Valerie Jean Conner, *The National War Labor Board: Stability, Social Justice, and the Voluntary State in World I* (1983); Carmen Brissette Grayson, "W. Jett Lauck: Biography of a Reformer" (Ph.D. diss., University of Virginia, 1975).)

Valerie Jean Conner

LAWRENCE TEXTILE STRIKE. On January 11, 1912, the textile mill owners in Lawrence, Massachusetts, announced drastic pay cuts and the workers walked out, shouting: "Better to starve fighting them than to starve working." In a town where three-quarters of the populace depended on the mills for a living, this was tantamount to a general strike. Joseph Ettor and William "Big Bill" Haywood,* organizers for the Industrial Workers of the World* (IWW), arrived in Lawrence to support the strikers. They also staged sympathy strikes in other cities; and on February 17, they hit upon an effective propaganda device, the evacuation of hungry strikers' children to foster homes in other cities. The obstinacy of the mill owners, the solidarity of the strikers, and the evident misery of the evacuated children turned public opinion against the employers, who capitulated on March 1 and offered a wage increase. The Lawrence strike marked the first victory for the IWW among immigrant workers in an eastern city, as this radical union had previously worked among American-born miners and lumbermen in the West. Though the events at Lawrence took on epic proportions in the legends of American labor, the victory proved short-lived, and the IWW did not strike deep roots in the East. (Donald B. Cole, *Immigrant City: Lawrence, Massachusetts* (1963); C. P. Neill, *Report on the Strike of Textile Workers in Lawrence, Massachusetts, 1912*, 62nd Cong., 2d sess., Senate Document 870 (1913); Patrick Renshaw, *The Wobblies* (1967).)

Edward R. Kantowicz

LAWSON, THOMAS W. (February 26, 1857–February 8, 1925). Born in Charleston, Massachusetts, and self-educated, Lawson started work early, first in a bank and then a broker's office, opened his own firm and made a large fortune, mainly through bearish manipulations on the stock exchange and by advertising for small investors. He served as president of Bay State Gas of Delaware and of various other gas and copper companies. In 1898, he managed Standard Oil's floating of the Amalgamated Copper Company in an operation that was very costly to public subscribers and profitable to the insiders. For reasons not known, he fell out with Standard Oil and "told all" in "Frenzied Finance" for *Everbody's Magazine** (1905–1906), one of the sensations of the muckrake era. His revelations of the use of money from the big life insurance companies, New York Life, Equitable, and Mutual Life, by the Standard Oil and J. P. Morgan* interests, led to New York State's Armstrong Investigations, which established the public reputation of Charles Evans Hughes.* Lawson promised but did not offer a solution to Wall Street manipulations and engaged in an unsuccessful pool while he wrote his denunciations. Eventually he lost his fortune and died in Boston, Massachusetts. (David M. Chalmers, *The Social and Political Ideas of the Muckrakers* (1964).)

David Chalmers

LAWSON, VICTOR FREMONT (September 9, 1850–August 19, 1925). Lawson was born in Chicago, and when ill-health delayed his entrance into college, he took up the management of his family's investments, including the Norwegian-language newspaper *Skandinaven*. He embarked on a career as a newspaper publisher in 1876, acquiring the fledgling *Chicago Daily News*, which he built into an influential and financially successful journal. Lawson published other papers for a time and, in 1894, helped found the Associated Press news service. Starting in 1898, he pioneered in establishing an extensive network of American news correspondents overseas.

Lawson was a deeply religious man who was involved in numerous church-related charities; the Chicago Theological Seminary and the YMCA* were two of the more notable recipients of his philanthropy. His social welfare–related work included sponsoring free adult education lectures in the public schools and the opening of a "fresh air sanitarium" for poor city children. Perhaps his most important accomplishment was spearheading the drive that led to the creation of the federal postal savings bank system* in 1910. In public affairs, Lawson was a political independent and clean government activist. He was an organizer of the Municipal Voters' League in 1896, served on various commissions, and championed the cause of civic reform. (Charles H. Dennis, *Victor Lawson: His Time and His Work* (1935); Robert Lloyd Tree, "Victor Fremont Lawson and His Newspapers, 1890–1900" (Ph.D. diss., Northwestern University, 1959).)

John R. Schmidt

LEAGUE OF NATIONS, THE. The idea was discussed many times before 1918 when it was made part of the Fourteen Points, a proposal offered by President Woodrow Wilson* as the basis for ending World War I.* Several progressives endorsed the idea, and some were part of the delegation which went to Paris to provide assistance to the American peace commissioners. Some saw the idea as an extension of the progressive idea into international politics. The Treaty of Versailles, with the league attached, was signed in the spring of 1919 and presented to the U.S. Senate by President Wilson shortly after.

Among the irreconcilables, the group of some fourteen Republican senators who opposed the treaty in any form were such leaders of the reform movement as Robert M. La Follette,* George Norris,* and Asle J. Gronna. Their opposition was based largely on the isolationist sentiments which had also predicated their vote against American entry into World War I. Other progressive opponents included William Borah* and Hiram Johnson.* Other progressives within the Republican party,* such as William Kenyon, Albert Cummins* and Irvine Lenroot,* supported the treaty with reservations. Within the Democratic party,* such progressives as Thomas Walsh, Henry Ashurst, Gilbert Hitchcock,* James Phelan,* Atlee Pomerene,* Robert Owen,* and Morris Sheppard* supported the treaty, although two of the document's most vocal critics were progressive Democrats James Reed* and Thomas Gore.* The Senate rejected the treaty twice, in November of 1919 and in March of 1920, and the American people followed suit in 1920 when ratification was one of the main points in the Democratic platform and in the campaign of James Cox* and Franklin Roosevelt.* (Thomas A. Bailey, *Wilson and the Peacemakers* (1947); Dennis F. Fleming, *The United States and the League of Nations, 1918–1920* (1968); Ralph A. Stone, *Wilson and the League of Nations* (1967).)

Thomas W. Ryley

LEAGUE OF WOMEN VOTERS. Founded as an independent organization in 1920, the League of Women Voters was originally formed as an auxiliary to the National American Woman Suffrage Association* at its 1919 national convention. Its stated goals were threefold; to expand voter education, to increase the electoral participation of women, and to support social welfare legislation. Maud Wood Park* led the organization in its early years and, in November 1920, was instrumental in forming the Women's Joint Congressional Committee (WJCC), an informational clearinghouse to coordinate legislative activity with other women's organizations. Originally viewed with hostility by political party leadership and opponents of woman suffrage, the league soon established respectable credentials, due in part to its nonpartisan stance. Red-baited in the 1920s, the league emphasized the need for extensive study prior to taking a position on controversial issues. Throughout the 1920s the league supported numerous reforms, including citizenship, social hygiene, child welfare, education reforms, women's legal status, and protection of women in industry. (J. Stanley Lemons, *The Woman Citizen: Social Feminism in the 1920s* (1973); Ida Husted

Harper, *History of Woman Suffrage*, vol. 5 (1922): Sara B. Brumbaugh, *Democratic Experience and Education in the National League of Women Voters* (1946).)

Marie Laberge

LEGISLATIVE REFERENCE LIBRARY. The origins of legislative reference lie in the efforts of Melvil Dewey,* then director of the State Library of New York, to inform lawmakers on major pieces of legislation both within and without the state. The real father of the movement, however, was Charles R. McCarthy,* who in 1901 was placed in charge of a small collection of legislative reference works held by the Wisconsin Free Library Commission and, within a decade, built it into a service that became a nationwide model. By 1911, he had assembled a staff of a dozen people operating on a $10,000 budget who provided lawmakers with statutes from other states and with all available information relating to the substance of contemplated legislation. In addition, they drafted thousands of bills per session.

McCarthy's announced goal was to apply "the scientific method to legislation" and to make Wisconsin* the "one state whose written law will be to some degree better than that of other states." He provided officials in other states with data on Wisconsin, aided other states in founding similar services, and provided them with staff whom he had conscientiously trained. McCarthy also served as a consultant to the Library of Congress when it contemplated the development of a similar institution. Although he saw himself as an apolitical, nonpartisan technician and a disinterested public servant, opponents charged McCarthy with running a "progressive bill factory" during the 1914 election. Riding out the storm, he eventually gained the confidence and respect of lawmakers of all political persuasions. By the end of the decade, at least twenty-seven states had adopted some form of legislative reference system based roughly on the Wisconsin model. (Charles R. McCarthy, *The Wisconsin Idea* (1912); Marion Casey, *Charles McCarthy: Librarianship and Reform* (1981).)

John D. Buenker

LENROOT, IRVINE L. (January 31, 1869–January 26, 1949). Born in Superior, Wisconsin, of Swedish immigrant parents, Lenroot attended a business college and read law. While acting as a stenographer, Lenroot entered politics as a progressive Republican. He served in the Wisconsin Assembly from 1901 to 1906, and as speaker from 1903 to 1906. Working with Governor Robert M. La Follette,* he helped secure the primary election law* and railroad tax and regulatory laws. In 1908 Lenroot was elected to the House of Representatives, where he served until 1918. An "insurgent,"* he helped win reform of the House rules in 1910. Later, he exerted strong influence respecting railroad and conservation legislation. After Lenroot voted for war in 1917, he broke with La Follette and in 1918 he won a special senatorial election as head of an anti–La

Follette, pro-war coalition of progressives and conservatives. In 1920, Lenroot was almost nominated for vice president; he won reelection to the Senate. There, he worked effectively with Secretary of Commerce Herbert Hoover* for a moderate progressive program of tariff and farm legislation. (Herbert F. Margulies, *Senator Lenroot of Wisconsin: A Political Biography, 1890–1929* (1977).)

                                                              Herbert F. Margulies

LIBERTY LOANS were government bonds issued to finance World War I.* Treasury Secretary William Gibbs McAdoo* proposed to pay for half of American participation in the war by increased taxation and half by borrowing, but he ended up relying more heavily on borrowing. The first Liberty Loan, as McAdoo titled it, passed Congress a few weeks after the declaration of war in April 1917. It provided for thirty year bonds totaling $2 billion and bearing an interest rate of 3.5 percent, slightly below the market rate. Three additional Liberty Loans were authorized during the war, at higher interest rates than the first, and a final bond issue, called a Victory Loan, was promoted after the war ended. McAdoo turned the marketing of government war bonds into a popular crusade, recruiting businessmen, church leaders, and even Boy Scouts* to sell bonds. "We went direct to the people," he wrote. "We capitalized the profound impulse called patriotism." This strategy succeeded, for all five loans were oversubscribed; but it also increased the propaganda and hysteria of wartime. (David M. Kennedy, *Over Here: The First World War and American Society* (1980); William G. McAdoo, *Crowded Years* (1931).)

                                                              Edward R. Kantowicz

LINCOLN-ROOSEVELT REPUBLICAN LEAGUE. The Lincoln-Roosevelt Republican League, created in 1907, provided the framework out of which the Progressive movement in California emerged. Sparked by Edward Dickson of the Los Angeles *Express* and Chester Rowell of the Fresno *Republican*, it drew its inspiration both from the experience of Los Angeles reformers in their municipal battles and from the success of Theodore Roosevelt* in demonstrating the possibilities of national reform. Attentive to national issues and active in local politics, it focused its energies on the possibilities of reform at the state level. Fundamental to that effort was the need to eliminate a political system dependent on boss rule and tied to the Southern Pacific Railroad and other large corporate interests.

Central to the success of the league was the active support provided by many of the state's major newspapers. In 1908–1909, the league, perfecting its organization at the local level and creating a "People's Lobby" in Sacramento financed by Dr. John R. Haynes, Edwin Earl, and Rudolph Spreckels* to publicize legislative proceedings, successfully pressured the legislature to adopt a direct primary.* In 1910, the league militantly entered the election campaign with a full slate of candidates, recruiting Hiram Johnson* as its choice for governor. Successful in the primary contest and the general election, Johnson and the new legislature moved swiftly to enact a series of reforms which included legislation undermining the old political order, securing regulation of railroads and public utilities, and extending protection to labor. (Joseph Gregg Layne, "The Lincoln-Roosevelt League; Its Origins and Accomplishments," *Historical Society of Southern California Quarterly* 25, no. 3 (September 1943): 156–171; George Mowry, *The California Progressives* (1951); Spencer C. Olin, Jr., *California's Prodigal Sons: Hiram Johnson and the Progressives, 1911–1917* (1968).)

Richard C. Lower

LINDBERGH, CHARLES A., SR. (January 20, 1859–May 24, 1924). Born in Stockholm, Sweden, Charles August (not Augustus, as often incorrectly cited) was the son of August Lindbergh Ola Monsson, a member of the Swedish parliament who emigrated to America in 1859. Lindbergh grew up on the Minnesota frontier and graduated from the University of Michigan Law School in 1883. A successful Little Falls, Minnesota, lawyer and businessman, he was the father of Charles Augustus, the aviator. C. A. Lindbergh, a foe of the "profiteers," served as a strong progressive Republican in the U.S. House of Representatives from 1907 to 1917, supporting banking and currency reform, the insurgent revolt, opposition to the European war, woman suffrage,* and the preservation of natural resources. Lindbergh ran unsuccessfully in the 1916 Republican primary for the U.S. Senate, the bitter 1918 Minnesota Republican gubernatorial primary with Nonpartisan League* endorsement, and the 1923 Farmer-Labor primary for the U.S. Senate. Stubbornly independent, he authored *Banking and Currency and the Money Trust* (1913), *Why Is Your Country at War?* (1917), and *The Economic Pinch* (1923). (Bruce L. Larson, *Lindbergh of Minnesota: A Political Biography* (1973); Richard B. Lucas, *Charles August Lindbergh, Sr.: A Case Study of Congressional Insurgency, 1906–1912* (1974); Lynn Haines and Dora B. Haines, *The Lindberghs* (1931).)

Bruce L. Larson

LINDSEY, BENJAMIN BARR (November 25, 1869–March 26, 1943). Nicknamed the "Kid's Judge," Lindsey was a crusader and reformer. Using imagination, grandstanding, and hard work, Judge Lindsey turned a county court in Colorado into a juvenile court* and a superior court in California into a divorce court. Born in Tennessee, he moved to Denver at sixteen, and passed the Colorado bar at twenty-five. In 1901 he launched a campaign to establish a juvenile court—a court where young male offenders became wards of the court and were thereby treated separately from hardened adult criminals. These juveniles could be placed on probationary status and given a chance for rehabilitation. Lindsey was clearly a "Boy's Judge"; he felt that girls—only 5 percent of the delinquents—were not good subjects for his rehabilitation program. One of the first in the country, Lindsey's Denver court became the preferred model. Even a Japanese delegation visited Denver to duplicate it—down to the actual dimensions and furnishings of the courtroom.

Lindsey served as judge of Denver's juvenile court from 1901 until 1927, when he was defeated for reelection, in large part because of his liberal views on companionate marriage. Lindsey's major contribution to the law was the Colorado Adult Delinquency Act of 1903, which made adults responsible for contributing to juvenile delinquency. Lindsey argued that Americans should practice birth control until their marriages were on a solid footing and that marriages which failed could be dissolved by mutual consent unless there were children involved. Lindsey wrote many books and articles including an autobiography, *The Problems of Children* (1903); *The Beast and the Jungle*, with Harvey O'Higgins (1910); and *The Companionate Marriage*, with Wainwright Evans (1927). (Charles Larsen, *The Good Fight: The Life and Times of Ben B. Lindsey* (1972).)

D'Ann Campbell

LIPPMANN, WALTER (September 23, 1889–December 14, 1974). Lippmann was born into a comfortable New York City, German-Jewish family, received an excellent education, and revealed at an early age two of his most notable lifelong characteristics: a lucid intelligence and a remarkable ability to express himself in writing. After a stunning career at Harvard (1906–1910), an apprenticeship in muckrake journalism, and a brief term as secretary to the socialist mayor of Schenectady, he was convinced that his talents lay in political analysis, speculation, and writing rather than in active affairs. He quickly published two important books—*A Preface to Politics* (1913) and *Drift and Mastery* (1914)— and when he was twenty-six, Theodore Roosevelt* was ready to describe him as "on the whole the most brilliant young man of his age in all the United States."

Except for government service during World War I* (in the War Department and then as an aide to Colonel Edward House*), Lippmann devoted himself to writing books, essays, editorials, and columns. He was with the *New Republic** (1917–1921), the New York *World* (1921–1931), the New York *Herald Tribune* (1931–1961), and the Washington *Post* (until 1967). He wrote more than two dozen books, some of them widely acclaimed; and his famous column, "Today and Tomorrow," was syndicated to 250 papers around the world. Regarded everywhere as the dean of American commentators on public affairs, he wielded an enormous influence for half a century. Lippmann died in New York City. (Ronald Steel, *Walter Lippmann and the American Century* (1980).)

David W. Levy

LLOYD, HENRY DEMAREST (May 1, 1847–September 28, 1903). The "millionaire radical," as he was known, was born in New York City and educated at Columbia College and Columbia Law School. Lloyd was admitted to the New York bar in 1869 and was soon known as an advocate of free trade and civil service reform.* In 1872, Lloyd joined the Chicago *Tribune*, becoming financial and chief editorial writer from 1875 to 1885. Too radical for the *Tribune*, he resigned in 1885 to devote himself full-time to reform.

Lloyd was an early muckraker, exposing the abuses of monopolistic power in the oil industry in "The Story of a Great Monopoly" (1881) and in his best known book, *Wealth against Commonwealth* (1894). Author of ten books, Lloyd advocated the public ownership of monopolies, including municipal utilities, the compulsory arbitration of labor disputes and labor copartnership, the Populist* platforms of the mid-nineties, and other measures which anticipated the welfare state of the twentieth century. As an activist, he defended the Haymarket anarchists in 1886, striking coal miners in Illinois in 1889, Milwaukee streetcar workers in 1893, and the anthracite coal miners in 1902. As a proponent of farmer-worker political unity, Lloyd ran unsuccessfully for Congress as a Populist in 1894 and supported Debsian socialism. (Charles M. Destler, *Henry Demarest Lloyd and the Empire of Reform* (1963); Jay E. Jernigan, *Henry Demarest Lloyd* (1976); Lloyd Caro, *Henry Demarest Lloyd, 1847–1903*, 2 vols. (1912).)

Peter J. Frederick

LOCHNER V. NEW YORK (198 U.S. 45) (1905). The underlying issue of *Lochner* was the degree to which a state could restrict the rights of property or freedom of contract and not violate the due process clause of the Fourteenth Amendment. A new statute limited labor in bakeries to ten hours a day and sixty hours a week. New York charged Joseph Lochner with requiring and permitting an employee to work more than sixty hours. Lochner was found guilty and appealed to the U.S. Supreme Court, arguing that the New York law violated freedom of contract and due process under the Fourteenth Amendment. Justice Rufus W. Peckham, speaking for the majority in a 5–4 decision, found for Lochner, arguing that the New York statute violated freedom of contract and due process under the Fourteenth Amendment.

The most effective attack on the majority decision was the dissent of Justice Oliver Wendell Holmes,* who charged the majority with basing its decision on social doctrine and declared, "The 14th Amendment does not enact Mr. Herbert Spencer's *Social Statics*," the latter refering to Spencer's social Darwinist* ideas of the survival of the fittest. Holmes further argued that the "constitution is not intended to embody a particular economic theory," including *laissez-faire*." (Felix Frankfurter, "Hours of Labor and Realism in Constitutional Law," *Harvard Law Review* 29 (February 1916): 35–73; Frank R. Strong, "The Economic Philosophy of Lochner: Emergence, Embrasure and Emasculation," *Arizona Law Review* 15 (1973): 419–55.)

John R. Aiken

LODGE, HENRY CABOT (May 12, 1850–November 9, 1924). Born in Boston, Massachusetts, of a prominent Boston family, Lodge attended Harvard, briefly taught American history, and published volumes of history, essays, and speeches throughout his life. He served in the U.S. House of Representatives from 1887 to 1893 and then in the Senate until his death in Cambridge. A conservative Republican, Lodge opposed free silver, direct election of senators,* woman suffrage,* and Prohibition;* he favored civil service reform,* federal protection of southern black voting rights, and the Sherman Antitrust and Pure Food and Drug Laws.* Lodge was a nationalist who feared compulsory international arbitration but advocated a protectionist tariff, immigration restriction,* a strong navy, annexation of Hawaii, the Spanish-American War,* annexation of the Philippines, and building of the Panama Canal.* A party loyalist, Lodge backed William Howard Taft* in 1912 and disliked most of Woodrow Wilson's* program. When war began in Europe, Lodge urged American preparedness* and proposed early entry into the war. Chairman of the Foreign Relations Committee, Lodge's "reservations" led to Senate defeat of the Versailles treaty. Lodge contributed to Warren G. Harding's* nomination and election and was a delegate to the Washington Disarmament Conference, but opposed American membership in the World Court. (Henry Cabot Lodge, ed., *Selections from the Correspondence of Theodore Roosevelt and Henry Cabot Lodge*, 2 vols. (1925); Henry Cabot Lodge, *The Senate and the League of Nations* (1925); John A. Garraty, *Henry Cabot Lodge: A Biography* (1953).)

Martin I. Elzy

LOEWE V. LAWLOR (208 U.S. 274 (1908). This case, better known as Danbury Hatters, was one of the critical judicial attacks on the use of the secondary boycott by labor unions. The Supreme Court ruled, for the first time, that labor unions which conducted boycotts were subject to the provisions of the Sherman Antitrust Act as combinations in restraint of trade and were liable for triple damages. The dispute originated between the D. E. Loewe Company of Danbury, Connecticut, and the Brotherhood of United Hatters. The union, as part of a national campaign, sought to win the closed shop against Loewe in July of 1902. Two hundred and fifty members walked out, and the union instituted a boycott of Loewe hats by attempting to influence the company's major customers not to deal with Loewe during the course of the dispute. During the previous five years the hatters had used the boycott effectively to unionize most of the industry. After a lower court found the union guilty and subject to damages of $232,240, the decision was overturned in 1911 by the Circuit Court of Appeals of the second district. A retrial beginning in 1912 led eventually to a Supreme Court decision in 1916 upholding the company and assessing damages against the union and its members of $252,000. The savings of individual members of the union were attached, and many were threatened with the loss of their homes. Only a nationwide campaign by the American Federation of Labor* and the Hatters Union prevented financial calamity for the Danbury hatters. This case, together with the Buck's Stove and Range Case,* effectively limited the use of one of labor's most effective weapons, the secondary boycott. (Harry W. Laidler, *Boycotts and the Labor Struggle, Economic and Legal Aspects* (1913); Charles

O. Gregory, *Labor and the Law* (1949); Leo Wolman, *The Boycott in American Trade Unions* (1916).)

Shelton Stromquist

LOMASNEY, MARTIN MICHAEL (December 3, 1859–August 12, 1933). A lifelong resident of Boston, the son of Irish immigrants, Lomasney was famous as the Mahatma of Ward 8, perhaps the most famous ward boss in the nation. For over forty years, he held court in the Hendricks Club, endorsing and slating candidates and dispensing such political wisdom as "the politican who thinks he can get away from the people who made him usually gets what's coming to him—a swift kick in his political pants." He and fellow Democratic ward bosses John F. Fitzgerald,* Patrick Kennedy, and James Michael Curley* jockeyed for political advantage, forming tenuous alliances for each election, although Lomasney and Curley generally remained bitter enemies.

Serving as an alderman and a state senator in the 1890s, Lomasney was elected to the lower house of the legislature on fourteen separate occasions between 1899 and 1929. As a legislator, he generally supported labor, welfare, and regulatory measures and those which increased urban political power. During the constitutional convention of 1917, he was hailed by its official historian as "conspicuously the most intense personal force in the convention." His support was vital to the elections and the legislative programs of Democratic governors Eugene Foss, David I. Walsh,* and Joseph B. Ely. (Leslie G. Ainley, *Boston Mahatma* (1949); John D. Buenker, "The Mahatma and Progressive Reform: Martin Lomasney as Lawmaker, 1911–1917," *New England Quarterly* 44 (1971): 397–419.)

John D. Buenker

LONDON, JACK (January 12, 1876–November 22, 1916). Realistic novelist and socialist born in San Francisco,* Jack London grew up in poverty on the Oakland waterfront. After attending public school and working odd jobs, he signed up as a sailor on a sealing vessel in 1893, then afterwards tramped across the United States as a hobo. During his wanderings, he read voraciously, became a socialist, then returned to California* and attempted to cram a college education into one year. He joined the Klondike gold rush in 1897, and the following year he began to write fictionalized accounts of his experiences. His first collection of stories was published in 1900, and in 1903 he wrote the novel *The Call of the Wild* which made him famous. He wrote over fifty books in all, including twelve about the Far North. He continued to travel widely, but after 1910 he devoted most of his time to his ranch in California. Like most naturalistic* writers, he stressed the dominance of brute force in nature; and his writings usually elaborated the theme of primitivism, a return to nature or savagery. Though his vision was dark and pessimistic, the vivid realism of his action adventure stories made him a writer of continuing popularity. (Franklin Walker, *Jack London and the Klondike* (1966); Andrew Sinclair, *Jack: A Biography of*

Jack London (1977); Charles N. Watson, *The Novels of Jack London: A Reappraisal* (1983).)

Edward R. Kantowicz

LONDON, MEYER (December 28, 1871–June 6, 1926). Born in the Russian-Polish province of Suwalki, Meyer came to the United States in 1891. He graduated from New York University Law School in 1898 and was admitted to the bar that same year. One of the founders of the Socialist party of America,* in 1914 he became the first Socialist elected to Congress from New York City. Reelected in 1916 and 1920, London attracted nationwide attention for his efforts in support of social reform and for his opposition to World War I.* During his three terms in Congress, he worked for the abolition of child labor, for old age pensions, unemployment insurance, and prohibition of injunctions in labor disputes, and he opposed the property qualification for voting in Puerto Rico, intervention in Mexico, restriction of immigration,* and the Fordney Tariff. Outspoken in urging neutrality in the war, London voted against the conscription and espionage* laws following America's entry. He was also active in the trade union field, representing striking workers in the "needle trades" in numerous injunction suits brought by employers, helping to found the International Ladies' Garment Workers Union,* and serving as general counsel for the Workmen's Circle. (Harry Rogoff, *An East Side Epic: The Life and Work of Meyer London* (1930).)

Frederick C. Giffin

LORIMER, WILLIAM (April 27, 1861–September 3, 1933). Born in Manchester, England, Lorimer emigrated with his family to the United States in 1865 and then moved to the West Side of Chicago* in 1870. Lorimer first became involved in politics in 1884 as a Republican and henceforth politics became his full-time occupation. He was primarily a "political entrepreneur" who regarded politics as a business and used his power for personal as well as party gain. By the early 1890s, Lorimer had become a powerful political force in the Illinois Republican Party. From 1894 to 1900, and then from 1902 to 1909, he also represented the Illinois Second District in Congress where he was best known for his devotion to local Chicago interests.

In 1909, a coalition of fifty-five Republicans and fifty-three Democrats in the Illinois General Assembly elected Lorimer to the U.S. Senate. In 1910, however, a Democratic state legislator confessed to having been bribed for his vote. A Senate subcommittee investigated the bribery charge and concluded that Lorimer's election was not corrupt, and the Senate voted to retain him in his seat. In 1912, however, after a second investigation, a Senate dominated by newly elected Republican and Democratic progressives voted 55 to 28 to oust him from the chamber. The removal of Lorimer undoubtedly played a role in the ratification in 1913 of the Seventeenth Amendment to the Constitution providing for the direct election of U.S. Senators.* After his expulsion from the Senate, Lorimer spent the rest of his life in politics and in business, but he never regained his former power. (Joel A. Tarr, *A Study in Boss Politics: William Lorimer of Chicago* (1971).)

Joel Tarr

LOS ANGELES. The population of Los Angeles, which had doubled in the 1890s, tripled in the first decade of the twentieth century as migrants, largely Protestant, middle-class, native-born, and midwestern, flooded into the multiplying suburbs and subdivisions of the city. Their backgrounds shaped and limited the reform movement that emerged. Reformist energies centered on the control exercised by utility interests, public works contractors, municipal employees, liquor dealers, and the Southern Pacific Railroad in determining city politics. In the mid-1890s Dr. John Randolph Haynes formed the Direct Legislation League, calling for the introduction of the initiative,* referendum,* and recall,* and in 1902 Los Angeles became the first city in the nation to adopt these measures. The city made history again in 1904 when a councilman was successfully recalled. A civil service commission and charter amendments shifting power from the council to mayor, adopted in 1902, together with changes in 1909 requiring citywide nonpartisan elections* and a direct primary* further contributed to the breakup of the older political order.

Throughout this period, reformers, often younger members of business and professional groups, sought not only structural reform* but political control of the city. In 1908, the threat of recall forced Mayor Arthur Harper to resign, and George Alexander, a septuagenarian member of the county board of supervisors, secured election. Alexander, the reformers' choice, promising an "honest business government," continued the already established programs for municipal development of the San Pedro port and the Owens Valley aqueduct, and for municipal ownership of electric and other utilities. Supporting the efforts of the city's business community to prevent the development of union labor, the progressive city council gave unanimous endorsement to a stringent antipicketing ordinance in July 1910. Class violence exploded that year—symbolized by the bombing of the Los Angeles *Times* building in October—and the reelection of Alexander seemed in doubt as Job Harriman, a socialist, faced Alexander in the 1911 mayoralty contest. Threatened from the left, progressives retreated to the right, drawing support from their longtime enemy, Harrison Gray Otis* of the *Times*, and placing direction of their campaign in the hands of their onetime enemies.

Reelected, Alexander continued to stress economy, efficiency, and morality, largely ignoring those who called for more socially oriented programs to respond to the problems of the underprivileged. Unable to broaden their support among the lower classes and the less affluent or to ease the suspicions of the city's prominent business leaders, the progressive movement floundered. In 1913, Harry Rose, the candidate of the conservatives, with support from many who had once supported Job Harriman, won election as mayor. (Robert M. Fogelson,

The Fragmented Metropolis: Los Angeles, 1850–1930 (1967); Albert H. Clodius, "The Quest for Good Government in Los Angeles 1890–1910" (Ph.D. diss., Claremont Graduate School, 1953); Martin J. Schiesl, "Politicians in Disguise: The Changing Role of Public Administrators in Los Angeles, 1900–1920," in Michael H. Ebner and Eugene M. Tobin, eds., *The Age of Urban Reform: New Perspectives on the Progressive Era* (1977).)

                                                                        Richard C. Lower

LOUISIANA. Progressivism was not a driving force in early twentieth-century Louisiana. Dominance in state politics remained in the hands of the Democratic conservative oligarchy that had taken power after Reconstruction. At the core of this coalition was the Choctaw Club of Louisiana, the Democratic machine in New Orleans. The Choctaws, under the leadership of Mayor Martin Behrman,* held the balance of power in the state legislature and controlled most nominations to high state office. Progressive reforms were consequently few. In 1904 the convict lease system ended. Two years later, the state instituted primary elections* to choose party nominees. Public education also received greater attention although appropriations remained exceedingly low. In New Orleans, Behrman initiated improvements in drainage, the city water supply, and streets; established the Public Belt Railroad; and in 1912 endorsed the adoption of a commission-council form of government. These innovations resulted from agreements with local businessmen and the absorption of some progressives into the New Orleans Democratic organization, but they did not substantially alter machine practices in local politics.

In 1912 Luther E. Hall, candidate of the Good Government League, an urban-based reform group, became governor, but his administration achieved few changes. In 1920 John M. Parker,* a former Bull Moose Progressive and long-time urban reformer, defeated the conservative candidate in the gubernatorial election. Parker's administration featured opposition to the Ku Klux Klan and the New Orleans machine, aid for education and roads, a new state constitution, and a severance tax on oil. Despite these successes, Parker's emphasis on pay-as-you-go financing, his lack of political aggressiveness, legislative disapproval, and compromises with oil interests undermined his programs. Further progressive reforms in Louisiana awaited the rise of Huey Pierce Long to the governorship in 1928. (John R. Kemp, ed., *Martin Behrman of New Orleans: Memoirs of a City Boss* (1977); George M. Reynolds, *Machine Politics in New Orleans, 1897–1926* (1936); Mark T. Carleton, *Politics and Punishment: A History of the Louisiana State Penal System* (1971); Matthew J. Schott, "John M. Parker of Louisiana and the and the Varieties of American Progressivism" (Ph.D. diss., Vanderbilt University, 1969).)

                                                                        Edward F. Haas

LOVEJOY, OWEN R. (September 9, 1866–June 29, 1961). Born in Jamestown, Michigan, Lovejoy received an A.B., M.A., and LL.D. from Albion College. After serving as a Methodist and Congregational minister, he became an investigator and later general secretary of the National Child Labor Committee.* For the next nineteen years, Lovejoy guided a sometimes a sometimes divided coalition of reformers through the difficulties attendant upon the establishment of the U.S. Children's Bureau*, the passage of the Keating-Owen Act* and the Child Labor Tax, and the campaign for ratification of the Child Labor Amendment. His search for national remedies represented the most advanced tactical thinking of progressivism. When the ratification campaign failed, Lovejoy resigned as general secretary rather than accede to reducing the committee's role to that of a clearinghouse for information collected by other agencies. He continued his work for children with the Children's Aid Society and the American Youth Commission. Lovejoy was also a director of Survey Associates and a president of the National Conference of Social Work. (*New York Times*, June 30, 1961, p. 27; Robert W. McAhren, "Making the Nation Safe for Childhood: A History of the Movement for Federal Regulation of Child Labor, 1900–1938" (Ph.D. diss., University of Texas–Austin, 1967); Stephen B. Wood, *Constitutional Politics in the Progressive Era: Child Labor and the Law* (1968).)

Robert W. McAhren

LOW, SETH (January 18, 1850–September 17, 1916). Good government reformer, president of Columbia University, mayor of Brooklyn and of New York, Seth Low was born in Brooklyn to a merchant family of New England Yankee stock. He was educated at Columbia College, then joined his father's firm, A. A. Low and Brothers, in 1870. He pursued both philanthropic and political activities and was elected mayor of Brooklyn twice (1881, 1883). After retiring from business, he served as president of Columbia from 1890 to 1901, greatly expanding the graduate and professional schools of the university and purchasing land on Morningside Heights for a new campus.

The Citizens Union,* a leading good government reform organization, chose him to run in the first mayoral election for Greater New York in 1897, but he was defeated by a Tammany Hall* Democrat. Tammany scandals led Low to wage a successful campaign for mayor in 1901 on a Fusion ticket which united all anti-Tammany forces under one banner. Low served one two-year term, but was defeated by a Tammany resurgence in 1903. He continued his reform activities, serving as president of the National Civic Federation* in 1907. Though Low's term as mayor was marked by honesty and efficiency, he was unable to excite the voters or enact any permanent reforms. He is a prime example of Tammany Hall boss George Washington Plunkitt's dictum: "Reformers were like morning glories—looked lovely in the mornin' and withered up in a short time." (Benjamin R. C. Low, *Seth Low* (1925); Gerald Kurland, *Seth Low: The Reformer in an Urban and Industrial Age* (1971).)

Edward R. Kantowicz

LOWDEN, FRANK O. (June 26, 1861–March 20, 1943). Born in Minnesota, Lowden was educated at Iowa State Agricultural College, the University of Iowa, and the Union College of Law. On April 29, 1896, he married Florence Pullman, daughter of George Pullman, sleeping car tycoon. The two men became close, combining the legal talents of Lowden with the money of Pullman to put together monopolistic companies, such as the National Biscuit Company (1898), American Radiator Company (1898–1899), and Shelby Steel Tube Company (1900). Lowden, on the board of several major corporations, became colonel of the 1st Infantry of the Illinois National Guard, regarded by business as a weapon against strikes. In 1906, with the help of Chicago* political boss William Lorimer,* Lowden was elected to Congress, serving two terms.

From 1917 to 1921 he served as governor of Illinois. Lowden shook off the influence of Lorimer and became a moderate reformer. Although his link to big business plagued him politically, he was seriously considered as presidential material by the Republicans in 1920. His main thrust as governor was for more efficiency. He promoted an administrative code which did away with the worst features of the patronage system, and a new constitution was written, although it was never adopted. He made some progress in highway building. During World War I,* Lowden was militarist and repressive toward dissent during the Red Scare.* The Lowden administration was also plagued with two disastrous race riots* in East Saint Louis and Chicago. (William T. Hutchinson, *Lowden of Illinois: The Life of Frank O. Lowden*, 2 vols. (1957).)

Donald F. Tingley

LOWELL, ABBOTT LAWRENCE (December 13, 1856–January 6, 1943). Born in Boston, Massachusetts, educated at private schools in Boston and in France, Lowell graduated from the Phillips Academy at Andover in 1873. He received the B.A. from Harvard College in 1877 and the LL.B from the Harvard Law School in 1880. He practiced law for several years before joining the faculty at Harvard in the Department of Government in 1897. In 1908, he published *The Government of England*, his most notable work. He also authored articles and books on government in the United States and in Europe.

In 1909, he was chosen as president of Harvard, suceeding Charles W. Eliot,* who had held the post for forty years. Lowell served as president of Harvard until 1933 and modified severely the free elective system that Eliot had brought to undergraduate studies at Harvard College. Under Lowell, distribution requirements and the requirement of a major area of concentration, plus general examinations for students in the college and a tutorial system, were introduced. In 1915, Lowell was active in founding the League to Enforce Peace, and after the war, he fought vigorously for American admission to the League of Nations.* In 1927, Lowell served on a committee appointed by the governor of Massachusetts to review the conviction for murder of Nicola Sacco and Bartolomeo Vanzetti. (Henry Aaron Yeomans, *Abbott Lawrence Lowell, 1856–1943* (1948);

Lawrence A. Lowell, *At War with Academic Traditions in America* (1934); Samuel Eliot Morison, *Three Centuries of Harvard* (1946).)

                                                                Wayne J. Urban

LUDLOW MASSACRE. This was the term applied to the killing of striking coal miners and their families by National Guard troops during a 1914 strike at Ludlow, Colorado. The coal strike of 1913–1914 and the ensuing massacre climaxed a generation of industrial warfare in Colorado,* which left the corporate mine owners, particularly the Colorado Fuel and Iron Company controlled by John D. Rockefeller,* in control of the mine districts. In September 1913, the United Mine Workers* struck for union recognition, higher wages, and an end to closed company camps. Nine thousand workers walked off their jobs and moved their families from the company camps to tent cities on the open prairie.

A virtual civil war ensued between state troops and the miners. On April 20, 1914, guardsmen attacked a tent city at Ludlow, raking the camp with machine guns and setting fire to the tents. Five strikers and one militiaman were killed in the fighting, but two women and eleven children suffocated in the smoke. Ten more days of fighting resulted in forty more deaths, until federal troops finally restored order. Numerous trials and investigations followed, and Rockefeller offered a conciliatory company union plan. Though the miners gained some improvements in wages and working conditions as a result of Ludlow, they did not win union recognition or change the balance of industrial power. (George P. West, *Report on the Colorado Strike* (1915); George S. McGovern and Leonard F. Guttridge, *The Great Coalfield War* (1972); Carl Abbott, *Colorado: A History of the Centennial State* (1976).)

                                                                Edward R. Kantowicz

LUSK COMMITTEE. The Lusk Committee was a joint committee of the New York State Legislature appointed in 1919 to investigate seditious activities. Clayton R. Lusk, the chairman of the committee, had been an outspoken advocate of Americanization* during World War I* and had led a propaganda campaign against German influence in America. When his attention shifted to the supposed danger of a communist revolution after the war, he was appointed to investigate the matter, and his committee produced a 4,500-page report in 1920. Largely due to his committee's propaganda, the New York legislature refused to seat five members of the Socialist party,* even though they belonged to a legal party and had been duly elected in November 1919. The Lusk Committee formed part of a much larger Red Scare,* a hysterical campaign against radicals, foreigners, and labor unionists which raged for about a year after the end of World War I. (New York Legislature, Joint Committee Investigating Seditious Activities, *Rev-*

olutionary Radicalism (1920); Julian F. Jaffe, *Crusade against Radicalism* (1972); John Higham, *Strangers in the Land* (1955).)

Edward R. Kantowicz

LYNCHING. Illegal capital punishment by mob action peaked in the 1890s, claiming 230 victims in 1892. In the first decade of the twentieth century, lynchings still averaged nearly a hundred per year. By that time, lynching had assumed a definite southern and racial character. Between 1904 and 1914, more than ten times as many blacks (650) were lynched as whites (58). Frenzied southern mobs often engaged in fiendish torture, such as dismemberment and burning at the stake. Although thousands witnessed these grisly spectacles, lynchers rarely were prosecuted. Powerful southern whites defended lynching as necessary to protect women from rape, even though less than a quarter of those lynched were accused of that crime.

Lynching, like the related race riots of the period, cannot be understood apart from the historical context of rampant popular and pseudoscientific racism or the collective imperative of southern whites to maintain the caste status of Afro-Americans. In the age of disfranchisment and Jim Crow, antilynching was the only racial cause that attracted substantial numbers of white progressives, many of whom held racist attitudes. The National Association for the Advancement of Colored People* (NAACP), organized in 1910, made federal antilynching legislation its top priority during the Progressive Era. (NAACP, *Thirty Years of Lynching in the United States, 1889–1918* (1919, reprint 1969); Walter White, *Rope and Faggot: A Biography of Judge Lynch* (1929); Robert L. Zangrando, *The NAACP Crusade against Lynching, 1909–1950* (1980).)

David W. Southern

M

McADOO, WILLIAM GIBBS (October 31, 1863–February 1, 1941). Born in Marietta, Georgia, McAdoo graduated from the University of Tennessee and in 1885 was admitted to the bar. In 1892, he sought his fortune in New York City.* Eventually a successful attorney, McAdoo saw the desirability of connecting Manhattan Island to New Jersey by tunnel, and arranged for the necessary capital and engineering skills to complete the task. Having earned a fortune and a reputation as a successful promoter, McAdoo entered politics as a supporter of the presidential candidacy of Woodrow Wilson,* serving as campaign manager in 1912. Appointed secretary of the treasury in 1913, McAdoo was considered one of Wilson's closest and ablest advisers. Widowed in 1912, he married Eleanor Randolph Wilson in 1914.

As a progressive cabinet officer, McAdoo voiced strong support for a public interest that transcended special interests, and he supported the president's New Freedom* measures. In banking reform, he failed to persuade Congress to establish a central bank operated by public officials in the Treasury Department. An internationalist in foreign policy, McAdoo was in charge of financing the war effort in 1917 and 1918, and he served as director-general of the railroads in 1918. Resigning from the cabinet in 1919, he moved to California in 1922. McAdoo unsuccessfully sought the Democratic presidential nomination in 1924. Elected to the U.S. Senate in 1932, he served one term. (John J. Broesamle, *William Gibbs McAdoo: A Passion for Change, 1863–1917* (1973); William G. McAdoo, *Crowded Years* (1931).)

K. Austin Kerr

McCARTHY, CHARLES R. (June 29, 1873–March 26, 1921). Born in Brockton, Massachusetts, the son of Irish immigrant parents, McCarthy worked his way through Brown University, graduating with honors in 1896, and earning all-American football honors. He received his Ph.D. from the University of

Wisconsin* in 1901, writing a dissertation that won the Justin Winsor Prize of the American Historical Association.* In 1901, he organized the nation's first Legislative Reference Library* (LRL), which researched and drafted every major piece of legislation that characterized the state's progressive reputation. He also taught courses in legislation at the university and, in 1912, wrote *The Wisconsin Idea*, which established Wisconsin's reputation as the most progressive state in the union.

For the remainder of the decade, he made Madison the center of a national reform network, advising Theodore Roosevelt* and Woodrow Wilson,* training public servants for other states, corresponding with a host of nationally renowned reformers, and serving in a myriad of national reformist organizations. Within the state, he was a staunch advocate of industrial and agricultural education, agricultural marketing cooperatives, budget reform, and government by commission. Charged by conservatives with running a progressive "bill factory," in 1914 McCarthy successfully defended the LRL when his adversaries took office. During 1914 and 1915 he served as the first director of the U.S. Commission on Industrial Relations* and, in 1918, made an unsuccessful bid for the Democratic nomination to the U.S. Senate. (Charles R. McCarthy, *The Wisconsin Idea* (1912); Edward A. Fitzpatrick, *McCarthy of Wisconsin* (1944); Marion Casey, *Charles McCarthy: Librarianship and Reform* (1981).)

John D. Buenker

McCLURE, SAMUEL (SIDNEY) (February 17, 1857–March 21, 1949). Born in County Antrim, Ireland, McClure came to America in 1866. After graduation from Knox College in 1882, he founded the *Wheelman*, a bicycling magazine. In 1884, he launched the Associated Literary Press, which circulated large amounts of Sunday supplement material, including the works of Henry George,* Edward Bellamy,* William T. Stead,* and Ida M. Tarbell.* In 1887, McClure began the first American publication of stories by Robert Louis Stevenson, Arthur Conan Doyle, and Rudyard Kipling. To these were added such American authors as Hamlin Garland,* Mark Twain, William Dean Howells,* and William James.*

In 1893, McClure established *McClure's*, a ten-cent magazine which a decade later became the leading Progressive journal. Lincoln Steffens's* *Shame of the Cities*, Ida Tarbell's* *History of Standard Oil*, and Ray S. Baker's* *Labor Unrest* were long series on what McClure called the American contempt of the law. The magazine was especially influential in promoting the antitrust suit against Standard Oil,* the passage of the Pure Food and Drugs Act,* and the Hepburn Act.* *McClure's* promoted the enfranchisement of women, the direct election of senators, prohibition, and the city manager and city commission forms of local government. In 1906 *McClure's* original staff resigned to form the *American Magazine*,* but McClure hired Willa Cather,* Burton J. Hendrick,* and Samuel Hopkins Adams* and continued his assaults on patent medicine, insurance frauds, and political corruption. Through financial difficulties in 1911, McClure lost control of his magazine and never successfully reentered publishing. (Peter Lyon,

Success Story: The Life and Times of S. S. McClure (1963); Samuel S. McClure, *My Autobiography* (1913); Harold S. Wilson, *McClure's Magazine and the Muckrakers* (1970).)

Harold S. Wilson

McCORMICK, JOSEPH MEDILL (May 16, 1877–February 25, 1925). Member of the *Chicago Tribune* newspaper family, Republican congressman and senator, McCormick was born in Chicago* to Robert Sanderson McCormick, diplomat, and Katherine Van Etta Medill, daughter of *Tribune* editor Joseph Medill. He was educated at Groton and Yale. He began working as a reporter for the *Tribune* in 1900 and eventually held nearly every job on the paper. He married Ruth Hanna, daughter of Republican political boss Marcus A. Hanna,* in 1904. He became actively involved in local reform politics in 1908, bolted to the Progressive party,* and was elected to two terms in the state legislature in 1912 and 1914. Returning to the Republican party,* he was elected congressman-at-large from Illinois* in 1916, then senator in 1918. He was defeated in the Republican primary in 1924 and died a few days before his Senate term expired. Though considered a maverick by the *Tribune* clan and the Republican establishment, he had become a thoroughly conventional Republican by the time of his service in the Senate, opposing the Treaty of Versailles and American entry into the League of Nations.* (*Dictionary of American Biography*, vol. II; *Biographical Directory of the American Congress*; Frank Waldrop, *McCormick of Chicago* (1966).)

Edward R. Kantowicz

McDOWELL, MARY ELIZA (November 30, 1854–October 14, 1936). Born in Cincinnati, Ohio, Mary McDowell grew up in Chicago where her father was an industrialist. Influenced by Methodism, she had an early interest in the everyday application of Christian tenets. She became associated with the Woman's Christian Temperance Union* in her early thirties and became the leader of its kindergarten activities. In 1890, she joined Jane Addams* at Hull House* and became active in its social reform activities. In 1894, she became director of the new University of Chicago* Settlement which became a social laboratory in an industrial, immigrant neighborhood.

Active in social reform in Chicago, McDowell promoted increased municipal services, such as improved sewers to the settlement's neighborhood. In 1904, McDowell joined a women's union in the Chicago stockyards, a controversial stance which lost contributors for the settlement. She was one of the founders of the National Women's Trade Union League* in 1903 and was active in efforts to secure federal and state legislation to protect women in the workplace. She was influential in creating a Women's Bureau in the U.S. Department of Labor* in 1920. As a social reformer, McDowell was active in local politics, in efforts to better race relations, and in the women's peace movement. (Edward T. James, et al., *Notable American Women*, vol. 2 (1971); Howard E. Wilson, *Mary*

McDowell, Neighbor (1928); Lea D. Taylor, "The Social Settlement and Civic Responsibility—The Life Work of Mary McDowell and Graham Taylor," *Social Service Review* 28, no. 1 (March 1954): 31–40.)

                                                                John M. Herrick

McGOVERN, FRANCIS E. (January 21, 1866–May 16, 1946). Born on a farm near Elkhart Lake, Sheboygan County, Wisconsin,* McGovern worked as a rural schoolteacher and was graduated from the University of Wisconsin* in 1890. After seven years as a high school principal, he was admitted to the bar and began law practice in Milwaukee. Elected district attorney in 1904, McGovern gained fame for his prosecution of the graft-ridden administration of Mayor David Rose. Denied the Republican nomination for reelection in 1906, he ran a successful campaign as an independent and became the leader of an urban-based reform faction of the GOP that was tenuously allied with the group headed by U.S. Senator Robert M. La Follette.*

After failing in a try for the U.S. Senate in 1908, McGovern was elected governor in 1910 in coalition with La Follette, who won reelection. Under McGovern's leadership, the 1911 legislature compiled one of the most progressive records ever, enacting an income tax, workmen's compensation,* an industrial commission, urban home rule,* a state life insurance fund, laws protecting women and children in factories, several conservation acts, and numerous measures to aid agriculture. Its also created a Board of Public Affairs to engage in economic planning.

But McGovern and La Follette had a falling out over the former's support of Theodore Roosevelt* in 1912, and La Follette's men stymied the governor's legislative program in 1913. They also helped cause McGovern's defeat in the 1914 race for the U.S. Senate. During World War I,* he served in the Judge Advocate General's office and then returned to private practice in Milwaukee. (Herbert F. Margulies, *The Decline of the Progressive Movement in Wisconsin, 1890–1920* (1968); Cyril C. Cavanaugh, "Francis E. McGovern and the 1911 Wisconsin Legislature" (M.A. thesis, University of Wisconsin, 1961).)

                                                                John D. Buenker

McKELWAY, ALEXANDER J. (October 6, 1866–April 16, 1918). Born in Sedburyville, Pennsylvania, Alexander was educated at Hampden-Sydney College and Virginia's Union Theological Seminary. He married the daughter of Dr. Benjamin Smith, president of Hampden-Sydney, and was the father of Benjamin M. McKelway, editor of the *Washington Star*, and St. Clair McKelway, editor of the *New Yorker*. McKelway was ordained a Presbyterian minister and was pastor of a large Fayetteville, North Carolina, congregation (1892–1898). From 1898 to 1905, he was editor of the most prominent Presbyterian newspaper in North Carolina.

He became the National Child Labor Committee's* assistant for the southern states in 1905 and directed the state campaigns for child labor laws.* After 1909 he was the committee's chief Washington lobbyist and was influential in obtaining President Woodrow Wilson's* support for a national child labor law. He framed twenty-two social welfare planks for the 1916 Democratic National Convention. Twenty were adopted. He led the successful fight in Oklahoma for a dependent children's bill and was instrumental in obtaining liberal features in the constitutions of Arizona and New Mexico. He aided in organizing the Southern Sociological Congress* and in enforcing the 1916 National Child Labor Law. (Hugh C. Bailey, *Liberalism in the New South* (1969); Elizabeth H. Davidson, *Child Labor Legislation in the Southern Textile States* (1939).)

Hugh C. Bailey

McKINLEY, WILLIAM (January 29, 1843–September 14, 1901). Born in Niles, Ohio, William McKinley completed only one term at Allegheny College because of family financial reverses. He enlisted in the Twenty-third Ohio Volunteer Infantry when the Civil War broke out in 1861, and participated in many of its major conflicts. He studied law for a short time, then was admitted to the bar in Canton, Ohio, in 1867. Between 1877 and 1891 McKinley served his district as a Republican member of the House of Representatives, where he developed a national reputation for his strong protectionism, and from his position on the Ways and Means Committee he pushed through the McKinley Tariff Act of 1890. When McKinley lost his reelection bid in 1890, he ran for the Ohio governorship with the support of Cleveland industrialist Marcus Hanna* and won two terms.

McKinley rebuffed initial attempts to nominate him for president in 1892, in part because he believed Republicans owed support to incumbent Benjamin Harrison. But in 1896, after four years of economic depression under Democrat Grover Cleveland, he welcomed Hanna's efforts to win him the nomination. Pitted against McKinley's dignified, relatively low-key front-porch campaign was the hyperactive William Jennings Bryan,* pro-silver Democratic candidate who gave hundreds of speeches across the country, many from the rear of a train. Despite Bryan's press appeal, however, McKinley carried a comfortable majority.

Ironically, McKinley's most profound impact on American history came in foreign affairs, when the sinking of the *Maine* forced him to ask an eager Congress to decide upon a declaration of war. Not only did he look to liberate Cuba from Spain, he also decided to acquire the Philippine Islands, Puerto Rico, and Guam. War lasted six months, but its conclusion brought the United States an overseas empire and a larger stake in world affairs. McKinley easily defeated Bryan a second time in his bid for reelection in 1900,* but died of an assassin's bullet. (Paul W. Glad, *McKinley, Bryan, and the People* (1964); Lewis L. Gould, *The*

Presidency of William McKinley (1981); Margaret Leech, *In the Days of McKinley* (1959); Wayne H. Morgan, *William McKinley and His America* (1963).)

Wayne A. Wiegand

McREYNOLDS, JAMES CLARK (February 3, 1862–August 25, 1946). The son of a medical doctor, McReynolds was born in Elkton, Kentucky. At age twenty-two, he graduated with first honors from Vanderbilt University and two years later earned his law degree from the University of Virginia. He settled in Nashville and established a prosperous career in law and real estate. In 1896 McReynolds ran unsuccessfully for the U.S. House of Representatives as a sound-money Democrat who favored antitrust action, low tariff, and limited government. Theodore Roosevelt* appointed McReynolds assistant to the attorney general in 1903 to work on antitrust proceedings. Four years later he joined a law firm in New York City, but returned to the Justice Department in 1910 at the request of William Howard Taft* to help prosecute the American Tabacoo Company* for antitrust violations. The next year McReynolds returned to New York City until Woodrow Wilson* named him attorney general in 1913 because of his antitrust reputation. In August 1914, Wilson nominated McReynolds to the Supreme Court, where he served until February 1, 1941. As a justice he consistently voted for limited government, found the New Deal an anathema, and left a record 310 dissents. A bachelor with a difficult temperament, McReynolds died in Washington, D.C. (Stephen T. Early, "James Clark McReynolds and the Judicial Process" (Ph.D. diss., University of Virginia, 1954); Arthur S. Link, *Wilson: The New Freedom* (1956); *Dictionary of American Biography*, supp. 4.)

Keith W. Olson

MACK, JULIAN W. (January 19, 1866–September 5, 1943). Mack was born in San Francisco, but spent most of his childhood in Cincinnati. He was educated at Harvard Law School and the universities of Berlin and Leipzig. He settled in Chicago* in 1890, working as an attorney and later a law professor, while becoming involved in the social settlement movement and in Jewish charities. Mack served as the city's civil service commissioner, and in 1903 was elected (as a Democrat) to the Circuit Court of Cook County.

Deeply interested in child welfare, he sought assignment to the pioneering county juvenile court,* where his work earned great renown. Mack was one of the initiators of the first White House Conference on Children (1909), which resulted in the establishment of the federal Children's Bureau.* He was active in the Juvenile Protective Association and other social welfare organizations, and served a term as president of the National Conference of Social Workers.* In 1911, he was appointed to the new U.S. Commerce Court. Spending his later years mainly in New York City as an ambulatory federal circuit court judge, Mack continued to devote his energies to various liberal and reform causes. He also became one of the leaders of American Zionism. (Harry Barnard, *The Forging of an American Jew: The Life and Times of Judge Julian W. Mack* (1974); Horace M. Kallen, "Julian William Mack, 1866–1943," *American Jewish Yearbook* 46 (1944–1945): 35–46.)

John R. Schmidt

MAHAN, ALFRED THAYER (September 27, 1840–December 1, 1914). Naval captain, author, and apologist for American imperialism,* Mahan was born at West Point, New York; he was educated at private schools and Columbia University before entering the Naval Academy at Annapolis, from which he graduated in 1859. He served on ships blockading the Confederacy during the Civil War, then rotated routinely between ship and shore duty for the next twenty years. Named captain in 1885, he was appointed to lecture at the newly established Naval War College in Newport, Rhode Island, and served as president of the College from 1886 to 1889.

His War College lectures, published in 1890 as *The Influence of Sea Power upon History*, became enormously influential, both in Europe and America. His ideas led to a rebuilding of the American fleet and a more aggressive, outward-looking naval policy. Mahan retired in 1896, though he served briefly in Washington during the Spanish-American War* and was later named an admiral in recognition of his wide influence on foreign policy. In his writings and lectures, he advocated control of the seas and commercial dominance of emerging markets in Latin America and Asia. Along with Theodore Roosevelt,* Brooks Adams,* and Henry Cabot Lodge,* he formed a coterie of imperialists who provided the intellectual rationale for the acquisition of overseas colonies and markets. (William D. Puleston, *Mahan: The Life and Work of Captain Alfred Thayer Mahan, USN* (1939); Howard K. Beale, *Theodore Roosevelt and the Rise of America to World Power* (1956); Walter LaFeber, *The New Empire* (1963).)

Edward R. Kantowicz

MANN, JAMES R. (October 20, 1856–November 30, 1922). Born in Bloomington, Illinois, Mann was educated at the University of Illinois and the Union College of Law and began legal practice in the Chicago* suburb of Hyde Park. After the village was annexed, he was elected to the Chicago City Council as a clean-government Republican, serving from 1892 to 1896. In 1896, he was elected to the U.S. House of Representatives. A staunch conservative, Mann became one of the more influential members of the Republican majority and a protégé of Speaker Joseph Cannon.* His most notable legislative accomplishments were two 1910 laws increasing the scope of the national government: the Mann-Elkins Act,* which greatly expanded the power of the Interstate Commerce Commission over communication; and the Mann "White Slavery" Act,* an early example of federal social welfare legislation.

He succeeded Cannon as Republican leader when the Democrats took control of the House in 1913, retaining the position for six years. Mann's conservatism doubtlessly cost him the speakership when the Republicans captured a House majority in the 1918 elections. After being defeated for the position by Frederick H. Gillett in the party caucus, Mann continued as an active member of the House leadership despite gradually declining health. He died in Washington. (Rena Shuping Mitchell, "The Congressional Career of James Robert Mann" (M.A. thesis, University of Chicago, 1938).)

John R. Schmidt

MANN ACT. Officially titled the White Slave Traffic Act, this 1910 law, introduced by Republican Representative James R. Mann* from Chicago,* outlawed the transportation of women across state lines for immoral purposes. Muckraking* journalist George Kibbe Turner set off a white slavery (prostitution) scare with his 1907 *McClure's** article exposing open vice and immorality in Chicago. This led to the appointment of a vice commission in Chicago, vice crusades* in other cities, and ultimately the passage of the Mann Act in 1910. The act employed the federal government's regulatory power over interstate commerce to stop the commercialized network of "white-slave rings" which were thought to control the supply of prostitutes. The law made transportation of women in interstate commerce "for the purpose of prostitution or debauchery, or for any other immoral purpose" a felony punishable by five years in jail or a $5,000 fine. If the girl transported was under eighteen years of age (such girls came to be known colloquially as "jail bait"), penalties were doubled. Over 2,000 convictions for white slavery, and only 323 acquittals, were obtained between 1910 and 1918.

The Mann Act drew on a general hostility to big-business interests (the "white-slave trust") and tapped deep currents of antiforeign sentiment (white slavers were usually portrayed as foreigners, often Jews). It was also part of the progressive campaign to preserve human resources, like the movement to improve working and housing* conditions of laborers. (Roy Lubove, "The Progressives and the Prostitute," *Historian* 24 (1962):308–30; Mark T. Connelly, *The Response to Prostitution in the Progressive Era* (1980).)

Edward R. Kantowicz

MANN-ELKINS ACT. This legislation was introduced by the William Howard Taft* administration to fulfill a platform pledge made in 1908 to further extend railroad control. Progressive elements in both House and Senate amended the bill in such a way as to strengthen railroad regulation far beyond that originally proposed by Taft. One of the important provisions of the act was to amend the Long- and Short-Haul Clause which had been made ineffective by a decision of the Supreme Court in 1897. The Mann-Elkins Act restored the Long- and Short-Haul Clause by eliminating the phrase "under substantially similar circumstances and conditions." The effect was to prohibit higher rates for shorter than for longer hauls unless the exception was made by the Interstate Commerce Commission. The act also allowed the commission to suspend a proposed rate change for 120 days while making an investigation into the reasonableness of the rate change. An additional suspension of six months was allowed if the 120-day period was not long enough. The burden of proof in justifying a change in rates was placed on the railroads. Two additional provisions of the act, the establishment of a Commerce Court and a Railroad Securities Commission, proved ineffective. The Commerce Court was abolished by Congress in 1913; the Railroad Securities Commission submitted its report to the president and went out of existence. (Phillip D. Locklin, *Economics of Transportation* (1966); Marvin L. Fair and Ernest W. Williams, Jr., *Economics of Transportation* (1959); I. L. Sharfman, *The Interstate Commerce Commission*, vol. 1 (1931).)

Curtis Richards

MARKHAM, EDWIN (April 23, 1852–March 7, 1940). Mystical poet laureate for many progressives, Markham was born in Oregon City, Oregon. Raised by his mother in California, he was educated at the Normal School in San Jose and Christian College in Santa Rosa. From 1872 to the mid-nineties, Markham was a schoolteacher and principal in several northern California communities. Influenced by Victor Hugo and the mystical utopian communitarian, Thomas Lake Harris, Markham discovered that his real love was writing "rebel poems."

After a decade of brooding over Jean François Millet's *Angelus* painting, Markham finally completed his masterpiece, "The Man with the Hoe," publishing it in the *San Francisco Examiner* on January 15, 1899. This one poem, written at the end of an intense decade of protests by farmers and workers, mourned the plight of the oppressed and celebrated the dignity of labor. Markham spent the next two decades writing and lecturing about the poem, which was translated into forty languages. In 1906–907 he wrote a series on child labor,* titled "The Hoe-Man in the Making" for *Cosmopolitan** magazine. Although Markham wrote other poems about "Brotherhood" and "common man" themes, none was as successful in arousing middle-class sympathy for the downtrodden as "The Man with the Hoe." (Don Chase, "Edwin Markham: California Prophet," *Pacific Historian* 20 (1976): 167–76; Louis Filler, *The Unknown Edwin Markham* (1966); Peter J. Frederick, *Knights of the Golden Rule* (1976).)

Peter J. Frederick

MARSH, BENJAMIN CLARKE (March 22, 1877–December 30, 1952). Born in Eski Zaghra, Bulgaria, Marsh was the son of New England Congregational missionaries. After graduation from Iowa (now Grinnell) College in 1898, he pursued graduate study at the University of Chicago* (1899–1900) and the University of Pennsylvania (1902–1905). A dynamic, outspoken social justice advocate, Marsh had spent five years in social work in Philadelphia by 1907, when the Committee on Congestion of Population (CCP) in New York hired him as executive secretary. He briefly emerged as the nation's most vocal proponent of foreign city planning and land-tax reform along the lines of Henry George* as answers to congestion.

Two trips to study European planning, especially German zoning, and the staging of anticongestion exhibits for the CCP culminated in 1909 when Marsh authored *An Introduction to City Planning* and organized the First National Conference on City Planning. Both challenged then prevalent City Beautiful* values. In 1910–1911, Marsh further highlighted the congestion issue while secretary of the New York City Commission on Congestion of Population. However, his tax radicalism cost him his support. In 1912–1913, he became a war correspondent for the First Balkan War. He ended his career operating a one-man People's Lobby in Washington. (Harvey A. Kantor, "Benjamin C. Marsh and the Fight over Population Congestion," *Journal of the American Institute of Planners* 40 (1974): 422–29; Roy Lubove, *The Progressives and the Slums: Tenement House Reform in New York City, 1890–1917* (1962); Benjamin C. Marsh, *Lobbyist for the People: A Record of Fifty Years* (1953); *Who Was Who in America with World Notables, 1969–1973*, 5 (1973): 460.)

Jon A. Peterson

MARSHALL, THOMAS R. (March 14, 1854–June 1, 1925). The twenty-eighth vice president of the United States was born in North Manchester, Indiana. After graduating from Wabash College in 1873, he read law and was admitted to the bar in 1875. In the next thirty years, Marshall worked actively in the Democratic party* rising to membership on the state committee in 1896 and 1898. Aloof from warring party factions, Marshall was the compromise candidate for governor in 1908. Focusing on Republican liquor control legislation and reemphasizing traditional Democratic theories of government, he won a narrow victory. As governor, he supported local autonomy on moral issues and won child labor* and employers' liability* legislation, but he failed to obtain regulation of banking and stocks. His major concern was making elections and government honest, efficient, and responsive. Although somewhat successful, his major reform vehicle—a new state constitution—was killed by the state supreme court.

His activities brought him national attention and, in 1912, the vice presidency. Reelected in 1916 (defeating former vice president and fellow Hoosier Charles W. Fairbanks*), Marshall competently performed the limited duties of his office. Briefly prominent in 1919, because of President Woodrow Wilson's* incapacity, Marshall prevented a constitutional crisis by deliberately refusing to assume or seek the president's powers. (Randall W. Jehs, "Thomas R. Marshall: Mr. Vice President, 1913–1921," in Ralph Gray, ed., *Gentlemen from Indiana: National Party Candidates, 1836–1940* (1977); Charles Marion Thomas, *Thomas Riley Marshall: Hoosier Statesman* (1939); John E. Brown, "Woodrow Wilson's Vice President: Thomas R. Marshall and the Wilson Administration" (Ph.D. diss., Ball State University, 1970).)

Philip R. VanderMeer

MARYLAND. In Maryland, progressive reform began in Baltimore,* then spread to the state. Administrative reforms began with Mayor Alcaeus Hooper, but the first significant change came with the new city charter of 1898, followed by more systematic city planning, all aimed at modernizing city government, especially after the devastating fire of 1904. Urban social reforms designed to help the poor were led by the Charity Organization Society,* James Cardinal Gibbons,* physicians from Johns Hopkins concerned with public health, and the Baltimore Federation of Labor. Urban reform climaxed in 1911 with the formation of the City-Wide Congress to discuss additional progressive reforms.

Although progressive reforms were regularly proposed and debated at the state capital, few were enacted before 1908. During the century's first decade, the Democratic party* was concerned with controlling the growing black vote and was dominated by two political bosses—U.S. Senator Arthur P. Gorman and Baltimore machine chief Isaac Freeman Rasin. At the state level reform Democrats Isaac Lobe Straus and David J. Lewis did push through the 1902 legislative session bills on compulsory education,* juvenile court,* and child labor.* After the racial issue was laid to rest and Rasin and Gorman died, the pace of reform quickened with the election of Governor Austin Lane Crothers. Crothers championed a number of reforms and signed many progressive bills into law dealing with corrupt practices,* public utilities regulation, primary elections,* pure food, suppression of prostitution, and an eight-hour workday for labor. This spate of legislation came at the cost of Democratic party solidarity, and Republican Phillips Lee Goldsborough won the gubernatorial election of 1912, although the legislature remained under Democratic control. The chief progressive measure enacted during his term was the establishment of the Industrial Accident Commission, subsequently renamed the Workmen's Compensation Commission, and passed largely through David Lewis's efforts. (James B. Crooks, *Politics and Progress: The Rise of Urban Progressivism in Baltimore, 1895–1911* (1968); James B. Crooks, "Maryland Progressivism," in Richard Walsh and William Lloyd Fox, eds., *Maryland: A History, 1632–1974* (1974); Nicholas C. Burckel, "Governor Austin Lane Crothers and Progressive Reform in Maryland, 1908–1912," *Maryland Historical Magazine* 76 (1981): 184–201.)

Nicholas C. Burckel

MASSACHUSETTS. The Progressive Era was a paradoxical time for Massachusetts. The state, which had a tradition of responsible, progressive government, continued in this pattern, compiling an impressive progressive legislative record in such critical areas as business regulation, social welfare, and responsive government. Massachusetts' achievements included a Public Service Commission, workmen's compensation* and insurance, minimum wage and maximum hour laws, and the direct primary.* These progressive initiatives were sponsored by factions of both major parties and occurred most notably in the administrations of Republican Governor Curtis Guild (1906–1908) and Democratic Governors Eugene Foss (1911–1913) and David I. Walsh* (1914–1915).

By contrast, the Progressive party* played little part in these achievements. Formed by insurgents within the Republican ranks, the Progressives never attracted major Republican leadership or voting strength beyond their Yankee base.

Their principal effect was to split the Republican vote and allow the election of Democratic governors from 1911 to 1915. Losing its principal supporters after 1913, the Progressive party became increasingly the vehicle for nativism and Prohibition until its demise in 1915. Yet, despite the progressive legislation and political activism, the period marked no new departures for Massachusetts. Progressive legislation modernized existing traditions but did not create a modern political system in the state. There was an encouraging beginning toward a pluralist, liberal Democratic party* under the leadership of Walsh, who created a coalition of Irish, newer immigrants, and liberal Yankees which seemed to prefigure the New Deal coalition. However, his leadership was challenged by the city machine led by James M. Curley,* and the fragmentation of the national party after 1919 created further difficulties.

The state was experiencing a critical erosion of its economic position, yet progressivism did not offer solutions. In the most dramatic case, Louis Brandeis* led a dogged battle against the merger of the New Haven Railroad with the Boston and Maine system, charging monopoly and financial chicanery and protesting that the merger was a conspiracy against the public interest. Others believed that it was in the public interest, necessary to provide Massachusetts with an effective transportation system. Although Brandeis was vindicated when the railroad went into bankruptcy and the merger failed, reformers left the system more crippled than before. (Richard M. Abrams, *Conservatism in a Progressive Era: Massachusetts Politics 1900–1912* (1964); John Buenker, "The Mahatma and Progressive Reform: Martin Lomasney as Lawmaker, 1911–1917," *New England Quarterly* 44, no. 3 (September 1971): 397–419; Richard M. Sherman, "Progressive Politics in Massachusetts: 1908–1916" (Ph.D. diss., Harvard University, 1959).)

Constance Burns

THE MASSES. Established in 1911, the magazine emerged as a leading journalistic vehicle for the political, literary, and pictorial radicalism that helped shape the decade before American entrance into World War I.* From late 1912 on, Max Eastman* served as the magazine's editor, and among the gifted artists and writers who contributed their efforts were John Sloan,* Art Young, Louis Untermeyer, Mary Heaton Vorse, Floyd Dell,* Mary White Ovington,* Upton Sinclair,* and John Reed.* The *Masses* was generally socialistic in viewpoint and consistently supported labor causes, but it was not formally connected to the Socialist party.* The magazine reflected a daring, rebellious, creative spirit, pursuing, as Reed announced, a broad purpose to "everlastingly attack old systems, old morals, old prejudices." Its pages included articles of sober social criticism, but there was also the light touch of humor expressed in writing and cartoons. The smugness of the upper classes and what the *Masses* saw as the hypocrisy of institutional religion were targets for satire.

The magazine repeatedly spoke out against militarism, and in 1917 it responded critically to President Woodrow Wilson's* decision for intervention, eventually falling victim to official repression. An issue of the magazine was excluded from the mails, and then Postmaster General Albert Burleson* withdrew mailing privileges on the grounds that the *Masses* was no longer a regularly issued periodical. In 1918 Eastman, Dell, Young, and Reed were among those indicated under the Espionage Act.* Two trials were held in New York, but the juries would not convict these defendants. (Leslie Fishbein, *Rebels in Bohemia: The Radicals of "The Masses"* (1982); William O'Neill, ed., *Echoes of Revolt: "The Masses," 1911–1917* (1966); Art Young, *Art Young, His Life and Times* (1939).)

Herbert Shapiro

MASTERS, EDGAR LEE (August 23, 1869–March 6, 1950). Born in Kansas, Masters grew up in Illinois. After failure at farming and in business, his father was admitted to the bar and became a highly successful lawyer, successively in Petersburg, Lewistown, and Springfield. Growing up in Petersburg and Lewistown near the Spoon River which figured in his literary life, Masters was educated at Knox College in Galesburg. After teaching briefly in the public schools, he studied law, moved to Chicago, opened a law office, and began to build a practice, made up, at first, of ill-paying personal injury suits. Some of his cases involved the defense of unions against injunctions. He also defended his brother-in-law, who was accused of dispensing birth control devices, and an anarchist who was threatened with deportation. Masters attended the 1896 Democratic National Convention, heard William Jennings Bryan's* "Cross of Gold" speech, and became a partisan.

From his student days, Masters wrote poetry, and his greatest fame came as a writer. At first he hid his talent as a writer because he thought it would hurt his law practice. But after publication of his third volume, *Spoon River Anthology* in 1915, he was thrust into fame. Masters was a tortured man, torn between his family and the many other women in his life, between the law and literature, and by the constant and increasing need for money, of which there was not enough. (Edgar Lee Masters, *Across Spoon River* (1936).)

Donald F. Tingley

MATTHEWS, NATHAN (March 28, 1854–December 11, 1927). Mayor of Boston* and government reformer, Matthews was born in Boston to an old-stock Yankee family. He graduated from Harvard in 1875, traveled and studied in Europe from 1875 to 1877, then passed the Massachusetts bar exam in 1880. He supported Grover Cleveland, the Democratic candidate for president, in the Mugwump election of 1884; then in 1888 he helped organize the Young Men's Democratic Club, which forged an alliance between a small number of Yankee Democrats and the growing masses of Irish* Catholic voters. He represented this alliance as reform mayor of Boston from 1891 to 1895, and he was the first to use the greatly enlarged mayoral powers granted by the 1885 city charter.

His cost-cutting measures during the depression of the 1890s,* however, alienated the Irish and broke up the Yankee-Irish coalition. Thereafter, Matthews practiced law, lectured on government at Harvard, and worked with the Good Government Association against the Irish ward bosses. He headed a finance commission that wrote a new city charter in 1909, reducing the size of the city council and providing for a nonpartisan, at-large* election of council members. (*Dictionary of American Biography*, vol. 12; Melvin G. Holli and Peter d'A. Jones, eds., *Biographical Directory of American Mayors*; Geoffrey Blodgett, "Yankee Leadership in a Divided City: Boston 1860–1910," in Ronald P. Formisano and Constance K. Burns, eds., *Boston 1700–1980: The Evolution of Urban Politics* (1984).)

Edward R. Kantowicz

MEAD, GEORGE HERBERT (February 27, 1863–April 26, 1931). Born at South Hadley, Massachusetts, Mead grew up in a household filled with the Christian ethics of brotherhood and social conscience, a similar experience of many members of the founding generation of American sociology. His childhood was spent at Oberlin College where his father taught theology. After a brief tenure as a schoolteacher, Mead worked on the railroad in the Pacific Northwest. He read omnivorously. While he was a Harvard graduate student in 1887, Josiah Royce* and William James* converted Mead to pragmatic philosophy. Like other founders of the American sociological tradition, Mead studied in Germany, where he met G. Stanley Hall.* Mead joined the Department of Philosophy at the University of Michigan and the academic company of Charles Horton Cooley,* James H. Tufts, and John Dewey.* In 1893, Mead joined Dewey in the Department of Philosophy at the University of Chicago,* where he stayed until his death.

Greatly influenced by Deweyan instrumentalism,* Mead's philosophy accepted Darwinian naturalism, but it emphasized the social basis of human reality, the evolution of human society. Mead's creed began with the self divided into the "I" and the "Me." The Significant Other created the context for the self and for Mind, which is the individual acceptance of the social process. The individual continually interacts with society, and Mead accepted that meaning arose from the subjective meaning actors give their actions. Mead had a meager publication record; students and colleagues published his lecture notes as *Mind, Self and Society* (1934), *Movements Of Thought in the Nineteenth Century* (1936), and *The Philosophy Of the Act* (1938). (David J. Miller, *George Herbert Mead: Self, Language and the World* (1973); Maurice A. Nathanson, *The Social Dynamics of George H. Mead* (1973); David J. Lewis and Richard L. Smith, *American Sociology and Pragmatism* (1980).)

Donald K. Pickens

MEAT INSPECTION ACT. This was a 1906 law mandating strict sanitary inspection of all meat products sold in interstate commerce. For years, Dr. Harvey W. Wiley,* chief chemist for the Department of Agriculture, had advocated a wide-ranging pure food and drug law; and Senator Albert Beveridge* had introduced a companion meat inspection act. The 1906 publication of socialist Upton Sinclair's* sensational novel *The Jungle*, which exposed the filthy conditions of the Chicago* stockyards, created sufficient public outcry to pass both laws.

President Theodore Roosevelt* ordered Commissioner of Labor Charles P. Neill and New York social worker James B. Reynolds to conduct an independent investigation of the meat packers, which largely corroborated Sinclair's revelations. Using a threat to release the damning Neill-Reynolds report, Roosevelt prodded Congress to pass both the Pure Food and Drugs Act* and the Meat Inspection Act. Sinclair, who had intended his novel as a step toward socialism, not government food regulation, remarked ironically: "I aimed at the public's heart, and by accident I hit it in the stomach." (Upton Sinclair, *The Jungle* (1906); Oscar E. Anderson, *The Health of a Nation* (1958); George E. Mowry, *The Era of Theodore Roosevelt* (1958).)

Edward R. Kantowicz

MENTAL HYGIENE. This was a movement to improve the treatment of the insane and to promote mental health. In 1900 businessman Clifford W. Beers had a breakdown, attempted suicide, and was confined to a Connecticut mental hospital for three years. After his recovery, he published a best-selling book called *A Mind That Found Itself* (1908) and launched a nationwide movement to improve mental health. The pioneering psychiatrist Adolf Meyer suggested the name "mental hygiene" to the Beers, who adopted it enthusiastically and founded a National Committee for Mental Hygiene in 1909. The phrase "mental hygiene" proved a fortunate choice, for it emphasized health rather than institutional reform and gave the movement a broader appeal, linking it to other reforms such as social hygiene* and the prohibition* of alcoholic beverages. Beers and Meyer eventually quarreled over the issue of lay versus medical control of the association; and after 1920 the emerging profession of psychiatry* won out, renaming their campaign the mental health movement. (Gerald N. Grob, *The Inner World of American Psychiatry, 1890–1940* (1985); Franz G. Alexander, *A History of Psychiatry* (1966); Albert Deutsch, *The Mentally Ill in America* (1946).)

Edward R. Kantowicz

MERRIAM, CHARLES EDWARD (November 15, 1874–January 8, 1953). Chicago* political science professor and reform politician, Merriam was born in Hopkinton, Iowa;* he was educated at Lenox College in Iowa and pursued graduate work at Columbia University. He taught at the University of Chicago* from 1900 onwards. Elected alderman in 1909, he headed a city council commission which exposed waste and graft in city expenditures. He won the Republican nomination for mayor in Chicago's first direct primary in 1911, but was defeated by Democrat Carter Harrison II.* He returned to the council in 1913 for one term and unsuccessfully sought the Republican mayoral nomination in 1919. He devoted the rest of his life to the organization of social science* as a public policy tool at the national level. He founded the Social Science Research Council in 1923 to advance the cause of scientific public administration. His former partner in Chicago reform politics, Harold I. Ickes,* secured his appointment to the New Deal's National Resources Planning Board, on which he served from 1933 to 1943. (Charles E. Merriam, *A More Intimate View of Urban Politics* (1929); Barry D. Karl, *Charles E. Merriam and the Study of Politics* (1974); Steven J. Diner, *A City and Its Universities: Public Policy in Chicago, 1892–1919.* (1980).)

Edward R. Kantowicz

MEYER, GEORGE VON LENGERKE (June 24, 1858–March 9, 1918). Born in Boston, graduate of Harvard (1879), Meyer used his blue-blood connections and his position as a prominent State Street merchant to launch a political career which took him into Boston* city politics (1889–1892), and then to the Massachusetts State House of Representatives (1892–1896), where he served three terms as speaker. In 1900 he was appointed ambassador to Italy, and five years later Theodore Roosevelt* made him ambassador to Russia. There he played an important role in the delicate negotiations leading to the Treaty of Portsmouth;* he also reported on the chaotic Russian internal situation between 1905 and 1907.

Meyer returned to the United States in 1907 to become Roosevelt's postmaster general, a position from which he led the fight for postal savings banks* and extension of parcel post. William Howard Taft* made him secretary of the navy in 1909, where he instituted as major reorganization scheme. After leaving office in 1913, he became the Republicans' chief critic of the new Democratic administration's navy policies. In 1915 he joined efforts to reunite Roosevelt with the Republican party* in hopes of recapturing the presidency for him in 1916. (DeWolfe M. A. Howe, *George von Lengerke Meyer* (1919); Wayne A. Wiegand, *Patrician in the Progressive Era: A Biography of George von Lengerke Meyer* (1987); Wayne A. Wiegand, "Ambassador in Absentia: George Meyer, William II and Theodore Roosevelt," *Mid-America* 51 (1974): 3–15.)

Wayne A. Wiegand

MICHIGAN. The Progressive Era in Michigan began with the governorship of Hazen S. Pingree* (1897–1901), who corrected the most flagrant tax evasion by large corporations and forced through the state legislature the first significant statewide appraisal of railroad and corporate property, which helped establish a rational basis for regulation and taxation, emulated by later progressive reformers in other states. Michigan's first two twentieth-century governors, Aaron T. Bliss (1901–1904) and Fred M. Warner (1905–1910), were conservative, but were carried along by the popular tide and permitted some progressive reforms. The fact that Bliss had virtually bought his nomination from a Republican convention brought about fierce pressures for direct primary elections,* which became law in 1909. During Warner's term, popular demand led to a new state constitution in 1908, which extended a partial franchise to women taxpayers on money issues; limited the hours and conditions of child labor;* gave cities a larger measure of home rule;* permitted the municipal ownership of utilities;* and enabled the state to undertake internal improvements such as highway construction.

Michigan's first twentieth-century progressive governor was Chase S. Osborn (1911–1912), a colorful leader and admirer of Pingree, who pushed for the vote for women (but failed); passed the state's first workmen's compensation law;* strengthened the enforcement of child labor laws; and wiped out the state's debt and left office with a surplus in the treasury. A progressive Democrat, Woodbridge Ferris (1913–1916) brought through an initiative* and referendum* measure; more effective state regulation of the utilities; a corrupt practices act* and ballot reform; and strongly supported a state prohibition* bill which passed in 1917. (F. Clever Bald, *Michigan in Four Centuries* (1954); Melvin G. Holli, *Reform in Detroit: Hazen S. Pingree and Urban Politics* (1969); V. L. Beal, "The Political Record of Michigan Governor Chase S. Osborn," Michigan Historical Collections *Bulletin no. 4* (January 1980).)

Melvin G. Holli

MILITARY REFORM. The military was not immune to the reform impulse of the Progressive Era; a number of institutional innovations during the period helped to transform the army and, to a lesser extent, the navy. The popular outcry against major miscalculations and errors in mobilization during the Spanish-American War,* as well as the army's assumption of a new role as a colonial garrison force, helped to create a political climate favorable to a number of long-delayed changes. Under the leadership of Secretary of War Elihu Root* (1899–1904), the so-called Root Reforms were authorized by Congress. The most important of these expanded the army's peacetime strength from 28,000 in 1897 to 80,000 in 1903 and created a General Staff, headed by a chief of staff. Root also greatly expanded the army's postgraduate educational system for officers and opened the Army War College.

As a result of lobbying by militia officers, Congress in 1902 officially designated the National Guard as the nation's ready reserve. From 1915 to 1917, a civilian-led "preparedness"* movement sought to replace the state militia with a national reserve force prepared through universal military training. Although Congress refused such a radical departure, the National Defense Act of 1916 provided for "federalization" of the National Guard during emergencies and created modern mechanisms for prewar training of large numbers of citizen officers through special camps and the Reserve Officers Training Corps. A Council of National Defense was established in 1916 to plan for wartime economic mobilization. In addition to obtaining a sizable battleship fleet, naval reformers, supported by a number of civilian groups, improved the promotion process and took the first steps toward creating a system of reserve officers as well as initiating centralized coordination. (Peter Karsten, "Armed Progres-

sives," in Fred Israel, ed., *Building the Organizational Society* (1972); Allan
R. Millett and Peter Maslowski, *For the Common Defense* (1984).)

John Whiteclay Chambers II

MILWAUKEE. The Progressive Era in Milwaukee was characterized by at least
four distinct, but frequently overlapping, movements. The first was a revolt
against the regular Republican leadership eventually headed by district attorney
and future governor Francis E. McGovern.* The second consisted of such bipartisan organizations as the Municipal League and Voters League, which were
galvanized by the graft trials prosecuted by McGovern against the Democratic
administration of five-time mayor David E. Rose. The third involved the widespread consumer rebellion against the Milwaukee Electric Railway and Light
Company (MER&LC) and other utilities. Finally, there was the Social Democratic party (SDP), headed by Victor Berger,* whose chief support lay with
organized labor and with German-Americans.* The SDP downplayed municipal
ownership and concentrated on providing a high level of public services through
honest, efficient administration.

In 1898, Rose was elected by a Democratic-Populist fusion on an anti-
MER&LC platform but quickly capitulated to the utility interests, ran a "wide-
open city," and undermined the civil service. Rose was eventually undone by
the McGovern graft prosecutions, lost to "boy mayor" Sherburn M. Becker in
1906, and regained office in 1908. In 1910, McGovern was elected governor,
and the SDP, led by Mayor Emil Seidel, captured city government. Although
the SDP administration pursued a moderate social welfare program and greatly
improved the caliber of government, a newly passed nonpartisan election law
facilitated the election of fusion mayor Gerhard A. Bading in 1912 and 1914.
In 1916, however, Seidel's district attorney Daniel W. Hoan was elected mayor,
inaugurating a twenty-four-year reign of "sewer socialism" and clean, efficient
government. (Bayard Still, *Milwaukee, The History of a City* (1965); Sally M.
Miller, *Victor Berger and the Promise of Constructive Socialism, 1910–1920*
(1973); Fred I. Olson, "The Milwaukee Socialists, 1879–1941" (Ph.D. diss.,
Harvard, 1952).)

John D. Buenker

MINNESOTA. Minnesota contributed both to the national development of reform thought and action, and to the tradition of American protest politics during
the Progressive Era. Both Republicans and Democrats variously contributed to
this reform tradition but the Grange, the Farmers Alliance, the Populists,* and
by the early twentieth century, the Nonpartisan League,* were also factors.
Unfair railroad rates, high interest charges on credit, and low prices and control
by Minneapolis millers were common grievances among farmers. Broader progressive issues were supported by Minnesota politicians and the legislature in
the early 1900s.

The 1898 gubernatorial election of Swedish-born John Lind, a Democrat-Populist, signaled the beginning of the Progressive Era in Minnesota. Although unsuccessful in gaining most of his reform program, Lind set the tone by advocating strong educational, social, and state administrative reform. Other progressive governors, including Samuel R. Van Sant, John A. Johnson, and Adolph Olson Eberhart, were more successful. Republican Van Sant, for example, secured passage of a state Board of Control bill for state institutions; but it was Democrat Johnson who championed such major issues as tax reform, an insurance code, and public utilities for cities. While legislative approval was not complete, Johnson nonetheless gained bipartisan support and was mentioned as a likely presidential candidate, but he died in 1909. Eberhart's administration enacted a nonpartisan legislature, school consolidation, a "Good Roads"* amendment, and a workmen's compensation bill. At the congressional level, Minnesota was represented by such strong progressives as Charles A. Lindbergh, Sr.,* a foe of the money trust and an unflinching House Republican insurgent, and Senator Moses E. Clapp, a longtime reformer. Republican Congressman Andrew Volstead authored the national Prohibition bill (1919).

Minnesota progressivism, as Carl H. Chrislock argues convincingly, changed from "consensus" politics to "conflict" politics about 1914. The old unifying themes of idealistic reform and distrust of the eastern interests were replaced by the debate on the Nonpartisan League, the farm protest movement, and the European war. However, German-Americans* and Scandinavian-Americans,* who had disagreed on county option, now joined on the war issue. Politically, the Nonpartisan League would merge with organized labor to form Minnesota's unique Farmer-Labor party. (Carl H. Chrislock, *The Progressive Era in Minnesota, 1899–1918* (1971); Winifred G. Helmes, *John A. Johnson, the People's Governor: A Political Biography* (1949); Theodore C. Blegen, *Minnesota: A History of the State* (rev. ed., 1975).)

Bruce L. Larson

MINNESOTA RATE CASE. This case, decided by the Supreme Court in 1913, grew out of litigation begun by several railroads operating in Minnesota which challenged maximum rates set by the Minnesota legislature and the State Railroad Commission. Although it was certain that the intrastate rates set by Minnesota had had an effect on interstate rates in the region, it was unclear whether the effect was significant enough to invalidate the rates set by the state. The Court therefore upheld the rates set by Minnesota but implied that had the rates been found discriminatory, the state would have had to yield to federal regulation and control. In a later case, decided in 1914, the Supreme Court upheld the Interstate Commerce Commission, which had found rates set by the Texas Railroad Commission unduly prejudicial to Shreveport, Louisiana, and preferential to Houston and Dallas. (Philip D. Locklin, *Economics of Transportation* (1966); Stuart Daggett, *Principles of Inland Transportation* (1955).)

Curtis Richards

MISSISSIPPI. From the turn of the century to the onset of World War I,* the Mississippi legislature enacted an impressive array of reform legislation. From 1902, when a popular primary law was passed, through the administration of Governor James K. Vardaman* (1904–1908), Edmund F. Noel (1908–1912), Earl Leroy Brewer (1912–1916), and Theodore G. Bilbo (1916–1920), Mississippi, perhaps more than any other southern state, illustrates the success of agrarian progressivism. Some of the most significant examples of Progressive reforms include the establishment of several eleemosynary institutions (tuberculosis sanitorium, school for the deaf and speechless), the creation of state regulatory agencies (Agriculture Commission, Highway Commission, bar examiners, Board of Pardons), penal reform (including a correctional school for white youths), a child labor law,* prohibition,* tax equalization, old age assistance, increased funding for white public schools, the expansion of health care facilities and adult education programs, an elective judiciary, abolition of the fee system for county officials, and several antimonopoly statutes. Although Mississippi blacks did not experience any significant improvement of their condition during the Progressive period, they did reap some short-term benefits. But most of those benefits were wiped out during the depression in southern agriculture following World War I. (William F. Holmes, *The White Chief: James Kimble Vardaman* (1970); Albert D. Kirwan, *Revolt of the Rednecks* (1951); William Alexander Percy, *Lanterns on the Levee* (1973).)

David G. Sansing

MISSOURI. Lincoln Steffens* wrote in *McClure's* magazine of "The Shamelessness of St. Louis," identifying Colonel Edward Butler as the political party boss of the city. Popular unrest with the growing arrogance of large companies, especially the traction and utilities companies, coupled with the blatant influence of Butler, eventually stirred reform-minded citizens, consumers, and politicians to action. The focal point for the reform impluse was circuit attorney Joseph W. Folk,* who owed his election in part to Butler's support. Folk became involved as a prosecutor in a bribery case involving the Suburban Railway Company and members of the Municipal Assembly.

Aided by favorable publicity in Joseph Pulitzer's* *St. Louis Post-Dispatch*, Folk's successful bribery prosecutions of 1902 led to wider investigations of corruption in the state legislature and to early support for Folk as a Democratic reform gubernatorial candidate. His platform became the "Missouri Idea"— emphasis on honesty in government, an involved electorate, and prosecution of corruption in either political party. With the strong support of the Saint Louis business community, Folk carried progressive reform to the state level with his election as governor in 1904. Although Folk had alienated many fellow Democrats, he was able to take credit for enactment of an antilobby law, a general primary law, a maximum railroad freight rate law, a two-cent passenger rate law, an antidiscrimination law forbidding unfair competition, and a public utilities corporation law, allowing cities to establish regulatory commissions. Social reform legislation included laws covering pure food, child labor,* compulsory education,* and labor.

Continuing division within the Democratic Party* allowed the leadership of progressive reform to shift to Republicans under Folk's gubernatorial successor, Herbert S. Hadley,* who had established a reform reputation as attorney general in prosecuting Standard Oil, International Harvester, and other corporations. Only two important reform bills became law, one dealing with limiting the hours women could work and the other preventing passenger rate discrimination on railroads, and Hadley himself gradually shifted from emphasizing prosecution to regulation of corporations through expert commissions and boards. In 1913 Elliott W. Major succeeded Hadley as governor, and the legislature created a public service commission, ratified direct election of senators,* and authorized commission or city manager forms of government for smaller cities. (David P. Thelen, *Paths of Resistance: Tradition and Dignity in Industrializing Missouri* (1986); Nicholas C. Burckel, "Progressive Governors in the Border States: Reform Governors of Missouri, Kentucky, West Virginia, and Maryland, 1900–1918" (Ph.D. diss., University of Wisconsin–Madison, 1971).)

Nicholas C. Burckel

MITCHEL, JOHN PURROY (July 19, 1897–July 6, 1918). Born in Fordham (Bronx), New York, Mitchel was educated at Columbia College and the New York Law School. A private attorney, Mitchel was appointed by the City of New York in 1907 to investigate charges of incompetency and corruption against several municipal officials. His success won him election as president of the Board of Aldermen in 1909 on an anti-Tammany* Republican-Fusionist ticket. Mitchel supported administrative and fiscal reform, an antivice crusade,* police neutrality during labor strikes and, unsuccessfully, a municipally owned and operated transit system.

After serving a few months as collector of the Port of New York, Mitchel was elected Fusion mayor of New York City on November 4, 1913. His progressive administration was effective in city appointments, fiscal and administrative reform, police efficiency, zoning, labor, and military preparedness, but proved ineffective in securing home rule* and significant reforms in education and public charities, removing the tracks of the New York Central Railway from city streets, and convincing the masses that the city government cared about the needs of ordinary people. In 1917 Mitchel was decisively defeated by Tammany candidate John F. Hylan. (Edwin R. Lewinson, *John Purroy Mitchel: The Boy Mayor of New York* (1965); Augustus Cerillo, Jr., "The Reform of Municipal

Government in New York City: From Seth Low to John Purroy Mitchel,'' *New York Historical Society Quarterly* 57 (January 1973): 51–71.)

Augustus Cerillo, Jr.

MITCHELL, JOHN (February 4, 1870–September 19, 1919). Mitchell attended Braidwood schools in Illinois but did not graduate, instead entering the coal mines in 1882. For the next several years he moved about the mines of Illinois, Colorado, and New Mexico. During the 1890s, he mined coal in northern Illinois, joined the United Mine Workers of America* (UMWA), and developed a reputation in Illinois as an effective union advocate and legislative lobbyist. He participated actively in Illinois during the 1897 national bituminous coal strike, and although relatively unknown outside the state, he was elected UMWA vice president in January 1898. After an unsuccessful stint at organizing West Virginia miners, Mitchell returned to Illinois, increased his union exposure, and was appointed acting UMWA president in September 1898.

In 1899 he was elected president and was reelected yearly until 1908, when he declined to run for health reasons. Under his leadership, Pennsylvania's anthracite mine workers won a strike in 1900. Two years later, some 150,000 mine workers struck for over five months and achieved a partial victory from a special commission appointed by President Theodore Roosevelt* to adjudicate the dispute. Along with other conservative labor leaders, Mitchell participated in the meetings of the National Civic Federation* (NCF), serving as salaried chairman of its trade agreement department from 1908 to 1911. From 1914 to 1915, he served as a member of the New York State Workmen's Compensation Commission, and as chairman of the New York State Industrial Commission from 1915 until his death. (Elsie Gluck, *John Mitchell: Miner* (1920); Joseph Gowaskie, ''John Mitchell: A Study in Leadership'' (Ph.D. diss., Catholic University of America, 1969); James O. Morris, ''The Acquisitive Spirit of John Mitchell, UMWA President (1899–1908),'' *Labor History* 20 (Winter 1979): 5–43.)

Joseph Gowaskie

MOBILE PLEDGE. In an address to the annual convention of the Southern Commercial Congress at Mobile, Alabama, on October 27, 1913, President Woodrow Wilson* promised to end the imperial domination of the United States over Latin America. He thus repudiated Theodore Roosevelt's* unilateral interpretation of the Monroe Doctrine and vowed that the United States ''will never again seek one additional foot of territory by conquest; nor will it, any longer, act the role of big brother, a role which protected Latin America from aggression from Europe but left it open to attack from the United States.'' In arguing that ''morality, not expediency'' must guide the United States, Wilson was establishing a new basis for inter-American relations, one that Secretary of the Navy Josephus Daniels* later described as ''foreshadowing the Good Neighbor policy'' of the 1930s. In practice, however, the Wilson administration was responsible for more interventions than any of its predecessors; morality and imperialistic expediency, no matter how different rhetorically, led to the same results in Mexico and Central America. If anything, Wilson's well-intentioned remarks at Mobile and in other addresses during his administration only made intervention more respectable. (Arthur S. Link, ed., *The Papers of Woodrow Wilson* (1966–), 28:448–52; Arthur S. Link, *Wilson: The New Freedom* (1956); N. Gordon Levin, *Woodrow Wilson and World Politics* (1968).)

Robert C. Hilderbrand

MODERNISM. Also known as liberalism, this major shift in Protestant theology arose in the last two decades of the nineteenth century and flourished in the first quarter of the twentieth. The main tenets of modernism are an adaptation of religious ideas to modern culture, the concept that God is immanent in human cultural development, and the belief that human society is moving toward the realization of the Kingdom of God. Modernism attempted to demonstrate these tenets in a time of profound social change which was made more complex by the intellectual shifts posed by modern science, comparative religion, and biblical criticism, and by the changing moral and religious attitudes of many Americans.

Modernism made significant inroads in most northern denominations including Congregationalists, Presbyterians, Methodists, Baptists, Episcopalians, Disciples, and Unitarians. Many ministers and lay leaders in these denominations supported such progressive reforms as direct primaries,* woman suffrage,* initiative,* referendum,* and recall,* regulation of interstate commerce, effective antitrust legislation, municipal ownership of public utilities,* income tax,* eighthour day, and prohibition of child labor* and of alcoholic beverages (*see* Prohibition). (William R. Hutchison, *The Modernist Impulse in American Protestantism* (1976); R. V. Pierard, "Liberalism, Theological" in Walter A. Elwell, ed., *Evangelical Dictionary of Theology* (1984), 631–35; Ferenc H. Szasz, "The Progressive Clergy and the Kingdom of God," *Mid-America* 55 (1973); 3–20.)

Paul C. Wilt

MODERNIZATION. Progressives sought to make the world less traditional and more modern. "Traditional" suggested old-fashioned, ignorant, wasteful, or corrupt practices that limited the capabilities of mankind. Modernization could overcome traditionalism and build a highly productive economy, an honest and effective government, a society in which the full potential of people could flourish, and a peaceful world order based on the rule of law. Defeat of traditionalism meant the overthrow of corrupt politics, the regulation of unwise corporate activity, the conquest of disease, and (in 1917–1919) the overthrow of reactionary empires.

Progressives looked to expert knowledge, as developed by scientists, engineers, and scholars; as publicized by crusading journalists; as supported by the new foundations and universities. The entire population had to be modernized through education, especially at the high school and college levels. The new-model modern American must purify his or her conscience before the commitment to social uplift would be truly effective. The more radical progressives lost their faith in modernization after the Great War, but it remained a popular middle-class credo until the disaster of the Great Depression suddenly challenged the implicit assumption that more modernization would always bring more progress and prosperity for everyone. (Richard Jensen, *Illinois: A Bicentennial History* (1978); Richard D. Brown, *Modernization: The Transformation of American Life, 1600–1860* (1976); Robert H. Wiebe, *The Search for Order, 1877–1920* (1967).)

Richard Jensen

MORGAN, JOHN PIERPONT (April 17, 1837–March 31, 1913). Born into a banking family in Hartford, Connecticut, and educated in the United States, Switzerland, and Germany, Morgan epitomized finance capitalism in America between the Civil War and World War I.* The Morgan firm made the major contributions of luring European investment into the United States and reorganizing by merger major American industries. By leading this effort, Morgan became the symbol of a "money trust" to the American public.

After some questionable business practices during the Civil War, Morgan acquired a share of the government's securities business during the 1870s, refinanced and reorganized the railroad industry during the 1880s, and helped finance the organization of General Electric, American Telephone and Telegraph, International Harvester, and United States Steel from 1892 to 1902. Morgan became so powerful that he was called upon during the 1890s to provide gold for the depleted U.S. Treasury and to coordinate the financial community response to the economic panic of 1907.* As fear of the money trust grew, Morgan and his industry were subjected to the congressional Pujo investigations* of 1912. Morgan died in Rome, Italy. (Frederick L. Allen, *The Great Pierpont Morgan* (1949); George Wheeler, *Pierpont Morgan and Friends: The Anatomy of a Myth* (1973); Andrew Sinclair, *Corsair: The Life of J. Pierpont Morgan* (1981).)

Martin I. Elzy

MOSKOWITZ, BELLE LINDNER ISRAELS (October 5, 1877–January 2, 1933). Born in Harlem, New York, Belle Lindner graduated from Horace Mann High School for Girls in 1894 and briefly attended Teachers College (Columbia University). After three years in settlement work at the Educational Alliance, on November 11, 1903, she married Charles Henry Israels; they had three children, but Charles Israels died in 1911.

As an active member of the Council of Jewish Women, Belle Israels led a dance hall reform campaign and was active in antiprostitution and other vice campaigns.* In 1912 she joined the New York Progressive party* and served as an associate leader of her home ward in Yonkers, New York. From 1913 to 1916, she worked as grievance clerk and later manager of the labor department of the Dress and Waist Manufacturers' Association. On November 22, 1914, she married Henry Moskowitz.*

Having supported Alfred E. Smith* in his first gubernatorial campaign, Belle Moskowitz established, and then became executive secretary of, the New York State Reconstruction Commission, which provided Smith with his policies on government reorganization, public health, labor and industrial relations, and housing reform. From 1923 on, as publicity director of the State Democratic Committee, she worked with Smith on legislation and masterminded his nomination for the presidency in 1928. (Elisabeth Israels Perry, *Belle Moskowitz: Social Reform and Politics in the Age of Alfred E. Smith* (1987).)

Elisabeth Israels Perry

MOSKOWITZ, HENRY (September 27, 1879–December 17, 1936). Born in Huesche, Rumania, he emigrated to America as a boy and grew up on New York's Lower East Side. In 1898, with friends from City College, he founded the Downtown Ethical Society, later Madison House. In 1906, he earned a Ph.D. in philosophy at the University of Erlangen. Involved in social reform since 1901, he helped bring abut the "Protocol of Peace" in the garment trade. Active in the City Club, the Citizens Union,* and in the movement to establish the New York State Factory Investigating Commission* after the fire at the Triangle Shirtwaist Company, he also helped found the National Association for the Advancement of Colored People.*

He held leadership posts in municipal fusion campaigns and in the national and New York State Progressive party* campaigns of 1912, running unsuccessfully for Congress himself. In 1913, Mayor John Purroy Mitchel* appointed him president of the Municipal Civil Service Commission. On November 22, 1914, he married Belle Israels.* The couple supported Governor Alfred E. Smith* throughout the 1920s. Moskowitz published several books on Smith, served as impartial chairman in labor arbitrations, and was active in Jewish philanthropy. (Hamilton Holt, "Henry Moskowitz: A Useful Citizen," *Independent* 77 (January 12, 1914): 66–67; J. Salwyn Schapiro, "Henry Moskowitz: A Social Reformer in Politics," *Outlook* 102 (October 26, 1912): 446–49; Elisabeth Israels Perry, *Belle Moskowitz: Social Reform and Politics in the Age of Alfred E. Smith* (1987).

Elisabeth Israels Perry

MOTHERS' PENSIONS ACTS. The mothers' pensions of the Progressive Era were the forerunner to Aid to Dependent Children (ADC) in the 1935 Social Security Act. Mothers' pensions reflected the new theory of poverty which argued that social inequities rather than personal defects were the principal causes of poverty. Reformers concluded that the state had to intervene to ensure social justice* and to overcome the results of impersonal forces. The pensions were state measures to prevent the breakup of families owing to poverty resulting from the death, desertion, and disablement of fathers. Progressives believed that for the normal child any home was better than any institution. A major agenda item of the Progressive Era was the child, as exemplified in the child labor* crusade; the campaigns for kindergartens and schools, parks and playgrounds; and juvenile court systems.*

In the first decade, the special needs of dependent children received increasing attention from Children's Aid Societies, from the Child Rescue League, and through the "child rescue" series published in *Delineator* magazine. The *Delineator* crusade led President Theodore Roosevelt* to call the 1909 Conference on Care of Dependent Children, which then gave considerable impetus to the mothers' pensions movement. In 1911 Missouri enacted a measure which applied only to Kansas City, and Illinois was the first to pass statewide legislation. By 1913, eighteen states had mothers' pensions acts, and the number reached thirty-nine states by 1919. The most determined opponents were the voluntary charity organizations which denounced the pensions as socialism and the "dole" which would pauperize the recipients. (Mark Leff, "Consensus for Reform: The Mothers' Pensions Movement in the Progressive Era," *Social Service Review* 47 (September 1973): 397-417; Roy Lubove, *The Struggle for Social Security, 1900–1935* (1968); David Rothman, "The State as Parent: Social Policy in the Progressive Era," in Willard Gaylin, ed., *Doing Good: The Limits of Benevolence* (1978).)

                                                                            J. Stanley Lemons

MOTION PICTURES. Though first demonstrated in 1889, this popular entertainment form did not begin to reach large audiences until 1896. Two years earlier, Thomas Edison and W. K. L. Dickson developed and began marketing the Kinetoscope, a peephole machine which showed a short filmstrip to one viewer at a time. To surmount the viewing limitations of the peep show, Dickson in America and others, particularly the Lumière brothers in France, worked simultaneously to perfect a motion picture projector that could show films to large audiences. The two projectors, debuting within months of each other in 1896, showed that moving pictures were commercially viable. The continued success of motion pictures, first shown as a separate act at vaudeville houses, led to the establishment of theatres that presented films exclusively. By 1905, the nickelodeon (named for its admission price) had begun to dominate motion picture exhibition, providing cheap entertainment to increasingly working-class and immigrant audiences.

Although some reformers, including Jane Addams,* considered film an important educational tool, vice crusaders saw the nickelodeons as unsafe centers of licentious behavior. Protests across the country peaked with the 1908 Christmas Day closing of New York City's 550 movie houses. The closing resulted in the formation of the National Board of Review,* which was assigned to preview pictures for proper moral standards. At the same time, exhibitors shifted away from cramped nickelodeons to movie "palaces," hoping to attract middle- and upper-class audiences by upgrading the theatres' appearance. Production companies, too, curried middle-class favor by emphasizing increasingly "wholesome" subject matter.

Throughout the era, the economic structure of the industry drifted toward monopoly. The major independents moved toward vertical integration, fighting for control over production, distribution, and exhibition of their films, and by the mid-1920s, the industry's oligopolistic structure had become firmly established. (Lewis Jacobs, *The Rise of the American Film: A Critical History* (1968); Lary May, *Screening Out the Past: The Birth of Mass Culture and the Motion Picture Industry* (1983); Tino Balio, ed., *The American Film Industry* (1985).)

Chris Foran

MUCKRAKING. The muckrakers were a group of Progressive Era journalists who wrote explicit accounts of the widespread national corruption. Their medium was the new, inexpensive popular magazine, whose development was the product of a growing national literacy, technological advances in printing, and a group of entrepreneurial editor-publishers such as S. S. McClure.* *Collier's,* *Cosmopolitan,* *McClure's, Everybody's,* and *American Magazine* were leading muckrake journals, and many newspapers offered similar accounts for their readers. Samuel Hopkins Adams* and Mark Sullivan* exposed fraudulent and dangerous patent medicines. Ray Stannard Baker* covered the railroads, industrial conflict, race relations, and the churches. Charles Edward Russell* wrote on the beef trust and on poverty and social conditions around the world. Christopher P. Connolly's beat was western land scandals, labor-management conflict, and judicial corruption. Alfred Henry Lewis and Burton J. Hendrick* examined the insurance industry and showed how the great American fortunes had been accumulated. Thomas Lawson* muckraked Wall Street. George K. Turner focused on municipal government, the white-slave trade, and the liquor interests. Will Irwin's specialties were the saloon and the press. The best-known series were Lincoln Steffens*, "Shame of the Cities"; David Graham Phillips,* "Treason of the Senate"; Ida Tarbell,* "History of the Standard Oil Company"; and Upton Sinclair's* account of immigrants and the Chicago meatpacking industry in *The Jungle*.

President Theodore Roosevelt* felt their stories were too one-sided and might stir up dangerous socialist discontent. He used the *Pilgrim's Progress* story of "the man with the muck-rake," who refused to lift his eyes from the corruption to see better things, to pin an unfavorable label on the journalists. Nevertheless, the muckrake accounts helped passage of his 1906 Meat Inspection*, Pure Food and Drugs,* and Hepburn* laws, and influenced public demand for honest elections; improved city and state government; direct election of U.S. senators;* better job and living conditions for women, children, and workingmen; provision for the unfortunate; and control of corporations. (Louis Filler, *Crusaders for*

American Liberalism (1939); Arthur Weinberg and Lila Weinberg, eds., *The Muckrakers* (1964); Arthur Weinberg and Lila Weinberg, eds., *The Muckrake Years* (1974).)

David Chalmers

MUGWUMPS. Used today, the term "Mugwump" is often employed as a synonym for political independence. Originally, however, it simply referred to those Republicans, most likely well-born and well-educated, who bolted their party during the 1884 presidential campaign to vote for the Democratic candidate, Grover Cleveland. These gentlemen reformers, never many in number and concentrated in urban areas in the states of Massachusetts, Connecticut, and New York, had as their main political concerns tariff reform, honesty in government, and the adoption of the merit system.

Both contemporaries and most historians have often dismissed Mugwumps, but individual Mugwumps did anticipate and participate in many progressive campaigns, especially those that advocated professionalism in public life. While affirming such traditional values as the responsibility of educated men to the community and the need for individual moral rectitude, they also accepted such elements of the modern order as scientific methods, national professional societies, and expanded municipal services. (Gerald W. McFarland, ed., *Moralists or Pragmatists? The Mugwumps, 1884–1900* (1975); Gerald W. McFarland, *Mugwumps, Morals, and Politics, 1884–1920* (1975); John G. Sproat, *"The Best Men": Liberal Reformers in the Gilded Age* (1968).)

Lloyd J. Graybar

MUIR, JOHN (April 21, 1838–December 24, 1914). Born in Dunbar, Scotland, Muir migrated with his family to a farm on the Wisconsin frontier. He attended the University of Wisconsin,* where he studied works of Ralph Waldo Emerson and Henry David Thoreau, and scientific theories of Louis Agassiz and Asa Gray. At the age of twenty-nine he walked 1,000 miles from Indiana to the Gulf of Mexico, then took a ship to California, arriving there in 1868. He made geological studies in Yosemite Valley and Sierra Nevada and published his observations in the *Overland Monthly* and *New York Daily News* during 1871–1872. He became increasingly interested in conservation* problems as he noted results of land and water misuse by commercial groups. His concern for this situation resulted in work to help initiate the magazine *Picturesque California*. He visited Yosemite in 1889 and presented his observations of forest destruction in articles for the *San Francisco Bulletin*.

His strong advocacy of conservation measures helped to bring legislation establishing the Sierra Forest Reserve in 1891 and Yosemite Park in 1906. In 1892 he helped to organize and became first president of the Sierra Club, which became a leading American conservation organization. He was unsuccessful in efforts to prevent authorization of a large reservoir in Hetch Hetchy Valley of Yosemite Park for water supply of San Francisco. In 1911 he submitted to

President William H. Taft* plans for a national park system. He wrote for many leading national magazines and was the author of a dozen books, including *The Mountains of California* (1894), *Our National Parks* (1901), and *The Yosemite* (1912). (Stephen Fox, *John Muir and His Legacy: The American Conservation Movement* (1981); Holway R. Jones, *John Muir and the Sierra Club: The Battle for Yosemite* (1965); Herbert F. Smith, *John Muir* (1965).)

Harold T. Pinkett

MULLER V. OREGON (208 U.S. 412) (1908). The issue was the extent of state police power to enact reasonable laws to protect health, safety, morals, and the general welfare while not violating the individual rights to property and freedom of contract that are protected by the Fourteenth Amendment. An Oregon statute prohibited women from working in a laundry more than ten hours during a one-day period. The case was ultimately appealed to the U.S. Supreme Court. Louis D. Brandeis* was retained to defend the constitutionality of the law. Brandeis's brief was precedent-setting. It contained over one hundred pages on the conditions of labor, legislation, hours, statistics, and only two pages of law.

In a unanimous decision upholding the law, Justice David J. Brewer, speaking for the court, argued "that a woman's physical structure and the performance of maternal functions place her at a disadvantage in the struggle for subsistence in obvious. This is especially true when the burdens of motherhood are upon her." Consequently, "healthy mothers are essential to vigorous offspring," and "the physical well-being of woman becomes an object of public interest and care in order to preserve the strength and vigor of the race." This decision is an interesting contrast to *Lochner v. New York** (1905). (Felix Frankfurter, "Hours of Labor and Realism in Constitutional Law," *Harvard Law Review* 29 (February 1916): 353–73; Ray A. Brown, "Police Power—Legislation for Health and Personal Safety," *Harvard Law Review* 42 (May 1929): 866–98.)

John R. Aiken

MUNICIPAL BATH MOVEMENT. Those urban Progressive reformers most concerned with the plight of slum-dwellers felt that city governments should provide for the poor a means to attain middle-class standards of personal cleanliness which their crowded tenements lacked. Citing the municipal bath systems of European cities, statistics indicating the dearth of bathing facilities in slums, and buttressed by public acceptance of the germ theory of disease, the advocates of municipal baths argued that the public health and the health of the individual would be safeguarded. The cleanliness made possible by public baths, they also felt, would stimulate a "feeling of self-respect and a desire for self-improvement," and help to Americanize* the immigrant.

Responding to these demands, thirty-one American cities either constructed at municipal expense or acquired through private philanthropy a system of public baths between 1890 and 1915. In 1912 bath reformers, led by Simon Baruch, a New York physician, founded the American Association for Promoting Hygiene and Public Baths. In spite of this achievement, municipal baths were never patronized as fully as their advocates hoped, and the need for them declined as tenement house legislation required private bathing facilities in low-income housing. (G. W. W. Hangar, "Public Baths in the United States," in U.S. Department of Commerce and Labor, *Bulletin of the Bureau of Labor* (1904), 1245–367; Marilyn Thornton Williams, "The Public Bath Movement in the United States, 1890–1915" (Ph.D. diss., New York University, 1972); Marilyn Thornton Williams, "New York City's Public Baths: A Case Study in Urban Progressive Reform," *Journal of Urban History* 7 (1980): 49–81.)

                                                                Marilyn Thornton Williams

MUNICIPAL OWNERSHIP OF UTILITIES. Most American cities have always owned "utilities," such as streets and parks. In the late nineteenth century, however, movements arose in many cities for the "municipalization" of what were then private businesses: gas, electric, and street railway companies. The movements grew in influence after 1900. In several large cities, including Chicago* in 1905, mayoral elections were won by candidates calling for little else but municipal ownership. By 1917, more than two-thirds of American cities owned waterworks, one-third owned electric plants, 5 percent owned gas plants, and a handful owned street railways.

In part, municipal ownership was simply one aspect of the broader interest in utility regulation.* But municipal ownership also had links to two other Progressive Era movements: socialism and municipal home rule.* For socialists, municipal ownership was the key to practical politics. The Socialist party* achieved its greatest electoral successes in this era, and nearly always utility regulation was the chief local issue. Municipal ownership was the perfect platform for Socialist coalition building because it touched everyone. The municipal ownership idea also gained prominence because it was associated with home rule, i.e., the independence of city governments from state control. Diverse groups—including the Conference of American Mayors, the National Civic Federation's* Commission on Public Ownership, and the National Municipal League*—insisted upon home rule in utility regulation, including the right of cities to acquire utility properties.

After 1907, however, states began to transfer control of utilities from city councils to state commissions. As a result, the municipal ownership movement gradually faded in most cities. Municipal ownership projects since World War I* have sprung more from unwelcome necessity (failed private enterprises) than from ideals of municipal reform. (National Civic Federation, Commission on Public Ownership and Operation, *Municipal and Private Operation of Public Utilities*, 3 vols. (1907); Carl D. Thompson, *Public Ownership* (1925).)

                                                                        David Paul Nord

MUNSEY, FRANK A. (August 21, 1854–December 22, 1925). Born on a farm near Mercer, Maine, and educated in public schools until the age of sixteen, Munsey could have been the prototype for the major character in a Horatio Alger novel. Penniless, he started his career as a telegraph operator. Then, with a capital of forty dollars, he began publication of a juvenile magazine in New York City in 1882. His ambition, shrewdness, avarice, and restlessness led him into heavy investments in U.S. Steel, and ownership of grocery stores, hotels, office buildings, magazines, and newspapers, including some storied ones. In forty years he amassed $40 million, while earning the unyielding enmity of newspapermen for his destruction of so many of his purchases.

Normally a class-conscious Republican, he became an ardent Progressive* in 1912. Stirred almost exclusively by hero worship for Theodore Roosevelt,* he joined his friend George W. Perkins* in underwriting the new party. After a dramatic decision in Chicago in June to open their coffers, they discovered that their money was more welcome than their advice. Their activities also stimulated anger among the more orthodox Progressives. The campaign over, Munsey abandoned the new party on January 8, 1913, with a signed front-page editorial in his New York *Press*. He urged the amalgamation of the Republicans and the Progressives. (George Britt, *Forty Years—Forty Millions* (1935); Amos R. E. Pinchot, *History of the Progressive Party, 1912–1916*, Helene M. Hooker, ed. (1958); John Allen Gable, *The Bull Moose Years: Theodore Roosevelt and the Progressive Party* (1978).)

Jules A. Karlin

MURDOCK, VICTOR (March 18, 1871–July 8, 1945). Born in Burlingame, Kansas, Murdock was educated in the Wichita public schools and at Lewis Academy. He learned the newspaper business with his father, worked for the *Inter Ocean* in Chicago, and returned to Wichita in 1894 to become managing editor of the family-owned *Daily Eagle*. Elected to Congress in 1903, he served until 1915. His disagreement with Speaker Joseph G. Cannon* over the method used to pay for mail carried by the railroads caused him to become increasingly critical of Republican leadership in the House. He began to support progressive reform in 1906 and was aligned with the reform faction in Kansas thereafter.

A leader of the Republican insurgency, he promoted much of the publicity that led to the downfall of the autocratic "Cannon rules." Not recognized as much as George Norris* for this achievement, he was much more despised by party regulars. Murdock was generally more radical in his beliefs than most Progressives, and although he opposed the bolt in 1912, he became an avid spokesman for the Progressive party.* He was its floor leader in the House in 1913. After an unsuccessful bid for the Senate on the Bull Moose ticket, he became chairman of the Progressive National Committee in 1914. He refused to follow Theodore Roosevelt's* advice in 1916 and supported Woodrow Wilson.* Murdock presided over the last meeting of the Progressive party at Saint Louis in 1917. Wilson appointed him to the Federal Trade Commission* that year, and he served until 1925, part of the time as its chairman. (George W. Norris, *Fighting Liberal: The Autobiography of George W. Norris* (1945); *The*

Autobiography of William Allen White (1946); Robert S. La Forte, *Leaders of Reform* (1974).)

Robert S. La Forte

MURPHY, CHARLES FRANCIS (June 30, 1858–April 25, 1924). The son of Irish immigrants, Murphy was born in New York City on June 20, 1858. Acquiring little formal education, he grew up living by his wits and physical prowess. In 1892 he became a Tammany Hall* district leader. Six years later Mayor Robert A. Van Wyck appointed him a dock commissioner. This office, which dispensed lucrative contracts, strengthened his political position, and by 1902 he had gained undisputed control of Tammany. Murphy secured the mayoralty election for George B. McClellan, son of the Civil War general, in 1903 and again in 1905, despite the vigorous opposition of reformers.

Murphy had become the dominant figure in New York State Democratic politics by 1906. He then obtained the election of William J. Gaynor* as mayor in 1907 and John A. Dix as governor in 1910. His candidate William Sulzer* also won the gubernatorial race in 1912. However, after Sulzer quarreled with him over patronage and tried to assert his independence, Murphy forced his impeachment from office. The enmity of President Woodrow Wilson* briefly weakened Murphy's position, but in 1918 he secured the nomination and subsequent election of Alfred E. Smith* as governor. He also helped to win the Democratic presidential nomination for James Cox* in 1920 and was hoping to do likewise for Smith four years later, but died unexpectedly. (Gustavus Myers, *The History of Tammany Hall*, 2d ed. (1917); Nancy Joan Weiss, *Charles Francis Murphy* (1968); Mark R. Werner, *Tammany Hall* (1928).)

Robert Muccigrosso

MURPHY, EDGAR GARDNER (August 31, 1869–June 23, 1913). Born near Fort Smith, Arkansas, Murphy graduated from the University of the South in 1889 and did a year's postgraduate study in New York City. He was ordained in 1893 and served churches in Chillicothe, Ohio (1893–1897); Kingston, New York (1897–1898); and Montgomery, Alabama (1898–1901). He wrote extensively on social issues for national magazines and organized the Southern Society to study race relations. At Tuskegee Institute he became friends with a number of northern philanthropists and southern educators who organized the Southern Education Board, and from 1901 to 1910 he served as its secretary. In ten years its campaigns aided in obtaining a 500 percent increase in state appropriations for education. Out of it grew the General Education Board, which promoted educational and health reforms internationally. In 1901–1902 he prepared the first extensive body of literature on child labor, and in 1904, under his leadership, the National Child Labor Committee* was organized. (Hugh C. Bailey, *Edgar*

Gardner Murphy, Gentle Progressive (1968); Maud K. Murphy, *Edgar Gardner Murphy, From Records and Memories* (1943).)

Hugh C. Bailey

MURRAY, WILLIAM H. (November 21, 1869–October 15, 1956). Born in Toadsuck, Texas, "Alfalfa Bill" Murray was educated at College Hill Institute and Mineral Wells College, graduating from the latter in 1893. Murray's political career in Texas and Oklahoma was dedicated to preserving the family farm and rural ideals. After moving to Indian Territory in 1898, he served as president of the convention which drew up a constitution for the new state of Oklahoma. Many of Murray's agrarian views were incorporated into that document. Murray served as the speaker of the first Oklahoma House of Representatives, where he continued to espouse his agrarian-Progressive views. From 1913 to 1917, he served in the U.S. House of Representatives, where he strove to put agrarianism into the federal statutes and worked on behalf of Indians. After living for a decade in Bolivia, where he was an agricultural colonizer, Murray won the governship of Oklahoma in 1930, from which he carried out an individualized campaign against the Great Depression. (Keith L. Bryant, Jr., *Alfalfa Bill Murray* (1968).)

Monroe Billington

MYERS, GUSTAVUS (March 20, 1872–December 7, 1942). Born in Trenton, New Jersey, Myers grew up in an impoverished family. Factory work as a teenager instilled in him a lifelong sympathy for the underprivileged, and in 1907 he joined the Socialist party.* As a journalist, his penchant for laborious research helped to make him an important and controversial writer during the Progressive Era. His *History of Public Franchises in New York City* (1900) and *History of Tammany Hall* (1901) were well-documented exposés of graft and corruption that stemmed from collusion between public officials and private businessmen. *The History of the Great American Fortunes* (1909–1910), published in three volumes, was Myers's most significant achievement. This study focused on wealthy individuals during the post–Civil War era, whose fortunes, while fraudulently obtained, ultimately derived from the nature of capitalism itself, which was responsible for the polarities of colossal wealth and grinding poverty. *The History of the Supreme Court* (1912) emphasized the power of capitalism to influence judicial thinking and decisions. Myers never recanted his radicalism, but in 1912 he quit the Socialist party and during World War I* served with the Committee on Public Information* that espoused American belligerency. The 1930s found him a supporter of the New Deal. His *History of Bigotry in the United States* (1943) appeared posthumously. (*Dictionary of American Biography*, Supp. 3; John Chamberlain, *Farewell to Reform*, 2d ed. (1933).)

Robert Muccigrosso

N

NATION, THE. Founded in 1865 by E. L. Godkin and Wendell Phillips Garrison, this weekly review championed the rights of black Americans and advocated free trade, civil service reform,* and other tenets of Manchester liberalism. Through a merger with the *New York Evening Post* in 1881, it became the weekly edition of that newspaper, but its policies remained unchanged. It appealed to a small, but influential, audience of conservative intellectuals who favored cautious trust-busting to restore economic competition, but who condemned labor militancy and all radical programs of social change. Under the direction of Paul Elmer More (1909–1914), the *Nation* was best known for its informed and trenchant commentary on literary, scientific, and cultural subjects.

When Oswald Garrison Villard* became editor in 1918, he severed the magazine's tie to the *Post* and transformed it into a powerful organ of political dissent. Temporarily suppressed in World War I* for criticizing Wilsonian violations of civil liberties, the *Nation* denounced the Treaty of Versailles, pleaded for pacifism and disarmament, urged recognition of the U.S.S.R., and defended the labor movement and the rights of racial and ethnic minorities. (Henry F. May, *The End of American Innocence: A Study of the First Years of Our Own Time, 1912–1917* (1959); Frank L. Mott, *A History of American Magazines, 1865–1885* (1938); Theodore Peterson, *Magazines in the Twentieth Century* (1956).)

Maxwell H. Bloomfield

NATIONAL AMERICAN WOMAN SUFFRAGE ASSOCIATION. The National American Woman Suffrage Association (NAWSA) was created in 1890 by the unification of two rival suffrage organizations. Although NAWSA's first two presidents were Elizabeth Cady Stanton and Susan B. Anthony, it developed in a conservative direction, separating itself from contemporary radical movements and advancing woman suffrage by political compromise. In 1900, Carrie

Chapman Catt* became president, but was unable to move the organization forward and in 1904 passed the leadership to Anna Howard Shaw,* who kept it for over a decade.

NAWSA was a federation of loosely affiliated state societies. Nominally committed to a federal amendment, NAWSA actually concentrated on amending state constitutions. By 1907, younger suffragists were bringing new energy into the movement, but NAWSA clung to its ways. In 1913, Alice Paul* became chairman of NAWSA's Congressional Committee and revived the drive for a federal amendment. NAWSA leaders, hostile to Paul's initiative, forced her to resign, and endorsed instead the Shafroth-Palmer Bill, authorizing state-by-state referenda. This ill-advised strategy, designed to avoid antagonizing southern Democrats who feared the votes of black women, finally ended Shaw's presidency.

In December 1915, Catt resumed the office. Her "Winning Plan" coordinated state campaigns with congressional support for a federal amendment. In 1917, under her leadership, NAWSA offered its services to the war effort, which split the suffrage movement. NAWSA's federated structure was crucial to the ratification process. In 1920, the Nineteenth Amendment was added to the Constitution, and NAWSA dissolved itself into the League of Women Voters.* (Mari Jo Buhle and Paul Buhle, eds., *The Concise History of Woman Suffrage: Selections from the Classic Work of Stanton, Anthony, Gage, and Harper* (1978); Aileen Kraditor, *The Ideas of the Woman Suffrage Movement, 1890–1920* (1965).)

Ellen Du Bois

NATIONAL ASSOCIATION FOR THE ADVANCEMENT OF COLORED PEOPLE (NAACP).

This organization, founded by blacks who were militantly opposed to racial discrimination and by racially liberal white Progressives, was established in 1910. The chain of events which led to the founding of the NAACP began with the race riot* in Springfield, Illinois, in August 1908. William English Walling* wrote an article for the *Independent** deploring the rising tide of racial violence and calling for a revival of the reform spirit associated with the abolitionist movement. Walling's article inspired an interracial group to form and to join Oswald Garrison Villard,* grandson of William Lloyd Garrison, in calling a meeting to discuss renewing the struggle for the civil and political rights of black Americans. The conference met in New York City in 1909 on Lincoln's birthday. During the second national conference in 1910, the NAACP was born.

The new organization brought together the black militants who had joined with W. E. B. Du Bois* in 1905 to form the Niagara Movement and a group of white progressives. Du Bois joined the staff of the NAACP in 1910 and founded and edited the *Crisis** magazine. From 1910 to 1917, he was the organization's only black officer. In 1915, with its attack on the grandfather clause in the Oklahoma constitution and the campaign against the racist film

Birth of a Nation,* the NAACP began its struggle for first-class citizenship for black Americans. (Charles Flint Kellogg, *NAACP: A History of the National Association for the Advancement of Colored People* (1967); Mary White Ovington, *The Walls Came Tumbling Down* (1947).)

Arvarh E. Strickland

NATIONAL ASSOCIATION OF MANUFACTURERS. This association was a businessmen's lobbying group best known for its vociferous opposition to labor unions. In 1895, 300 industrialists met in Cincinnati to organize the National Association of Manufacturers (NAM). The new association did not represent big business, but rather the middle ranks of manufacturers. It did not initially give much attention to labor matters. Rather the major concerns of its founders were the deep economic depression of the 1890s* and the recently lowered protective tariff. These issues, however, did not unite business, for manufacturers were not suffering equally from the depression, and some businessmen benefited from lower tariffs while others did not. After the end of the depression, the organization sought to unite around an effort to increase foreign trade. This did not stir any excitement, and the association languished until three midwestern industrialists, David Parry, John Kirby, Jr., and James W. Van Cleave, rose to prominence.

David Parry, an Indianapolis manufacturer, became president of the NAM in 1902, and he directed the association to an issue which united all businessmen, antiunionism. Labor unions had increased their membership fourfold since 1897 and were increasingly active in politics. Therefore, the NAM adopted a militant stance against strikes and in favor of the open shop. Its political efforts against labor-backed candidates were especially noteworthy in the 1912 election,* leading to congressional investigation of its activities. Besides its opposition to unions, the NAM also took a consistently negative stance on all major reforms of the Woodrow Wilson* presidency. (Robert H. Wiebe, *Businessmen and Reform* (1962); Albert K. Steigerwalt, *The National Association of Manufacturers* (1964); Richard W. Gable, "Birth of an Employers' Association," *Business History Review* 33 (1959): 535–45.)

Edward R. Kantowicz

NATIONAL ASSOCIATION OPPOSED TO WOMAN SUFFRAGE. The Massachusetts Association Opposed to the Further Extension of Suffrage to Women (MAOFESW), the oldest and most active antisuffragist state organization, formed in the 1880s, organized a convention in 1911. Delegates from several state antisuffrage organizations convened in New York to form the National Association Opposed to Woman Suffrage (NAOWS). Its express goals were to help coordinate efforts among states, to organize new state associations, and to inform public opinion through literature distribution. Mrs. Arthur M. Dodge (Josephine Marshall Jewell) served as president from 1911 until 1917. When the suffrage strategy shifted its emphasis to Congress, NAOWS followed and moved its national headquarters to Washington, D.C., where Mrs. J. W.

Wadsworth (Alice Hay), wife of Senator James Wadsworth of New York, became president.

NAOWS argued that only by keeping women free from economic and political concerns could women make a contribution to society as wives and mothers, and effectively blocked introduction of suffrage legislation. The organization was an arena for middle- and upper-class women to actively protect women's traditional roles as wives and mothers, which they saw as threatened by the vote. Although the organization dissolved in 1920, with the ratification of the Nineteenth Amendment, the NAOWS newspaper the *Woman Patriot* (formerly the *Woman's Protest*) was maintained by a small committee and continued to red-bait numerous women's organizations in the 1920s. (Jane Jerome Camhi, "Women against Women: American Antisuffragism, 1880–1920" (Ph.D diss., Tufts University, 1973); James J. Kenneally, "The Opposition to Woman Suffrage in Massachusetts, 1868–1920" (Ph.D diss., Boston College, 1963); Ida Husted Harper, *History of Woman Suffrage*, vol. 5 (1922); J. Stanley Lemons, *The Woman Citizen: Social Feminism in the 1920s* (1973).)

Marie Laberge

NATIONAL BOARD OF FARM ORGANIZATIONS. After the 1890s, many farmers felt that they had been ill-served by the partisanship of the populist era. They saw business and labor interests organizing and lobbying Congress in the early 1900s, but they had no similar representation. The National Grange concentrated most of its efforts on social and educational activities. The Farmers Union* (NFU) and the American Society of Equity,* both founded in 1902, sought to increase income by commodity-withholding actions. Only in 1911 did a group of insurgent state granges send a lobbyist to Washington, but progressive farmers were slow to act. Finally, with the impetus of American entry into war, a conference representing the NFU, Gifford Pinchot's* conservationists, a group of midwestern editors and educators interested in better farm credits, and several commodity groups, formed the National Board of Farm Organizations (NBFO) on July 20, 1917.

The immediate goal of the NBFO was to get draft exemptions, higher commodity prices, control over railroad rates, and protection of cooperatives from antitrust laws. The moderate successes of the NBFO led to great exuberance about the postwar period, but the group soon foundered over disagreements among its interest groups. Radical elements of the NFU broke off toward the left, and conservatives soon opted for the business-oriented American Farm Bureau Federation.* Despite the remembrance of the 1910–1914 period as the "Golden Age of Parity," the late appearance and the rapid failure of the NBFO demonstrated the inability of the nation's farmers to agree on common goals. (James L. Guth, "The National Board of Farm Organizations: Experiment in

Political Cooperation,'' *Agricultural History* 48 (1974): 418–40; Lowell K. Dyson, *Farmers' Organizations* (1986).)

Lowell K. Dyson

NATIONAL BOARD OF REVIEW OF MOTION PICTURES. (Also the National Board of Censorship of Motion Pictures.) Formed in March 1909 by the People's Institute of New York City in response to local concern about the content of motion pictures, under the name of the National Board of Censorship of Motion Pictures and in cooperation with the Motion Picture Patents Company, this organization attempted to assuage the developing tide of social and religious outcries. While its public position was "review," its private stance was "censorship."

Working clearly from the assumption that motion pictures were protected under the First Amendment, board members worked to negotiate for the showing of films in New York City. Using a group of volunteers to screen all films submitted to them, the board tried to establish what was "moral" or "immoral" by New York City standards. By June of 1909 the board members found their scope had been expanded to include all of the United States and that they were being financed by a fee producers would pay to have their films screened by them. While they had no real power, they could suggest changes in the films.

Because of the board's financial ties to the film industry, it was never able to become the public voice. In 1915 the name was changed to the National Board of Review of Motion Pictures. As a social pressure organization, the board began to perceive its function as improving both the quality of motion pictures and the public's taste, but it ultimately failed to stop the distribution and exhibition of what many social and religious leaders considered to be objectionable motion pictures. (Lewis Jacobs, *The Rise of the American Film* (1968); Garth Jowett, *Film: The Democratic Art* (1976).)

Michael T. Marsden

NATIONAL CATHOLIC WELFARE COUNCIL. A national coordinating body for American Catholicism headquartered in Washington, D.C., from 1917 to 1966, the National Catholic Welfare Council (NCWC) began its life as the National Catholic War Council, founded at a meeting of 115 delegates from 68 American dioceses in August 1917. A Paulist priest, Rev. John J. Burke, spearheaded the council's organization and placed it under the jurisdiction of an administrative board of bishops. During the war, NCWC provided material support to chaplains and Catholic servicemen and cooperated with such groups as the YMCA,* the Salvation Army, and the Jewish Welfare Board in fundraising efforts for home-front activities. After the war, the NCWC reorganized as a permanent welfare council. The Vatican nearly dissolved it in 1921–1922, fearful of "conciliar" bodies that infringed on individual bishops' prerogatives, but the organization survived by changing its name from "Council" to "Conference." It played a twofold role: an informational clearinghouse for American

Catholic leaders and a Washington lobby to protect Catholic interests in the political arena. (Michael Williams, *American Catholics in the War* (1921); Elizabeth McKeown, "War and Welfare" (Ph.d. diss., University of Chicago, 1972); James Hennessey, *American Catholics* (1981).)

Edward R. Kantowicz

NATIONAL CHILD LABOR COMMITTEE. In 1900, children under fourteen constituted 7.7 percent of the northern industrial work force and 25 percent of southern mill workers. Edgar Gardner Murphy* organized the Alabama Child Labor Committee and in 1901–1902 issued a series of nationally distributed anti-child labor pamphlets. Increased concern led to the formation of a New York committee in 1903 and 1904 of the National Child Labor Committee by twenty-five national leaders. In 1906–1907, the committee temporarily supported a national child labor bill which was defeated in Congress. From 1907 until his death in 1918, the committee's most effective political strategist was the former North Carolina Presbyterian editor Alexander J. McKelway.*

By 1914, the committee had 8,733 members and had been instrumental in obtaining a fourteen-year age limit in thirty-five states and other reforms. It pressured Congress into extensively studying the condition of women and children and establishing the Children's Bureau* in 1912. Discontented with slowness and unevenness of state actions, the committee again supported a national child labor law in 1914. It was deeply involved in advising the government on enforcement of the 1916 and 1918 acts until their nullification in 1918 and 1922. (Elizabeth H. Davidson, *Child Labor Legislation in the Southern Textile States* (1939); Hugh C. Bailey, *Liberalism in the New South* (1969).)

Hugh C. Bailey

NATIONAL CITIZENS' LEAGUE. This was a businessmen's group organized in 1911 to lobby for reform of the banking system. The panic of 1907* had revealed numerous flaws in the national banking system, so Congress passed the Aldrich-Vreeland Act* in 1908 authorizing temporary reforms and establishing a National Monetary Commission* to recommend more permanent measures. The commission reported in 1911, recommending the establishment of a central bank. Paul M. Warburg,* a New York investment banker and the principal author of the commission's report, worked to unite business behind the drive for a central bank. In order to defuse resentment against Wall Street influence, he asked the Chicago Association of Commerce to take the lead. This association organized the National Citizens' League for the Promotion of a Sound Banking System on June 6, 1911. It incorporated in Illinois; invited merchants and manufacturers, not bankers, to serve on its board; and hired J. Laurence Laughlin, an economist from the University of Chicago,* to act as its executive director. Despite all these precautions, the Pujo Committee* of the House of Representatives, investigating the "money trust," revealed the Wall Street dominance of the National Citizens' League. As a result, it played only a minor role in the final drive for passage of the Federal Reserve Act* in 1913. (J. Laurence Laughlin, *The National Citizens' League for the Promotion of a Sound Banking System* (1911); J. Laurence Laughlin, *The Federal Reserve Act* (1933); Robert H. Wiebe, *Businessmen and Reform* (1962).)

Edward R. Kantowicz

NATIONAL CIVIC FEDERATION (NCF). Organized by Ralph M. Easley in June 1900, the NCF drew its membership equally from organized labor, big business, and the public, and carried on its work through a number of special departments, national conferences, publications, model bills, and political lobbying. Positioned between anticapitalist socialists and radicals on the left and antiunion small businessmen on the right, the progressive NCF accepted business combinations and trade unions as permanent and integral parts of the nation's economic structure, and sought industrial harmony and justice within the framework of the American capitalist system.

From 1900 to 1916, the NCF mediated several labor disputes and promoted trade agreements between corporations and unions, company welfare programs, and uniform state laws in the areas of workmen's compensation,* factory safety,* child labor,* and public utilities.* It secured the Newlands Act (1913) for the mediation of railroad labor disputes and provided ideological support for the Federal Trade Commission Act* (1914), but failed to obtain the federal licensing and incorporation of interstate business or the legalization of reasonable restraints of trade through an amendment to the Sherman Act. After 1916, the NCF, guided by the superpatriotic Easley, crusaded against pacifists, socialists, radicals, communists, and other subversives. (Marguerite Green, *The National Civic Federation and the American Labor Movement, 1900–1925* (1956); James Weinstein, *The Corporate Ideal in the Liberal State: 1900–1918* (1968); Gerald Kurland, *Seth Low: The Reformer in an Urban and Industrial Age* (1971).)

Augustus Cerillo, Jr.

NATIONAL CONFERENCE OF CHARITIES AND CORRECTION. Meeting in 1874 in association with the American Social Science Association (ASSA), representatives of state boards of charities formed the Conference of Boards of Public Charities (renamed Conference of Charities in 1875). Delegates found even the ASSA's limited theorizing insufficiently practical and began meeting separately in 1879. Control of the group, renamed the National Conference of Charities and Correction (NCCC) in 1884, passed in the 1890s to leaders in the charity organization societies* and other nongovernmental agencies. Each year the NCCC elected as president a prominent individual, such as Jane Addams* (1910) or Homer Folks* (1911 and 1923).

The annual conferences brought together leaders in varied lines of social work; many specialized associations met concurrently. The sessions and widely circulated *Proceedings* served as sounding boards for current ideas, from condemnation of alcohol to debate over cooperative fund-raising and from Mary

Richmond's 1897 call for professional education in social work to Abraham Flexner's 1915 argument that social work was not a profession. "Social Standards for Industry,"* composed by an NCCC committee, may have influenced the 1912 Progressive party* platform. With practical problems and remedies paramount, sessions on social and economic issues were common from 1910 onward. In 1917 the NCCC renamed itself the National Conference of Social Work (National Conference on Social Welfare, 1956). (Frank J. Bruno, with Louis Towley, *Trends in Social Work, 1874–1956: A History Based on the Proceedings of the National Conference of Social Work* (1957); Clarke A. Chambers, *Seedtime for Reform: American Social Service and Social Action, 1918–1933* (1963); National Conference of Charities and Correction/National Conference of Social Work, *Proceedings*.)

David I. Macleod

NATIONAL CONFERENCE ON CITY PLANNING (NCCP). This was an umbrella group composed of professional planners and social reformers concerned with urban problems. In 1907, social settlement residents in New York formed a Congestion Committee, with Benjamin C. Marsh* as secretary. This committee organized a traveling Congestion Exhibit to illustrate New York's overcrowded slums, and issued a call for a National Conference on City Planning and Congestion. The conference brought together architects, engineers, social reformers, charity workers, and politicians on May 21, 1909, in Washington, D.C. Annual conferences were held thereafter in different cities.

The architects and engineers engaged in day-to-day planning work soon took over the conference from the social reformers.* They dropped the word *congestion* from the title, wrote a model enabling act for the establishment of a department of city planning, and in 1917 organized the American City Planning Institute (now the American Institute of Planners) as a professional organization for active planners. The National Conference continued as a vehicle for public education on city problems. Though viewed today primarily as a stepping-stone toward the professionalization of city planning, the original NCCP was typical of many Progressive Era reform groups in its broad-based composition and wide-ranging concerns. (Mel Scott, *American City Planning since 1890* (1969); John L. Hancock, "Planners in the Changing American City, 1900–1940," *Journal of the American Institute of Planners* 33 (1967): 290–304; Donald A. Krueckeberg, ed., *Introduction to Planning History in the United States* (1983).)

Edward R. Kantowicz

NATIONAL CONSERVATION ASSOCIATION. This organization was created by Gifford Pinchot* in 1909 to stimulate public support of conservation principles that he had championed during the administration of President Theodore Roosevelt.* Its first president was Charles W. Eliot,* outgoing president of Harvard University, and its staff work was entrusted mainly to close associates of Pinchot. Eliot was succeeded by Pinchot in 1910, after he had been discharged by President William H. Taft* as chief of the U.S. Forest Service.* Financial support of the association came mainly from its founder and a few friends.

Its principal efforts, directed by Pinchot, included a campaign to prevent transfer of control over national forests to the states and work for legislation to control the development of water power on federal government property. These efforts contributed to defeat of proposed legislation seeking state control of national forests and aided the passage of the Water Power Act of 1920 establishing broadly the principle of federal government regulation of hydroelectric power. Meanwhile, the association conducted an unsuccessful campaign for federal legislation to regulate private forestry. It was dissolved in 1923, when Pinchot became governor of Pennsylvania. (Samuel P. Hays, *Conservation and the Gospel of Efficiency: The Progressive Conservation Movement, 1890–1920* (1959); M. Nelson McGeary, *Gifford Pinchot; Forester-Politician* (1960); Harold T. Pinkett, *Gifford Pinchot, Private and Public Forester* (1970).)

Harold T. Pinkett

NATIONAL CONSERVATION COMMISSION. This organization was appointed by President Theodore Roosevelt* in June 1908 in response to recommendations of the White House Conference of Governors of that year. It was chaired by Gifford Pinchot,* ardent conservationist and chief of the U.S. Forest Service,* and composed of representatives of federal government natural resource agencies and congressional supporters of the conservation movement. It was organized in four sections: water resources, forest resources, resources of the land, and mineral resources. Members of the commission were asked by the president to investigate the condition of America's natural resources, advise him on their findings, and cooperate with other organizations created for similar purposes. The commission was without government funds, but was able to use the assistance of staffs of government resource agencies.

Each of its sections reported on the amount of the nation's natural resources, their rate of use, and the probable date of their exhaustion. The findings constituted the most comprehensive inventory of the country's resources that had yet been prepared. The commission recommended that the federal government lease certain public lands, undertake soil and water conservation measures, and evaluate public lands. Roosevelt approved the findings and recommendations of the commission and asked Congress to provide funds for continuation of its work. Although Congress did not comply with this request and the commission's work ended in 1909, the work was publicized in three printed volumes and gave important stimulus to the conservation movement. (U.S. Government, 60th Congress, 2d Session, Senate Document No. 676, *Report of the National Conservation Commission* (1909); Gifford Pinchot, *Breaking New Ground* (1947); Henry Clepper, *Professional Forestry in the United States* (1971).)

Harold T. Pinkett

NATIONAL CONSERVATION CONGRESS. This group was organized in Seattle, Washington, in September 1909, mainly under the auspices of the Washington (State) Conservation Association. It was created to serve as an annual forum for exchange of ideas, experiences, and problems of interest to state, federal, and private conservation leaders. At its first session the congress declared that its purpose was "to act as a clearing house for all allied social forces" and "to seek to overcome waste in natural, human, or moral forces." The congress soon became an arena for annual debates between Gifford Pinchot* and his followers, who advocated charging federal fees to utility companies using hydroelectric power sites, and members who opposed fees because of their possible determent of private power development.

Some members frequently complained that Pinchot sought to use the congress mainly to promote his ideas concerning national conservation issues and that he lacked interest in state and regional conservation questions. There was wide dissatisfaction with his efforts to absorb the congress into the National Conservation Association,* which he controlled, and his continual debating of the water power issue at each annual meeting. Controversy over Pinchot's ideas and actions led to the disbanding of the congress after 1916. (National Conservation Congress, *Proceedings* (1909, 1913); Samuel P. Hays, *Conservation and the Gospel of Efficiency: The Progressive Conservation Movement, 1890–1920* (1959); M. Nelson McGeary, *Gifford Pinchot: Forester-Politician* (1960).)

Harold T. Pinkett

NATIONAL CONSUMERS' LEAGUE. This was an organization devoted to the improvement of working conditions for women and children through direct action by consumers and the passage of protective legislation. The first Consumers' League was founded in New York* in 1891 to improve the conditions of female salesclerks in department stores. The New York League, under the presidency of Maud Nathan, published a "white list" of stores which adhered to fair labor practices and urged consumers to patronize only those stores. Similar leagues arose in Brooklyn, Philadelphia,* Boston,* Syracuse, and Chicago;* and in 1898, an organizing convention formed the National Consumers' League. Florence Kelley* became the national secretary and guided the organization until her death in 1932. By 1905 there were sixty-four local leagues in twenty states.

Kelley and the Consumers' League followed a strategy best summed up in four words: "investigate, educate, legislate, enforce." Though the league's distinctive method was the consumer boycott, this often proved ineffective. Both the New York white list and a national label for products made in approved factories were eventually discontinued. Kelley devoted most of her efforts to lobbying for protective legislation. The Consumers' League advocated child labor* bans, minimum wage laws, maximum hours and other special legislation for working women, and the formation of both a Women's and a Children's Bureau* in the Department of Labor.* The league attained most of its goals with the passage of a network of state protective laws. (Josephine Goldmark, *Impatient Crusader* (1953); Irwin Yellowitz, *Labor and the Progressive Movement in New*

York State, 1897–1916 (1965); Louis L. Athey, "The Consumers' League and Social Reform" (Ph.D. diss., University of Delaware, 1965).)

Edward R. Kantowicz

NATIONAL COUNCIL OF COMMERCE. This was a short-lived organization which attempted to unite all business lobbying organizations in one umbrella group. In 1907 Gustav H. Schwab, the American agent for the North German Lloyd Steamship Company, approached Secretary of Commerce and Labor Oscar Straus* with a proposal for a general business organization to promote foreign trade. Straus held the council's organizational meeting in December 1907 and appointed Schwab the chairman. Too close an identification with low-tariff advocates and foreign-trade interests doomed the council, which passed out of existence in 1910. The organizational effort, however, was part of a greater movement to unite all business lobbying groups in an "association of associations." This movement succeeded with the founding of the U.S. Chamber of Commerce* in 1912. (Robert H. Wiebe, *Businessmen and Reform* (1962); Harwood L. Childs, *Labor and Capital in National Politics* (1930).)

Edward R. Kantowicz

NATIONAL EDUCATION ASSOCIATION. This organization, known widely by the acronym NEA, was the principal educational organization in the United States from the 1880s to the mid-twentieth century. Started in 1857 as a loose federation of state teachers' organizations, by the turn of the century the NEA had become the country's largest association of educators, embracing teachers, administrators, college professors, university presidents, and educational reformers. Despite the efforts of some reform-minded teachers to have the NEA agitate for better teachers' wages and working conditions, the organization was dominated by school administrators through the opening four decades of the twentieth century. Its primary goal was to establish a high standard of professionalism and expertise at all levels of the educational system. This meant better working conditions for teachers, but it also strengthened the power of administrators to run schools more economically.

The NEA's most important historical role revolved around its service as a forum for debates and discussion of educational ideas, and as a vehicle for the promotion of educational reform. In 1892 a "Committee of Ten" was commissioned to recommend reform of the nation's secondary schools. Headed by Harvard University president Charles W. Eliot,* it recommended the adoption of an elective system of studies designed to make the high school accessible to a wider range of students. Later, commissions were established to study educational problems and publish recommendations for their resolution. The most famous of these was the Commission on the Reorganization of Secondary Education, appointed in 1913 and headed by Clarence Kingsley, which endorsed the ideal of the comprehensive high school. A membership drive launched in 1917 increased the NEA's size from 8,000 to over 50,000 in just a few years.

(Theodore D. Margin, *Building a Teaching Profession: A Century of Progress, 1857–1957* (1957); Erwin S. Selle, *The Organization and Activities of the National Educational Association* (1932); Wayne Urban, *Why Teachers Organized* (1982).)

John L. Rury

NATIONAL FEDERATION OF SETTLEMENTS. Settlement houses brought college-educated women and men into working-class neighborhoods, where they organized clubs and classes, undertook social research, and advocated reforms. By 1900, the College Settlements Association counted 103 settlements; Robert A. Woods* and Albert J. Kennedy described 413 in 1911, of which almost half supported religious programs. This growth in numbers led first to citywide federations and then in 1911 to formation of the National Federation of Settlements with Woods of South End House in Boston as secretary, followed in 1914 by Kennedy. The federation held large annual conferences but remained organizationally weak. Exclusion of sectarian settlements limited membership; the budget was small; there was no full-time executive secretary before the 1930s; and the federation did not expand the number of settlements.

The federation's foremost undertaking in the 1910s was a series of studies of youth—notably *Young Working Girls* (1913)—based on settlement workers' reports and advocating improved neighborhood conditions. In the early 1920s, the federation campaigned unavailingly for housing reform,* but caution and cultural activities tended to displace reformism by mid-decade. The federation greeted prohibition* enthusiastically and sponsored a basically favorable study, *Does Prohibition Work?* (1927). (Clarke A. Chambers, *Seedtime for Reform: American Social Service and Social Action, 1918–1933* (1963); Allen F. Davis, *Spearheads for Reform: The Social Settlements and the Progressive Movement, 1890–1914* (1967); Judith Ann Trolander, *Settlement Houses and the Great Depression* (1975).)

David I. Macleod

NATIONAL GRANGE (PATRONS OF HUSBANDRY). The Grange is the oldest general farmers' organization in the United States. It exercised great influence briefly in the mid-1870s and then almost collapsed. From its low point of 58,000 members in 1888, it rose to 98,000 in 1900 and 297,000 by 1917. During this rebirth, the Grange reflected much of the philosophy of the Progressive Era and the conflicts played out between conservatives and insurgents. Cautious Grange leaders tried to remain apolitical and to emphasize neighborly social intercourse, but most grangers saw needed changes and had come to believe in the concept of the disinterested professional. The organization, therefore, fought for a tariff commission,* a fair food and drug commission,* fair labeling laws, and better education. It supported woman suffrage* and opposed American imperialism.* State and local groups built economically sound and increasingly powerful cooperatives.

Those who had pulled the Grange through its drought years, however, opposed bolder measures such as public ownership and more direct democracy. In 1911, insurgent Granges established a parallel organization and sent a lobbyist to Washington. For a time schism seemed probable, but war, compromise, and death mixed an elixir of reconciliation. The Grange emerged from the Progressive Era as the strongest farm group, but it soon faced the federally encouraged American Farm Bureau Federation, which would surpass it. (Thomas C. Atkeson, *Outlines of Grange History* (1928); Charles W. Gardner, *The Grange— Friend of the Farmer* (1949); Lowell K. Dyson, *Farmer's Organizations* (1986).)

Lowell K. Dyson

NATIONAL HOUSING ASSOCIATION, THE. The National Housing Association (NHA) (1910–1936) was born the brainchild and creation of Lawrence Veiller* (1872–1959), the prominent New York City* tenement house reformer. Veiller gained a national reputation as secretary of both the New York Charity Organization Society's* Tenement House Committee and the New York State Tenement House Committee, deputy commissioner of the New York City Tenement House Department, and author of the New York State Tenement House Law of 1901. Other cities and states sought Veiller's assistance. By 1910 there existed an informal national housing movement, and Veiller decided that it required formalization. In that year he persuaded the Russell Sage Foundation to finance the movement, and the National Housing Association was born. Former New York City Tenement House Commissioner Robert W. deForest was the first president; however, Veiller, as the NHA's director throughout its entire existence, dominated the organization.

The NHA's primary function during the Progressive Era reflected Veiller's philosophy that private housing could provide living quarters for all Americans and that it only needed to be regulated by restrictive legislation. Thus the NHA assisted municipalities and states in establishing minimum requirements for sanitation, ventilation, and density. Veiller's books, *A Model Tenement House Law*, *A Model Housing Law*, and *Housing Reform*, served as handbooks for state and local reformers, as did the NHA's journal, *Housing Betterment*. The NHA conducted seminars and conferences for reformers and housing officials across the country. NHA activity receded in the twenties as changing attitudes and strategies left it behind; Veiller opposed both subsidized and public housing during the New Deal. In 1936 the National Housing Association formally disbanded. (Peter Romanofsky, ed., *Encyclopedia of American Institutions*, vol. 2: *Social Service Organizations* (1978); Roy Lubove, *The Progressives and the Slums: Tenement House Reform in New York City, 1890–1917* (1962).)

John F. Sutherland

NATIONAL INDUSTRIAL CONFERENCE BOARD. Founded in 1916, the National Industrial Conference Board (NICB) was a research and propaganda organization controlled by the nation's leading employers' organizations and large business firms. Headquartered in Boston, the NICB was initially administered by corporate liberals who had close ties with the National Civic Federation* and the National Association of Manufacturers.* Between 1917 and 1920 the NICB responded to the trend toward more government regulation of working conditions and labor relations by studying proposals for health insurance and the eight-hour day, which the board decided to oppose, by evaluating the operation of worker's compensation* systems and by developing a labor policies program that emphasized increased productivity, criticized union interference with employer autonomy, and opposed government regulation of collective bargaining.*

The NICB published books and pamphlets to disseminate the findings of its investigations. Walter Drew, the counsel to the NICB, explained its mission as that of "developing the intelligent class-consciousness of the business man and giving to him a voice with which to make himself heard." Drew noted (in 1917) that "big business interests, by their very nature, cannot well organize for protection against the politician and demagogue." The NICB, as an ostensibly neutral research organization, "presents an opportunity for big business interests . . . to have a widespread maintenance and progress and the use of . . . effective machinery in making those principles a part of public opinion and legislative policy." (Clarence E. Bonnett, *A History of Employers' Associations in the United States* (1956); Robert H. Wiebe, *The Segmented Society: An Introduction to the Meaning of America* (1975).)

Robert Asher

NATIONAL MONETARY COMMISSION. Established by the Aldrich-Vreeland Act* (1908), this commission studied banking and currency systems in the United States and Europe and issued a forty-volume report in 1910–1913. Senator Nelson W. Aldrich* of Rhode Island chaired the commission of nine senators and nine representatives. After the commission completed its European study, Aldrich was convinced that the United States needed a centralized banking system and a broad-based asset currency backed by sound commercial paper, gold, bonds, and other restricted reserves. Many New York financiers who shared his views noted that the panic of 1907* had revealed the deficiencies inherent in decentralized monetary reserves.

In 1910 Aldrich held a secret conference at his estate on Jekyll Island, Georgia, with four influential New York bankers: Paul M. Warburg,* Frank Vanderlip,* and Charles Norton of the First National Bank; and Henry Davison of the House of Morgan. From this meeting emerged a plan for a National Reserve Association in Washington to preside over fifteen regional banking districts. The bankers in the districts would elect thirty of the thirty-nine board members in Washington. The association would issue currency based on gold and commercial paper and hold deposits of the federal government. The association also could buy and sell on the open market, determine discount reserves, and carry some of the reserves of member banks. On the surface, this plan provided for more flexible currency and banking systems and avoided Wall Street domination.

Anticipating that Democrats and Insurgent* Republicans would label this plan as a Wall Street scheme, Aldrich and his advisers chose James B. Forgan, president of the First National Bank of Chicago, to coordinate a program to win support of bankers and other businessmen. The American Bankers Association's endorsement of the Aldrich plan in 1911 was indicative of widespread business support for the proposal. However, President William H. Taft's* concern over the lack of government supervision in the Aldrich plan severely undermined its progress in Congress. In 1912, the Aldrich bill was submitted to Congress but never came to a vote. Thus, the question of devising a centralized banking system was left for the Wilson* administration in 1913. (*National Monetary Commission*, Sen. Doc. 243, 62d Cong., 2d sess. (1912); Arthur S. Link, *Woodrow Wilson and the Progressive Era, 1910–1917* (1963); Gabriel Kolko, *The Triumph of Conservatism: A Reinterpretation of American History, 1900– 1916* (1963).)

David Alsobrook

NATIONAL MUNICIPAL LEAGUE. In response to the perceived evils of city government in late nineteenth-century America, urban reformers established the National Municipal League (NML) in May 1894. The organization emerged from the first National Conference for Good City Government, which had been sponsored by municipal reform clubs from Philadelphia* and New York City.* Clinton Rogers Woodruff,* secretary of the Municipal League of Philadelphia, became the secretary and moving force of the NML for over twenty years. By the mid-1890s, some 260 local civic reform groups had been established, but their efforts were isolated and unfocused until the NML facilitated a convergence of energy and a sense of direction.

The NML reflected the ideas and interests of "structural" reformers,* who sought to improve municipal administration through reforms in city charters and in the constitutional structure of urban government. The NML's first "model" city charter, adopted in 1899, built on such established reforms as the strong mayor plan and the civil service* principle. It also incorporated a number of innovative structural reforms: nonpartisan elections,* the secret ballot,* at-large elections* for city councilmen, a unicameral city council, the short ballot principle,* extensive "home rule"* without state legislative interference, an independent fiscal authority, specific debt and taxation limitations, and short-term utility and transit franchises.

Through its publications, annual meetings, and other activities, the NML sought to educate the public about the need for better city government. The NML reformers worked from the conviction that the cities had to be saved from the corrupt political machines* and that urban government must be made more honest, efficient, and businesslike. By 1910, the NML supported the commission form* of city government as an improvement over mayor-council government. By 1915, however, the NML had abandoned commission government and strongly endorsed the city manager plan,* which spread quickly after its adoption in Dayton in 1913. The city manager plan centralized administrative decision making in the hands of an appointive, expert public administrator. When linked to the short ballot, at-large elections, and the nonpartisan city council, the new plan provided a model of technical expertise and administrative control. In 1918, the NML officially incorporated the city manager plan in a revised model charter, along with recommendations for a city planning board and such measures of direct democracy as the initiative,* referendum,* and recall.* (Frank M. Stewart, *A Half Century of Municipal Reform: The History of the National Municipal League* (1950); Ernest S. Griffith, *A History of American City Government: The Progressive Years and Their Aftermath, 1900–1920* (1974); Martin J. Schiesl, *The Politics of Efficiency: Municipal Administration and Reform in America, 1880–1920* (1977).)

Raymond A. Mohl

NATIONAL NEGRO BUSINESS LEAGUE. Founded in Boston* on August 23-24, 1900, by Booker T. Washington,* the National Negro Business League represented concepts of self-help and racial solidarity prevalent in the ideologies of both black accommodationists and radicals. Indeed, Washington organized black entrepreneurs and professionals into national conferences and local chapters according to ideas first expounded in 1899 by future rival W. E. B. Du Bois.* By the time of Washington's death in 1915, the league's original 300 delegates had mushroomed to 3,000, representing 600 local organizations in thirty-six states and revealing an increase of black enterprises from 20,000 to 40,000.

Under Washington's presidency, the league emerged as an instrument of his Tuskegee machine and a base for black conservatism. Hence it provided an alternative to protest for civil and political rights by the Niagara Movement (1905) and the National Association for the Advancement of Colored People* (1909), while promoting Horatio Alger models and group economy among the self-made, segregated urban middle class. The league never addressed basic problems facing small, black operators in an era of economic expansion and white competition. Yet it continued beyond the 1920s as ghettos formed and white politicians, like earlier progressives, ignored black well-being. (Louis R. Harlan, "Booker T. Washington and the National Negro Business League," in William G. Shade and Roy C. Herrenkohl, eds., *Seven on Black: Reflections on the Negro Experience in America* (1969); August Meier, *Negro Thought in America, 1880–1915: Racial Ideologies in the Age of Booker T. Washington* (1963); Booker T. Washington, *The Negro in Business* (1971).)

Dominic J. Capeci, Jr.

NATIONAL PARK SERVICE. This agency evolved from purposes in creating national parks and monuments that began to be achieved with the establishment of Yellowstone Park in Wyoming, Montana, and Idaho in 1872. After that year other areas, such as Yosemite, California; Mount Rainer, Washington; and Mesa Verde, Colorado, were set aside as parks by Congress to preserve them from commercial exploitation, because their unique scenic qualities made them important to all Americans. Similarly established were national monuments—areas of diverse size and interest that are notable for scientific or historic reasons. These varied areas were administered by the U.S. Department of the Interior and other federal agencies.

Secretary of the Interior Franklin K. Lane* and two assistants, Stephen T. Mather and Horace M. Albright, convinced the public and Congress of the need for coordinated administration of the areas. Accordingly, the National Park Service* was created in the Department of the Interior by an act of August 25, 1916, and to it were transferred functions pertaining to the administration of national parks and monuments. Under Mather's direction from 1916 to 1929, the National Park Service won increasing public support and funding and received authority to expand the national park system into new areas of unique scenic quality, including deserts of the Southwest and mountains of the eastern United States. (William C. Everhart, *The National Park Service* (1972); John Ise, *Our National Park Policy: A Critical History* (1961); Alfred Runte, *National Parks: The American Experience* (1979).)

Harold T. Pinkett

NATIONAL PROGRESSIVE REPUBLICAN LEAGUE. Following the 1910 elections, in which regular Republican candidates suffered major setbacks at the hands of both insurgent Republicans and Democrats, Senator Robert M. La Follette* of Wisconsin organized the National Progressive Republican League as a vehicle for challenging President William Howard Taft* for control of the Republican party.* Publicly announced in Chicago in January 1911, with Senator Jonathan Bourne* of Oregon as its president, the league had the active support of most of the insurgent Republican senators, representatives, and governors. Their strength was magnified by the fact that they held the balance of power in the Senate. But the National Progressive Republican League was always troubled. The key members disagreed on many issues. La Follette's platform had to be limited to a series of procedural reforms: primaries,* the initiative* and referendum,* and direct election of senators* and national convention delegates. The league's strength was also too obviulsy confined to the Midwest. Theodore Roosevelt,* in particular, remained aloof, although he was the preferred choice of many league members. La Follette formally announced his candidacy in June 1911, and at first his campaign progressed well. But when Roosevelt, too, declared for the presidency in February 1912, La Follette was quickly overshadowed and the ranks of the league hopelessly divided. (George E. Mowry, "Election of 1912," in Arthur Schlesinger, Jr., ed., *The Coming to Power: Critical Presidential Elections in American History (1972); David P. Thelen, Robert M. La Follette and the Insurgent Spirit* (1976).)

Keith Ian Polakoff

NATIONAL SECURITY LEAGUE. The largest and most influential of the groups that lobbied for military preparedness after 1914, the National Security League was organized by S. Stanwood Menken with the support of many of the

famous and influential in New York society. The initial aim of investigating the
state of the armed forces was soon broadened to include the tasks of "patriotic
education" and the advocacy of universal military training. During 1915, the
league spread its influence and carried on a spirited campaign of press releases,
magazine articles, pamphlet mailings, public speeches, and conferences to drive
home its point of the need to strengthen the army and navy. With many of its
leaders drawn from the ranks of Republicans or Roosevelt* nationalists, some
league spokesmen turned to an attack of the Wilson* administration for its failure
to act on military matters. Menken held the organization to a bipartisan course,
and a group of Republican defectors formed the more extreme American Defense
Society in August of 1915. When Wilson sought to establish his own military
program, the league fought for the enactment of Secretary of War Lindley K.
Garrison's Continental Army plan, but saw few of its goals realized in the
National Defense Act of 1916.

With the advent of war, the league became more avowedly nationalistic in
fostering conformity and "100 percent Americanism." The league planned a
postwar program of "teaching the meaning and value of our constitution as
opposed to mass rule." Before the congressional elections in 1918 it began direct
political action to ensure the defeat of congressmen who had voted "wrong"
on preparedness or wartime measures. In December 1918, the House of Representatives established a special committee to investigate the league and concluded that the league had violated the Corrupt Practices Act, but recent scholars
stress difficulties in financial support and the league's general lack of influence
in military matters. (John Carver Edwards, *Patriots in Pinstripe: Men of the
National Security League* (1982); John Patrick Finnegan, *Against the Specter of
a Dragon: The Campaign for American Military Preparedness, 1914–1917*
(1974); Robert David Ward, "The Origin and Activities of the National Security
League, 1914–1919," *Mississippi Valley Historical Review* 47 (June 1960): 51–
65.)

Robert David Ward

NATIONAL TAX ASSOCIATION. Originally designated "State and Local
Taxation," representing local tax reform groups throughout the Northeastern
and North Central states, plus various lobbies commenced in the late 1860s, the
National Tax Association (NTA) emerged as a coalition organization in 1907.
Its roots, "national" or not, were in the Northeastern states, where changes due
to industrialization, urbanization, and new forms of wealth unreached by the
standard source of revenue, the direct property tax, produced widespread feelings
of inequity. The founder of the national organization was Allen Ripley Foote,
who already had forty years experience in state and local tax reform in New
York, Michigan, Ohio, Illinois, Maryland, and Washington, D.C. A staunch
Republican, Foote feared threats to private enterprise, but recognized traditional
tax structures were unjust and in decay.

The prime purposes of the NTA were to improve state and local fiscal affairs, to stimulate communication through local tax reformers, to disseminate the best scientific tax information, and to bind tax officials of the country together. Organizationally distinct from the NTA, its *Annual Proceedings* brought together forums for experts such as E. R. A. Seligman,* Milo Maltbie, Lawson Purdy, among many others of similar repute, including Single Taxers,* followers of Henry George.* NTA publications continued to present, and influence professional and administrative awareness of, old inequities and new fiscal necessities. (Allen Ripley Foote, "Birth, Work, and Future of the National Tax Association," *Proceedings of the National Tax Association* (1916); Clifton K. Yearley, *The Money Machines* (1970); Roy Blakey and Gladys Blakey, *National Tax Association Digest and Index, 1907–1925* (1927).)

Clifton K. Yearley and Kerrie L. MacPherson

NATIONAL URBAN LEAGUE. This interracial organization was formed in 1911 by consolidating the National League for the Protection of Colored Women (1906), the Committee for Improving the Industrial Conditions of Negroes in New York (1906), and the Committee on the Urban Conditions among Negroes (1910). The National Urban League quickly became the principal agency for easing the process of urbanization for rural black migrants, offering services of social uplift and acculturation already available to foreign white immigrants through settlement houses. Chiefly concerned with procuring jobs for blacks, the Urban League sponsored vocational training and fought discrimination in labor unions. Additionally, it trained black social workers and acted as the major social service agency for black urbanites, most of whom were poor, unskilled, and uneducated. The league sought decent housing and recreational and health facilities for such people, and, in the tradition of Booker T. Washington,* gave them meticulous advice on personal hygiene, good manners, proper speech, and hard work. It depended on moral suasion, research, and education to accomplish its economic and social objectives.

By 1918 the parent organization in New York had twenty-seven affiliates, located mostly in the large eastern cities. Never a mass organization, the Urban League's small membership was drawn from the well-educated and professional elite of both races. Dependent almost entirely on white philanthropists for financing, the league was often hampered by lack of funds. The sociologist George Edmund Haynes, the first black Ph.D. at Columbia University, served as the league's first executive secretary. The Urban League and the slightly older National Association for the Advancement of Colored People (NAACP)* had an agreement that assigned the protest for civil rights and social equality to the latter and economic and social service concerns to the former.

While smoothing the transition to city life somewhat and providing valuable research about the urban black minority, the Urban League failed to change employment patterns that confined Negroes primarily to domestic work, nor could it stem the rising tide of racial tension and violence. World War I* temporarily bolstered Negro employment, but it also brought enlarged northern ghettos full of the very pathology that the league was established to combat. (Guichard Parris and Lester Brooks, *Blacks in the City: A History of the National Urban League* (1971); Nancy J. Weiss, *The National Urban League, 1910–1940* (1974); Jesse Thomas Moore, Jr., *A Search for Equality: The National Urban League, 1910–1961* (1981).)

David W. Southern

NATIONAL WOMAN'S PARTY, THE. Though comprised of a small minority of women working for the vote, the National Woman's Party revitalized a stagnant American woman suffrage* campaign. The party actually began in 1913 as the congressional committee of the National American Woman Suffrage Association* (NAWSA). Headed by Alice Paul* and Lucy Burns,* who had served apprenticeships with the Pankhurst militant suffragists in England, it soon separated from NAWSA (1914) to become the Congressional Union (CU) and to work for a federal amendment. Union strategy included pressuring the Democrats (the party in power), beginning with the 1914 elections. In June 1916, the CU organized western women who could vote for president into an affiliate called the Woman's Party to campaign against Woodrow Wilson.* On March 2, 1917, the CU and the Woman's Party united to form the National Woman's Party (NWP). The NWP frequently staged colorful parades, pageants, and large demonstrations. Its most controversial activities, picketing the White House and burning copies of the president's speeches, brought arrests, hunger strikes, and forced feedings. After the passage of the Nineteenth Amendment, the NWP continued to crusade for woman's equality by introducing the Equal Rights Amendment into Congress in 1923, and reinjecting it every year thereafter until its proposal in 1972. (Eleanor Flexner, *Century of Struggle: The Woman's Rights Movement in the United States* (1959); Susan Becker, *The Origins of the Equal Rights Amendment: American Feminism between the Wars* (1981); Loretta Zimmerman, "Alice Paul and the National Woman's Party, 1912–1920" (Ph.D. diss., Tulane University, 1964).)

Sidney Bland

NATIONAL WOMEN'S TRADE UNION LEAGUE (NWTUL). This was a reform group dedicated to the organization of women wage workers into trade unions. Modeled after a British Women's Trade Union League founded in 1874, the American league was organized in 1903 at the American Federation of Labor* (AFL) convention in Boston.* William English Walling* had discovered the Women's Trade Union League on a trip to England, and he convinced Mary Kenney O'Sullivan* to join him in organizing an American counterpart. The league's main purpose was to stimulate organization of working women and to support existing women's unions. Its most effective action came during a series of garment workers' strikes in New York,* Philadelphia,* and Chicago* from 1909 to 1911. Secondarily, the NWTUL joined with other groups of social progressives, such as the National Consumers' League,* in advocating protective legislation for working women.

The NWTUL was marked by a continuing tension between the middle-class women who supported it and the working-class women who formed the object of its efforts. The league's constitution mandated that a majority of its board members be working union members, but most of the financial support came from middle-class "allies" of the unionists. The AFL and individual unions, such as the International Ladies' Garment Workers Union,* never fully trusted the NWTUL and resented its attempts to control union activities. The league's duality was symbolized by the two women who guided it for most of its history. Margaret Dreier Robins,* a wealthy society woman, served as president from 1907 to 1922; her working-class collaborator, garment worker Rose Schneiderman,* held the same office from 1926 to 1950. (*Toward Better Working Conditions for Women: Methods and Policies of the National Women's Trade Union League*, Bulletin No. 252 of the Women's Bureau, Department of Labor (1953); Alice Henry, *Women and the Labor Movement* (1923); Gladys Boone, *The Women's Trade Union Leagues in Britain and America* (1942); Nancy Schrom Dye, *As Equals and as Sisters: Feminism, The Labor Movement Women's Trade Union League of New York* (1980).)

                                                                    Edward R. Kantowicz

NATURALISM. The term is sometimes used to label literature that reflects an absorption with nature that reflects an intense realism. The expression, however, more particularly describes the late nineteenth- and early twentieth-century literary movement, beginning in France and spreading to the United States and Britain, that sees human beings not as autonomous agents who can exercise free will, but as creatures at the mercy of depressing environmental and innate forces which, in an indifferent universe, control human action. Naturalism represents an artistic construction of the ideas of such social determinists as Hippolyte Taine, Auguste Comte, Karl Marx, and Herbert Spencer, and such scientific ones as Issac Newton, Sigmund Freud, and Charles Darwin above all. Chiefly centered in the novels and shorter fiction of such writers as Emile Zola and the Brothers Goncourt; Frank Norris,* Stephen Crane,* Jack London,* and Theodore Dreiser;* Thomas Hardy (who tended to call the deterministic forces "fate") and George Eliot, the naturalistic view affects much poetry of the period, too— the poems of Stephen Crane, for example.

The handling of the secular determinism in fiction is often heavy-handed: Crane's heroine in *Maggie: A Girl of the Streets* moves inexorably to her destruction, unable to overcome the squalor of her environment. Clyde Griffith's death at the hands of the law is inevitable in Dreiser's *An American Tragedy*, and there is no cosmic ombudsman or court of appeal; when a person announces his existence in Crane's poem "A man said to the universe," the universe coldly replies, "The fact has not created in me / A sense of obligation." Naturalism remained influential in twentieth-century literature, notably affecting the novels of James T. Farrell, James Jones, John Steinbeck, and even Saul Bellow. (June Howard, *Form and History in American Literary Naturalism* (1985); Donald Pizer, *Realism and Naturalism in Nineteenth-Century American Literature* (1966); Christopher P. Wilson, *The Labor of Words: Literary Professionalism and the Progressive Era* (1985).)

Alan Shucard

NEARING, SCOTT (August 6, 1883–August 24, 1983). Born in Morris Run, Pennsylvania, Nearing graduated from the University of Pennsylvania in 1905 and received a doctorate in economics there in 1909. From 1909 to 1915, he taught economics at the University of Pennsylvania's Wharton School of Finance, during which time he attracted widespread attention for crusading against child labor* and criticizing capitalism. His dismissal by the university in 1915 was nationally publicized, and the case spurred the attempt to define the proper role and rights of the teacher. Nearing joined the Socialist party of America* shortly after the United States intervened in World War I,* but resigned in 1922 because of the party's hostility to Bolshevism. In the meantime, his opposition to the war resulted in his dismissal from the University of Toledo, where he had served since 1915 as dean of the College of Arts and Sciences, and in his indictment under the Espionage Act.* Although acquitted at his 1919 trial, he was for many years thereafter blacklisted by universities and mainstream publishers. Nearing authored or coauthored numerous books, among them *Social Adjustment* (1911), *Women and Social Progress* (1912), *Social Sanity* (1913), and *Education in Soviet Russia* (1926). (Scott Nearing, *The Making of a Radical: A Political Autobiography* (1972); Stephen J. Whitfield, *Scott Nearing: Apostle of American Radicalism* (1974).)

Frederick C. Giffin

NEBRASKA. The Progressive Era in Nebraska flowed out of concerns raised by the Populists* in the 1890s and ebbed as a result of conflicts raised by statewide prohibition* and World War I* loyalty issues. The reformist impulse was a bipartisan one, personified by the leadership of Republican George W. Norris* and Democrat William Jennings Bryan.* Fusion between Populists and Democrats in gubernatorial elections persisted through 1902 as progressives in both parties emphasized regulation of railroads and other utilities. Elected on an antirailroad platform in 1906, Governor George L. Sheldon persuaded the legislature to abolish free passes, reduce passenger fares to two cents per mile, and enact a state railway commission. He also brought about the establishment of a statewide system of direct primary elections.* Sheldon was defeated in 1908 by Democrat Ashton C. Shallenberger, who helped inaugurate a state guarantee of bank deposits law and the "Oregon System" of expressing a U.S. senatorial preference in the primary election.

However, Shallenberger's signing of the controversial "daylight saloon" law that mandated 8:00 P.M. closing so alienated German and Czech voters that he lost his bid for renomination in 1910. Successful Republican Chester H. Aldrich helped enact an initiative* and referendum* measure, blocked a telephone merger bill pushed by the Bell Company, pressed for the commission form of municipal government,* and lobbied for a good roads bill. Despite those achievements, Aldrich lost to Democrat John H. Morehead in 1912, who appointed the first members of the State Board of Control, signed a workmen's compensation* act, and instituted the budget system. In 1917, he was succeeded by fellow Democrat M. Keith Neville, who alienated many of his party by his vigorous enforcement of prohibition. (Robert W. Cherny, "Populism and Progressivism in Nebraska: A Study of Nebraska Politics, 1885–1912" (Ph.D. diss., Columbia University, 1972); Paul W. Glad, *The Trumpet Soundeth: William Jennings Bryan and His Democracy, 1896–1912* (1960); Richard Lowitt, *George W. Norris: The Making of a Progressive, 1861–1912* (1963).)

John D. Buenker

NEIGHBORHOOD IDEA. The neighborhood idea was perhaps the animating idea of the settlement house movement. Its pioneers held that a viable sense of community could flourish in the modern city; that this community ethos could unite people across class, ethnic, and religious lines; and that this new spirit could imbue immigrants with a sense of civic pride and responsibility which could then be invoked to break the hold of political machines* on urban government. Many settlement workers and other social progressives were the children of Protestant clergy. Still others were themselves ministers or had studied for the ministry. They saw the working-class urban neighborhood, once it had been transformed by a social settlement, as a secular analogue to the traditional parish. This was especially true in those cities, like New York, where established congregations had abandoned their old downtown sites and moved out toward the suburban fringes. The neighborhood idea was their answer to what they saw as the failure of the church to minister to the needs of the old neighborhoods' new residents.

In addition, sociologists such as E. A. Ross* argued that the United States was rapidly changing from a network of communities characterized by mutuality and face-to-face contact into a contractual society characterized by so-called secondary relations, i.e., the reliance upon formal roles to define social interactions. Many progressives saw the neighborhood as a key to moderating the effects of this shift in that it could both foster the trust and respect supposedly characteristic of earlier communities and encourage democracy by providing an arena where ordinary people could still determine their own conditions. (Jane Addams, *Twenty Years at Hull House* (1910); Arthur C. Holden, *The Settlement Idea: A Vision of Social Justice* (1922); Allen Davis, *Spearheads of Reform: The Social Settlements and the Progressive Movement, 1890–1914* (1967).)

John F. McClymer

NELSON, KNUTE (February 2, 1843–April 28, 1923). Born in Voss Parish, Norway, Knute Nelson emigrated with his mother, Ingeborg Johnson, to Chicago in 1849. Moving to Dane County, Wisconsin, in 1850, Knute took the surname

of his stepfather and attended common schools and Albion Academy, and served
as an officer during the Civil War. In 1867 Nelson passed the bar examination
and set up practice in Cambridge, Wisconsin; moreover, he won election to the
Wisconsin Assembly. In 1871 the family moved to Alexandria, Minnesota, and
Nelson served as county attorney, state senator, and University of Minnesota
regent.

Elected governor in 1892, Nelson, the state's first Scandinavian chief executive, championed agrarian reform such as farm land drainage. He resigned in
1895 to accept appointment to the U.S. Senate. Independent, honest, and politically wise, Nelson was neither clearly an insurgent* or a stand-patter, opposing
the Payne-Aldrich Tariff* yet supporting Taft* in 1912. (Martin W. Odland,
The Life of Knute Nelson (1926); Millard L. Gieske, "The Politics of Knute
Nelson, 1912–1920" (Ph.D. diss., University of Minnesota, 1965); Rolfsrud
Erling Nicolai, *Scandinavian Moses: The Story of Knute Nelson* (1986).)

                                                                  Bruce L. Larson

NELSON, WILLIAM ROCKHILL (March 7, 1841–April 13, 1915). Born in
Fort Wayne, Indiana, Nelson claimed to be a "natural insurgent" whose early
flouting of authority led to his expulsion from Notre Dame College for disciplinary reasons. After a brief legal career, Nelson became a successful contractor,
then turned to journalism, but a disastrous investment wiped out most of his
fortune. With his partner, Samuel E. Morss, he managed the *Fort Wayne Sentinel*,
a Democratic paper, for two years before founding the *Kansas City Evening Star*
on September 18, 1880.

Under Nelson's vigorous direction the *Star* crusaded for civic improvements
and nonpartisan politics and became a leading organ of midwestern progressivism
by the early twentieth century. Rejecting sensationalism and vulgarity—including
the use of comics—Nelson appealed to his readers through low prices, human
interest features, and constant calls for the restoration of democratic values in
American politics. Besides such majoritarian reforms as the initiative,* the referendum,* and public ownership of utilities,* he advocated programs of social
control* and managerial efficiency,* including prohibition* and city commission
government.* A weekly edition of the *Star*, begun in 1890, carried his ideas to
farmers throughout the Southwest. In 1912 he helped to launch the abortive
Progressive party.* (Staff of the *Kansas City Star*, *William Rockhill Nelson: The
Story of a Man, a Newspaper, and a City* (1915); Icie F. Johnson, *William
Rockhill Nelson and the "Kansas City Star"* (1935); Frank L. Mott, *American
Journalism: A History, 1690–1960* (1962).)

                                                              Maxwell H. Bloomfield

NEUTRALITY. When World War I* began, the United States declared itself
neutral. Initially, this position rested on the tradition of noninvolvement in European conflicts, horror at the war's carnage, and conflicting foreign propaganda,
as well as ethnic, class, and regional antagonisms toward the various European

participants. However, the economy, the nature of this conflict, and adherence to traditional international maxims made it impossible to remain unaffected or to avoid influencing the outcome. The British blockade cut off trade with Germany, but trade with the Allies tripled in compensation. Since prohibiting loans denied profits to American bankers and hurt only the Allies, the policy was abandoned after August of 1915.

Although some Americans argued that neutrality meant total noninvolvement, by 1916 many wanted to protect the right to trade and travel. President Wilson* stressed this issue and in May of 1916 forced Germany to abandon submarine warfare. American neutrality changed further as the preparedness movement* led to military reorganization and expansion. Debate over preparedness was overwhelmed when Germany resumed submarine warfare in 1917. American reaction was sharply critical, but the decision to abandon neutrality was ultimately Woodrow Wilson's. When he opted for war, it became too dangerous for most politicians to disagree. (Patrick Devlin, *Too Proud to Fight: Woodrow Wilson's Neutrality* (1975); John M. Cooper, Jr., *The Vanity of Power: American Isolationism and the First World War, 1914–1917* (1969); John M. Cooper, Jr., and Ross Gregory, *The Origins of American Intervention in the First World War* (1971).)

Philip R. VanderMeer

NEWELL, FREDERICK HAYNES (March 5, 1862–July 5, 1931). Born in Bradford, Pennsylvania, and graduated from MIT in 1885, Newell worked on state surveys until 1888, when John Wesley Powell appointed him assistant hydraulic engineer in the U.S. Geological Survey (USGS). Appointed chief hydrographer in the USGS's Irrigation Survey in 1890, he directed stream measurements and selection and survey of reservoir sites in the Far West. A strong supporter of federal financing for reclamation of the arid lands, he worked to secure passage of the Reclamation Act* in 1902. After the creation of the Reclamation Service in the USGS, Newell became chief engineer, and he was appointed director of the independent Bureau of Reclamation in 1907. Newell supervised the construction of nearly $100 million in irrigation works in eighteen states. After the inauguration of Wilson,* Interior Secretary Franklin K. Lane* undercut Newell's authority, and Newell resigned in disgust in 1915 and moved to the University of Illinois. He returned to Washington, D.C., in 1920 and organized a private research and consultation service in 1924. (Lawrence B. Lee, *Reclaiming the American West: An Historiography and Guide* (1980); Michael C. Robinson, *Water for the West: The Bureau of Reclamation, 1902–1977* (1979); "Newell, Frederick Haynes," *National Cyclopedia of American Biography* 23 (1933): 162–63; Arthur Powell Davis, "Newell, Frederick Haynes," *Dictionary of American Biography* 7 (1934): 456–57.)

Thomas G. Alexander

NEW FREEDOM was Woodrow Wilson's* domestic program in the presidential election of 1912; often contrasted with his opponent, Theodore Roosevelt's,* program, the New Nationalism.* Under the influence of Louis D. Brandeis,*

Wilson launched a full-scale attack on industrial monopoly and corporate special privilege during the 1912 campaign. He proposed to restore competition and unleash individual economic enterprise by reducing tariff protection for business, breaking the control of Wall Street over banking, and splitting up corporate monopolies. He ridiculed Roosevelt's belief that corporate monopolies were more efficient than small businesses and could serve the public interest if regulated by government. In the early days of his first term, Wilson put his program into effect with the Underwood Tariff Act* of 1913 and the Federal Reserve Act* and Clayton Antitrust Act* of 1914.

The distinction between the New Freedom and the New Nationalism was often confused in practice; both programs opposed the unbridled power of big business. Yet, philosophically, the distinction marked an important duality in the progressive movement. New Freedom advocates feared bigness in itself and wished to restore an economy of individual enterprises; New Nationalists accepted big business as an inevitable development and wished merely to regulate it. (Woodrow Wilson, *The New Freedom* (1913); Louis D. Brandeis, *Other People's Money* (1914); Arthur S. Link, *Woodrow Wilson and the Progressive Era* (1954); Arthur S. Link, *Wilson: The New Freedom* (1956).)

Edward R. Kantowicz

NEW HAMPSHIRE. The progressive movement is central to the history of New Hampshire politics in the forty years prior to America's entry into World War I.* Three Republicans dominate the drama: William E. Chandler,* Winston Churchill,* and Robert P. Bass. Chandler (secretary of the navy, 1882–1885; U.S. senator, 1887–1901) launched reformism in the state in the nineteenth century with his attempts to eliminate railroad influence in political affairs. Although unsuccessful, Chandler's efforts paved the way for the 1905–1906 gubernatorial candidacy of Winston Churchill, author of the reformist novels *Coniston* and *Mr. Crewe's Career*. Continuing Chandler's antirailroad thrust, the unsuccessful Churchill campaign also espoused greater participation by the working class in the political process, what Churchill considered a restoration of "popular government."

Encouraged by the Churchill campaign, a number of reformers were subsequently elected to the General Court. Among these was Robert Bass, a wealthy businessman and legislative leader of the successful effort in 1909 to pass the East's first direct primary law.* Catapulted into prominence by these activities, Bass won the 1910 race for the governorship. Under the Bass leadership, much progressive legislation was enacted in 1911. But, in 1912, Bass led the bolt to Theodore Roosevelt's* Progressive party,* thereby destroying reformism in Republican ranks. (Thomas R. Agan, "The New Hampshire Progressive Movement" (Ph.D. diss., State University of New York at Albany, 1975); Jewel Bellush, "Reform in New Hampshire: Robert Bass Wins the Primary," *New*

England Quarterly 35 (December 1962): 469–88; James Wright, *The Yankee Progressives: Republican Reformers in New Hampshire, 1906–1916* (1987).)

Thomas R. Agan

NEW HISTORY, THE. The New History identifies a conception of scholarship that sought to expand the scope of historical writing beyond its traditional political and institutional base to encompass every aspect of human culture. From Edward Eggleston's *The Transit of Civilization from England to America in the Seventeenth Century* (1900) to perhaps its apogee in Charles and Mary Beard's* *The Rise of American Civilization* (two volumes, 1927), the New History claimed a place for itself with psychology, sociology, anthropology, and political science, as a truly scientific discipline that would stimulate reform as it explained the present in relation to the past.

As set forth by James Harvey Robinson* *(The New History*, 1912), professor of European history at Barnard College and Columbia University; and further developed by Robinson's students such as Harry Elmer Barnes and Preserved Smith, the New History displayed a strongly elitist tendency, with its emphasis on the role of behavioral psychology and psychoanalysis in explaining the irrational component of human behavior manifested in social history. (Morton G. White, *Social Thought in America: The Revolt against Formalism* (1949); John Higham, *History: Professional Scholarship in America* (1965); Dorothy Ross, "The 'New History' and 'New Psychology': An Early Attempt at Psychohistory," in Stanley Elkins and Eric McKitrick, eds., *The Hofstadter Aegis: A Memorial* (1974).)

Morey Rothberg

"NEW IMMIGRATION." During the 1800s, a series of economic and demographic changes swept through Europe, creating a mobile work force of itinerant laborers searching for jobs or the opportunity to buy cheap land. Improvements in diet, hygiene, and sanitation, the smallpox vaccine, and the lack of a major war between 1815 and 1914 created a population explosion in Europe just as the Industrial Revolution was eliminating home manufacturing and consolidating peasants were being pushed off ancestral lands and forced to find work in the larger Atlantic economy. These economic changes hit Britain, Germany, and Scandinavia first, and between 1820 and 1880 nearly nine million of their citizens came to the United States. Historians have labeled them the "old immigrants." Except for the Irish Catholics, most of them were Protestants from northern and western Europe who settled on farms or small towns in the North and Midwest.

Later in the 1800s, similar demographic and economic changes reached the rest of Europe, triggering a "new immigration" of more than twenty-six million people between 1880 and 1940. These "new immigrants" were Roman Catholics (Poles, Czechs, Slovaks, Italians, Slovenes, Croatians, Ruthenians, Lithuanians, and Magyars), Eastern Orthodox (Russians, Bulgarians, Greeks, Romanians,

Armenians, Syrians, and Serbians), and Jews (Russian, Hungarian, and Polish). Usually they settled in cities of the Midwest and Northeast where they could be close to jobs in the factories, mines, and mills. The large-scale influx of the "new immigrants" triggered another wave of nativism, anti-Catholicism, and anti-Semitism. Racist and ethnocentric groups like the American Protective Association and the Ku Klux Klan began demanding immigration restriction,* and they were supported by labor unions worried about unemployment and declining wage levels.

After the Chinese were exluded in 1882, Congress passed a series of increasingly restrictive immigration laws designed to keep paupers, criminals, prostitutes, and the illiterate out of the country. The immigration restriction movement reached fruition in 1924, when Congress passed the National Origins Act, imposing nationality quotas on future immigration. The quotas were biased in favor of the "old immigration" and against the "new immigration." The National Origins Act of 1924 effectively ended the "new immigration." (John Higham, *Strangers in the Land: Patterns of American Nativism 1860–1925* (1963); James S. Olson, *The Ethnic Dimension in American History* (1979); James S. Olson, *Catholic Immigrants in America* (1987).)

James S. Olson

NEW JERSEY. From the 1880s onward, New Jersey so favored corporate organization that by the turn of the century the state was known as "the mother of trusts." The smooth relationship between corporate leaders and political bosses like Democrat James Smith, Jr., and Republican Carl Lentz began to slip in 1901 with the election of Mark Fagan,* an Irish-Catholic Republican, as mayor of Jersey City. Fagan's program to rebuild the schools, parks, baths, and water and sewer systems ran into trouble when he and his associate, George L. Record,* found that much of the private property in the city was exempt from local taxes because it was owned by railroads. Taking the fight to the state legislature, they interested Everett L. Colby, an Essex Republican whose constituents were facing efforts by the Public Service Corporation, a giant utility, to grab franchises through suburban areas. In 1905 Colby won election to the state senate on a "New Idea" platform—the new idea being essentially that the people should control the government and the government the corporate interests.

Other industrialized counties now began to support the "New Idea" and young, urban, new-stock Democrats rallied to the cause. Stiff battles in the legislatures of 1906 through 1910 brought passage of some reform laws: a revised railroad tax structure, limitations on utility franchises, and stiffer regulation of the insurance industry. More importantly, a core of reformers in both parties developed a program of political reform on which they agreed. When, in the 1910 gubernatorial campaign, the boss-backed Woodrow Wilson* declared his support for reform, the scene was set for a dramatic turnaround. The legislative session of 1911 saw the passage of radical election reform and corrupt practices measures,* the creation of a strong Public Utilities Commission, the passage of a workmen's compensation law,* and the establishment of commission government* for cities in order to combat bossism.

The Bull Moose split in the campaign of 1912* and Wilson's election to the presidency left New Jersey progressivism divided and practically leaderless. In the legislative session of 1913 the lame-duck governor forced through passage of the Seven Sisters laws—a series of measures to destroy the trusts and enhance fair competition in industry—and returned briefly from Washington to help reform a corrupt jury system. But, in 1915, a woman suffrage* amendment lost in a statewide referendum;* soon the antitrust legislation was dismantled, and political leaders like Frank Hague* learned how to use the new political structures to their own purposes. A small coterie of reformers continued active in the state, but their immediate influence upon legislation proved minimal after 1914. (Ransom E. Noble, Jr., *New Jersey Progressivism before Wilson* (1946); Arthur S. Link, *Wilson: The Road to the White House* (1947); Joseph F. Mahoney, "New Jersey Politics after Wilson: Progressivism in Decline" (Ph.D. diss., Columbia University, 1964).)

Joseph F. Mahoney

NEWLANDS, FRANCIS G. (August 25, 1848–December 24, 1917). Born in Natchez, Mississippi, Newlands was educated at Yale and at Columbia University. In 1870, he moved to San Francisco, where he practiced law. He was elected to Congress in 1891, serving in the House until 1901 and in the Senate from 1901 until 1917. Newlands was a consistent advocate of progressive reform, a firm believer in the efficacy of government regulation. His proposal for federally sponsored irrigation projects in the arid west, the Reclamation Act,* is considered one of the first major pieces of national progressive reform legislation. As a member of the Inland Waterways Commission, Newlands worked to apply the Reclamation Act's principles of multipurpose development to the nation's river systems.

In 1911, he introduced a bill to create an interstate trade commission, and as chairman of the Senate Committee on Interstate Commerce he worked for the creation of the Federal Trade Commission.* He wrote the 1913 arbitration amendment to the Interstate Commerce Commission Act (the "Newlands Arbitration Act"), supported the passage of the Adamson Eight-Hour Act,* and at the time of his death had nearly completed a draft of the U.S. Railroad Administration Act.* (William D. Rowley, "Francis G. Newlands: A Westerner's Search for a Progressive and White America," *Nevada Historical Society Quarterly* 17 (1974): 69–79; Arthur B. Darling, ed., *The Public Papers of Francis G. Newlands* (1932); William Lilley, "The Early Career of Francis G. Newlands, 1848–1897" (Ph.D. diss., Yale, 1965).)

Kathryn M. Totton

NEW NATIONALISM, THE. This was the slogan used to capsulize the philosophy and program of Theodore Roosevelt* in the campaign of 1912;* it was set in opposition to the philosophy and program of Woodrow Wilson,* which was called "the New Freedom."* The term itself came from Herbert Croly's* book of 1909, *The Promise of American Life* (p. 169). Roosevelt read that book in the summer of 1910 and, finding that Croly's views echoed and systematized many of his own, wrote the author in late July that he would be using the book's ideas in his speeches. On August 31, in an important address in Osawatomie, Kansas, the former president first used the slogan. As with all such appellations, however, its various components were far from precisely defined.

Principally, the designation meant Roosevelt's proposal to use the federal government as an active agent, both in the regulation of American industry and in the protection of various elements of American society. The consolidation of industry was inevitable, Croly and Roosevelt argued, and in most cases beneficial, driven by the desire for greater efficiency. The state must be prepared, however, to intervene in the economic life of the nation in order to ensure fair play and the public interest—even to the point of insisting that traditional prerogatives of private property might occasionally be contravened for the welfare of the community. For this purpose, quasi-judicial commissions composed of impartical experts would be required to define and ensure the public good.

In addition to its well-publicized proposals for handling the problem of large corporations, the New Nationalism was also thought to include Rooseveltian positions on other issues: legislation on behalf of workers; lower tariffs; an active program of conservation;* the referendum,* initiative,* and recall* (including recall of judicial decisions); and a far more assertive and energetic foreign policy. In each of these realms, a reinvigorated and thoroughly democratic nation, commanding the loyalty of the American people, would be the chief instrument of economic prosperity and social justice. Despite Roosevelt's defeat, the principles of the New Nationalism were quickly embodied in the programs of Wilson and in the programs of other twentieth-century liberal administrations. (Theodore Roosevelt, *The New Nationalism* (1910); John M. Cooper, Jr., *The Warrior and the Priest: Woodrow Wilson and Theodore Roosevelt* (1983).)

David W. Levy

NEW POLITICS. The term "new politics" has at least two meanings for the Progressive Era. For political reformers of the time, new politics meant opposition to "boss politics," to the control of elections by parties dominated by traditional political elites. At the local level, new organizations such as the Municipal Voters' League (MVL) in Chicago* gained a great deal of political power by operating outside the regular party system. The MVL and similar groups elsewhere pioneered in the direct mobilization of public opinion, through mass meetings, public information campaigns, and mass-circulation newspapers. At the state level, insurgent politicians such as Robert M. La Follette* used similar tactics of direct appeal to the voters outside the organizational structure of their party. In both cases, the architects of the new politics sought to build coalitions around specific issues that directly touched great numbers of people, such as public utility regulation.* While the new politics was probably no less dominated by elites, the tactics were new. Issue-based associations, popular candidates, public opinion mobilization, and mass communication all became part of the style of American electioneering. When New York Republican boss Thomas Platt died in 1910, editorial writers celebrated his passing, declaring that he "represented a kind of politics which has fortunately passed out of fashion."

But politics had changed even more profoundly than anyone at the time could know—and this is the second meaning of "new politics." The Progressive Era marked a major change in electoral behavior: many people stopped voting. Nationwide voter turnout in 1890, for example, was 65 percent; in 1970 it was 45 percent. And this is typical of the differences between ninetieth-century and twentieth-century turnout rates. For a variety of reasons, parties ceased to be efficient institutions for the generation of votes. Perhaps equally important, new nonelectoral routes to political participation began to open up. Civic leagues, issue lobbies, and interest groups of every sort became part of the political scene. In short, "new politics" meant not only new styles of election campaigning, but also new methods of politicking that would tend to make elections themselves less important in a new century of political influence. (David P. Thelen, *The New Citizenship: Origins of Progressivism in Wisconsin, 1885–1900* (1972); David Paul Nord, *Newspapers and New Politics: Midwestern Municipal Reform, 1890–1900* (1981); Richard L. McCormick, *From Realignment to Reform: Political Change in New York State, 1893–1910* (1981); Paul Kleppner, *Who Voted? The Dynamics of Electoral Turnout, 1870–1980* (1982).)

David Paul Nord

NEW REPUBLIC, THE. This illustrious "journal of opinion" began publication in November 1914. It was created and sustained by generous contributions from Dorothy and Willard Straight*—she, the idealistic heir of the Whitney fortune, and he, an Asian expert with J. P. Morgan.* Impressed by Herbert Croly's* *Promise of American Life*, the couple agreed to help him found a weekly magazine. Croly gathered a brilliant editorial board and consistently attracted an extraordinary array of contributors and reviewers. The journal immediately faced the issues raised by the European war. After advocating neutrality, the editors ended by urging U.S. entry. Domestically, the magazine advocated Croly's reform program and supported Theodore Roosevelt.* By 1916, however, it had broken with him and grew ever closer to Woodrow Wilson.* For a time the journal was thought to be a mouthpiece for Wilsonian domestic and foreign policies, and it enjoyed considerable influence and popularity until breaking decisively and bitterly with Wilson over the Treaty of Versailles.

During the 1920s, the embattled editors tried to keep the torch of progressive reform burning, but subscriptions fell and the magazine devoted more attention to cultural matters. Throughout Croly's editorship the journal was known for its lucid (if sometimes pretentious), logical (if sometimes patronizing), and intelligent (if sometimes elitist) views. Thanks to Dorothy Straight, the *New Republic* survived Croly's death and continued, under a series of editors, down to the present day. (Frank L. Mott, *"The New Republic,"* in *A History of American Magazines* (1968); Charles Forcey, *The Crossroads of Liberalism: Croly, Lippmann, and Weyl and the Progressive Era, 1900–1924* (1961); Charles Forcey and David W. Levy, *Herbert Croly of "The New Republic": The Life and Thought of an American Progressive* (1985).)

David W. Levy

NEW SOUTH is a term descriptive of the ideas and proposals of Henry W. Grady (1850–1889) and other advocates of industrialization in the post-Reconstruction South. By the early 1880s several editors began to urge Southerners to invest in manufacturing enterprises and to reform their agriculture. Grady's reasoning was that the South possessed the resources vital to a northern-style industrial economy, but was forced by its single-crop economy to purchase manufactured goods from outside. The South's experience of defeat by a better-armed foe was proof of the need for home production; the South would never regain its position within the nation by holding fast to faded glories. Moreover, New South proponents argued that the rise of cities such as Atlanta* would provide a market for foodstuffs grown in present cotton-producing districts, which had been suffering from the declining price of the staple since the panic of 1873.

New South themes were congenial to Bourbon Democrats* and to northern entrepreneurs, who in the 1870s and 1880s developed the lumber, coal-mining, iron-making, cotton-manufacturing, and transportation industries of the region. Soon, New South journalists were claiming that the Southern economy had been transformed and that prosperity had returned. They were right, to the extent that much of the Appalachian South had been transformed from an area of yeoman farming to a "colonial" extension of the North. Workers in the extractive industries were paid very low wages, and in many cases had sold their lands to developers. Southerners still had to buy finished goods elsewhere; but the industrialization-prosperity myth was long-lived, persisting until the Great Depression of the 1930s. The New South program had little to offer southern blacks, though Booker T. Washington* attempted to make Tuskegee Institute into an "industrial training" school. Nor did industrialization break the one-crop system, as leaders of the Farmers' Alliance and the People's party were well aware. Overall, the New South movement developed an optimistic attitude among a growing urban middle class, and so helped prepare the way for Southern progressivism. (Paul Gaston, *The New South Creed: A Study in Southern Mythmaking* (1970); Ronald D. Eller, *Miners, Millhands, and Mountaineers: Industrialization of the Appalachian South, 1880–1930* (1982); and C. Vann Woodward, *Origins of the New South, 1877–1913* (1951).)

Paul M. Pruitt, Jr.

NEW YORK. A cauldron of the political and social evils the reformers decried, New York was in many respects a model progressive state and the home of many of the most influential men and women who called themselves progressives. Nowhere did the reformers and their enemies do battle more fiercely than in New York City. Home of Tammany Hall,* the nation's most infamous political machine, the downstate metropolis also included putrid tenements, grasping street-railway corporations, and the worst excesses of the urban, industrial conditions against which progressives crusaded. Theodore Roosevelt,* Charles Evans Hughes,* Al Smith,* and Robert F. Wagner* first gained fame as reform-minded New York politicians and later went on to national careers. Lillian D. Wald* and Robert Hunter* stood among the foremost leaders of the settlement house movement, just as Lawrence Veiller* did among tenement house reformers and Frances Kellor* among those who crusaded to improve the living and working conditions of immigrants. Although no unified progressive movement ever emerged within the state, New York produced almost all the varieties of progressivism seen in the nation at large. Often New York's adoption of a reform provided a catalyst for other states to act. New York's legislative life insurance investigation* of 1905, its Factory Investigating Commission* of 1911–1915, and its campaigns for woman suffrage* in 1915 and 1917 all attracted national attention and were emulated elsewhere.

The course of progressivism in New York may be traced in roughly three stages. In the 1890s, urban independents made significant political gains against the entrenched party machines. The reformers' wholesale desertion of the Republican party* in the off-year city elections of 1897 made independence a potent political creed and led directly to Theodore Roosevelt's election as governor in 1898, as well as to a series of reforms in the electoral machinery and the civil service.* Then, in 1905, an investigation of the life insurance industry disclosed the intimate connections between business and politics and brought forth calls for state regulation of the offending corporations. Under Governor Charles Evans Hughes (1907–1910) significant advances were made, although corporations often found the new regulations to be beneficial. Finally, the tragic Triangle Shirtwaist Company fire of 1911, in which nearly 150 women died, stimulated an avalanche of social and industrial reforms, enacted on the recommendation of the Factory Investigating Commission. Just as in other states, progressivism in New York had begun with an urban, elitist concern to change the political rules; it had focused next on the regulation of business corporations; and finally it had come to address the conditions in which industrial laborers lived and worked. Just as in other states, too, the results of progressivism were often incomplete and ironical. (Richard L. McCormick, *From Realignment to Reform: Political Change in New York State, 1893–1910* (1981); Robert F. Wesser, *Charles Evans Hughes: Politics and Reform in New York, 1905–1910* (1967); Roy Lubove, *The Progressives and the Slums: Tenement House Reform in New York City, 1890–1917* (1962).)

Richard L. McCormick

NEW YORK CITY. The largest city in the United States as early as 1820, New York counted 1.5 million inhabitants in 1890, when its boundaries included only Manhattan Island and parts of the Bronx. In 1898, New York consolidated with Brooklyn, then the fourth largest U.S. city, and with the lightly settled areas of Queens and Staten Island, to create a Greater New York of five boroughs, 299 square miles, and nearly 3.5 million people. By 1930 its population had grown to nearly 7 million. Approximately 80 percent of New York's people at the turn of the century were immigrants or the children of immigrants, primarily Irish,* Germans,* Italians,* and East European Jews.* The Germans were well-established in business and commerce and the Irish in construction and government employment, whereas the Italians and the Jews found niches in the garment industry and shopkeeping.

Poverty and overcrowding were widespread in immigrant ghettos such as the Lower East Side, but a host of reformers attacked the social ills of the metropolis, often living and working in social settlements,* such as the University Settlement* or the Henry Street Settlement.* Reporter Jacob Riis* exposed the dreadful housing* conditions of the tenement districts in his 1890 book *How the Other Half Lives*. A committee of the Charity Organization Society,* led by Lawrence Veiller,* conducted a thorough investigation of housing conditions and organized a tenement house exhibition in 1900 which led to a landmark tenement regulation law in 1901. Other New York reformers concentrated on improving wages and working conditions in sweatshops through such organizations as the International Ladies' Garment Workers Union* and the National Women's Trade Union League.* The Jewish community supported a vigorous socialist* movement, electing Meyer London* to Congress in 1914.

The Tammany Hall* Democratic machine dominated New York politics from the 1870s until the Great Depression. Tammany bosses traded jobs and favors for votes, fending off numerous assaults by upper- and middle-class reformers. A reform wave in New York followed a standard script: first, a sensational investigation of Tammany corruption, then the formation of a nonpartisan reform committee and the mounting of a Fusion campaign for mayor, in which Republicans, independents, and anti-Tammany Democrats all fused in support of a single reform slate. Typically, Fusion mayors would serve only one term, then when public outrage dissipated, Tammany would return to power. This pattern held true with the election of William L. Strong* in 1894, Seth Low* in 1901, and John Purroy Mitchel* in 1913. As Tammany ward boss George Washington Plunkitt phrased it: "Reformers were mornin' glories—looked lovely in the mornin' and withered up in a short time, while the regular machines went on flourishin' forever, like fine old oaks." (Milton Klein, *The Centennial Years* (1976); Roy Lubove, *The Progressives and the Slums: Tenement House Reform in New York City, 1890–1917* (1962); Melvyn Dubofsky, *When Workers Organize: New York City in the Progressive Era* (1968); Irwin Yellowitz, *Labor and the Progressive Movement in New York State, 1897–1916* (1965); William L. Riordon, *Plunkitt of Tammany Hall* (1963); Moses Rischin, *The Promised City: New York's Jews* (1962).)

Edward R. Kantowicz

NEW YORK STATE FACTORY INVESTIGATING COMMISSION. Popularly known as the Triangle Fire Commission, the body was founded as a result of the tragic Triangle Shirtwaist sweatshop fire on March 25, 1911, in which 147 employees, mostly young women of Italian or Jewish origin, died either from smoke inhalation or by leaping to their death on the pavement several stories below. Most of them died because the existing fire safety regulations for loft factories were totally inadequate. When the owners and proprietors were exonerated, the National Women's Trade Union League* (WTUL) organized a public funeral demonstration in which 100,000 people, including many labor, business, civic, and religious leaders, marched through the city to the Metropolitan Opera House. There a meeting delegated a Committee of Fifty to deliver a petition to the state legislature demanding an investigation of working conditions in the state.

The legislature responded by establishing the commission, with Senator Robert F. Wagner* and Assemblyman Alfred E. Smith* as cochairmen and including Mary E. Dreier,* president of the WTUL, Samuel Gompers,* and two prominent business leaders. During the four years of its existence, the commission, aided by an expert staff, held scores of public hearings, made site visits to dozens of factories, heard the testimony of several hundred witnesses, and produced thirteen volumes of reports. Ultimately, it drafted sixty bills dealing with health, safety, sanitation, fire prevention, and wages and hours of labor, fifty-six of which were enacted into law, giving New York the best system of factory legislation in the Union. None of these laws was ever overturned by the courts. (Leon Stein, *The Triangle Fire* (1962); J. Joseph Huthmacher, *Senator Robert F. Wagner and the Rise of Urban Liberalism* (1968); Thomas J. Kerr IV, "The New York Factory Investigating Commission and the Minimum Wage Movement," *Labor History* 12 (1972): 373–91; Nancy Schrom Dye, *As Equals and As Sisters: Feminism, the Labor Movement, and the Women's Trade Union League of New York* (1980).)

John D. Buenker

NONPARTISAN LEAGUE. The Nonpartisan League, a farmers' political organization, originated in North Dakota. Under the direction of Arthur C. Townley, a disenchanted "Flax King" and former Socialist, the National Nonpartisan League (NPL) was formed in 1915, spread rapidly to Minnesota, and ultimately organized in thirteen farm states. Using paid memberships to gain support, its program was primarily a protest by small wheat farmers against existing grain-marketing procedures. With the aid of its *Leader* newspapers, the league called for major reforms, demanding grain inspection laws and state-owned elevators, mills, and meat-packing plants. Its greatest success came in North Dakota, where Lynn Frazier was elected governor in 1916, and the 1919 league-controlled legislature set up a state elevator and state bank. Other NPL leaders included Congressmen William Lemke, John M. Baer, and Henry G. Teigan.

But the league, with many Scandinavians and Germans as members, came under sharp attack during World War I* on charges of disloyalty and Bolshevism. The league declined, and by the early 1920s it was absorbed by the major parties. In Minnesota, the NPL and organized labor formed the Farmer-Labor party, while in North Dakota the league heritage continued to influence state politics. The NPL has been the subject of the films *Prairie Fire* (1977) and Cannes award-winning *Northern Lights* (1978). (Robert L. Morlan, *Political Prairie Fire: The Nonpartisan League, 1915–1922* (1955); Patrick K. Coleman and Charles R. Lamb, comps., *The Nonpartisan League, 1915–1922: An Annotated Bibliography* (1986); Elwyn B. Robinson, *History of North Dakota* (1966).)

Bruce L. Larson

NORRIS, FRANK (March 5, 1870–October 25, 1902). Born Benjamin Franklin Norris, he was the son of a wholesale jeweler in Chicago. When Frank was fourteen, the family moved to San Francisco, where he experienced the life that he would describe in his best novel. He attended the University of California and Harvard, and discovered Zola, before he went to South Africa as a correspondent for the San Francisco *Chronicle*. There he suffered an attack of tropical fever from which he never really recovered. In 1898, he was in New York working for *McClure's Magazine* in its period of real muckraking.* The journal sent him to Cuba as a war correspondent where he suffered another attack of African fever. Back in New York, he became a reader for Doubleday, Page before returning to California. In his capacity for Doubleday, his claim to fame was that he was the discoverer of Theodore Dreiser's* *Sister Carrie*.

Norris is generally considered to be one of the great pioneers in American literary realism. His most important works include *McTeague, Vandover and the Brute*, and the "Wheat Series," *The Octopus* and *The Pit*. Critics are generally agreed that, while Norris attempted to portray life as it really was, his characters (except perhaps in *McTeague*) are never fully realized and his philosophical framework is rather sophomoric. There is little development from his first writings until his last. (Don Graham, ed., *Critical Essays on Frank Norris* (1980); Robert W. Schneider, *Five Novelists of the Progressive Era* (1965); Franklin Walker, *Frank Norris: A Biography* (1963).)

Robert W. Schneider

NORRIS, GEORGE WILLIAM (July 11, 1861–September 2, 1944). Born in Sandusky County, Ohio, Norris attended Baldwin University and then Northern Indiana Normal School and Business Institute, where he received his law degree. He moved to Nebraska in 1885 and practiced law in Furnas County. Norris entered politics as a Republican in the 1890s and served for seven years as a district court judge. Elected to Congress in 1902, he spent the first part of his House career as an organization Republican. Then, in 1909, he joined a group of insurgents* who were seeking to limit the power of House Speaker Joseph G. Cannon.* Their effort was abortive, but the next year Norris, taking umbrage at the rebels' loss of patronage and convinced that President William Howard Taft* was allied with the Old Guard speaker, led them in a second move to curb Cannon's authority. The insurgents, with Democratic help, succeeded in passing the Norris resolution, which provided that the House Rules Committee be elected and that the Speaker not sit on it. Norris viewed this as a necessary first step toward the passage of genuine progressive legislation by Congress. From 1913 to 1943, Norris served as a U.S. senator from Nebraska, and authored many liberal measures, including the Tennessee Valley Authority Act of 1933. (Richard Lowitt, *George W. Norris: The Making of a Progressive* (1963); Norman L. Zucker, *George W. Norris: Gentle Knight of American Democracy* (1966); George W. Norris, *Fighting Liberal: The Autobiography of George W. Norris* (1945).)

Robert P. Wesser

NORTH AMERICAN CIVIC LEAGUE FOR IMMIGRANTS. The mass migration of millions of South and East Europeans late in the nineteenth and early in the twentieth century caught most native Americans off guard. The new immigrants, usually Catholic or Jewish in religion, crowded into urban ghettos and into the Democratic party* and threatened the status quo that Anglo Protestants had long since established. Upper-class businessmen were alarmed at the strange cultures of the new arrivals but, at the same time, opposed immigration restriction* laws which would have reduced their labor pool. One solution seemed to be education and Americanization,* and in 1908 a group of New England businessmen established the North American Civic League for Immigrants, an organization committed to helping the immigrants find jobs, teaching them English, and inculcating them with patriotic values. A New York branch of the league was organized by Frances Kellor* in 1909.

Between 1909 and 1924, the two wings of the North American Civic League for Immigrants evolved in different directions. In New York, Kellor pushed the league toward social welfare goals, trying to lobby for more state and federal legislation to assist immigrants with health, education, and employment needs. The Boston branch retained an antigovernment business flavor, preferring philanthropic paternalism to state action. The New York group broke away in 1914 and became the Committee for Immigrants in America. The North American Civic League for Immigrants continued with its Americanization campaigns, eventually opting for immigration restriction. (John Higham, *Strangers in the Land: Patterns of American Nativism 1860–1925* (1963); Barbara Solomon, *Ancestors and Immigrants* (1956).)

James S. Olson

NORTH AMERICAN REVIEW, THE. First published in 1815, the *North American Review* was edited by a series of prominent Bostonians that included Edward T. Channing, Edward Everett, Andrew P. Peacock, Richard H. Dana, and Henry Cabot Lodge.* James Russell Lowell moved from his post as the first editor of the *Atlantic Monthly** to the *North American Review* (1863–1872). Henry Adams* edited the *Review* while he held his teaching position at Harvard. By the turn of the century, the *Review* was considered to be on a par with the established literary reviews in Great Britain.

George Harvey* purchased the *Review* in 1899 and edited the magazine until 1926. Harvey's editorship throughout the Progressive Era continued the *Review's* tradition as a forum for public issues no less than as a showcase for main currents in the international art and literary communities. Harvey published a cross section of writers from Europe such as William Butler Yeats, William Henley, Leo Tolstoi, Gabriele D'Annunzio, and Maurice Maeterlinck, and serialized U.S. writers like Mark Twain, William Dean Howells,* and Henry James.* In fact, James's *The Ambassadors* was first published in the *Review*. Harvey introduced political controversy by the inclusion of lead editorial articles that alternatively boosted and undermined the political fortunes of Theodore Roosevelt* and Woodrow Wilson.* (Frank Luther Mott, *A History of American Magazines* (1957).)

Salme H. Steinberg

NORTH CAROLINA. Between 1898 and 1920, the Old North State took the identity "The Wisconsin of the South," and ever since this period North Carolinians have considered themselves distinctively "progressive" within the section. Indeed, the accomplishments were impressive, with significant road building, school building, and economic diversification as well as fundamental reform of the judicial systems and of municipal government. From this era emerged the most famous postbellum governor, Charles Brantley Aycock; the most famous postbellum jurist, Walter Clark; and the most famous journalist, Josephus Daniels.* There was also the development of the University of North Carolina, North Carolina State University, and Duke University into major academic institutions which played political as well as educational roles in the nation.

For all that, however, North Carolina progressivism was clearly more "of the South" than it was "Wisconsin." Governors Aycock and Locke Craig, State Supreme Court Judge Clark, Assemblyman Henry Govers Connor, and Raleigh *News and Observer* editor Daniels campaigned hard to bring the previously very rural and very poor state into line with contemporaneous national economic development. Aycock authorized construction for thousands of miles of farm-to-market roads and took special pride in building "a school a day" for every day the general assembly was in session; Connor and Craig cooperated to implement industrial and other business regulation; Clark presided over a massive overhaul of the judicial apparatus; and Daniels supported all of this reformism in the pages of the most prestigious newspaper in the South Atlantic.

But Progressives in Carolina were essentially conservative Southerners, with considerable prejudice against black people and little regard for structural poverty suffered by both races within the evolving industrial and metropolitan areas and in the increasingly isolated rural areas of the eastern coastal plain. Thus, the most important improvements in education and in transportation occurred strictly for middle-class whites in the larger cities of the Piedmont region, while poverty persisted "down east" and blacks endured constitutional disfranchisement, segregated and deeply inferior schools, and a vicious negrophobic race riot* in Wilmington (1898). (Connor, Aycock, and Clark Papers in North Carolina State Archives, Raleigh; Louis R. Harlan, *Separate and Unequal: School Campaigns and Racism in the Southern Seaboard States* (1968); J. Morgan Kousser, *The Shaping of Southern Politics: Suffrage Restriction and the Establishment of the One-Party South, 1880–1910* (1974); Joseph F. Steelman, "The Progressive Era in North Carolina, 1899–1917" (Ph.D. diss., University of North Carolina at Chapel Hill, 1956).)

John H. Roper

NORTH DAKOTA. When the northern prairie state entered the Union in 1889, its "model" constitution provided limited woman suffrage,* universal public education, and prohibition.* In the three succeeding decades, immigration tripled the population to 640,000, and a dependent economic status created a climate favorable to political insurgency. North Dakotans supported a Populist-Democrat fusion in 1892, but stalwart Republicans again dominated after 1894. In 1906, GOP progressives bolted to elect Democrat John Burke, inaugurating a reform era characterized by advances in public health,* agricultural research, and political change. Milestones included the Pure Food and Drugs Law* (1903), the nation's first presidential primary* (1912), the initiative* and referendum* (1914), authorization of state-owned business enterprises (1914, 1919), and recall* (1918). Cooperative movements, such as the American Society of Equity,* also proliferated.

The Progressive movement culminated in the Nonpartisan League* (NPL), an agrarian insurgency formed in 1915 that modernized state government and steadfastly defended civil liberties during World War I.* Among its major social initiatives were rural school consolidation, improvement of library services, prohibition enforcement, and full suffrage for women (1917, 1919); the NPL also created state-owned businesses, including a bank and mill. By 1919, North Dakota was known as the nation's "laboratory of democracy," a reputation stemming from the response of its rural people to progressive ideals. (Elwyn B. Robinson, *History of North Dakota* (1966); Thomas B. Howard, ed., *The North Dakota Political Tradition* (1981); Robert L. Morlan, *Political Prairie Fire: The Nonpartisan League, 1915–1922* (1955).)

Larry Remele

NORTHERN SECURITIES CO. v. UNITED STATES (193 U.S. 187). This 1904 Supreme Court decision helped to revitalize the Sherman Antitrust Act, which had been drastically constrained in the *E. C. Knight Case* (1895). At the turn of the century, a number of railroad managers and financiers had sought to strengthen the industry through consolidations and by purchasing stock in competing roads to maintain a common pricing policy toward large and small shippers and thus make the railroads profitable and attractive to investors. The policy halted declining freight rates between 1899 and 1904. In 1901, a battle of the Chicago, Burlington and Quincy (CB&Q) pitted E. H. Harriman and his Union Pacific system against the controllers of the CB&Q, J. P. Morgan* and James J. Hill with their Northern Pacific and Great Northern railways. After Harriman's attempt at domination led to frenzied bidding and a brief panic on Wall Street, the two sides created the Northern Securities Company, a holding company with Morgan, Hill, and Harriman on the board, which created a railroad monopoly in the Northwest.

Following a public outcry, President Theodore Roosevelt* had the Justice Department file suit in 1902 to dissolve the corporation as an illegal restraint of commerce under the Sherman Act.* In the majority opinion in the 5–4 vote, Justice John Marshall Harlan* largely ignored the *Knight* case and took a broad view of the federal government's superior power to regulate interstate commerce. He rejected defense counsel's arguments that Northern Securities was simply a holding company, not directly engaged in interstate commerce, and that its dissolution was an invasion of New Jersey's state sovereignty, contending that such a principle would paralyze the power of the federal government to act where empowered by the Constitution. In dissent, Chief Justice Melville Fuller's opinion saw no grounds for such a radical departure from *Knight*. (B. H. Meyer, *History of the Northern Securities Case* (1906); Albro Martin, *Enterprise Denied: Origins of the Decline of American Railroads, 1897–1917* (1971); Alfred H. Kelly and Winfred A. Harbison, *The American Constitution: Its Origins and Development* (1983).)

John Whiteclay Chambers II

NORTON, CHARLES ELIOT (November 16, 1827–October 21, 1908). The descendant of a pioneering New England family, Norton was born and died in Cambridge, Massachusetts. After graduating from Harvard in 1846, he worked in international trade and traveled abroad for nine years. Then he spent the period from 1857 to 1874 as a writer and editor. In 1874, after a residence of five years in Europe, he accepted a position as professor of fine arts at Harvard, remaining at that institution until his retirement in 1897. As a scholar, Norton was an expert in medieval studies and an acknowledged translator of Dante. In teaching, he emphasized the relationship between the arts and social progress, arguing that the more intellectual and moral a society, the greater its artistic achievements.

Norton was a severe critic of American society in the late nineteenth century. He complained that Americans had gone astray from their Puritan origins and European heritage, the "best" in their culture. Advocating tradition and order, he opposed the mass production, materialism, labor strikes, literary realism, and stylistic innovations in architecture. He protested U.S. involvement in the war against Spain and the policy of imperialism.* (Sara Norton and M. A. DeWolfe, eds., *Letters of Charles Eliot Norton with Biographical Comment* (1913); Kermit Vanderbilt, *Charles Eliot Norton: Apostle of Culture in a Democracy* (1959); Robert L. Beisner, *Twelve against Empire: The Anti-Imperialists, 1898–1900* (1968).)

James A. Zimmerman

O

O'GORMAN, JAMES A. (May 5, 1860–May 17, 1943). Born to Irish immigrants in New York City, O'Gorman graduated from City College and studied law at New York University. He practiced law and was active in the Democratic party;* nevertheless, he supported Henry George* for mayor and ran unsuccessfully as an Independent Labor candidate for civil justice. Resuming his Democratic allegiance, O'Gorman rose in the ranks of Tammany Hall* and was rewarded with election to judgeships on the municipal court and the New York State Supreme Court in the 1890s. He entered the U.S. Senate in 1911 after a dramatic impasse in the legislature in which Franklin D. Roosevelt* presided over the insurgents who challenged the Democratic organization and its candidate, William F. Sheehan, and eventually compromised on O'Gorman. He served on Woodrow Wilson's* campaign committee in 1912.

In the new administration FDR and O'Gorman led opposing forces that were competing for control of Democratic patronage and party in their state. Although he favored direct election of senators,* the income tax,* and tariff reduction, a quantitative analysis of the senatorial record rates him among the least progressive of Democrats. He defied the president to delay passage of the Federal Reserve Act* but ultimately voted for it. Anglophobia placed the senator at loggerheads with Wilson on foreign policy with regard to Panama Canal tolls and the arming of merchant ships. When he retired after a single term, O'Gorman concentrated on his legal practice. (Frank Freidel, *Franklin D. Roosevelt: The Apprenticeship* (1952); Arthur S. Link, *Wilson* (1947–1965); *New York Times.*)

Paula Eldot

O'HARE, KATE RICHARDS (March 26, 1876–January 10, 1948). Born in Ottawa County, Kansas, Carrie Katherine Richards was educated in elementary grades and at a normal school and briefly taught school herself until her family lost its homestead. In Kansas City, Missouri, she engaged in religious and temperance activities while working as a machinist. She was attracted to socialism after hearing Mary Harris "Mother" Jones, and enrolled in a socialist training school in Girard, Kansas, where she married a fellow student, Francis P. O'Hare, in 1902. The two worked with Eugene V. Debs* on socialist periodicals such as the widely read *Appeal to Reason* and the *National Rip-Saw*. Meanwhile, Kate O'Hare became a popular speaker and social critic, especially at the summer socialist encampments in the Southwest.

Within the Socialist party,* O'Hare served on the National Executive Committee and the Woman's National Committee, ran for the House of Representatives and U.S. Senate, and represented her party at the International Socialist Congress in London. During World War I,* she was indicted for an antiwar speech which she gave throughout the country and was convicted under the Espionage Act.* She served fourteen months in the Missouri State Penitentiary, after which she focused on the cause of penal reform. She was eventually recognized for her work and won an appointment as assistant director of the California department of penology in 1938. (Philip S. Foner and Sally M. Miller, eds., *Kate Richards O'Hare: Selected Writings and Speeches* (1982), Sally M. Miller. "Kate Richards O'Hare: Progression toward Feminism," *Kansas History* 8 (Winter 1984–1985): 263–79; Neil K. Basen, "Kate Richards O'Hare: 'First Lady' of American Socialism, 1901–1917," *Labor History* 21 (1980): 165–99.)

Sally M. Miller

OHIO. Centered in the large cities, the Ohio reform movement focused on the problems of an urban-industrial society. In Toledo, Cleveland, Columbus, Cincinnati, and elsewhere leaders such as Samuel "Golden Rule" Jones,* Tom L. Johnson,* Washington Gladden,* and Herbert Bigelow advocated a new governmental order. Mostly middle-class businessmen and professionals, the early twentieth-century reformers found allies in the print media and among representatives of special interest groups seeking redress of grievance. Suffragists, ethnic leaders, labor organizers, and school reformers stand out. They were united by a belief in social justice* and a confidence in expertise.* Jones, as mayor of Toledo, worked to improve the quality of urban life by encouraging trade unions, promoting publicly owned utilities, and providing improved services through public works. In Cleveland, Mayor Johnson similarly sought to control utilities and to expand and improve services. He added the reliance upon experts to guarantee fairness and efficiency in taxation, expenditure of funds, and the administration of justice. Gladden, as a clergyman and later as a city councilman in Columbus, promoted the interest of unions, fought discrimination, and sought control of public utilities. In Cincinnati,* described by Lincoln Steffens* as the worst boss-ridden city in the nation, Bigelow, a protégé of Johnson and a minister by vocation, built a diverse coalition in an effort to unseat "Boss" George B. Cox.

On the state level, beginning in 1902, Tom Johnson developed a program to redirect the Democratic party* to the cause of reform. Focusing on tax revision, home rule for cities, and utility reform, Johnson's coalition precipitated a fifteen-year struggle that led to the modernization of state government. The Democrats gained control of the governorship in 1905 and, in a piecemeal way, began to regulate utilities, to restructure local government operations, and to revise the tax code. In the midst of revelations of financial corruption in state government, the political mood began to change. Within a few years Ohio politicians were divided, according to historian Hoyt Landon Warner, "between progressives, as the reformers were called, and conservatives within each party." Bigelow took the initiative and successfully organized an electoral campaign leading to a state constitutional convention which modernized Ohio's constitution. The 119 delegates, chosen on a nonpartisan basis, elected Bigelow president and after nearly six months of debate and compromise submitted forty-two amendments to the electorate. The proposed changes dealt with education, liquor regulation, penal reform, and woman suffrage* as well as taxation, capital-labor relations, political institutions, administrative centralization, and the judiciary. The voters approved thirty-four of the amendments. The amendments were implemented by the new Democratic party–controlled General Assembly and the newly elected Democratic governor, James M. Cox.* Cox also successfully promoted a short ballot law* and the creation of a state highway system, two proposals which the electorate had rejected in 1912. World War I* slowed reform in Ohio, but after the war Ohio approved the woman suffrage and prohibition* amendments to the U.S. Constitution. The convention had rejected the latter proposal, and the voters had opposed extending voting rights to women. (Hoyt Landon Warner, *Progressivism in Ohio, 1897–1917* (1964); John D. Buenker, "Cleveland's New Stock Lawmakers and Progressive Reform," *Ohio History* 78 (1969): 116–37; Stephen M. Hurst, "Progressive Government: Administrative Reorganization and Bureaucratic Tradition in Ohio, 1880–1921" (Ph.D. diss., Miami University, 1977); Lloyd L. Sponholz, "Progressivism in Microcosm: An Analysis of the Political Forces at Work in the Ohio Constitutional Convention of 1912" (Ph.D. diss., University of Pittsburgh, 1969).)

James Cebula

OKLAHOMA. Oklahoma was once the land of Indian tribes such as the Kiowa, Comanche, Apache, and Osage. As a result of the policy of removal, the Five Civilized Tribes (Cherokee, Chickasaw, Choctaw, Creek, and Seminole) joined these earlier groups. White settlers moved onto the land, and in 1907 Oklahoma was admitted to the Union. Oklahoma's new state constitution reflected the progressivism of the times. It revealed a lack of faith in legislative wisdom, a mistrust of executive officials, and a skepticism of the power of uncontrolled courts. It provided for the protection of agriculture and farmers and for the control of railroads and other monopolies. It contained social provisions concerning child labor,* the eight-hour day, and mine safety. Its agricultural economy was tied to cotton, corn, wheat, and cattle. Lead, zinc, and coal dominated its mining industries. The discovery of rich oil and gas fields in the mid-1920s drastically altered both agriculture and mining in Oklahoma. The state moved from being primarily rural to being both urban and industrial. (H. Wayne Morgan and Anne Hodges Morgan, *Oklahoma: A Bicentennial History* (1977); James R. Scales and Danny Goble, *Oklahoma Politics: A History* (1982); Roy Gittinger, *The Formation of the State of Oklahoma* (1939).)

Monroe Billington

OLMSTED, FREDERICK LAW, JR. (July 24, 1870–December 25, 1957). Born on Staten Island, New York, Olmsted grew up in New York City and Brookline, Massachusetts. Travel and private study under his father's aegis, before and after his graduation from Harvard College in 1894, prepared him for his career in landscape architecture and public service. Highlights included work under Daniel H. Burnham* on the Chicago World's Fair, summer 1891, and thirteen months, 1894–1895, assisting his ailing father develop George Vanderbilt's immense Biltmore Estate in North Carolina. In 1898, he and his half-brother, John C. Olmsted, formed Olmsted Brothers, perpetuating the nation's most eminent landscape architecture firm. Olmsted served on the U.S. Senate Park Commission to redesign the nation's capital in 1901–1902. As Harvard University faculty member (1900–1914), he devised the nation's first curriculum in landscape architecture and in city planning.* Olmsted strongly encouraged the growth of city planning as a technical endeavor, authoring or coauthoring six city plans (1908–1913), chairing the National Conference on City Planning (1910–1918), and serving as first president of the American City Planning Institute (1917–1919). (Olmsted Associates Papers, Box 176, Library of Congress; Laura Wood Roper, *FLO: A Biography of Frederick Law Olmsted* (1973); Edward Clark Whiting and William Lyman Phillips, "Frederick Law Olmsted, 1870–1957: An Appreciation of the Man and His Achievements," *Landscape Architecture*, 48 (1958): 145–57.)

Jon A. Peterson

OPEN DOOR POLICY. In 1899, Secretary of State John Hay launched a diplomatic initiative commonly known as the open door policy to protect American commercial opportunities in China. The British had been seeking an international agreement to cooperate in the exploitation of Chinese territorial resources and trade. Hay sent notes to Germany, England, Russia, Japan, Italy, and France asking assurances that each within its own sphere of influence or leasehold would not interfere with business interests of citizens of other countries nor discriminate against citizens of other countries concerning harbor and railroad fees and that Chinese tariff alone would prevail and would be collected by the Chinese government. Although the responses were evasive, Hay announced in early 1900 that the nations to which he had written had agreed.

Later in 1900, Hay used the same method to extend the agreements to protect Chinese territorial and administrative integrity. For the next two decades, the United States continued to advocate the open door policy and occasionally sought to further specific American business interests in China. The Nine-Power Treaty of 1922 formalized the open door agreement but made it no more effective in protecting China from depredation. (Charles Vevier, *United States and China, 1906–1913: Finance and Diplomacy* (1955); Paul Varg, *Making of a Myth: The United States and China, 1879–1912* (1968); Jerry Israel, *Progressivism and the Open Door: America and China, 1905–1921* (1971).)

Martin I. Elzy

OREGON. In the adoption of democratic political reforms during the Progressive Era, Oregon was the undisputed leader. It was the famous legislative "Holdup of '97" which occurred when a coalition of Republican, Democratic, and Populist legislators, organized by Jonathan Bourne,* blocked the reelection of Senator John Mitchell* by preventing the House of Representatives from permanently organizing that paved the way. The thirteen Populists in the House, under the leadership of an obscure young lawyer, William S. U'Ren,* agreed to participate in the "holdup" in exchange for the support of Bourne and other Republican co-conspirators in the passage of a constitutional amendment providing for the initiative* and referendum.* They lived up to this "corrupt bargain," and in 1902 the amendment was approved, Oregon being the third state to adopt the initiative and referendum.

During the next ten years, almost entirely by means of the initiative, U'Ren and fellow reformers were successful in obtaining voter approval for a series of additional democratic reforms. The first of these was a direct primary law* in 1904. Although Wisconsin had adopted this reform the previous year, Oregon's law included a unique feature, Statement No. 1., providing, in effect, for the popular election of U.S. senators.* In 1907, by means of this reform, Bourne would become the first member of the U.S. Senate to be elected by popular vote. In 1906, initiatives were passed providing for municipal home rule,* prohibiting free railroad passes, and extending the initiative and referendum to local legislation. Among the reforms adopted in 1908 were a corrupt practices act* and a means of recalling* elected officials. In 1910, Oregon became the first state to adopt a presidential preferential primary, and two years later, after a long campaign by Abigail Scott Duniway, granted women the vote.

In the meantime, under the leadership of Democratic governors George Chamberlain (1903–1909) and Oswald West (1911–1915), Oregon, by either legislative action or initiative, also adopted a series of labor and economic reforms including the taxation of private utilities, employers' liability* and child labor laws,* and laws providing for an eight-hour day in public works, a ten-hour day for women, an Industrial Welfare Commission with power to set minimum wages for women, a public utility commission,* and a state forestry commission. It was this long list of reforms, particularly the political ones, that Frederic C. Howe* had in mind when he described Oregon as "the most complete democracy in the world." (Allen H. Eaton, *The Oregon System: The Story of Direct Legislation in Oregon* (1912); James D. Barnett, *The Operation of the Initiative, Referendum and Recall* *in Oregon* (1915); Tony Howard Evans, "Oregon Progressive Reform, 1902–1914" (Ph.D. diss., University of California–Berkeley, 1966); Warren M. Blankenship, "Progressives and the Progressive Party in Oregon, 1906–1916" (Ph.D. diss., University of Oregon, 1966).)

Thomas C. McClintock

O'REILLY, LENORA (February 16, 1870–April 3, 1927). Born in New York City, O'Reilly was committed to the labor movement, and her commitment grew steadily after age sixteen when she accompanied her mother to meetings of a local assembly of the Knights of Labor and began to meet influential reformers who encouraged her widening interests. Working in a shirtwaist factory, O'Reilly organized a women's local of the United Garment Workers of America and developed a talent for public speaking. She graduated in 1900 from Pratt Institute in Brooklyn, where she prepared to teach vocational courses. After working in settlement houses, including Henry Street,* O'Reilly founded in 1903 an organizational center for her activities, the National Women's Trade Union League* (WTUL). In 1909 league "ally" Mary Dreier* gave O'Reilly a lifetime annuity to support her organizational work. O'Reilly rose to the leadership of the WTUL and served effectively during the shirtwaist makers' strike of 1909–1910. O'Reilly was a socialist, an active suffragist, and a founding member of the National Association for the Advancement of Colored People.* She attended the International Congress of Women at the Hague in 1915 and the International Congress of Working Women at Washington in 1919. (Lenora O'Reilly Papers, Schlesinger Library, Radcliffe College; Ellen C. Lagemann, *A Generation of Women: Education in the Lives of Progressive Reformers* (1979); Nancy Schrom Dye, *As Equals and as Sisters: Feminism, Unionism, and the Women's Trade Union League of New York City* (1980).)

Mari Jo Buhle

OSTROGORSKI, MOSEI (Yakovlevich) (1854–1919). Born in Grodno, Russia, of Jewish parents, he was educated in the law faculty in Saint Petersburg and also studied in France. Ostrogorski wrote a number of histories of Russia aimed at the elementary and secondary student and served in the Russian ministries of finance and justice. In 1906, Ostrogorski was a member of the First Duma. In 1902, he published his major work, *Democracy and the Organization of Political Parties*, which was divided into two volumes—the first on Great Britain and the second on the United States. His thesis was that democracy was corrupted by the *organization* of politics. He believed the "caucus" rule sapped the independent judgment of party members. Although his work is generally unknown now, it had some impact on progressive thought in the United States and on the studies of politics undertaken by Max Weber and Robert Miche. He also wrote about and advocated equal rights for women. (Rodney Barker and

Xenia Howard Johnson, "Politics and Political Ideas of Mosei Ostrogorski," *Political Studies* 23 (1975): 415–29.)

David J. Maurer

O'SULLIVAN, MARY KENNEY (January 8, 1864–January 18, 1943). Women's labor union organizer and social reformer, O'Sullivan was born in Hannibal, Missouri,* to Irish* immigrant parents; she moved to Chicago* and worked as a bookbinder, while becoming active in union activities. She worked with Florence Kelley* of Hull House* on an investigation of sweatshop conditions, then served as an assistant to Kelley when the latter was named Illinois factory inspector in 1893. Samuel Gompers* appointed her the first woman organizer for the American Federation of Labor* in 1892; and while on union business in Boston,* she met fellow-organizer John F. O'Sullivan, whom she married in 1894. Taking up residence at Denison House in Boston, the O'Sullivans continued their union activities. Mary O'Sullivan collaborated with William English Walling* in founding the National Women's Trade Union League* in 1903, and she served as state factory inspector for Massachusetts* from 1914 to 1934. (Alice Henry, *Women and the Labor Movement* (1923); Allen F. Davis, *Spearheads for Reform* (1967); James, Edward T., et al., *Notable American Women*, vol. 2 (1971).)

Edward R. Kantowicz

OTIS, HARRISON GRAY (February 10, 1837–July 30, 1917). Harrison Gray Otis was born near Marietta, Ohio. His formal education was limited to common school, to a five-month course at Wetherby's Academy at Lowell, Ohio, and a three-month commercial course at Granger's College, Columbus, Ohio. A delegate from Kentucky to the 1860 Republican convention, Otis enlisted as a private in the 12th Ohio Volunteers in 1861. Twice wounded, he advanced through the ranks and was mustered out as a brevet lieutenant colonel. In 1866, he served as the reporter of the Ohio House and the following year secured appointment as a compositor and then foreman in the U.S. Government Printing Office. Between 1871 and 1876, Otis worked as a clerk in the U.S. Patent Office. In 1876 he moved to California to edit the Santa Barbara *Press*, but returned to public work as a Treasury Department agent in Alaska in 1879. Otis moved to Los Angeles in 1882, acquiring a quarter interest in the recently founded Los Angeles *Times*. By 1886, he had acquired full control. Otis returned briefly to military service during the Spanish-American War* when he saw action in the Philippines.

A community booster, he was a founding member of the Los Angeles Chamber of Commerce. A conservative Republican, he fought the attempt of the Southern Pacific Railroad to prevent harbor development at San Pedro, supported the construction of the Owens River Aqueduct, and championed the effort to eliminate union labor from Los Angeles. In 1910, twenty-one *Times* employees were killed and the *Times* building destroyed by a bomb set in retaliation for his open-shop stance. Both emotionally and politically he was tied to the established order and aggressively fought the efforts of progressives in the city and state to alter that order. (Richard C. Miller, "Otis and His Times: The Career of Harrison Gray Otis of California" (Ph.D. diss., University of California–Berkeley, 1961); Robert Gottlieb and Irene Wolt, *Thinking Big: The Story of the Los Angeles "Times"* (1977).)

Richard C. Lower

OUTLOOK, THE. This weekly magazine, under the title *Christian Union*, was from 1869 to 1881 a principal forum for the Rev. Henry Ward Beecher, the noted Congregational minister. In 1881, Beecher ended his association with it and the Rev. Lyman Abbott,* who had joined the periodical in 1876, led the magazine in title as well as in fact. Retaining a foundation of liberal religion, the magazine expanded into secular news and comment; its name change to the *Outlook* in 1893 reflected its expanded interests. At the turn of the century and for twenty years thereafter, it enjoyed a weekly circulation of over 100,000. It serialized Booker T. Washington's* *Up from Slavery* and Jacob Riis's* *The Making of an American*.

Not given to muckraking* journalism, the *Outlook* covered literature and the arts well, but with the passage of time treated current issues more extensively. An early believer in civil service,* tariff, and tax reform, Abbott later became concerned with industrial and labor topics. Theodore Roosevelt* was named contributing editor in 1908; the magazine backed the Bull Moose ticket in 1912. It supported an early American entry into World War I.* After the war, circulation declined slowly but steadily, and in 1923, Lyman Abbott died. (Lyman Abbott, *Reminiscences* (1923); Frank Luther Mott, *A History of American Magazines, 1865–1885* (1967); Theodore Roosevelt, *"Outlook" Editorials* (1909).)

Lloyd J. Graybar

OVINGTON, MARY WHITE (October 11, 1865–July 15, 1951). Born in Brooklyn, New York, Ovington was raised in a well-to-do family with an abolitionist tradition. A social worker, journalist, feminist, and peace advocate, Ovington embraced many progressive causes. Her chief significance, however, lies in her civil rights work. The white reformer first became interested in the plight of blacks when she heard Booker T. Washington* speak in 1903, but soon thereafter she came under the influence of W. E. B. Du Bois,* the black protest leader. In 1904 she began an in-depth study of the Negro, published in 1911 as *Half a Man: The Status of the Negro in New York*. In 1909 she and a handful of white progressives, galvanized by a vicious race riot* in Springfield, Illinois, took steps that led to the formation of the interracial National Association for the Advancement of Colored People* (NAACP, 1910).

Firmly situated in the inner circle of the NAACP, Ovington subordinated her socialist views and worked courageously and untiringly for complete legal and civil equality for blacks. She held many high positions in the NAACP before her retirement in 1947, presiding as chairman of the board from 1919 to 1932. For several years she was an invaluable conciliator between the irascible Du Bois and other influential members of the organization, ensuring the survival of the NAACP until it achieved institutional momentum. (Mary White Ovington, *The Walls Came Tumbling Down* (1947); B. Joyce Ross, *J. E. Spingarn and the Rise of the NAACP, 1911–1939* (1972); Daniel W. Cryer, "Mary White Ovington and the Rise of the NAACP" (Ph.D. diss., University of Minnesota, 1977).)

David W. Southern

OWEN, ROBERT L. (February 2, 1856–July 19, 1947). Born in Lynchburg, Virginia, Owen was of Scotch-Irish and Cherokee Indian ancestry. He was educated at Washington and Lee University, graduating in 1877. He moved to Indian Territory in 1879, where he was a teacher, newspaper owner and editor, lawyer, banker, cattleman, and federal Indian agent. He was an organizer of the Democratic party* in Indian Territory and helped include in the constitution of Oklahoma* the direct primary,* the initiative* and referendum,* and the recall.* When Oklahoma became a state in 1907, Owen was elected one of its senators, and he remained in the Senate until 1925. He favored the direct election of U.S. senators,* lower tariffs, and the regulation of trusts. He devoted attention to Indian affairs, rural problems, the wage earner, and health and education. His major contributions were in banking and monetary and economic reform. Serving as chairman of the Senate Banking and Currency Committee, he was cosponsor of the Federal Reserve Act of 1913.* (Edward Elmer Keso, *The Senatorial Career of Robert Latham Owen* (1938).)

Monroe Billington

P

PAGE, WALTER HINES (August 15, 1855–December 21, 1918). Journalist, New South* advocate, American ambassador to England during World War I,* Page was born in Cary, North Carolina.* He attended Trinity College (now Duke University) in North Carolina,* Randolph-Macon College in Virginia,* and Johns Hopkins in Maryland.* He began work as a journalist for the Saint Joseph, Missouri,* *Gazette* in 1880, then worked for the New York *World*. In 1883 he bought the Raleigh, North Carolina, *State Chronicle* and used it to advocate a modern, industrialized New South. The paper failed financially, so Page then wrote for the *Forum** and in 1898 became editor of the *Atlantic Monthly.** In 1900 he founded his own national journal, *World's Work,** which he edited until 1913.

He was one of many Southerners living up North who gathered around Woodrow Wilson's* successful presidential campaign in 1912. Wilson appointed him ambassador to England, where he served until ill health forced his resignation in 1918. Page was unabashedly pro-English during the time when America remained neutral in World War I,* so much so that President Wilson found him unreliable and often did not consult him on sensitive matters. Wilson relied instead on his personal adviser, Colonel Edward M. House,* to transmit peace proposals to Great Britain and Germany. (Walter Hines Page, *A Publisher's Confession* (1923); John Milton Cooper, *Walter Hines Page: The Southerner as American, 1855–1918* (1977); Arthur S. Link, *Woodrow Wilson and the Progressive Era* (1954).)

Edward R. Kantowicz

PALMER, A. MITCHELL (May 4, 1872–May 11, 1936). Attorney General of the United States at the time of the Red Scare* after World War I.* Palmer was born in Pennsylvania to devout Quaker parents. He graduated from Swarthmore College in 1891 and was admitted to the bar in 1893. He served three terms as a progressive Democratic congressman from Pennsylvania (1909–1915) and acted as Woodrow Wilson's* floor manager at the Democratic convention in 1912. Due to his Quaker background, he declined Wilson's offer of a cabinet post as secretary of war, but he later served as alien property custodian during the war years of 1917 and 1918. He succeeded Thomas Gregory as attorney general on March 4, 1919.

In late 1919 and early 1920, Attorney General Palmer orchestrated a series of arrests and deportations of alien radicals which came to be called the "Palmer Raids." These actions fanned the flames of the Red Scare in the months after the end of World War I. Palmer's antiradical activities were partly motivated by political ambition, and he contended strongly for the Democratic presidential nomination in 1920, finally losing to James M. Cox.* Palmer's combative personality and his role in the Red Scare earned for him the ironic nickname of "The Fighting Quaker." (Stanley Coben, *A. Mitchell Palmer* (1963); Robert K. Murray, *Red Scare: A Study in National Hysteria* (1955).)

Edward R. Kantowicz

PANAMA CANAL. The Panama Canal, connecting the Atlantic and Pacific coasts by waterway, opened on August 14, 1914. The canal remains the major achievement of the Theodore Roosevelt* administration. Under an 1878 concession to Ferdinand de Lesseps, builder of the Suez Canal, construction began but was interrupted in 1889 due to undercapitalization and tropical disease. In 1901, British objections, based on the Clayton Bulwer Treaty, were eliminated by the Hay-Pauncetote Treaty and the assets of the canal company offered to the United States for $40. The Spooner Act of 1902 approved purchase contingent upon a treaty with Colombia. After Colombia rejected the Hay-Herran Treaty, Panama declared independence on November 3, 1903. The United States recognized Panama and signed a treaty for the right to construct the canal. After the canal's completion, Panama, in several treaties and negotiations over the next half century, sought to free the canal from U.S. control and to increase its own revenue. Finally, on September 7, 1977, the United States agreed in two treaties to Panamanian control and neutralization of the canal by the year 2000. (Walter LaFeber, *The Panama Canal* (1977); D. McCullough, *Path between the Seas: The Creation of the Panama Canal, 1870–1914* (1977); D. C. Miner, *The Fight for the Panama Route* (1940); George C. Mowry, *The Era of Theodore Roosevelt* (1963).)

C. David Tompkins

PANIC OF 1907. This minor depression, also known as the "Rich Man's Panic," followed a period of general economic prosperity during the early 1900s. This panic resulted from industrial overproduction, irresponsible speculation, and financial mismanagement, particularly by banking institutions in the East and Midwest. In mid-March 1907, after a sharp drop in New York Stock Exchange prices, J. P. Morgan* asked President Theodore Roosevelt* about possible government assistance in the impending crisis. The president assured Morgan and other financiers that he would act responsibly in all economic matters and would not interfere with recovery efforts by business leaders. The U.S. Treasury deposited customs receipts in various banks and restricted its normal withdrawals of government funds.

Nevertheless, the crisis deepened in the fall of 1907. By mid-October, a nationwide panic had appeared, characterized by bank failures, frozen deposits, and tightened credit. In New York and Chicago, commercial loans became virtually nonexistent. Morgan hastily arranged a pool of the assets of several influential New York banks to bolster shaky financial institutions across the nation. The government also plunged over $38 million into New York banks and trust companies. Roosevelt permitted Morgan's U.S. Steel Corporation to acquire the Tennessee Coal and Iron Company, with the understanding that no antitrust litigation would be instituted.

Although a total economic collapse was averted in 1907, recovery would not come until 1915. Revelations of serious deficiencies in the banking and credit systems led to passage of the Aldrich-Vreeland Act* (1908). To increase the flexibility of the currency, this law authorized national banks for six years to issue circulating notes based on commercial paper and state, county, and municipal bonds. This act also created the National Monetary Commission,* with a mandate to investigate U.S. and European financial systems and report on its findings. (William H. Harbaugh, *Power and Responsibility: The Life and Times of Theodore Roosevelt* (1961); John Chamberlain, *The Enterprising Americans: A Business History of the United States* (1963); Gabriel Kolko, *The Triumph of Conservatism: A Reinterpretation of American History, 1900–1916* (1963); Robert H. Wiebe, *Businessmen and Reform: A Study of the Progressive Movement* (1962).)

David Alsobrook

PARK, MAUD WOOD (January 25, 1871–May 8, 1955). Born in Boston, Massachusetts, Park was class valedictorian at Saint Agnes School in 1887 and, in 1898, after only three years, graduated summa cum laude from Radcliffe College. While at Radcliffe, she joined the Massachusetts Woman Suffrage Association (MWSA). As the chair of MWSA in 1900, Park attended the National American Woman Suffrage Association* (NAWSA) national convention, where she became aware of the lack of young women in the suffrage movement. As a result, Park and Inez Haynes Gillmore (Irwin) formed the Massachusetts College Equal Suffrage League (MCESL) in 1901. Seven years later, the National College Equal Suffrage Association formed and elected Park as vice president. Active in the unsuccessful 1915 Massachusetts state suffrage referendum, in 1917 she became coordinator of the NAWSA Congressional Committee, lobbying for congressional support for suffrage. After ratification of the Nineteenth Amendment, NAWSA formed the National League of Women Voters,* and Park served as its first president and legislative chair. In this position, she helped establish the Women's Joint Congressional Committee (WJCC).

Park devoted her life to social reform activities, emphasizing the need for legislation to improve the lives of women and children, as well as issues of world peace, civic responsibility, and public health. She believed that the vote was an important means to achieve these goals. Park also helped found the Boston Equal Suffrage Association for Good Government (BESAGG) and the Boston Parent Teachers Association. (James, Edward T., et al., *Notable American Women*, vol. 3 (1971); *Dictionary of American Biography*, Supplement 5; Sharon Hartman Strom, "Leadership and Tactics in the American Woman Suffrage Movement: A New Perspective from Massachusetts," *Journal of American History* 62 (September 1975): 372–92.)

Marie Laberge

PARKER, ALTON BROOKS (May 14, 1852–May 10, 1926). Born near Cortland, New York, Parker followed a short term as a teacher with studies at Albany Law School. He set up practice in Kingston, New York, in 1873. Over the next two decades he branched out into Democratic politics, managing various successful campaigns while being elected to a succession of county and state judicial offices. In 1897 he became chief justice of the New York Court of Appeals. Although Parker had declined repeated attempts to slate him for governor or U.S. senator, his probity, noncontroversial background, and electoral victories made him the leading contender of his party's anti-Bryan conservatives for the 1904 Democratic presidential nomination. He easily defeated William Randolph Hearst* on the first convention ballot.

As a candidate, Parker conducted a restrained front-porch campaign, attracting attention only with his fervent declaration of support for the gold standard and his charge that the Republicans had extorted corporate contributions. His tactics failed, and he was decisively beaten by Theodore Roosevelt.* Parker spent his later years building a considerable legal practice in New York City,* active in civic and professional affairs. (John Randolph Grady, *The Lives and Public Services of Parker and Davis* (1904); Irving Stone, *They Also Ran* (1943); Leonard Schlup, "Alton B. Parker and the Presidential Campaign of 1904," *North Dakota Quarterly* 49 (1981): 48–60.)

John R. Schmidt

PARKER, JOHN MILLIKEN (March 16, 1863–May 20, 1939). Born in Bethel Church, Mississippi, Parker was educated in private academies in Mississippi and Virginia and Eastman's Business College, Poughkeepsie, New York. Parker was a cotton planter and cotton factor in New Orleans and president of the Board of Trade (1893), New Orleans Cotton Exchange (1897), Southern Commercial Congress (1908), and Mississippi Valley Association. An advocate of business principles and elite rule in government, he became active in municipal reform in the 1890s. Parker favored federal flood control and protective tariffs.

A supporter of Theodore Roosevelt's* New Nationalism,* he endorsed the Bull Moose party in 1912.

In 1916, he was an unsuccessful gubernatorial candidate on the Progressive party* ticket. When Roosevelt shunned the third party, Parker accepted its vice presidential nomination, but later admitted the hollowness of his bid and campaigned for Woodrow Wilson.* During World War I,* he was state food administrator. In 1920, Parker became Democratic governor of Louisiana. His administration featured opposition to the Ku Klux Klan and the New Orleans machine, aid for education and roads, and a severance tax on oil. Parker's emphasis on pay-as-you-go financing, legislative opposition, and compromises with oil interests undermined his programs. (Matthew J. Schott, "John M. Parker of Louisiana and the Varieties of American Progressivism" (Ph.D. diss., Vanderbilt University, 1969); John M. Parker Papers, University of North Carolina at Chapel Hill and the University of Southwestern Louisiana.)

Edward F. Haas

PATERSON TEXTILE STRIKE. On January 27, 1913, workers at a silk mill in Paterson, New Jersey, walked out to protest the firing of their union representatives. The strike spread to the whole town; and in February, organizers from the Industrial Workers of the World* (IWW), who had recently won a similar strike in Lawrence,* Massachusetts, arrived to support the Paterson workers. The strike lasted into the summer. The IWW attracted sympathy by evacuating the hungry strikers' children to foster homes, as they had done in Lawrence.* John Reed,* a young reporter arrested while covering the strike, dreamed up a further propaganda device: the Paterson pageant. Supported by New York literary friends, Reed rented Madison Square Garden and produced a pageant in which a thousand workers depicted the story of the Paterson strike. Despite these efforts, the strike failed and the workers returned in July without any gains in wages or bargaining status. The Lawrence strike had marked the high point of the IWW's influence as an industrial union. After the failure of the Paterson strike, however, industrial unionism had to wait until the Great Depression of the 1930s. (Patrick Renshaw, *The Wobblies* (1967); Philip S. Foner, *A History of the Labor Movement in the United States*, vol. 4: *The Industrial Workers of the World, 1905–1917* (1965); Joyce L. Kornbluh, *Rebel Voices* (1964).)

Edward R. Kantowicz

PATTEN, SIMON N. (May 1, 1852–July 24, 1922). Born in rural De Kalb County, Illinois, Patten was educated at Jennings Seminary in nearby Aurora and received a Ph.D. degree at Halle University in Germany in 1878. After returning from Germany, he taught in rural Illinois schools before assuming a position at the University of Pennsylvania in 1888, where he gave form to the newly created Wharton School of Commerce and Finance, remaining there until his retirement in 1917. The school embarked on the first effort to train business students in an academic setting.

Like several other younger American scholars who had been trained in Germany, Patten rejected the orthodoxies of classical economics and their gloomy forebodings. He foresaw a world of abundance that offered everyone opportunities for comfort and leisure. Such opportunities could become realities only through additional public expenditures. Though he was not an original thinker, his emphasis upon abundance inspired reformers from the Progressive Era to Lyndon Johnson's Great Society. (Daniel M. Fox, *The Discovery of Abundance and the Transformation of Social Theory* (1967); Joseph Dorfman, *The Economic Mind in American Civilization*, vol. 3 (1959); Scott Nearing, *Educational Frontiers* (1925).)

Benjamin G. Rader

PAUL, ALICE (January 11, 1885–July 9, 1977). Perhaps the most charismatic leader of the woman suffrage* movement, Paul was born to Quakers in Moorestown, New Jersey. She was educated at Swarthmore, the University of Pennsylvania (Ph.D., 1912), Washington College of Law (LL.B., 1922), and American University (LL.M and D.C.L., 1927–1928). Paul worked for woman suffrage with the Pankhursts in England and Scotland (1909–1912). She injected their militant tactics into the American woman suffrage movement, initially as chairman of the Congressional Committee of the National American Woman Suffrage Association,* formed in 1913, then as head of her own organization, the Congressional Union (after 1917 the National Woman's Party).*

Paul campaigned for a federal suffrage amendment, castigated the Democrats and President Woodrow Wilson* for not achieving it, and paraded and picketed throughout the war. Like the Pankhursts, Paul endured arrests, hunger strikes, and forced feeding. Paul reorganized the Woman's Party after suffrage was won and, in 1923, introduced the Equal Rights Amendment. In Europe in the twenties and thirties, Paul worked for international women's rights and founded a World Woman's Party in 1938. (Inez Haynes Irwin, *The Story of the Woman's Party* (1921); Susan Becker, *The Origins of the Equal Rights Amendment: American Feminism between the Wars* (1981); Loretta Zimmerman, "Alice Paul and the National Woman's Party, 1912–1920" (Ph.D. diss., Tulane University, 1964).)

Sidney Bland

PAYNE-ALDRICH TARIFF. This tariff was named for Representative Sereno E. Payne of New York and Senator Nelson W. Aldrich* of Rhode Island. During the 1908 election, tariff reform had been a major issue of the campaign. Popular opinion ascribed a persistent rise in the cost of living* to import duties. During the last years of Theodore Roosevelt's* presidency, a desire had grown for some downward revision of the Dingley Tariff* of 1897. William Howard Taft* wanted perhaps the lowest tariff of any major Republican of his time. Leading GOP speakers in the fall of 1908, moreover, had promised that their party would alter

359

import duties if returned to office. Taft consequently called Congress into special session in March 1909, asking for a new tariff.

In the ensuing evolution of the new bill in the House, the president, hoping to avoid acrimony in his relations with Congress, played a less active role than Republican progressives would have preferred. Taft did use his influence to defy the old-guard leadership and secure free hides, coal, and iron, but Senate changes in the bill distressed many reformers. Although not enthused about the upper chamber's version, Taft thought that the differences had been exaggerated by the press and that he could improve the final law by making use of his influence during the deliberations of the House-Senate Conference Committee. The process of negotiation continued during June and July 1909 and was not completed until the beginning of August. The more militant progressives in the GOP, furious with the compromises the administration had made with the regular Republican leadership, wished Taft to veto the bill. He refused to do so, feeling that the Payne-Aldrich Tariff was the best measure he could obtain under the circumstances.

The new law's rates did mark a modest retreat from the rigid high protectionism of the existing duties. Taft interpreted a technical aspect of the law as authorizing him to appoint a tariff commission.* He felt that if impartial experts could collect enough data, it would be possible to have a more equitable revision of import duties in the future. The provision for free trade with the Philippines also appealed to the president. He was aware of the bitter criticism opponents had of the bill, but he underestimated the strength of the feeling. Taft's defense of the law alienated many Republican progressives, especially from the Middle West, and became a significant factor in the division of the GOP. (Paolo E. Coletta, *The Presidency of William Howard Taft* (1973); David W. Detzer, "The Politics of the Payne-Aldrich Tariff of 1909" (Ph.D. diss., University of Connecticut, 1970); Stanley D. Solvick, "William Howard Taft and the Payne-Aldrich Tariff," *Mississippi Valley Historical Review* 50 (1963): 424–42.)

Stanley D. Solvick

PEACE MOVEMENT, THE. Clearly linked to the increasing American economic and political involvement in international affairs, the peace movement evolved from a marginal reform into a respectable and popular establishment. The new peace supporters promoted the extension of American moral influence and institutions through standardized conciliation procedures, peace research, international congresses and laws, and a world court. The post-1900 peace advocates, many of whom were lawyers and businessmen, represented a social, economic, and educational elite, indifferent to public support. Not comprehending the extent of the nationalistic rivalries in Europe, they accepted the premise that civilized man had progressed beyond the resort to war.

The outbreak of World War I* shattered the confident assumptions of the prewar peace advocates. Opposition to the war came from individuals who had previously eschewed the peace movement as less critical than the social and economic injustices in American society. Determined to keep the United States out of the war and fearful of its impact on the "social fabric," social justice reformers,* feminists,* students, labor leaders, Social Gospel clergy,* religious pacifists, and antiwar socialists formed new antiwar organizations and coalitions. Peace workers during the period from 1914 to 1917 promoted neutral mediation and opposed military preparedness, conscription, intervention, and the abridgement of civil liberties. The Woman's Peace party,* the American Union Against Militarism, and the Fellowship of Reconciliation all joined the movement. After the break in diplomatic relations with Germany in February 1917, many peace advocates ceased their activities; following American intervention in April 1917, there was further erosion in the peace organizations' memberships.

Many liberals feared that continued opposition to the government would be futile and would jeopardize their effectiveness in achieving other reforms. Organizations divided over wartime policies, especially the issue of support for conscientious objectors* to war. Many of the peace advocates became firm supporters of the war effort, but those who remained pacifists refused to accept the notion that the United States was fighting an idealistic war that would promote freedom and justice. (David S. Patterson, "An Interpretation of the American Peace Movement, 1898–1914," in Charles Chatfield, ed., *Peace Movements in America* (1973); Charles Chatfield, *For Peace and Justice: Pacifism in America, 1914–1941* (1971); C. Roland Marchand, *The American Peace Movement and Social Reform, 1898–1918* (1972).)

Barbara J. Steinson

PENAL REFORM. Penal reform in the Progressive Era established the indeterminate sentence, probation, parole, and the juvenile court as basic institutions in the American criminal justice system. The new institutions embodied the concept of rehabilitation, or reforming offenders through individualized treatment. In 1900, only six states permitted probation, a handful used the indeterminant sentence and parole, and only one had a juvenile court. By 1915, over thirty states had the indeterminate sentence, parole, and adult probation, while over forty states had juvenile probation and/or separate juvenile courts. Under the indeterminate sentence, judges could impose a sentence within a statutory minimum and maximum. The parole board would then determine the actual release date, based upon its determination that the offender was successfully rehabilitated. This approach was designed to tailor prison terms to the perceived needs of particular offenders. Juvenile court* judges also had broad discretion in determining sentences, since proceedings were designed to avoid the legalistic formalities and terminology of the adult criminal process. Both probation and parole involved supervision of the offender in a community setting.

A complex mixture of humanitarian, scientific, and social control motives prompted these reforms. The nonlegalistic style of the juvenile court was thought to be a more humane way of handling young offenders. Probation was also thought to be more humane than prison. Individualized treatment was also intended to be more scientific, since decisions were to be based on a diagnosis of the circumstances of particular offenders. These reforms were buttressed by the simultaneous rise of the science of criminology and also permitted greater social control. Under the indeterminate sentence offenders could be kept in prison for very long periods of time, while juvenile court statutes permitted legal intervention in a broad range of behavior that was not criminal when committed by an adult. (Anthony Platt, *The Child Savers: The Invention of Delinquency* (1969); David J. Rothman, *Conscience and Convenience: The Asylum and Its Alternatives in Progressive America* (1980); Samuel Walker, *Popular Justice: A History of American Criminal Justice* (1980).)

Samuel Walker

PENNSYLVANIA. Pennsylvania in the early twentieth century was governed by a powerful Republican machine headed by U.S. Senator Boies Penrose,* which grew more efficient even as the state experienced both the Progressive critique and reforms. Muckrakers like Ida Tarbell* and Lincoln Steffens* exposed industrial corruption and corrupt municipal politics, but the state's reforms resulted from uneasy cooperation between reformers and competing urban machine factions. In 1906 a treasury scandal led Governor Samuel W. Pennypacker to push through reform legislation which included reapportionment, corrupt practices* legislation, and a uniform primary law. Reform Democrat William H. Berry, the state treasurer, exposed corruption in the building of a new state capitol in 1906. Progressives (with the help of Pittsburgh Republican boss William Flinn) carried the state for Theodore Roosevelt* in 1912.

The most prominent social reform activity was associated with Paul U. Kellogg's* *Pittsburgh Survey* of 1907–1908, which focused attention on working and living conditions and child labor. Housing legislation in Pittsburgh and Philadelphia prevented some of the worst tenement conditions, although too few inspectors could never adequately enforce it, and the problem of insufficient low-income housing was never addressed. A series of child labor* laws set fourteen as the minimum working age, established a fifty-one–hour week, required a sixth-grade education, and limited the entry of children into dangerous occupations. Women's labor legislation and a workmen's compensation* law were also passed. (Philip S. Klein and Ari Hoogenboom, *A History of Pennsylvania* (1980); Joseph M. Speakman, "Unwillingly to School: Child Labor and Its Reform in Pennsylvania, 1889–1915" (Ph.D. diss., Temple University, 1976); Sylvester K. Stevens, *Pennsylvania: Birthplace of a Nation* (1964).)

John F. Sutherland

PENROSE, BOIES (November 1, 1860–December 31, 1921). Born in Philadelphia of a wealthy physician's family on November 1, 1860, Penrose was educated at Harvard University, from which he graduated magna cum laude in 1881. Of exceptional intelligence, he was nevertheless lazy, self-indulgent, and cynical. Standing six feet four inches tall and ultimately weighing 350 pounds,

Penrose satiated his enormous appetites without restraint. In 1882, he joined the law firm of Page, Allinson, and Penrose. With his partner, Edward P. Allinson, he published *Philadelphia, 1681–1887: A History of Municipal Development* in 1887.

The law bored Penrose, and he quickly entered politics in Philadelphia's eighth district, which he represented in the state House of Representatives from 1884 to 1886, and in the state Senate from 1887 to 1897. With the support of Pennsylvania Republican boss Matthew Quay, Penrose was elected to the U.S. Senate in 1897, where he served continuously until his death in 1921. Following Quay's death in 1904, he became the leader of Pennsylvania's Republican party.

Unlike previous party bosses, Penrose did not speculate with the state's money. Independently wealthy, he sought only power, and he became a champion of big-business interests. As chairman of the Senate Finance Committee, Penrose constantly supported high tariffs. Normally a foe of Progressives (he suffered his only defeat when Theodore Roosevelt's* Progressive party* carried Pennsylvania in 1912), he would nevertheless support them and their measures when it was to his advantage and when such measures would not impact negatively upon big business. Thus he endorsed reform charters for both Pittsburgh* and Philadelphia* in order to minimize the power of local bosses. (Robert Douglas Bowden, *Boies Penrose: Symbol of an Era* (1937); Walter Davenport, *Power and Glory: The Life of Boies Penrose* (1931); Philip S. Klein and Ari Hoogenboom, *A History of Pennsylvania* (1980).)

John F. Sutherland

PERKINS, FRANCES (April 10, 1880–May 14, 1965). The first woman cabinet member in U.S. history, Fannie Coralie Perkins was born in Boston. She changed her name to Frances, her year of birth to 1882, her religion to Episcopalian, but did not change her surname after marriage to Paul C. Wilson. A Mount Holyoke graduate, Frances Perkins taught, did settlement work, studied economics under Simon Patten,* and social work at the New York School of Philanthropy. With Florence Kelley* of the National Consumers's League,* she fought for labor laws to protect women and children, and ended up opposing the Equal Rights Amendment. On March 25, 1911, she witnessed human torches jumping from the flame-engulfed eighth and ninth floors of the Triangle Shirtwaist Factory, and shortly thereafter headed the New York State Factory Investigating Commission.* In 1919, New York Governor Al Smith* appointed the "fiery young idealist" to the State Industrial Commission, and upon reelection in 1926, named her chairman. Two years later, Governor Franklin D. Roosevelt* appointed her commissioner of the largest state's Department of Labor. Despite furor over her sex, president-elect Roosevelt named her secretary of the Department of Labor.* (George Martin, *Madam Secretary: Frances Perkins* (1976);

Lillian H. Mohr, *Frances Perkins: "That Woman in FDR's Cabinet"* (1979); Frances Perkins, *People at Work* (1934); Frances Perkins, *The Roosevelt I Knew* (1946).)

Lillian H. Mohr

PERKINS, GEORGE W. (January 31, 1862–June 18, 1920). Born in Chicago, Illinois, Perkins left grammar school at age fifteen to work in his father's insurance office. Perkins's success in the international insurance market brought him to the attention of J. P. Morgan, Sr.,* who made him a partner in February of 1901. Large financial contributions and political lobbying also brought Perkins to the attention of the Republican party.* In 1900 Perkins supported Theodore Roosevelt's* candidacy for vice president at the GOP convention, and he contributed large amounts of money to the Republican campaign of that year. At Morgan, Perkins was instrumental in solving the financial problems of United States Steel and in the creation of the International Harvester Corporation. As a businessman and as a contributor to Republican political causes, Perkins advocated a policy of government-business cooperation and federal regulation to replace the enforcement of the Sherman Antitrust Act.

In 1912, he broke with the Taft* administration over the administration's antitrust suits against U.S. Steel and International Harvester, and played a key role in organizing and financing Roosevelt's bid for the 1912 Republican presidential nomination. When that effort failed, he pledged his organizational skills and financial support to Roosevelt and the new Progressive party.* From the New York campaign headquarters, Perkins unleashed a flood of publications that paid most of the bills. Following Roosevelt's defeat in 1912, Perkins attempted unsuccessfully to revive the Progressive party in the 1914 congressional elections, and in 1916, after failing to get Roosevelt the GOP nomination, he reluctantly joined the Hughes campaign. By 1918 he was once again a Republican. (John A. Garraty, *Right Hand Man: The Life of George W. Perkins* (1957); Perkins Papers, Columbia University; Morton Keller, *The Life Insurance Enterprise 1885–1910* (1963).)

Jack D. Elenbaas

PERSHING, JOHN JOSEPH (September 13, 1860–July 25, 1948). Born near Laclede, Missouri, Pershing graduated from the U.S. Military Academy in 1886. After seeing brief action in the Indian Wars, he was appointed professor of military science at the University of Nebraska in 1891, where he received a law degree. Six years later he returned to West Point as instructor of tactics and received from the cadets a nickname that stuck—"Black Jack." During the war with Spain,* Pershing served in Cuba, then commanded troops in the Philippines Insurrection. He attended the Army War College in 1904–1905.

After catching the attention of Theodore Roosevelt* for his reports on the Russo-Japanese War, Pershing was promoted to brigadier general in 1906 over more than 800 senior officers. He commanded the punitive expedition into Mex-

ico in 1916, and although failing to capture Pancho Villa, won the favor of
Woodrow Wilson* and Secretary of War Newton Baker.* When the United
States entered the World War* in 1917, Pershing was made commander of the
American Expeditionary Forces in France. In difficult battles, he demonstrated
his own mettle as a commander as well as that of his men. In September 1919
he was named general of the armies, the nation's highest military rank; two years
later he became army chief of staff. He remained active as an adviser on military
affairs following his retirement in 1924. His memoir, *My Experiences in the
World War* (1931), won the Pulitzer Prize for history. (Richard O'Connor, *Black
Jack Pershing* (1961); Donald Smythe, *Guerrilla Warrior: The Early Life of
John J. Pershing* (1973); Frank E. Vandiver, *Black Jack: The Life and Times
of John J. Pershing* (1977).)

                                                                    Robert C. Hilderbrand

PHELAN, JAMES DUVAL (April 20, 1861–August 7, 1930). Born in San
Francisco, California, the only son of a wealthy merchant, Phelan graduated
from Saint Ignatius College. His early interests included Democratic politics,
exclusion of Orientals, ballot reform, and civic improvement. Following his
father's death in 1892, he managed his family's extensive land and banking
interests. Phelan served as reform mayor of San Francisco* from 1897 to 1902.
He helped pass a new city charter and supported efforts to establish a municipally
owned water supply. In 1906 he became one of the principal financial backers
of the graft prosecution. Following the San Francisco earthquake and fire, he
was appointed administrator of all relief funds.

An early Woodrow Wilson* supporter in 1912, Phelan declined appointment
as minister to Austria-Hungary in order to run for the U.S. Senate in 1914. Once
elected, he concerned himself chiefly with California interests: naval protection,
wine growing, oil production, and exclusion of Japanese workers. He only briefly
identified himself with preparedness, Irish independence, and the League of
Nations.* (Robert E. Hennings, *James D. Phelan and the Wilson Progressives
of California* (1985); Roy Swanstrom, "Reform Administration of James D.
Phelan, Mayor of San Francisco, 1897–1902" (M.A. thesis, University of California, 1947); Roger Daniels, *The Politics of Prejudice: The Anti-Japanese
Movement in California and the Struggle for Japanese Exclusion* (1978).)

                                                                    Robert E. Hennings

PHILADELPHIA. Lincoln Steffens* labeled Philadelphia "corrupt and con-
tented," but the Quaker city did experience modest reform activity. The city's
Republican organization was the bailiwick, first of state insurance commissioner
Israel Durham, and later of state senator James P. ("Sunny Jim") McNichol,
although South Philadelphia was usually controlled by the brothers George,
Edwin, and William Vare. In 1905, Durham attempted to grant a seventy-five–
year lease to the U.S. Improvement Company for $25 million. The "gas steal"
led to an outcry by good government reformers in the Committee of Seventy,

and by *North American* editor Edwin Van Valkenburg, and the bill was defeated in the city councils.

In 1911, Philadelphians elected Mayor Rudolph Blankenburg on a fusion "Keystone Party" ticket, due primarily to a split between U.S. Senator Boies Penrose,* McNichol, and the Vares. Blankenburg brought efficiency to Philadelphia's public services, but he never formed an effective coalition in the city councils. In 1915, the Republican organization returned to power. In 1919, Penrose joined good government reformers in pushing through the legislature a charter revision which abolished the two-house, 146-member city councils in favor of a unicameral 21-member council. The structural reformers* frequently showed little concern for social issues, but activists like Anna Davies of College Settlement, Helen Parrish and Hannah Fox of the Octavia Hill Association, and Mary Richmond of the Society for Organizing Charity did. The reformers guided tenement legislation through the state legislature in 1907 and 1913. However, councils never appropriated enough funds to staff the city's Division of Tenement House Inspection, the law didn't cover thousands of nontenement properties, and the issue of insufficient low-income housing was never adequately addressed. (Lloyd M. Abernathy, "Progressivism: 1905–1919," in Russel F. Neigley, ed., *Philadelphia: A Three Hundred Year History* (1982); Donald W. Disbrow, "The Progressive Movement in Philadelphia: 1900–1916" (Ph.D. diss., University of Rochester, 1956); John F. Sutherland, "A City of Homes: Philadelphia Slums and Reformers, 1880–1918" (Ph.D. diss., Temple University, 1973).)

John F. Sutherland

PHILLIPS, DAVID GRAHAM (October 31, 1867–January 24, 1911). A muckraking* journalist and novelist, Phillips was born in Madison, Indiana, attended a Methodist college in Indiana, then Princeton University for two years. His father, a local banker with a large private library, had inspired in David a love of the printed word. In 1887, he began his career as a journalist in Cincinnati, then he moved to New York in 1890. He apprenticed at Charles A. Dana's *New York Sun* and Joseph Pulitzer's* *New York World*, finally launching out on his own as a free-lance writer in 1902.

Phillips is best known for his "Treason of the Senate" series published by William Randolph Hearst's* *Cosmopolitan** in 1906. This sensational exposé of "The Millionaires' Club," as the U.S. Senate had become known, increased political pressure for the direct election of senators.* President Theodore Roosevelt's* rebuttal to "The Treason of the Senate," delivered in an address to the Gridiron Club on March 15, 1906, gave Phillips and his brand of journalists their nickname of "muckrakers." Phillips's novels focused on women and feminist* issues. His most important novel, *Susan Lenox*, was published posthumously; for on January 24, 1911, Phillips was assassinated by a man who believed he had defamed womanhood. (George E. Mowry and Judson A. Grenier, Introduction to *The Treason of the Senate* by David Graham Phillips (1964); Eric F.

Goldman, *Rendezvous with Destiny: A History of Modern Reform* (1952); Isaac F. Marcosson, *David Graham Phillips and His Times* (1932).)

Edward R. Kantowicz

PINCHOT, AMOS R. E. (December 6, 1873–February 18, 1944). Born in Paris, France, on December 6, 1873, Pinchot was educated at Yale, Columbia, and New York law schools. Following service in the Spanish-American War,* he returned to New York City* and worked briefly as a deputy assistant district attorney. He first entered public life in 1909 during the Ballinger-Pinchot affair,* which divided the Republican party* between supporters of ex-president Theodore Roosevelt* and President William Howard Taft.* In 1911, Pinchot joined GOP insurgents* in creating the National Progressive Republican League* and vigorously supported the presidential hopes of Senator Robert M. La Follette.* The following year, he switched his allegiance to Roosevelt, played a key role in founding the new Progressive party,* and campaigned for Congress as a Bull Moose progressive advocating antimonopoly and public ownership. In 1914–1915 Pinchot organized a labor defense fund for the editors of the *Masses** in a libel suit brought by the Associated Press. He also testified before the U.S. Commission on Industrial Relations* on the causes of labor unrest and served on the New York (City) Unemployment Commission.

With the outbreak of war in Europe, Pinchot joined the American Union Against Militarism and urged President Woodrow Wilson* to reject universal military training and needless preparedness* propaganda. During the 1916 campaign, he joined the "Wilson Volunteers" and barnstormed New York State in behalf of the president's reelection. On the eve of U.S. involvement in the war, Pinchot organized the Committee for Democratic Control and advocated armed neutrality as the best means of avoiding war. (Amos R. E. Pinchot, *History of the Progressive Party, 1912–1916*, ed. Helene M. Hooker (1958); Otis L. Graham, Jr., *An Encore for Reform: The Old Progressives and the New Deal* (1967); Eugene M. Tobin, *Organize or Perish: America's Independent Progressives, 1913–1933* (1986).)

Eugene M. Tobin

PINCHOT, GIFFORD (August 11, 1865–October 4, 1946). Chief forester and leading advocate of conservation* during the Theodore Roosevelt* administration, Pinchot was born in Simsbury, Connecticut.* He graduated from Yale University in 1889 then studied at the French National Forestry School. He worked for a variety of clients as a private forester, then in 1898 became chief of the Division of Forestry, a small research bureau in the U.S. Department of Agriculture. In 1905 he was instrumental in transferring the national forests from the Department of Interior to a greatly expanded Forest Service in the Agriculture Department.

Pinchot administered the timber and mineral resources under his jurisdiction in a scientific and efficient manner, believing in controlled and regulated use of natural resources rather than passive preservation. After President Roosevelt left office, Pinchot engaged in a sharp controversy with Interior Secretary Richard Ballinger, charging him with laxity in conservation matters (*See* Ballinger-Pinchot controversy). President William Howard Taft* forced Pinchot's resignation in 1910, and the forester bolted to the Progressive party.* Pinchot and Roosevelt together laid a firm foundation for the management and conservation of natural resources by the federal government. (Gifford Pinchot, *Breaking New Ground* (1947); M. Nelson McGeary, *Gifford Pinchot: Forester-Politician* (1960); James Penick, Jr., *Progressive Politics and Conservation: The Ballinger-Pinchot Affair* (1968).)

Edward R. Kantowicz

PINGREE, HAZEN S. (August 30, 1840–June 18, 1901) was born near Denmark, Maine, and had less than eight years of schooling in local rural schools. From humble beginnings as a leather cutter and cobbler, Pingree moved on to Detroit where, by 1890, he had become the proprietor of a shoe factory whose sales exceeded $1 million annually. In 1889, Pingree, running as a Republican, won the Detroit mayoral election and held that office until 1897. Pingree's mayoralty elections transformed Detroit from its normal Democratic majorities to Republican victories with the help of foreign-born and ethnic voters, whom he assiduously courted.

As a "social reformer"* and preprogressive, Pingree began a new depression relief program (urban farming in 1893) and engaged in heated controversies with Detroit's traction, gas, electric light, and telephone companies, forcing rate reductions. He won public approval for a citizen-owned electric plant, brought into being a competitive transit system to drive down fares, became an outstanding spokesman for both municipal ownership* and state regulation of utilities,* and achieved national acclaim as one of the preeminent social reformers of this time. As governor of Michigan, Pingree corrected the most flagrant tax evasion by large corporations and forced through the state legislature the first significant statewide appraisal of railroad and corporate property which helped establish a rational basis for regulation and taxation. (Melvin G. Holli, *Reform in Detroit: Hazen S. Pingree and Urban Politics* (1969); C. R. Starring, "Hazen S. Pingree: Another Forgotten Eagle," *Michigan History* 32 (June 1948): 129–49 Hazen S. Pingree, *Facts and Opinions* (1895).)

Melvin G. Holli

PITTMAN, KEY (September 12, 1872–November 10, 1940). Pittman was born in Vicksburg, Mississippi. Between 1890 and 1902, after attending Southwestern Presbyterian University in Clarksville, Tennessee, he lived in Seattle, Dawson, Nome (where he married Mimosa Gates on July 8, 1900), and San Francisco before settling in Tonopah, Nevada. In Tonopah, Pittman practiced law, invested in mining claims, and became involved in state politics, first as a member of the Silver party and then in 1904 as a Democrat. He was elected to the U.S. Senate to fill a vacancy in January 1913.

Pittman entered the Senate supporting progressive reform, and in addition to working for a silver purchase act for the benefit of his constituents, he voted for the Federal Reserve Act,* the Keating-Owen Child Labor Act,* the Farm Loan Act,* the Adamson Act,* prohibition,* and woman suffrage.* In 1916, he was appointed to the Senate Foreign Relations Committee and in 1933 became chairman of the committee, was elected president pro tempore of the Senate, and served as a member of the U.S. delegation to the International Monetary Conference in London. (Betty Glad, *Key Pittman: The Tragedy of a Senate Insider* (1986); Fred L. Israel, *Nevada's Key Pittman* (1963).)

Kathryn M. Totton

PITTSBURGH. Situated where the Allegheny and Monongahela rivers join to form the Ohio, Pittsburgh was incorporated as a city in 1806 (population 6,000). The Ohio connected it with the Old Northwest and the Mississippi Valley, making it a commercial gateway to much of the West. It also early developed an industrial base, particularly iron and glass manufacture. By 1860, Pittsburgh produced 40 percent of the nation's iron. By the 1880s steel surpassed iron both in Pittsburgh and in the nation. In 1892, the Carnegie Steel Company broke the Amalgamated Steel Workers Union, and in the years following the panic of 1893, Carnegie consolidated his control of much of the country's steel production, consolidating Pittsburgh's preeminence as an industrial center in the process. The city grew from 49,217 inhabitants in 1860 to 156,389 in 1880, 321,616 in 1900, and 533,905 in 1910. By 1900, almost a quarter (24.7 percent) of its population had been born abroad with an additional third (35.1 percent) being the children of immigrants.

Pittsburgh was the "shock city" of the age. Its immense wealth, purchased by the highly visible destruction of the environment (not for nothing was Pittsburgh described as "Hell with the lid off"), its bitterly contested labor wars, culminating in the triumph of the steel trust in the great strike of 1919,* its polyglot population; its questionable politics (Lincoln Steffens* called it "A City Ashamed"), all combined to make Pittsburgh seem the somewhat ominous prototype of modern America. This prototypic quality also provided a national audience for the researches of the *Pittsburgh Survey* (1907–1914).* (Roy Lubove, *Twentieth-Century Pittsburgh: Government, Business, and Environmental Change* (1969); David Brody, *Steelworkers in America: The Nonunion Era* (1960); Samuel P. Hays, "The Politics of Reform in Municipal Government in the Progressive Era," *Pacific Northwest Quarterly* 55 (1964): 157–69.)

John F. McClymer

PITTSBURGH SURVEY. This was the first systematic study of the combined impact of urbanization, industrialization, and immigration on the nature and character of American society. It was undertaken by social experts of various sorts—social workers, economists, and efficiency experts—and sponsored by the National Publication Committee of the New York Charity Organization Society* (COS) and the newly created Russell Sage Foundation, the prototype of the new all-purpose foundations.*

The *Survey* was first published in three special issues of *Charities and the Commons*,* the journal of the New York COS, and subsequently in six volumes (1910–1914). It exerted considerable influence over contemporary discussions of the dislocations accompanying social change, and it has remained a basic source of information about the nature of those dislocations and the progressive response to them, as well as about the history of Pittsburgh. While the *Survey* aimed to be encyclopedic in scope, its primary foci were the nature of industrial work, the living and cultural standards of working-class families, the frequency and causes of industrial accidents, the effects of immigration on the city's civic life, and the new roles of women. Its goal, according to editor Paul U. Kellogg,* was to promote those reforms the "facts" showed to be necessary. (John F. McClymer, "The Pittsburgh Survey, 1907–1914: Forging an Ideology in the Steel District," *Pennsylvania History* 41 (1974): 169–86; Samuel P. Hays, Introduction to the reprint of Margaret Byington, *Homestead: The Households of a Mill Town* (1974; originally published as volume 4 of the *Survey*, 1910); Clarke A. Chambers, *Paul U. Kellogg and the Survey: Voices for Social Welfare and Social Change* (1971).)

John F. McClymer

PLATT, THOMAS C. (July 15, 1833–March 6, 1910). A U.S. Senator (1881, 1897–1909) and boss of the Republican party* in New York State, Platt practiced, and in time came to symbolize, the very forms of politics against which progressives crusaded. Platt was born in Owego, New York; joined the Republican cause in the 1850s; and, by the 1870s, had become a behind-the-scenes leader of Roscoe Conkling's Stalwart wing of the state GOP. Inheriting the machine's leadership upon Conkling's retirement from politics, Platt skillfully carried on the work of party boss: the management of conventions, the collection of campaign contributions, the domination of legislators, and the distribution of patronage. Not blatantly corrupt by Gilded Age standards, Platt and his allies nonetheless profited from the boss's political influence. So did the railroads, insurance companies, and other corporations that bankrolled the Republican organization.

Although he despised the "mugwumps"* and civil service reformers* who assailed his kind of politics, Platt proved flexible in accommodating at least some of their demands. In 1898, he supported the nomination of Theodore Roosevelt* for governor in order to win back the votes of rebellious urban independents, and during Roosevelt's term at Albany (1899–1900) Platt often supported measures demanded by the ambitious young Rough Rider. After 1900, Platt's power waned, and he became a supreme negative symbol for progressives. Although reelected to the Senate in 1903, Platt had little influence there. (Harold

F. Gosnell, *Boss Platt and His New York Machine* (1924); Richard L. Mc-Cormick, *From Realignment to Reform: Political Change in New York State, 1893–1910* (1981).)

Richard L. McCormick

PLATTSBURGH TRAINING CAMP MOVEMENT. This was a campaign to promote universal military training, which resulted in the establishment of officers' training camps for business and professional men in the summers of 1915 and 1916. Even before the outbreak of World War I,* Theodore Roosevelt* and Major General Leonard Wood,* senior officer in the U.S. Army, had campaigned for compulsory military service. Advocates of the strenuous life, Wood and Roosevelt hoped that military training would promote physical fitness, Americanize* the immigrant masses, and enhance national security. The War Department sponsored two voluntary camps which enrolled 222 college and high school students in 1913. After the outbreak of war, the training camp movement expanded and merged with the larger campaign for preparedness.*

Wood opened a training camp at Plattsburgh, New York, in August 1915 which enrolled 1,300 business and professional men to train at their own expense. In 1916 the school and professional camps merged to form the Military Training Camps Association of the United State. Over 16,000 men enrolled at nine camps that summer. Though the Plattsburgh camps proved nearly useless in a military sense, they did serve as effective propaganda measures in the campaign to ready America for entrance into World War I. (John G. Clifford, *The Citizen Soldiers* (1972); Francis Russell, *The Great Interlude* (1964); Chase C. Mooney and Martha E. Layman, "Some Phases of the Compulsory Military Training Movement, 1914–1920," *Mississippi Valley Historical Review* 38 (1952): 633–56.)

Edward R. Kantowicz

PLAYGROUND ASSOCIATION OF AMERICA. A prime example of the social control impulse among progressives, the playground movement was both an antimodernist response to life that had apparently grown soft and an effort to prepare urban, immigrant, street youths for corporate citizenship. With the organization of the Playground Association in 1906, the movement went far beyond the 1880s efforts simply to provide play space for street waifs. Through conferences and publications, the association disseminated an entire philosophy of play and advocated enlarged state responsibility—whether through municipal playgrounds or physical education courses at school. Founders of the organization included wealthy Bostonian Joseph Lee, physical education instructor Luther H. Gulick, Jr., and child psychologist Henry S. Curtis.

According to the association, carefully supervised recreation would teach proper behavior and habits; play, as a shaper of character, would be a weapon against poverty and vice. "A boy without a playground is father to the man without a job" was one motto. In this spirit, play experts in numerous cities developed highly structured, and often elaborately scheduled, children's recreation programs. They hoped to replace autonomous street games that were escapist, individualistic, and aggressive with well-organized "play factories," stressing rules, self-control, group loyalty, and a cooperative team spirit. (Dominick Cavallo, *Muscles and Morals: Organized Playgrounds and Urban Reform, 1880–1920* (1981); Cary Goodman, *Choosing Sides: Playground and Street Life on the Lower East Side* (1979); Paul Boyer, *Urban Masses and Moral Order in America, 1820–1920* (1978).)

LeRoy Ashby

PLESSY v. FERGUSON (163 U.S.). In this historic case, handed down in 1896, the Supreme Court established the doctrine of "separate-but-equal" and provided judicial sanction for the system of racial segregation that came into being throughout the South during the first two decades of the twentieth century. The Louisiana legislature passed a law in 1890 requiring railroad companies to provide separate accommodations for black and white passengers. While traveling between two Louisiana cities, Homer Adolph Plessy refused to ride in the coach designated for black passengers and was arrested. Plessy challenged the constitutionality of the Louisiana law on the grounds that it violated the Thirteenth and Fourteenth Amendments.

The Supreme Court held that the Fourteenth Amendment "could not have been intended to abolish distinctions based on color, or to enforce social, as distinguished from political equality, or a commingling of the races upon terms unsatisfactory to either." Consequently, state laws requiring separate accommodations did not violate the equal protection clause if the separate accommodations were "substantially equal." In a prophetic dissent, Justice John Marshall Harlan* said that the majority decision would "in time, prove to be quite as pernicious as the decision made by this tribunal in the Dred Scott case." (Richard Bardolph, *The Civil Rights Record: Black Americans and the Law, 1849–1970* (1970); Albert P. Blaustein and Robert L. Zangrando, *Civil Rights and the American Negro: A Documentary History* (1968).)

Arvarh E. Strickland

PLUMB PLAN. Proposed soon after World War I* by Glenn E. Plumb, an attorney for the railroad unions, it proposed permanent federal ownership and operation of the railroad industry. Treated favorably by the wartime Railroad Administration,* which had increased wages substantially and granted a measure of worker control over labor policies, the unions mounted a campaign to have Congress accept nationalization. Under the scheme, a public corporation, comprised equally of representatives of labor, management, and the public, would be responsible for the nation's vital rail carriers. Advocates of the Plumb plan claimed that it would result in more efficient and cheaper service while harmonizing the often conflicting interests of the rail corporations, their employees, investors, and customers under private operation and federal regulation.

Although the Plumb plan attracted considerable attention in 1919 and won the favor of railroad workers, Congress never seriously considered the proposal. Instead, the Senate passed a bill, not accepted by the House of Representatives, that would have enforced harmony between the railroads and labor by outlawing strikes. In the midst of new troubles of bankruptcy and declining service in the railroad industry during the 1970s, the railroad unions again proposed the Plumb plan to help solve the nation's transportation problems. (K. Austin Kerr, *American Railroad Politics, 1914–1920* (1968).)

K. Austin Kerr

POINDEXTER, MILES (April 22, 1868–September 21, 1946). A U.S. Senator from the state of Washington, Miles Poindexter was born in Virginia and moved to Washington in 1891. Poindexter was elected in 1908 to the House of Representatives and to the U.S. Senate in 1910. He backed Theodore Roosevelt's* effort to wrest the Republican nomination from William Howard Taft* in 1912, and he followed Roosevelt into the Progressive party.* Poindexter supported the domestic legislative program of Woodrow Wilson,* and he established a reputation as one of the more strident and vocal supporters of progressive causes in the Senate. In 1915 Poindexter returned to the Republican party* and was re-elected in 1916 by a substantial majority.

On foreign policy matters Poindexter championed a strong national defense and favored increased U.S. intervention in Latin America. He strongly favored U.S. intervention in World War I* in 1917, and he opposed ratification of the Treaty of Versailles. Poindexter ran unsuccessfully for the Republican nomination for president in 1920, and after he lost his bid for reelection to the Senate in 1922, President Warren G. Harding* appointed him ambassador to Peru, a post which he held until 1928. (Howard W. Allen, *Poindexter of Washington: A Study in Progressive Politics* (1981).)

Howard W. Allen

POLICE REFORM. The movement to professionalize the American police began during the Progressive Era. Reform goals included elimination of political influence, introduction of modern management techniques, and the improvement of police personnel standards. The rhetoric of professionalism* masked the political interests of the business and professional figures who led the reform movement. Eliminating political influence over the police was part of a larger effort to reduce the political power of the working-class–based urban political machines.*

Leadership of the professionalization movement came primarily from civic reformers outside the police occupation, notably Raymond B. Fosdick, author of *American Police System* (1920) and *European Police System* (1914). The leading police chief was August Vollmer of Berkeley, Calfornia (1905–1932). National organizations sponsoring reform included the National Conference of Charities and Corrections,* the International Association of Chiefs of Police, and the Bureau of Municipal Research.* Reform enjoyed only scattered success during the period. Most departments resisted even piecemeal reform. Some instituted reforms, only to slide backward in subsequent years. The major achievement was establishing the idea of policing as a profession and defining a specific reform agenda. (Robert Fogelson, *Big City Police* (1977); Raymond B. Fosdick, *American Police System* (1920); Samuel Walker, *A Critical History of Police Reform: The Emergence of Professionalism* (1977).)

Samuel Walker

POLISH-AMERICANS. Over two million people immigrated to the United States from Poland between 1890 and 1914. Though Poland was politically oppressed, having been wiped from the map by the partitioning powers, Russia, Prussia, and Austria, this mass migration was economically, not politically, motivated. Most Polish immigrants were peasants, pushed off the land by the forces of agrarian reform and economic modernization. They came, in the phrase of the day, *za chlebem*, after bread. Most intended only a temporary stay in America, long enough to earn money to buy land back in the old country. Eventually, the majority remained permanently, but about 30 percent did return to Poland. Polish peasant immigrants gravitated to the newest and rawest industrial cities of the Northeast and the Midwest, where machine technology had reduced most tasks to a routine requiring little skill but much strength. Thus Chicago alone attracted over 400,000 Polish-Americans. Other large industrial cities, such as Detroit, Cleveland, Pittsburgh, and Buffalo, also attracted large numbers, as did the many smaller mill and mining towns of Pennsylvania.

Polish-Americans were fervent Roman Catholics, and they built their communities in America around their churches. The earliest Polish settlers in an area would form a mutual benefit society, named for a saint, in order to provide death benefits to members and to buy land for a church. Then they would petition the bishop for a Polish-speaking priest, build a large church and a parochial school, and organize numerous parish societies. A Polish Catholic parish was more than a place for religious services; it was a community center, a partial re-creation of the Polish peasant village. The communal solidarity of the peasant Poles eased their transition into the working class in America and made them good union members.

Initially, their seeming docility and their willingness to work for low wages put them at cross-purposes with union organizers. But once the union leaders broke through the linguistic and cultural barriers, they realized that the Poles' communal loyalties made them fierce allies in a strike situation. Polish workers played leading roles in the Chicago stockyard strikes of 1904 and 1921, the New Jersey refinery strikes of 1915–1916, and numerous anthracite strikes in Pennsylvania. Polish-Americans took relatively little part in the politics of the Progressive Era. Those who did become citizens voted overwhelmingly for Democratic candidates, because of that party's identification with the working class and its greater sensitivity to cultural diversity. (Victor Greene, "The

Poles,'' in Stephen Thernstrom, ed., *Harvard Encyclopedia of American Ethnic Groups* (1980); Victor Greene, *The Slavic Community on Strike* (1968); Edward R. Kantowicz, *Polish American Politics in Chicago, 1888–1940* (1975); Joseph Parot, *Polish Catholics in Chicago* (1981); Paul Wrobel, *Our Way: Parish and Neighborhood in a Polish-American Community* (1979).)

Edward R. Kantowicz

POLITICAL MACHINES. During the Progressive Era "political machine," a commonly used pejorative term since at least the time of Andrew Jackson, also had a more specific meaning, referring to a new type of urban politics that emerged in the last third of the nineteenth century. Although ultimately controlled from the top down, the new political machines grew from the bottom up. Since the Civil War, industrialization and immigration had lured millions of rural people from Southern and Eastern Europe, Ireland, and the American countryside to the densely crowded slums of the burgeoning cities, where they congregated in distinctive ethnic neighborhoods.

Gradually, politically active individuals or small groups of men developed reliable followings, usually based on ethnic ties, among the voters of those neighborhoods. The ability to deliver a predictable number of votes at primary meetings and elections gave a local political leader leverage to negotiate with the city's other politicians. Ward "bosses" and precinct captains maintained the loyalty of their following through a combination of personal recognition—they attended every christening, bar mitzvah, wedding and funeral, distributed free turkeys on Thanksgiving, and staged public fireworks shows and barbecues on July 4—and assistance in time of need. These small favors were highly effective because the cities themselves were unequipped to provide welfare services on a regular basis.

The activities of the ward bosses cost money, of course, but money was seldom a problem. There were whole new neighborhoods to build, streets to pave, public buildings to construct, franchises to be awarded for horsecar, trolley, and elevated lines, and for water, gas, electric, and telephone connections. An organization that controlled city hall was in a position to extract cash payments and promises of jobs in return for providing access to these rewarding opportunities. Urban politicians could also profit from their insider's knowledge of future projects likely to enhance property values and from protection afforded gamblers, prostitution rings, and after-hours saloons. This undeniable element of corruption infuriated educated, middle-class reformers. The rise of urban machines represented a transfer of power from the native-born Protestant elite to the conscious champions of the predominantly immigrant and Catholic lower classes. This circumstance explains both the determination of the reformers to break the machines and the ability of the strongest machines to adapt to new conditions without significant loss of popular support. (John M. Allswang, *Bosses, Machines, and Urban Voters* (1977); William L. Riordan, *Plunkitt of*

Tammany Hall (1963); Zane L. Miller, *Boss Cox's Cincinnati: Urban Politics in the Progressive Era* (1968).)

Keith Ian Polakoff

POLLOCK v. FARMER'S LOAN AND TRUST (158 U.S.). This is the controversial 1895 Supreme Court decision that invalidated the income tax section of the Wilson-Gorman Tariff and provided much of the impetus for the adoption of the Sixteenth Amendment. The plaintiff's attorneys based their arguments primarily upon the direct tax clause, despite the fact that the Court had ruled, in the 1880 Springer Case, that the Civil War income taxes were not direct and did not need to be apportioned among the states on the basis of population. They buttressed their arguments by stigmatizing the tax as a plot by populists, anarchists, and communists to destroy property rights.

With Justice Howell Jackson absent, the Court ruled 6–2 that a tax on the income from land was direct and therefore unconstitutional. On the larger question of whether that invalidated the entire income tax section, the justices divided 4–4. They were unanimous in their opinion that Congress lacked the power to tax state and municipal bonds and evenly divided on the questions of whether a levy on the income from personal property was direct and of whether any part of the tax, if indirect, lacked uniformity. When Jackson returned, the Court proceeded to invalidate the entire income tax section on a 5–4 vote, ruling that there was no real difference between income from land and from other sources. (Edward S. Corwin, *Court over Constitution* (1938); Arnold M. Paul, *Conservative Crisis and the Rule of Law: Attitudes of Bar and Bench, 1887–1895* (1969); E. R. A. Seligman, *The Income Tax: A Study of the History, Theory and Practice of Income Taxation at Home and Abroad* (1911).)

John D. Buenker

POMERENE, ATLEE (December 6, 1863–November 12, 1937). Part of the Tom Johnson* coalition in early twentieth-century Ohio politics, Pomerene typified its middle-class, professional orientation toward political reform. Born in rural Berlin, Ohio, the son of a physician, Pomerene graduated from Princeton University and the Cincinnati Law School. Admitted to the bar in 1886, he moved to Canton, Ohio, to practice law with Charles Russel Miller, the nephew of then Republican Congressman William McKinley.* Pomerene entered politics as a Democrat and eight months after arriving in Canton was elected city solicitor. He was elected prosecuting attorney of Stark County in 1896, the only Democrat to win in president-elect McKinley's home county.

From 1903 on he was part of the Johnson coterie of bright, young professionals committed to modernizing Ohio's government. Governor John Pattison appointed him to the Ohio Tax Commission, a blue-ribbon panel established to recommend changes in Ohio's tax code. In 1908 Johnson unsuccessfully promoted Pomerene for governor, and two years later, incumbent Governor Judson Harmon* slated the Canton lawyer as his choice for lieutenant governor. Both men won easily.

With political alliances that transcended the various regional coalitions in Ohio politics, Pomerene decided to challenge Party Chairman Ed Hanley for the U.S. Senate seat. Hanley was a utility magnate, and Pomerene favored regulation. When the Democratic legislative caucus met in January 1911, Pomerene was chosen by a two-vote margin.

In the Senate, Pomerene emerged as a moderate on the economic, political, and social issues of the era. He supported the direct election of senators,* the Underwood Tariff,* the Adamson Act,* and the eight-hour day for workers on federally funded public works. On woman suffrage,* prohibition,* and government ownership of the railroads, he was steadfastly opposed. The best known legislation which he sponsored, the Webb-Pomerene Act* (1918), allowed for the exemption of antitrust laws through cooperative export arrangements. His support for Henry Cabot Lodge's* amendments to the Versailles treaty demonstrated his independence of action. In 1922, in the midst of Republican party* ascendancy on the national level and upon the heels of an economic downturn, Pomerene was defeated in his bid for a third term in the Senate. (*Dictionary of American Biography*, Supplement 2; Thomas Howard Smith, "The Senatorial Career of Atlee Pomerene of Ohio" (Ph.D. diss., Kent State University, 1966).)

James E. Cebula

POPULIST PARTY. The agricultural crisis of the late nineteenth century was one of the worst in American history. Falling profits, soaring debt, and exorbitant shipping costs drove many farmers to the edge of despair. This was especially true in the improverished states of the South and the Great Plains. But in the late 1880s hope arrived in the form of an organization called the Farmers' Alliance. By 1891, the alliance claimed several million members. Its Saint Louis Demands called for government ownership of the railroads, the free and unlimited coinage of silver, an end to national banks of issue, and a graduated income tax.* Later the alliance endorsed the subtreasury plan, a scheme by which the farmers would receive government loans based on their produce stored in federal warehouses. Conservatives denounced such ideas as at best misguided and at worst communistic.

When the Republican and Democratic parties failed to champion these reforms, the more militant Alliancemen met in Omaha in 1892. There they created the People's party—or, as it was more commonly called, the Populist party. They endorsed the Saint Louis Demands and the subtreasury plan, and nominated James B. Weaver for president. Although Weaver was defeated, he demonstrated considerable strength in the hard-pressed states of Texas, Georgia, North Carolina, Kansas, Nebraska, and the Dakotas. In 1896, the Democrats endorsed— the Populists would say "stole"—the third-party demand for free silver and nominated William Jennings Bryan* for president against Republican William McKinley.* Caught in a quandary, the Populists arrived at a compromise: they endorsed Bryan for president, but tried to maintain their party identity by nominating a Populist, Tom Watson,* for vice president. Such machinations proved futile; on election day McKinley was triumphant. In 1900, the Populists nominated Wharton Barker for president, and in 1904 and 1908 they nominated Tom Watson. (Lawerence Goodwyn, *Democratic Promise: The Populist Movement in America* (1976); John D. Hicks, *The Populist Revolt: A History of the Farmers' Alliance and the People's Party* (1931); Robert F. Durden, *The Climax of Populism: The Election of 1896* (1965).)

Barton C. Shaw

POST, LOUIS FREELAND (November 15, 1859–January 10, 1928). Post was a journalist who was involved in radical Reconstruction in South Carolina, where he worked as a stenographer in the Ku Klux Klan cases of 1871–1872. Here he developed liberal views on the race question which he was to hold all his life. The major influence on Post's life was Henry George* and his single tax movement.* Post campaigned for George in the 1886 New York mayoral race and, after George's death, became the leader of the movement. In 1898 Post founded the *Public* in Chicago, an important voice of progressivism. Post worked closely with William Jennings Bryan,* Brand Whitlock,* Tom L. Johnson,* John P. Altgeld,* and many others.

His support for the Democratic party* brought Post into the newly formed Department of Labor* as assistant secretary to William B. Wilson* (1913–1921). He helped establish procedures for the new department including the Division of Negro Economics and the U.S. Employment Service. He is most famous for his opposition to the Red Scare* tactics of Attorney General A. Mitchell Palmer* and his younger assistant, J. Edgar Hoover. Convinced that they had overstepped their authority, Post cancelled most of the deportation orders they requested for aliens arrested in the January 1920 Palmer Raids. Post was the author of *Deportations Deliriums of 1920* (1923), *The Prophet of San Francisco* (1930), *Ethics of Democracy* (1905), and an unpublished autobiography in the Post Papers, Library of Congress. (Dominic Candeloro, "Louis F. Post: Carpetbagger, Singletaxer, Progressive" (Ph.D. diss., University of Illinois at Urbana-Champaign, 1970); Dominic Candeloro, "L.F. Post's Development from the Single Tax to Broad Progressivism," *American Journal of Economics and Sociology* 37, no. 3 (July 1978): 325–35.)

Dominic Candeloro

POSTAL SAVINGS BANKS were savings banks established by the federal government in local post offices to encourage thrift among the poorer classes. The Populist party* of the 1890s had advocated postal savings banks, and the panic of 1907* brought the proposal new attention as a measure to reassure small depositors. In 1910 President William Howard Taft* recommended their establishment in order to head off a Democratic demand for deposit insurance and to facilitate further banking reform. Taft hoped that deposits in the postal banks would be invested in low-interest government bonds, currently held by the national banks, thus clearing the way for a central banking system based on higher-interest bonds. This proposal became embroiled in the factional political disputes between Taft and Insurgent* Republicans.

The Postal Deposit Savings Act, passed on June 25, 1910, stipulated a 2 percent interest cap on postal savings and limited to 30 percent the amount of deposits which could be invested in government bonds. Despite their rural roots in populism, postal savings banks were patronized largely by the foreign-born population of cities, who trusted the government more than they did bankers. Federal deposit insurance, established during the New Deal, eventually outmoded postal savings banks, and they were abolished by Congress in 1966. (Edwin W. Kemmerer, "Six Years of Postal Savings in the U.S.," *American Economic Review* (1917): 460–90; George E. Mowry, *Theodore Roosevelt and the Progressive Movement* (1942); Henry F. Pringle, *The Life and Times of William Howard Taft* (1939).)

Edward R. Kantowicz

POUND, (NATHAN) ROSCOE (October 27, 1870–July 1, 1964). Law professor, jurist, and botanist born in Lincoln, Nebraska, to a judge and a former schoolteacher, Pound was graduated from the University of Nebraska at age eighteen. His interest in botany and in law led him to attend Harvard Law School (1889–1890) and, while practicing law in Lincoln and teaching law at the University of Nebraska, to earn a doctorate in botany. Concern with adaptation to change also contributed to Pound's development of a theory of "sociological jurisprudence."* After legal practice and service as an intermediate appellate judge on the Nebraska Supreme Court and subsequently, dean of the Nebraska College of Law (1903–1907), Pound served on the law school faculties of Northwestern University (1907–1909) and the University of Chicago* (1909–1910), before beginning his long career at Harvard University (1910–1947, including the deanship, 1916–1936).

In a series of articles, including "The Scope and Purpose of Sociological Jurisprudence," *Harvard Law Review* 25 (1911), 591; and books such as *Interpretations of Legal History* (1923) and *Law and Morals* (1924), Pound criticized the prevailing deterministic legal philosophy with its emphasis on law as a closed system based on already existing principles and the determination by judges of presumably self-evident answers based heavily upon deduction and precedent, as an unrealistic, mechanical theory of judicial decision making which Pound in 1913 ridiculed as a "slot-machine theory" of law. Instead, as in the legal realism propounded by Oliver Wendell Holmes,* Pound argued for a more practical and pragmatic approach to the law which stressed the dependency of legal rules on changing social conditions. With its emphasis on flexible responses to changing circumstances, this approach contributed to and supported the pragmatic and progressive thought of the era. (Paul Sayre, *The Life of Roscoe Pound*

(1948); David Wigdor, *Roscoe Pound* (1974); *Dictionary of American Biography*, Suppl. 7.)

John Whiteclay Chambers II

PRAGMATISM. The term *pragmatism* was introduced by Charles Sanders Peirce, most notably in "How to Make Our Ideas Clear" (1878), to signify his conviction that knowledge is a function of human activity and that the meaning of a conception emerges from consideration of its practical consequences. Peirce and those who followed his lead sought ways of reconciling old social and religious ideals with evolutionary science and technologically driven mass society. Occupying what John Dewey* aptly called the "Via Media," pragmatism, William James* explained, rejected both "tender-minded" acceptance of absolute ideals and the "tough-minded" insistence that there is nothing except material facts. Instead, pragmatists posited a contingent universe where meaning and truth are measured in terms of experience, which can contain subjective elements of art, emotion, and supernatural faith, as well as objective substance. James's essays on will and humanism, his *Principles of Psychology* (1890), and his *Varieties of Religious Experience* (1902) showed how pragmatism conduced to self-defined freedom.

Subsequently, in accord with the Progressive movement, pragmatism moved toward a more social view of action. John Dewey's "instrumentalism"* contended that individuals fulfill themselves through relationships with others and thus stressed the value of action leading to a "good community." To discern the inner workings of persons within the community, George Herbert Mead* developed the field of social psychology, concentrating on the semiotic "conversation of gestures" which governs social interaction. The pragmatic movement promoted numerous progressive causes—including the child-centered school, settlement house efforts to acculturate immigrants and other disadvantaged urban folk, the advancement of industrial democracy through shared decision making among owners and workers, a school of economics that explained economic activity according to institutional structure rather than classical laws, and an American art that expressed lived experience rather than formal canons of style.

Pragmatism underwent a decline in reputation in World War I.* By trying to use the occasion for bringing instrumentalist principles to bear on a large scale for the world's betterment, Dewey and other leaders made themselves vulnerable to criticism that they condoned the evils of war. An influential group of critics, including Randolph Bourne,* Van Wyck Brooks,* and Lewis Mumford, developed the further charge that pragmatism too often favored social control over people rather than organic inner impulse and that it lacked refined aesthetic sensitivity. (James Campbell, *Pragmatism and Reform* (1979); Charles Morris, *The Pragmatic Movement in American Philosophy* (1970); Richard Rorty, *Con-*

sequences of Pragmatism (1978); Morton G. White, *Social Thought in America: The Revolt against Formalism* (1949).)

R. Alan Lawson

PREPAREDNESS. A movement to strengthen America's military forces during the period after World War I* broke out before the United States entered the war. On December 1, 1914, the National Security League* organized and spearheaded a campaign to build up the army and navy. At this point, preparedness was both a partisan and an ideological issue, with Republican businessmen and capitalists prominently in favor and agrarian Democrats and progressive reformers opposed. Germany's submarine warfare, and particularly the sinking of the liner *Lusitania*, broadened public support for preparedness; and on November 4, 1915, President Woodrow Wilson* announced his conversion to a program of military and naval expansion.

Wilson made a speaking tour of the country in January and February 1916 to build popular support for preparedness, but the administration's army and navy bills still met strong opposition. Finally, in May 1916, Congress authorized a doubling of the regular army's troop strength and the integration of the National Guard into the defense command structure. In August 1916, Congress passed a huge construction program for the navy. Though divisive politically, the preparedness campaign of 1915–1916 resulted in a greater state of military readiness when the United States declared war in April 1917. (Arthur S. Link, *Woodrow Wilson and the Progressive Era* (1954); Horace C. Peterson, *Propaganda for War* (1939); Robert D. Ward, "The Origins and Activities of the National Security League, 1914–1919" *Mississippi Valley Historical Review* 47 (June 1960):51–65.)

Edward R. Kantowicz

PRIMARY ELECTIONS. The most enduring political reform of the Progressive Era, a primary is a preliminary intraparty election in which the voters themselves select the candidates who will run in the general election. The origin of primary elections, however, is rooted in shrewd calculation more than idealism. During the 1880s and 1890s the supremacy of the Democratic party* in the South was challenged in state after state by a coalition of Republicans, Populists, and splinter Democrats. What the regular Democrats needed was a nominating mechanism that would ensure the continuing loyalty of the defeated candidates and their supporters. Thus, the first gubernatorial primary was held in faction-ridden Louisiana in 1892. Between 1896 and 1907, statewide Democratic primaries were introduced in ten more southern and border states.

Meanwhile, the idea gained popularity among insurgent midwestern Republicans as a means of taking the selection of candidates out of the hands of party "bosses," that is, the conservatives. Governor Robert M. La Follette* of Wisconsin trumpeted the introduction of the primary in his state in 1904 so loudly that he left many people believing the idea began there. Similarly, presidential preference primaries received a major boost from the Taft*-Roosevelt* battle for the Republican nomination in 1912.* With Taft commanding the loyalty of most party regulars, Roosevelt's followers in the state legislatures, cheered on by the Democrats, demanded primary elections as a test of public opinion. (J. Morgan Kousser, *The Shaping of Southern Politics: Suffrage Restriction and the Establishment of the One-Party South 1880–1910* (1974), chapter 3; David P. Thelen, *Robert M. La Follette and the Insurgent Spirit* (1976).)

Keith Ian Polakoff

PROFESSIONALIZATION. Professionalization is a social movement that grew rapidly in the later nineteenth century and reached a stage of maturity in the Progressive Era. A new middle class expressed its aspiration for democratic opportunity and mobility in the form of every man a trained and dedicated professional. Institutionally, ever more specialized professional associations appeared both in traditional occupations such as medicine and in new ones such as the scientific and critical writing of history. In theory, professionalization meant that (a) unaided senses or the common sense of laymen were inadequate to understand the "unseen" and perverse worlds in which expertise* and systematic analysis were required; (b) both the substance and technical skill of an individual professional performance were judged by means of corporate standards accepted within a self-regulating community of competent peers; and (c) fiduciary relationships rather than contractual or commercial ones bound together ministering practitioners and clients desiring valued services.

Identified neither with the provincialism and emotionalism of the masses nor with the partisanship and idiosyncratic ways of the upper classes, the professionalized individual ideally was committed to conducting himself in an autonomous, ethical, and efficient manner. A professionally disciplined mind was a socialized one, both cooperative and independent. But professionals tended to display little awareness of the ideological implications and unintended consequences of their pronouncements. In helping professions like social work, a disinterested scientific approach conveniently turned clients into cold objects of management in systems of bureaucratic control. Professional associations conventionally discriminated in their membership on the grounds of race, gender, and religion. Holding monopolistic power, an insider "community of the competent" could discourage skeptical inquiry and criticism with which it disagreed. Patriotic biases—heard, for instance, from academics participating in U.S. government propaganda campaigns during World War I*—were presented as the informed opinion of professional expertise. Nevertheless, despite these documented criticisms, the undeniable opportunities and real achievements made possible within the structures and processes of professionalization in twentieth-century America served the middle class exceptionally well in its rise to importance. (Robert H. Wiebe, *The Search for Order, 1877–1920* (1967); Burton J. Bledstein, *The Culture of Professionalism: The Middle Class and the Development of Higher Education in America* (1967); Thomas L. Haskell, *The Emerg-*

ence of Professional Social Science: The American Social Science Association and the Nineteenth-Century Crisis of Authority (1977).)

Burton J. Bledstein

PROFESSIONAL SPORT. The only professional sport that was widely respected and universally permitted was baseball, a clean, exciting game that epitomized the finest attributes of the core culture (democracy, rural society, traditional values) and was believed to promote boosterism, facilitate social integration, and teach values like hard work, competitiveness, individuality, and cooperation. Virtually every city had a professional team. Players were increasingly coming from middle-class backgrounds, and the crowds were also predominantly middle-class.

Prize fighting was still barred nearly everywhere, and the turf was temporarily banned in major cities outside Maryland and Kentucky. Both sports relied on the gambling nexus for their popularity, and contests were often presumed to have been fixed. The historic elite image of the turf had been destroyed by the rise of proprietary tracks in the 1880s operated by bookmakers and machine politicians who were both very active in illegal off-track betting. New York poolrooms were controlled by Tammany* boss Big Tim Sullivan and his allies in the gambling trust. Professional boxing was legal nowhere before 1890 and seldom thereafter until the 1920s. It was appreciated as an amateur sport by Theodore Roosevelt* and other Strenuous Life advocates, but was detested when professionalized because of the brutality, corruption, gambling, and ties to urban machine politics.* Combatants were still mainly Irish, but competition developed from impoverished new immigrants and blacks.

Federal involvement in sports was virtually nonexistent, and organized baseball freely operated as a monopsony. However, state governments under pressure from progressives and rural constituents did try to bar or at least supervise horse racing and boxing. Racing in New York was regulated by the state after 1895 through the elite Jockey Club, and tracks were closed from 1909 to 1912 because of the crusade by Governor Charles E. Hughes* to halt horse-race betting. In New York, where Tammany support was essential in legalizing prize fighting (1910–1917, 1920–   ), the sport was supervised by a State Athletic Commission. On the municipal level, politicians controlled baseball as well as the gambling sports, and they used their clout to prevent interference from competitors or the police, to secure inside information, and to obtain cheap public services that enhanced profitability. (Steven A. Riess, *Touching Base: Professional Baseball and American Culture in the Progressive Era* (1980); Steven A. Riess, "In the Ring and Out: Professional Boxing in New York, 1896–1920," in Donald Spivey, ed., *Sport in America: New Historical Perspectives* (1985); William H. P. Robertson, *History of Thoroughbred Racing in America* (1964).)

Steven A. Riess

PROGRESSIVE PARTY. This was a third party organized in 1912 by a faction of the Republican party* under the leadership of Theodore Roosevelt.* Within two years after Roosevelt handed over the presidency to William Howard Taft* in 1909, the Republican party split into two warring camps, and in 1912 Taft's renomination was challenged, first by his angry critics in the Congress, then by Roosevelt himself. The divisions in the Congress which precipitated the crisis were essentially sectional in nature; western senators and congressmen from agrarian states demanded a reduction in the protective tariff, which they felt favored eastern corporate and financial interests, and more effective regulation of railroads and other corporations. Roosevelt assumed leadership of the Insurgent* or progressive movement against Taft in 1912, but Taft controlled the Republican convention and was easily renominated. Roosevelt then called for the organization of a new Progressive ("Bull Moose") party.

Few of the professional politicians who had backed Roosevelt's efforts to win the Republican nomination joined him in this third-party experiment, but he was supported by many enthusiastic middle- and upper-class reformers from all parts of the nation eager to join in creating a new political era. Roosevelt accepted the Progressive party nomination in a rousing "Confession of Faith" in which he denounced the old parties, endorsed most of the progressive reform proposals of the time, including labor, health, and welfare legislation. In the election in 1912,* the division of the "expected" Republican vote between Roosevelt and Taft almost certainly made it possible for Woodrow Wilson,* the Democratic nominee, to win. The vote for Roosevelt was substantial; but otherwise the Progressive party did not do well. With even less success, the party ran candidates again in 1914.

When it met in convention in 1916, Roosevelt tried to use the party as a bargaining chip to persuade the Republicans to nominate him. Instead the Republican convention nominated Charles Evans Hughes,* and Roosevelt declined the Progressive nomination. After the convention, on Roosevelt's recommendation, the Progressive National Committee endorsed Hughes, its last important act. A great many of the measures proposed by the Progressive platform in 1912 eventually became law, and that is perhaps the party's most important contribution. On the other hand, the grand dream of forming a new national party that would unify progressives of all partisan affiliations failed. (John Allen Gable, *The Bull Moose Years: Theodore Roosevelt and* the Progressive Party (1978); William H. Harbaugh, *Power and Responsibility: The Life and Times of Theodore Roosevelt* (1961); George E. Mowry, *Theodore Roosevelt and the Progressive Movement* (1947).)

Howard W. Allen

PROHIBITION. The Eighteenth Amendment to the Constitution, which took effect on January 16, 1920, forbade the "manufacture, sale, or transportation of intoxicating liquors" in the United States. The Volstead Act, the congressional enabling act which put the amendment into effect, defined as "intoxicating" any beverage containing more than .5 percent alcohol. This prohibition of alcoholic beverages remained the law of the land until repealed by the Twenty-First Amendment in 1933. The prohibition movement had deep roots in the evangelical Protestant tradition. The first effective prohibition law was passed by the state of Maine in 1851. In 1872 a National Prohibition Party fielded a presidential ticket for the first time, and in 1879 Frances Willard* began a vigorous campaign as president of the Women's Christian Temperance Union.*

The movement for national prohibition did not make much impact, however, until the founding of the Anti-Saloon League* (ASL) in 1895. Avoiding simple moralism, it focused its publicity on the threat of the rowdy, working-class saloon to home and family and built an efficient grass-roots organization which mounted a pragmatic, step-by-step campaign, starting with local option laws, that permitted counties and municipalities to vote themselves dry, then moving on to lobby for statewide prohibition. By 1916, twenty-three states, mostly in the South and West, were legally dry, and the Webb-Kenyon Act,* passed by Congress in 1913, banned interstate shipment of liquor from wet states to dry ones. Finally, in 1913, the ASL mounted a well-financed campaign to elect dry congressmen and bring about national prohibition. This campaign bore fruit with the passage of the Eighteenth Amendment by Congress on December 22, 1917. Ratification by the states was completed in January 1919, and the amendment took effect a year later.

Prohibition reflected a deep division between rural and small-town Protestants, who opposed liquor and the saloon, and urban, immigrant Catholics and Jews, who saw no harm in them. The very real social problems surrounding the saloon gave the movement a broader appeal and helped it transcend this division. The Anti-Saloon League rode a tide of wartime unity to victory and enshrined prohibition in the Constitution as a "noble experiment," an experiment which failed and was ultimately repealed. (Norman H. Clark, *Deliver Us from Evil: An Interpretation of American Prohibition* (1976); Andrew Sinclair, *The Era of Excess* (1962); James H. Timberlake, *Prohibition and the Progressive Movement, 1900–1920* (1963); Joseph R. Gusfield, *Symbolic Crusade: Status Politics and the American Temperance Movement* (1963).)

Edward R. Kantowicz

PSYCHIATRY. The medical specialty which studies and treats mental illness and insanity, psychiatry developed empirically in the state mental hospitals which were established in the mid-nineteenth century. The profession gradually shifted its emphasis from administrative matters to clinical treatment of the insane. The Association of Medical Superintendents of American Institutions for the Insane, founded in 1844, permitted attending physicians to join in 1885, changed its name to the American Medico-Psychological Association in 1892, then finally to the American Psychiatric Asociation in 1921.

Psychiatrists at the turn of the century ascribed mental illness to physical causes, such as lesions on the brain, but they also believed that many of these physical causes were self-induced, so psychiatry remained a mixture of medicine and moralism. Sigmund Freud revolutionized psychiatry by providing it with a dynamic theory of personality and an effective means of treatment, called psychoanalysis. The pioneering experimental psychologist G. Stanley Hall* invited Freud to lecture at Clark University in 1909. Though Freud did not like America, his work had its greatest influence in this country, particularly after World War I.* Psychiatry developed greatly during the war as many psychiatrists served as consultants to the surgeon general. (Walter E. Barton, *The History and Influence of the American Psychiatric Association* (1987); Nathan G. Hale, *Freud and the Americans* (1971); Gerald N. Grob, *The Inner World of American Psychiatry, 1890–1940* (1985).)

Edward R. Kantowicz

PUBLIC HEALTH MOVEMENT. The movement for public health reform made unprecedented advances in the Progressive Era. The enormous population growth, urban congestion, contamination of food and water supplies, and spread of epidemics made reform all the more urgent. The progress of the revolution in preventive medicine allowed the movement to stop the spread of diseases that, until the late nineteenth century, had gone largely unchecked. The greatest progress in public health reform occurred at the state and municipal levels. Crusades supported substantially by private philanthropy attacked the hookworm menace and discovered the cause of pellagra. Led by Kansas, states fought such communicable diseases as tuberculosis and typhoid and inaugurated programs of public health education. Some states strengthened their boards of health and expanded their functions to provide free vaccination for some diseases.

Many municipalities set impressive health records. They passed laws regulating milk and water supplies, providing for quarantines and for medical inspection of schoolchildren. Milwaukee undertook reforms that later brought distinguished awards as the nation's healthiest city, while Newark, listed by the federal census of 1890 as the nation's unhealthiest city, made remarkable improvement. The impressive decline of mortality statistics for several major diseases by the end of the Progressive Era partially attested to the accomplishments of the public health movement. (John Ettling, *The Germ of Laziness: Rockefeller Philanthropy and Public Health in the New South* (1981); Judith Walzer Leavitt, *The Healthiest City: Milwaukee and the Politics of Health Reform* (1982); Stuart Galishoff, *Safeguarding the Public Health: Newark, 1895–1918* (1975); James G. Burrow, *Organized Medicine in the Progressive Era: The Move toward Monopoly* (1977).)

James G. Burrow

PUBLIC INTEREST. Urban reformers of the Progressive Era often used the term "public interest" to justify their battles against corrupt corporations and institutions (including utilities and governmental bodies) that allegedly subverted the will of "the people." In other words, from the reformers' viewpoint, such campaigns of "good" versus "evil" were clearly in the "public interest." Many historians have accepted this interpretation of urban reform shaped by contemporary participants, journalists (including "muckrakers"), and academics. Eugene M. Tobin's case study of Jersey City, New Jersey, raises several cogent questions about various competing public interests. For example, whose public interests were more important—those of the citizens of a single community whose tax-equalization efforts often stifled economic growth, or those of the railroads which provided jobs and services for citizens of a broader market? Jersey City reformers, frustrated by the railroad's domination of state politics and exemption from full taxation, turned to the courts for relief. Yet, not all of the Jersey City lawsuits were introduced to protect the public interest, nor did the reformers consistently act out of genuine concern over tax inequities. Such political interests usually were more important than ideology for the reformers. Moreover, residents of the city generally evinced an ambivalent attitude toward tax reform and the railroad. Such paradoxes suggest that the urban reform process was one of political give-and-take rather than simply a morality play involving angels and villains. (Eugene M. Tobin, " 'Engines of Salvation' or 'Smoking Black Devils': Jersey City Reformers and the Railroads, 1902–1908," in Michael H. Ebner and Eugene M. Tobin, eds., *The Age of Urban Reform: New Perspectives on the Progressive Era* (1977); Robert W. Harbeson, "Railroads and Regulation, 1877–1916: Conspiracy or Public Interest?" *Journal of Economic History* 27 (June 1967): 230-42; Melvin G. Holli, "Urban Reform in the Progressive Era," in Lewis L. Gould, ed., *The Progressive Era* (1974).)

David E. Alsobrook

PUBLIC LIBRARIES. Between 1890 and 1915, public librarians attempted to make their institutions a generally useful social center for the material and cultural elevation of their users. Through the development of new services, including reference, and programming for children, adults, and immigrants, provision was made for the general reader as well as for special classes of users. By the end of the nineteenth century, most large public libraries had designated reference personnel who worked in distinct departments. Reference service in main libraries was supplemented by work in branches. The adoption of children's services also occurred at this time and included provision for book lending, story hours, and book clubs. The library also supported university extension work and the Chautauqua movement* through the development of special collections of books for adult learners. Service to immigrants included the provision of reading matter in native tongues and English classes in the library. The ability of public libraries to offer such services was enhanced by the philanthropy of Andrew Carnegie,* who gave grants to 1,408 American communities between 1886 and 1919 for the construction of public library buildings. (George S. Bobinski, *Carnegie Libraries: Their History and Impact on American Public Library Development* (1969); D. W. Davies, *Public Libraries as Cultural and Social Centers: The*

Origin of the Concept (1974); Rosemary Ruhig Du Mont, *Reform and Reaction: The Big City Public Library in American Life* (1977).)

Rosemary Ruhig Du Mont

PUBLIC UTILITY REGULATION. The modern era of utility regulation began in the late nineteenth century with the linking of the old legal concept of "public interest"* with the new economic concept of "natural monopoly." Promoted by progressive academics such as Richard Ely,* the idea that some businesses—gas, water, electricity, transportation—were most efficiently operated as regulated monopolies became an accepted principle of political economy by the turn of the century. The chief issue for the Progressive Era, then, was *how* to regulate. On one side of the issue were those who favored *popular* control of utilities, ranging from regulation by local franchise (ordinance) to complete public ownership. On the other side were those who favored *expert* control, especially regulation by nonpolitical independent commissions. Each side included a mixture of politicians, reformers, and academics.

Throughout the Progressive Era, utility regulation was the major political issue in most large cities. Gradually, the commission idea triumphed, at least in part because the utility corporations began to consider it the lesser of evils. In 1907, both New York* and Wisconsin* set up modern state public service commissions to regulate a wide range of utilities. By 1920, more than two-thirds of the states had followed suit. And the idea of regulation by independent commission became one of the most enduring legacies of the Progressive Era. (David Paul Nord, "The Experts versus the Experts: Conflicting Philosophies of Municipal Utility Regulation in the Progressive Era," *Wisconsin Magazine of History* 58 (1975): 219–316; Bruce W. Dearstyne, "Regulation in the Progressive Era: The New York Public Service Commission," *New York History* 58 (1977): 331–47; Richard L. McCormick, "The Discovery That Business Corrupts Politics: A Reappraisal of the Origins of Progressivism," *American Historical Review* 86 (1981): 147–74.)

David Paul Nord

PUJO COMMITTEE. House Banking and Currency Committee Chairman Arsène Pujo (Louisiana) headed a subcommittee to investigate the concentration of control of money and credit. Hearings from May 16, 1912, to June 13, 1912, and again from December 9, 1912, to February 26, 1913, were actually conducted by counsel to the committee Samuel Untermeyer,* a leading New York lawyer. Three Wall Street firms, J. P. Morgan and Company, George F. Baker's National Bank, and James Stillman's National City Bank, made up the "inner or primary group," occasionally joined by Kuhn, Loeb and Company; Boston allies included Lee, Higginson and Kidder, Peabody together with three major banks. The three largest Chicago banks rounded out the roster of the "few leaders of finance" whose "community of interest" constituted "a vast and growing concentration of control of money and credit."

In their report dated February 28, 1913, the subcommittee majority acknowledged that they had no proof of oppressive use of this power. Nevertheless, they described "the arteries of credit" as "clogged well-nigh to choking by the obstructions created through the control of these groups." In a best-selling popularization of the majority's findings, *Other People's Money and How the Bankers Use It* (1914), Louis D. Brandeis* wrote that "a few men control the business of America." Already in March 1911 Governor Woodrow Wilson* had told an Atlanta audience, "The most serious thing facing us today is the concentration of money power in the hands of a few."

The 1912 Democratic platform proposed to revise the banking laws in order to protect the people from the "money trust." The 1916 platform hailed the Federal Reserve Act of 1913* as having supplanted an "archaic banking and currency system...long the refuge of the money trust." Even prior to the opening of the twelve Federal Reserve banks in 1914, however, Wall Street institutions were declining relative to those in other financial centers. Moreover, interlocking directorates were not synonymous with harmony of business conduct. (Louis D. Brandeis, *Other People's Money and How the Bankers Use It* (1967); Benjamin J. Klebaner, "The Money Trust Investigation in Retrospect," *National Banking Review* 3 (1966): 393–403; Vincent P. Carosso, *Investment Banking in America* (1970): 137–55.)

Benjamin J. Klebaner

PULITZER, JOSEPH (April 10, 1847–October 29, 1911). Born in Mako, Hungary, the originator of yellow journalism immigrated to the United States in 1864. After the Civil War, Pulitzer edited the *Westliche Post* and the *Post-Dispatch* in Saint Louis and entered politics as a supporter of Horace Greeley (1872) and Samuel J. Tilden (1876). Using a personal style of midwestern journalism, Pulitzer conducted his paper on combative partisan lines. He sensationalized scandals, attacked the rich, defended hard currency, and demanded lower tariffs and more civil service reform.*

In 1883, Pulitzer purchased the New York *World*. For the next decade he entertained the growing mass of literate immigrant and native readers with sordid literature, well written and illustrated, mixed with lovelorn advice, sports, and women's interest stories. The *World*'s circulation rose tenfold in two years. The Sunday supplement sold 600,000 copies on Easter, 1896. Written in colloquial English, with multicolumned advertisments, headlines or cartoons dominating the front page, the *World* provided a steady diet of sex, crime, and tragedy for one cent a day. His competitors, especially William Randolph Hearst,* labeled him "Jewseph Pulitzer," but imitated his style and lured away his editors and patrons. And in 1896 Pultizer lost politically by opposing William Jennings Bryan.* Racked by a debilitating illness and blindness, he retired. From afar he ordered the jingoistic campaigns of the 1890s and attacks upon Theodore Roosevelt's* administration. (George Juergens, *Joseph Pulitzer and the New York World* (1966); Julian S. Rammelkamp, *Pulitzer's "Post-Dispatch," 1878–1883* (1967); Don C. Seitz, *Joseph Pulitzer: His Life and Letters* (1924).)

Harold Wilson

PULLMAN STRIKE. George Pullman, manufacturer of railroad sleeping cars, dreamt of utopia when he created a company town south of Chicago in 1881, but his dream became a nightmare when his workers went on strike in 1894. Pullman ruled his town and factory like a feudal lord. As one worker told an investigator: "We are born in a Pullman house, fed from the Pullman shop, taught in the Pullman school, catechized in the Pullman church, and when we die we shall be buried in the Pullman cemetery and go to the Pullman hell." During the depression of the 1890s,* Pullman slashed wages but did not reduce rents. The workers walked off their jobs on May 11, 1894, and the fledgling American Railway Union, headed by Eugene Debs,* supported them by boycotting all trains with Pullman cars.

The strike idled 100,000 men nationwide, disrupted rail service, and sparked sporadic violence. President Grover Cleveland's attorney general, Richard Olney, obtained an injunction against the boycott on July 2 then broke the strike with federal troops on July 4, vowing to prevent obstruction of the mails and of interstate commerce. The Pullman strike illustrated vividly the sharp class conflicts in America and pushed the embittered union leader Debs towards the Socialist party,* which he ably served as perennial presidential candidate for the next twenty years. (Stanley Buder, *Pullman: An Experiment in Industrial Order and Community Planning* (1967); Almont Lindsey, *The Pullman Strike* (1942); Ray Ginger, *The Bending Cross: A Biography of Eugene Victor Debs* (1949).)

Edward R. Kantowicz

PURE FOOD AND DRUGS LAW. In the latter part of the nineteenth century, when the nation moved from an agricultural to an industrial society, and Americans became factory workers in cities, people became dependent on manufactured food. Vast amounts of food were adulterated by manufacturers using dubious substances as preservatives or to make unfit food look appetizing. Beef contained boric acid, for example, and pork and beans, formaldehyde. Starting in 1879, numerous measures were introduced to protect the consumer, but languished in a Congress responsive to big business. The major advocate of pure food, Dr. Harvey W. Wiley,* chief chemist of the Department of Agriculture, did experiments in which he fed volunteers the dubious preservatives, noting the harmful effects. The group was quickly dubbed the "poison squad," generating wide publicity.

Passage of the act was also facilitated by the backing of President Theodore Roosevelt* and by Upton Sinclair's* novel, *The Jungle*, a grisly story of the meat-packing industry which aroused consumer concern. The Pure Food and Drugs Act, signed on June 30, 1906, made it unlawful to manufacture, sell, or transport any adulterated, misbranded, poisonous, or deleterious food, drug, medicine, or liquor. Responsibility for enforcement was placed in the Bureau of Chemistry and Dr. Wiley, who discovered that a turbulent fight for pure food and drugs was just beginning. After thousands of court proceedings, the law was strengthened by legal interpretations and later by amendments. An extensive revolution in food processing resulted during the period 1907–1912. (Harvey W. Wiley, *Harvey W. Wiley: An Autobiography* (1930); Henry Welch and Felix Marti-Ibanez, *The Impact of the Food and Drug Administration on Our Society* (1956); Gerald H. Carson, "Consumer Protection: The Pure Food and Drugs Act," in John Garraty, ed., *Historical Viewpoints*, vol. 2: *Since 1865* (1976).).

Betsy B. Holli

R

RACE RIOTS. Between the race riot in Wilmington, North Carolina, in 1898 and the one in Tulsa, Oklahoma, in 1921, urban racial violence increasingly erupted in American cities. Some riots were one-sided affairs in which white mobs sadistically battered and murdered fleeing blacks and destroyed their property. In most cases, however, blacks armed themselves and exacted substantial casualties on marauding whites. Race riots occurred in New Orleans and New York in 1900; in Statesboro, Georgia, and Springfield, Ohio, in 1904; in Atlanta, Georgia, and Greensburg, Indiana, in 1906; and in Springfield, Illinois, in 1908. World War I* brought forth more and deadlier riots. In 1917, thirty-nine blacks and nine whites died in racial strife in East Saint Louis, and in Houston black soldiers killed seventeen whites. In the summer of 1919 some twenty-five outbreaks took place. Five days of conflict in Chicago left 23 blacks and 15 whites dead and 537 wounded. In many places federal troops or state militias had to be summoned to restore order. Like lynching, race riots constituted an extreme manifestation of white racism and a form of social control in the face of rising black militancy.

The subordination of blacks in the South through disfranchisement,* segregation, and terror, plus the anguish of southern agriculture, sparked a massive migration of Afro-Americans to northern cities. Reaching half a million during the war, the migration threw blacks and whites into bitter competition for jobs and housing. Black immigrants faced a highly prejudiced white police force that constantly gave offense to the minority community. Whites especially resented the black vote and the use of blacks as strikebreakers. On either side of the Potomac, irresponsible journalists sensationalized alleged rapes of white women by black men, the ostensible reason given for several of the riots. The promiscuous use of racist imagery by the media, best exemplified by D. W. Griffith's* classic film *The Birth of a Nation** (1915), and the zenophobic mania of the war further fanned the racial flames.

The Springfield, Illinois, riot led to the formation of the National Association for the Advancement of Colored People* (1910), and collectively the riots inspired the founding of the Commission on Interracial Cooperation* (1919). Black resistance to white attacks also generated racial pride and defiance of caste, traits associated with the "New Negro" of the postwar era. (Arthur I. Waskow, *From Race Riot to Sit-In, 1919 and the 1960s: A Study in the Connection between Conflict and Violence* (1966); Allen D. Grimshaw, ed., *Racial Violence in the United States* (1969); William M. Tuttle, *Race Riot: Chicago in the Red Summer of 1919* (1970).)

David W. Southern

RAILROAD ACT (February 28, 1920) returned the railroads to private operation after wartime federal control. Although reformers, led by Senator Albert Cummins,* had called for a new federal policy of promoting more "scientific" management* through a new federal agency empowered to superimpose its views on the Interstate Commerce Commission (ICC), the railroads, their customers, and railroad workers, Congress instead chose to modify the regulatory path outlined in the Progressive Era. The law enlarged membership in the ICC from nine to eleven members and granted the commission new authority over railroad service, finances, and rates. The commission was to draw up a consolidation plan for the railroad industry that would ensure its financial strength while preserving the benefits of competition to shippers and passengers. Congress instructed the ICC over a two-year period to set railroad rates so that efficient carriers would earn between a 5.5 and 6 percent return on their physical value, setting aside "excess" earnings to assist weaker railroad companies in improving their efficiency. In general, then, the act tried to strike a balance between the need of the railroads for the revenue necessary for capital improvements and efficient service and their customers' need for leverage in ensuring fair treatment. (K. Austin Kerr, *American Railroad Politics, 1914–1920* (1968); Ari Hoogenboom and Olive Hoogenboom, *A History of the ICC* (1976).)

K. Austin Kerr

RAILROAD ADMINISTRATION. By December 1917 the nation's transportation system was failing under the unusual burdens of war traffic, and the Interstate Commerce Commission and reformers urged federal operation to improve the efficiency of service and reduce pressures for freight rate increases. President Woodrow Wilson* announced federal railroad control and created the Railroad Administration to supervise the operation of the vital transportation system for the duration of the war. The Railroad Administration was in charge of 532 companies with 366,000 miles of track valued at $18 billion. Congress arranged to lease the corporations' property for the duration of the war.

Director-General William G. McAdoo,* Walker D. Hines, and career railroad executives appointed to the Railroad Administration launched a management reorganization to ensure the efficient coordination of train, freight, and passenger movements, as well as operating economies. Granted power by Congress over wages and freight rates, in response to wartime inflation the Railroad Administration raised both in 1918. The efficiencies imposed on the railroad industry effectively solved the wartime traffic burdens, but the Railroad Administration proved unpopular among influential shippers disappointed by the wage and rate increases, and after the Armistice, pressures mounted from those businessmen for a return to private operation. (K. Austin Kerr, *American Railroad Politics, 1914–1920* (1968); Walker D. Hines, *War History of American Railroads* (1928).)

K. Austin Kerr

RAILROAD REGULATION, FEDERAL. The first U.S. railroads began operation in 1830. For the next forty years the railroads were relatively free to run their businesses with little intervention from public authorities, state or federal. Not only did the railroads generally have liberal charters, they were also the recipients of extensive land grants and large subsidies. Beginning in the 1870s a tide of resentment began to build against the railroads particularly in the Midwest. Farmers attacked the railroads for setting rates on agricultural commodities which they felt were too high, a sentiment made worse by a severe decline in agricultural prices.

The result of this agitation was the enactment by the legislatures of Illinois, Iowa, Minnesota, and Wisconsin of a series of laws intended to regulate railroads. These Granger laws provided the legal basis for later federal legislation. Although the U.S. Supreme Court affirmed the rights of states to regulate industries including railroads "affected with public interest" in *Munn v. Illinois* (1877), the Court in the *Wabash* case (1886) limited state jurisdiction to intrastate traffic. Because the majority of traffic moving on the rails was interstate in nature, the *Wabash* decision had the effect of eliminating from regulation most of the traffic carried by the railroads.

In 1886, a report issued by a special joint council congressional committee emphasized abuses of monopoly power and discriminatory practices by the railroads. A compromise was worked out between the House and Senate, and the Act to Regulate Commerce was signed into law by the president on April 5, 1887. The law consisted of six sections: (1) reasonableness of rates, (2) personal discrimination, (3) undue preference or prejudice, (4) long- and short-haul clause, (5) pooling, and (6) publication of rates. The act also created the Interstate Commerce Commission to administer the act. Several weaknesses in the law and a series of adverse decisions by the Supreme Court made additional legislation necessary.

The Elkins Act* (1903) outlawed rebates and made it unlawful to depart from published rates; the Hepburn Act* (1906) extended commission jurisdiction over railroad related services, such as refrigeration, and gave the commission the power to prescribe maximum rates. The surge in rail traffic caused by World War I* resulted in a breakdown in the ability of railroads to move traffic to eastern ports. In December 1917, the federal government assumed temporary control of the railroads, and the Transportation Act of 1920 (*see* Esch-Cummins Act) was passed. The act revised many rail regulations and for the first time recognized the need for railroads to earn a fair rate of return on their investment. (Philip D. Locklin, *Economics of Transportation* (1966); Roy J. Sampson and Martin T. Farris, *Domestic Transportation—Practice, Theory, and Policy* (1979); I. L. Sharfman, *The Interstate Commerce Commission*, vol. 1 (1931).)

Curtis Richards

RANKIN, JEANNETTE (June 11, 1880–May 18, 1973). Born near Missoula, Montana, Rankin was educated at the University of Montana, the New York School of Philanthropy, and the University of Washington. Active in the suffrage movement, Rankin organized in the 1910 Washington State campaign, and she worked in Montana and several other states. In 1913, she served as field secretary for the National American Woman Suffrage Association* and helped win passage of woman suffrage in Montana in 1914. In 1916, Rankin became the first woman elected to the House of Representatives, after running on a platform of woman suffrage, protective legislation, prohibition,* tariff revision, and "preparedness."* After only four days in office, Rankin voted against U.S. entry into World War I.* Defeated in a 1918 campaign for the Senate, Rankin later served as field secretary and board member of the Women's International League for Peace and Freedom, field secretary of the National Consumers' League,* and founded the Georgian Peace Society in 1928. Elected again to the House of Representatives in 1940 on a pacifist platform, she cast the sole vote against U.S. entry into war. Barbara Sicherman et al., *Notable American Women: The Modern Period* (1980); Hannah Josephson, *Jeannette Rankin: First Lady in Congress* (1974).)

Marie Laberge

RAUSCHENBUSCH, WALTER. (October 4, 1861–July 25, 1918). Born in Rochester, New York, Rauschenbusch was educated in Germany, at the University of Rochester, and the Rochester Theological Seminary. He spent most of his ministry as a professor at the Rochester Theological Seminary, but his early experience as pastor of an immigrant church in New York was what shaped his perception of the need to reconcile social problems to Christian teachings. In 1892, he organized the Brotherhood of the Kingdom, a body of liberal clergymen interested in reform. He traveled abroad and studied economics at the University of Berlin and British industrial conditions with Sidney and Beatrice Webb. His *Christianity and the Social Crisis*, published in 1907, is considered the most important explanation of the Social Gospel.* He identified with the Christian Socialist faction of the movement, contending that there was a fundamental ethical error in capitalism. He believed the industrial system was wrong and laissez-faire a denial of the Christian message. His latter years saw his reputation diminished by his opposition to World War I.* (Walter Rauschenbusch, *Christianity and Social Crisis* (1907); Ronald C. White and Charles Howard Hopkins, *The Social Gospel: Religion and Reform in Changing America* (1976).)

Thomas W. Ryley

RECALL. Recall is a governmental mechanism permitting a percentage of registered voters to demand a special election and remove an elected official before the end of his term. Along with the initiative* and the referendum,* the recall was one of the direct democracy reforms borrowed from Switzerland and widely adopted by state and local governments. Reformers wished to break the control of corrupt political machines* over the government by appealing directly to the people. In reply to pessimists, who claimed that democracy had failed, they asserted that "the cure for democracy is more democracy." The recall was first adopted in the 1903 city charter of Los Angeles,* then shortly thereafter by the state of Oregon,* ten other states, and over a thousand municipalities. In 1904 Los Angeles voters recalled a corrupt councilman, and in 1906 an attempt to recall that city's mayor led to his resignation. Theodore Roosevelt* and the Progressive party* advocated the recall of judicial decisions during the 1912 presidential campaign, but none of the direct democracy reforms was adopted at the national level. (William B. Munro, *The Initiative, Referendum and Recall* (1912); Frederick L. Bird and Frances M. Ryan, *A Study of the Operation of the Recall in California* (1930); Ernest S. Griffith, *A History of American City Government*, vol. 4 (1974).)

Edward R. Kantowicz

RECLAMATION ACT. One of the first major pieces of progressive legislation for the conservation of natural resources, the Reclamation Act, passed in 1902, provided that funds from the sale and disposal of public lands in sixteen western states and territories would be placed into a special reclamation fund to be used to finance irrigation projects on the arid lands of those states and territories. Public lands in the projects were to be opened to entry under the Homestead Act and all holdings receiving water limited to 160 acres. As the cost of the projects was repaid by the settlers, they would gain title to the land and a voice in managing the project, but the irrigation works would remain under government control. Implementation of the act was assigned to the Department of the Interior.

In January 1901, Representative Francis Newlands* of Nevada introduced a draft of the bill, and in December, Theodore Roosevelt,* an ardent advocate of conservation and reclamation, provided crucial support, urging federal assistance for irrigation in his first State of the Union Message. The following month a final draft of the bill was entered in the House by Newlands and in the Senate by Henry C. Hansborough of North Dakota. A compromise bill passed both houses in June and was signed into law by Roosevelt on June 17, 1902. (Lawrence B. Lee, *Reclaiming the American West: An Historiography and Guide* (1980);

Paul W. Gates, *History of Public Land Law Development* (1968); William E. Smythe, *The Conquest of Arid America* (1969).)

Kathryn M. Totton

RECLAMATION BUREAU. The Reclamation Bureau was created July 8, 1902, as part of the plan of operation approved by the secretary of the interior for the implementation of the Reclamation Act.* Its creation represented the initial accomplishment of one portion of the progressive agenda: federal management of natural resources in the states for the purpose of conservation. Originally named the Reclamation Service, the bureau was part of the Geological Survey's Division of Hydrography directed by Frederick H. Newell* and staffed by professional engineers. This branch of the Geological Survey, which had begun conducting irrigation surveys in the arid West in 1888 under the leadership of John Wesley Powell, was now charged with the selection of sites and construction and operation of dams and irrigation projects to reclaim arid western lands.

After two years of preliminary surveys and site selection, work on the first projects began in Arizona, Idaho, Montana, and Nevada, and by late 1906, the service had projects underway in all but one (Oklahoma) of the sixteen states and territories included in the act. In 1907 the service became an independent agency under the Department of the Interior. The name was changed to Bureau of Reclamation, and the position of commissioner of reclamation was created by the secretary of the interior in 1923. The most significant achievement of the bureau during its first thirty years was the construction on twenty-two projects of technologically advanced dams, which provided not only water for irrigation but hydroelectric power, flood control, and recreational facilities. (Lawrence B. Lee, *Reclaiming the American West: An Historiography and Guide* (1980); Paul W. Gates, *History of Public Land Law Development* (1968); Marc Reisner, *Cadillac Desert: The American West and Its Disappearing Water* (1986).)

Kathryn M. Totton

RECORD, GEORGE L. (March 13, 1859–September 27, 1933). Born in Auburn, Maine, Record was educated at Bates College and studied law in New York City. Following his admission to the bar in 1887, he started a law practice in Jersey City (New Jersey) and earned an early reputation for honesty and integrity. Record served on the Jersey City Board of Education and as counsel for the State Riparian Commission. He drafted an unsuccessful primary* reform bill and became a leading proponent of direct democracy and Henry George's* single tax* as the best means of redistributing economic and political power. Tired of battling Hudson County's Democratic political machine* and unwilling to support William Jennings Bryan* for president in 1896, Record joined the Republican party.* Though defeated in a 1901 campaign for state senate, he caught the eye of Jersey City's progressive Republican mayor Mark Fagan.*

Over the next six years (1902–1908) Record's fight for utility regulation,* equal taxation of railroad property, and an end to corporate arrogance inspired a statewide progressive Republican movement known as the "New Idea." In 1910, he played a key role in legitimizing Woodrow Wilson's* progressive credentials and had a hand in drafting most of the major legislation passed during Governor Wilson's first year in office. The following year Record helped create the National Progressive Republican League* and advised Senator Robert M. La Follette* in the preconvention maneuvering. In 1912, he shifted his support to Theodore Roosevelt's* third-party movement. Following the collapse of the Progressive party,* Record continued to work for direct democracy through a succession of educational but unsuccessful candidacies. Between 1918 and 1924 he organized several efforts in behalf of a liberal-labor third-party movement. (Ransom E. Noble, Jr., *New Jersey Progressivism before Wilson* (1946); Ransom E. Noble, Jr., "George L. Record's Struggle for Economic Democracy," *American Journal of Economics and Sociology* 10 (July 1950): 71–83; Eugene M. Tobin, *George Record and the Progressive Spirit* (1979).)

Eugene M. Tobin

RED SCARE. An hysterical fear that a Communist revolution might break out in the United States raged briefly after the end of World War I.* In March 1919, the revolutionary government in Russia organized the Third International, a body dedicated to spreading the revolution worldwide. In September, two factions of the prewar Socialist party of America* reorganized as the American Communist party and the Communist Labor party, both affiliated with the Third International. When three sensational strikes broke out that same month—the Boston police strike,* the steel strike,* and the United Mine Workers'* bituminous coal strike—many Americans assumed they were Communist-inspired. A series of widely scattered terrorist bombings throughout 1919 added to the tension.

The Democratic attorney general, A. Mitchell Palmer,* launched a campaign to arrest and deport alien Communists and other radicals. On November 7, 1919, the first of the "Palmer Raids" occurred, a coordinated sweep of the Union of Russian Workers in a dozen American cities. On December 21, Palmer deported 249 aliens to Russia on an army transport which was nicknamed the "Soviet Ark." In January 1920, federal agents arrested more than 4,000 Communist party members in a coast-to-coast raid in thirty-three cities. Eventually, cooler heads prevailed. The Labor Department,* legally required to certify aliens for deportation, adopted strict rules of evidence which resulted in the release of many netted by the Palmer Raids.

The rash action of the New York State Legislature in expelling five duly elected Socialist party members turned public opinion against the Red hunters. Then, finally, Attorney General Palmer overreached himself. He predicted a Communist bomb plot for May Day of 1920, but May 1 came and went without a single detonation. The brief but intense Red Scare was due to Palmer's opportunistic and politically motivated actions, continuation of wartime hysteria,

398 REED, JAMES A.

and a deep longing for a simpler, more homogeneous, more racially pure America. (Robert K. Murray, *Red Scare: A Study in National Hysteria* (1955); Stanley Coben, "A Study in Nativism: The American Red Scare of 1919–1920," *Political Science Quarterly* 79 (1964): 52–75; William E. Leuchtenberg, *The Perils of Prosperity* (1958).)

Edward R. Kantowicz

REED, JAMES A. (November 9, 1861–September 8, 1944). Born near Mansfield, Ohio, Reed was educated at Coe College (Iowa) and read law in the offices of a Cedar Rapids, Iowa, law firm. After a brief stint as counselor and prosecuting attorney of Jackson County, Missouri, he won election in 1900 as mayor of Kansas City and secured major reforms in city transportation, utility services, paving contracts, and the police department. In 1910 Missourians elected Reed, a Democrat, to the first of three consecutive terms in the U.S. Senate, where he generally supported President Woodrow Wilson's* reform program and voted for the war resolution of 1917. He feared centralized federal power and opposed the creation of the wartime Food Administration.* He broke with Wilson over U.S. membership in the League of Nations,* becoming one of the "irreconcilables." Reed strongly opposed social reforms such as prohibition* and maternity legislation. (Jan A. Hults, "The Senatorial Career of James Alexander Reed" (Ph.D. diss., University of Kansas, 1986); Franklin D. Mitchell, "The Reelection of Irreconcilable James A. Reed," *Missouri Historical Review* 60 (1966): 416–35.)

Franklin D. Mitchell

REED, JOHN (October 22, 1887–October 17, 1920). A native of Portland, Oregon, Reed received his formal education at Morristown and Harvard and went on to become a legendary figure of American journalism and radicalism. Having become acquainted with muckraker Lincoln Steffens* while still a student at Harvard, Reed was assisted by the older journalist in beginning a highly successful career as magazine writer in New York. He was moved by the Paterson* and Ludlow* strikes to ardent sympathy for labor's cause, going on from these experiences to write *Insurgent Mexico*, a brilliant account of his encounter with revolutionary Mexico. With the onset of World War I* Reed turned to European events, and in the fall of 1917 he was in Petrograd, a firsthand witness of the dramatic Soviet advance to power. In April 1918, he returned to the United States where, in the face of wartime repression, he lectured in support of the Bolshevik Revolution and wrote the classic *Ten Days That Shook the World*. He was drawn to participation in founding the Communist Labor party and committed himself to the task of revolutionizing American society. In the fall of 1919, he returned to Russia, where he took part in debates of the Communist International. He died there and was buried in the wall of the Kremlin. (Robert A. Rosenstone, *Romantic Revolutionary: A Biography of John Reed* (1975);

Granville Hicks, *John Reed: The Making of a Revolutionary* (1936); John Reed, *Insurgent Mexico* (1914); John Reed, *Ten Days That Shook the World* (1919).)

                                                                                    Herbert Shapiro

REFERENDUM. A referendum is a policy proposal submitted to the voters for approval or disapproval. Along with the initiative* and the recall,* the referendum was one of the direct democracy reforms borrowed from Switzerland and widely adopted by state and local governments. South Dakota* was the first state to adopt the referendum as an ordinary agency of government, authorizing it in the state constitution in 1898. Approximately twenty other states adopted it shortly thereafter. The referendum is used most frequently in city government, where charter amendments, tax increases, and bond issues are routinely submitted to the voters. California,* where Dr. John R. Haynes was the leading advocate of direct democracy, and Oregon,* where William S. U'Ren* led the way, have made the most extensive use of referenda. (William B. Munro, *The Initiative, Referendum and Recall* (1912); V. O. Key and Winston W. Crouch, *The Initiative and Referendum in California* (1939); Ernest S. Griffith, *A History of American City Government*, vol. 4 (1974).)

                                                                                    Edward R. Kantowicz

REFORM DARWINISM. A subdivision of Darwinism which claimed that society followed the laws of a competitive nature that is "red in tooth and claw." Conservative Darwinists argued that the forces of nature, such as natural selection and instincts, dictated human behavior. Conservative Darwinism offered a naturalistic explanation of history, allowing a very slow evolutionary change via slow racial improvement. Innately superior individuals created progress. Reform Darwinists believed that human legislation, by changing the economic environment, would result in a better society. Progress was quicker because it was expressed in collective and cultural institutions or cooperative endeavors.

An economic interpretation of human events was a vital element in the reform Darwinists' philosophy of history. While Darwinism allowed reformers an opportunity to dismiss supernaturalism and to be scientific and modern, human needs, aspirations, and values shaped their reformism. Reform Darwinism influenced Lester Frank Ward,* Henry George,* Richard T. Ely,* Edward A. Ross,* Charles A. Beard,* and John Dewey,* among other progressive thinkers. Reform Darwinism made a significant contribution to the philosophic development of instrumentalism* and pragmatism.* (Eric F. Goldman, *Rendezvous with Destiny: A History of Modern Reform* (1952); Morton G. White, *Social Thought in America: The Revolt against Formalism* (1949); Robert C. Bannister, *Social Darwinism: Science and Myth in Anglo-American Social Thought* (1979).)

                                                                                    Donald K. Pickens

REPUBLICAN PARTY. The Republican party entered the Progressive Era as the newly entrenched majority party in American politics. In the congressional elections of 1894, the electorate blamed the Democrats for the severe depression* that followed the panic of 1893. Then, in the highly sectional presidential contests of 1896* and 1900,* Republican William McKinley,* defending the gold standard, tariff protection, and the nation's belated entry into the imperialist scramble for overseas territories, triumphed decisively over Democrat William Jennings Bryan.* McKinley swept New England, the Middle Atlantic states, and the Midwest—the creditor regions characterized by stronger financial institutions, industry, more diversified agriculture, and lower transportation costs.

Although the national leadership of the Republican party appeared to be responsive principally to the desires of northeastern business, the GOP was anything but monolithic. Following the lead of Hazen S. Pingree* of Michigan,* urban reformers sought to meliorate the worst effects of rapid industrialization. Politicians like Robert M. La Follette* of Wisconsin,* Albert B. Cummins* of Iowa,* and later Hiram Johnson* of California* wanted to increase the voice of ordinary citizens in the political process and thus gain more influence for their states in setting the national agenda. Even in the business community, there were those like George W. Perkins* who believed stable economic growth depended on government action to curb cutthroat competition.

Progressive Republicans received a big boost when McKinley's assassination in 1901 brought the intellectually restless Theodore Roosevelt* to the presidency. During his seven years in the White House, Roosevelt maneuvered a modest reform program past the conservative congressional leadership, then began advocating far more extensive changes he knew he could not achieve. Roosevelt's hand-picked successor, William Howard Taft,* was far more conventional. In 1912, Roosevelt grabbed the leadership of the progressive revolt against Taft. But that split in party ranks allowed the Democrats to gain control of Congress and the presidency, and when the split was finally healed, the Republicans immediately resumed their earlier ascendancy, albeit as a much more conservative party.

Throughout the Progressive years, the Republicans drew the main body of their strength from the alignment established in 1896, consisting of farmers, skilled workingmen, aspiring professionals, ambitious merchants, and manufacturers, primarily of pietistic Protestant background, but increasingly Lutheran or Catholic as well, in the economically dominant northeastern quarter of the country. By contrast, in the southern and border states, where the majority of poor black and white voters were now disfranchised, the party was reduced to a mere shadow of its former self, a series of rotten boroughs to be voted in presidential nominating conventions and otherwise forgotten. (Keith Ian Polakoff, *Political Parties in American History* (1981); Horace S. Merrill and Marion G. Merrill, *The Republican Command* (1971); Lawrence James Holt, *Congressional Insurgents and the Party System* (1967).)

Keith Ian Polakoff

REVENUE ACT OF 1916. This act represented a major victory for those in both political parties who wanted the cost of preparedness* to be borne mainly by more affluent citizens. Spurred by a group calling itself the Association for an Equitable Federal Income Tax and headed by John Dewey,* Frederick C. Howe,* George L. Record,* and Benjamin C. Marsh,* southern and western congressmen rejected the plan of President Woodrow Wilson* and Secretary of the Treasury William G. McAdoo* to finance preparedness through the existing tax structure which relied heavily upon import duties and excise taxes. Instead, the House raised the income tax rates from 1 percent to 2, raised the surtax on incomes over $40,000 to a maximum of 10 percent, imposed a graduated tax on estates exceeding $50,000, and levied a graduated tax on the gross receipts of munitions makers reaping net profits of over 10 percent. The Senate version, sponsored by George W. Norris* and Robert M. La Follette,* imposed an additional surtax of up to 13 percent on incomes over $20,000; levied a tax on corporation capital, surplus, and undivided profits; raised the estate tax to 10 percent, and increased the tax on munitions makers to 12.5 percent. (Sidney Ratner, *A Political and Social History of Federal Taxation* (1942); John W. Hillje, "The Progressive Movement and the Graduated Income Tax, 1913–1919" (Ph.D. diss., University of Texas, 1966).)

John D. Buenker

REVIEW OF REVIEWS. This monthly magazine began as the American edition of a British periodical of the same title founded by William T. Stead* in 1890. The American editor, historian and political economist Albert Shaw* brought out the first number in April 1891. Within a few years, however, Shaw had assumed control, and each edition developed separately thereafter. Before the advent of weekly newsmagazines, the *Review of Reviews* was a pioneer among popular magazines in the trend toward current affairs content with accompanying commentary. It bore the strong personal stamp of the highly regarded Shaw, a Johns Hopkins Ph.D., who wrote the editorial section "The Progress of the World" of some twenty to thirty pages.

While covering a wide variety of topics in his editorials, Shaw was a consistent advocate of municipal betterment and progressive Republican reforms of the sort championed by Theodore Roosevelt.* The magazine's format also included contributed pieces, selected political cartoons, and summaries of leading articles from other periodicals. From 1897 to 1910, the *Review of Reviews* enjoyed a monthly circulation of over 200,000 with a readership several times higher. Circulation began to slide, however, after World War I,* and in 1932 it merged with *World's Work.* (Lloyd J. Graybar, *Albert Shaw of the "Review of Reviews": An Intellectual Biography* (1974); Lloyd J. Graybar, "Albert Shaw's Search for the Ideal City," *Historian* 34 (1972); 421–36; Lloyd J. Graybar, "Albert Shaw and the Founding of the *Review of Reviews*, 1891–97," *Journalism Quarterly* 49 (1972): 692–96, 716.)

Lloyd J. Graybar

RHODE ISLAND The Progressive Era in Rhode Island was characterized primarily by efforts of the Democratic party* as "the spokesman for the underdog and the disfranchised immigrants" to challenge hegemony of the rural-based, pro-business Republican organization of General Charles R. Brayton. Secured in power by one of the most blatant cases of legislative malapportionment in the nation, Brayton's GOP was a "representative of business interests and rural Yankees," a constituency that controlled the state legislature, which regularly sent Brayton's friend and business partner Nelson W. Aldrich* to the U.S. Senate. His power was also protected by "Brayton's Law," which gave the legislature veto power over all gubernatorial appointments and denied the governor similar leverage over legislation.

Allied with organized labor and with their strongest backing in Providence, Woonsocket, Pawtucket, and other large cities, the Irish-led Democrats gained legislative reapportionment, the repeal of Brayton's Law, and an end to property qualifications for voting in local elections. The Democrats also fought in vain for woman suffrage,* a federal income tax,* and the direct election of U.S. senators,* while opposing prohibition* and Sunday blue laws.* They also sponsored a myriad of labor, welfare, and regulatory measures, most of which failed of enactment. Although Woodrow Wilson* carried the state in 1912, the legislature remained solidly in conservative, Republican hands until the late 1920s. (John D. Buenker, "Urban Liberalism in Rhode Island, 1909–1919," *Rhode Island History* (1972): 35–52; Duane Lockard, *New England State Politics* (1959); Elmer E. Cornwell, "Party Absorption of Ethnic Groups: The Case of Providence, Rhode Island," *Social Forces* 38 (1960): 205–10; Murray S. Stedman and Susan W. Stedman, "Rise of the Democratic Party of Rhode Island," *New England Quarterly* 24 (1951): 329–39.)

John D. Buenker

RIIS, JACOB AUGUST (May 3, 1849–May 26, 1914). New York* journalist, leading advocate of housing reform,* and author of the phrase "How the Other Half Lives," Jacob Riis was born in Ribe, Denmark. He apprenticed as a carpenter in Copenhagen, then emigrated to the United States in 1870. After many odd jobs around New York, he became a police reporter for the *New York Tribune* in 1877, moving to the *New York Evening Sun* in 1888. While tracking down crime stories, he discovered how the "other half" lived in squalid tenements on the lower part of Manhattan; and he set out to expose their conditions to the public. With both pen and camera he documented the housing problems of the immigrant poor, culminating in the publication of his landmark book, *How the Other Half Lives*, in 1890. His efforts led directly to the razing of the Mulberry Bend tenement block and its replacement by a park. Indirectly, his exposés sparked a housing reform movement which led to a drastic revision of the building codes in 1901. Riis retired from the newspaper world in 1899 and spent the remainder of his life writing and lecturing. (Jacob A. Riis, *The Making of an American* (1901); Donald N. Bigelow, Introduction to the 1957 paperback edition of *How the Other Half Lives*; Roy Lubove, *The Progressives and the Slums: Tenement House Reform in New York City, 1890–1917* (1962).)

Edward R. Kantowicz

ROBINS, MARGARET DREIER (September 6, 1868–February 21, 1945). Social reformer and supporter of women's trade unions, Robins was born in Brooklyn to a German* merchant family. She was educated privately then engaged in a variety of volunteer activities considered suitable for an upper-class lady. In 1904, she and her sister Mary* joined the New York branch of the National Women's Trade Union League* (WTUL), Margaret becoming president. In 1905 she moved to Chicago and married Raymond Robins,* the head resident of Northwestern University Settlement House. From 1907 to 1922 she served as national president of the WTUL. She provided her greatest service to the labor movement during a series of garment workers' strikes in New York,* Philadelphia,* and Chicago* from 1909 to 1911. She supported Rose Schneiderman* and other working-class organizers with moral and financial support during the protracted strikes and helped gain favorable publicity and a certain amount of respectability for the strikers. (Mary Dreier, *Margaret Dreier Robins* (1950); Barbara Sicherman, et al., *Notable American Women: The Modern Period* (1980); *Dictionary of American Biography*, supplement 3.)

Edward R. Kantowicz

ROBINS, RAYMOND (September 17, 1873–September 26, 1954). Social reformer, social settlement* resident, and internationalist, Robins was born on Staten Island, New York, and worked his way across the country after his parents died, supporting himself with a series of mining jobs. He became a lawyer in California* in 1896 but abandoned the law for the Alaska gold fields, where he earned a fortune and underwent a religious experience. Dedicating his life to the downtrodden, he moved to Chicago* and served as superintendent of the Municipal Lodging House from 1901 to 1905, then as head resident of Northwestern University Settlement. With his wife, Margaret Dreier Robins,* whom he married in 1905, he supported a variety of political reform and trade union causes. President Woodrow Wilson* appointed him a member of the Red Cross mission to Russia after the Russian Revolution in 1917, and he became a friend of Lenin and Trotsky. Thereafter, he worked tirelessly to promote American recognition of the Soviet Union. (William Hard, *Raymond Robins' Own Story* (1920); Elizabeth Robins, *Raymond and I* (1956); William Appleman Williams, *American-Russian Relations, 1781–1947* (1952).)

Edward R. Kantowicz

ROBINSON, EDWIN ARLINGTON (December 22, 1869–April 6, 1935). Robinson, usually acknowledged as one of the great American poets, was born and raised in Maine. A descendant of Anne Bradstreet, he demonstrated his precocity by writing verse by the time he was eleven. He attended Harvard until his father's death forced him to quit and return home to Maine. Following the death of his mother in 1896, he moved to New York, where he developed a reputation as a melancholy hermit; his poetry was virtually ignored except for a modest reputation in England. Theodore Roosevelt* became interested in his work, however, and appointed him to the New York Custom House in 1905. Robinson endured the job until 1909 when he resigned, finding his home at the MacDowell Colony in Petersborough, New Hampshire, in 1913.

His most creative period came between 1915 and 1923, when his famous medieval narrative poems were conceived and written. Soon he became the acknowledged king of the colony, his reputation as a great American poet shared only with Robert Frost. As his fame spread, legends concerning his celibacy and probable alcoholism developed. It is generally agreed that his most celebrated poems (*Merlin*, 1917; *Lancelot*, 1920; and *Tristram*, 1927) are not his best or most enduring works. That honor is bestowed on his shorter works in which he generally dealt with the defeat of his characters by their society. (Hermann Hagedorn, *Edwin Arlington Robinson: A Biography* (1938); Wallace L. Anderson, *Edwin Arlington Robinson: A Critical Introduction* (1968); Louis Coxe, *Edwin Arlington Robinson: The Life of Poetry* (1969).)

Robert W. Schneider

ROBINSON, JAMES HARVEY (June 29, 1863–February 16, 1936). James Harvey Robinson, historian, educator, and popularizer, was born in Bloomington, Illinois, and attended the State Normal School in nearby Normal, where he developed a life-long interest in biology. He entered Harvard University in 1884, earning a bachelor's degree in 1887 and a master of arts degree in 1888. Study at the universities of Strassburg and Freiburg in Germany earned Robinson a doctorate from the latter institution in 1890, after he produced a dissertation on *The Original and Derived Features of the Constitution of the United States.* Following his education in Germany, Robinson taught history at the University of Pennsylvania from 1891 to 1895 before accepting the professorship of European history at Barnard College and Columbia University. Here Robinson developed a reputation as both a captivating lecturer and the leading exponent of the "New History"* that argued for the broadening of historical research beyond political concerns to include social, cultural, and intellectual subjects and that insisted on joining history with the social sciences as an agent of social reform.

Robinson resigned from Columbia in 1919, having written singly, or in collaboration with James Henry Breasted and Charles A. Beard,* a series of successful textbooks in European history. He joined Beard, Herbert Croly,* and Alvin Johnson, among others, in founding the New School for Social Research in 1919. Disagreements over the purpose of the New School led Robinson to resign from its faculty in 1921 and to devote himself to popular writing. (Luther

V. Hendricks, *James Harvey Robinson: Teacher of History* (1946); James Harvey Robinson, *The New History: Illustrating the Modern Historical Outlook* (1965).)

Morey Rothberg

ROCKEFELLER, JOHN DAVIDSON (July 8, 1839–May 23, 1937). Born in Richford, New York, Rockefeller invested in an oil refinery in 1863 and, by 1870, was president of Standard Oil Company of Ohio. Rockefeller was disturbed by intense competition and sought to bring order to the industry through virtual monopoly, first by control of oil refineries and then through vertical integration. Rockefeller found his vehicle for control with the first use of a trust in 1882, but it was found illegal by the Ohio Supreme Court in 1892. He next turned to the holding company in 1899, but it was also ordered dissolved by the U.S. Supreme Court in 1911 (*see Standard Oil v. U.S.*). Rockefeller was not content to settle for control of the American oil industry alone, as his company became the major international petroleum corporation. As is suggested by the judicial decisions against his activities, Rockefeller became a villain to much of the American public. First Henry Demarest Lloyd* (*Wealth against Commonwealth*, 1894) and then Ida M. Tarbell* (*History of the Standard Oil Company*, two volumes, 1904) published stinging critiques. Rockefeller devoted much of his later life to philanthropy. (Allan Nevins, *John D. Rockefeller: The Heroic Age of American Enterprise* (1940); Earl Latham, *John D. Rockefeller* (1949); David Freeman Hawke, *John D.: The Founding Father of the Rockefellers* (1980).)

Martin I. Elzy

ROOSEVELT, FRANKLIN DELANO (January 30, 1882–April 12, 1945). Born in Hyde Park, New York, of a prominent, wealthy family, Roosevelt was educated at home by tutors before attending Groton School, Harvard University, and Columbia Law School. Roosevelt clerked in a New York City law firm until his 1910 election to the New York State Senate. A candidate of the reform wing of the state's Democratic party,* Roosevelt endorsed the direct primary and spoke against machine control and corruption in the state legislature. In office, Roosevelt gave tepid support to labor and social reform, warmly endorsed political and government reform, and enthusiastically promoted conservation. He vigorously campaigned for Woodrow Wilson* in 1912 and was rewarded with the position of assistant secretary of the navy in 1913. Favoring a strong navy and often representing the views of the admirals, Roosevelt served throughout World War I* until resigning in August 1920, after accepting the Democratic nomination for vice president. James M. Cox* and Roosevelt endorsed progressivism and the League of Nations,* but were soundly defeated. Following a bout with polio in 1921, Roosevelt recovered to serve as governor of New York and president of the United States before his death in Warm Springs, Georgia. (Frank Freidel, *Franklin D. Roosevelt: The Apprenticeship* (1952);

James MacGregor Burns, *Roosevelt: The Lion and the Fox* (1956); Kenneth S. Davis, *FDR: The Beckoning of Destiny, 1882–1928* (1971).)

Martin I. Elzy

ROOSEVELT, THEODORE (October 27, 1858–January 6, 1919). When President William McKinley* died from an assassin's bullet on September 14, 1901, his vice president, Theodore Roosevelt, succeeded him. Though noisy and belligerent in temperament, Roosevelt was far more than a "damn cowboy." He was the most important publicist for progressive reform in the first decade of this century and one of the creators of the modern presidency. Born in New York City,* he was a sickly youth with asthma and poor eyesight; he overcompensated for his infirmities and became a physical fitness faddist, a sportsman, and something of a bully himself. Educated at Harvard and Columbia Law School, he plunged into politics, serving two terms in the New York state legislature from 1881 to 1884. After the death of his first wife in 1884, he temporarily withdrew from politics and headed out West, where he worked as a cowboy. Returning to New York, he ran unsuccessfully for mayor in 1886, was appointed civil service commissioner by President Benjamin Harrison in 1889, and police commissioner by New York mayor William Strong* in 1894. Serving as assistant secretary of the navy when the Spanish-American War* broke out, he volunteered for the Rough Rider cavalry regiment and earned a national reputation at the battle of San Juan Hill.

As president from 1901 to 1909, Roosevelt used his enormous gifts for gaining publicity to focus day-to-day attention on the White House for the first time, thus strengthening the office of the presidency. He believed that the president alone represented the national interest as a whole. As spokesman for the public interest, he arbitrated the 1902 anthracite coal strike,* instructed his Justice Department to prosecute the Northern Securities* railroad combine for antitrust* violations, and pushed the Pure Food and Drugs Act* through Congress. His crowning achievement was the Hepburn Act* of 1907, which empowered the Interstate Commerce Commission to regulate railroad rates. Though reputed to be a "trust-buster," Roosevelt actually preferred to regulate large corporations rather than break them up. His philosophy, which he later called the New Nationalism,* envisioned a vigorous economy of large corporations with a strong federal executive protecting the public interest. He worked toward a similar balance of power in foreign affairs, policed by advanced nations such as England and the United States acting in concert. Accordingly, he won the Nobel Peace Prize for his role in negotiating the Treaty of Portsmouth,* which ended the Russo-Japanese War in 1905.

Roosevelt declined to run for a third term in 1908, went off to Africa for a big game safari, then took a triumphal tour of Europe. Finding the Republican party* divided by the conservatism of his successor, William Howard Taft,* he threw himself into the 1910 off-year elections on the side of Insurgent* candidates, then challenged Taft for the presidential nomination in 1912. Failing to win the Republican nomination, he bolted the party and ran unsuccessfully on the third-party Progressive* ticket. (Theodore Roosevelt, *An Autobiography* (1913); Richard Hofstadter, "The Conservative as Progressive," in *The American Political Tradition* (1948); George E. Mowry, *The Era of Theodore Roosevelt* (1958); Howard K. Beale, *Theodore Roosevelt and the Rise of America to World Power* (1956); John Morton Blum, *The Republican Roosevelt* (1954).)

Edward R. Kantowicz

ROOSEVELT COROLLARY. In his annual message to Congress in December 1904, President Theodore Roosevelt* significantly altered the basic meaning of the Monroe Doctrine. Roosevelt transformed the doctrine from one which warned against intervention by foreign powers in the Western Hemisphere to one which sanctioned U.S. intervention in this region. As early as 1896, Roosevelt had argued that the Caribbean and Latin America must be protected from European intervention. Although he was alarmed over British involvement in Venezuela in the mid-1890s, Roosevelt was more disturbed about the threat of a German presence in the Caribbean. Like President William McKinley* and Secretaries of State John Hay and Elihu Root,* Roosevelt believed that Latin American republics, with their weak, inefficient governments and chaotic finances, presented inviting targets for European intervention.

In December 1902, Britain, Germany, and Italy, in an attempt to collect debts owed by Venezuela, blockaded five ports and shelled the fortress of Puerto Cabello. Since Britian and Germany had notified Washington of their proposed action and disclaimed any intention of seeking territorial compensation, the United States lodged no objection. Although the Venezuelan crisis was settled by the Hague Tribunal, this episode deepened Roosevelt's suspicions of German aims in the Caribbean. Following this crisis, the Dominican Republic was unable to pay its debts ($32,280,000)—two-thirds of which was owed to European nationals. During the winter of 1903–1904, France, Germany, and Italy threatened to intervene in the Dominican Republic. The president of the republic asked the United States to establish a protectorate over his country, but Roosevelt refused.

After careful consultation with Root, Roosevelt delivered his annual message to Congress on December 6, 1904. In 1905 the United States installed an American customs collector in the Dominican Republic to apportion all customs receipts according to current expenses and foreign debts. Roosevelt enforced this arrangement by executive agreement until 1907, when a treaty to that effect received Senate approval. The Taft administration, under the name of "dollar diplomacy," pursued a similar interventionist policy in Haiti and Nicaragua. Although Woodrow Wilson* denounced dollar diplomacy during the 1912 presidential campaign, his Latin American policy closely followed the pattern established under Roosevelt and William Howard Taft.* (Dexter Perkins, *The Monroe Doctrine, 1867–1907* (1937); Howard K. Beale, *Theodore Roosevelt and the Rise of America to World Power* (1956); Seward W. Livermore, "Theo-

dore Roosevelt, the American Navy, and the Venezuelan Crisis of 1902–1903,''
American Historical Review 51 (April 1946): 452–72.)

David E. Alsobrook

ROOT, ELIHU (February 15, 1845–February 7, 1937). Born in Clinton, New
York, Root received a law degree in 1867 and soon became prominent by
representing wealthy corporate clients. As a conservative New York Republican,
he often opposed the state's Republican machine and developed a long alliance
with Theodore Roosevelt.* Root also helped run the state constitutional conventions of 1894 and 1915. Serving as secretary of war from 1899 to 1903, Root
modernized the army through reorganizing and dealt with the recently acquired
territories of Puerto Rico, Cuba, and the Philippines. Becoming secretary of
state in 1905, he sought to improve relations with Latin America and Japan,
increase the use of arbitration treaties, and professionalize the State Department.
He received the Nobel Peace Prize in 1912 for his various international efforts.

Root represented New York in the U.S. Senate from 1909 to 1915. He sought
to prevent the rift between William Howard Taft* and Roosevelt, but presided
over the 1912 Republican national convention and supported Taft. He opposed
most of Woodrow Wilson's* foreign and domestic programs. Root was president
of the Carnegie Endowment for International Peace from 1910 to 1925. (Robert
Bacon and James Brown Scott, eds., *Addresses on International Subjects by
Elihu Root* (1916); Phillip C. Jessup, *Elihu Root* (1938); Richard W. Leopold,
Elihu Root and the Conservative Tradition (1954).)

Martin I. Elzy

ROSENWALD, JULIUS (August 12, 1862–January 6, 1932). Rosenwald was
born in Springfield, Illinois. After attending the local public schools, he entered
the clothing business, first in New York and then in Chicago. In 1895, he
purchased a one-quarter share in the young Sears, Roebuck and Company. A
supporter of political reform in Chicago, Rosenwald became one of the founders
of the Municipal Voters' League in 1896. He later served as chairman of the
city's Bureau of Public Efficiency and as a member of such semiofficial agencies
as the Chicago Plan Commission and the Chicago Vice Commission. At Sears,
meanwhile, he helped guide the company's tremendous growth, becoming president of the firm after 1910. In 1916, he instituted a pioneering profit-sharing
plan for his employees.

In the wider world, he became a major philanthropist, noted both for his own
contributions and for his stimulation of contributions from others. Though much
of this work was in his own Jewish community, Rosenwald actively championed
the advancement of American blacks, particularly in education and housing;
financed the founding of Chicago's Museum of Science and Industry; and gave
large sums to the University of Chicago. In 1917, he established the Julius
Rosenwald Fund to carry out his philanthropies; according to his wishes, the
agency spent itself out of existence by 1948. (M. R. Werner, *Julius Rosenwald:*

The Life of a Practical Humanitarian (1939); Alfred Q. Jarrette, *Julius Rosenwald: Benefactor of Mankind* (1975); Pauline Angell, "Julius Rosenwald," *American Jewish Yearbook* 34 (1932–1933): 141-76.)

John R. Schmidt

ROSS, EDWARD A. (December 12, 1886–July 22, 1951). A pioneer sociologist, Ross was born in Virden, Illinois; orphaned at an early age, he grew up in small-town Illinois and Iowa, areas he remembered for their intense, moralistic Protestantism. His academic interests took him to Coe College, to Germany for graduate study, and to the Johns Hopkins University for his Ph.D. degree. His first major academic appointment, at Stanford University, terminated in 1900 in a celebrated academic freedom case. After other university assignments, Ross arrived at the University of Wisconsin* in 1906, bringing with him a reputation, albeit an inflated one, for radicalism. Wisconsin had already established a record of academic progressivism, and Ross reinforced the work of Richard T. Ely,* his former teacher at Hopkins, and John R. Commons,* a former fellow student there.

Among Ross's prolific writings his famous study of 1904, *Social Control*, was the most influential, winning praise from Theodore Roosevelt.* Ross worried considerably about the many signs of social disintegration in America and of the attending "neurasthenia" that increasingly described the inner disorientation of people under conditions of modern technology and the rapid pace of urban life. Ross was also paranoid about the "new immigration"* to the United States, and his writings even show his distaste for the physical features of East Europeans. Always advocating the ideals of self-discipline and self-control, Ross strongly championed the Prohibition* movement and endorsed what he called "social religion" as a necessary vehicle of social cohesiveness and harmony. *Sin and Society* (1906) expresses with wit and sarcasm Ross's disdain for the moral corruption of modern business and its arrogant defiance of public ethics. (Julius Weinberg, *Edward Alsworth Ross and the Sociology of Progressivism* (1972); Edward A. Ross, *Seventy Years of It: An Autobiography* (1936); Arthur J. Vidich and Stanford Lyman, eds., "Secular Evangelicalism at the University of Wisconsin," in *American Sociology: Worldly Rejections of Religion and Their Directions* (1985).)

J. David Hoeveler, Jr.

ROYCE, JOSIAH (November 20, 1855–September 14, 1916). The last great champion of nineteenth-century religious idealism, Royce was the main philosophic opponent of pragmatism* and other forms of relativism. His idealism owed much to his youth in the pioneer settlement of Grass Valley, California, to the evangelical faith of his mother, and to the transcendental philosophy of Immanuel Kant and Hermann Lotze which he absorbed as a student in Germany. In 1882, armed with a Johns Hopkins Ph.D. and sponsorship by William James,* Royce began a lifelong career as a member of Harvard's preeminent philosophy department. His massive scholarship, most importantly displayed in *The World and the Individual* (1901), *The Philosophy of Loyalty* (1908), and *The Problem of Christianity* (1913), propounded an "idealistic socialism" in which an informed citizenry would sacrifice individual interest for the general welfare.

Royce used his breadth in theology, logic, mathematics, and history to argue for an Absolute, to which all meaning must ultimately relate, and stressed loyalty to that cosmic whole as the logical and moral basis for his readers to transform the flawed society around them into a "beloved community." Royce himself preferred to stress the spiritual rather than the reformist implications of his thought and so steadily lost ground to pragmatist opponents allied to progressive social action. World War I* completed Royce's eclipse, when loyalty to any absolute authority likewise became suspect. (John J. McDermott, ed., *The Basic Writings of Josiah Royce* (1969); John Clendenning, *The Life and Thought of Josiah Royce* (1985); Bruce Kuklick, *Josiah Royce: An Intellectual Biography* (1972).)

Alan Lawson

RUBINOW, ISSAC M. (April 19, 1875–September 1, 1936). Born in Grodno, Russia, Rubinow emigrated to the United States in 1893, received an A.B. degree from Columbia University in 1895, and a medical degree from New York University in 1898. From 1900 to 1903, Rubinow was a student of political science, receiving a Ph.D. from Columbia University in 1914. Practicing medicine among the poor, he became convinced that ill health was as much an economic as a medical problem.

In 1903, Rubinow abandoned his medical practice and became an expert in economics and statistics and a pioneer in the social security movement in the United States. His book, *Social Insurance*, published in 1913, became a standard in the field, and Rubinow spent his career campaigning on behalf of worker's compensation,* unemployment insurance, old-age pensions, and health insurance.* During his career, Rubinow held a number of positions with federal government agencies, including the U.S. Civil Service Commission, the Department of Agriculture, the Department of Labor,* and the Department of Commerce. He was a consultant on President Franklin Roosevelt's* Committee on Economic Security, which drafted the Social Security Act, and was active in the Zionist movement.* (J. Lee Kraeder, "Issac Max Rubinow: Pioneering Specialist in Social Insurance," *Social Science Review* 50 (1976): 402–25.)

Leon Applebaum

RULE OF REASON. The Sherman Antitrust Act of 1890 declared, in its opening sentence, "Every contract, combination in the form of trust or otherwise . . . in restraint of trade . . . is hereby declared to be illegal." Although the language of the act seemed remarkably clear and to the point, the phrase "restraint of trade" was nowhere defined in the text. It therefore devolved upon the judiciary to give the law operational meaning. Meanwhile, the profound economic movement which had produced large corporations in the first place actually intensified, and the judiciary's task grew commensurately more difficult. On the one hand, judges did not wish to condone the ruthless methods of big business; on the other hand, they were not about to construe the Sherman Act so literally as to dismember all of the firms that were bringing unprecedented growth to the American economy.

Thus, in the landmark *Standard Oil* case* (1911), the Supreme Court enunciated a "rule of reason," which magically allowed the economy to have it both ways. While ordering the breakup of Standard Oil into more than thirty separate parts, the Court went on to modify the stringency of the 1890 act by declaring that not every restraint of trade was illegal, only "unreasonable" ones. Chief Justice Edward White's* tortuous prose in the *Standard Oil* decision spawned a virtual new industry of interpretation; yet such circumlocution may have been necessary as a means of providing business managers, judges, and prosecutors with the maneuvering room to exercise their common sense in promoting competition. (Robert H. Bork, *The Antitrust Paradox* (1978); René Joliet, *The Rule of Reason in Antitrust Law* (1967); William Letwin, *Law and Economic Policy in America* (1965).)

Thomas K. McCraw

RURAL POST ROAD ACT. Enacted July 11, 1916, this act made federal money available on a dollar-matching basis to the states for the purpose of building roads within the states. The amount of federal money given a state was dependent upon the ratio that state bore to all other states in population, area, and the mileage of rural delivery and star route roads. The law was originally sponsored by agrarians in Congress who sought federal aid for the improvement of farm-to-market roads. Indispensable to their argument for such legislation was the development of the rural delivery of mail. Because the Post Office Department refused to deliver the mail to farmers whose roads were impassable, congressmen argued that it was the national government's duty to aid the farmers in the upkeep of their rural delivery roads. Constitutional scruples against the act were overcome by asserting that Congress had the authority to give aid to the states because rural route roads were post roads.

Bills proposing federal aid for the building and repair of rural route roads submitted to Congress in the early 1900s were resisted by urban members of Congress and by automobile enthusiasts who preferred building major highways to improving rural, farm-to-market roads. Compromise between the farmers and automobilists came in 1916 when the proposed law was altered to permit the building or improving of either rural roads or major highways. (Wayne E. Fuller, *RFD: The Changing Face of Rural America* (1964); W. Stull Holt, *The Bureau of Public Roads* (1923); Frederic L. Paxson, "The Highway Movement, 1916–1935," *American Historical Review* 51 (1946): 236–53.)

Wayne E. Fuller

RUSSELL, CHARLES EDWARD (September 25, 1860–April 23, 1941). Born in Davenport, Iowa, Russell was educated at the Saint Johnsbury Academy, Vermont. Russell was a writer and editor, working successively for the New

York *World*, the *New York American*, and Hearst's* *Chicago American* between 1894 and 1902. The author of numerous books on social questions, he wrote muckraking* articles for a variety of magazines and was esteemed among the finest of reform journalists. His articles on the "Beef Trust," convict labor in Georgia, and the tenements of New York's Trinity Church attracted particular acclaim.

He joined the Socialist party* in 1908 and always held to the tenets of democratic socialism even after the party expelled him in 1917 over his support of the American war effort. In 1909, Russell became one of the five founders of the National Association for the Advancement of Colored People.* He was twice the Socialist candidate for governor of New York and also ran for mayor of New York City* and for the U.S. Senate on the Socialist ticket. In 1917, he served with Elihu Root's* mission to Russia and was named to the president's Industrial Commission in 1919; the same year he was appointed the Committee on Public Information's* commissioner to Great Britain and Ireland. (Charles E. Russell, *Bare Hands and Stone Walls* (1933); David M. Chalmers, *The Social and Political Ideas of the Muckrakers* (1964); Charles F. Kellogg, *The National Association for the Advancement of Colored People, 1909–1920* (1967).)

Lloyd J. Graybar

RYAN, JOHN A. (REV.) (May 25, 1869–September 16, 1945). A Roman Catholic priest-scholar, defender of the rights of labor unions, intellectual godfather of the minimum wage law, Ryan was a spokesman for what could be called a Catholic Social Gospel.* The oldest of eleven children born on a Minnesota farm, Ryan imbibed the spirit of Populism* preached by Ignatius Donnelly. In the seminary of the Saint Paul Archdiocese, his social conscience was further aroused by a reading of Pope Leo XIII's encyclical *Rerum Novarum*. Ordained by Archbishop John Ireland in 1898, Father Ryan received a doctorate in moral theology from the Catholic University of America in Washington, D.C., then began a career of teaching and scholarship, first at Saint Paul Seminary, then after 1915, at Catholic University. His doctoral dissertation, published as *The Living Wage* (1906), provided the intellectual underpinning for minimum wage laws. Ryan's phrase "the living wage" turned up in the Progressive party's* 1912 national platform, and the priest served on the committee of the National Consumers' League,* which wrote the model state minimum wage law. (John A. Ryan, *Social Doctrine in Action: A Personal History* (1941); Francis L. Broderick, *Right Reverend New Dealer: John A. Ryan* (1963); Andrew M. Greeley, *The Catholic Experience* (1965).)

Edward R. Kantowicz

RYAN, THOMAS FORTUNE (October 17, 1851–November 23, 1928). Born in Nelson County, Virginia, Ryan was orphaned at an early age, and his rise from penniless youth to multimillionaire epitomized the "rags-to-riches" ethos. He worked as a messenger for firms in Baltimore and New York City, and purchased a seat on the New York Stock Exchange the following year. His rapidly developing business acumen, genius for organization, and adroit manipulation of persons, legalities, and circumstances soon made him a dominant figure in the development of New York's metropolitan street railway system. Building on success as a public utilities magnate, Ryan played an immensely profitable role in the formative stages of the American Tobacco Company;* purchased a controlling interest in the Equitable Life Assurance Company in 1905; speculated in banks, railroads, and coal mines; and acquired lucrative mining concessions in the Congo Free State (1906) and Portuguese Angola (1912).

A conservative, states' rights Democrat and longtime associate of Tammany Hall,* he sought to prevent the national Democratic party* from succumbing to Bryanite "free silver" agitation in the 1890s and to "centralizing," antibusiness propensities in subsequent decades. He helped to engineer Alton B. Parker's* successful bid for the 1904 Democratic presidential nomination and contributed $400,000 to Parker's ill-fated campaign against Theodore Roosevelt.* Maintaining a residence in Virginia, Ryan established close ties to political leaders there and served as one of the state's delegates to Democratic national conventions in 1904 and 1912. On the latter occasion he was vehemently criticized by William Jennings Bryan,* who obtained passage of a resolution denouncing the influence of Ryan and other capitalists on the party. (*Dictionary of American Biography* vol. 16; R. Carlyle Buley, *The Equitable Life Assurance Society of the United States, 1859–1964* (1967); William Larsen, *Montague of Virginia: The Making of a Southern Progressive* (1965).)

James Tice Moore

S

SABATH, ADOLPH JOSEPH (April 4, 1866–November 6, 1952). Born in Zabori, Bohemia, Sabath emigrated to America in 1881 and earned a law degree in Chicago, but soon found politics to be his main vocation. In the 1890s, he served as police magistrate in the municipal courts and for four years was chairman of the Cook County Democratic Executive Committee. Sabath's political involvement was intertwined with his Bohemian-Czech ancestry and his Jewish religion. Along with several other nationality leaders in Chicago, he emerged as an ethnic spokesman who helped bridge the immigrant's assimilation gap in his adopted country. Sabath was difficult to label: he refused to accept progressive reform because of some of its antiethnic implications, but at the same time he stood apart from traditional machine politicians whose methods he often deplored. In 1907, Sabath was elected to Congress and served for nearly a half century. He gained his greatest notoriety by leading the fight against the 1924 immigration restriction* bill. He built and financed a home for the poor in his native Czechoslovakia and wrote and talked about the need for understanding the ethnic experience in America. (John M. Allswang, *A House for All Peoples* (1971); Alex Gottfried, *Boss Cermak of Chicago* (1963); Daniel Droba, ed., *Czech and Slovak Leaders in Metropolitan Chicago* (1934).)

Paul Michael Green

SABBATARIANISM was the movement to keep Sunday as the Lord's Day by attendance at church and abstention from work and public amusements. Laws banning the sale of liquor on Sundays had been passed by nearly all states and municipalities in the early nineteenth century under the influence of evangelical Protestant revivals. Sabbatarians lobbied the federal government in the 1830s to stop running mail trains on Sundays, and protested the opening of the 1876 Centennial Exposition in Philadelphia on Sundays. By the turn of the century,

Sabbatarianism was fighting a rearguard, holding action, aimed at the retention and enforcement of Sunday-closing laws for saloons.

This issue pitted middle-class, Anglo-Saxon Protestants against working-class immigrant Catholics and Jews, who saw no harm in drinking beer or wine on Sunday. German-Americans,* in particular, had a long tradition of Sunday merriment called the ''Continental Sabbath.'' Sunday-closing laws posed sharp dilemmas for city politicians and police, who often evaded the law by allowing side doors of saloons to remain open. They also presented opportunities for corruption, as many policemen demanded bribes from saloonkeepers before they would relax the law. Sabbatarianism formed part of the moral reform wing of progressivism, along with Prohibition* and social hygiene.* (Perry R. Duis, *The Saloon* (1983); Sydney E. Ahlstrom, *A Religious History of the American People* (1972).)

Edward R. Kantowicz

SAINT LOUIS. Saint Louis had battled Chicago* throughout the nineteenth century in an urban rivalry for dominance of the heartland, but the triumph of the railroad over water transport earned the victory for Chicago. Still, Saint Louis remained the nation's fourth largest city at the turn of the century, counting 451,770 inhabitants in 1890 and growing to 772,897 by 1920. It had a heavy concentration of German-Americans* and the third largest black* population in the nation. The city hosted the Louisiana Purchase Exposition in 1903–1904 and the Democratic National Convention in 1916. A bipartisan ''Combine'' of corrupt officeholders, directed by Democratic boss Edward Butler, the ''millionaire blacksmith,'' dominated Saint Louis politics at the turn of the century. Muckraker* Lincoln Steffens* brought notoriety to the city with his 1902 article, ''Tweed Days in St. Louis,'' later included in his book *The Shame of the Cities*.

The Jefferson Club, an association of reform Democrats, elected Rolla Wells mayor and Joseph W. Folk* circuit attorney in 1900. Folk refused to hire the assistant attorneys recommended by Boss Butler, and he swiftly brought indictments for vote fraud against seventeen Democrats and fifteen Republicans. In 1902 he convicted Butler of bribery, but the state supreme court overturned the verdict. Folk served as governor of Missouri from 1904 to 1908 and secured many progressive reforms. In 1914 a new city charter abolished the bicameral city council which had led to so much inefficiency and corruption. Moderate Republican Henry W. Kiel presided over the streamlined city government from 1913 to 1925, the longest mayoral tenure up to that time. Saint Louis was a mature city with a low percentage of foreign-born and a relatively stagnant economy, but it remained an important regional marketing and manufacturing center. (Ernest Kirschten, *Catfish and Crystal* (1960); Louis G. Geiger, *Joseph*

W. *Folk of Missouri* (1953); Selwyn K. Troen and Glen E. Holt, *St. Louis: A Documentary History* (1977).)

Edward R. Kantowicz

SAN FRANCISCO. The largest city and the dominant port on the West Coast, San Francisco in 1890 counted 298,997 inhabitants and occupied forty-two square miles, draped across steep hills on a peninsula between ocean and bay. By 1920, it had grown to a population of 506,676; but Los Angeles* had edged ahead of it to assume first rank on the Pacific Coast. The Bay City had a sizable immigrant community, with the Irish,* Germans,* and Italians* most prominent, and it was heavily Catholic, Democratic, and unionist. The Democratic machine of Christopher A. Buckley dominated San Francisco politics in the late nineteenth century; but in 1896 James D. Phelan,* a wealthy Democratic reformer, won the first of his three two-year terms as mayor. Phelan secured a revised city charter in 1898, administered the city honestly and economically, and struggled for municipal ownership of utilities.* During the 1901 union campaign for the closed shop, however, he sided with the employers and hired special police to break a strike. The outraged unionists bolted the Democratic party* and organized the Union Labor party, which was cynically manipulated by Republican boss Abraham Ruef. Ruef and the Labor party elected a popular member of the musicians' union, Eugene Schmitz, as mayor in 1902.

On April 18, 1906, a massive earthquake rocked the Bay City. Fires raged until April 21, killing over 400 people and destroying 28,000 buildings. The year before, former mayor Phelan had invited Daniel Burnham* to prepare a plan for the city; but it was largely ignored as Mayor Schmitz rallied the business community to rebuild the city rapidly. Only a few boulevards and an impressive civic center were built according to Burnham's monumental plan.

Six months after the quake, James Phelan and newspaper publisher Fremont Older, with the connivance of President Theodore Roosevelt,* mounted a legal attack on the corrupt Ruef-Schmitz machine. Special prosecutor Francis J. Heney* hired nationally famous detective William J. Burns to investigate; and on November 7, 1906, they indicted Ruef and began two years of graft prosecution trials, which broke Ruef's power and resulted in his imprisonment. The final years of the period were more placid politically, as a bipartisan coalition of business interests supported James ''Sunny Jim'' Rolph, who administered city government from 1912 to 1930, longer than any other San Francisco mayor. (George E. Mowry, *The California Progressives* (1951); Walton Bean, *Boss Ruef's San Francisco: The Story of the Union Labor Party, Big Business, and the Graft Prosecution (1952);* Judd Kahn, *Imperial San Francisco: Politics and Planning in an American City, 1897–1906* (1979); William Issel and Robert W.

Cherny, *San Francisco, 1865–1932: Politics, Power, and Urban Development* (1986).)

Edward R. Kantowicz

SANGER, MARGARET (née HIGGINS) (September 14, 1879–September 6, 1966). Born in Corning, New York, Sanger emerged between 1913 and 1917 as the charismatic leader of the birth control movement in the United States. The third daughter in a family of eleven, she resented the poverty of her family and blamed the death of her mother at the age of forty-nine on the burdens of parenthood. In 1910, Sanger sought an alternative to life as a suburban housewife and tubercular mother of three by moving to Manhattan and participating in radical politics. She first gained notoriety in 1912–1914 as an organizer for the Industrial Workers of the World* and a radical journalist.

Influenced by her experience as a home nurse, Sanger decided that women needed special advocacy in the struggle for social justice* and used the limitations on access to contraception as the primary symbol of female oppression. She developed the strategy of justifying contraception by publicizing the number of working-class women who died from septic abortion and kept her cause before the public through flamboyant defiance of the Comstock laws. Her arrest in 1916 for operating a contraceptive advice center led to a 1918 New York State court decision that found contraceptive advice by a physician legal.

In response to this decision, and influenced by society women who proved her most consistent sources of support, Sanger gradually abandoned the posture of militant woman rebel and developed a new image as a married mother lobbying among legislators and professional elites. She founded the American Birth Control League in 1921, opened the first doctor-staffed birth control clinic in the United States in 1923, and, in the *One Package* decision of 1936, finally won the right of physicians to give contraceptive advice. (James Reed, *The Birth Control Movement and American Society* (1984).)

James Reed

SCANDINAVIAN-AMERICANS. The four Scandinavian countries contributed over 2.5 million immigrants to the United States between the 1840s and the 1920s. Most came from backgrounds as farm tenants or laborers, though farm owners and professionals, and increasingly after 1890, urban laborers, also joined the immigrant stream. Settlement was heaviest on the farms of the Middle West and Plains states with urban and other rural concentrations scattered across the country.

Politically, most of the Scandinavians moved into the Republican party,* in part because of agreement with its stand on cultural issues such as Prohibition* and Sunday blue laws* and in part due to the Democratic party's* identification with what for them were negative reference groups such as urban Catholic Irish and proslavery, antiunion Southerners. An exception to this pattern would be the significant minority of Finnish voters who backed socialist parties. Defections from this pattern occurred when legislatures in Wisconsin* and Illinois* tried to force English language use on church-related schools and when both major parties ignored the concerns of the farmers in the 1890s. The Populist party* and later the Nonpartisan League* made major inroads into Scandinavian Republicanism especially in western Minnesota* and the Dakotas.

The progressive movement of the early twentieth century drew even more strongly from Scandinavian voters. Affected by a traditional distrust of big business and resentment of Yankee control of the regular Republican party, a majority of Scandinavian voters turned to progressive leaders like Robert La Follette* of Wisconsin. This move was solidified when prominent Scandinavians received recognition in progressive leadership ranks and even more, by mid-western and western progressive opposition to World War I,* a war Scandinavians saw as representing the interests of big business and munitions makers. These same voters gave strong support to La Follette's presidential campaign in 1924, an election which served as a bridge for many of them to the Democratic party. (Stephan Thernstram, ed., *Harvard Encyclopedia of American Ethnic Groups* (1980) (See especially pp. 362–70, 273–82, 750–61, and 971–81); David L. Brye, "Wisconsin Scandinavians and Progressivism, 1900–1950," *Norwegian American Studies* 27 (1977): 163–93.)

David L. Brye

SCHNEIDERMAN, ROSE (April 6, 1882–August 11, 1972). Born in Saven, Poland, Rose Schneiderman immigrated to the United States in 1890. At work since age thirteen, she helped form the first women's local of the Jewish Socialist United Cloth Hat and Cap Makers' Union in 1903. Two years later she joined the capmakers' successful strike and emerged a seasoned and militant labor activist. Despite initial reservations about the middle- and upper-class "allies," Schneiderman made the National Women's Trade Union League (WTUL)* her organizational home after 1907. In 1910, she became a full-time organizer, played a major role in the 1909–1914 organizing drive in the garment industry, and remained active in the New York league for thirty-five years.

Although the condition of wage-earning women remained her primary interest, Schneiderman participated in the campaigns for woman suffrage* and in 1919 attended the Paris Peace Conference. As president of the New York WTUL (1918–1949) she opposed the Equal Rights Amendment and continued to lobby for protective legislation for women workers. She served as the only woman on the labor advisory board of the National Recovery Act from 1933 until its dismantlement in 1935. (Rose Schneiderman, *All for One* (1967); Nancy Schrom Dye, *As Equals and as Sisters: Feminism, the Labor Movement and the Women's Trade Union League of New York* (1980); Ellen C. Lagemann, *A Generation of*

Women: Education in the Lives of Progressive Reformers (1979); Schneiderman's papers are located at the Tamiment Library, New York University.)

Mari Jo Buhle

SCHOOL AND SOCIETY. A weekly founded, owned, and edited by Columbia psychologist James McKeen Cattell,* *School and Society* first appeared on January 2, 1915. Reflecting Cattell's desire to link theory and application, *School and Society*, while not primarily a research journal, extensively covered pedagogy, educational philosophy, learning theory, testing, and science teaching. It also included many features to keep teachers professionally current: reviews, organizational reports, excerpts from press and periodicals, addresses by educators, and wide coverage of educational trends and events—everything from "The Salaries of Teachers in the District of Columbia" to "University Reform in India."

The journal covered all levels of education; it particularly registered the growing sense of professional identity among college professors. Cattell's *University Control* (1913) had urged more faculty power, and he helped found the American Association of University Professors* (AAUP). *School and Society* was one of the few educational journals consistently to side with professors and criticize the Carnegie Foundation's pension system; kept tabs on governance issues, the AAUP, and academic freedom (Cattell himself was fired from Columbia in 1917—in part for his stand against military conscription), and, particularly in 1919–1920, after five years of falling real salaries, reported on the pay situation at dozens of institutions. (William C. Brickman, "A Half-Century of *School and Society*," *School and Society* (January 23, 1965): 34–39; Richard Hofstadter and Walter P. Metzger, *The Development of Academic Freedom in the United States* (1955).)

Frank Stricker

SCIENTIFIC MANAGEMENT. Scientific management was the name given to Frederick W. Taylor's* system of management which he developed over the years 1880–1910. Taylor saw his system at first principally as a method of business therapy, then as a science of work, and ultimately as a social program. Actually, all of these components were inherent in his scheme almost from the beginning. When Taylor first proposed his piece-rate system, he insisted that it be "scientific." That insistence led him to a complete reorganization of the factory, men and machines, into a planned and integrated arrangement that would yield maximum productivity. Taylor thought his program was scientific because it was based upon careful observation, measurement, experiment, and generalization. He thought it would bring social harmony because it promised to free the productive powers of society, making the economic surplus so large that quarrels over its division would become innocuous.

It was Louis D. Brandeis,* in his argument before the Interstate Commerce Commission at the Eastern Rate Case (1910–1911), who brought the Taylor system to the attention of a broad public and fixed the name Scientific Management upon it. Brandeis put Taylor and his disciples on the witness stand to show that the railroads were inefficient, that they could cut costs and even raise wages without any rate increase. Brandeis's presentation captured the imagination of a wide assortment of progressive reformers and Socialists, ranging from Ida Tarbell,* Herbert Croly,* and Walter Lippmann,* to John Spargo* and Algie Simons.* Scientific Management could be used to point to the inefficiencies in society, to suggest a new role for experts and planning, and even to indicate the possibilities of a future social harmony.

The Eastern Rate Case touched off an "efficiency craze," lasting almost until American entry into World War I,* in which reformers attempted to apply Taylor's methods to a wide variety of political and social issues. The favorable response of reformers to Scientific Management also affected Morris Llewellyn Cooke,* who took an active part in reform politics and urged cooperation between Scientific Management and the trade unions. However, there was an unavoidable conflict between Scientific Management's assertion of expert authority and received notions of democracy. One of Taylor's principal dicta was that the man who does the work cannot understand its science and therefore must submit to the direction of the expert who can. Such assertions made Scientific Management attractive to many at home and abroad who wished to revamp traditional notions of democracy and helps explain, in part, Lenin's enthusiastic adoption of Taylorism. In broadest terms, Scientific Management epitomized the entry of scientific technique and authority into the factory and the world beyond. (Frank Barkley Copley, *Frederick W. Taylor: Father of Scientific Management* (1923); Samuel Haber, *Efficiency and Uplift: Scientific Management in the Progressive Era, 1890–1920* (1964); Judith A. Merkle, *Management and Ideology: The Legacy of the International Scientific Management Movement* (1980).)

Samuel Haber

SCUDDER, VIDA (December 15, 1861–October 9, 1954). Educator and social activist, Scudder was born of missionary parents in India. A graduate of Smith College (1884), she did postgraduate work at Oxford before accepting a teaching position at Wellesley in 1887, where she remained the rest of her life. Imbued with a sense of social justice* and a deep faith in Episcopalianism, Scudder advocated the application of Christian principles to social and industrial relations. Her inspiring course on "Social Ideals in English Literature" was the basis for several books on literary, religious, and social issues.

With other Smith graduates in 1887, Scudder founded the College Settlements Association, and was a leader of Denison House in Boston, where she lived in the mid-1890s. She also helped organize the National Women's Trade Union League* in 1903 and was a delegate to the Boston Central Labor Union. Her stirring speech at the Lawrence textile strike* in 1912 brought her into conflict with Wellesley trustees. Long a member of the Society of Christian Socialists and the Christian Social Union, Scudder joined the Socialist party,* founded the

Episcopal Church Socialist League in 1911, and later joined the Church League
for Industrial Democracy and the Intercollegiate Socialist Society. (Theresa S. C.
Corcoran, "Vida Dutton Scudder: The Progressive Years" (Ph.D. diss., Georgetown University, 1973); Peter J. Frederick, "The Professor as Social Activist,"
New England Quarterly 43 (1970): 407–33; Vida Scudder, *On January* (1937).)

Peter J. Frederick

SEASONGOOD, MURRAY (October 27, 1878–February 21, 1983). The
leader of the celebrated Cincinnati* progressive municipal reform movement of
the 1920s, Murray Seasongood was born of German-Jewish immigrant parents.
After receiving his A.B. with honors from Harvard in 1900 and his LL.B. from
Harvard Law School in 1903, Seasongood soon established himself as a leading
trial lawyer in Cincinnati. Although a "Roosevelt Republican," the lawyer took
little interest in politics, until he became aroused by deteriorating conditions in
his city under the political domination of Rudolph K. "Rud" Hynicka, the
successor to the famous "boss" George B. Cox.

After 1915, Seasongood became an increasingly vocal critic of Hynicka's
political organization, until in 1923 in a speech labeled "The Shot Heard 'Round
the Ward," he opposed a tax levy submitted by Hynicka's city administration.
This 1923 campaign led to the formation of the City Charter Committee in 1924.
In an exciting campaign in 1924, Seasongood led a successful effort to bring
the council-manager system to Cincinnati, and in 1924 the reformers captured
the city, with Seasongood serving two terms as mayor from 1926 to 1930.
Seasongood epitomized the "urban gentry" type of progressivism, with an un-
yielding reform philosophy that emphasized efficiency, businesslike administration of local government, faith in civil service,* and a highly moral judgment
of political corruption. After leaving the mayoralty, he became a champion for
this progressive ideal as president of the National Municipal League* from 1931
to 1934. (William A. Baughin, *Murray Seasongood and Cincinnati Reform in
the 1920s* (forthcoming, 1988).)

William A. Baughin

SEATTLE. Two of the dominant reform issues in Progressive Era Seattle had
emerged in the turbulent politics of the 1890s when the Populist party* provided
a means by which reformers of various persuasions could unite. Populists, Single-
Taxers,* Prohibitionists, and advocates of a labor party found common cause
in the municipal ownership* of public utilities* and the democratization of
government through direct legislation. Reform leaders emphasized the economic
advantages of municipal ownership and the effect direct legislation would have
in empowering labor and the lower middle class. But as they experienced great
difficulty in carrying these issues in elections, reformers attempted to broaden
their political base.

Adopting nonpartisanship as a third reform objective, they sought voter support
on issues unimpeded by traditional party affiliations. They successfully enlisted

the backing of middle-class voters who were attracted to municipal ownership as a means to eradicate the corruption and bribery popularly associated with public utilities and who saw direct legislation as a way to secure honest and efficient government by making officeholders responsible to the voters. A nonpartisan City party led in securing charter amendments to provide for the initiative,* referendum,* and recall* in city affairs (1908) and the designation of city elections as nonpartisan (1910). (Roger Sale, *Seattle, Past to Present* (1976); Robert D. Saltvig, "The Progressive Movement in Washington" (Ph.D. diss., University of Washington, 1966).)

Robert D. Saltvig

SEATTLE GENERAL STRIKE. In February 1919, Seattle was a strong, closed-shop, American Federation of Labor* (AFL) town, its Central Labor Council lending class-consciousness and solidarity to the labor movement. In January, the Metal Trades Council requested a wage increase for shipyard workers that exceeded the maximum allowed by the Emergency Fleet Corporation's Macy Board. When their request was disallowed, shipyard workers not only struck, but asked the Central to call a general strike in sympathy. Regarding the interests of all organized labor at issue and anticipating the opening of an open-shop campaign, the Central Labor Council cooperated. A General Strike Committee was organized and, without stating the objectives of the strike or under what circumstances it would end, called for the strike to begin on February 6.

When the day came, some 60,000 AFL workers walked off their jobs, and the economic life of the city came to a halt. To many in the community, though, the strike represented not a labor weapon but a revolutionary act, an impression supported by statements of some labor radicals. Although the Strike Committee officially ended the strike on February 11, many workers had already drifted back to their jobs. Labor had been highly successful in organizing the strike, maintaining order, and providing essential services, but failed to secure the demands of the shipyard workers or any other stated objectives. (Robert Friedheim, *The Seattle General Strike* (1964).)

Robert D. Saltvig

SEDITION ACT. Enacted on May 16, 1918, this law expanded the Espionage Act of 1917,* a relatively narrow measure which prohibited intentional interference with the military. Some U.S. attorneys and district judges construed the law more broadly, however, and the sedition law was intended to provide a legal basis for punishing "disloyal" statements. The Wilson* administration also claimed this law was necessary for deterring vigilantism and for defeating a proposal in Congress to try war critics in military courts.

The new law prohibited any statement which interfered with the war effort or was abusive toward the U.S. government, constitution, military, or flag. Punishment included fines of up to $10,000 and twenty years in prison. Despite token warnings, officials applied the law in wildly uneven fashion: half the prosecutions came from thirteen of the eighty-seven districts. People were convicted for anticapitalist, prewar, or private statements. By 1921, when the sedition law expired, the Justice Department had brought 2,168 cases and won 1,055 convictions under this and the espionage laws. In 1919 the Supreme Court upheld the law, in *Abrams v. United States*, but the case prompted a notable dissent by Justice Oliver Wendell Holmes, Jr.,* which stimulated public support of free speech and civil liberties. (Paul L. Murphy, *World War I and the Origin of Civil Liberties in the United States* (1979); Harry N. Scheiber, *The Wilson Administration and Civil Liberties, 1917–1921* (1960); H. C. Peterson and Gilbert C. Fite, *Opponents of War, 1917–1918* (1957).)

Philip R. VanderMeer

SEGREGATION. Segregation, a system of separate public facilities for whites and blacks, was decreed by the so-called Jim Crow laws in the southern states after the Civil War. Slavery, of course, had provided a complete system of social control over the black race. Slaves enjoyed no legal rights, they could not vote, and they were excluded from public facilities. When the Thirteenth Amendment to the Constitution emancipated the slaves in 1865, the entire fabric of race relations needed to be reconstructed. The states granted freedmen a modicum of legal rights: they could own property, validly marry, and testify in court. While the radical Republicans in Congress controlled the process of reconstruction, blacks were also allowed to vote and hold office. White Southerners, however, had no intention of letting blacks mix freely with whites in public places, so they attempted to exclude blacks altogether from schools, public transportation, theatres, and parks. Congress responded by passing the Fourteenth Amendment (1868), which decreed "equal protection of the laws" for all citizens, and the Civil Rights Act (1875), providing for equal access to public accommodations.

However, after the president withdrew the last federal troops from the South in 1877 and the Supreme Court found the Civil Rights Act unconstitutional, the South had a free hand to devise its own rules for race relations. The southern states passed Jim Crow segregation laws in the last two decades of the nineteenth century and the first decade of the twentieth, decreeing "separate but equal" accommodations for blacks and whites. When blacks challenged a Louisiana* law mandating segregated railroad cars, the U.S. Supreme Court upheld the separate but equal doctrine in the case of *Plessy v. Ferguson** (1896). In practice, the separate facilities provided in southern states tended to be unequal. Blacks were assigned to inferior seats in theatres and railcars, often in the smoking section; and states spent far less money on black schools than white schools.

Jim Crow segregation formed just one part of a total system of race control. States disfranchised* blacks through a series of devices, such as poll taxes, discriminatory literacy tests, and all-white primaries. They also attempted to retain a cheap, repressed labor force with unfair sharecropping contracts, vagrancy laws, and widespread use of convict labor on chain gangs. In sum, white

Southerners constructed a system of segregation, disfranchisement, and labor control as a substitute for slavery, a means of maintaining white supremacy without slavery. This system was sanctioned by law in the 1890s and remained intact until challenged by the civil rights movement in the mid-twentieth century and overturned by federal law in the 1960s. (C. Vann Woodward, *The Strange Career of Jim Crow* (1955); Howard Rabinowitz, *Race Relations in the Urban South* (1978); George M. Fredrickson, *White Supremacy* (1981).)

Edward R. Kantowicz

SELECTIVE SERVICE. The modern American military draft—selective national conscription operated through a Selective Service System—was first established in the United States during World War I.* In 1915–1917, a movement to authorize a national reserve force based upon a permanent system of short-term universal military training and service failed, but this "preparedness"* movement helped to convince many Americans of the efficacy of a selective draft over a purely volunteer system for raising mass wartime armies equitably and with minimal disruption to the economy. Thus, the Wilson* administration, despite considerable hostility toward the war and the draft in the agrarian South and West, was able to obtain from Congress a selective national wartime draft in 1917.

Brig. Gen. Enoch H. Crowder, the army's chief legal officer, devised an organization of "supervised decentralization" called the Selective Service System. Some 4,000 local draft boards composed of civilian members of the community decided on the induction or deferment of particular individuals within overall guidelines established by Congress, the administration, and military officials in Crowder's office. During the war, Selective Service effectively registered 23.9 million Americans and drafted 2.8 million men. In all, 72 percent of the 4-million-man wartime army was raised through conscription, the constitutionality of which was upheld by the Supreme Court in *Arver v. U.S.* (1918). Some 338,000 men (12 percent of those actually drafted) failed to report or deserted after arrival at training camp, but despite such evasion, there was little overt resistance. A number of potential resisters became conscientious objectors.* Compared to the Civil War, Selective Service in 1917–1918 proved highly successful in raising a mass army. (John W. Chambers II, *Draftees or Volunteers* (1976); John W. Chambers II, *To Raise an Army: The Draft Comes to Modern America* (1987).)

John Whiteclay Chambers II

SELIGMAN, EDWIN R. A. (April 25, 1861–July 18, 1939). Born in New York and educated at Columbia University, Seligman received his A.B. in 1879, A.M. and LL.B in 1884, Ph.D. in 1885, and LL.D in 1904. Seligman spent his entire academic life at Columbia University, commencing as a lecturer in 1885 and becoming the first McVickar Professor of Political Economy, a chair he held from 1904 to 1931. Seligman was known for his pioneering work in taxation and public finance and was an advocate of the progressive income tax.* At Columbia, he taught mainly political economy and the history of economic doctrines.

Seligman took an active interest in public affairs and lent his expertise to numerous local, state, and national committees and commissions. He was a founder of the American Economic Association* and served as its president from 1902 to 1904. He served as president of the National Tax Association* from 1913 to 1915 and played an instrumental role in the founding of the American Association of University Professors,* serving as its president from 1919 to 1920. Seligman served as editor of the Columbia Series in History, Economics and Public Law and the *Political Science Quarterly*, and as editor in chief of the prestigious fifteen-volume *Encyclopedia of the Social Sciences*. (Clifton K. Yearley, *The Money Machines* (1970).)

Leon Applebaum

SHAW, ALBERT (July 23, 1887–June 28, 1947). Born in Paddy's Run (later Shandon), Ohio, Shaw graduated from Iowa (now Grinnell) College in 1879. His early career included a valuable period on the *Grinnell Herald* and then the post of chief editorial writer on the *Minneapolis Tribune*, which he left to undertake postgraduate studies. At the Johns Hopkins University, where in 1884 he took the Ph.D. in history and political economy, he also began a lifelong friendship with Woodrow Wilson.* Shaw, a Republican, was a scholar of urban reform, writing acclaimed monographs and articles on European and British municipal government.

From 1891 to 1937, Shaw was editor and publisher of the *Review of Reviews*,* one of the first American magazines to concentrate on reporting and commentary on the events of the day. A respected public figure, he spoke widely and participated in many civic and charitable causes. Shaw was a friend and frequent adviser to Theodore Roosevelt,* supporting his stands on most public issues and joining him in the Progressive party* in 1912, but was still able to support many of Wilson's early reforms. After World War I,* he endorsed American entrance into the League of Nations.* (Lloyd J. Graybar, *Albert Shaw of the "Review of Reviews": An Intellectual Biography* (1974); Lloyd J. Graybar, "Albert Shaw's Search for the Ideal City," *Historian* 34 (1972): 421–36; Lloyd J. Graybar, "Albert Shaw's Ohio Youth," *Ohio History* 74 (1965): 29–34.)

Lloyd J. Graybar

SHAW, ANNA HOWARD (February 14, 1847–July 2, 1919). One of the few prominent suffragists who rose from the lower classes, Shaw was the most outstanding orator produced by the woman's rights movement. Born in Newcastle-on-Tyne, England, she was raised in Massachusetts and on the Michigan frontier. After two years at Albion College, she enrolled at Boston University, where she earned degrees in divinity (1878) and medicine (1886). The first woman ordained by the Methodist Protestant church, she filled pastorates and won renown as a temperance lecturer during the 1870s and early 1880s.

Deciding about 1885 to give her life to the struggle for the vote rather than to medicine or theology, she was persuaded by Susan B. Anthony to work full-time as a suffrage lecturer and organizer. Traveling tirelessly and speaking in every state in the Union, Shaw rose to the National American Woman Suffrage Association's* presidency, serving from 1904 to 1915. Often tactless and a poor administrator, she resigned the presidency in 1915. Shaw continued to lecture for suffrage and combined that work during World War I* with her chairmanship of the Woman's Committee of the Council of National Defense, for which she received the Distinguished Service Medal. (Anna Howard Shaw, *The Story of a Pioneer* (1915); William L. O'Neill, *Everyone Was Brave* (1969); James R. McGovern, "Anna Howard Shaw: New Approaches to Feminism," *Journal of Social History* 3 (Winter 1969): 135–53.)

Paul E. Fuller

SHEPPARD, JOHN MORRIS (May 28, 1875–April 9, 1941). Son of a Texas judge and Democratic congressman, educated at the University of Texas and at Yale, Sheppard was elected to the U.S. House of Representatives in 1902 to fill his father's vacant seat. In 1913, he was elected to the U.S. Senate and remained a member until his death in 1941. Sheppard's career is evidence of the compatibility of prohibitionism* and advanced Progressive views. A supporter of the Anti-Saloon League* at a time when Prohibition was becoming a dominant issue of Texas politics, he supported Woodrow Wilson's* reform agenda and in addition campaigned for woman suffrage* and other ultra-Progressive causes. Sheppard's 1917 Senate resolution was the basis of the Eighteenth Amendment, and he became famous as the "Father of National Prohibition." He was also cosponsor of the Sheppard-Towner Act* of 1921. He continued to be a Progressive throughout the 1920s; he was subsequently a loyal New Dealer. (Escal F. Duke, "Political Career of Morris Sheppard, 1875–1941" (Ph.D. diss., University of Texas, 1958); David C. Roller and "Robert W. Twyaman, eds., *The Encyclopedia of Southern History* (1979); George B. Tindall, *The Emergence of the New South, 1913–1945* (1967).)

Paul M. Pruitt, Jr.

SHEPPARD-TOWNER ACT. The Sheppard-Towner Act of 1921 was the first social welfare measure enacted by the federal government, the first national dividend of woman suffrage,* and a continuation of the reform thrust into the 1920s. Social feminists'* efforts resulted in the White House Conference on Care of Dependent Children* in 1909 and the creation of the U.S. Children's Bureau* in 1912. The bureau's investigation of infant and maternal mortality showed that the nation had unusually high rates and that few women received prenatal care. In 1917, Julia Lathrop,* the bureau chief, recommended federal aid to states to provide public protection for maternity and infancy.

America's first congresswoman, Jeannette Rankin,* introduced the bill in 1918, but it was not acted upon. Reintroduced by Senator Morris Sheppard* (D-Texas) and Representative Horace Towner (R-Iowa) in the next Congress, the proposal languished until women won the vote in 1920. Passed in November 1921, the Sheppard-Towner Act called for a modest appropriation of $1,470,000 to be distributed to cooperating states on a matching basis to be expended on instruction in the hygiene of maternity and infancy through public health nurses, visiting nurses, consultation centers, child-care conferences, and literature distribution. Forty-five states eventually joined the program despite the vigorous opposition of the American Medical Association* and a variety of conservative organizations and individuals who denounced it as Bolshevistic, un-American, and paternalistic. (J. Stanley Lemons, "The Sheppard-Towner Act: Progressivism in the 1920s," *Journal of American History* 55 (March 1969): 776–86; Joseph B. Chepaitis, "Federal Social Welfare Progressivism in the 1920s," *Social Service Review* 46 (June 1972): 213–29; J. Stanley Lemons, *The Woman Citizen: Social Feminism in the 1920s* (1973).)

J. Stanley Lemons

SHIPPING ACT OF 1916. A preparedness* measure of the Wilson* administration, the Shipping Act established a Shipping Board to own and operate commercial vessels. Immediately after the outbreak of World War I,* Treasury Secretary William G. McAdoo* proposed a ship-purchase bill to build up the American merchant marine. McAdoo and Wilson intended to purchase German ships interned in American ports and use them to increase foreign trade, particularly with Latin America. Great Britain protested the transfer of belligerent vessels to a neutral nation for the purpose of capturing her traditional markets. This diplomatic controversy combined with Republican opposition to a government-owned shipping line to defeat the bill in 1915.

A second shipping bill, introduced in January 1916, authorized a U.S. Shipping Board to spend $50 million to purchase or construct merchant ships, and granted the board power to regulate rates and services of all U.S. commercial vessels. The administration presented this new bill primarily as a preparedness measure, calling the authorized ships "naval auxiliaries." Congress amended the bill to forbid the purchase of belligerent ships and to require the return of all government-operated ships to private ownership five years after the war. The Shipping Act became law on September 7, 1916. (Arthur S. Link, *Woodrow Wilson and the Progressive Era* (1954); David M. Kennedy, *Over Here: The First World War and American Society* (1980); Jeffrey Safford, *Wilsonian Maritime Diplomacy* (1978).)

Edward R. Kantowicz

SHORT BALLOT. At the turn of the century, civic reformers attempted, without much success, to shorten the long, confusing "blanket ballots" used in American elections by making most secondary political offices appointive. The essence of the short ballot idea was that only top executive and legislative offices should be elective, all others appointive, thus shortening the ballot, decreasing voter confusion, and lessening the power of political bosses who slated candidates for minor offices. In 1909, reformer Richard S. Childs* founded the National Short Ballot Organization, with Woodrow Wilson* as president and Childs himself as secretary-treasurer. The organization merged with the National Municipal League* in 1921. The short ballot idea has made little progress. Though most observers acknowledge that voters are confused by long ballots and know little about the candidates for minor offices, the tradition of electing public officials by popular vote is so strong that attempts to shorten the ballot have generally failed. (Austin P. MacDonald, *American State Government and Administration* (1940); Richard S. Childs, *Short Ballot Principles* (1911); Edna D. Bullock, *Short Ballot* (1915).)

Edward R. Kantowicz

SIMKHOVITCH, MARY MELINDA KINGSBURY (September 8, 1867– November 15, 1951). This social economist who founded Greenwich House, in New York City,* was born in Chestnut Hill, a suburb of Boston,* Massachusetts, on September 8, 1867. After receiving her A.B. degree from Boston University in 1890, the Phi Beta Kappa scholar did graduate work at Radcliffe College, the University of Berlin, and Columbia University. While working in New York City settlement houses, she married Professor Vladimir Gregorievitch Simkhovitch, a Russian-born history professor at Columbia. In 1902 the couple founded Greenwich House, lived in and entertained international notables in an apartment on the upper floor, and for forty years provided help and opportunity to the underprivileged in the area. Mary Simkhovitch taught social economics at Barnard College, Columbia Teachers College, and the New York School of Social Work.

Motivated by the settlement house concept of people living and working together, of understanding their neighbors' problems and helping them to build better lives, she promoted humanitarian ideals as a member of the State Board of Social Welfare, as vice chairman of the New York City Housing Authority, and in her books. *The City Worker's World in America* (1917), a sociological study, includes her religion as the "heart of life, the inner assurance of the truth that only by living into the life of others can one truly live . . . the capacity for service and surrender." Coauthored by Elizabeth Ogg, *Quicksand: The Way of Life in the Slums* (1942) contains vignettes of the poor, including their graphic speech. *Neighborhood: My Story of Greenwich House* (1938) combines biography with history, anecdotes, and philosophy. A fitting sequel, *Here Is God's Plenty* (1949), reflects her living faith in a developing society. (*Woman's Who's Who of America, 1914–1958*; Allen F. Davis, *Spearheads for Reform: The Social*

Settlements and the Progressive Movement (1967); Mary M. K. Simkovitch, *Here Is God's Plenty: Reflections on American Social Advance* (1949).)

Lillian H. Mohr

SIMONS, ALGIE MARTIN (October 9, 1870–March 11, 1950). One of the leaders of the American Socialist party* during the early twentieth century, Simons was best known early in his career as an editor and theorist for the party's left wing. Over the years, he crossed the ideological spectrum and ended as a spokesman for the right. Several factors in his early life led him to socialism. These included the frontier traditions of his family, his education at the University of Wisconsin,* his exposure to the Christian Socialist movement, and the experiences of his charity work prior to the turn of the century. Simons was deeply influenced by the economic, social, and religious ideas of Social Gospel* advocate Richard T. Ely,* whose principles were based upon a notion of the marriage of ethics and economics.

While administering charity work in Cincinnati* and Chicago* before 1900, Simons came to believe that industry and poverty were interrelated and that socialism was truth, scientific fact, and demonstrated logic. Simons's goal was to arouse the class consciousness of the people, so that they would act politically in their own interest through the Socialist party. He was the head of the Chicago edition of a weekly newspaper known as the *Worker's Call*, and in 1900 he founded the *International Socialist Review*. His most famous work was a book entitled *Social Forces in American History* (1911). His commitment to the Socialist party came to an end as a result of the great debate over American entry into World War I* when he joined with the minority who supported President Woodrow Wilson.* (The Algie and May Wood Simons Papers, State Historical Society of Wisconsin, Madison; Robert Huston, "Algie Martin Simons and the American Socialist Movement" (Ph.D. diss., University of Wisconsin, 1965); Kent Kreuter and Gretchen Kreuter, *An American Dissenter: The Life of Algie Martin Simons* (1969).)

Kenneth E. Hendrickson, Jr.

SINCLAIR, UPTON BEALL (September 20, 1878–November 25, 1968). This famous author and public figure was born in Baltimore to the unsuccessful branch of a powerful aristocratic family. He worked his way through the College of the City of New York and Columbia University by writing stories for pulp magazines. After his marriage, he lived in a grinding poverty that affected his entire life. His first novels brought him a minimal income, and he was ripe for socialism by the age of twenty, although he was never an orthodox Marxist.

It was in 1906 that he published his most influential novel, *The Jungle*, which was a study not only of the Chicago* meat-packing industry but also of an immigrant Lithuanian family. It is open to question how much influence the book had on the subsequent meat-packing reform, but it is clear that it had little impact on the lives of the workers about whom he was most concerned. Although

he never considered himself to be an influential writer, he spent years trying to
"educate" the Progressive Era's most popular novelist (Winston Churchill)*
about the issues that he found most pressing. He ran for office as a socialist
candidate in both New Jersey and California, but abandoned his socialist associates when he supported American's participation in World War II. (Leon Harris,
Upton Sinclair: American Rebel (1975); William A. Bloodworth, Jr., *Upton
Sinclair* (1977); Floyd Dell, *Upton Sinclair: A Study in Social Protest* (1970).)

Robert W. Schneider

SINGLE TAX. When Henry George* ran for mayor of New York in 1886, he
was supported by Henry George Clubs as well as labor unions. It was not until
late 1887 that he accepted the "single tax" as a name and slogan for his social
philosophy. The Manhattan Single Tax Club was not founded until 1889, but
by the end of that year 131 such organizations were set up. After the election
of 1892, single taxers claimed four congressmen.

The movement lost momentum, however, later in the 1890s. Henry George
had antagonized many labor supporters by accepting the verdict of the Illinois
courts in the Haymarket affair. His death in 1897 and divisions among single
taxers on key issues further weakened the cause. On the basic doctrine of con-
fiscating rent, George's followers differed on the proper degree of taxation.
Although many supported William Jennings Bryan* in the election of 1896,*
others adamantly opposed him. On municipal ownership of public utilities,* they
divided, in George's terms, into "individualistics" and "socialistics."

Nonetheless, such publications as the *Public* and a variety of individual single
taxers contributed substantially to reform. Tom Johnson* and Brand Whitlock*
were active on the municipal level. William S. U'Ren* in Oregon led the movement for direct democracy on the state level. In Wilson's administration Franklin
K. Lane,* Newton D. Baker,* Louis Post,* and Frederic C. Howe* occupied
important positions on the national level. Ultimately, bitter splits over Woodrow
Wilson's* war policies led to collapse of the movement. (Charles Albro Barker,
Henry George (1955); Dominic Candeloro, "The Single Tax Movement and
Progressivism, 1880–1920," *American Journal of Economics and Sociology* 38
(1979): 113–27; Dominic Candeloro, "Louis F. Post and the Single Tax Movement, 1872–1898," *American Journal of Economics and Sociology* 35 (1976):
415–30.)

Herbert H. Rosenthal

SLOAN, JOHN (August 2, 1871–September 7, 1951). John Sloan was born at
Lock Haven, Pennsylvania, but his family moved to Philadelphia.* Before grad-
uation, he was forced to seek work, but he continued to study art, attending
drawing classes and (from 1892 to 1893) evening classes at the Philadelphia
Academy of Fine Arts. From 1892 to 1902 he worked in art departments of the
Philadelphia *Inquirer* and *Press*, meeting other young artists, including William
Glackens, Everett Shinn, and George Luks. Robert Henri* attracted this group

to discussions in his studio, inspiring them to paint the life around them. They were to form the nucleus of a progressive art movement in New York City* which led to the exhibitions of "The Eight" (1908), the Independent Artists (1910), the Armory Show* (1913), and the Society of Independent Artists (1917 and following). Sloan was actively involved throughout.

From the time he moved to New York (1904), Sloan portrayed the human comedy of city life in paintings and etchings which were frequently criticized as vulgar. From 1910 to 1916 he belonged to the Socialist party,* and he became art editor for the *Masses*,* contributing notable drawings. In his paintings he avoided political subjects, turning increasingly to landscapes and figure studies. Eventually disillusioned with the party, he and his first wife, Dolly, continued their independent support of liberal causes. Sloan taught at the Art Students League in New York between 1916 and 1938, influencing an entire generation of students. (John Sloan, *New York Scene: From the Diaries, Notes and Correspondence, 1906–1913* (1965); John Sloan, *Gist of Art* (1939); Van Wyck Brooks, *John Sloan: A Painter's Life* (1955); David Scott, *John Sloan* (1975).)

David W. Scott

SMALL, ALBION W. (May 11, 1854–March 24, 1926). Born in Buckfield, Maine, Small grew up in an evangelical Protestant environment. After graduating from Colby College in 1876, he entered the Newton Theological Seminary and did graduate work in the social sciences in Germany. Small taught at Colby and completed his Ph.D. at Johns Hopkins University in 1879. The next year, he taught the first course in sociology and compiled his first book, *Introduction to a Science of Society*. He became chairman of the Department of Sociology at the University of Chicago* in 1892. In 1895, he established the *American Journal of Sociology*.

Subscribing to the Wisconsin Idea, Small agreed with Lester Frank Ward's* goal that the discipline of sociology would contribute to social improvement in the future. Disliking Herbert Spencer's* work, Small accepted the challenge of Darwinian biology for society, but he feared that it would co-opt sociology into a type of substructure. His *General Sociology* (1905) was his response to the Darwinian challenge and secured the participation of European scholars at the Saint Louis World's Fair. Over the years, Small shifted his orientation from a nonscientific Christian position to accept the Hegelian social process with its stress on a collective organic society. Small distrusted businessmen's motives and urged governmental regulation to control their behavior; he desired social control directed by the expert of society, the sociologist. (George Christakes, *Albion W. Small* (1978); Ernest Becker, *The Lost Science of Man* (1971); Vernon K. Dibble, *The Legacy of Albion Small* (1975).)

Donald K. Pickens

SMITH, ALFRED EMANUEL (December 30, 1873–October 4, 1944). Tammany Hall* Democrat, governor of New York,* first Catholic candidate to run for president, Smith was born on the Lower East Side in New York, of Irish,*

German,* and Italian* stock. He dropped out of parochial school in the eighth grade and worked at a variety of odd jobs, including wholesale clerk at the Fulton Fish Market. Befriended by Tom Foley, a Tammany district leader, he was elected to the state assembly in 1903, becoming majority leader of the assembly in 1911 and speaker in 1913. Under the tutelage of Tammany's Grand Sachem, Charles Francis Murphy,* Smith remained a loyal machine* politician, but he also promoted progressive measures if they were of practical value to his immigrant constituency.

After the disastrous fire at the Triangle Shirtwaist Company in 1911, he chaired the New York State Factory Investigating Commission* and formed close friendships with many reformers and social workers. Smith and his vice chairman on the commission, Robert F. Wagner,* were the finest products of Charley Murphy's Tammany: loyal Democrats but liberal on social issues. Smith was elected governor of New York four times, in 1918, 1922, 1924, and 1926. He earned the Democratic nomination for president in 1928, but lost to Herbert Hoover* in a campaign marked by anti-Catholicism.* (Oscar Handlin, *Al Smith and His America* (1958); Matthew Josephson and Hannah Josephson, *Al Smith: Hero of the Cities* (1959); John D. Buenker, *Urban Liberalism and Progressive Reform* (1973).)

Edward R. Kantowicz

SMITH, HOKE (September 2, 1855–November 27, 1931). Born in Newton, North Carolina,* Smith was the son of a University of North Carolina professor. As a young man, he read law in Atlanta* and was admitted to the bar in 1873. Five years later he bought the Atlanta *Journal*. In 1892, his newspaper enthusiastically endorsed Grover Cleveland in his successful campaign for the presidency. Cleveland rewarded Smith by appointing him secretary of the interior, a position he held until 1896. In 1906, Smith was elected governor of Georgia,* serving from 1907 to 1909. In 1911 he was again elected governor; but the legislature appointed him to the U.S. Senate in the same year, an office he held until 1921.

In the 1890s, Smith was in some respects conservative, but by the time he was governor, he had clearly crossed into the progressive camp. He strengthened the railroad commission, ended convict lease, improved roads, and instituted statewide prohibition.* As a senator he was coauthor of the Smith-Lever Act* (1914), which established the agricultural extension service, and the Smith-Hughes Act* (1917), which encouraged the teaching of vocational courses in public schools. In 1908, however, he helped lead the campaign that disfranchised blacks* in Georgia. Still, most historians consider Smith to have been Georgia's first progressive governor. (Dewey W. Grantham, Jr., *Hoke Smith and the Politics of the New South* (1958); *Dictionary of American Biography*, Vol. 17 280–82; Numan V. Bartley, *The Making of Modern Georgia* (1983).)

Barton C. Shaw

SMITH, J. ALLEN (May 5, 1860–January 30, 1924). J. Allen Smith was born in Pleasant Hill, Missouri, and received a B.A. in 1886 and an LL.D. in 1887 from the University of Missouri. After practicing law for five years in Kansas

City, Missouri, he began graduate work at the University of Michigan under the guidance of Henry Carter Adams, a leading spokesman of the "New Economics." Upon completion of his dissertation, "The Multiple Money Standard," he received his Ph.D. in 1894. In 1895, he joined the faculty at Marietta College. In 1897, his appointment at Marietta having been terminated because of his opposition to the gold standard, he was invited to the University of Washington as a professor of political economy. Although eventually he again would come under conservative attack, he remained at Washington until his death. He immediately became involved in municipal reform in Seattle* and in the pages of national municipal reform journals.

In 1907, he published his first book, *The Spirit of American Government*. In the most influential as well as controversial section of this book, he charged not only that the Constitution was undemocratic but also that it was so because its authors feared democracy. However, in a second book, nearing completion at the time of his death, Smith revealed growing disillusionment about democratic reforms as panaceas. The book, *The Growth and Decadence of Constitutional Government*, was completed by his daughter Elfreda Allen Smith and, with an introduction by his colleague and close friend Vernon Louis Parrington, was published in 1930. (Eric F. Goldman, "J. Allen Smith: The Reformer and His Dilemma," *Pacific Northwest Quarterly* 35 (1944): 195–214; Thomas C. McClintock, "J. Allen Smith and the Progressive Movement: A Study in Intellectual History" (Ph.D. diss., University of Washington, 1959); Thomas C. McClintock, "J. Allen Smith, A Pacific Northwest Progressive," *Pacific Northwest Quarterly* 53 (1962): 49–59; Cushing Strout, Introduction to *The Spirit of American Government* by J. Allen Smith (1965).)

                                                              Thomas C. McClintock

SMITH-HUGHES ACT. By this law Congress provided aid to the states on a dollar-matching basis for the purpose of paying teachers of agricultural, trade, home economics, and industrial subjects, and for preparing teachers to teach such subjects. Following the Philadelphia Centennial Exposition, pedagogical reformers and businessmen, anxious to employ the skilled workers no longer being supplied by the apprentice system, avidly supported vocational instruction in the schools. In the early 1900s, a movement to secure federal aid for such training found ready acceptance among progressive educational theorists, farmers, and businessmen. Organized labor, wary of the plan at first, also eventually gave its support.

Nevertheless, the early vocational education bills in Congress failed of passage because professionals in the colleges of agriculture objected to combining agricultural extension work with general vocational education as originally planned. Upon the enactment of the Smith-Lever Act* in 1914, however, which provided separately for extension work, and the promise of Senator Hoke Smith* of Georgia* to work for a general vocational bill, the way was cleared for the passage of the Smith-Hughes Act on February 23, 1917. (Marvin Lazerson and

W. Norton Grub, eds., *American Education and Vocationalism: A Documentary History, 1870–1970* (1974); Arthur F. McClure, James Riley Chrisman, and Perry Mock, *Education for Work: The Historical Evolution of Vocational and Distributive Education in America* (1985); Dewey W. Grantham, Jr., *Hoke Smith and the Politics of the New South* (1958).)

Wayne E. Fuller

SMITH-LEVER ACT. This law provided for cooperative agricultural extension work between the agricultural colleges and the Department of Agriculture, funded by a dollar-matching arrangement with the states in which federal money would be apportioned among the states according to their rural populations. Inspired by the efforts of professionals in agricultural science to teach farmers to farm scientifically, the law reflected confidence in the efficacy of science and education to improve farming and farm life and led to the development of the nation's county demonstration system.

Passage of the law was delayed by supporters of a general vocational education bill and by professional jealousy between the Department of Agriculture and the colleges of agriculture. Professionals in the colleges of agriculture sought control over the program and insisted on the use of experts to conduct farmers' institutes and conferences as a method of teaching farmers. But demonstration work in the South, supported by the Department of Agriculture and conducted by county agents without college degrees, had been too successful to ignore. The removal of the general vocational education feature from the proposal and a compromise between the Department of Agriculture and the colleges of agriculture, which allowed the latter to administer agriculture extension but made their programs dependent upon the Department of Agriculture's approval, smoothed the way for the passage of the law, May 8, 1914. (Roy V. Scott, *The Reluctant Farmer: The Rise of Agricultural Extension to 1914* (1970); Alfred Charles True, *A History of Agricultural Extension Education in the United States, 1785–1925* (1969); Edmund des Brunneer and E. Hsin Pao Yang, *Rural America and the Extension Service: A History and Critique of the Cooperative Agricultural and Home Economics Extension Service* (1949).)

Wayne E. Fuller

SMOOT, REED OWEN (January 10, 1862–February 9, 1941). Born in Salt Lake City and reared in Provo, Smoot graduated from Brigham Young Academy (now University). He engaged in business ventures ranging from woolen manufacture, a cooperative store, and a drug store to lumber sales, livestock, banking, mining, railroading, and electricity. Ordained an apostle in the Church of Jesus Christ of Latter-day Saints in 1900, he served as a member until his death. Opposed to the Mormon-Gentile division in politics, Smoot became a Republican largely because of the protective tariff. Elected a senator in January 1903, he was challenged because of his position in the Latter-day Saints hierarchy. Extended (1904–1907) Senate hearings finally resulted in his retention, in part because of his support of the Roosevelt* administration and the Senate leadership.

Although Smoot was best known for the tariff, his principal service during the Progressive Era was as a member and chairman of the Senate Committee on Public Lands and Surveys. A strong supporter of the Forest Service,* he opposed the Hetch Hetchy project, worked for passage of the National Park Service* Act, and coauthored the Federal Minerals Leasing Act. (Milton R. Merrill, "Reed Smoot, Apostle in Politics" (Ph.D. diss., Columbia University, 1950); Thomas G. Alexander, "Senator Reed Smoot and Western Land Policy, 1905–1920," *Arizona and the West* 13 (Autumn 1971): 245–64; Thomas G. Alexander, "Teapot Dome Revisited: Reed Smoot and Conservation in the 1920s," *Utah Historical Quarterly* 45 (Fall 1977): 352–68.)

Thomas G. Alexander

SOCIAL AND INDUSTRIAL JUSTICE PLATFORM. This section of the Progressive* party program of 1912 was the culmination of decades of agitation. For example, such disparate labor organizations as the Workingmen's party of America, the Knights of Labor, the short-lived American Railway Union, and the American Federation of Labor* had fruitlessly pressed for the establishment of an eight-hour day and the abolition of child labor.* Ultimately, labor drew support from allies like the Populists,* the Socialists,* the National Conference of Charities and Corrections,* and adherents of the Social Gospel.* During his presidency, Theodore Roosevelt* was angered by the "malefactors of great wealth," and frightened of the potential ability of the Socialists to capitalize on the abuses publicized by the muckrakers.*

In 1910, Roosevelt's reformist and Hamiltonian tendencies persuaded him to proclaim the necessity of enacting federal statutes encompassing a host of socioeconomic objectives. Two years later, Albert J. Beveridge* urged the delegates to the Progressive convention to adopt the motto "Pass prosperity around." The resolutions committee approved the doctrine of the general-welfare state, and then adopted fourteen specific recommendations. These included the abolition of child and convict contract labor, and the establishment of minimum wage standards for working women. In 1934, Paul U. Kellogg* defended this section of the Progressive platform, saying that nationally, " 'more social legislation . . . was passed in the two following years than in ten years preceding.' " (John Allen Gable, *The Bull Moose Years: Theodore Roosevelt and the Progressive Party* (1978); Allen F. Davis, *Spearheads for Reform: Social Settlements and the Progressive Movement 1890–1914* (1967); Philip Taft, *The A.F. of L.* (1957–1959).)

Jules A. Karlin

SOCIAL CONTROL. The term "social control" refers to any coercive, manipulative, or conditioning technique that serves to promote acceptance of the dominant social order of a given society. During the Progressive Era, concern about social control was prompted by widespread fears among middle- and upper-class Americans that the slums, urban political machines,* and labor-capital conflict that characterized the new industrial society were threatening traditional rural and small-town American values. Social control through coercion—i.e., the forceful suppression of gambling, drinking, and prostitution—was advocated by those who believed that all modern social problems originated with slum dwellers who lacked sufficient self-control to behave responsibly.

Against this view, environmentalists argued that it was not individual immorality but appalling slum conditions that explained working-class people's rejection of middle-class values and that the solution was to provide parks, playgrounds,* model tenements, free concerts, and clean streets in slum districts. Radical scholars extended the definition of social control to include such pro-labor ideas as unionization and workmen's compensation,* which, radicals claimed, were sops given workers to prevent them from demanding truly revolutionary changes in the American economic system. (Paul Boyer, *Urban Masses and Moral Order in America, 1820–1920* (1978); James Weinstein, *The Corporate Ideal in the Liberal State, 1900–1918* (1968); Robert H. Wiebe, *The Search for Order, 1877–1920* (1967).)

Gerald W. McFarland

SOCIAL DARWINISM. "Social Darwinism" describes social theories that draw analogies between biological processes and human social developments. In a strict sense, the term applies to arguments couched in the explicitly Darwinian phrases "struggle for existence," "natural selection," and the "survival of the fittest." More loosely, it has been used to characterize any appeals to the "natural" order, whether in references to society as a "social organism" or to the "natural laws of trade." Historically, the phrase "social Darwinism" first surfaced in the 1880s in debates between continental socialists and their opponents, in particular the Englishman Herbert Spencer,* whose defense of laissez-faire these defenders of increased state action found an anathema. Although virtually unknown in the United States when it first appeared in the late nineties, the phrase was soon the stock-in-trade of proponents of state activism, who applied it to Spencer and such American disciples as Andrew Carnegie* and William Graham Sumner.*

Gradually, however, the term was applied ubiquitously to progressives themselves, whether eugenicists, social controllers such as the sociologist Lester Frank Ward,* or overseas expansionists such as the historian John Fiske and the clergyman Josiah Strong.* In individual cases, including those of Sumner, Carnegie, and Strong, use of Darwinian analogies was infrequent, and when taken in context, not a defense of brutal struggle, selection, and survival. Applied to defenders of laissez-faire, individualism, and the free market, the epithet "social Darwinism" was thus caricature rather than characterization—typically as preface for an argument in favor of governmental action or other social controls to curb the evils of the "natural" order. So, also, it was universally a term of abuse when used in debates among varieties of progressive reformers, as, for example, when advocates and opponents of eugenic legislation* accused each other of espousing inhumane policies in Darwin's name. Although inaccurate in a literal sense, the phrase was nonetheless an important marker on the emotional and ideological roadmap of American progressivism, setting limits and boundaries to the quest to make social policies "scientific." (Richard Hofstadter, *Social Darwinism in American Thought* (1944); Robert C. Bannister, *Social Darwinism: Science and Myth in Anglo-American Social Thought* (1979); Donald C. Bellomy, " 'Social Darwinism' Revisited," *Perspectives in American History*, n.s. 1 (1984): 1–129.)

Robert C. Bannister

SOCIAL ENGINEERING. The term describes an analysis of social conditions and an approach to reform and change generated in the late 1890s and of considerable influence into the 1920s. Social engineering consists of a movement toward the engineering of human beings rather than machines, a turn away from force and the state as mechanisms of authority, and a practical discipline based on the recently articulated "science" of society. Among its advocates were Jane Addams,* Luther Gulick, Joseph Lee, George Creel,* Edward T. Devine,* Frank Parsons, and sociologist Edward A. Ross,* whose *Social Control* (1901) was the movement's foremost text. Besides Ross, academics of influence included John Dewey,* William James,* Charles Horton Cooley,* and Simon Patten.*

The range of activities and institutions promoted by its proponents included public libraries,* child labor laws,* museums of safety, pensions, profit-sharing, model tenements, personnel management, playgrounds,* settlements, vocational guidance, employment exchanges, benefit associations, home economics courses, Bible classes, recreation programs, wartime propaganda, certain participatory styles of scientific management* and—quite prominently—public health.* Social engineering emerged from certain shared assumptions or observations: that industrialization, the machine, the congested city, and an outmoded competitive individualism had heightened class tensions, increased friction between capital and labor, destabilized families, undermined the claim of religion to social leadership, created gross inefficiency, and encouraged a debilitating fatalism about the possibilities of progress.

With unremitting optimism, social engineers held out the project of forging a new social bond and facilitating adjustment to industrial society through primarily nonpolitical, decentralized, indirect, and ostensibly noncoercive and democratic methods based on psychology and sociology and including public opinion, art, advertising, film, leadership, suggestion, and small group discussion. They called for the participation of the objects of control in discussion and decision-making processes, but generally conceded that responsible analysis of social conditions and social engineering itself were properly the function of professionals. (Christopher Lasch, *The New Radicalism in America, 1889–1963: The*

Intellectual as a Social Type (1965); David F. Noble, *America by Design: Science, Technology, and the Rise of Corporate Capitalism* (1977); Paul Boyer, *Urban Masses and Moral Order in America, 1820–1920* (1978).)

William Graebner

SOCIAL FEMINISM. The term ''social feminism'' describes the broad mainstream of feminism in the United States in the late nineteenth century and first several decades of the twentieth century. In general, it was a moderate, nonideological women's movement which sought women's rights, emancipation, opportunity, and equality, but accepted the general economic, social, political, and cultural system of the United States. Social feminists, for example, favored divorce law reform,* but not free love or the abandonment of family institutions. They favored greater social justice,* consumer protection, and regulation of business, but not the overthrow of capitalism. From 1870 to 1920, the great crusade was to win the right to vote, but social feminists wanted the franchise not as a matter of justice but for the social good they could accomplish with the power of the vote. Many social feminists either accepted or used the notion that women were the ''better half'' (the belief that women had a higher moral nature than men), and demanded a greater voice in the schools, the town, the state, and the nation. They wanted, as Frances Willard* said, ''to make the whole world more homelike.''

In addition to clear women's issues of purity, suffrage,* and economic rights, social feminists led or supported a wide range of reforms, including pure food and drugs;* national parks and conservation;* health, education, and welfare programs; Prohibition;* peace;* and political improvements. The principal women's leaders of the Progressive Era, such as Jane Addams,* Carrie Chapman Catt,* Lillian Wald,* or Florence Kelley,* were social feminists; and the social feminist organizations included the National Council of Women, General Federation of Women's Clubs,* Congress of Mothers, Parent Teachers Association, National Consumers' League,* National Women's Trade Union League,* Women's Christian Temperance Union,* and the National American Woman Suffrage Association* and its offspring, the National League of Women Voters.* (J. Stanley Lemons, *The Woman Citizen: Social Feminism in the 1920s* (1973); William L. O'Neill, *Everyone Was Brave: The Rise and Fall of Feminism in America* (1969); Nancy Woloch, *Women and the American Experience* (1984).)

J. Stanley Lemons

SOCIAL GOSPEL. The Social Gospel was the effort of Protestant clergymen to apply the doctrines and teachings of Christ to social, economic, and political problems. It was an important intellectual aspect of the era and had a profound effect upon Woodrow Wilson* and William Jennings Bryan.* It arose at a time when American Protestantism seemed to be wedded to the existing order and churches frequently apologized for social and economic conditions as a reflection of the way God had designed the world. Protestant reformers were aided in their departure from their conventional role as shepherds of flocks rather than as social activists by the liberating influence of the evolutionists, whose attacks on mainline Christian thinking made major inroads in theological thought.

Social Gospelers were divided into two major groups: the social Christians, who believed that the industrial system and laissez-faire were contrary to God's plan and urged moderate changes, and the Christian Socialists, who contended that the existing order was in need of wholesale revision. The most prominent figures in the Social Gospel movement were Washington Gladden,* the most representative of the former group, and Walter Rauschenbusch,* sometimes called the philosopher of the Social Gosepl, who best represents the latter. Both men, orthodox in theology, were converted to social activism by their experiences as pastors of urban churches. Other clergymen who were identified with the movement were William Dwight Porter Bliss, George Herron,* Lyman Abbott,* Josiah Strong,* R. Heber Newton, Jesse Jones, Samuel Dan Huntington, and W. W. Rainsfort. Most of these men were active in the Federal Council of Churches,* which was the movement's most important voice.

Social Gospel clergymen were supportive of labor unions, championing higher wages and safer working conditions. They supported tax reform,* the breakup of monopolies, and the use of the state as a factor in the control of social and economic conditions. They also supported political reform, calling for direct election of senators* and direct primaries,* civil service reform,* and the restriction of immigration.* (Robert T. Handy, ed., *The Social Gospel in America, 1870–1920* (1966); Ronald C. White and Charles Howard Hopkins, *The Social Gospel: Religion and Reform in Changing America* (1976).)

Thomas W. Ryley

SOCIAL HYGIENE. A movement to stop prostitution and the spread of venereal disease, social hygiene was a more scientific version of the nineteenth-century campaign for "social purity." It shared with that earlier movement a desire to regulate and outlaw vice through such laws as the Mann Act* and to promote self-control and a single standard of sexual morality for men and women. Social hygienists, however, focused primarily on the medical prevention and treatment of venereal disease. When the Wasserman blood test for the detection of venereal disease became available in 1906, social hygienists campaigned to make it mandatory for all marriage license applicants. The American Social Hygiene Association was established in 1913, in a merger of two earlier groups, the National Vigilance Committee and the American Society for Sex Hygiene. It enjoyed considerable success in lobbying against prostitution near military bases during World War I* and in convincing state governments to adopt the Wasserman test. By 1921 twenty states required the test for marriage licenses.

Along with the prohibition* of alcoholic beverages, social hygiene formed part of the moral reform wing of progressivism. (Ruth Rosen, *The Lost Sisterhood* (1982); David J. Pivar, *Purity Crusade: Sexual Morality and Social Control, 1868–1900* (1973); Mark T. Connelly, *The Response to Prostitution in the Progressive Era* (1980).)

Edward R. Kantowicz

SOCIAL INSURANCE. This term encompasses a variety of government programs that are designed to provide protection against the continuing hazards that workers face, e.g., old age dependency, unemployment, job-related injuries, sickness, and disability. While social insurance is similar to commercial insurance in that it is a method of distributing among the many the losses of a few, there are significant differences. Social insurance is designed to provide incomes that maintain a minimum standard of living rather than to supplement earnings or make up an income loss. The level of benefits is determined by social policy, with benefits a matter of right and not based on need. In social insurance, benefits are deliberately established in favor of those receiving lower incomes with premiums related to income rather than benefits. Social insurance is usually compulsory, while commercial insurance is voluntary. In social insurance, premiums are either paid by the employer (e.g., unemployment insurance and workmen's compensation*) or are shared by employer and employee (e.g., Old Age Survivors and Disability Insurance). Development of social insurance programs in the United States lagged behind such developments in Europe due to the laissez-faire economic philosophy espoused in the United States. With the exception of state worker's compensation laws, which first appeared in 1911, it was not until the Great Depression of the 1930s that social insurance legislation was enacted by the federal government. (Eveline M. Burns, *Social Security and Public Policy* (1956); Domenico Gagliardo, *American Social Insurance* (1955).)

Leon Applebaum

SOCIALISM, AGRARIAN. Agrarian socialism flourished in parts of the Southwest and Midwest from 1901 to 1914. Drawing initial support from former Populists, Socialist party of America* organizers appealed to yeomen farmers, tenants, lumberjacks, railroad men, and miners. Leaders such as Thomas Hickey in Texas and Oscar Ameringer in Oklahoma sought with some success to create a Populist-style movement culture. Thousands traveled to yearly encampments to hear Eugene V. Debs,* Mother Jones, Kate R. O'Hare,* and others describe the "cooperative commonwealth" of the future. Successful socialist newspapers included the Girard, Kansas, *Appeal to Reason* (which sustained a subscription rate of over 100,000) and the Hallettsville, Texas, *Rebel*.

Southwestern socialists disagreed over party organization, the role of blacks, and the attitude which party members should adopt toward "direct action" groups such as the Industrial Workers of the World.* Still, the socialist message reached an increasing constituency; in 1912, Deb's combined presidential vote in Texas,

Oklahoma, Arkansas, and Louisiana was over 80,000. Repression at state and federal levels had destroyed the effectiveness of the Socialist party by the end of the World War.* (James R. Green, *Grass-Roots Socialism: Radical Movements in the Southwest, 1895–1943* (1978); Seymour Martin Lipset, *Agrarian Socialism* (rev. ed., 1968).)

Paul M. Pruitt, Jr.

SOCIALISM, URBAN. The Socialist party of America* was founded in 1901 as the result of a merger of several Marxist factions which had been active in the United States for some time. During its early period of development the party's major centers of activity were New York City* and Chicago,* although party organizations were to be found in numerous industrial towns and cities throughout the nation, where they participated in the electoral process along with the established parties. In two rather important industrial cities, Milwaukee,* Wisconsin, and Schenectady, New York, they actually gained control of municipal government for a time, while in other localities they elected numerous individuals to office, even though they did not control city government.

Usually coming to power as a result of voter reaction to corruption within major party administration, and realizing that they could not realistically expect to destroy the capitalist system, they generally sought to win elections, stay in power, and work for reform within the existing framework. As a result, they advocated clean, efficient government and were interested in such things as cost-accounting systems, central purchasing programs, sound credit ratings, and the extension of municipal services, as well as public ownership of transportation and utilities, and the rights of workers. Socialists were most successful in winning power when they presented themselves as Progressives espousing democracy rather than revolution. But in doing so they left much of their potential constituency on the left—miners, factory workers, immigrants, and blacks—dissatisfied and disillusioned.

In 1912, the Socialist party held some 1,200 public offices in 340 cities coast to coast. Among these were 79 mayors in 24 states. During this period the best-known leaders of the party were Eugene V. Debs* of Terre Haute, Indiana; Morris Hillquit* of New York City; George R. Lunn of Schenectady, New York; and Victor Berger,* Emil Seidel, and Daniel W. Hoan of Milwaukee, Wisconsin. (Bruce M. Stave, *Socialism and the Cities* (1975); David A. Shannon, *The Socialist Party of America* (1955); John H. M. Laslett and Seymour Martin Lipset, *Failure of a Dream? Essays in the History of American Socialism* (1974).)

Kenneth E. Hendrickson, Jr.

SOCIALIST LABOR PARTY. The Socialist Labor party, an uncompromising and ideologically rigid Marxist Socialist party, dominated left-wing politics in the 1890s. Socialism first came to America with German immigrants, some of whom had worked with Karl Marx in the fatherland. After 1864 they organized a number of sections of the First International, which united in 1876 as the

Workingman's party. The name was changed to the Socialist Labor party (SLP) in 1877. The SLP found its greatest support among German and Jewish skilled workers in New York. Its numbers remained small, and it was wracked by continual splits and factional disputes.

In 1890 Daniel De Leon,* a Jewish immigrant from the Dutch West Indies, joined the party and became its dominant figure until his death in 1914. During the early 1890s, De Leon's party attempted to "bore from within" the established craft unions of the American Federation of Labor* and the Knights of Labor, in order to convert them to socialist principles; but in 1895 they changed to a strategy of "dual unionism" by organizing the Socialist Trade and Labor Alliance as a revolutionary industrial union. The foreign character of the SLP and De Leon's dogmatism alienated many socialists, who broke off and founded the Socialist party of America* in 1901. The SLP became more of an ideological sect than a full-blown political party. (Ira Kipnis, *The American Socialist Movement* (1952); Morris Hillquit, *History of Socialism in the U.S.* (1903); Donald D. Egbert and Stow Persons, *Socialism and American Life* (1952).)

Edward R. Kantowicz

SOCIALIST PARTY OF AMERICA. Founded in Indianapolis, Indiana, in July 1901, the Socialist party of America was a vigorous force in the nation's politics during the first quarter of the twentieth century. A broad organization representing all varieties of leftist conviction, it was committed to obtaining its objective—the cooperative commonwealth—through the ballot box. Although New York City* and Chicago* were strong Socialist centers in terms of membership and votes in presidential elections, until 1918 the party's greatest relative voting strength was in states west of the Mississippi River (Oklahoma* had the largest state organization).

By 1912, the party had a membership of 118,000, was publishing more than 300 periodicals, had a substantial following in the trade union membership, and had elected well over 1,000 public officials throughout the United States. In the presidential election of that year, Eugene V. Debs* received 6 percent of the popular vote. While the party ceased to grow after 1912 and by 1922 had all but ceased to exist, it still enjoyed a membership of approximately 80,000 at the time the United States entered World War I.* The party and its leaders played an extremely important role as the focal point for all those who objected to the war and America's participation in it.

By the war's end, almost a third of the Socialists' National Executive Committee was behind bars. It was the Bolshevik Revolution in Russia, however, that led to the party's loss of authenticity as a movement of radical action. The Socialist party's left wing succumbed to the illusion that revolution in the United States was imminent, while the leaders of the party neither accepted the view that America was ripe for revolution nor gave in to demands that the party be restructured along Leninist lines. By the late summer of 1919, there were three parties were there had been one—the Socialist party of America, the Communist party, and the Communist Labor party—and none of them was very strong. Within a year after the split, they had only 36,000 members among them; within a decade the Socialist party had dwindled to less than 10,000 members. (David A. Shannon, *The Socialist Party of America* (1955); James Weinstein, *The Decline of Socialism in America, 1912–1925* (1967).)

Frederick C. Giffin

SOCIAL JUSTICE. The social justice movement arose at the end of the nineteenth century in response to the social consequences of unregulated capitalism. In factories, mills, and mines, millions of unskilled laborers worked twelve hours a day and longer; child labor* was widespread; disabling and fatal accidents were commonplace; wages were abysmally low; and wretched poverty was the norm. The fetid urban slums were horribly overcrowded and without sanitary facilities of any sort. Disease, crime, delinquency, "vice," and family instability were epidemic.

By the 1890s a growing number of well-born Americans, profoundly moved by the plight of the poor and, at the same time, profoundly frightened by the possibility of social upheaval among them, sponsored a wide array of reforms intended to correct this situation. Boldly, they dismissed the prevailing argument that social evils were the products of flawed individuals, insisting instead that they were the symptoms of a flawed social environment that was susceptible to improvement. At the local level, they pressed for housing codes, supported programs for mass inoculation against communicable diseases, and often sought to "improve" the behavior of the poor. At the state level they sponsored laws to modify the industrial order by regulating factory conditions, by limiting the working hours and establishing minimum wages for women, and by abolishing child labor. After 1910, they advocated compensation for work-related accidents and were beginning to call for a system of old-age pensions. A few of the most daring even proposed health insurance.*

By 1912 most of them were looking to the federal government as the guarantor of these reforms. Although many states passed laws regulating housing, public health, child labor, factory safety, and the wages and hours of women, these laws were often riddled with loopholes, stymied in the courts, and poorly enforced by the very agencies and individuals assigned to police them. Several states enacted workmen's compensation* laws which fared somewhat better, but little headway was made with other forms of social insurance.* (Robert H. Bremner, *From the Depths: The Discovery of Poverty in the United States* (1956); Allen F. Davis, *Spearheads for Reform* (1967); Don S. Kirschner, *The Paradox of Professionalism* (1986).)

Don S. Kirschner

SOCIAL REFORM. The social reform tradition was first illustrated and exemplified in the Detroit* mayoralty of Hazen S. Pingree* (1889–1897) and was compared by Melvin G. Holli to a distinctly different reform tradition, which he called "structural reform."* Social reform mayors such as Pingree, Samuel "Golden Rule" Jones* (1897–1903), Tom Johnson* (1901–1909), Mark Fagan* (1901–1907), Brand Whitlock* (1906–1913), and Newton D. Baker* (1912–1916) shared the view that big business and its quest for preferential treatment had corrupted city government and that moral reforms that sought to root out gambling, drinking, and prostitution were mere attempts to treat the symptoms of the disease and left the fundamental problems of the urban masses untouched. Social reform programs aimed at lower gas, light, telephone, and street railway rates for the community and higher taxes for railroads and corporations. When they were unable to obtain regulation of the public utilities, these mayors fought for muncipal ownership,* the only technique then available to redistribute economic power. The establishment of free public baths,* expansion of parks, schools, and public relief were similar attempts by the social reformers to distribute the amenities of middle-class life to the masses.

The whole tone of the social reform movement was populistic and empirical. It did not attempt to prescribe standards of personal morality nor to draft social blueprints of city charters which had as their goals the imposition of middle-class morality or patrician values upon the masses. Social reformers sought to find the basic causes of municipal misgovernment in the social and economic conditions of the urban masses. (Melvin G. Holli, *Reform in Detroit: Hazen S. Pingree and Urban Politics* (1969); J. Joseph Huthmacher, "Urban Liberalism and the Age of Reform," *Mississippi Valley Historical Review* 49 (September 1962): 23–41; Martin J. Schiesl, *The Politics of Efficiency: Municipal Administration and Reform in America, 1880–1920* (1977); John D. Buenker, *Urban Liberalism and Progressive Reform* (1973).)

Melvin G. Holli

SOCIAL SCIENCE. The study of collective human behavior, how men and women act in groups, social science developed in the mid-nineteenth century as a response to the growing problems of industrial society. Hoping to endow their study of social conditions with the same intellectual rigor as the natural sciences, a group of reformers founded the American Association for the Promotion of Social Science in 1865, changing its name to the American Social Science Association (ASSA) in 1869. The two sides of social science, reform advocacy and scientific objectivity, soon began to go separate ways. Practical amateurs, many from the charities organizations, continued to dominate the ASSA under the leadership of Frank B. Sanborn, the association's secretary for nearly half a century. Meanwhile, the universities began differentiating the subject matter of social science into separate disciplines of history, political science, economics, and sociology, organizing graduate departments for each subject. Academic social scientists broke off from the ASSA to form their own professional associations: the American Historical Association* in 1886, the American Economic Association* that same year, the American Political Science Association* in 1904, and the American Sociological Society* in 1905.

By the first decade of the twentieth century, therefore, separate academic social sciences had taken over the theoretical study of society, whereas the rapidly professionalizing field of social work assumed the practical tasks of serving the needy. Though academic objectivity and specialization had triumphed as the dominant feature of social science, many individual social scientists still harbored a strong reform impulse during the Progressive Era. Historian Charles A. Beard,* economist Richard T. Ely,* and sociologist Edward A. Ross* believed passionately that ideas were weapons and information was power. They belonged to a "factual generation" who believed that unearthing knowledge about society would lead to an improvement of society. (Mary O. Furner, *Advocacy & Objectivity* (1975); Eric F. Goldman, *Rendezvous with Destiny: A History of Modern Reform* (1952); Henry Steele Commager, *The American Mind* (1950); Luther L. Bernard, *Origins of American Sociology* (1943).)

Edward R. Kantowicz

SOCIAL SERVICE STATE. In response to industrialization and urbanization* in the early 1900s, a loose coalition of people called upon government to assume responsibility for the economic and social well-being of its citizens. This coalition included middle-class social activists, settlement house workers, academics from the new social sciences* such as sociology, economics, and social work, as well as trade unionists, Social Gospel* Christians, and women's organizations. Some were motivated by social Christian and secular humanistic values, others by anxiety about unrest among the poor. Most believed that poverty and economic insecurity were primarily caused by environmental and structural factors. As a result, they favored governmental regulation and economic aid where the free market failed to provide for a minimum standard of living.

This social progressive coalition was successful in pressuring a number of large industrial cities and states to enact laws that they hoped would ameliorate the worst conditions that created poverty and dependency. Such efforts included minimum wage and maximum hours law for women, child labor regulations,* compulsory education* requirements, tenement house regulations (*see* housing reform), special courts for children, mothers' pensions,* and workmen's compensation.* Despite these important advances during the Progressive Era, a full comprehensive national social service state did not develop in the United States as it did in Western Europe. Nevertheless, the endeavors of social progressives during the early part of the twentieth century laid the foundation for the American version of a partial social service state that was finally formulated in the 1930s during the New Deal and extended in the 1960s. (Sidney Fire, *Laissez-Faire and the General Welfare State* (1966); Richard L. McCormick, *From Realignment to Reform: Political Change in New York State, 1893–1910* (1981).)

Anthony Travis

SOCIAL SETTLEMENTS. These were social service and community centers located in the worst slums of large cities. The distinctive feature of a social settlement was that those who worked in the settlement house also lived there.

A social settlement worker gloried in the title of "resident." The idea of living with the lower classes originated in England, with Samuel A. Barnett, a London vicar, who opened the first settlement house, Toynbee Hall, in 1884. Stanton Coit brought the idea to New York, where he opened Neighborhood Guild (later renamed University Settlement)* in 1886 on the Lower East Side. In 1897 there were 74 settlements in America, including Lillian Wald's* Henry Street Settlement* in New York,* Robert Woods's* Andover House (later renamed South End House) in Boston,* Jane Addams's* Hull House,* and Graham Taylor's* Chicago Commons* in Chicago.* By 1910 the number of settlements had grown to 400, mostly in the cities of the Northeast and the Midwest.

Settlement life appealed to young, well-educated, middle-class men and women; it particularly attracted the first generation of college-educated women, who lacked outlets for their newly acquired skills and independence. Though American settlement houses were usually nondenominational, most settlement residents responded to a religious impulse growing out of the Social Gospel* movement. They generally worked for a short time, then moved on to other careers; but a nucleus of head residents, such as Jane Addams, stayed for life. Social settlements offered many services to their neighbors: day care for working mothers, language classes for immigrants, lectures and discussion groups, playgrounds and recreation programs. In addition, settlement residents engaged in political action to change the environment of the working class and the immigrants.

Many settlements sponsored reform candidates to run against local political bosses (see Political machines), and settlements became virtual think-tanks for reform movements of all kinds. Typically, a settlement activist would follow an issue all the way up the "stepladder of reform," lobbying first at city hall, then in the state legislature, and finally in Washington. Accordingly, settlement residents took a leading part in the formation of the Progressive party* in 1912, writing the most advanced portions of the party platform, the "Social Standards for Industry."* Hampered by their reliance on voluntary financial donations and sometimes limited by their own middle-class, Anglo-Saxon prejudices, settlement residents, nevertheless, brought sympathy and hope to the poorest neighborhoods and made a major impact on numerous reform movements. (Allen F. Davis, *Spearheads for Reform: The Social Settlements and the Progressive Movement* (1967); Allen F. Davis, *American Heroine: The Life and Legend of Jane Addams* (1973); Louise C. Wade, *Graham Taylor: Pioneer for Social Justice, 1851–1938* (1964); Jane Addams, *Twenty Years at Hull House* (1910); Lillian Wald, *Windows on Henry Street* (1934).)

Edward R. Kantowicz

SOCIAL STANDARDS FOR INDUSTRY. In 1910 the National Conference of Charities and Corrections* appointed a Committee on Occupational Standards, whose name was subsequently changed to the Committee on Standards of Living and Labor. Chaired at first by Paul U. Kellogg* and then by Florence Kelley* and Owen R. Lovejoy,* all leading social progressives, the committee developed and presented to the 1912 convention of the National Conference a position paper, "Social Standards for Industry," which called for a living wage and minimum wage commissions; biweekly wage payments; an eight-hour day and a six-day week; restrictions on night work, especially for women and minors; federal safety, health, and sanitation standards—enforced by inspection—for all industrial work; regulation of the employment of women and children in dangerous occupations; a prohibition on home work; safe and sanitary housing; a version of Henry George's* land tax on real estate held for speculative purposes; a ban on all wage-earning employment of children under sixteen years of age; care and retraining for the unemployed in private relief agencies and government labor colonies; worker's compensation for accidents and occupational diseases; old age pensions; and unemployment insurance. This program was endorsed by the convention.

Paul Kellogg, Henry Moskowitz,* and John Kingsbury* then persuaded Theodore Roosevelt* to endorse the essential planks of this program and include them in the Progressive party* platform on which he ran for president in 1912.* Roosevelt's stance led many prominent settlement house and private charity organization leaders, state and city charity administrators, and social progressives who were active in various reform organizations to campaign enthusiastically for his election. (Clarke A. Chambers, *Paul U. Kellogg and "The Survey": Voices for Social Welfare and Social Justice* (1971); Clarke A. Chambers, *Seedtime for Reform: American Social Service and Social Action, 1918–1933* (1963).)

Robert Asher

SOCIAL STATISTICS. Progressives relied heavily on empirical, often statistical, investigations to reveal the flaws of the economy, society, and polity, and to point the way to efficient solutions. Massive investigations into working conditions, vice, trusts, prices, the banking system, and the immigration problem, and thousands of local surveys of school systems and municipal government provided the facts. The results, usually presented in graphic form for broad public impact, often did form the basis for significant reforms. The assumption that facts were neutral and numerical data irrefutable directed progressives away from theory. They typically believed there was only one best solution, which left little incentive for compromise and consensus. The data they collected were limited to observable, quantifiable "facts." The opinions and attitudes of the people at large, not being grounded on scientific facts, did not have to be listened to. (Joseph Dorfman, *The Economic Mind in American Civilization, vol. 3: 1865–1918* (1949); Pauline Young, *Scientific Social Surveys and Statistics* (1939).)

Richard Jensen

SOCIOLOGICAL JURISPRUDENCE. Reformers attacked traditional declaratory jurisprudence, which held that law was a consistent and objective body of rules and principles that the courts applied impartially. The advocates of sociological jurisprudence rejected the idea that the law was a body of unchanging rules and principles. For them, the law, like other social institutions, was formed by society and was relative to a particular time and place. Social forces and experience, not abstract principles, shaped the law. Judges, as products of their own time, place, and social class, adapted law to social conditions as they understood society. Reformers saw the courts enforcing the prevailing conservative morality, which reformers sought to change. Declaratory legal theory, in the minds of many reformers, was a system that defended conservative social forces against the general welfare. They saw in sociological jurisprudence a democratic, humane, and realistic way of advancing social justice.*

The leading proponent of sociological jurisprudence was Roscoe Pound.* While recognizing the relative element in judicial decisions, he also recognized that judges adhering to declaratory jurisprudence believed in the ideal of an abstract, unchanging system of rules and principles. Other jurists of the time, such as Oliver Wendell Holmes, Jr.,* who did not consider themselves legal reformers were influenced by sociological factors. In *The Common Law* (1880), Holmes argued that the law was experience and practical invention, not logic. While not a progressive reformer, in *Lochner v. New York** (1905), *Hammer v. Dagenhart** (1918), and elsewhere he expressed some ideas compatible with sociological jurisprudence. Louis Brandeis* in *Muller v. Oregon** (1908) founded his arguments on an ocean of social and economic facts. Later, as a U.S. Supreme Court Justice, he analyzed the social background of the issues that appeared before him. (Roscoe Pound, *Contemporary Juristic Theory* (1940); Lawrence Friedman, *The Legal System: A Social Science Perspective* (1975); Alan Hunt, *The Sociological Movement in Law* (1978).)

John R. Aiken

SOUTH CAROLINA. As in Alabama* and Mississippi,* the race issue dominated South Carolina's political affairs during the 1890s and early 1900s. Governor Benjamin R. ("Pitchfork Ben") Tillman, the chief architect of disfranchisement,* established a pattern of demagoguery in the 1890s which shaped the state's political history prior to World War I.* Playing on the economic hardships and racial prejudice of rual South Carolinians, he had captured control of the old Bourbon Democratic party machinery by the early 1890s. During his tenure in the U.S. Senate (1895–1918), he often belied his populist past by seeking support from the Bourbons* he had fought to win office. During the early 1900s, bitter public debate frequently erupted over the operation of the state liquor dispensary, a Tillman legacy. His gubernatorial successors faced rigorous opposition from independent legislators and popularly elected state officials.

Nevertheless, a few public-spirited South Carolinians sought educational and prison reform, child labor legislation,* and municipal improvements. N. G. Gonzales, editor of the Columbia *State*, condemned lawlessness, lynching,* and convict leasing, and championed educational reform and industrial and urban development. Between 1910 and 1914, Governor Coleman L. Blease, a self-professed heir of Tillmanism, won the support of textile workers by catering to their fears of child labor laws and compulsory education.* Unabashedly racist in his appeals, Blease brought a dramatic increase in the voting turnout of white South Carolinians. His successor, Richard I. Manning, broadened state social services and increased the state's administrative efficiency. He established a board of charities and corrections, a state tax commission, and a highway department. He also secured school attendance and child labor laws and a workmen's compensation act.* Despite his efforts, no effective reform coalition existed in South Carolina. (Robert M. Burts, *Richard Irvine Manning and the Progressive Movement in South Carolina* (1974); David L. Carlton, *Mill and Town in South Carolina, 1880–1920* (1982); Ernest McPherson Lander, Jr., *A History of South Carolina, 1865–1960* (1960).)

David E. Alsobrook

SOUTH DAKOTA. South Dakota resembled its neighboring states in actively participating in the Progressive movement, but differed in that it had earlier been more deeply involved in the populist crusade of the 1890s. As late as 1898, a "Popocrat," Andrew E. Lee, won election to the governorship. Although the People's party disappeared after the turn of the twentieth century, progressive activities emerged about 1903. Early efforts involved antimachine Republicans who sought to depose a powerful clique led by Alfred B. Kittredge, a Sioux Falls attorney and legal counsel for the Chicago, Milwaukee & St. Paul Railroad. For most of the 401,570 residents of this prairie state, "boss rule" meant acts of corporate arrogance perpetrated by several large corporations. While South Dakota's growing progressive forces, under the generalship of Huron attorney Coe I. Crawford,* failed initially to get a direct primary* law, they won control of the dominant Republican organization in this largely one-party state in June 1906, and then swept the November general elections.

Between 1906 and 1914, a series of progressively oriented governors did much to uplift the state: Crawford (1906–1908), Robert S. Vessey (1908–1912), and Frank M. Byrne (1912–1916). During this period, the legislature passed meaningful antilobbying and railroad-pass restrictions and subsequently increased assessments on corporate property, including the railroads. South Dakota reformers moved to the political left after 1916, when a prosperous Redfield well-driller, Peter Norbeck, leading a new united GOP, assumed the governor's chair. During the era of World War I,* South Dakota embarked on the most advanced form of progressivism, "state socialism." Desiring to reduce costs to consumers, the Norbeck administration entered into hail insurance, cement, and coal businesses, and seriously considered publicly owned stockyards, packing plants, terminal elevators, flour mills, and hydroelectric plants. Because of the crushing post–World War I farm depression, South Dakota progressives and their ideas did not become unpopular until the latter 1920s. (Calvin Perry Armin, "Coe I. Crawford and the Progressive Movement in South Dakota," *South Dakota His-*

torical Collections 32 (1964): 26–330; Gilbert C. Fite, *Peter Norbeck: Prairie Statesman* (1948); Herbert S. Schell, *History of South Dakota* (1961).)

H. Roger Grant

SOUTHERN PROGRESSIVISM. At the end of the 1890s, and for more than a decade afterwards, progressive political leaders, drawing upon and channeling popular discontent, rose to power in the South. Conspicuous among the group were a number of outstanding governors including Charles Brantley Aycock (North Carolina), Andrew Jackson Montague (North Carolina), James K. Vardaman* (Mississippi), Napoleon Bonaparte Broward (Florida), Braxton Bragg Comer (Alabama), Hoke Smith* (Georgia), James B. McCreary (Kentucky), Locke Craig (North Carolina), and Ben W. Hooper (Tennessee). In general, Southern Progressives were members of the substantial middle class who sought through the proper utilization of individualism and free enterprise to perfect "the American way of life." They used the "New South"* philosophy as justification for legislation which would bring equality of opportunity.

Backed by many of the region's editors, businessmen, affluent farmers, educators, and professional men, progressive politicians sought pragmatic and, in many instances, mechanical solutions to many problems. They established primary elections,* the initiative,* the referendum,* and the commission system* of government, often before other sections did so. Drawing on a ferocity derived from the agrarian revolt, each tended to emphasize a specific reform. Collectively, they attacked basic injustices and obtained varying degrees of railway regulation; control over insurance companies and their investments; overthrow, in most states, of the convict lease system; child labor laws;* and, for the first time since Reconstruction, systems of universal education.

Edgar Gardner Murphy,* an Alabama minister, developed the first effective body of anti–child labor material, was instrumental in organizing the National Child Labor Committee,* and served as the first executive secretary of the Southern Education Board. Alexander McKelway,* a North Carolina clergyman and editor, became the most effective political strategist of the National Child Labor Committee and helped convert President Woodrow Wilson* to supporting a national child labor law. Walter Hines Page* gave significant support to promoting public education and aided in engineering Wilson's selection as the Democratic nominee for president in 1912. T. Thomas Fortune and Booker T. Washington* influenced much of America's attitude on race relations. Unfortunately, the Southern reformers emerged in an era when race repression was reaching its crest, and most of them at least acquiesced in it. (Dewey W. Grantham, *Southern Progressivism: The Reconciliation of Progress and Tradition* (1983); C. Vann Woodward, *Origins of the New South, 1877–1913* (1951); George B. Tindall, *The Emergence of the New South, 1913–1945* (1967).)

Hugh C. Bailey

SOUTHERN SOCIOLOGICAL CONGRESS. This organization was one of those forces which spread progressivism among Southerners. Organized in 1912 in Nashville, Tennessee, after a call by Oklahoma charity commissioner Kate

Barnard, the Southern Sociological Congress (SSC) was not an academic association. Rather it was a clearinghouse in which social workers, professors,
clergymen, journalists, and others could exchange information and make plans,
a forum for discussion of racial problems by both blacks and whites. SSC
conventions were often organized around themes—the Houston meeting of 1915
discussed public health, for example, while the Birmingham meeting of 1918
was dominated by discussion of the World War.*

Yet SSC members interested themselves in Prohibition,* housing,* mobilizing
churches for social service, care of delinquents and the handicapped, and such
causes as the crusade against lynching.* In 1916, the SSC sponsored an extension
service which sought to improve health standards in small cities. A product of
the most optimistic days of progressivism, the SSC faded in the postwar atmosphere. Still its supporters had to some degree successfully challenged the
individualism of southern society, carrying the message that society was an
"organic" and "interdependent" thing. (Dewey W. Grantham, *Southern Progressivism: The Reconciliation of Progress and Tradition* (1983); E. Charles
Chatfield, Jr., "The Southern Sociological Congress, 1912–1920" (M.A. thesis,
Vanderbilt University, 1958); E. Charles Chatfield, "The Southern Sociological
Congress: Organization of Uplift" *Tennessee Historical Quarterly* 19 (1960):
328–47; E. Charles Chatfield, "The Southern Sociological Congress: Rationale
of Conflict" *Tennessee Historical Quarterly* 20 (1961): 51–64.)

Paul M. Pruitt, Jr.

SPANISH-AMERICAN WAR. Americans considered their war with Spain,
waged for four months in 1898, a glorious victory against a corrupt, Old World
colonial power. Historian Richard Hofstadter has ascribed the exultant public
opinion surrounding the war to "the psychic crisis of the 1890s." Americans
felt frustrated by the closing of the frontier, which ended territorial expansion,
and the rise of big business combinations, which stifled individual economic
aspirations. A sharp depression which struck in 1893 and divisive political agitation by the Populist party* further increased the mood of edginess. In such a
climate, "the primary significance of the war," Hofstadter concluded, "was
that it served as an outlet for aggressive impulses while presenting itself, quite
truthfully, as an idealistic and humanitarian crusade."

Cuba was Spain's last major colony in the New World, but revolutionary
feelings had been simmering there for years. "Yellow journalists," spurred by
the newspaper rivalry between Joseph Pulitzer* and William Randolph Hearst,*
published inflammatory stories of Spanish atrocities in Cuba. Then on February
15, 1898, the U.S. battleship *Maine*, on a courtesy visit to Cuba, exploded and
sank in Havana Harbor. Though the destruction of the *Maine* was probably
accidental, President William McKinley* submitted to popular indignation and
asked Congress for a declaration of war on April 11, 1898.

The war had many tragicomic overtones, for neither Spain nor America was
prepared for battle; and ultimately more soldiers died of tropical diseases than

from enemy bullets. The decisive engagements of the war were the destruction of two Spanish naval squadrons, one at Santiago in Cuba, the other at Manila in the Philippines. The U.S. Army occupied the environs of Manila, the eastern half of Cuba, and all of Puerto Rico. Spain sued for peace in August 1898; and the Treaty of Paris, signed on December 10, 1898, granted the United States possession of the Philippines, Puerto Rico, and Guam. The United States assumed an informal protectorate over Cuba, but Congress prevented Cuban annexation by the self-denying Teller Amendment. Though short and probably unnecessary, the war signaled a more active U.S. role in world affairs and resulted in the acquisition of the first noncontiguous U.S. possessions. (Richard Hofstadter, "Manifest Destiny and the Philippines," in Daniel Aaron, ed., *America in Crisis* (1952); Frank Freidel, *The Splendid Little War* (1958); David F. Trask, *The War with Spain in 1898* (1981).)

Edward R. Kantowicz

SPARGO, JOHN (January 31, 1876–August 17, 1966). Born in England, Spargo emigrated to the United States in 1901 and soon established an active career as author of pamphlets, newspaper articles, and books. In Socialist party* affairs he was aligned with the right-wing group that de-emphasized class struggle and urged a gradualist policy. In 1912 he played a key role in the Socialist convention that denied membership to those justifying recourse to violence.

During his Socialist years Spargo wrote a book of enduring worth, *The Bitter Cry of the Children* (1906), which documented for the American reading public the conditions of exploitation, poverty, and hunger afflicting millions of children. This work, an important contribution to a growing child welfare movement, went beyond exposure to offer a broad range of reforms that would at least partially remedy existing evils. Extracts from the book were read to the U.S. Senate, and Spargo's message spurred the formation of public agencies focused on the problems he raised. By 1912 the federal government had established the U.S. Children's Bureau.*

Spargo, long a mixture of reformer and radical, became increasingly more conservative in later years. He abandoned the Socialist party to support American entrance into World War I* and vehemently opposed Communism in the wake of the Russian Revolution. (*New York Times*, August 18, 1966; Walter I. Trattner, Introduction to John Spargo, *The Bitter Cry of the Children* (1968); Ronald Radosh, "John Spargo and Wilson's Foreign Policy, 1920," *Journal of American History* 52 (1965): 548–65.)

Herbert Shapiro

SPENCER, HERBERT (April 27, 1820–December 8, 1903). Born in Derby, England, Spencer was a sickly lad whose father educated him at home. Interested in a scientific career, he soon drifted into radical journalism, arguing an extreme laissez-faire social philosophy. Over the years he published such books as *Social Statics* (1851), *The Principles of Psychology* (1855), *First Principles* (1862),

The Study of Sociology (1873), *The Man Versus the State* (1884), and his *Autobiography* (1904). Spencer used biological analogies in describing human society; his evolutionary social theory, however, emerged independently of Darwin. Force was behind reality, and conception of economic competition served the same function as natural selection did in Darwin's analysis. Social laws operated in the same deterministic fashion as those governing nature.

Thomas Malthus and Adam Smith were the greatest influences on Spencer, who was the high spokesman for classical liberalism in Victorian England. It was that designation that made his reputation in the United States. As a system-building philosopher, Spencer desired to answer all questions with his books. Other people, such as Henry George,* were less complimentary; however, the writings of William Graham Sumner* and Thorstein Veblen* reveal an influence from the Englishman, particularly his ideas concerning industrial and militant societies. On a more popular level, Spencer's doctrines of negative theory of state competence and poverty resulting from improvidence pleased a readership who accepted the self-made man ideal and the rags-to-riches myth. By 1900, the rise of the social sciences, various reformers contributing to welfare liberalism, and the growth of democracy meant that Spencer's extreme version of laissez-faire was going out of fashion. (David Wiltshire, *The Social and Political Thought of Herbert Spencer* (1978); J. W. Burrow, *Evolution and Society* (1966); David Duncan, *Life and Letters of Herbert Spencer*, 2 vols. (1908).)

Donald K. Pickens

SPRECKELS, RUDOLPH (January 1, 1872–October 4, 1958). Born in San Francisco,* California, the youngest son of Claus Spreckels, a self-made West Coast sugar magnate, Rudolph received a sketchy education before entering his father's business at the age of seventeen. Observing the unethical practices used by the "Sugar Trust" which challenged his family's interests, he beat his opponents without using their methods. He soon feuded with his father, but succeeded in becoming a millionaire on his own. After 1900 he established himself as a San Francisco banker and utility promoter.

His identification with political reform began in 1905 when he became the principal financial backer of the San Francisco graft prosecution. He supported Hiram Johnson* as reform governor of California in 1910, but broke with him over Johnson's repudiation of Robert La Follette* for the presidency in 1912. Spreckels then backed Woodrow Wilson.* Spreckels opposed the military buildup in 1916 and believed labor radicals Tom Mooney and Warren K. Billings innocent of complicity in the San Francisco preparedness parade bombing. During the 1920s Spreckels supported state regulation of water and electric power while amassing another fortune from questionable trading in radio stock. (Lincoln Steffens, *Upbuilders* (reprint ed., 1968); Bean Walton, *Boss Ruef's San Fran-*

cisco: *The Story of the Union Labor Party, Big Business, and the Graft Prosecution* (1952); *New York Times*, October 5, 1958.)

Robert E. Hennings

SQUARE DEAL. This was a slogan used to describe Theodore Roosevelt's* domestic reform policies. Roosevelt first used the phrase during his 1904 presidential reelection campaign while defending his mediation of the 1903 anthracite coal strike.* Roosevelt said he had simply given a "square deal" to both mine workers and company owners. His negotiated settlement granted the miners a pay raise but did not force the companies to accept a closed-union shop. The square deal came to characterize Roosevelt's general approach to economic policymaking. He sought a balance between big labor and big business. He did not want to outlaw or break up either business combinations or labor unions, but attempted instead to use the executive branch of the federal government to regulate them in the public interest. When Roosevelt ran for the presidency again on the Progressive party* ticket in 1912, he advocated virtually the same program under a different name, the New Nationalism.* (John Braeman, "The Square Deal in Action: A Case Study in the Growth of the 'National Police Power,' " in John Braeman, ed., *Change and Continuity in Twentieth Century America* (1964); John M. Blum, *The Republican Roosevelt* (1967); George E. Mowry, *The Era of Theodore Roosevelt* (1958).)

Edward R. Kantowicz

STANDARD OIL OF NEW JERSEY ET AL. V. U.S. (221 U.S. I (1911)). *Standard Oil of New Jersey v. U.S.* was decided by the U.S. Supreme Court on May 15, 1911. The Court ruled that Stndard Oil was a monopoly in restraint of trade under the provisions of the Sherman Antitrust Act. The judgment upheld lower federal courts' rulings that Standard Oil should be dissolved, but modified those rulings to allow an extension of the deadline for dissolution and allowed Standard Oil to engage in interstate commerce during that period. The significance of the opinion, written by Chief Justice Edward White,* was to define the concept of "restraint of trade," and in doing so, it stated that the act of forming a trust was illegal only if it engaged in "unreasonable" restraint of trade.

In 1882 Standard Oil had created a trust capitalized at $70 million. Within a few years it controlled 90 percent of the petroleum refining industry in the country. In 1890 Congress enacted an antitrust law which declared illegal "every contract, combination in the form of trust or otherwise, or conspiracy, in restraint of trade, commerce, among the several states, or with foreign actions." The first federal attack on Standard Oil was made by the Theodore Roosevelt* administration in 1907, but it was dismissed by the U.S. Court of Appeals. The William Howard Taft* administration renewed the attack, culminating in the 1911 Supreme Court decision. John D. Rockefeller,* the founder and largest stockholder of Standard Oil, accepted the court's decision because he felt it meant very little, and ties among the various branches of Standard Oil continued into the 1920s. (Robert H. Bowie, Eugene V. Rostow, and Robert Bork, *Government Regulation of Business* (1963); Bruce Bringhurst, *Antitrust and the Oil Monopoly: The Standard Oil Cases* (1979).)

Albert Erlebacher

STARR, ELLEN GATES (March 19, 1859–February 10, 1940). Starr centered her career at Hull House in Chicago, the social settlement she cofounded with her close friend and confidante, Jane Addams.* Born near Laona, Illinois, to Caleb Allen and Susan Gates Starr, she attended Rockford Female Seminary in 1877–1878. There she met Addams. Their correspondence during the following ten years forms the insight into the development of their personal philosophies before they became public figures. Starr, the more introspective, became a voice for the aesthetic dimensions of life, the cause of labor unionization, and religious expression. Industrial society, having lost touch with personal expression through craft, needed to have beauty and harmony restored.

At Hull House, Starr led the reading group studying Shakespeare, Dante, and Browning; organized art exhibits of loaned works from wealthy Chicagoans; created the Labor Museum to preserve immigrants' spinning and weaving arts; and donated framed photographs of artworks for the Public School Art Society over which she first presided. Because of her belief in the nobility of labor, she spoke and wrote against child labor* and in favor of unionizing. She joined in several strikes, suffering arrest. By 1913, she had joined the Socialist party* to further labor's cause, running for office under its banner. Starr's life as a social reformer was grounded in a religious quest. Beginning as a Unitarian and then an Episcopalian, she converted to Roman Catholicism and spent several years writing and speaking on art and liturgy. (Ellen Gates Starr, "Art and Labor," in *Hull House Maps and Papers* (1895); Jane Addams, *Twenty Years at Hull House* (1910); Allen F. Davis, *Spearheads for Reform: The Social Settlements and the Progressive Movement 1890–1914* (1967).)

Mary Ellen H. Schmider

STATUS REVOLUTION. By interpreting class motivation in society, some historians have evolved a provocative and challenging theory to explain the rise of the Progressive movement. Both George W. Mowry in his study of 47 California progressives and Alfred Chandler, who described 260 members of the 1912 Progressive party,* stated that reform was the product of young, Yankee, Protestant, professional, or business classes who felt "hemmed in" by the rising power of the large corporations. In 1955 Richard Hofstadter's *The Age of Reform* suggested that these middle-class progressives saw themselves pushed aside by the "new rich" who now had the standing and prestige in the community that formerly had resided with the "old gentry."

While the status theory still holds favor with many historians, others have been quick to challenge its worth, particularly for ignoring the class position of the opposition. Richard B. Sherman compared Massachusetts progressives with their counterparts and discovered that all "had essentially similar class characteristics." In separate surveys of state leaders in Iowa and Washington, E. D. Potts and William T. Kerr found no occupational or other major differences. A class analysis of progressives and conservatives in Toledo, Ohio, by Jack Tager demonstrated that those factors supposedly determining status were identical between the two, and that vague class definitions overlooked the complexities of individual motivation. David Thelen's study of Wisconsin* doubted that social tensions were useful parameters to diagnose group behavior. Others have argued that both the lower and upper classes had a major role to play in supporting progressivism. Yet for all the criticism of the status theory, a 1977 study by quantitative methodologists Jerome Clubb and Howard Allen make the case that the "control group" critics were "unscientific," and that the status revolution formulation remains "an intriguing and . . . untested and undeveloped-conceptual scheme." (Richard Hofstadter, *The Age of Reform* (1955); Jack Tager, "Progressives, Conservatives, and the Theory of the Status Revolution," *Mid-America* 48 (1966): 162–75; Jerome Clubb and Howard Allen, "Collective Biography and the Progressive Movement: The 'Status Revolution' Revisited," *Social Science History* 1 (Summer 1977): 518–34.)

Jack Tager

STEAD, WILLIAM T. (July 5, 1849–April 15, 1912). Born in Embleton, Northumberland, England, Stead became a newspaper reporter in the 1870s. He joined the staff of the *Pall Mall Gazette* in 1880. As the paper's editor (1883–1890), he was a crusading journalist who proposed reforms that ranged from eliminating prostitution to modernizing the British navy. Stead left the *Gazette* in 1890 to found a monthly magazine, the *Review of Reviews*. In 1893 he came to Chicago* for the World's Fair and stayed on through the winter of 1893–1894. He called a public meeting at which he decried the prevalence of saloons, brothels, and gambling halls in Chicago's slum districts and condemned local politicians who profited from those conditions. His widely read book, *If Christ Came to Chicago* (1894), also described the city's seamy side and called for civic regeneration. Largely due to Stead's urging, the Chicago Civic Federation was formed in 1894. This watchdog organization campaigned vigorously against vice and for fiscal reform and improved municipal services throughout the Progressive Era. Stead wrote extensively on spiritualist phenomena in the 1890s and from 1898 onward was active in the international peace movement. He died aboard the *Titanic*. (Frederic Whyte, *The Life of W. T. Stead* (1925); William Thomas Stead, *If Christ Came to Chicago* (1894); David F. Burg, *Chicago's White City of 1893* (1976).)

Gerald W. McFarland

STEEL STRIKE OF 1919. In 1918, officers of major unions in the steel crafts established a National Committee for Organizing Iron and Steel Workers. Their requests included an eight-hour day, elimination of the seven-day week, higher pay, and doubletime for overtime, but recognition of independent unions ranked as the most important demand. When the steel industry, long a bastion of the open shop, proved intractable, the National Committee called a strike which began on September 22, 1919. About a quarter of a million workers walked out, shutting down steel plants all over the country. In several locations, notably Pennsylvania and Indiana, antiunion law enforcement agencies prohibited strike meetings, suppressed freedom of speech, and harassed strike leaders.

With telling effectiveness, management spokesmen took advantage of the prevailing fear that a "Red Menace" threatened America by claiming that they were combatting Bolshevism within the labor movement. William Z. Foster, secretary of the National Committee, became the favorite target of attacks because of his former Industrial Workers of the World* membership and syndicalist writings. Management's successful use of strikebreakers plus defections and internal dissension within labor's ranks so weakened the workers' cause that by January 8, 1920, the National Committee called off the strike. While labor lost this battle, the strike heightened public awareness of working conditions in the steel industry which, in part, impelled management to accept the eight-hour day by 1923. (David Brody, *Labor in Crisis: The Steel Strike of 1919* (1965); William Z. Foster, *The Great Steel Strike and Its Lessons* (1920); Interchurch World Movement of North America, Commission of Inquiry, *Report on the Steel Strike of 1919* (1920).)

Graham Adams, Jr.

STEFFENS, JOSEPH LINCOLN, JR. (April 6, 1866–August 6, 1936). Born into an advantaged San Francisco* family, the future muckraking* journalist took his degree at the University of California (1889) before studying psychology and philosophy at Munich and the Sorbonne. Upon his return to the United States in 1892 Steffens joined Edwin L. Godkin's *New York Evening Post*; he mastered the "slice of life" genre of human interest story and discovered the ethnic communities of the Lower East Side. He trained as a financial and police court reporter interested in the psychological nuances of his beat, while following the careers of Rev. Charles Parkhurst and Theodore Roosevelt.* Steffens's *Autobiography* exaggerates his influence over these men.

After serving briefly as city editor for the New York *Commercial Advertiser*, Steffens began his muckraking career for *McClure's Magazine*. Instructed to write on machine politics, Steffens prepared "Tweed Days in St. Louis" (October, 1902), and then muckraked New York, Chicago, and other cities. The collected essays, *The Shame of the Cities* (1904), gave a classic description of the "invisible government" which brought together unscrupulous businessmen (like Chicago's traction magnate Charles T. Yerkes)* and urban machine politicians (like William Marcy Tweed). Subsequent studies of the states, *The Struggle for Self-Government* (1906), and reformers, *The Upbuilders* (1909), established his reputation. Steffens left *McClure's* in 1906 for a partnership in the new *American Magazine.*

In 1911 he entered an activist phase of his career. He attempted to mediate at the trial of the McNamara brothers, charged with bombing the San Francisco *Times*; intervened with Woodrow Wilson* on behalf of Venustiano Carranza in the Mexican Revolution; and participated as Wilson's peace emissary to the new Bolshevik government in Russia. Upon his death, Steffens was widely acclaimed as a radical, having been the mentor of such writers as John Reed* and Walter Lippmann.* (Patrick F. Palermo, *Lincoln Steffens* (1978); Lincoln Steffens, *The Autobiography of Joseph Lincoln Steffens* (1931); Robert Stinson, *Lincoln Steffens* (1979).)

Harold Wilson

STEICHEN, DAVID (Eduard Jean) (March 27, 1879–March 25, 1973). Steichen was born and raised in Milwaukee, Wisconsin. Starting photography in 1895, exhibited nationally by 1899, and a painter since childhood, he was a successful portrait photographer in Paris and later in New York. Until the 1920s, however, his standing as a photographic giant was based primarily on amateur work. During this period, he was closely associated with Alfred Stieglitz* in the quarterly, *Camera Work*, in the Photo-Secession, and in the Stieglitz-run New York gallery they cofounded in 1905 (later called "291"), for which Steichen procured avant-garde paintings and sculpture from 1907 to 1914. By 1914, quarrels over cubism, futurism, amateurism, and World War I* had eroded their friendship, which ended in 1917.

Pioneering aerial photography in the Signal Corps in France (1917–1919), Steichen perfected thereafter the sharp, dramatic images that made him Condé Nast's and advertising's star from 1923 to 1938. By then he was famous also as a delphinium culturist. Head of combat photography for the navy (1943–1945), Steichen directed the photography department of New York's Museum of Modern Art from 1947 to 1962. Among his shows was the 1955 *Family of Man*, acclaimed worldwide for its scope and compassion. He continued photographing until 1960. (William Innes Homer, *Alfred Stieglitz and the American Avant-Garde* (1977); Sue Davidson Lowe, *Stieglitz: A Memoir/Biography* (1983); Carl Sandburg, *Steichen the Photographer* (1929).)

Sue Davidson Lowe

STIEGLITZ, ALFRED (January 1, 1864–July 13, 1946). Born in Hoboken, New Jersey, Stieglitz lived principally in New York City and Lake George, New York. From 1881 to 1890, living in Berlin, he traveled widely and attended the Polytechnikum and Berlin University. In 1885, he exchanged engineering studies for photography. The first American photographer known worldwide as both a technical pioneer and a creative giant, Stieglitz arranged international shows in Europe in 1889, and at home and abroad from 1890 to 1910, promoting photography as an art. Co-editor for a year of the *American Amateur Photographer*, he helped found the Camera Club of New York in 1896 and, until 1902, edited its *Camera Notes*. In 1902, he launched the Photo-Secession; in 1903, he founded, edited, and published the nonpareil arts quarterly *Camera Work*; and in 1905, he opened the Fifth Avenue gallery, 291, to give photography a show-place.

Although he remained an active photographer and introduced others until 1938, Stieglitz began a crusade to gain acceptance in the United States of modern art in 1908. *Camera Work* became the voice, and 291 the home, of the avant-garde. Before 1913, he had given American debuts to Auguste Rodin, Henri Matisse, Paul Cézanne, and Pablo Picasso. By 1917 (when both *Camera Work* and 291 ended), he was featuring also the American modernists John Cheri Marin, Arthur Garfield Dove, and Georgia O'Keeffe, whose mainstay he became at his sub-sequent galleries. An antiestablishment moralist-educator, Stieglitz had a pro-nounced influence on American writers as well as artists, advocating the search for individual truth, in life as in art, to foster a pluralistic, sensitive, and non-materialistic society. True to his principles, he worked throughout most of his life as a full-time unpaid volunteer. (Waldo Frank, ed., *America and Alfred Stieglitz: A Collective Portrait* (reprint ed., 1975); Sarah Greenough and Juan Hamilton, *Alfred Stieglitz, Photographs and Writings* (1983); Sue Davidson Lowe, *Stieglitz: A Memoir/Biography* (1983); Dorothy Norman, *Alfred Stieglitz: An American Seer* (1973).)

                                                                      Sue Davidson Lowe

STIMSON, HENRY LOUIS (September 21, 1867–October 20, 1950). Born in New York City* to an aristocratic New England family, Stimson joined the law firm of Elihu Root* in 1891. Continuing representation of wealthy corporate clients, Stimson formed his own law firm in 1899. Appointed a U.S. attorney by Theodore Roosevelt* in 1906, Stimson prosecuted companies for violating the Sherman Antitrust and Elkins Railroad* acts. Stimson unsuccessfully ran for governor of New York in 1910 as a Republican. In 1915, he was a delegate to the reform-minded New York constitutional convention. Stimson had shifted his primary attention from domestic matters to foreign policy by 1911, when he was appointed secretary of war by President William Howard Taft.* Serving till 1913, Stimson endeavored to reorganize the military for the modern world. As a private citizen from 1914 to 1917, Stimson advocated American preparation for entry into the European war, and in 1917 he briefly served in the military. For the rest of his life, Stimson alternated private legal practice with government service in the foreign policy field, notably as secretary of state under President Herbert Hoover* and secretary of war under President Franklin Roosevelt.* (Henry L. Stimson and McGeorge Bundy, *On Active Service in Peace and War* (1949); Richard N. Current, *Secretary Stimson: A Study in Statecraft* (1954); Elting E. Morison, *Turmoil and Tradition: The Life and Times of Henry L. Stimson* (1960).)

                                                                      Martin I. Elzy

STOKES, JAMES GRAHAM PHELPS (March 18, 1872–April 8, 1960) and **STOKES, ROSE PASTOR** (July 18, 1879–June 20, 1933). This couple con-sisted of a "millionaire socialist" from New York and his immigrant socialist wife. Heir to a merchant and industrial fortune, J. G. Phelps Stokes was born in New York and educated at Yale and Columbia. He served as president of the Nevada Central Railroad from 1898 to 1938. He became interested in social and political causes, backing Hearst's* Municipal Ownership* campaign to 1905, and living at University Settlement* for a time. Rose Pastor, a journalist for the *Jewish Daily News*, interviewed J. G. at the settlement house in 1903 and they were married in 1905. Rose was an immigrant from Russian Poland who had worked at a cigar factory in Cleveland before moving to New York for a writing career.

Mr. and Mrs. Phelps Stokes both joined the Socialist party* in 1906, and J. G. was elected to the national executive committee in 1908. Both quit the party in 1917 when the socialists opposed American entry into World War I,* but Rose soon rejoined and was jailed for antiwar activities. Her radicalism estranged her from an increasingly conservative J. G., and the couple were divorced in 1925. But while their marriage lasted, the millionaire and his immigrant wife earned considerable publicity as the "odd couple" of the socialist cause. (*New York Times* Obituary, April 9, 1960; *Dictionary of American Biography* vol. 18; David A. Shannon, *The Socialist Party of America* (1955).)

Edward R. Kantowicz

STRAIGHT, WILLARD DICKERMAN (January 31, 1880–December 2, 1918). The son of Henry H. and Emma May (Dickerman) Straight of English background, Straight was born in Oswego, New York, and educated there, graduating from Cornell University in 1901. Having learned Chinese and Japanese while his father served as a missionary, he returned to the Far East to work for the Chinese Imperial Maritime Customs Service until becoming a Reuters News correspondent during the Russo-Japanese War. He served as vice-consul and secretary to the American minister in Seoul, and after a brief stint in Cuba, returned to Mukden as consul general.

Subsequently, as acting chief of the Division of Far Eastern Affairs at the State Department in 1908–1909, he was extremely pro-Chinese and an advocate of dollar diplomacy* to prevent Japanese expansion at China's expense. He left the State Department to head a consortium to increase American trade and investment opportunities, especially in the Hukuang and Manchuria railroads. His dollar diplomacy effort collapsed due to Russian and Japanese opposition in 1911. Straight returned to the world of U.S. finance, marrying Dorothy C. Whitney, daughter of Wall Street magnate William C. Whitney. The Straights later founded *New Republic** magazine. (H. D. Croley, *Willard Straight* (1925); *Dictionary of American Biography*; Warren I. Cohen, *America's Response to China* (1971); *New York Times*, December 2, 1918.)

C. David Tompkins

STRAUS, OSCAR S. (December 23, 1850–May 3, 1926). Born in Otterburg, Rhenish Bavaria, Straus, whose family had emigrated to the United States, received his undergraduate and legal education at Columbia University. After practicing law for eight years, he became a partner in the family mercantile business. Its burgeoning prosperity enabled Straus to devote himself to diplomacy, government service, and Jewish causes. He served as minister to Turkey in three different administrations. In 1902, Theodore Roosevelt* conferred upon Straus the appointment he most esteemed: a six-year term to the Court of Arbitration at the Hague, which was renewed four times.

Straus's role in Roosevelt's "kitchen cabinet" and his service as secretary of commerce and labor from 1906 until 1909 transformed him into an ardent, dedicated Rooseveltian, whose "blind devotion" to his leader was unquestioned. In 1912, Straus was "captured by the moral aura engulfing the Progressive cause, the fervor of the new party, and Roosevelt's personal leadership." He was a conspicuous delegate to the August convention. The following month the New York Progressives averted factional strife by bestowing the gubernatorial nomination upon Straus. From 1912 until 1916 Straus followed Roosevelt's shifting policies toward the Progressive party.* Straus's return to the GOP was celebrated by his appointment to its fifteen-man campaign committee as one of six former Progressives. Straus ended his public career appropriately as a prominent member of the League to Enforce Peace. (Naomi W. Cohen, *A Dual Heritage: The Public Career of Oscar S. Straus* (1969); Oscar S. Straus, *Under Four Administrations* (1922); Ruhl J. Bartlett, *The League to Enforce Peace* (1944).)

Jules A. Karlin

STRONG, JOSIAH (January 19, 1847–April 28, 1916). Social Gospel* minister and author born in Naperville, Illinois, Strong was educated in Ohio, at Western Reserve College, and Lane Theological Seminary. He was ordained a Congregationalist minister in 1871; then in 1885 he published *Our Country*, the book which won him his reputation as a Social Gospel publicist and earned him a job as general secretary of the Evangelical Alliance. In *Our Country* and subsequent books, Strong described the squalid living conditions of industrial cities and lamented that the working class was either unchurched or else belonged to nonevangelical faiths such as Roman Catholicism and Judaism. He advocated a Social Gospel, that is, a reinterpretation of the Christian Gospel that emphasized the improvement of social conditions and the coming of the Kingdom of God *in this world*. When his views forced his resignation from the mainstream Evangelical Alliance in 1898, he founded the League for Social Services. Strong's liberal Christianity was a major force for social reform, but it was also heavily tinged with Anglo-Saxon superiority, making Strong an apologist for imperialism and immigration restriction.* (Dorothea R. Muller, "The Social Philosophy of Josiah Strong: Social Christianity and American Progressivism," *Church History* 28 (1959): 183–201; Henry F. May, *Protestant Churches and Industrial America*

(1967); Sydney E. Ahlstrom, *A Religious History of the American People* (1972).)

Edward R. Kantowicz

STRONG, WILLIAM LAFAYETTE (March 22, 1827–November 2, 1900). Businessman and reform mayor of New York,* Strong was born in Ohio* of New England stock, worked in a country store, moved to New York, and clerked in a wholesale dry goods house. In 1869, he founded his own wholesale firm; Strong was reputedly worth $5 million at the time of his death. He ran unsuccessfully for Congress in 1882; then in 1894, following sensational disclosures of Tammany Hall* corruption by the Lexow Committee of the New York state legislature, he was chosen by a reform Committee of Seventy as the nonpartisan candidate for mayor.

Most of the anti-Tammany forces united behind Strong in a Fusion campaign, and he was elected on a good government platform. The disparate politicians supporting him, however, soon fell to quarreling; and Tammany came back to power in 1897, arrogantly chanting the ditty: "Well, well, well, Reform has gone to hell." Strong's brief tenure as mayor was most noted for two outstanding appointments he made: Theodore Roosevelt* as police commissioner, and Colonel George E. Waring as street commissioner. (*Dictionary of American Biography vol. 18; Melvin G. Holli and Peter d'A Jones, eds., Biographical Dictioinary of American Mayors*; George F. Knerr, "The Mayoral Administration of William L. Strong" (Ph.D. diss., New York University, 1957).)

Edward R. Kantowicz

STRUCTURAL REFORM. Structural reform mayors, according to Melvin G. Holli, sought to reform cities by changing the structures of municipal government, eliminating petty crime and vice, and by introducing the business system of the contemporary corporation into municipal government. Charter tinkering, elaborate audit procedures, and the drive to impose businesslike efficiency upon city government were the stock-in-trade of this type of urban executive. Mayors of this reform persuasion could be found in New York, Buffalo, San Francisco, and countless other cities at the turn of the century. They all shared a certain style and a number of common assumptions about the causes of municipal misgovernment and, in some instances, a conviction about which class was best fit to rule the city. None of the structural reformers had unqualified faith in the ability of the masses to rule themselves as did their counterparts, social reformers.*

The structural reform tradition represented the first wave of prescriptive municipal government which placed its faith in rule by upper-class Americans and later municipal experts rather than the lower orders. Efficiency,* honesty, and merit selection of employees were the tocsin calls of structural reform. The putting into office of men of character, substance, and integrity was an effort to impose middle-class, patrician, and business ideals upon the urban masses. The movement reached its height in the second and third decades of this century with the city manager and commission forms of government. Mayors Seth Low* (1902–1903), William F. Havemeyer (1872–1874), James D. Phelan* (1897–1902), and Grover Cleveland (1882) are exemplars of the structural reform tradition. (Melvin G. Holli, *Reform in Detroit: Hazen S. Pingree and Urban Politics* (1969); Melvin G. Holli and Peter d'A. Jones, eds., *Biographical Dictionary of American Mayors, 1820–1980* (1981); M. G. Holli, "Urban Reform in the Progressive Era," in Lewis L. Gould, ed., *The Progressive Era* (1974).)

Melvin G. Holli

STUBBS, WALTER ROSCOE (November 7, 1858–March 25, 1929). Born near Richmond, Wayne County, Indiana, Stubb was educated in rural schools. He was elected to the Kansas House of Representatives in 1902, 1903, and 1906. After losing a U.S. senatorial race in 1906, he was chosen governor in 1908 and 1910. He fell victim to the Progressive party* bolt of 1912, losing a Senate bid to the Democratic candidate, William H. Thompson. He also failed in subsequent elections when he ran for the Senate in 1918 and for governor in 1922 and 1924. He helped form the Kansas Republican League in 1904, the Square Deal Movement of 1906, and the progressive-Republican faction in 1908.

As speaker of the house (1905) and governor (1909–1913), he promoted the entire range of state progressivism. He was in part responsible for the elective state printer and state-owned printing plant laws in 1903; the railroad antipass law, two-cent passenger fare law, and state tax commission law in 1907; the primary election* law of 1908; the bank depositors' guaranty law,* corrupt practices* act, antilobbying law, campaign expenditures acts, inheritance tax law, and senatorial preference primary law in 1909. He also secured the employer's liability law,* workmen's compensation act,* public utilities commission, the first-ever state "Blue Sky" investment law, woman suffrage* amendment to the Kansas constitution, and various educational, health, and human welfare laws, in 1911. A Quaker, Stubbs was an ardent backer of Prohibition. He was one of the governors who called on Theodore Roosevelt* to seek the nomination in 1912 and was prominent in the Progressive party.* (Robert S. La Forte, *Leaders of Reform* (1974); William Elsey Connelley, ed., *Kansas and Kansans* (1918); *The Autobiography of William Allen White* (1946).)

Robert S. La Forte

SULLIVAN, LOUIS H. (September 13, 1856–April 11, 1924). Generally considered to be the first modern American architect, Sullivan was born in Boston* and attended public schools there. His professional education was brief, including a year's study at the Massachusetts Institute of Technology (1872–1873) and at the renowned École des Beaux Arts (1874–1876) in Paris. He achieved fame in partnership with Dankmar Adler of Chicago; from 1881 to 1885 the firm produced many of the best early "skyscrapers" of the so-called Chicago school of architecture, including the Wainwright Building (1890) in Saint Louis and the Guarantee Building (1894) in Buffalo. In his writing, he promoted the idea of an American architecture, somehow evolving naturally out of a romantic, Whitmanesque belief in democracy, and free of "feudal" references to past historical styles.

Although Sullivan is best known for his earlier large works like the Auditorium Building (1890) and the Transportation Building (1893) at the World's Columbian Exposition in Chicago, his philosophy is better represented by the series of small banks that he designed in the early twentieth century for farm communities in the Midwest. He is considered to be the father of the midwestern Prairie school of architects, which included Frank Lloyd Wright,* who had worked briefly for Adler & Sullivan. Seeing himself as alone in his struggle against the more popular classical design of his time and unable to attract commissions, he died bitter and destitute in Chicago. (David S. Andrew, *Louis Sullivan and the Polemics of Modern Architecture* (1985); Hugh Morrison, *Louis Sullivan, Prophet of Modern Architecture* (1935); Louis Sullivan, *The Autobiography of an Idea* (1956).)

Diane Filipowicz

SULLIVAN, MARK (September 10, 1876–August 15, 1952). Mark Sullivan was born to Irish immigrants in Chester County, Pennsylvania, the youngest of nine children. While a student at Harvard (A.B., 1900; LL.B., 1903) he wrote occasional travel and political pieces for the Boston *Transcript* and the *Atlantic Monthly*.* In 1904 as an investigator for the *Ladies' Home Journal*,* he made a small but useful contribution in exposing patent medicine frauds, such as Dr. Peirce's Favorite Prescription, a proprietary medicine adulterated with morphine. After legal research for *McClure's*, Sullivan joined *Collier's Weekly** in 1906. In twelve years he progressed from writing articles, to preparing his own editorial page, and finally to editing the magazine from 1914 to 1919.

Although not a muckraker, Sullivan wrote pointedly on behalf of the insurgent Republicans: Senator Nelson W. Aldrich* was a "sinister figure," William Howard Taft's* tariff was business "graft," and Theodore Roosevelt* was the chosen leader for Armageddon. Sullivan applauded much in Woodrow Wilson's* domestic reforms, but was extremely critical of the president's foreign policy. He joined the New York *Evening Post* in 1919 and three years later became a syndicated columnist for the *Herald Tribune*. His final tribute to the Progressive Era was the monumental history, *Our Times*, published in six volumes. (Mark Sullivan, *The Education of an American: An Autobiography* (1938); Mark Sullivan, *Our Times: The United States, 1900–1925* (1926–1936); Edward LaRue Weldon, "Mark Sullivan's Progressive Journalism, 1876–1925: An Ironic Persuasion" (Ph.D. diss., Emory University, 1970).)

Harold Wilson

SULLIVAN, ROGER CHARLES (February 3, 1861–April 14, 1920). Sullivan came to Chicago* from Belvidere, Illinois, in 1879 and worked at various odd jobs, but soon found himself drawn to politics. He was not a gifted speaker, but he was a good social mixer who did not mind performing the tedious tasks ("grunt work") of political organizing. Sullivan became inseparable pals with future Chicago mayor John Hopkins, and together, this Irish tandem took on the Carter Harrison* family for control of the local Democratic party and eventually the city itself. Sullivan held only one public office in his life, probate court clerk, but planted the seeds behind the scenes for the growth and development of the mighty Chicago Democratic machine.

He took advantage of the city's historic rapid growth by recognizing the economic possibilities and advantages of combining political "clout" with business entrepreneurship. He and his associates became citywide villians to reformers in both parties for their efforts to use their political muscle to influence the awarding of expanded public utility franchises and lucrative city contracts. Though Sullivan, or his allies, could never win city hall, they did manage to become rich and powerful. In 1912, however, Sullivan helped win the Democratic nomination for Woodrow Wilson* by swinging the Illinois delegation at the Baltimore convention. In 1914 Sullivan attempted an image change by running a respectable, but losing, race for U.S. Senate. (Paul Micheal Green, "Irish Chicago: The Multi-Ethnic Road to Machine Success," in Melvin G. Holli and Paul M. Green, eds., *Ethnic Chicago* (1984); Alex Gottfried, *Boss Cermak of Chicago* (1962); Samuel A. Lilly, "The Political Career of Roger C. Sullivan" (M.A. thesis, Eastern Illinois University, 1964).)

Paul Micheal Green

SULZER, WILLIAM (March 18, 1863–November 6, 1941). Independent-minded New York Democrat who was impeached as governor by Tammany Hall* opponents, Sulzer was born in Elizabeth, New Jersey, of Dutch and German stock. He moved to the Lower East Side of New York with his family, clerked in a wholesale grocery, took night classes at Cooper Union, and became a lawyer in 1884. After two terms in the state assembly, he served in Congress from 1895 to 1912. He was a noted orator, speaking out passionately in defense of the common man. In 1912, Tammany boss Charles Francis Murphy,* who often chose honest and independent Democrats for important positions in order to co-opt reform forces, slated Sulzer for governor of New York. Once elected, he proved too independent for Tammany, trying to introduce direct primary* elections which would dilute Tammany influence. Murphy retaliated by ordering his impeachment and removal, which was carried out by the legislature on October 17, 1913. The Sulzer impeachment became the main issue in municipal politics and led to the election of a reform mayor, John Purroy Mitchel.* (Jacob A. Friedman, *The Impeachment of Gov. William Sulzer* (1939); Nancy Joan Weiss, *Charles Francis Murphy* (1968); Edwin R. Lewinson, *John Purroy Mitchel: The Boy Mayor of New York* (1965).)

Edward R. Kantowicz

SUMNER, WILLIAM GRAHAM (October 30, 1840–April 12, 1910). The son of English working-class immigrants, Sumner studied at Yale (class of 1863), and later prepared for the Episcopalian clergy at Geneva, Göttingen, and Oxford.

After serving in pastorates in the New York area, he accepted a chair of political economy at Yale in 1872, and was soon active in the academic reforms of the Young Yale movement. During the 1880s, he won a reputation as a leading defender of laissez-faire with such works as *What Social Classes Owe to Each Other* (1883).

Branded "conservative" and worse by proponents of positive state action, Sumner in his way wished also to reform the political corruption and economic abuses of his day, notably by eliminating the protective tariff. During the 1890s, he condemned America's imperialism in a widely read essay "The Conquest of the United States by Spain." In the final decades of his life, Sumner turned from economics to sociology, the result in part of his inability to influence the course of affairs. The result was *Folkways* (1906), which added the terms "folkways" and "mores" to the sociologists' lexicon and moved the debate over social controls and the limits of state action to a new level. (Harris E. Starr, *William Graham Sumner* (1925); Robert C. Bannister, "Sumner's 'Social Darwinism,' " *History of Political Economy* 5 (1973): 89–109; Bruce Curtis, *William Graham Sumner* (1981).)

Robert C. Bannister

SURVEY, THE. The *Survey* magazine provided the major link between a wide variety of reforms and the new profession of social work. The magazine was the result of the mergers of the journals of several social work agencies, most notably New York City's Charity Organization Society,* whose journal *Charities* merged with the *Commons*, published by Chicago Commons* settlement house, to become in 1905 *Charities and the Commons*. By 1909, when the magazine adopted the name the *Survey*, it was national in scope. The key person in its development was Paul Underwood Kellogg,* who began as an assistant editor of *Charities* in 1902. The Charities Publication Committee selected Kellogg to direct the massive Pittsburgh survey* and edit its investigations for publications.

The Pittsburgh Survey was a detailed investigation of the interrelationships among various social problems and became the model for similar, if less intensive, investigations in other cities. As editor of the *Survey* from 1912 to 1952, Kellogg believed that publicizing bad conditions would prompt people to come up with solutions. The *Survey* ran everything from analyses of ethnic neighborhoods to a pioneering article on syphilis in 1905, and many key reformers contributed to its pages. (Clarke A. Chambers, *Paul U. Kellogg and "The Survey"* (1971); Edward T. Devine, *When Social Work Was Young* (1939); Paul U. Kellogg, ed., *The Pittsburgh Survey* (1909–1914).)

Judith Ann Trolander

SWIFT 7 CO. v. U.S. (196 U.S. 375). This 1905 Supreme Court case infused new power into the Sherman Antitrust Act by directly expanding the limited definition of interstate commerce which had been put forward in the E. C. Knight case (1895). As part of the great merger movement of the turn of the century, three of the nation's largest meat-packing companies—Swift, Armour, and Morris—formed the National Packing Company in 1902 in an effort by these Chicago-based firms to control livestock and manipulate meat prices in stockyards and slaughtering centers in East Saint Louis, Kansas City, and Omaha. Responding to public outcry, President Theodore Roosevelt* ordered the Justice Department to file suit against these and three other meat packers, charging them with using monopolistic practices to restrain trade and control the sale of meat in interstate commerce.

Although it failed to order dissolution of the National Packing Company, the Court unanimously accepted the opinion written by Oliver Wendell Holmes,* which enunciated a broader definition of interstate commerce than in the Knight case, in which the Court had drawn a sharp distinction between "manufacturing" and "commerce" and had declared that the Sherman Act applied only to the latter. In the Swift case, Holmes first formulated the "stream of commerce" doctrine, which emphasized the degree to which the animals and the processed meat products moved through the local stockyards in a current of interstate commerce. Although the packers' control of the stockyards was not curtailed until 1920, the Court in 1905 gave up making distinctions between interstate and local aspects of giant industries. (Hans B. Thorelli, *The Federal Antitrust Policy* (1955); David Gordon, "Swift & Co. *v.* United States: The Beef Trust and the Stream of Commerce Doctrine," American Journal of Legal *History* 28 (July 1984): 244–79.)

John Whiteclay Chambers II

T

TAFT, CHARLES PHELPS (December 21, 1843–December 31, 1929). Born in Cincinnati, Ohio, Charles was the eldest of three half-brothers including William Howard.* After completing his education in the local public schools, he attended the universities of Yale, Columbia, and Heidelberg and the Sorbonne. After traveling in Europe and practicing law for a decade, he purchased and edited several local newspapers, managed extensive properties left to him by his father-in-law, codified Ohio's school laws, and edited the *Reports* of the Cincinnati Supreme Court.

Charles served as one of William Taft's closest advisers, counseling him not to keep all of Theodore Roosevelt's* cabinet, to support Richard A. Ballinger rather than Gifford Pinchot* on the conservation issue, and, after the elections of 1910, to pay some heed to insurgent Republicans. Charles spent a year on William's preconvention campaign and also helped him financially. William's saying that he owed his election as president as much to Charles as to Roosevelt sat badly with the latter and was in part responsible for the Taft-Roosevelt break in 1912. (Henry F. Pringle, *The Life and Times of William Howard Taft* (1939); Ishbel Ross, *An American Family: The Tafts, 1678–1964* (1964); Mrs. William Howard Taft, *Recollections of Full Years* (1914).)

Paolo E. Coletta

TAFT, WILLIAM HOWARD (September 15, 1857–March 8, 1930). Born in Cincinnati, Ohio, Taft obtained his higher education at Yale University and until elected president in 1910 filled only appointive offices including those of civil governor of the Philippines and secretary of war. As a judge, he early earned the dislike of organized labor; on the race question he followed the policies of Booker T. Washington.* Taft met Theodore Roosevelt* when he himself was the solicitor of the United States. They established a close friendship that lasted until 1912. Deciding not to run in 1908, Roosevelt supported Taft as his successor even though the latter preferred an appointment to the Supreme Court.

A coolness quickly developed with Roosevelt over his dropping some members of Roosevelt's cabinet and filling it with rich corporation lawyers. If the two men agreed on progressive policies, they disagreed on methods. Taft exerted little leadership over Congress and failed to use the patronage or the press effectively. The victories of Democrats and "insurgents,"* or progressive Republicans, in 1910, put these in control of the House during his last two years. Taft obtained more progressive legislation in four years than Roosevelt had in seven: tariff reform (of a sort); a tariff commission* to establish "scientific" rates; postal savings bank,* parcel post, and federal budget systems; the federal incorporation of corporations engaged in interstate commerce; and a prohibition against corporation contributions to political parties. He also put the postal system upon a paying basis, tightened up railroad regulations, improved government administration, and favored the direct election of senators.*

On the other hand, he interpreted the Constitution so narrowly that he would not act unless he found authority therein to do so. He also failed to obtain tariff reciprocity with Canada* and arbitration treaties with Great Britain and France. Taft's support for his secretary of the interior, Richard A. Ballinger, against the reformer Gifford Pinchot* made it appear that he endorsed the corporate exploitation of the nation's natural resources rather than the Roosevelt-Pinchot way of regulated use. He so displeased Roosevelt that the latter created his own party in 1912 and, by dividing the Republican vote, made possible Woodrow Wilson's* victory. After his defeat he accepted a professorship of law at Yale, wrote about the presidency, and was appointed Chief Justice of the Supreme Court by Warren Harding.* (Paolo E. Coletta, *The Presidency of William Howard Taft* (1973); George E. Mowry, *The Era of Theodore Roosevelt, 1900–1912* (1958); Henry F. Pringle, *The Life and Times of William Howard Taft* (1939).)

Paolo E. Coletta

TAGGART, THOMAS (November 17, 1856–March 6, 1929). Democratic boss of Indiana,* a "kingmaker" at Democratic National Conventions, Taggart was born in Ireland; he emigrated with his family in 1861, settling in Xenia, Ohio. He was educated in public schools, moved to Indiana in 1874, and went into the hotel and restaurant business, eventually building the resort hotel at French Lick Springs. He served as mayor of Indianapolis from 1895 to 1901, then chaired the Democratic National Committee from 1900 to 1908. He attended every Democratic National Convention from 1900 to 1924 and played a major part in securing the vice presidential nomination for Indianans John Worth Kern in 1908 and Thomas Marshall* in 1912.

At the 1912 convention in Baltimore, Taggart and Roger Sullivan* of Illinois joined with the Tammany Hall* bosses of New York in trying to stop the nomination of Woodrow Wilson.* Failing in this, Taggart threw Indiana's twenty-nine votes to Wilson, starting a series of vote shifts that finally nominated him. Taggart was appointed to fill a vacancy in the U.S. Senate on March 20, 1916, but he failed to hold the seat in the election later that year. (*Biographical Directory of the American Congress*; William E. Wilson, *Indiana: A History* (1966); Arthur S. Link, *Wilson: The Road to the White House* (1947).)

Edward R. Kantowicz

TAMMANY HALL. Founded in 1789 as the "Society of St. Tammany, or Columbian Order," Tammany Hall initially was a benevolent society but soon turned to politics. During the nineteenth century it became the preeminent Democratic club in New York City* and, arguably, the most powerful political machine* in the nation. After the Civil War, from the reign of "Boss" William Marcy Tweed (1867–1871) onwards, Tammany Hall became synonymous with graft and corruption: purchased and stolen votes, bribery, blackmail, prostitution, gambling, extortion. Additionally, it promoted "honest graft," whereby public officials used prior knowledge of business transactions to further their personal interests. Yet it also offered needed public services during an age of rapid urban change and gave both sympathy and tangible benefits to the city's native and immigrant poor, who, in turn, gratefully provided the votes that made machine rule possible.

Attacks by reform groups such as the Citizens Union,* dissident Democrats like William Randolph Hearst,* as well as investigations and adverse publicity, occasioned some diminution of popularity. The elections for mayor of Seth Low* in 1901 and John Purroy Mitchel* in 1913 demonstrated that substantial reform victories were possible. Nonetheless, Tammany continued as a successful political establishment, reaching the zenith of its power during the long tenure of Charles F. Murphy* (1902–1924). (Gustavus Myers, *The History of Tammany Hall* (1917); Roy V. Peel, *The Political Clubs of New York City* (1935).)

Robert Muccigrosso

TARBELL, IDA MINERVA (November 5, 1857–January 6, 1944). Ida Tarbell was born in Erie County, Pennsylvania. Her father, Frederick Tarbell, a small producer, was economically disadvantaged when Cleveland financiers consolidated this oil-producing region under their control. Tarbell graduated from Allegheny College in 1880, the sole female in her class. She taught school, managed the *Canutauquan*, and in 1890 went to Paris to prepare a biography of Madame Marie Jeanne Roland, the French revolutionary. After translating short pieces for the American press, she was invited by Samuel McClure* to write for his newspaper syndicate. Upon the founding of *McClure's Magazine* in 1893, she joined the staff as an editor. Her biography of Napoleon was an immediate success, and in 1896 she commenced her study of Abraham Lincoln. These series did much to ensure the financial success of *McClure's*. Her *History of Standard Oil* was a model of muckraking journalism. She used court cases, interviews, and government investigations, and her treatment, although marked by a personal animus against John D. Rockefeller,* was free of the ideological bias which colored Henry D. Lloyd's* *Wealth Vs. Commonwealth*. In 1906 Miss Tarbell left *McClure's* to help found the *American Magazine*.* Her subsequent writings focused on the tariff, business biography, and women's rights, although she opposed woman suffrage. (Kathleen Brady, *Ida Tarbell: Portrait of a Muckraker* (1984); Mary E. Tomkins, *Ida M. Tarbell* (1974); Ida M. Tarbell, *All in a Day's Work: An Autobiography* (1939).)

Harold S. Wilson

TARIFF COMMISSION. The Tariff Commission, a bipartisan board of economic experts, was established in 1916 to make "scientific" and "objective" recommendations for revising the federal tariffs on imported goods. Tariff-making was traditionally a highly partisan and divisive process in Congress, with Democrats* favoring lower tariffs and Republicans* advocating high tariffs. Final tariff bills always represented many compromises and much "log-rolling." Progressive Republicans of the New Nationalism* persuasion advocated an expert commission in order to "take the tariff out of politics." President William Howard Taft* appointed a commission in 1911, but it lapsed with the end of his administration.

The Progressive party* platform of 1912 called for a permanent tariff commission. Finally, President Woodrow Wilson* embraced the New Nationalism views of his political opponents and included the authority for a tariff commission in the Revenue Act of 1916.* Though the commission held only advisory authority and did not remove politics from the process of tariff-making, its technical advice did prove useful to Congress when drafting the next general revision of the tariffs in 1922. (Frank W. Taussig, *The Tariff History of the United States* (1931); Arthur S. Link, *Woodrow Wilson and the Progressive Era* (1954).)

Edward R. Kantowicz

TAUSSIG, FRANK WILLIAM (December 28, 1859–November 11, 1940). Born in Saint Louis, Missouri, Taussig was Harvard A.B. (Highest Honors) 1879, Ph.D. 1883, and LL.B. 1886. He was secretary to Harvard's president, Charles W. Eliot,* before joining the Harvard faculty, on which he served from 1882 to 1935. He edited the *Quarterly Journal of Economics* (1896–1937) and was president of the American Economic Association* (1904–1905). As first chairman of the U.S. Tariff Commission,* he shaped its fact-finding role. He served on the War Industries Board* and as an adviser on trade as a member of the U.S. delegation to the Paris Peace Conference.

A traditional but not doctrinaire economist, concerned with policy application, inequality, international trade, and comparative advantage, he published 13 books and over 200 articles; his highly influential text, *Principles of Economics*, went through four editions (1911–1939), and his *Tariff History of the United States* went through eight editions (1888–1931). (Frank W. Taussig, ed., *Explorations in Economics, Notes and Essays: Contributed in Honor of F. W. Taussig* (1936); J. A. Schumpeter, A. H. Cole, and E. S. Mason, "Frank William Taussig,"

Quarterly Journal of Economics 55 (May 1941):337–63; Howard S. Ellis, "Frank William Taussig, 1859–1940," *American Economic Review* 31 (1941): 209-11.)

David Chalmers

TAX REFORM, STATE. Despite acknowledged absurdities in state tax systems prior to the late nineteenth century and Pennsylvania's attempts, commenced in 1824, to derive all revenues from corporate taxation rather than general properties, reforms in other states occurred primarily between 1895 and 1916. Inspiration came first from David A. Well's *Reports on Taxation to New York State* (1871, 1872, 1875), furthered by Richard Ely's* *Report to the Maryland Tax Commission* (1883). Middle-class, general property taxpayers everywhere complained of unjust burdens which were escaped largely by varieties of corporate wealth and personality. Thus, state reforms concentrated on several complex issues, most corrected but not resolved before 1916.

Reforms primarily called for were the separation of revenues, with corporate wealth falling mainly to the states and property taxation remaining the province of localities. Second, without intent to inhibit capital formation, other reforms sought more equitable forms of corporate and personality taxation, such a complex of issues that expert equivocations as well as evasion continued. But, by 1916, one-third of the states secured, as Massachusetts claimed, fairer taxation of most forms of corporate and personal wealth. Pioneers in these reforms were E. R. A. Seligman,* Walter E. Weyl,* and Robert La Follette's* Wisconsin Tax Commission (1903), all recognizing that the problem of corporate taxation was the key to establishing a system of equitable levies. (E. R. A. Seligman, *Essays in Taxation* (rev. ed., 1913); Clifton K. Yearley, *The Money Machines* (1970); Edward Moore, *Taxation of Corporations* (1909).)

Clifton K. Yearley and Kerrie L. MacPherson

TAYLOR, FREDERICK W. (March 20, 1856–March 21, 1915). Born in Philadelphia, Taylor was educated at Phillips Exeter Academy and the Stevens Institute of Technology, where he received an engineering degree in 1883. Taylor drew on his family's extensive contacts to establish himself as an engineer and manager at the Midvale Steel Company in the 1880s. When the company was sold to outsiders, he became a partner in the Manufacturing Investment Company, a pulp and paper concern (1890–1893), and then spent the rest of his business career (1893–1901) as an independent consultant, engineer, and inventor.

His most important client was the Bethlehem Steel Company (1898–1901), where he conducted important technical research and completed the system of managerial methods that he would later call "scientific management."* The major features of that system were (1) various improvements in machinery and production management similar to the "systematic management" techniques of his contemporaries, (2) a specific planning department, (3) function foremanship, (4) stopwatch time study, and (5) an incentive wage plan. Taylor became well-known, especially to progressives, as a result of the Eastern Rate Case before the Interstate Commerce Commission (1910) and the publication of *The Principles of Scientific Management* (1911). Independently wealthy since the 1890s, Taylor devoted himself wholly to the cause of publicizing scientific management during his later years. (Frank Barkley Copley, *Frederick W. Taylor: Father of Scientific Management* (1923); Daniel Nelson, *Frederick W. Taylor and the Rise of Scientific Management* (1980).)

Daniel Nelson

TAYLOR, GRAHAM (May 2, 1851–September 26, 1938). Social Gospel minister, educator, founder of Chicago Commons* settlement house and Chicago School of Civics and Philanthropy, Taylor was born in Schenectady, New York. He graduated from Rutgers College and a Dutch Reformed seminary in New Brunswick. Taylor served a rural conservative church in New York in the 1870s and Hartford's more liberal Fourth Congregational Church in the 1880s, where he combined urban missionary work with teaching at the local Congregational seminary. In 1892, he agreed to organize a Department of Christian Sociology at the Chicago Theological Seminary. Impressed by Hull House,* he moved his wife and four children into a spacious, old house on the near northwest side of the city and opened Chicago Commons in 1894. Two years later he started a monthly settlement house magazine, the *Commons*, which later merged with *Charities** in New York. From 1902 to the end of his life Taylor wrote a weekly column of social commentary in the Chicago *Daily News*.

His experiences training ministers and settlement residents led to courses in the University of Chicago* extension program, and in 1908, he established the School of Civics and Philanthropy. Faculty members included Charles R. Henderson, Alexander Johnson, Julian Mack,* Raymond Robins,* Julia Lathrop,* Edith Abbott,* and Sophonisba Breckinridge.* In 1920 Taylor's school became the Graduate School of Social Service Administration at the University of Chicago. Taylor was president of the National Conference of Charities and Corrections* in 1914 and the National Federation of Settlements* in 1918. In addition to numerous articles, Taylor published *Religion in Social Action* (1913), *Chicago Commons through Forty Years* (1936), and an autobiography, *Pioneering on Social Frontiers* (1930). (Graham Taylor, *Pioneering on Social Frontiers* (1930); Lea D. Taylor, "The Social Settlement and Civic Responsibility—The Life Work of Mary McDowell and Graham Taylor," *Social Service Review* 28, no. 1 (March 1954): 31–40; Louise C. Wade, *Graham Taylor: Pioneer for Social Justice, 1851–1938* (1964).)

Louise C. Wade

TENNESSEE. Tennessee entered the Progressive Era troubled not by utility corporations or political bosses, but by the urban evil of alcohol. Rural people, 86 percent of the state population, had achieved small-town prohibition* with their Four Mile Law prohibiting the sale of intoxicants within four miles of a country school. The twentieth-century struggle promoted prohibition for the cities—Memphis, Nashville, Chattanooga. When an urban local option advocate killed prohibitionist editor and politician Edward Ward Carmack in a Nashville gunfight, the legislature responded by banning the sale and manufacture of intoxicants in 1909. Tennessee cities ignored the new law until the first Republican governor since Reconstruction, Ben W. Hooper, pushed through an ouster law in 1915, to remove city officials by court action if they failed to enforce state prohibition law, thus forcing Memphis Mayor E. H. Crump from office.

Memphis, the largest city in the state and third largest in the South with 103,000 in population at the turn of the century, represented saloons, bossism, and corruption to rural voters. The city's progressive middle class had pushed for increased government efficiency with two new city charters, but organized a machine financed by the underworld of gambling, prostitution, and alcohol. A popular crusade for a state support of high schools, teacher training institutes and a compulsory school attendance law made education the number two issue of Tennessee progressives. Relieving industrial distress aroused much less passion, although maximum hours of labor for women and children were established. (Dewey W. Grantham, *Southern Progressivism: The Reconciliation of Progress and Tradition* (1983); Paul E. Isaac, *Prohibition and Politics: Turbulent Decades in Tennessee* (1965).)

David M. Tucker

TEXAS. The state was home to a diverse population, including numerous Mexican-Americans. Cotton and cattle-raising dominated agriculture. There was a marked tendency toward concentration of landholdings; over 50 percent of farms were tenant-operated by 1910. During the period, Texans witnessed dramatic growth in oil, lumber, and transportation industries. Democrats controlled politics despite factional divisions. Conservatives, led by Congressman (later Senator) Joseph W. Bailey, were favorably disposed toward "outside" corporations such as Standard Oil. Progressives, led by governors James S. Hogg (1891–1895) and Thomas M. Campbell (1907–1911), enacted antitrust and regulatory legislation.

By the 1910s prohibition was a major issue. Governor James E. Ferguson (1915–1917) promoted farm tenancy reforms, but was impeached for improper use of state funds and on suspicion of bribery by liquor interests. Outside the mainstream of politics, thousands of small landowners, tenants, artisans, and workers responded to the appeals of the People's party (*see* Populist party) and the Socialist party of America.* Democrats ensured the supremacy of their party by enacting a disfranchising poll tax, by race-baiting and red-baiting, and by co-opting the radicals' ideas. (Dewey W. Grantham, *Southern Progressivism: The Reconciliation of Progress and Tradition* (1983); James R. Green, *Grass-Roots Socialism: Radical Movements in the Southwest, 1895–1943* (1978); and

James A. Tinsley, "The Progressive Movement in Texas" (Ph.D. diss., University of Wisconsin, 1953).)

Paul M. Pruitt, Jr.

THOMAS, WILLIAM ISAAC (August 13, 1863–December 5, 1947). Born in Russell County, Virginia, Thomas was the son of a Congregational minister who later moved to Tennessee. In 1880, he enrolled at the University of Tennessee where, six years later, he received the university's first Ph.D. in English and modern languages. Thomas taught at the university for the next four years and, after a year in Germany studying folk psychology and ethnology, spent the next three as a professor of English at Oberlin College. Influenced by Herbert Spencer's* theories, Thomas became a graduate student in the Department of Sociology at the University of Chicago* in 1893. Within a year, he taught his first course in sociology and was on the faculty at the University of Chicago until 1918.

His early academic orientation was toward instinct theory, as expressed in his article "The Scope and Method of Folk Psychology," *American Journal* 1 (1895–1896). His research, based on wide reading and primary sources, soon moved toward the importance of habit, crisis theory, and the situation concept. In 1918–1920, along with Florian Znaniecki (1882–1958), he published *The Polish Peasant in Europe and America*, a landmark study in empirical sociology, which set the standard for sociological scholarship from the University of Chicago for the next twenty years. With Thomas's arrest for violating the Mann Act,* the president of the University of Chicago dismissed him. Although the charges were dropped, Thomas's formal academic career was ended. During the balance of his life and writing career, he lived in New York City.* (Martin Bulmer, *The Chicago School of Sociology* (1984); Fred H. Matthews, *Quest for an American Sociology: Robert E. Park and the Chicago School* (1977); Morris Janowitz, ed., *W. I. Thomas on Social Organization and Social Personality* (1966).)

Donald K. Pickens

THORNDIKE, EDWARD LEE (August 31, 1874–August 9, 1949). Born in Williamsburg, Massachusetts, Thorndike received a B.A. degree from Wesleyan University (1895), A.B. and A.M. degrees from Harvard (1896, 1897), and a Ph.D. from Columbia (1898). During his career (1899–1940) at Columbia and after, he published more than 40 books or monographs and more than 400 articles. Thorndike is considered the "father" of modern scientific educational psychology and was one of the earliest and strongest advocates of developing a science of education. His standing as a scientist can be seen from his membership in the National Academy of Sciences, his election to the American Academy of Arts and Sciences, and his presidency of the American Association for the Advancement of Science in 1935.

In some ways Thorndike was a typical progressive. He had a strong, even exaggerated, belief in science and education, especially as manifested in his faith in the power of measurement, for example. However, it is also possible to interpret much of Thorndike's work, growing out of his studies of individual differences, in ways that now seem to be the antithesis of many progressive ideas. He was a very strong believer in inherited traits, especially intelligence, attributing a much smaller role to the effects of environment than did someone like John Dewey.* Thorndike also held very unsophisticated views on economic matters that led to a somewhat naive acceptance of social class relationships that could not be labeled progressive. (Merle Curti, *The Social Ideas of American Educators* (1935); Geraldine Joncich, *The Sane Positivist* (1968).)

Chris Eisele

TRACTION REGULATION. This was the idea that a city should exercise some control over mass transit, based on the principle that such systems operated over public rights-of-way for the public good. Beginning in 1832 with the London Stage Carriage Act, early regulation was very loose, often no more than the granting of a franchise. With the consolidation into monopolies of many urban systems, the actions of such traction tycoons as Charles T. Yerkes* (detailed in "muckraking" novels like *The Titan*) reinforced popular perceptions of poor service, overcrowding, high fares, and insensitive management. Some Progressives believed that properly controlled urban transit could be an agent for social progress, by making less congested outlying districts accessible for living and for recreation. The most extreme view advocated complete municipal ownership* of city systems.

Regulation was considered a middle position, a way for municipalities to guarantee efficient service and hold down fares while avoiding the physical, financial, and ideological burdens of adopting "socialized" transit. A prime example of this approach was the 1907 Chicago Settlement Ordinances, which granted the private carriers twenty-year franchises in return for 55 percent of company profits, a stable fare structure, and annual route extensions. Urban mass transit went into decline after the 1920s, resulting in financial reversals for many private carriers and a renewed movement toward city ownership. (Paul Barrett, *The Automobile and Urban Transit* (1983); Mark S. Foster, *From Streetcar to Superhighway* (1981); Charles W. Cheape, *Moving the Masses* (1980).)

John R. Schmidt

TRADE ASSOCIATIONS were advisory bodies bringing together all the companies in the same industry, e.g., the American Iron and Steel Institute. Numerous trade associations, or industrial institutes, organized in the late nineteenth and early twentieth century as part of a larger trend toward order, efficiency, and professionalization in American society. They conducted industrial and commercial research, provided uniform accounting procedures, exchanged price information, and engaged in public relations and lobbying. Trade associations had an ambiguous relationship with federal antitrust* laws. By providing to all members benefits that would otherwise be available only to large companies, they may have aided competition. But when their activities crossed over into overt price-fixing, as they sometimes did, they engaged in restraint of trade. Depending on how they interpreted their mandate from industry, trade associations ranged from mere information clearinghouses to virtual cartels.

During World War I,* the Wilson* administration swept aside antitrust concerns and encouraged industry to organize, in conjunction with the War Industries Board,* to stabilize prices and allocate production resources. During the 1920s, Secretary of Commerce Herbert Hoover* further encouraged associational activities. The New Deal's National Industrial Recovery Act virtually adopted trade associations as part of the government mechanism to restore production during the depression. (Arthur R. Burns, *The Deadline of Competition* (1936); National Industrial Conference Board, *Trade Associations* (1925); Robert D. Cuff, *The War Industries Board* (1973).)

Edward R. Kantowicz

TREATY OF PORTSMOUTH. Signed by Japan and Russia on September 5, 1905, the Treaty of Portsmouth ended the Russo-Japanese war in which Japan inflicted severe defeats on the Russians in Korea and Manchuria. Eager to maintain a balance of power between Japan and Russia in the Far East to protect American interests, President Theodore Roosevelt,* after informal assurances from both sides, offered his good offices to mediate between Japan, bereft of further resources to continue the war, and Russia, pressured by international bankers and confronted with internal turmoil. At Portsmouth, under Roosevelt's surveillance, Russia recognized Japan's primary interest in Korea and with China's consent, agreed to transfer Kwantung, Port Arthur, Dairen and the Chinese Eastern Railroad in South Manchuria to Japan.

Both parties agreed to the territorial integrity of China, and Russia ceded the southern half of Sakhalin to Japan instead of paying an idemnity. Much weaker, Russia was effectively eliminated as an Oriental power, and the stage was set for the Russian Revolution of 1917. Korea was eventually absorbed by Japan, to which the United States acquiesced in the Taft-Katsura memorandum. Because the Japanese people and rulers perceived the terms as hostile and unfair to Japan, the treaty represented another building block of American anti-Japanese actions. (Howard K. Beale, *Theodore Roosevelt and the Rise of American to World Power* (1956); Eugene P. Trani, *The Treaty of Portsmouth* (1969); Frederick W. Marks III, *Velvet on Iron: The Diplomacy of Theodore Roosevelt* (1979); Raymond A. Ethus, *Theodore Roosevelt and Japan* (1966).)

C. David Tompkins

TRUSTS. "The term '*trust*,' " Louis D. Brandeis* wrote in the 1890s, "is commonly used in a broad, and perhaps inaccurate, sense as including all kinds of combinations of concerns engaged in the same line of business. Its general purpose is usually and mainly one of monopoly." The trust represented a convenient adaptation of an old legal device (the exercise of authority over property by an expert agent, usually on behalf of some elderly or minor person) to new business conditions such as scale economies and industrial overcapacity. The voting trust, which allowed all stockholders to turn over to an individual or a small group the control represented by their shares, while retaining the economic interest, had been used in some earlier corporate mainpulations, but it was not until the 1880s that the device began to be employed in really important new ways.

In 1882, John D. Rockefeller* and his associates used the voting trust to reorganize their loose confederation of oil-related companies into a tighter horizontal combination. The resulting new speed and coordination of decisions helped the company shut down inefficient plants and gain enormous cost advantages over its competitors both in the United States and abroad. There quickly followed a series of legal innovations such as the holding company (1889), all designed to enhance market power and tighten administrative control within the new enterprises. In the great merger movement of 1897–1904, some 4,227 American firms combined into 257 corporations, many of which dominated their industries: General Electric, International Harvester, United States Steel. By 1904, 318 "trusts" were alleged to control about 40 percent of all American manufacturing assets.

The American legal prohibition against loose horizontal combinations (cartels) promoted tighter intergration in the form of mergers. Moreover, numerous trusts and mergers failed altogether, because tight combination into very large enterprises works well only in a minority of industries characterized by substantial economies of scale or scope. Finally, even the successful combinations lost substantial market share during the decades following the merger movement. Never before in American history had any institution (with the exception of the national government in time of war) achieved such size and power as did big business at the turn of the century. Because the phenomenon was so new and so threatening to the nation's democratic ideals, it became *the* central political concern of the Progressive Era. (Alfred D. Chandler, Jr., *The Visible Hand* (1977); Naomi R. Lamoreaux, *The Great Merger Movement in American Business, 1895–1904* (1985); Thomas K. McCraw, *Prophets of Regulation* (1984).)

Thomas K. McCraw

TUMULTY, JOSEPH P. (May 5, 1879–April 8, 1954). Born in Jersey City, New Jersey, Tumulty graduated from Saint Peter's College in 1899 and was admitted to the bar in 1902. Tumulty early became a Democratic party regular in the Hudson County machine, but endorsed numerous social and political reform measures. In the State assembly (1907–1910), he supported civil service reform* and measures to improve working conditions and to effect state regulation of railroad and utility rates. In Woodrow Wilson's* gubernatorial campaign of 1910, Tumulty stressed issues important to urban and suburban voters and served as liaison to the machine. As secretary to the new governor, he built support within the party for Wilson's program and for his 1912 nomination for the presidency, influenced patronage, and recruited Irish- and Italian-Americans to the Wilson cause.

In the presidential campaign of 1912, Tumulty served very effectively as press secretary and in the White House continued to handle press relations, analyze public opinion, advise on patronage, and keep the president's calendar. Tumulty's advice that Wilson postpone his second marriage until after the election of 1916* shook the president's trust in his secretary. An expanded executive office during World War I* assumed most of Tumulty's earlier tasks, and his advice rarely prevailed. After Wilson's administration, Tumulty established a law practice in Washington. (John Morton Blum, *Joe Tumulty and the Wilson Era* (1951); John D. Buenker, "Urban, New-Stock Liberalism and Progressive Reform in New Jersey," *New Jersey History* 87 (1969): 79–194.)

Joseph F. Mahoney

TURNER, FREDERICK JACKSON (November 14, 1861–March 14, 1932). Born in Portage, Wisconsin, and graduated from the University of Wisconsin* (B.A., 1884; M.A., 1888), Turner chose to pursue the new career of professional historian after working in the archieves at the Wisconsin State Historical Society. In 1890 his doctoral dissertation, "The Character and Influence of the Fur Trade in Wisconsin," was accepted and published by the Johns Hopkins University. In 1893 Turner delivered a brief paper, "The Significance of the Frontier in American History," at the American Historical Association* meetings held in Chicago* at the World's Fair. His proposition establishing the availability of free land and socioeconomic opportunity on a wave of Western frontiers, from explorer to farmer, in turn defined the unique process and distinctive character of the American experience. Emphasizing geography and environmental influences, Turner's reading was a broader one than allowed for by the earlier "germ theory" of Anglo-Saxon institutions. From 1892 to 1910, he taught at the University of Wisconsin, then at Harvard until 1924. He was very active professionally, serving as president of the American Historical Association in 1909–1910. Turner's scholarship never strayed far from the theme and methods of his early work: *Rise of the West* (1906); *The Frontier in American History* (1920); *The Significance of Sections in American History* (1932). (Ray Allen Billington, *Frederick Jackson Turner: Historian, Scholar, Teacher* (1973); Wilbur R. Jacobs, *The Historical World of Frederick Jackson Turner* (1968); Lee Benson, *Turner and Beard: American Historical Writing Reconsidered* (1969).)

Burton J. Bledstein

U

UNDERWOOD, OSCAR WILDER (May 6, 1862–January 28, 1929). Born in Louisville, Kentucky, Underwood attended the University of Virginia (1881–1884). He was admitted to the bar in 1884 and briefly practiced law in Saint Paul, Minnesota, before joining a firm in Birmingham, Alabama. He served as a congressman from the Birmingham district, 1896–1915. He was elected to the U.S. Senate in 1914 and served nine consecutive terms, retiring in 1927. After the Democrats gained control of the House in 1910, he became majority leader (1911–1915) and chairman of the Ways and Means Committee. He drafted rate reductions in the Payne-Aldrich Tariff,* vetoed by President William Howard Taft.*

Underwood was a leading contender for the Democratic presidential nomination in 1912. William Jennings Bryan* bitterly contested his nomination, and he declined consideration as Woodrow Wilson's* running mate. After Wilson's election, he promoted much of the new president's program—the Underwood-Simmons Tariff* (1913), the Federal Reserve Act* (1913), and the Clayton Antitrust Act* (1914). As a senator, he continued to serve as one of Wilson's leaders, but opposed the Eighteenth and Nineteenth Amendments to the Constitution. As a presidential candidate in 1924, his opposition to the Ku Klux Klan and the Eighteenth Amendment severely damaged his conservative southern political base. (Evans C. Johnson, *Oscar W. Underwood: A Political Biography* (1980); Oscar W. Underwood, *Drifting Sands of Party Politics* (1928); Jack E. Kendrick, "Alabama Congressmen in the Wilson Administration," *Alabama Review* 24 (October 1971): 243–60.)

David E. Alsobrook

UNDERWOOD-SIMMONS TARIFF (1913). The Underwood-Simmons Tariff was the first major piece of legislation introduced (by Oscar W. Underwood*-

D. Ala. and Furnifold McLendel Simmons-D. N. C.) under Woodrow Wilson's* New Freedom.* Wilson used the tariff issue as an excuse to personally address a joint session of Congress on April 8, 1913, the first time a president had done so since Jefferson. In his address, Wilson called for a reduction of the tariff as a means of reintroducing competition and efficiency and ending the system of privilege that had encouraged the growth of trusts.

The debate on the tariff was highlighted by the president's charge that "special interests" had descended on Washington and jeopardized the reform effort. A subsequent congressional investigation failed to validate this charge, yielding instead the finding that the most persistent critics of the administration's proposal were the lesser competitors of the major producers, thereby casting some doubt on the "reformist" nature of the final legislation. The bill Wilson signed on October 3, 1913, reduced the rates on average from 40 percent to 29 percent, increased the items on the free list, and included the first income tax* made possible by the passage of the Sixteenth Amendment. (Arthur S. Link, ed., *The Papers of Woodrow Wilson* (1978); Lewis L. Gould, *Reform and Regulation: American Politics, 1900–1916* (1978); Frank Burdick, "Woodrow Wilson and the Underwood Tariff," *Mid-America* 50 (1968): 273–90).)

Frank Burdick

UNEMPLOYMENT CONFERENCES. In an effort to obtain public attention for the necessity of improving unemployment relief,* the American Association for Labor Legislation* organized two conferences in 1914. At the First National Conference on Unemployment in New York, February 27–28, social workers, government officials, academics, and other reform-oriented participants from twenty-five states discussed questions of public responsibility and possible remedies. Resolutions demanded the creation of a nationwide system of public employment exchanges and steps toward better statistics, the regularization of industrial production, and the introduction of unemployment insurance. As a followup, a Second National Conference on Unemployment was held with smaller participation in Philadelphia, December 28–29.

The conferences had no immediate practical results, but the public had taken notice and, perhaps more importantly, those concerned about unemployment had been able to sort out the problem and to strengthen their own resolve to urge remedial action. During the war, joblessness receded, but with the depression of 1921 renewed efforts seemed to be called for. This time the initiative for a fact-finding conference came from federal Secretary of Commerce Herbert Hoover.* The President's Conference on Unemployment met in Washington, D.C., intermittently from September 26 to October 13, 1921, gathering over a hundred participants from business, unions, government, academia, social work, and other interests. Little more than a strong call for local initiatives resulted, but the very fact that the federal government had for the first time involved itself in the unemployment problem made the conference a milestone. (*American Labor Legislation Review* 4 (1914): 209–387; ibid., 5 (1915): 167–70, 195–456; Carolyn Grin, ''The Unemployment Conference of 1921: An Experiment in National Cooperative Planning,'' *Mid-America* 55 (1973): 83–107.)

Udo Sautter

UNEMPLOYMENT RELIEF. In the nineteenth century, Poor Law tradition, laissez-faire convictions, and social Darwinist* notions all insisted that work should and could be found by the individual to provide for his living. Increasing industrialization, however, rendered this assumption questionable. From the depression of the mid-nineties,* a growing number of reform-oriented minds began to perceive a social obligation to help those who were unable to secure work because of external circumstances. While the old forms of poor relief, which essentially consisted of handouts, still remained the predominant form of aid beyond World War I,* new ways of help were being discussed and experimentally implemented. The most important lesson learned during the Progressive period was doubtless insight that the traditional dispensers of relief, private charity and local authorities, were not able to cope with widespread unemployment during depression periods.

Some state governments, notably in Massachusetts, New York, Wisconsin, Illinois, and Ohio, and also the federal government, began in a hesitant and cautious manner to explore the form and cost of remedial action. Taking various cues from European (in particular English and German) experiences, efforts were made to count the unemployed, to provide them with job information through public employment agencies, and, though rarely, to undertake public works projects. The merits of unemployment insurance were debated, but only some insignificant private endeavors (trade union and company plans) were in evidence. (Daniel Nelson, *Unemployment Insurance: The American Experience, 1915–1935* (1969); Irwin Yellowitz, ''The Origins of Unemployment Reform in the United States,'' *Labor History* 9 (1968): 337–60; Udo Sautter, ''North American Government Labor Agencies before World War One: A Cure for Unemployment?'' *Labor History* 24 (1983): 366–93.)

Udo Sautter

UNITED MINE WORKERS OF AMERICA (UMWA). Founded in Columbus, Ohio, on January 25, 1890, by representatives from competing unions in the bituminous coal fields, the UMWA was an industrial union chartered by the American Federation of Labor* with jurisdiction over all workers in and about the country's coal mines. Nearly destroyed by the 1893 depression,* the union rebounded and conducted a successful national bituminous coal strike in 1897 with less than 10,000 members. In 1898, the union and coal operators from the Central Competitive Field (western Pennsylvania, Ohio, Indiana, and Illinois) negotiated a joint contract which propelled the UMWA into a period of tremendous growth. Industry-wide strikes in 1900 and 1902 in Pennsylvania's anthracite coal fields* provided for a strong UMWA presence among hard-coal mine workers. During the 1900s, UMWA leaders promoted the joint agreement between operators and the union as the most democratic and equitable solution to the labor problem and the most effective way to produce stability in an industry characterized by low wages, overproduction, and cutthroat competition.

The UMWA's successes in organizing mine workers in the Central Competitive Field and the anthracite industry were not matched in the growing and increasingly crucial fields of West Virginia, Kentucky, Colorado, and elsewhere. In these areas, the UMWA faced the combined forces of autocratic and hostile coal operators assisted by local and state judicial, police, and military authorities. Union organizing efforts spawned armed resistance by private and public bodies, producing violent confrontations in West Virginia in 1912–1913 and the Ludlow massacre* in Colorado in 1914. Although World War I* swelled the ranks of the UMWA, the failure to organize miners in Appalachia and other coal fields would present insurmountable difficulties during the 1920s and 1930s. (McAlister Coleman, *Men and Coal* (1943); Melvyn Dubofsky and Warren Van Tine, *John L. Lewis* (1977); John Brophy, *A Miner's Life* (1964).)

Joseph Gowaskie

UNIVERSITY OF CHICAGO. Opened in 1892 as one of the nation's first institutions of higher education oriented toward graduate studies and research, the University of Chicago quickly assumed a central role in American higher education because of the visionary educational leadership of William Rainey Harper and the generous financial support of John D. Rockefeller.* Harper dedicated the university both to the advancement of knowledge in a wide variety of fields and to the dissemination of knowledge not only through graduate, undergraduate, and professional school degree programs, but through correspondence courses, extension programs, public lectures, and extensive involvement with the Chicago public schools.

The new university played a significant role in the social and intellectual movements of the Progressive Era in several ways. First, in its vigorous intellectual environment, it spawned a variety of significant intellectual movements, including pragmatic philosophy, modernist Protestant theology,* progressive education,* urban sociology and ecology, empirically based study of urban politics, and the study of social welfare policy, among others. Second, in its efforts to bring knowledge and enlightment to the entire Midwest and its optimistic faith in scientifically directed progress, the university was itself a characteristically progressive institution. Finally, key members of the university's faculty played important roles in progressive reform. For example, Harper and philosopher George Herbert Mead* led the movement to reform the Chicago public schools. Political scientist Charles E. Merriam* led the movement for efficiency and scientific management* in urban government, served a term on the Chicago City Council, and ran twice for mayor against machine candidates. Sociologist and clergyman Charles R. Henderson worked to improve poor relief correctional methods and to protect workers from the effects of unemployment. Legal scholar Ernst Freund* and political economists Sophonisba P. Breckenridge* and Edith Abbott* were major figures in progressive battles for the protection of immigrants, children, women, and factory workers. (Richard J. Storr, *Harper's University: The Beginnings* (1966); Thomas W. Goodspeed, *A History of the University of Chicago: The First Quarter Century* (1916); Steven J. Diner, *A City and Its Universities: Public Policy in Chicago, 1892–1919* (1980).)

Steven J. Diner

UNIVERSITY OF WISCONSIN, THE. Founded in 1846 before Wisconsin itself had achieved statehood, this university became, in the late nineteenth and early twentieth centuries, one of the major academic centers of the Progressive movement. The expression the "Wisconsin Idea" referred, first, to the new initiatives taken by the university to extend its programs beyond the confinements of the campus to the boundaries of the state itself. University Extension and Farmers' Institutes brought professors of agriculture and the sciences to farms and county fairs to demonstrate applications of their research. The university was not the sole pioneer in this aspect of the Progressive ideal of service, but it became a national model, especially after the reformer-journalist Lincoln Steffens* celebrated its work in his essay "Sending a State to College" in the February 1909 issue of *American Magazine.**

Second, the "Wisconsin Idea" referred to the political experiment in Wisconsin led by the reform governors Robert La Follette* and Francis E. McGovern.* Through the close cooperation of university professors, and through the *Legislative Reference Library** of Charles McCarthy,* the Wisconsin Progressive movement gained from the working input of academics, most notably John R. Commons.* At one point, more than forty faculty in the School of Economics, Political Science, and History, directed by Richard T. Ely,* served as advisers and helped write legislation for the reform administration. (Merle Curti and Vernon Carstensen, *The University of Wisconsin: A History, 1848–1925* (1949); Laurence Veysey, *The Emergence of the American University* (1965); J. David Hoeveler, Jr., "The University and the Social Gospel: The Intellectual Origins of the 'Wisconsin Idea,' " *Wisconsin Magazine of History* 59 (Summer 1976): 282–98.)

J. David Hoeveler, Jr.

UNIVERSITY SETTLEMENT. The social settlement movement had strong ties to American institutions of higher education, many of which established university settlements. The earliest American settlements were inspired by London's Toynbee Hall, founded in 1883 by a minister and students at Oxford to bring the culture of the university to the slums. American professors and college students, like their English counterparts, devoted considerable volunteer time to the settlements' clubs, classes, and community services, but the most important university connection with the settlements, and one of the things that distinguished it from the English pattern, was the use, by professors and graduate students, of the settlements for social research.

In 1887, Dr. Stanton Coit, stimulated by a short residence at Toynbee Hall, established Neighborhood Guild (renamed University Settlement in 1891) on New York's Lower East Side to bring college men in contact with the people of the neighborhood. In 1889, a group of Smith College alumnae opened the College Settlement on Rivington Street, and the next year they organized the College Settlement Association with chapters in Wellesley, Smith, Vassar, and Bryn Mawr. The most famous settlements, like Jane Addams's* Hull House* and Lillian Wald's* Henry Street Settlement* had close ties with university professors and students, but many settlements had direct university affiliations. Among these were the University of Chicago* Settlement House in the Chicago stockyards district, opened in 1894; the Northwestern University Settlement on West Division Street in Chicago, opened in 1891; Denison House (Boston College Settlement), established in 1892 under the auspices of the College Settlements Association; the Wisconsin University Settlement in Milwaukee, founded in 1902 to serve as a sociological laboratory for the University of Wisconsin;* and the University Settlement in Philadelphia, established in 1898 by the University Christian Association of the University of Pennsylvania. (Allen F. Davis, *Spearheads for Reform: The Social Settlements and the Progressive Movement* (1967); Robert A. Woods and Albert J. Kennedy, *The Settlement Horizon: A National Estimate* (1922).)

Steven J. Diner

UNTERMYER, SAMUEL J. (June 6, 1858–March 14, 1940). Samuel J. Untermyer was born in Lynchburg, Virginia. He was educated in the public schools of New York City and graduated from City College of New York and Columbia Law School in 1878. After substantial professional and financial success, he began to develop doubts about the power and goals of major corporations, and gradually he emerged as a vigorous foe of corporate abuse. He led stockholder fights against an insurance company and worked for greater state and federal regulation of corporations. In 1911 he decried the existence of a "money trust" which led to the concentration and control of wealth in Wall Street. In 1912–1913 he served as counsel to the Pujo Committee* of the U.S. House of Representatives. Its recommendations led to the Federal Reserve Act,* the Federal Trade Commission Act,* and the Clayton Antitrust Act.*

In addition, Untermyer wrote many articles calling for corporate regulation to maintain fair competition and opportunity to individual initiative. He ardently supported every Democrat from Woodrow Wilson* through Franklin D. Roosevelt.* In World War I,* he became a vigorous and effective supporter of the federal government's efforts and served as a special adviser to the Treasury Department on the writing and interpretation of tax legislation. After the war Untermyer served on several New York City and state investigating commissions dealing with housing and the centralization of private urban transit firms. Despite his enormous wealth, he advocated a graduated income tax* and public ownership of utilities.* Firmly opposed to socialism, he frequently defended the civil liberties of individual socialists and radicals. (*Dictionary of American Biography* Supplement 2; *New York Times*, March 17, 1940; Samuel Untermyer manuscripts are located at Hebrew Union College, Cincinnati, Ohio.)

Albert Erlebacher

URBANIZATION. Urbanization is the process by which rural land becomes urban and people become city dwellers. Between 1890 and 1920, the process of urbanization proceeded vigorously throughout the United States, as small towns grew into cities, and as cities and urban regions pushed out their boundaries to encompass formerly rural areas. Urban population rose dramatically during these three decades, increasing by 29 to 39 percent per decade, or about twice as rapidly as the rate of national population increase. In 1890, about 35 percent of the American people lived in cities and urban places; by 1920, the proportion had grown to over 51 percent. The number of big cities of over 100,000 population rose rapidly as well, from 28 in 1890 to 68 in 1920.

Some cities had grown to enormous size by 1920; New York City* with 5.6 million people, Chicago* with 2.7 million, and Philadelphia* with 1.8 million were the nation's largest cities. Smaller cities and towns were also growing in size and number during this period, and by 1920, about half of America's 54 million urban dwellers lived in places smaller than 100,000. In the Midwest and the Far West, the urban proportion of population approximated the national average in 1890 (35.1 percent) and again in 1920 (51.2 percent). However, the Northeast far surpassed the national average of urbanization, while the South lagged behind substantially. American cities were also swelling in size physically as a result of a succession of transportation innovations (electric streetcar, electric interurban trains, and, by 1920, the automobile), which facilitated the expansion of the residential urban/suburban periphery. This process reached its peak in Los Angeles,* whose 29 square miles in 1890 had increased to 364 square miles by 1920.

Urbanization stemmed in the first instance from rapid population increases in cities and urban regions. High rural birthrates and the mechanization of agriculture, along with the economic and social lure of the city, resulted in a massive flow of rural Americans to urban centers. Similarly, net immigration amounted to 12.5 million during the 1890–1920 period—the peak years of European immigration to the United States. Natives and immigrants alike were attracted to urban life because of the expanding economic opportunities in the industrializing city. Local or regional political, social, and cultural factors mediated this process and often produced divergent urban outcomes in different parts of the nation. In the final analysis, however, it was the interaction of economic development, new technologies, and population concentration that propelled the process of urbanization. (Blake McKelvey, *The Urbanization of America, 1860–1915* (1963); Raymond A. Mohl, *The New City: Urban America in the Industrial Age,*

1860–1920 (1985); Kenneth T. Jackson, *Crabgrass Frontier: The Suburbanization of the United States* (1985).)

Raymond A. Mohl

UNITED STATES CHAMBER OF COMMERCE. The U.S. Chamber of Commerce, a national umbrella organization, was formed in 1912 to unite local business groups into one "association of associations." Business had long desired to speak with one voice on matters of national importance, but the previously organized National Council of Commerce* had failed and the National Association of Manufacturers* (NAM) had proven too controversial and partisan. So Secretary of Commerce and Labor Charles Nagel suggested that President William Howard Taft* publicly recommend the founding of a new national body.

A group of businessmen met with government officials in February 1912, then Taft formally invited 1,000 business associations to a founding convention on April 22, 1912, in Washington, D.C. Under the leadership of its first two presidents, Harry A. Wheeler of Chicago and John H. Fahey of Boston, the chamber adopted a nonpartisan political stance and avoided the rabid antiunion rhetoric of the NAM. Launched upon this moderate course, the chamber ably represented business interests and worked successfully with federal regulatory bodies, such as the Federal Trade Commission,* to make their decisions more favorable to business. (Robert H. Wiebe, *Businessmen and Reform* (1962); Harwood L. Childs, *Labor and Capital in National Politics* (1930).)

Edward R. Kantowicz

U.S. V. AMERICAN TOBACCO CO. (221 U.S. 106 (1911)). On July 19, 1907, James C. McReynolds* of the Justice Department's antitrust division filed the government's petition against the American Tobacco Company, its subsidiaries, and its British partners, in New York's circuit court for the southern district. With the approval of Attorney General Charles J. Bonaparte,* McReynolds asked the court to place the tobacco combine in receivership to force conformity with the Sherman Act. Although exempting the British partners, the lower court found American Tobacco and its partners here guilty and enjoined them from further anticompetitive activities. The court rejected the receivership proposal and suspended its own injunction pending appeal.

Under the terms of the Expedition Act of 1903, the government enjoyed the right of appeal to the Supreme Court. Chief Justice Edward D. White,* who announced the court's decision in May 1911, upheld the circuit court in part and, applying the "rule of reason,"* said that the intent of the combination was "to acquire dominion and control of the tobacco trade." White overruled the lower court's exclusion of the two British partners and, to McReynolds's satisfaction, ordered the tobacco trust into receivership and dissolved. (John Quentin Feller, *Theodore Roosevelt, the Department of Justice, and the Trust Problem:*

A Study in Presidential Policy (1968); Earl W. Kintner and Mark R. Joelson, *An International Antitrust Primer* (1974).)

John Quentin Feller

U.S. V. UNITED STATES STEEL CORPORATION (251 U.S. 417 (1920)). The suit to break up the U.S. Steel Corporation was originally filed in 1911. In 1915 the District Court dismissed the government's case, but the government appealed the decision. The U.S. Supreme Court heard the case in 1919 and rendered a decision on March 1, 1920. The 4–3 decision upheld the lower court, but two justices (Louis Brandeis* and James McReynolds*) did not participate. The author of the majority opinion, Justice Joseph McKenna, relied on the "rule of reason"* in his verdict. He acknowledged that the large size of the corporation made it possible for it to operate as a monopoly, but he argued that the Sherman Antitrust Act did not make sheer size illegal. He also asserted that the company had not engaged in any illegal activities to gain its size, nor was it using tactics such as price-fixing or manipulating the market in order to gain business. McKenna stated "that an industrial combination is formed with the expectation of monopoly is not enough to make it a monopoly within the meaning of the Anti-Trust Act." The dissenters, led by Justice William Day, argued that the way in which U.S. Steel was organized and the tactics it used in the marketplace violated the antitrust laws. Because the William Howard Taft* administration had instituted the suit over the objections of Theodore Roosevelt,* the case contributed significantly to the irreparable break between the two Republican leaders. (Melvin I. Urofsky, *Big Steel and the Wilson Administration* (1969); *United States v. United States Steel Corporation et al.*, 251 U.S. 417–466.)

Albert Erlebacher

U'REN, WILLIAM S. (January 10, 1859–March 8, 1949). Known as "the father of the Oregon System," William S. U'Ren was born in Lancaster, Wisconsin. Moving to Colorado in 1876, he worked first as a miner and blacksmith and later as a lawyer and newspaper editor. While there, he read Henry George's* *Progress and Poverty* and became a lifelong single taxer.* Arriving in Oregon in 1889, he soon became involved in Portland in the campaign for the Australian ballot,* adopted in 1891. That year, he became a partner in the nursery business of the pioneer horticulturist, Seth Lewelling, in Milwaukee, Oregon. With the Lewellings, he joined the Farmers' Alliance and Populist party* and launched a ten-year campaign for the initiative* and referendum.*

As a Populist, he was elected to the Oregon House of Representatives in 1896, the only public office to which he ever would be elected. Although he was a participant in the legislative "Holdup of '97," he used it to bring about the adoption of an initiative and referendum constitutional amendment in 1902. During the next ten years, using the initiative, he was primarily responsible for the adoption of a remarkable series of political reforms that became known as the "Oregon System." However, he was unsuccessful as the sponsor of singletax initiatives several times between 1908 and 1920 and as a Republican candidate for governor in 1914 and for the legislature in 1932 and 1934. (Lincoln Steffens, "W. S. U'Ren, The Lawgiver," in *Upbuilders* (1909); Robert C. Woodward, "William S. U'Ren: A Progressive Era Personality," *Idaho Yesterdays* 4 (Summer 1960): 4–10; Robert C. Woodward, "William S. U'Ren and the Single Tax in Oregon," *Oregon Historical Quarterly* 61 (1960); 46–63; Thomas C. McClintock, "Seth Lewelling, William S. U'Ren and the Birth of the Oregon Progressive Movement," *Oregon Historical Quarterly* 68 (1967): 197–220.)

Thomas C. McClintock

UTAH. Utah experienced integration of its economy with national business, secularization of its politics, and mixed results with progressive legislation. Tending to lead in social legislation, Utahans lagged behind in political reform and economic regulation. Laws limiting miners to eight hours and prohibiting the employment of boys under fourteen and of women in underground mines passed in 1896. Utah adopted pure food regulation in 1903, and in 1911, it regulated child labor* in street trades (the eighth state to do so), prohibited the employment of children in dangerous occupations, and limited women to nine hours per day. In 1913, Utah adopted a minimum wage for women. It adopted the commission form of city government* (1911). The legislature declined to ratify either the income tax* or direct election amendments* and was one of the last to adopt public utilities regulation.*

Reed Smoot's* "Federal Bunch" political machine, which had strong ties to the Latter-day Saints church hierarchy, tended to dominate from 1903 through 1916. While Smoot favored utilities regulation, his opposition to direct election, the income tax, and prohibition,* which emerged as the principal issue in the state between 1909 and 1917, led eventually to a division in the Republican party in 1912 and, in 1916, brought about the election of Simon Bamberger, a German Jew, as governor. The Democratic party passed legislation such as prohibition and utility and stock market regulation. (Richard Poll et al., *Utah's History* (1978); Jean B. White, "Utah State Elections, 1895–1899" (Ph.D. diss., University of Utah, 1968); Brad E. Hainsworth, "Utah State Elections, 1916–1924" (Ph.D. diss., University of Utah, 1968); Thomas G. Alexander, *Mormonism in Transition: A History of the Latter-day Saints, 1890–1930* (1986).)

Thomas G. Alexander

V

VANDERLIP, FRANK ARTHUR (November 17, 1864–June 29, 1937).
Newspaper editor, banker, self-made man, Vanderlip was born on a farm near
Aurora, Illinois,* of Dutch and New England Yankee stock; he went to work
in a machine shop at age thirteen after his father died. Largely self-educated,
he became a skillful writer and a financial prodigy. He started working as city
editor of the *Aurora Evening Post* in 1885, then was hired as financial reporter
for the *Chicago Tribune* in 1889. Treasury secretary Lyman Gage appointed him
assistant secretary in 1897, and Vanderlip was instrumental in floating the $200
million Spanish-American War* loan the following year. In 1901 he joined National City Bank of New York, serving as president from 1909 to 1919. He greatly
expanded that bank's foreign investments; and as a dedicated internationalist, he
opposed the Republican foreign policy of isolationism after World War I.* (*New
York Times* obituary, June 30, 1937; *Dictionary of American Biography* supplement
2; Frank Vanderlip, *From Farm Boy to Financier* (1935).)

Edward R. Kantowicz

VAN HISE, CHARLES R. (May 29, 1857–November 19, 1918). Scientist,
conservationist, and university president, Van Hise presided over the University
of Wisconsin* from 1903 to 1918. Born in Fulton, Wisconsin, Van Hise graduated from the state university in 1879, along with classmate Robert La Follette.*
He did graduate work in geology and worked for a period with the U.S. Geological Survey. A distinguished academic career at his alma mater led to Van
Hise's appointment as president in 1903. His inaugural address became a famous
statement of the course in American higher education, celebrating the ideals of
the university's service to the state and its support of the widest range of educational programs, from the new natural and physical sciences to the humanities
and fine arts. It was during Van Hise's presidency that the university developed
its close ties with the state and with the reform movements of Governors La

Follette* and Francis E. McGovern.* His book *The Conservation of Natural Resources in the United States* showed the concerns of this noted scientist for preservation and careful use of natural resources. Like most progressives, Van Hise strongly supported American involvement in World War I* and fully committed the university's resources and programs to the war effort. (Maurice M. Vance, *Charles Richard Van Hise: Scientist Progressive* (1960); Merle Curti and Vernon Carstensen, *The University of Wisconsin: A History, 1848–1925* (1949); Lincoln Steffens, "Sending a State to College" (1909), in James C. Stone and Donald P. De Nevi, eds., *Portraits of the American University, 1890–1910* (1971).)

J. David Hoeveler, Jr.

VARDAMAN, JAMES KIMBLE (July 26, 1861–June 25, 1930). Born in Texas, Vardaman moved to Mississippi in 1868. He received a public school education and then devoted his early career to practicing law and editing newspapers, first in Winona and then in Greenwood. In 1889, he entered politics and served three terms in the Mississippi legislature (1889–1895), one term as governor (1904–1908), and one term as U.S. senator (1913–1919). Throughout most of his political career, Vardaman combined appeals for racism and reform. In addition to upholding racial segregation* and the disfranchisement* of blacks,* he also called for the abolition of Negro education.

For the white people of Mississippi, especially the small farmer class, he worked for programs that would improve their socioeconomic standing. As governor, he helped to achieve larger public school appropriations, a uniform textbook law, stricter regulation of corporate wealth, abolition of convict leasing, and reform of the penitentiary system. In the Senate, he supported every major reform passed by Congress between 1913 and 1916. His senatorial voting record closely resembled those of such Midwestern progressives as Robert M. La Follette* and George W. Norris.* In 1917, he became one of six senators who voted against entry into World War I,* and Vardaman lost in his bid for reelection in 1918. (William F. Holmes, *The White Chief: James Kimble Vardaman* (1970).)

William F. Holmes

VAUDEVILLE. Vaudeville developed out of the need for a flexible form of entertainment which could adapt to the changing public tastes while at the same time providing an affordable and enjoyable evening's entertainment for the large immigrant audiences populating the urban areas. Its prime years of vaudeville were from 1890 to 1920 when one chain owned 400 theatres and one booking agency had 20,000 entertainers under contract. With an average billing consisting of twenty to thirty acts, vaudeville provided a platform for all sorts of unusual acts from parodies of Shakespeare to specialty acts such as rope dancers and mechanics who disassembled automobiles on stage. Vaudeville simultaneously focused on broad middle-class culture, and on ethnic and racial humor, thus offering both acculturation and cultural retention to immigrant audiences. Vaudeville served to celebrate city life and was virtually the first mass-produced entertainment form to do so.

Many of the great stars of vaudeville were drawn from the ranks of the lower and immigrant classes, conveying the great promise of America to all who would be entertained. By reflecting significant cultural patterns and traditions and by offering similar experiences to audiences from coast to coast, vaudeville provided an important cultural and social glue for a pluralistic and rapidly changing society. Vaudeville also served the music publishers by advertising their new songs from coast to coast. Vaudeville served as a social and cultural index to the society, carried city culture to the rural areas, created new markets for American song and humor, and offered both escape from the day-to-day anxieties and a promise of a better tomorrow. Through its humor vaudeville offered links to older traditions, and through its songs it offered a vision of future traditions. (John E. DiMeglio, *Vaudeville as Ritual* (1965); Russel B. Nye, *The Unembarrassed Muse* (1970).)

Michael T. Marsden

VEBLEN, THORSTEIN B. (July 26, 1861–June 25, 1930). Born in Manitowoc County, Wisconsin, Veblen received a bachelor's degree from Carleton College, a doctorate from Yale University in philosophy, and doctorate in political economy from Cornell University. He advanced from a teaching fellow (1892) to an assistant professorship at the University of Chicago* before being forced to leave in 1905; from 1906 to 1909, he taught at Stanford, losing both positions because of extramarital liaisons. He taught at the University of Missouri from 1911 to 1918. From 1918 to 1926, he resided in New York, writing and serving as an instructor at the New School of Social Research.

Veblen may have left the most creative body of social thought that any single American has produced. He broke with static formulations in classical economics and criticized businessmen as a social class. His sardonic analysis of contemporary culture, especially in *The Theory of the Leisure Class* (1899), influenced an entire generation of social reformers. Yet Veblen was more pessimistic about the potentialities of reform than most progressives. A complete evolutionist, he believed that institutions, which he defined as habits of thought (sometimes manifested in such legal devices as private property), and inherited instincts determined most of human behavior. (John P. Diggins, *The Bard of Savagery: Thorstein Veblen and Modern Social Theory* (1978); Joseph Dorfman, *Thorstein Veblen and His America* (1934); David Reisman, *Thorstein Veblen: A Critical Appraisal* (1953).)

Benjamin G. Rader

VEILLER, LAWRENCE TURNURE (January 7, 1872–August 30, 1959). Born in New York City,* Veiller graduated from the City College of New York in 1890. Veiller's acquaintance with urban poverty began during the depression of 1893, when he served as the head of the East Side Relief Work Committee.

He also worked as a caseworker for the New York Charity Organization Society*
(COS). It was while he was secretary of the COS's Tenement House Committee
that Veiller arranged a tenement house exhibition of maps, photographs, and
cardboard models which attracted nationwide attention and ultimately led to the
passage of the New York State Tenement House Law of 1901, which provided
minimum standards for tenement house construction. Veiller became secretary
of the New York State Tenement House Commission in 1900, and in 1901,
Mayor Seth Low* appointed him deputy commissioner of the new New York
Tenement House Department under Commissioner Robert W. deForest.

In 1910, Veiller organized and became the first director and secretary of the
National Housing Association* (NHA). From this position he was able to assist
other cities in housing reform, and the NHA's publications became textbooks
for urban reformers. In 1910 Veiller wrote a model tenement house law which
guided the legislative efforts of over forty cities. Veiller was unenthusiastic about
model tenements and opposed public housing during the New Deal. He brought
the technicians' badly needed expertise to reform, but he lacked the broader
neighborhood reconstruction vision of colleagues like Jacob Riis.* His solution
for poor housing was to enact and enforce good laws. (Robert W. deForest and
Lawrence T. Veiller, eds., *The Tenement House Problem* (1903); Anthony Jackson, *A Place Called Home: A History of Low-Cost Housing in Manhattan* (1976);
Roy Lubove, *The Progressives and the Slums: Tenement House Reform in New
York City, 1890–1917* (1962).)

                                                                        John F. Sutherland

VICE CRUSADES. Moral purity campaigns were typically the work of Americans who feared that urbanization* was leading to a rapid deterioration of the
nation's moral standards. Their goal was coercive social control,* and prostitution, liquor consumption, obscene literature, and gambling were the vice crusaders' most common targets. Earlier examples could be cited, but the antivice
movements launched by the Reverend Charles H. Parkhurst in New York City*
in 1892 and by William T. Stead* in Chicago in 1893 exemplify the moral fervor
of the late nineteenth-century reformers. Crusades against brothels and saloons
gained particularly widespread support. Public criticism, journalistic exposés,
and police action were used in city after city to close red-light districts, albeit
often only temporarily. Similar agitation led to the passage of the Mann Act*
(1910), which made participation in the so-called white-slave trade a federal
offense. Prohibitionists* enjoyed even greater political success in their attacks
on the saloon. With the Anti-Saloon League* promoting the cause, state after
state adopted prohibition laws, and in 1917 Congress passed the Eighteenth
Amendment. (Paul Boyer, *Urban Masses and Moral Order in America, 1820–
1920* (1978); David J. Pivar, *Purity Crusade: Sexual Morality and Social Con-*

trol, 1868–1900 (1973); Norman H. Clark, *Deliver Us from Evil: An Interpretation of American Prohibition* (1976).)

Gerald W. McFarland

VILLARD, OSWALD GARRISON (March 13, 1872–September 29, 1949). Born in Wiesbaden, Germany, Villard grew up in New York City and graduated from Harvard University, where he also earned an M.A. degree in history. After a brief apprenticeship with the *Philadelphia Press*, he joined the staff of the *New York Evening Post* in 1897. Three years later he inherited his father's controlling interest in the *Post*, and shaped its policies. An old-fashioned liberal who believed in free trade and limited government, Villard championed the rights of women and racial minorities, and played a major role in the founding of the National Association for the Advancement of Colored People* in 1909.

While he applauded the domestic reforms of Woodrow Wilson,* he denounced American involvement in World War I* as a betrayal of Progressive principles. Villard's outspoken pacifism in wartime brought him into conflict with the authorities and his own editors. In 1918 he sold the *Post*, but took over its weekly supplement, the *Nation*,* which he transformed into the leading liberal magazine in the country during the 1920s. (Oswald Garrison Villard, *Fighting Years: Memoirs of a Liberal Editor* (1939); D. Joy Humes, *Oswald Garrison Villard: Liberal of the 1920's* (1960); Michael Wreszin, *Oswald Garrison Villard: Pacifist at War* (1965).)

Maxwell H. Bloomfield

VIRGINIA. Progressivism in Virginia emerged within the context of a newly consolidated system of one-party rule. As Populist and Republican strength waned in the late 1890s, antagonisms against political manipulation and corrupt practices began to surface within Democratic ranks, pitting various "independent" or antimachine elements against the inner circles of the party leadership (headed by U.S. Senator Thomas S. Martin). Determined to revive traditional, "Old Virginia" standards of patrician rule and political probity, antimachine Democrats soon gained the advantage in this intraparty struggle and spearheaded the movement that led to the drafting of the state constitution of 1902. In addition to creating a state corporation commission to regulate railroads and other business enterprises, this new fundamental law disfranchised* tens of thousands of presumably corruptible black and poor white voters through poll tax and literacy requirements.

Meanwhile, "independent" spokesman Andrew J. Montague captured the governorship in 1901, and the Democratic state convention of 1904 secured another antimachine goal by endorsing the use of primary elections* to choose party nominees. With "courthouse cliques" in every county to muster votes in a drastically reduced electorate, machine candidates ironically swept to victory in the statewide primary of 1905. Martin retained his senate seat, defeating Montague, while organization stalwart Claude A. Swanson won the gubernatorial nomination by a resounding margin. However, the reinvigorated but chastened Democratic machine proved surprisingly receptive to reform proposals, expanding educational appropriations, beginning a state highway system, and creating a state board to ameliorate conditions in prisons, reformatories, and asylums.

The gubernatorial administrations of William H. Mann (1910–1914) and Henry C. Stuart (1914–1918) provided still more evidence of the Democratic organization's receptivity to reformist initiatives. Responding to demands from rural pressure groups, the legislature established two state-owned lime-grinding plants, provided enhanced support for agricultural education, encouraged the growth of cooperatives, and created a legislative reference bureau. The Anti-Saloon League* gained influence during this period as well, prompting the 1914 General Assembly to authorize a referendum* on statewide prohibition of alcoholic beverages. The measure was approved by a 30,000-vote majority, and the Old Dominion became officially "dry" in 1916. Bitter disputes over Prohibition* and woman suffrage* gradually eroded Virginia's progressive consensus, and the outbreak of World War I* also served to divert attention from reformist undertakings. (Raymond H. Pulley, *Old Virginia Restored: An Interpretation of the Progressive Impulse, 1870–1930* (1968); William Larsen, *Montague of Virginia: The Making of a Southern Progressive* (1965); Jack T. Kirby, *Westmoreland Davis: Virginia Planter-Politician, 1859–1942* (1968); Henry C. Ferrell, Jr., *Claude A. Swanson of Virginia: A Political Biography* (1985).)

James Tice Moore

VOTER TURNOUT. Turnout, the rate at which eligible citizens vote, averaged 65 percent in presidential races from 1900 through 1916 (only 50 percent in off-year congressional elections). The trend was steadily downward, from 73 percent in 1900 to 49 percent in 1920 and 1924. Turnout was higher in the North (74 percent, versus 32 percent in the South), in rural areas, and among men, older people, the middle class, whites, and old stock. However, the decline affected all groups. Eligibility was set by state laws. During the Progressive Era, 90 percent of southern blacks were effectively excluded from general and primary elections. Literacy and registration requirements reduced turnout among immigrants; poll taxes did the same for poor whites in the South. The spread of woman suffrage* doubled the potential electorate, but women took a decade or so to become accustomed to voting.

Why did people bother to vote? The excitement of elections and their sense of civic duty pushed them, and the parties pulled. The Progressive ethos emphasized civic duty and understanding of "issues." The goal was not high turnout per se, but an electorate comprised exclusively of well-informed people who had not been bribed or herded to the polls by bosses. Political parties, which had previously concentrated their efforts on maximizing turnout among their loyalists, changed strategies after 1900. Restraints on party action (including cutbacks on patronage and enforcement of antibribery laws) weakened their ability to get out the vote. Their new campaign style of advertising the candidates' positions to voters appealed to independents more than loyalists. Perhaps most important was the decline of interparty competition. Most elections before 1900 had been close, and differential turnout decided the winner. Now most elections were lopsided, and efforts to increase turnout were more difficult and less necessary. (Paul Kleppner, *Who Voted? The Dynamics of Electoral Turnout, 1870–1980* (1982).)

Richard Jensen

W

WAGES AND HOURS LEGISLATION. With the exception of the substantial legislation passed in the Progressive period to limit the hours of work for women, the regulation of wages and hours had to await the New Deal. Earlier legislation to limit hours, while ineffective, made such laws seem less extreme. Moreover, state court decisions had been divided on the constitutionality of hours laws for women, and thus the positive decision of the U.S. Supreme Court in *Muller v. Oregon** (1908) was not unprecedented. Organized labor's opposition to the regulation of wages and hours by law was weakest with regard to women. Finally, the reformers created the image of women as weaker people who therefore needed the protection of the state. However, it had the concomitant result of strengthening the traditional view of women which fortified long-standing barriers to wider employment opportunities and was also used against laws for men who supposedly lacked the weakness attributed to women.

In contrast, minimum wage legislation for women had few precedents in the United States. The labor movement offered stronger opposition even though the unions divided on this issue based on whether the organization represented large numbers of women workers as well as its capacity for independent economic action. Moreover, the constitutional question was murky, and ultimately the U.S. Supreme Court in *Adkin v. Children's Hospital* (1923) refused to apply the weakness principle to minimum wage laws for women. Legislation to protect men was passed only in special cases. For example, laws to regulate the hours of railroad workers were based on public safety, and the hours of miners were regulated because of the extreme danger and unhealthiness of the work.

Many leaders of the American Federation of Labor* feared legislation could replace unions as the means for gains in wages and hours. They also believed that since workers did not control the government, state oppression was as likely as state support. Clearly, legislation in the area of wages and hours was possible only under the best of conditions, and these emerged only for the limitation of hours for women. (John R. Commons et al., *History of Labour in the United States*; Alice Kessler-Harris, *Out to Work: The History of Wage-Earning Women in the United States* (1982); Irwin Yellowitz, *Labor and the Progressive Movement in New York State, 1897–1916* (1965).)

Irwin Yellowitz

WAGNER, ROBERT F. (June 8, 1877–May 4, 1953). Born in Nastätten, Germany, Wagner migrated as a child to New York City, where he graduated from City College and New York Law School. Wagner practiced law, campaigned for Democrats, and was elected in 1904 to the New York State Assembly, defeated in 1905 by a candidate of William Randolph Hearst's* Municipal Ownership League, but returned to his seat at the next election. Elevated to the state senate in 1908, he overcame a lack of seniority to become, by his second term, majority or minority leader, depending on the fortunes of his party. In his selective support of reform, he exemplified the progressivism of new-stock urban politicians and of Charles F. Murphy's Tammany Hall,* which Wagner dubbed "the cradle of modern liberalism."

The legislator who sponsored utility regulation, the Sixteenth Amendment, and woman suffrage* made his greatest contribution as chairman of the New York State Factory Investigating Commission* that transformed the labor law of the Empire State into a model for expert administration, workplace safety, workmen's compensation,* and maximum hours for women and children. Between 1919 and 1926 he served on state courts, where his decisions upholding the rights of labor embodied the jurisprudence of legal realism. In the U.S. Senate from 1927 to 1949 he took the lead in supporting the New Deal, welfare and labor legislation, including the National Labor Relations Act that bears his name, and the civil rights of blacks. (J. Joseph Huthmacher, *Senator Robert F. Wagner and the Rise of Urban Liberalism* (1968); John D. Buenker, *Urban Liberalism and Progressive Reform* (1973); Thomas Jefferson Kerr IV, "New York Factory Investigating Commission and the Progressives" (D.S.S. diss., Syracuse University, 1965).)

Paula Eldot

WALD, LILLIAN D. (March 10, 1867–September 1, 1940). Lillian D. Wald, one of the founders of the settlement house movement in the United States and of the field of public health nursing, was born in Cincinnati of Jewish immigrant parents. Her father became a successful dealer in optical goods, and the family moved first to Dayton and then to Rochester. Wald spent several years as a young woman of fashion before entering the New York Hospital Training School for Nurses in 1889. After graduation, she worked at the New York Juvenile Asylum and then, in 1893, enrolled in the Women's Medical College. While there, she agreed to organize home nursing classes for immigrant women on the Lower East Side of New York and found the meaningful work she had been seeking.

Later, in 1893, she and Mary Brewster moved into the College Settlement to inaugurate the practice of public health nursing in the United States. In 1895, Wald opened the famous "House on Henry Street." By 1913 there were ninety-two visiting nurses working out of the settlement, making 200,000 visits each year. Wald also helped create the first public school nursing program. She and Florence Kelley* helped found the National Child Labor Committee* in 1904. The next year she helped persuade President Theodore Roosevelt* to propose a federal Children's Bureau.* In 1914, she, Jane Addams,* and Kelley set up the American Union Against Militarism, but once the United States entered the war, she headed the committee on home nursing of the Council of National Defense.* (Lillian Wald, *The House on Henry Street* (1915); R. L. Duffus, *Lillian Wald: Neighbor and Crusader* (1938); Allen F. Davis, *Spearheads for Reform: The Social Settlements and the Progressive Movement, 1890–1914* (1967).)

John F. McClymer

WALKER, FRANCIS A. (July 2, 1840–January 5, 1897). Born in Boston, Massachusetts, Walker obtained the A.B. degree from Amherst College and studied law for two years. In 1866, he became a deputy to the special commissioner of revenue, David A. Wells, and later was appointed chief of the Bureau of Statistics. He served as the superintendent of the tenth census (1879–1881); the results immediately established the reputation of Walker as a world leader in the gathering of statistics. From 1873 to 1881, he served as a professor of political economy and history in the Sheffield Scientific School of Yale and as president of the Massachusetts Institute of Technology from 1881 to 1897. Walker served as the first president of the reform-inclined American Economic Association* from 1885 to 1892 and as president of the American Statistical Association from 1882 to 1892. In these roles he was a senior mentor of an entire younger generation of economists, who sought to abandon or move beyond classical economic formulations and to examine how historical forces shaped the economy and society.

As a theorist, Walker was best known for his attack on the wages-fund theory which had been used to refute the utility of labor unions and to defend existing wage rates. In brief, Walker argued that the final value of the product rather than the capital invested determined wages. Like many other progressives, Walker feared that unrestrained immigration would result in low wages and increased violence among American workers. (Joseph Dorfman, *The Economic Mind in American Civilization* (1959); Bernard Newton, *The Economics of Francis Amasa Walker: American Economics in Transition* (1968); J. P. Munroe, *The Life of Francis Amasa Walker* (1923).)

Benjamin G. Rader

WALLACE, HENRY CANTWELL (May 11, 1886–October 25, 1924). Born in Rock Island, Illinois, Wallace spent most of his boyhood on a farm in Winterset, Iowa. In 1892, he graduated from Iowa State Agricultural College (today

Iowa State University). Two years later, he and his father—Henry Wallace (1836–1916)—moved to Des Moines, where they founded a journal that was soon to gain national attention: *Wallaces' Farmer*. Although normally Republicans, both father and son bolted the party in 1912 and supported Theodore Roosevelt's* Progressive* campaign for the presidency. During World War I,* Henry C. Wallace served as an adviser to the Food Administration,* and in 1921 President Warren G. Harding* appointed him secretary of agriculture. As a member of the cabinet, Wallace sought to preserve the Forest Service* and aid farmers in the marketing of crops. Wallace was the father of Henry Agard Wallace (1888–1965). (Russell Lord, *The Wallaces of Iowa* (1947); Donald L. Winters, *Henry Cantwell Wallace as Secretary of Agriculture, 1921–1924* (1970).)

Barton C. Shaw

WALLING, WILLIAM ENGLISH (March 14, 1877–September 12, 1936). Socialist* writer and reformer, Walling was born in Louisville, Kentucky;* he was educated at private schools in Kentucky and Scotland, then graduated from the University of Chicago* in 1897. Inheriting wealth, he dedicated his life to social reform, serving as factory inspector for the state of Illinois* from 1900 to 1901, then working at University Settlement* in New York* from 1901 to 1905. At the 1903 convention of the American Federation of Labor,* he organized the National Women's Trade Union League* along with Mary Kenney O'Sullivan.* He went to Russia for two years after the abortive 1905 Russian Revolution, marrying socialist Anna Strunsky while there.

Back in the United States, he and his wife witnessed the 1908 race riot* in Springfield, Illinois. Shocked by the brutal racism in the home of Abraham Lincoln, Walling called a series of meetings with New York social worker Mary White Ovington* which led to the founding of the National Association for the Advancement of Colored People (NAACP)* in 1910. Walling joined the Socialist party of America* in 1910 and fought against conservative socialists who tried to create a reformist labor party. He resigned from the party in 1917 to support American entry into World War I.* After the war, he became more conservative, working as a writer for the American Federation of Labor and rejecting socialism. (Anna Strunsky Walling, *William English Walling: A Symposium* (1938); David A. Shannon, *The Socialist Party of America* (1955); Allen F. Davis, *Spearheads for Reform* (1967).)

Edward R. Kantowicz

WALSH, DAVID IGNATIUS (November 11, 1872–June 11, 1947). Born in Leominster, Massachusetts, the ninth of ten children of Irish immigrant parents, Walsh graduated from Holy Cross College, Worcester, Massachusetts, in 1893 and from Boston University Law School in 1897. He established a law practice in industrial Fitchburg, Massachusetts, and became active in Democratic politics. Walsh was elected lieutenant governor in 1912 and governor in 1913 and 1914, the first Irish Catholic to attain these offices in Massachusetts. In 1918, he was elected to the U.S. Senate. Narrowly defeated for reelection in 1924, Walsh was returned to the Senate in 1926. Walsh was identified with the progressive wing of the Democratic party,* and during his governorship, he sponsored measures to strengthen important state agencies, including the Industrial Accident Board, the Department of Public Utilities, the Department of Health, and University Extension.

Allied with the national progressive Democrats, Walsh ran for senator in 1918 as a supporter of Woodrow Wilson.* Although he broke with Wilson over the League of Nations* in 1919, he continued to support liberal legislation in the 1920s. Walsh's enduring political success derived from a coalition of Irish, newer immigrants, and Yankee Democrats which prefigured the New Deal coalition. (William J. Grattan, "David I. Walsh and His Associates: A Study in Political Theory" (Ph.D. diss., Harvard University, 1957); David I. Walsh, Papers, Holy Cross College, Worcester, MA; Dorothy G. Wayman, *David I. Walsh, Citizen, Patriot* (1952).)

Constance Burns

WALSH, FRANCIS P. (July 20, 1864–May 2, 1939). Born in Saint Louis, Missouri, "Frank" Walsh studied law in Kansas City and was admitted to the bar in 1889. Walsh began his public career in 1892 as assistant corporation counsel and subsequently served on the Tenement Commission (1906–1908), as president of the Board of Civil Service (1911–1913), and as architect of Kansas City's acclaimed Board of Public Welfare. In 1913, President Woodrow Wilson* chose Walsh to chair the U.S. Commission on Industrial Relations* investigation of labor unrest. His spectacular cross-examination of such prominent individuals as J. P. Morgan,* John D. Rockefeller,* Sr., and Jr., and Andrew Carnegie* captured public attention, but the commission's pro-labor recommendations fell on deaf ears. Subsequent passage, however, of the La Follette Seamen's Act* (1915), Keating-Owen National Child Labor Act* (1916), Adamson Eight-Hour Day Act* (1916), and Kern-McGillicuddy Workmen's Compensation Act* (1916) all reflected commission goals.

In 1918, as cochairman of the War Labor Board,* Walsh fought for workers' right to organize, a "living wage," and equal pay for women for comparable work. In the postwar years he divided his time between the struggle for Irish independence and the defense of civil liberties. Walsh was mentioned as a presidential candidate in 1920 by liberals in the Committee of Forty-Eight and the Farmer-Labor party. (Graham Adams, Jr., *Age of Industrial Violence, 1910– 1915: The Activities and Findings of the United States Commission on Industrial Relations* (1966); James Weinstein, *The Corporate Ideal in the Liberal State: 1900–1918* (1968); Eugene M. Tobin, *Organize or Perish: America's Independent Progressives, 1913–1933* (1986).)

Eugene M. Tobin

WALSH, THOMAS JAMES (June 12, 1859–March 2, 1933). Born in Two Rivers, Wisconsin, Walsh was educated in the public schools of Two Rivers and at the University of Wisconsin law school. Walsh practiced law in Dakota

Territory from 1884 to 1890, then continued in Helena, Montana, attaining a reputation as one of the ablest attorneys in the West. A Democrat, he ran in 1906 for a seat in the U.S. House of Representatives but was defeated. With many others, Walsh objected to the intrusions of the Anaconda Copper Mining Company into governmental affairs and sought to broaden popular authority. As a leader of this movement and benefiting from divisions in the Republican party,* he was elected to the U.S. Senate in 1912.

In Washington, Walsh gained recognition as a hardworking legislator and an "advanced progressive" in his support of social and economic legislation. He led the fight in the Judiciary Committee in 1916 to confirm the nomination of Louis D. Brandeis* to the Supreme Court. Essentially a Jeffersonian liberal, Walsh changed with the times and became an advocate of enlarged federal programs including the retention of public lands and their management through a leasing system. He was a true "progressive" in his optimism concerning national development and the mission of the United States in world affairs. (J. Leonard Bates, "T. J. Walsh: His 'Genius for Controversy,' " *Montana* 19 (October 1969): 3–15; Michael P. Malone and Richard B. Roeder, *Montana: A History of Two Centuries* (1976).)

J. Leonard Bates

WARBURG, PAUL MORITZ (August 10, 1868–January 24, 1932). A New York* investment banker, and a founder of the Federal Reserve System,* Warburg was born into a famous banking family in Hamburg, Germany; he was educated at German universities then went to work for the M. M. Warburg banking house. He joined Kuhn, Loeb investment banking house in 1902, settling in New York, and he became a U.S. citizen in 1911. After the panic of 1907* he took an active role in the movement to reform the banking system and establish a central bank. He was the principal author of the National Monetary Commission's* report, the so-called Aldrich Plan, in 1911; and he helped organize the National Citizens' League,* a business lobby for passage of the Aldrich Plan. This plan was much amended by the Democratic administration of Woodrow Wilson,* but it still served as the basis of the Federal Reserve Act passed in 1913. Wilson named Warburg a member of the first Federal Reserve Board, where he served from 1914 to 1918 and acted as liaison to the Wall Street banking community. (*New York Times* obituary, January 25, 1932; Paul M. Warburg, *The Federal Reserve System* (1930); H. Parker Willis, *The Federal Reserve System* (1923).)

Edward R. Kantowicz

WAR INDUSTRIES BOARD. The War Industries Board was an executive agency in the Woodrow Wilson* administration that coordinated home-front production policies during World War I.* American entry into the war posed a harsh dilemma for Wilson. He had been elected as a champion of the New Freedom* and an opponent of business influence over government, yet mobilization of the economy for war required business expertise and central direction. Accordingly, in July 1917 Wilson created an ambiguous, hybrid agency, called the War Industries Board (WIB), which attempted to coordinate production through voluntary cooperation of business and government, through persuasion and negotiation rather than compulsion. The six-man board supervised numerous "dollar-a-year men" from business who headed "commodity sections" and negotiated production and price agreements in their respective industries.

The WIB floundered for a time under weak leadership and inadequate enforcement authority; but when Wilson appointed Bernard Baruch,* a shrewd Wall Street speculator, as chairman in March 1918, the board took on a new life. Baruch effectively bullied, cajoled, and finessed businessmen into cooperating for the duration of the war. The WIB was dissolved immediately after the Armistice, but during the depression of the 1930s, President Franklin D. Roosevelt* used it as a model for his National Recovery Administration. (Robert D. Cuff, *The War Industries Board* (1973); David M. Kennedy, *Over Here: The First World War and American Society* (1980); William E. Leuchtenberg, "The New Deal and the Analogue of War," in John Braeman, ed., *Change and Continuity in Twentieth Century America* (1966).)

Edward R. Kantowicz

WAR LABOR BOARD. An executive agency in the Woodrow Wilson* administration that coordinated labor policy during World War I,* the War Labor Board was organized early in 1918; it continued policies that Wilson had followed throughout the war. In order to ensure an uninterrupted supply of labor for maximum industrial production, the board navigated a middle course between the compulsion of labor on the one hand, and the outright legitimizing of labor union authority on the other. Accordingly, the board discouraged strikes by underwriting high wages with generous cost-plus contracts for industry. It protected the unions' right to organize and bargain collectively, but did not insist on closed-union shops.

This labor policy proved effective for the duration of the wartime crisis—the government commandeered factories that violated the rules and discouraged labor unions from disruptive strikes—but it led to mixed results in the long run. Many workers were exposed to union organizers for the first time, and the American Federation of Labor* made gains during the war, but the government's refusal to impose the closed shop led to the growth of many tame company unions. (Gordon S. Watkins, *Labor Problems and the Labor Administration in the United States during the World War* (1920); Alexander M. Bing, *War-time Strikes and Their Adjustment* (1921); David M. Kennedy, *Over Here* (1980).)

Edward R. Kantowicz

WARD, LESTER FRANK (June 18, 1841–April 18, 1913). Ward was born in Joliet, Illinois, the son of an itinerant mechanic. After serving in the Civil War, he joined the growing federal bureaucracy in Washington, in successive positions at the Treasury Department, the Geological Survey, and the Smithsonian. His major contribution, however, came in *Dynamic Sociology* (1883), an early defense of the theory of the positive state guided by science, which he termed "sociocracy," and also a seminal text for American sociology. Begun as a defense of universal education, the work combined Auguste Comte and Herbert Spencer* to argue that evolution is not a blind process beyond human control, but "telic" since the emergence of mind at the higher stages allows control of the evolutionary process. "Feeling" (subjective desire) is the starting point and final test of all human activity.

In later works such as *Pure Sociology* (1903) and *Applied Sociology* (1906), Ward tempered the potentially radical implications of these views, emphasizing the value of religion and other social controls. Meanwhile, a younger generation of academic sociologists led by Albion Small* of the University of Chicago* brought the discipline more in line with the pragmatic perspectives of progressivism. Although Ward had lost much of his influence and audience by the time he accepted a professorship at Brown in 1906, his reputation as the nestor of American sociology and pioneer of modern liberalism has survived his many critics. (John C. Burnham, *Lester Frank Ward in American Thought* (1956); Samuel Chugerman, *Lester Frank Ward: The American Aristotle* (1939); Clifford H. Scott, *Lester Frank Ward* (1976).)

                                                                     Robert C. Bannister

WAREHOUSE ACT. Established to provide the credit farmers needed to temporarily withhold their crops from market and to prevent fraud in marketing, the Warehouse Act authorized the secretary of agriculture to license bonded warehousemen who agreed to comply with Department of Agriculture's regulations to receive, grade, and weigh farm products and issue warehouse receipts for them. Farmers might use these receipts as collateral to secure loans. The law bore a resemblance to the subtreasury plan included in the Populist* platform of 1892, and reflected the continuation of Populist thought into the Progressive period. As proposed by southern members of Congress in 1914 during the cotton crisis of that year, the Warehouse Act provided only for storing of cotton and was presented as an emergency measure.

Attacked on the grounds that it was unconstitutional, an invasion of states' rights, and that it would lead to the inclusion of all farm products, the bill failed in the House of Representatives. In 1916, however, the climactic year for progressive farm legislation, cherished southern constitutional scruples were set aside. The Warehouse Act, altered to include grains, wool, tobacco, and flaxseed, as well as cotton, that entered into interstate commerce, was attached to the Agricultural Appropriation bill for 1917, and enacted August 11, 1916. (Theodore Saloutos, *Farmers Movements in the South, 1865–1933* (1960); David D.

Houston, *Eight Years with Wilson's Cabinet* (1926); Murray R. Benedict, *Farm Policies of the United States, 1790–1950* (1953).)

Wayne E. Fuller

WARREN, FRANCIS EMROY (June 20, 1844–November 24, 1929). Born in Hinsdale, Massachusetts, Warren volunteered to fight for the Union in the Civil War at the age of eighteen. Moving West, he settled in 1868 in Cheyenne, Wyoming, where he involved himself in the developing cattle- and sheep-raising industries. Upon the creation of the National Wool Growers' Association in 1901, he became its first president. Warren's interest in Wyoming politics and efforts on behalf of the Republican party* resulted in his appointment as territorial governor by Chester Arthur in February 1885. In 1890, he was elected the new state's first governor but resigned a few days later to become U.S. senator, an office he held until 1893 and again from 1895 until his death. Before the World War,* he served as chairman of the Senate Committee on Military Affairs and, later, of the Committee on Appropriations. Warren labored in the Senate for legislation to provide for the reclamation of arid lands and, as a representative of the first state to give women the vote, supported the equal-suffrage amendment to the Constitution. (Frank B. Beard, *Progressive Men of the State of Wyoming* (1903); *Dictionary of American Biography* vol. 19.)

Robert C. Hilderbrand

WASHINGTON, BOOKER T. (1865–November 14, 1915). Born in Hale's Ford, Virginia, Washington lived in slavery until his ninth year. In 1875, he was graduated from Hampton Institute, a Virginia industrial school based on the conservative ideology of its white founder, Samuel Chapman Armstrong. Washington was called to Tuskegee, Alabama, to head Tuskegee Normal and Industrial Institute, the child of a political compromise between white politicians and the black majority of Macon County. When Washington arrived, the school consisted only of a $2,000 state appropriation, but due to his political and fund-raising skills was the second best endowed black school by 1900. It was patterned after Hampton except in being staffed completely by blacks. Most of its graduates became teachers in the rural South; several founded schools.

In 1895, Washington spoke at the Cotton States Exposition in Atlanta, articulating the accommodationist approach to race relations. Called the "Atlanta Compromise," the speech asked blacks to concentrate on educational and economic advancement and to defer temporarily agitation for political and civic equality. In return, white southerners were asked to hire blacks and to contribute to black education. Coming in the era of black disfranchisment* and racial violence, his words reflected the temper of the times, thus catapulting Washington to the position of "spokesman" for Afro-Americans. As such, he wielded considerable power over political appointments and the distribution of philanthropic funds. He also established the National Negro Business League* and controlled much of the black press. His autobiography, *Up from Slavery*, published in 1901, further enhanced his influence.

By 1905, however, accommodationism's failure to stem the tide of racism, Washington's sometimes ruthless use of power, and his advocacy of industrial schools at the expense of higher education provoked an organized revolt by some black intellectuals, who united under W. E. B. Du Bois* and William Monroe Trotter to form the Niagara Movement, a forerunner of the National Association for the Advancement of Colored People.* (Louis R. Harlan, *Booker T. Washington: The Making of a Black Leader, 1856–1901* (1972); Louis R. Harlan, *Booker T. Washington: The Wizard of Tuskegee, 1901–1915* (1983); August Meier, *Negro Thought in America, 1880–1915: Racial Ideologies in the Age of Booker T. Washington* (1963).)

Linda O. McMurry

WASHINGTON (STATE). The Republican party* had long dominated Washington State except for the Populist interlude of the 1890s, but its harmony was disrupted in 1906 by the emergence of self-described insurgents. With the support of labor and farm organizations as well as urban reformers, they succeeded in the next several sessions of the legislature in securing the direct primary;* an advisory ballot in U.S. Senate elections; a constitutional amendment providing for the initiative,* referendum,* and recall;* a local option prohibition* law; an eight-hour day for women workers; provision for a commission to establish a minimum wage for women; and an industrial insurance law. In national politics, the insurgents supported the election of progressive Republican Miles Poindexter* to the House of 1908 and to the Senate in 1910.

In 1912, the newly launched Progressive party* fielded a state as well as a national ticket, and although the Progressive candidate for president, Theodore Roosevelt,* carried the state and two Progressive candidates won seats in Congress, other Progressive party candidacies failed. The successful candidate for governor, Democrat Ernest Lister, played down his party affiliation and emphasized his record of efficiency and economy in the Populist administration. Four years later, though, like President Woodrow Wilson,* he actively sought the support of those who had voted Progressive in 1912. (Howard W. Allen, *Poindexter of Washington: A Study in Progressive Politics* (1981); Robert D. Saltvig, "The Progressive Movement in Washington" (Ph.D. diss., University of Washington, 1966).)

Robert D. Saltvig

WATER POWER ACT. During the Taft* administration, various groups pushed for a legislation to regulate hydroelectric power sites. The administration proposal would have allowed state development under federal supervision. In 1914, the Wilson* administration began to press for an act, introduced by Scott Ferris of Oklahoma, for exclusive federal regulation of such sites. The inability to compromise with those who wanted some measure of state control and security for business blocked passage. In 1919, the Senate Commerce and Public Lands committees began to consider new legislation. The bill passed in 1920, establishing a federal power commission consisting of the secretaries of war, interior, and agriculture.

Exercising general control over all water-power sites located on navigable waters and on public lands, the commission could grant fifty-year permits for development. The law passed largely because of a compromise between conservatives and progressives which allowed business to feel secure in investing money, gave the states revenue from the sites within their boundaries, and provided for federal regulation. At the same time, the charge for development was divided between the reclamation* fund (50 percent), the state with the power site (37.5 percent), and the federal treasury (12.5 percent). (Thomas G. Alexander, "Senator Reed Smoot and Western Land Policy, 1905–1920," *Arizona and the West* 13 (Autumn 1971): 245–64; James G. Kerwin, *Federal Water Power Legislation* (1926); Milton Conover, *The Federal Power Commission* (1923); Richard Lowitt, "Federal Power Commission," in Donald R. Whitnah, ed., *Government Agencies* (1983), 233–38.)

Thomas G. Alexander

WATSON, THOMAS EDWARD (September 5, 1856–September 26, 1922). Born near Thomson, Georgia, Watson attended Mercer University from 1872 to 1874. Afterward he became a lawyer and a charismatic champion of the farmers, who elected him to Congress in 1890. Frustrated by his inability to bring about reform within the Democratic party,* Watson joined the Populist party* two years later. His three unsuccessful attempts to regain his congressional seat earned him national attention, and in 1896, the Populists nominated Watson for vice president. After yet another defeat, he retired from politics and devoted himself to law. He also edited the popular reform journal, *Tom Watson's Magazine*.

In 1906, he helped elect Hoke Smith,* Georgia's first Progressive governor. Although in many respects still a reformer, Watson had also become a vicious racist and anti-Catholic. His attacks on Leo Frank,* an Atlanta Jew accused of murdering a gentile girl, undoubtedly contributed to Frank's lynching in 1915. Watson vigorously opposed American involvement in World War I,* and he later denounced the League of Nations.* In 1920 Georgia elected him to the U.S. Senate. (C. Vann Woodward, *Tom Watson, Agrarian Rebel* (1938); William W. Brewton, *The Life of Thomas E. Watson* (1926); Barton C. Shaw, *The Wool-Hat Boys: Georgia's Populist Party* (1984).)

Barton C. Shaw

WEBB-KENYON ACT (1913). Bearing the name of a North Carolina Democrat (Edwin Y. Webb) and an Iowa Republican (William S. Kenyon), the act ensued from the nearly insuperable challenge of enforcing local dry laws in one area while a wet community existed nearby. As long as the commerce clause of the

Constitution permitted shipment of liquor into dry states, prohibition* was a sometime thing. In 1902, a dry coalition proposed national legislation regulating interstate liquor shipments. In 1911, a Democratic House of Representatives drafted the act, and in February 1913, the House version prohibiting transportation of liquor in interstate commerce in conflict with local dry laws secured acceptance by the Senate. Following the advice of Attorney General George W. Wickersham,* lame-duck President William Howard Taft* vetoed the legislation on grounds that it delegated power to the states. Within two hours, the Senate overrode the veto 63 to 21 and the next day the House did likewise, 246 to 95.

Enforcement, however, lacked vigor and system. In 1917, the Supreme Court, despite refusal by the Woodrow Wilson* administration to argue the case, upheld its constitutionality (*Clark Distillery Company v. Western Railway Company* 242 US 311 [1917]). A link in the chain from local option to state dry laws to the Eighteenth Amendment (1919), the law was revived, after repeal of federal prohibition, as Section 2 of the Twenty-First Amendment forbidding importation of intoxicants into dry states. (K. Austin Kerr, *Organized for Prohibition: A New History of the Anti-Saloon League* (1985); David E. Kyvig, ed., *Law, Alcohol, and Order: Perspectives on National Prohibition* (1985); Peter H. Odegard, *Pressure Politics: The Story of the Anti-Saloon League* (1928); James H. Timberlake, *Prohibition and the Progressive Movement: 1900–1920* (1963).)

Henry C. Ferrell

WEBB-POMERENE ACT (1918). Introduced by Edwin Y. Webb (D-North Carolina in August 1916 after a long gestation, the bill contained provisions to augment American foreign trade advantages for small and mid-sized firms competing against overseas cartels. By freeing them from the constraints of existing antitrust laws (the Sherman Act, Federal Trade Commission Act,* and Clayton Act*) and placing them outside the jurisdiction of the Federal Trade Commission and Antitrust Division of the Department of Justice, the bill permitted formation of collusive associations to secure the economies of scale enjoyed by larger corporations. In contrast, the bill failed to describe the forms of these cooperative associations, leaving their organization to private officials.

A two-year delay followed, engendered primarily by midwestern senators who questioned the dichotomy of domestic antitrust laws juxtaposed with foreign trade collectivist policies, who feared the beginning of repeal of antitrust legislation, and who considered it a boon to large corporations intent upon controlling domestic markets. Events of World War I* stimulated further economic integration between private business and government, however, and in April 1918, bearing an additional name, that of Atlee Pomerene* (D-Ohio), chairman of the Senate Interstate Commerce Committee, the bill became law. (Michael J. Hogan, *Informal Entente: The Private Structure of Cooperation in Anglo-American Economic Diplomacy, 1918–1928* (1977); Burton I. Kaufman, *Efficiency and Expansion: Foreign Trade Organization in the Wilson Administration* (1974); Carl P. Parrini, *Heir to Empire: United States Economic Diplomacy,*

1916–1923 (1969); Davis A. Larson, "An Economic Analysis of the Webb-Pomerene Act," *Journal of Law and Economics* 13 (1970): 461–500.)

Henry C. Ferrell

WEST VIRGINIA. The Mountain State experienced gradual progressive reform under Republican leadership, beginning first with efforts by Governor Albert B. White in 1901 to revise the tax system, increasing corporate taxation and reducing personal property taxes. Although he advocated other reforms, including a pure food law, an antibody law, election reforms, and increased railroad regulation, he worked hardest on tax reform.* By the time he left office, however, he had failed to achieve one of his most important goals—a tax on coal, oil, and gas leases and options. Under his successor, former Secretary of State William O. Dawson, the state nudged closer to the reform pattern of other states during the period, adopting a corrupt practices* act and a law to protect the state's mine workers. Dawson subsequently played an active role on behalf of Theodore Roosevelt* in 1912, even following him out of the Republican party.*

Governor William E. Glasscock came to office in 1909 with the support of the state's leading political boss, Stephen B. Elkins,* but succeeded in securing creation of a public service commission, revamping the state's educational system, and providing for workmen's compensation.* Glasscock also supported Roosevelt for the Republican presidential nomination in 1912, but remained within the party after William Howard Taft* won the nomination. Progressive reform activity reached its peak under physician-turned-politician Henry D. Hatfield, when the state endorsed woman suffrage,* the direct election of U.S. senators,* a child labor law,* and an eight-hour day for labor. Fighting within the Republican party between prominent industrial and political leaders spelled an end to further reform and opened the door for the election of Democrat John D. Cornwell. (John Alexander Williams, *West Virginia and the Captains of Industry*, (1976); Nicholas C. Burckel, "Publishing Progressivism: William M. O. Dawson," *West Virginia History*, 42 (1901): 222–48; Carolyn Karr, "A Political Biography of Henry Hatfield," *West Virginia History* 28 (1966–1967): Part 1, 35–63; Part 2, 137–70.)

Nicholas C. Burckel

WEYL, WALTER EDWARD (March 11, 1873–November 9, 1919). Few would challenge Walter Lippmann's assertion that Weyl was "by far the best trained economist in the progressive movement." Born in Philadelphia, a member of a large family of German-Jewish immigrants, Weyl won a scholarship to the Wharton School, where he gained the attention of the prominent economist, Simon N. Patten.* After three years of European study and travel, he returned to America in 1896, finished his Ph.D. dissertation, and then proceeded to drift aimlessly for a decade—travel, various assignments for the Bureau of Labor Statistics, a stint in the settlement house movement, and a three-year association as an aide to John Mitchell,* the embattled leader of the United Mine Workers.*

Weyl wrote on many topics, but was at his best on labor, railroads, and immigration. His most important book, *The New Democracy*, appeared in 1912 and was an admirable and influential study of American conditions and a plea for progressive measures. He supported Theodore Roosevelt* in 1912, and in 1914, at Herbert Croly's* invitation, became a founding editor of the *New Republic.** He combined a hard-headed pragmatism with profound social compassion and gentle humanity. "He looked like a saint," Alvin Johnson once wrote, "and fundamentally was one." (Charles Forcey, *The Crossroads of Liberalism: Croly, Weyl, Lippmann and the Progressive Movement, 1900–1925* (1961); Charles Forcey, *Walter Weyl: An Appreciation* (1922).)

David W. Levy

WHEELER, BURTON KENDALL (February 27, 1882–January 7, 1975). Wheeler was born and educated in Hudson, Massachusetts, and graduated from the University of Michigan Law Department in 1905. After working a variety of jobs, he passed the bar in Butte, Montana. Wheeler won election in 1911 to the State House of Representatives and worked for improved working conditions for miners. Wheeler served as U.S. district attorney, and lost as the nonpartisan gubernatorial candidate in 1920, but was elected by the farmers and miners to the U.S. Senate as a Democrat in 1922.

His political philosophy of action was a rich molding of old-fashioned populism and progressivism; his enemies called him "Bolshevik Burt." Wheeler, outraged by the conservatism of the Democrats in 1924, ran as vice presidential nominee on Robert La Follette's* Progressive ticket. An early advocate of Franklin D. Roosevelt's* election, Wheeler supported New Deal reforms except for the National Industrial Recovery Act and the Court Packing scheme, but was an ardent isolationist. (B. K. Wheeler, *Yankee from the West* (1962); *Current Biography* (1940); Richard T. Ruetten, "Burton K. Wheeler of Montana: A Progressive between the Wars" (Ph.D. diss., University of Oregon, 1961); *New York Times*, January 8, 1975.)

C. David Tompkins

WHITE, EDWARD DOUGLAS, JR. (November 3, 1845–May 19, 1921). Born into a politically prominent family, reared in the antebellum South, and educated in Jesuit schools, White remained unreflectively attached to the conservative faith and habits of thought inculcated during his youth. After Civil War service as a Confederate soldier, he read law and rose swiftly in state politics, eventually being chosen a U.S. senator in 1888. He was appointed to the U.S. Supreme Court by President Grover Cleveland. As an associate justice (1894–1910), White displayed notable analytical skill, usually attributed to his scholastic training, while his judicial philosophy harmonized readily with the principal constitutional doctrines of the laissez-faire majority. In particular, he sought to limit congressional power, developing the famous rule of reason* and helping to elaborate the doctrines of dual federalism as protections of property.

Nevertheless, he occasionally deviated from conservative jurisprudence, as in the *Pollock** and *Lochner** cases.

When Chief Justice Melville Fuller died unexpectedly, President William Howard Taft* advanced White, an older man, thereby practically assuring himself one last chance for elevation to the position he dearly wanted. As Chief Justice during the height of the Progressive Era (1910–1921), White managed creditably as the Court's administrator but was unable to exert doctrinal influence over its liberal core of justices. The static principles of law he espoused took little account of reality, often blinding him to social change and the need for political and economic reform. (Robert B. Highsaw, *Edward Douglas White: Defender of the Conservative Faith* (1981); Sister Marie Caroly Klinkhamer, *Edward Douglas White* (1943).)

Stephen B. Wood

WHITE, SUE SHELDON (May 25, 1887–May 6, 1943). Born in Henderson, Tennessee, White was the daughter of a lawyer and Methodist minister. Her education included both teacher training and business courses. While a court reporter in Jackson, Tennessee (1907–1918), she developed a consuming interest in law and politics. An active participant in the suffrage movement, she served as secretary and organizer for the state suffrage association. She defended and approved the militant agitation of the Alice Paul* suffragists and, in 1918, became Tennessee chairman for the National Woman's Party.* She engaged in no militant agitation in Tennessee, but was one of several women arrested and jailed for burning an effigy of President Woodrow Wilson* in front of the White House on February 9, 1919. A strong supporter of the federal woman suffrage* amendment, she took an active part in the campaign to gain Tennessee's ratification in August 1920. (James P. Louis, "Sue Shelton White and the Woman Suffrage Movement in Tennessee, 1913–1920," *Tennessee Historical Quarterly* 22 (1963): 170–190; A. Elizabeth Taylor, *The Woman Suffrage Movement in Tennessee* (1957); Inez Haynes Irwin, *The Story of the Woman's Party* (1921); Doris Stevens, *Jailed for Freedom* (1920).)

A. Elizabeth Taylor

WHITE, WILLIAM ALLEN (February 10, 1868–January 29, 1944). Born in Emporia, Kansas, White was educated at the College of Emporia and the University of Kansas. His friendship with Theodore Roosevelt* and his writings—novels, essays, biographies, editorials, etc.—made him nationally renowned. He began his newspaper career in Kansas but was most influenced by his years as editorial writer for William Rockhill Nelson's* Kansas City, Missouri *Star*. In 1895, he purchased the Emporia *Gazette*, a journal that he would convince the public was the authentic voice of rural, small-town America. His political involvement began in the nineties through membership in the so-called Leland Machine, and with the antipopulist editorial "What's the Matter with Kansas?"

He became a progressive as a result of his association with Theodore Roosevelt,* once writing that "he bit me and I went mad." White was a leader of the antirailroad movement in Kansas in 1906, organized the progressive-Republican faction in 1908, and managed Joseph L. Bristow's* senatorial election in 1909. He was the driving force of the Progressive party* in the state after the 1912 bolt and one of its significant national strategists. Although he never seriously sought public office, his editorials, political dealings, and general influence placed him in the forefront of the movement. (Walter Johnson and Alberta Pantle, "A Bibliography of the Published Works of William Allen White," *Kansas Historical Quarterly* 15 (February 1947): 22–41; Walter Johnson, *William Allen White's America* (1947); *The Autobiography of William Allen White* (1946); Robert S. La Forte, *Leaders of Reform* (1974).)

Robert S. La Forte

WHITE HOUSE CONFERENCE ON CARE OF DEPENDENT CHILDREN. On Christmas Day 1908, President Theodore Roosevelt* invited more than 200 interested persons to a White House Conference on Care of Dependent Children which would meet on January 25 and 26, 1909. Roosevelt acted at the behest of a group of social workers who, holding to a typical progressive belief in the efficacy of fact finding, hoped the conference might persuade Congress to establish a Federal Children's Bureau* which would gather and publish data about the condition of American children. The president addressed the opening session, and after two days, the conference adjourned with a call for protection of the family and a recommendation for the establishment of the Children's Bureau. In a special message to Congress, Roosevelt endorsed the conference recommendation; he was, however, a lame duck, and it required three more years of intensive lobbying before President William Howard Taft* signed the Children's Bureau into law. In subsequent years the bureau worked closely, but cautiously and conservatively, with reformers outside the government. (Dorothy Bradbury, *Five Decades of Action for Children: A History of the Children's Bureau* (1962); Robert H. Bremner, *From the Depths: The Discovery of Poverty in the United States* (1956).)

Robert W. McAhren

WHITLOCK, BRAND (March 4, 1869–May 24, 1934). Born in Urbana, Ohio, he worked as a reporter in 1890s Chicago,* joined the administration of Illinois governor John Peter Altgeld* from 1893 to 1897, and became a convinced social reformer. In 1897, Whitlock began a law practice in Toledo, Ohio, and the writing of "realist" fiction, an avocation that resulted in thirteen novels. His penal reform activities brought him into close contact with Toledo's charismatic reform mayor, Samuel "Golden Rule" Jones.* After Jones's death, Whitlock was elected to the mayoralty for four two-year terms (1905–1913). In Toledo, he tackled environmental problems, created public works projects for the unemployed, and was most successful in his campaign against traction* monopolists. Statewide, he worked for home rule,* the singletax,* and the abolition of capital punishment. From 1914 to 1919 he was minister-ambassador to Belgium. Disenchanted after the war, he stayed in Europe. (Brand Whitlock, *Forty Years of It* (1920); Allan Nevins, ed., *The Letters and Journals of Brand Whitlock* (1936); Jack Tager, *The Intellectual as Urban Reformer: Brand Whitlock and the Progressive Movement* (1968).)

Jack Tager

WICKERSHAM, GEORGE WOODWARD (September 19, 1858–January 25, 1936). Born to wealthy parents, Wickersham studied civil engineering at Lehigh (1873–1875), then became private secretary to Pennsylvania Senator Matthew Quay in 1878. He graduated from the University of Pennsylvania Law School in 1880 and was admitted to the bar in Philadelphia that same year. In 1883 he joined the New York firm of Strong and Cadwalader to specialize in business litigation of railroads and metropolitan transportation. Over subsequent decades Wickersham became an active Republican, friend of Elihu Root,* and law partner with the brother of William Howard Taft,* who as president-elect nominated Wickersham for attorney general in 1909.

Wickersham quickly became a close Taft adviser and acquired a national reputation by pressing the Sherman Antitrust Law to break monopolies, including Standard Oil,* United States Steel,* and International Harvester. He returned to private practice in 1913, but showed continued commitment to public affairs by accepting numerous appointments to local, state, and national committees and investigative bodies. He fought hard but in vain to get the United States into the League of Nations.* (David A. Booth, "On Crime Commission Reports," *Polity* 2 (1969): 92–99; Paolo E. Coletta, *The Presidency of William Howard Taft* (1973); James C. German, Jr., "The Taft Administration and the Sherman Anti-Trust Act," *Mid-America* 54 (1972): 172–86.)

Wayne A. Wiegand

WILCOX, DELOS FRANKLIN (April 2, 1873–April 4, 1928). Born in Ida, Michigan, Wilcox was educated at the University of Michigan, Ann Arbor, later receiving a Ph.D. at Columbia University. A "public utilities" expert, a term requiring increasingly precise definition during the Progressive Era, Wilcox was more in the mold of the academic, administrative, specialist mode of Woodrow Wilson,* Louis Brandeis,* or Milo Maltbie than of Herbert Croly,* Walter Lippmann,* or Ida Tarbell.* Between 1902 and 1925, Wilcox authored ten books, plus numerous articles, emphasizing reforms in city government, drawing sources from a score of American cities. He also testified before hearings of the U.S. Industrial Commission of 1911–1912 and served as chief of the Bureau of Franchises of the Public Service Commission of the City of New York (First District).

Muncipal Franchises (two volumes, 1910–1911) was his major work, stressing with precision redefinitions of the public interest in respect of urban franchises pertaining to electric, light, heat, and power utilities; to telephone, telegraph, messenger, and signal services; to electrical conduits, water works, sewers, oil pipelines, gas, and street transportation franchises; and the public control and taxation of these utilities. Not opposed to private operation of utilities, he sought legislative and legal safeguards to preclude or end monopolies and indeterminate franchises. He regarded the Minneapolis Gas Settlement Ordinance of 1910 a model, but all his efforts concentrated upon the public's right to control their streets through contractual, legislative, and judicial safeguards in the grant of any franchise. (Milo R. Maltbie, "Taxation of Public Service Corporations," *Proceedings of the National Tax Association Conference* (1908); Harry J. Carmen, *The Street Surface Railway Franchises of New York City* (1919); Delos F. Wilcox, *Municipal Franchises* (1910–1911).)

Clifton K. Yearley and Kerrie L. MacPherson

WILEY, HARVEY W. (October 18, 1844–June 30, 1930). The "Father of the Pure Food Law," Wiley was born in a log cabin in Kent, Indiana. Following service in the Civil War, he received an A.B. from Hanover College in 1867, his M.D. from Indiana Medical College in 1871, and a B.S. from Harvard in 1873. After teaching at Indiana Medical College and at Northwestern Christian University, he served for nine years as professor of chemistry at Purdue University, studying food adulteration. In 1883, Wiley became chief of the Division of Chemistry of the Department of Agriculture in Washington, beginning a long and distinguished career as a pure food reformer.

In 1902, he established what became known as the "poison squad," twelve young men who volunteered to test the effects of chemicals and adulterated foods on themselves. Wiley fought for passage of the Pure Food and Drugs Act,* which became law in 1906. Although the Bureau of Chemistry and Wiley were responsible for enforcement, within three months an appointed Board of Food and Drug Inspection usurped his authority. Wiley discussed the assaults against the law and the bureau in his book, *The History of a Crime against the Food and Drugs Act* (1929). (Harvey W. Wiley, *Harvey W. Wiley: An Autobiography* (1930); Henry Welch and Felix Marti-Ibanez, eds., *The Impact of the Food and Drug Administration on Our Society* (1956); *New York Times* Obituary, July 1, 1930.)

Betsy B. Holli

WILLARD, FRANCES ELIZABETH CAROLINE (September 28, 1939–February 17, 1898). Frances Willard was born in Churchville, New York, grew up in Ohio, and was graduated from North Western Female College, Evanston, Illinois, in 1859. After teaching for several years, she was appointed president of Evanston College for Ladies in 1871. In 1873, she became dean of women and professor of English and art at Northwestern University and vice president of the Association for the Advancement of Women. She was elected corresponding secretary of the National Woman's Christian Temperance Union (WCTU)* in 1874, president of the Illinois state WCTU in 1878, and national WCTU president in 1879, a position she retained for twenty years.

Willard's interest in temperance and prohibition* paralleled her desire to advance the cause of women and to promote reform generally in the immediate pre-Progressive period. Under her leadership the WCTU expanded into a major reform organization. Willard engaged the WCTU in general political activity and party politics in the 1880s and 1890s. She stressed the need to unite the campaigns for Prohibition* and woman suffrage.* (Mary Earhart Dillon, *Frances Willard: From Prayer to Politics* (1944); Willard Memorial Library, National WCTU headquarters, Evanston, Illinois; Ruth Borden, *Woman and Temperance* (1981).)

Norton Mezvinsky

WILSON, WILLIAM BAUCHOP (April 2, 1862–May 25, 1934). Labor leader, congressman, first secretary of labor, Wilson was born in Scotland; he emigrated with his parents in 1870, settling in the Pennsylvania* coalfields. He worked in the mines from 1871 to 1898, then served as secretary-treasurer of the United Mine Workers* from 1900 to 1908. He was elected to three terms as a Democratic congressman from Pennsylvania (1907–1913), but was defeated for reelection in 1912 by a sharp antilabor campaign spearheaded by the National Association of Manufacturers.* As chairman of the House Labor Committee during his final term in Congress, he wrote the bill establishing a cabinet-level Department of Labor.* Appointed first secretary of labor in 1913, he held that office throughout President Woodrow Wilson's* two terms, until 1921. He took a special interest in the mediation of labor disputes during his tenure as labor secretary. (*Biographical Directory of the American Congress*; Roger Babson, *William B. Wilson and the Department of Labor* (1919); John Lombardi, *Labor's Voice in the Cabinet: A History of the Department of Labor from Its Origins to 1921* (1942).)

Edward R. Kantowicz

WILSON, (THOMAS) WOODROW (December 28, 1856–February 3, 1924). Though Wilson's administration did pass major domestic legislation in its first term, Wilson is best remembered as an international leader who transformed World War I* into a crusade to "save the world for democracy." Born Thomas Woodrow Wilson in Staunton, Virginia,* he followed an unconventional road to the White House, pursuing a full career as a professor before entering politics. Educated at Davidson College, Princeton University, and University of Virginia Law School, he earned a Ph.D. at Johns Hopkins University in 1886. After several junior appointments, he became professor of jurisprudence and politics at Princeton in 1890, rising to the presidency of that institution in 1902. When his plans to reorganize the academic and social life of Princeton were stymied, he resigned his presidency in 1910 and rode a wave of progressive reform sentiment to election as governor of New Jersey* that same year.

The Democratic National Convention of 1912 chose Wilson as its candidate for president on the forty-sixth ballot. He was elected, the first Democratic president since 1896, because of a split in Republican ranks. When the Republicans renominated conservative William Howard Taft,* Theodore Roosevelt* bolted the party to run on the third-party Progressive* ticket. Wilson called his program the New Freedom,* an attempt to unleash individual enterprise and restore competition by curbing the power of big business. Accordingly, his administration drastically lowered tariff protection for industry and strengthened the antitrust laws. Wilson had opposed Roosevelt's New Nationalism,* which envisioned a strong regulatory apparatus in the federal government; but once elected he enacted much of Roosevelt's program as well, establishing a Federal Trade Commission,* a Federal Reserve Board,* and a Tariff Commission.*

When World War I broke out in August 1914, Wilson asked his countrymen to remain neutral in thought as well as in deed, and he ran successfully for reelection in 1916 on the slogan "he kept us out of war." The German declaration of unrestricted submarine warfare in January 1917, however, resulted in the sinking of numerous American merchant ships and forced America to declare war on April 7, 1917. Wilson attempted to redeem the slaughter of war by transforming the conflict into an idealistic crusade. He called for a "peace without victory" and, in his Fourteen Points peace plan, outlined a new world order. At the end of the war, he succeeded in making the Fourteen Points the basis for negotiations at the Versailles Peace Conference, and he convinced his allies to establish a League of Nations.* He failed, however, to convince the U.S. Senate to ratify the Versailles treaty, so the U.S. did not join the League. Wilson suffered a crippling stroke while on a speaking tour in favor of ratification in September 1919, and he lay incapacitated for the remainder of his term. (Richard Hofstadter, "The Conservative as Liberal," in *The American Political Tradition* (1948); Arthur S. Link, *Woodrow Wilson and the Progressive Era* (1954); Arthur S. Link, *Woodrow Wilson: Revolution, War, and Peace* (1979); John M. Blum, *Woodrow Wilson and the Politics of Morality* (1956).)

Edward R. Kantowicz

WILSON V. NEW (243 U.S. 332) (Argued January 8-10, 1917; decided March 19, 1917). Their expectations heightened by progressive achievements that advanced labor's interests, the national railway unions pressed the carriers in 1916 to adopt the eight-hour day, "labor's supreme objective," while retaining existing compensation, accompanying their demands with threats of a nationwide strike. When management adamantly refused, President Woodrow Wilson* intervened, asking Congress to impose emergency legislation to avert the impending "tragical national calamity." The resulting Adamson Act,* hurriedly enacted, permanently established the eight-hour day but only provisionally, subject to study, adjusted wage scales. The railway companies rushed test litigation to the Supreme Court, for government price-fixing attacked the heart of constitutional laissez-faire.

Faced with a devastating strike by the militant operating brotherhoods on the eve of American entrance into World War I,* the Supreme Court's five-man majority bent to the progressive interpretation of the commerce power, pragmatically finding a justification in history and public necessity to sustain the pioneering legislation. Writing for the Court, Chief Justice Edward White* found "not disputable" Congress's power to regulate hours and the "expressly limited" fixing of wages essential to prevent imminent "infinite injury to the public interest." Among the dissenters, William R. Day conceded Congress's authority to enact emergency legislation, but condemned the statute as confiscatory in nature. (Thomas Reed Powell, "The Supreme Court and the Adamson Act," *University of Pennsylvania Law Review* 65 (1917): 607–747.)

Stephen B. Wood

WISCONSIN. No state won such fame for progressive achievement as Wisconsin in the period from 1901 to 1914. Wisconsin's reform legislation was not radical, but it was abundant, sometimes innovative, and usually well drawn. The expertise that informed legislation and administration often came from University of Wisconsin* faculty, preeminently John R. Commons.* Important too was Charles McCarthy,* who virtually created the *Legislative Reference Library** to provide legislators information and bill-drafting services.

Much of Wisconsin's fame and success is attributable to the leadership of Robert M. La Follette,* who, heading a fragile coalition within the Republican party,* held the governorship from 1901 to 1906, then went to the U.S. Senate. La Follette appealed strongly to Scandinavians,* farmers in poorer rural counties, and ambitious young politicians. He allied with men of wealth and influence, and benefited also from a municipal reform movement that gained strength and unity during the depression of the 1890s,* especially in Milwaukee.* During La Follette's term as governor, Wisconsin adopted a system of statewide primary elections,* an ad valorem railroad tax measure, and a moderate railroad commission law.

Under James O. Davidson, a mild progressive who overcame La Follette's early opposition and served as governor from 1906 to 1911, the regulatory functions of the railroad commission were extended and insurance came under regulation. When Francis E. McGovern* became governor, in 1911, the pace of reform quickened. McGovern, a Milwaukeean, responded to the growing socialist challenge among urban workers and the reformist spirit of the period 1910–1912. Legislation limited hours for women and children, and provided for factory safety and workmen's compensation;* aid went to farmers through loans, courses, and assistance to cooperatives; the state created an insurance fund and imposed an income tax.* Forest reserves were established, and waterpower use was regulated.

But McGovern and La Follette were uncertain allies, and factional division contributed to the triumph in 1914 of the "stalwart" leader, Emanuel Philipp. Philipp capitalized, too, on voter discontent with high spending and taxing and with a swelling bureaucracy. Under John Blaine, the progressives did regain the governorship in 1920, and La Follette continued in the Senate until his death in 1925, to be succeeded by his son Robert. (David P. Thelen, *The New Citizenship: Origins of Progressivism in Wisconsin, 1885–1900* (1972); Robert S. Maxwell, *La Follette and the Rise of the Progressives in Wisconsin* (1956); Herbert F. Margulies, *The Decline of the Progressive Movement in Wisconsin, 1890–1920* (1968).)

Herbert F. Margulies

WISE, STEPHEN S. (Rabbi) (March 17, 1874–April 19, 1949). Rabbi of the Free Synagogue in New York and spokesman for what could be called a Jewish Social Gospel,* Wise was also a leader of the American Zionist* movement. He was born in Budapest, Hungary, in 1874 and brought to America a year later. Graduated from Columbia University in 1892, Wise began his career as a Reform rabbi, first at B'nai Jeshurun in New York then at Temple Beth Israel in Portland, Oregon. In 1906 he was called to New York's Temple Emanu-El, the leading Reform Jewish synagogue in America; but he differed with the trustees over freedom of speech in the pulpit, so in 1907 he founded the Free Synagogue, which provided a platform for many Jewish and Christian speakers to discuss a wide range of religious, political, and economic issues.

Wise remained the guiding light of the Free Synagogue for over forty years. An ardent advocate of a Jewish homeland in the Mideast, he served as president of the Zionist Organization of America in 1917 and helped organize the American Jewish Congress, an umbrella organization for all of American Jewry, in 1915–1916. A close collaborator of Louis Brandeis,* confidant of Presidents Woodrow Wilson* and Franklin Roosevelt,* Wise remained active both in Zionist affairs and reform politics until his death. (Melvin I. Urofsky, *A Voice That Spoke for Justice: The Life and Times of Stephen S. Wise* (1982); Carl Hermann Voss, *Rabbi and Minister: The Friendship of Stephen S. Wise and John Haynes Holmes* (1964).)

Edward R. Kantowicz

WISTER, OWEN (July 14, 1860–July 21, 1938). Wister, the foremost "cowboy" novelist, was born in Philadelphia; attended schools in New Hampshire, England, and Switzerland; graduated from Harvard with honors in music in 1882; and took two more years of musical training in Paris. Upon his return, he attended Harvard Law School from 1885 to 1888, became a member of the Philadelphia bar, and practiced law for two years. During the 1890s, he made fifteen trips to the West and published a few short stories before his meteoric ascent to fame in 1902 with the publication of *The Virginian: A Horseman of the Plains*—which was dedicated to the nation's number one horseman, Theodore Roosevelt.*

It has been argued that Wister had a keen ear for dialogue and that the book has a dignity and strength that has not been surpassed by its hundreds of imitators.

Perhaps Wister, more than anyone else, made the western cowboy a respectable topic for American fiction. It is also clear that he made the figure of the Anglo-Saxon cowboy (a staple of the dime novel of the late nineteenth century and a gross distortion of reality) a staple of fictional depictions of the West from that time to the present. (John J. Cobbs, *Owen Wister: Chronicler of the West, Gentleman of the East* (1985); Ben Merchant Vorpahl, *My Dear Wister: The Frederic Remington–Owen Wister Letters* (1972).)

Robert W. Schneider

WOMAN'S CHRISTIAN TEMPERANCE UNION. Influenced by the women's crusades against saloons and retail liquor sellers, which had erupted first in Ohio and then had swept through other states during the winter of 1873–1874, 135 women delegates, representing sixteen states, established the Woman's Christian Temperance Union (WCTU) as a national organization in Cleveland, Ohio, on November 18, 1874. By the 1880s the WCTU, which banned men from membership, was the largest organization of women that had ever existed in the United States. WCTU chapters were established in every state and territory, all major cities, and thousands of communities.

Highlighting prohibition,* the WCTU became the nation's leading temperance organization between 1874 and 1900. Creatively led by Frances Willard,* national president from 1879 until her death in 1898, the WCTU also dedicated itself to a host of other reforms and provided women with the means for organized political activity. This broad-based approach and "do-everything" policy resulted in the WCTU's developing into one of the most important reform organizations in American society by the beginning of the Progressive period. Although gradually declining in significance, it remained a major force of reform activity until the 1920s. (Ruth Bordin, *Woman and Temperance* (1981); Joseph R. Gusfield, *Symbolic Crusade: Status Politics and the American Temperance Movement* (1963); Mary Earhart Dillon, *Frances Willard: From Prayer to Politics* (1944).)

Norton Mezvinsky

WOMAN'S PEACE PARTY. The formation of the Woman's Peace party (WPP) in January 1915 signaled the emergence of a new peace movement. Critical of the ineffectual male-dominated peace societies, the women elected Jane Addams* as their president and approved a platform calling for neutral mediation, limitation of armaments, democratic control of foreign policy, removal of the economic causes of war, and extension of the franchise to women. WPP members believed that, as "the mother half of humanity," they had a special stake in opposing war and thus needed a voice in their government. Over forty American women, most of them WPP members, participated in the International Congress of Women at the Hague in April 1915. After the International Congress, delegates visited belligerent and neutral capitals to present peace resolutions and promote a neutral mediation conference.

Although he received the women, Woodrow Wilson* did not endorse their mediation plan. WPP members were also disappointed by his support for military preparedness* and, along with the American Union Against Militarism, waged active antipreparedness campaigns. WPP branches, which had formed in several states and cities, educated citizens on the implications of universal military training in schools and helped to defeat such programs on both state and national levels. Following the February 1917 break in diplomatic relations with Germany, many branches ceased their activities, some disbanded, and the national WPP leaders avoided decisions by deferring matters to the remaining branches. Only the militant New York City branch, led by Crystal Eastman,* continued to challenge government policies after the United States entered the war in April. National WPP leaders focused on plans for an international women's peace conference after the war. The conference, held at Zurich in May 1919, attacked the vindictive Versailles peace proposals, but supported the League of Nations.* The women at Zurich created the Women's International League for Peace and Freedom, of which the WPP became the American branch. (Marie L. Degen, *History of the Woman's Peace Party* (1939); Barbara J. Steinson, *American Women's Activism in World War I* (1982).)

                                                                    Barbara J. Steinson

WOMAN SUFFRAGE. In 1890, the territory of Wyoming, where women had voted since 1869, became the first woman suffrage state; in 1896, Utah also joined the union with women voters. Simultaneously, the rise of the Populist party* brought woman suffrage before male voters in a series of western referenda; as a result women won full suffrage in two more states (Colorado, 1893, and Idaho, 1896). Beginning about 1907, in cities from San Francisco to New York, women wage earners and college graduates joined together to form small, innovative suffrage societies, independent of the National American Woman Suffrage Association (NAWSA).* These new recruits admired the heroism of British "suffragettes," and borrowed their tactics—open-air parades, aggressive publicity, street-corner speaking.

At the same time, the rise of urban progressivism led to a second series of state referenda; by 1912, women had won the vote in Washington, California, Oregon, Arizona, and Kansas. After 1912, these successes at the city and state level began to build toward national victory. Women's votes in the "suffrage states" were a weapon to force established parties, especially the Democrats after Woodrow Wilson's* victory, to support woman suffrage. At the same time, insurgent suffragists started to pressure Anna Howard Shaw,* president of NAWSA since 1904, to yield her office to someone with better political instincts. In 1913, two young American "suffragettes," Alice Paul* and Lucy Burns,* took over NAWSA's Congressional Committee to work for a federal amendment prohibiting the disfranchisement of women. Their use of suffragette tactics and the excitement they generated threatened NAWSA's leadership, and in early 1914 they resigned to form their own organization, the Congressional Union

(CU), later the National Woman's party (NWP).* The CU's tactics, including its campaign to get women voters to vote against Democrats, produced spectacular publicity; meanwhile, the NAWSA, after 1915 headed by Carrie Chapman Catt,* concentrated on state referenda.

The combination of public challenges to Wilson's moral leadership and increasing numbers of congressmen obligated to women voters eventually led to victory. This process, slowed down by southern Democrats' opposition to votes for black women, and accelerated by suffragists' skillful use of popular divisions over U.S. entry into the war, culminated, on August 26, 1920, in the Nineteenth Amendment to the U.S. Constitution. (Eleanor Flexner, *Century of Struggle: The Woman's Rights Movement in the United States* (1959); Carrie Chapman Catt and Nettie Rogers Shuler, *Woman Suffrage and Politics: The Inner Story of the Suffrage Movement* (1932).)

Ellen Du Bois

WOMEN'S PROTECTIVE LEGISLATION. Progressive reformers were appalled at the working conditions of women and turned to state legislatures to stop the abuses of employers. By 1917, thirty-nine states and the District of Columbia had enacted women's hour laws, and more than a dozen states had passed minimum wage laws. Yet, in 1905, the U.S. Supreme Court declared a New York law which limited bakers' hours unconstitutional (*Lochner v. New York,* 1905). This defeat led to a new tactic: to limit protective legislation to women with the underlying assumption that it is better to have legislation helping some workers than no legislation at all. Louis Brandeis* was hired to defend an Oregon law limiting hours for women. In his now famous "brief," Brandeis argued that women workers were different than men in physical strength and that overwork would harm women's health. Because women bore children, the "health and vigor of the race" was at stake, so women must be protected.

The Supreme Court accepted Brandeis's rationale and upheld the state law in *Muller v. Oregon* (1908). In stereotyping the different roles of men and women, Brandeis and fellow reformers inadvertently opened the door for discriminating against female workers. After 1920, increasing wealth and technological improvements substantively improved working conditions and thereby reduced the need for protection, yet the protective legislation continued to restrict job opportunities for women. Since an Equal Rights Amendment would strike down gender-specific protective legislation, these reformers opposed it from the 1920s through the 1960s. (Judith A. Baer, *The Chains of Protection: The Judicial Response to Women's Labor Legislation* (1978).)

D'Ann Campbell

WOOD, LEONARD (October 9, 1860–August 7, 1927). Leonard Wood was born and reared in small-town New England, graduated from Harvard Medical School in 1883, and entered the Army Medical Corps in 1885. After serving two years on the frontier and at several small posts, he received an appointment, in 1895, as assistant surgeon to the president of the United States. In Washington, he made many important connections and became close friends with assistant secretary of navy Theodore Roosevelt,* leading to his appointment as commander of the First Volunteer Regiment (the Rough Riders) during the Spanish-American War.* At the close of the fighting, he was appointed governor of Santiago Province and, in 1900, military governor of Cuba. It was in this latter position that Wood began carrying out reforms that one historian calls a "workshop" for progressivism.

What Cuba needed above all else, Wood wrote Roosevelt in 1899, was a "decent, candid, courageous government, good courts, good schools, and all the public works we can pay for, and a businesslike way of doing things." Wood was convinced that the use of intelligent, rational methods would make social and political institutions more efficient and more responsive to social needs, and to Wood, rational institutions meant American ones. With this attitude, he proceeded to replace the Spanish judicial system with an Anglo-American jury system, create a school system based on Ohio's, and a municipal government based on American systems. Wood's methods were authoritarian, and his attitude toward the Cubans was paternalistic and insensitive; he left the Cubans with the form but without the substance of reform. (Jack C. Lane, *Armed Progressive: Leonard Wood* (1974); Howard Gillette, Jr., "The Military Occupation of Cuba, 1899–1902: Workshop for American Progressivism," *American Quarterly* 25 (October 1973): 410–25.)

Jack C. Lane

WOODRUFF, CLINTON ROGERS (December 17, 1868–January 24, 1948). Municipal reformer in Philadelphia,* longtime secretary of the National Municipal League,* Woodruff was born in Philadelphia. He earned a law degree from the University of Pennsylvania Law School, served two terms in the state legislature, and held a variety of appointive positions in city government. When the National Municipal League was organized in 1894, to fashion a model program for the reform of city government, Woodruff became the organization's general secretary, serving until 1920. In 1912 he became editor of the league's journal, the *National Municipal Review*, and also edited or authored many studies of city government. He served as civil service commissioner of Philadelphia from 1920 to 1924. (*New York Times* obituary, January 25, 1948; Frank M. Stewart, *A Half Century of Municipal Reform: The History of the National Municipal League* (1950); Kenneth Fox, *Better City Government* (1977).)

Edward R. Kantowicz

WOODS, ROBERT ARCHEY (December 9, 1865–February 18, 1925). A settlement house leader, Woods was born into a Scotch-Irish Presbyterian family in Pittsburgh. The Calvinist strain accompanied him to Amherst College and Andover Theological Seminary, where it was transmuted into a need to discern the flow of God's intention for humanity and to change human relationships to conform to it. Sent to study Toynbee Hall in 1890, William Jewett Tucker installed Woods as head resident of Boston's first settlement, soon known as South End House. Woods's ideas on training for citizenship in the Irish and Jewish neighborhoods of the South End led to group-based manipulation of ward bosses and officials for community facilities, such as public baths, playgrounds,* gymnasia, a branch library, and improved educational access. Residents on scholarship from Andover, Amherst, Dartmouth, Harvard, and Radcliffe conducted significant published studies of the area and established an early child guidance clinic.

The strategic sense of the needs of the moment carried over into his role in founding the National Federation of Settlements* and presidency of the National Conference of Social Work. In his last decade, Woods supported the Progressive party,* prohibition,* the war effort, immigration restriction,* and vocational education.* His support of craft unionism was lifelong, although he condemned the syndicalist role in the Lawrence strike.* He coauthored two major works on settlements, and his addresses were published as *The Neighborhood in Nation-Building*. (Eleanor H. Woods, *Robert A. Woods, Champion of Democracy* (1929); "Walter Trattner, ed., *Biographical Dictionary of Social Welfare in America* (1986); Edward S. Shapiro, "Robert A. Woods and the Settlement Impulse," *Social Service Review* 52 (June 1978): 215–26.)

Jacqueline K. Parker

WORKMEN'S COMPENSATION. In the late nineteenth century, industrially advanced European nations, led by Germany, had passed various forms of compensation legislation providing for automatic payments to workers and their families for injury or death sustained in the course of their employment. The idea caught on slowly in the United States largely because certain common-law defenses—the fellow servant rule and the doctrines of the assumption of risk and contributory negligence—had been incorporated into state laws that required workers to seek recourse only through the courts. At first, those wishing to reform the system concentrated on agitating for so-called employers' liability laws* designed to liberalize the application of these doctrines and make it easier for injured employees to win suits for damage in the courts. By 1907, this effort had resulted in some changes in twenty-six states.

However, studies showing large numbers of workers injured or killed in industrial employment each year with little recompense to them or their families impelled social and middle-class progressives, in particular, to push for the automatic payment, no-fault system. Beginning about 1907, the campaign was spearheaded by the American Association for Labor Legislation* and the National Civic Federation.* Even certain large corporations adopted modest voluntary plans for their workers, while most spokesmen for organized labor continued (at least through 1910) to work for modifications in the old liability system. In order to meet the objections of conservative courts, some states adopted an elective system, or, as in the case of New York in its first law in 1910, mixed an elective system with automatic compensation in certain hazardous trades.

The movement was dealt a temporary setback when, in 1911, the New York measure was declared unconstitutional by the State Court of Appeals on the grounds that it violated not only a provision of the state constitution but also the Fourteenth Amendment. Gradually, state courts assumed a more liberal attitude and, in 1917, the U.S. Supreme Court upheld the constitutionality of the compulsory version of compensation. By 1920, all but six states in the nation had workmen's compensation laws, but these varied widely in terms of funding, coverage, and benefits. (Robert Asher, "Workmen's Compensation in the United States, 1880–1935" (Ph.D. diss. University of Minnesota, 1971); Robert F. Wesser, "Conflict and Compromise: The Workmen's Compensation Movement in New York, 1890s–1913," *Labor History* 12 (1971): 345–72; Carl Hookstadt, *Comparison of Workmen's Compensation Laws of the United States and Canada up to January 1, 1920* (1920).)

Robert F. Wesser

WORLD WAR I. The effect of America's participation in World War I on the Progressive movement has been hotly debated by historians. The first inclination was to see the war as diverting the nation's attention and energy away from domestic reform toward the processes of war mobilization. The war effort, moreover, was seen as generating undemocratic attitudes which led to the restriction of fundamental rights and freedoms. These historians based their arguments on the early criticism of such leftist intellectuals as Randolph Bourne,* on the war and postwar illiberalism of the progressive Woodrow Wilson* administration, on the Republican effort to return the nation to "normalcy," and on the rise in the 1920s of racist and illiberal movements as immigration restriction,* prohibition,* fundamentalism,* and the Ku Klux Klan.

A more recent interpretation, however, depicts Wilson's call for a "war to make the world safe for democracy" as a logical extension of the crusading themes of the moralist-reformist branch of the Progressive movement, one that believed that government was a proper instrument for shaping moral social behavior and that was successful in the passage of the Pure Food and Drugs Act,* the child labor* acts, and the Mann Act.* As Arthur S. Link has argued, moreover, this brand of progressivism lived on into the twenties as shown by the popularity of the progressive effort in the election of 1924.

Other historians have come to see the war as a kind of workshop for the corporatist-management branch of the Progressive movement, which, by 1917, they argue, had become the predominant thrust of progressivism. These progressives believed that the greatest reform goal was economic prosperity and the greatest moral achievement would be to establish equality of opportunity through the efficient, scientific organization of society. Such efforts, they maintained, required cooperation between government and business, new government agencies to direct that cooperation, and professional experts to guide society toward this cooperative ideal. In the government's success during the war in rationalizing American industry, in creating harmonious labor-management relations, and in its effective use of businessmen and professional experts, the national governmental system of war management was a logical outcome of progressive principles. (Arthur S. Link, "What Happened to the Progressive Movement in the 1920s?" *American Historical Review* 64 (July 1959): 833–51; Hawley Ellis, *The Great War and the Search for a Modern Order* (1979); Barry D. Karl, *The Uneasy State: The United States from 1915–1945* (1983); Carl Resek, ed., *War and the Intellectuals* (1964).)

Jack C. Lane

WORLD'S WORK, THE. This magazine was published monthly by Doubleday, Page & Company and its successor from November 1900 to July 1932. Its founding editor was Walter Hines Page* who, in 1913, became U.S. ambassador to Great Britain. The *World's Work* encompassed a wide scope of topics, most often presenting articles on technological progress, social reform, industrial relations, and international and domestic politics. Handsomely illustrated, it featured after 1907 a "portrait gallery" which complemented its editorial section, "The March of Events," a forerunner in style to the modern newsmagazine. Often running personality sketches of prominent figures in business and finance, it reflected a widely held optimism that the rise of an increasingly successful and altruistic class of entrepreneurs would be the key to improvement of the general welfare. Politically, the *World's Work* spurned both the agrarian radicalism of William Jennings Bryan* and Old Guard conservatism to align with the mainstream of progressivism, in turn supporting Theodore Roosevelt,* William Howard Taft,* and particularly Woodrow Wilson.* Its circulation in its prime years hovered around 100,000, with a peak of 140,000 during World War I.* (John Milton Cooper, Jr., *Walter Hines Page: The Southerner as American, 1855–1918* (1977); Frank Luther Mott, *A History of American Magazines: 1885–1905* (1957); Burton J. Hendrick, *The Life and Letters of Walter Hines Page* (1922–1925).)

Lloyd J. Graybar

WRIGHT, CARROLL DAVIDSON (July 25, 1840–February 20, 1909). First chief of the U.S. Bureau of Labor Statistics, a pioneer in the use of social statistics as tools for reform, Wright was born in Dunbarton, New Hampshire;* he was educated in public schools, read law, volunteered for Civil War duty, then passed the bar and settled in Reading, Massachusetts.* He served two terms in the state senate and then was appointed chief of the Massachusetts Bureau of Statistics of Labor, serving from 1873 to 1888. Massachusetts had been the first state to establish an official body to gather labor statistics, and Wright urged other states to follow suit, organizing a convention of state labor statisticians in 1883.

He was appointed first commissioner of the U.S. Bureau of Labor when that agency was created in 1885. The annual reports of the bureau were a gold mine of facts for contemporary reformers and a rich resource for later historians. Wright was appointed in 1893 to complete work on the 1890 census reports, which had been lagging. He also chaired the commission investigating the Pullman Strike* in 1894 and served on the commission of inquiry into the Anthracite Coal Strike* of 1902. He resigned his post as commissioner of labor statistics in 1905 due to ill health. Progressive reformers have often been described as a "factual generation," who believed that the gathering and dissemination of social data would lead to reform. (Horace A. Wadlin, *Carroll Davidson Wright: A Memorial* (1911); James Leiby, *Carroll Wright and Labor Reform* (1960).)

Edward R. Kantowicz

WRIGHT, FRANK LLOYD (June 8, 1869–April 9, 1959). Acclaimed as the greatest American architect to date and among the most influential in history, Frank Lloyd Wright was a figure whose genius still exerts its influence on his profession today. Born in Richland Center, Wisconsin,* he conceived and forcefully promoted an "organic" architecture imbued with the "spririt of man" and having within it the power to reshape civilization. After a short stint in the engineering school at the University of Wisconsin* at Madison, he served an inspiring apprenticeship with architects Louis H. Sullivan* and Dankmar Adler of Chicago from 1888 to 1893. With Sullivan, he shared a nineteenth-century Romantic faith in democracy and the ability of architecture to express it, but Wright also saw his profession as capable of producing necessary social reform.

Working and living in the progressive consciousness of Chicago* at the turn of the century, he developed a concept of architecture and planning that glorified the independence of the American spirit and necessitated the decentralization of American cities. His "Prairie" houses, designed low to profile the midwestern landscape and constructed of "natural" native materials, were the basis for the international reputation that he achieved; his flamboyant personality and scandalous lifestyle resulting from a series of marriages and personal tragedies, as well as his brilliant work, ensured his celebrity status for life. Among his best-known works are the Robie House (1908) in Chicago; Taliesin (1911–1925) and Taliesin West (1938–1954), his home and studio complexes in Wisconsin and Arizona; "Fallingwater" (1936), the Edgar Kaufmann house, built over a creek in Bear Run, Pennsylvania; and the Solomon R. Gugenheim Museum (1957) in New York. (Henry-Russell Hitchcock, *In the Nature of Materials: The Architecture of Frank Lloyd Wright* (1973); Robert L. Sweeney, *Frank Lloyd Wright: An Annotated Bibliography* (1978); Frank Lloyd Wright, *The Natural House* (1954).)

Diane Filipowicz

WRIGHT BROTHERS. Wilbur (April 6, 1867–May 30, 1912) and Orville (August 19, 1871–January 30, 1948), the sons of Bishop Milton Wright of the United Brethren Church, early became interested in the dynamics of flight. While designing and manufacturing bicycles in their small shop in Dayton, they avidly read all available literature on the topic and corresponded with such leading authorities as Octave Chanute. At the turn of the century, the Wright brothers began experimenting with gliders, eventually becoming expert pilots. These efforts, together with aerodynamic tests in a self-designed and constructed wind tunnel, led to the development of efficient wing shapes and the first practical control system. Skilled mechanics, they next built a twelve-horsepower gasoline engine and designed a propeller.

Their labors were rewarded at Kill Devil Hills (near Kitty Hawk), North Carolina, on December 17, 1903, when Orville made the first controlled mechanical flight, covering 120 feet in twelve seconds. The Wrights avoided publicity for several years as they worked to perfect their new invention. In 1908–1909, they demonstrated the airplane in the United States and Europe, winning worldwide acclaim. Wilbur died of typhoid fever in the midst of a bitter patent fight that eventually was resolved in favor of the Wrights. (Marvin W. Mc-Farland, *The Papers of Wilbur and Orville Wright* (1953); Fred C. Kelly, *The Wright Brothers* (1943); Richard P. Hallion, ed., *The Wright Brothers: Heirs of Promethus* (1978).)

William M. Leary

Y

YELLOW-DOG CONTRACT. Nothing illustrates better the Progressive Era dilemma concerning the definition of "freedom" than the yellow-dog contract in which workers pledged themselves not to join unions. The first significant challenge to the yellow-dog contract was made in Section 10 of the Erdman Act (1898), which forbade the yellow dog because it deprived an employee of his ability to negotiate freely with an employer. In *Adair v. U.S.* (1908), the Supreme Court declared Section 10 of the Erdman Act unconstitutional because it violated the freedom of contract for the employer. Justices Joseph McKenna and Oliver Wendell Holmes* dissented. In *Coppage v. Kansas* (1915), the court again upheld the yellow-dog contract. Justices Holmes and William R. Day dissented. In *Hitchman Coal & Coke Co. v. U.S.* (1917), the Court upheld the yellow-dog contract by forbidding the United Mine Workers* to organize a contracted company. Justices Holmes and Louis D. Brandeis* dissented, declaring that yellow-dog contracts violated the Fourteenth Amendment. In these cases, the Supreme Court handed down decisions which offended progressive definitions of free negotiations. The yellow-dog contract was finally forbidden by the National Labor Relations Act (1935). (Bruno Ramirez, *When Workers Fight: The Politics of Industrial Relations in the Progressive Era, 1898–1916* (1978); Philip S. Foner, *History of the Labor Movement, in the United States, vol. 5: The AFL in the Progressive Era, 1910–1915* (1980); Supreme Court *Reporter* (1854–1985).)

Frank Grubbs

YERKES, CHARLES TYSON (June 25, 1837–December 29, 1905). Street railway tycoon in Philadelphia,* Chicago,* and London, Yerkes was born in Philadelphia to Quaker parents, left school at age seventeen, clerked in a brokerge house, then opened his own investment banking firm in 1862. A financial crisis in 1871 destroyed his finances and resulted in a brief imprisonment. Though he later recouped his fortune, he had lost his social position in Philadelphia so he moved to Chicago in 1882.

He began buying up street railray companies and planned to unify all the streetcar lines in Chicago into one grand system. By 1896 he controlled all the lines on the north and west sides of the city, and he lobbied the state legislature and the city council to extend the franchise rights of his companies for fifty years. He was defeated by vigorous opposition from Chicago Mayor Carter Harrison II* and civic reformers who resented his use of bribery and his authoritarian business practices. He left Chicago in 1899, settling in London as head of a syndicate financing that city's underground railways. His name became a synonym for robber baron, and writer Theodore Dreiser* modeled the central character of his novels *The Titan* and *The Financier* after him. (Sidney I. Robertys, "Portrait of a Robber Baron," *Business History Review* 35 (1961): 344–71; Robert D. Weber, "Rationalizers and Reformers: Chicago Local Transportation in the Nineteenth Century" (Ph.D. diss., University of Wisconsin, 1971); John A. Fairlie, "The Street Railway Question in Chicago," *Quarterly Journal of Economics* 21 (1907): 371–404.)

Edward R. Kantowicz

YOUNG MEN'S CHRISTIAN ASSOCIATION (YMCA). Founded 1844, in London, England, YMCAs first appeared in North America in the 1850s. Originally highly evangelistic, they limited voting membership to evangelical Protestants until 1933. By 1900, though, evangelism was only one of many character-building activities; city YMCAs in large buildings provided fee-paying men (mainly white-collar workers) and boys with gymnastics, swimming, sports, clubs, Bible study, and self-improvement classes. Separate YMCAs served college students, railroad workers, and blacks. Local associations, state committees, and an International Committee (United States and Canada) were dominated by paid secretaries who raised funds for widely varied projects; YMCA building drives pioneered the high-speed fund-raising campaign. Membership boomed: 238,000 men and 31,000 boys in 1900; 669,000 men and 200,000 boys by 1920. Rapid turnover and makeshift training prevented the secretaryship from becoming a full-fledged profession, however.

By the 1910s, Social Gospel* ideas flourished in student YMCAs, some International Committee staff were moderately liberal, moralism displaced heaven versus hell in YMCA evangelism, and YMCA secretaries cautiously promoted reformist causes such as playgrounds* and prohibition.* But most local associations and YMCA laymen remained conservative. YMCA "foreign work" planted dozens of American-style YMCAs in China and India. During World War I,* the International Committee provided relief for European prisoners of war, ran canteens for U.S. soldiers, and founded YMCAs in Eastern Europe after the war. Under John R. Mott, the International Committee's general secretary from 1915 to 1928, the national leadership became fervently internationalist and increasingly supported social and religious liberalism. (C. Howard Hopkins, *History of the Y.M.C.A. in North America* (1951); David I. Macleod, *Building Character in the American Boy: The Boy Scouts, YMCA, and Their Forerunners, 1870–1920* (1983); Owen E. Pence, *The Y.M.C.A. and Social Need: A Study of Institutional Adaptation* (1946).)

David I. Macleod

Z

ZIONISM. Zionism was the movement to reestablish a Jewish homeland in the Middle East. Jews had been expelled from their homeland of Israel by the Romans in A.D. 70. Though scattered in the diaspora for nearly 2,000 years, they kept alive the hope of an aliya, or return, to Israel. Until the late nineteenth century, however, this remained merely a messianic dream. After the Russian pogroms of 1881, Jews in Eastern Europe, under the leadership of Theodor Herzl, launched the Zionist movement to save Jews from Russian persecution. A small band of Jewish settlers migrated to the territory of Palestine in the Ottoman Empire, supported by financial aid from Zionists. The movement grew, and Herzl convened the First International Zionist Congress in 1897 at Basle, Switzerland.

Zionism received a lukewarm response, at first, from Jewish-Americans.* German Jews in America, like those in Germany, were prosperous and assimilated and showed little interest in Israel. The newly arrived immigrant Jews from Russia had already uprooted themselves for the arduous journey to America, and many considered the New World their promised land, their Zion. Though a loose Federation of American Zionists was organized in New York in 1898, other movements, particularly socialism* and labor unionism,* overshadowed it.

After 1914, the movement gathered momentum, due to the efforts of Louis Brandeis,* a leading lawyer and political adviser to President Woodrow Wilson.* Brandeis emphasized the democratic and humanitarian aspects of Zionism and showed American Jews how it could be reconciled with loyalty to their new country. Brandeis appealed to moderate Zionists who had no intention of migrating to Israel themselves but who supported the cause as a means of fulfilling their religious aspirations and spreading democracy as well. Brandeis, Stephen S. Wise,* and others reorganized the American movement in 1917 as the Zionist Organization of America. That same year the international movement scored a great coup when it persuaded the British government to issue the Balfour Declaration, favoring the "establishment in Palestine of a national home for the Jewish people." (Melvin I. Urofsky, "Zionism: An American Experience," *American Jewish Historical Quarterly* (1974); Melvin I. Urofsky, *A Mind of One Piece: Brandeis and American Reform* (1971); Melvin I. Urofsky, *A Voice That Spoke for Justice: The Life and Times of Stephen S. Wise* (1982); Irving Howe, *World of Our Fathers* (1976).)

Edward R. Kantowicz

ZUEBLIN, CHARLES (May 4, 1866–September 14, 1924). Sociologist, social settlement* resident, writer and lecturer on municipal reform, Zueblin was born in Pendleton, Indiana,* of Swiss stock; he was educated at public schools and at the University of Pennsylvania, graduated from Northwestern University in 1887, then pursued graduate study at Yale and at Leipzing in Germany. Settling in Chicago,* he lived at Hull House* for a time, then in 1891 he founded the Northwestern University Settlement in a Polish* and German* neighborhood on the northwest side of the city.

Appointed an instructor in sociology at the University of Chicago* in 1892, he became a professor in 1902 and lectured extensively on civic reform for the university extension department. University president Harry Pratt Judson demanded Zueblin's resignation in 1908 after he publicly denounced Chicago businessmen. Thereafter, he earned his living as a writer and lecturer. Always an outspoken and forceful advocate of political and economic reform, Zueblin was a virtual one-man Chautauqua,* dedicated to public education in the broadest and most practical sense. (*New York Times* obituary, September 16, 1924; *National Cyclopedia of American Biography* (1910); Steven J. Diner, *A City and Its Universities: Public Policy in Chicago, 1892–1917* (1980).)

Edward R. Kantowicz

Chronology of the Progressive Era

1890

Sherman Antitrust Act passed

Wounded Knee Massacre perpetrated in South Dakota

General Federation of Women's Clubs organized in New York City

William Dean Howells published *A Hazard of New Fortunes*

National American Woman Suffrage Association founded

Wyoming became the first state to grant women to right to vote in its constitution

Hazen Pingree became mayor of Detroit

Mississippi disfranchised blacks

1891

University of Chicago founded

Review of Reviews founded

Hamlin Garland published *Main-Travelled Roads*

Northwestern University Settlement established

Washington Gladden authored *Who Wrote the Bible?*

1892

Mississippi adopted direct primary

Homestead Steel Strike crushed

People's party (Populists) formed

John Peter Altgeld became governor of Illinois

Richard T. Ely headed School of Economics, Political Sciences and History at the University of Wisconsin

1893

National Education Association founded

Anti-Saloon League established in Ohio

Governor Altgeld pardoned three remaining convicted Haymarket conspirators

Fredrick Jackson Turner presented "The Significance of the Frontier in American History"

Sherman Silver Purchase Act repealed

Samuel McClure established *McClure's Magazine*

Stephen Crane authored *Maggie: A Girl of the Streets*

Stock market panic initiated depression

Henry Street Settlement founded by Lillian Wald

Eugene V. Debs established American Railway Union

1894

William T. Stead wrote *If Christ Came to Chicago*

Coxey's Army marched on Washington

Pullman Strike crushed

Henry Demarest Lloyd published *Wealth against Commonwealth*

Wilson-Gorman Tariff Act (including first graduated income tax law) passed

Graham Taylor opened Chicago Commons Settlement House and published the *Commons*

1895

Stephen Crane published *Red Badge of Courage*

Income tax provision of Wilson-Gorman voided by Supreme Court in *Pollock v. Farmer's Loan and Trust*

Booker T. Washington gave "Atlanta Compromise" address

U.S. v. E. C. Knight decided by Supreme Court

Utah wrote woman suffrage into its constitution

National Association of Manufacturers established

American Historical Review founded by American Historical Association

Daniel De Leon founded Socialist Trade and Labor Alliance

Sophonisba Breckenridge of Kentucky became first woman admitted to bar

1896

Plessy v. Ferguson proclaimed "separate but equal" doctrine

Rural Free Delivery established by U.S. Post Office

William McKinley defeated William Jennings Bryan for the presidency

First moving picture shown in public in New York City

Municipal Voters League of Chicago established

Alfred Stieglitz founded Camera Club of New York

1897

William Allen White wrote "What's the Matter with Kansas?," attacking Populists

Samuel "Golden Rule" Jones elected mayor of Toledo, Ohio

Eugene V. Debs and Victor L. Berger led the formation of the Social Democracy of America

James Duval Phelan elected reform mayor of San Francisco

Citizens Union established in New York City

1898

Greater New York City established

Louisiana ratified constitution including "grandfather clause" to disfranchise blacks

New York State Tenement House Committee established

Hawaii annexed to United States

Anti-Imperialist League established

Race riots rocked Wilmington, North Carolina

Spanish-American War fought

1899

National Consumers' League founded

John Dewey published *The School and Society*

Thorstein Veblen published *Theory of the Leisure Class*

Everybody's Magazine founded

First American juvenile court established in Chicago

Open door policy initiated by Secretary of State John Hay

1900

Benjamin C. Marsh organized the first National Conference on City Planning

Galveston, Texas, adopted commission plan of city government

Theodore Dreiser published *Sister Carrie*

Thirty-first state adopted compulsory school attendance law

International Ladies' Garment Workers Union formed

Robert M. La Follette elected governor of Wisconsin

National Civic Federation founded

National Negro Business League created in Boston

World's Work founded by Walter Hines Page

1901

Ford Motor Company organized

Florida enacted first presidential primary law

Mark Fagan became the youngest mayor in the history of Jersey City

U.S. Steel Corporation formed

Platt Amendment established Cuba as a quasi-protectorate of the United States.

President McKinley shot at Pan-American Exposition and Theodore Roosevelt became president

Tom L. Johnson, single tax advocate, elected mayor of Cleveland

Northern Securities Company created

Andrew Carnegie donated $5.2 million for the first public library system

Frank Norris published *The Octopus*

Seth Low elected mayor of New York City

Legislative Reference Library founded in Madison, Wisconsin

Gustavus Myers wrote *History of Tammany Hall*

American Medical Association reorganized

New York State Tenement House Law enacted

Socialist party founded by Morris Hillquit

Benjamin Barr Lindsey, the "Kid's Judge," established second juvenile court in Denver

Maude Wood Park, with Inez Gillmore, formed Massachusetts College Equal Suffrage League

Ida Tarbell had *The History of the Standard Oil Company* serialized in *McClure's Magazine*

Edward A. Ross wrote *Social Control*

1902

Anthracite Coal Strike settled

Oregon adopted initiative and referendum

Lincoln Steffens' "Tweed Days in St. Louis" published in *McClure's Magazine*

Oliver Wendell Holmes appointed to Supreme Court

Mississippi adopted direct primary

Maryland adopted first workmen's compensation law

Albert B. Cummins became governor of Iowa

National Farmers' Union established in Texas

John D. Rockefeller established the General Education Board

1903

James K. Vardaman elected governor of Mississippi

Elkins Act passed

Department of Commerce and Labor established

Wisconsin adopted direct primary

The Great Train Robbery, first narrative film, exhibited

Jack London published *Call of the Wild*

First heavier-than-air machine flown by Orville Wright at Kitty Hawk, North Carolina

Oregon passed ten-hour law for women in industry

The Souls of Black Folk by W. E. B. Du Bois published

Los Angeles became the first city to adopt initiative, referendum, and recall

National Women's Trade Union League founded

Rose Schneiderman formed first women's local of Jewish Socialist United Cloth Hat and Cap Maker's Union

Charles R. Van Hise became president of the University of Wisconsin

Lester Frank Ward published *Pure Sociology*

1904

Work began on Panama Canal

Supreme Court ruled that Northern Securities Company violated Sherman Antitrust Act

Roosevelt Corollary to the Monroe Doctrine proclaimed

Lincoln Steffens published *The Shame of the Cities*

Joseph W. Folk, prosecutor of the "boodlers" of Saint Louis, elected governor of Missouri

Frank Lloyd Wright designed Unity Temple, Chicago

Harvey W. Wiley revealed "poison squad" experiments

Frank J. Goodnow became president of the American Political Service Association

Chautauqua traveling curcuit begun

Alexander J. McKelway named secretary for the southern states of the National Child Labor Committee

1905

Charlotte Perkins Gilman wrote *Women and Economics*

Industrial Workers of the World founded by Eugene V. Debs and William Haywood

Armstrong Insurance Investigating Committee began hearings in Albany, New York

Swift and Co. v. U.S. decided

Thomas Dixon wrote *The Clansman*

W. E. B. Du Bois established the Niagara Movement

Edward F. Dunne elected mayor of Chicago as advocate of municipal ownership of traction system

Forest Service established under the Department of Agriculture

Edward Steichen and Alfred Stieglitz founded "291"

Supreme Court decision in *Lochner v. New York* handed down

Brand Whitlock elected mayor of Todedo, Ohio

Upton Sinclair wrote *The Jungle*

Roosevelt received Nobel Peace Prize for negotiating Treaty of Portsmouth that ended Russo-Japanese War

Robert La Follettte elected U.S. senator from Wisconsin

McClure's Magazine published George Kibbe Turner's article "Galveston: A Business Corporation"

Mayor Eugene Schmitz and "Abe" Ruel, political bosses of San Francisco, indicted for extortion

1906

Jonathan Bourne from Oregon is first senator elected by popular vote

Theodore Roosevelt coined the term "muckraker"

Coe Crawford elected governor of South Dakota

Winston Churchill published *Coniston*

National Education Association chartered by Congress

Playground Association of America founded

Rev. John A. Ryan's *The Living Wage* published

John Spargo authored *The Bitter City of the Children*

Ida Tarbell took control of *American Magazine*

Walter Fisher named president of Chicago Municipal Voters League

John F. Fitzgerald elected mayor of Boston

American Association for Labor Legislation established

American Sociological Association founded

Congress passed Hepburn Railway Rate Regulation Act

Cosmopolitan serialized David Graham Phillips's "The Treason of the Senate"

Charles Evans Hughes elected governor of New York

Thomas W. Lawson published *Frenzied Finance*

1907

George L. Sheldon elected governor of Nebraska

Hoke Smith elected governor of Georgia

Lincoln-Roosevelt Republican League founded in California

Chicago Settlement Ordinances for traction regulation adopted

Japanese laborers excluded from continental United States by presidential order

Oklahoma adopted state constitution including prohibition

Robey House, Chicago, one of Frank Lloyd Wright's Prairie houses, built

Ray Stannard Baker's "Following the Color Line" appeared in the *American Magazine*

First Bank Depositors Guaranty Law passed in Oklahoma

Harriot Stanton Blatch formed Equality League of Self-Supporting Women

Henry Bruere organized Bureau of Municipal Research

Ty Cobb led American League in batting

Clarence Darrow defended Bill Haywood against charges of murder in the assassination of the governor of Idaho

Thomas Gore, "the blind orator," elected first senator from Oklahoma

National Tax Association founded

Panic of 1907 triggers depression

New York and Wisconsin established public service commissions

Walter Rauschenbusch published *Christianity and the Social Crisis*

J. Allen Smith authored *The Spirit of American Government*

Burton J. Hendrick published "The Story of Life Insurance"

William Graham Summer published *Folkways*

Gustavus Myers wrote *History of Great American Fortunes*

1908

"Ash Can School" of modern realist painters formed in New York City

Leowe v. Lawlor (Danbury Hatters Case) decided

Henry Ford introduced first Model T automobile

Winston Churchill published *Mr. Crewe's Career*

Oregon adopted recall principle for all elected officials

Muller v. Oregon upheld ten-hour day for women

Gary School Plan established

White House Conservation Conference held

Adair v. U.S. upheld yellow-dog contracts

Commission on Country Life established by Theodore Roosevelt

Andrew Furuseth became president of International Seamen's Union

"Jack" Johnson became first black heavyweight champion

Keller v. U.S. decision rendered

National Monetary Commission created by the Aldrich-Vreeland Act

William Howard Taft elected president of the United States

National Board of Censorship of Motion Pictures formed

National Conservation Commission appointed by Theodore Roosevelt, chaired by Gifford Pinchot

1909

Robert Henri organized and John Sloan participated in art exhibit "The Eight" in New York City

Payne-Aldrich Tariff passed

Congress proposed Sixteenth Amendment for federal income tax

Ballinger-Pinchot controversy divided Republicans

Herbert Croly authored *The Promise of American Life*

La Follette's Magazine published

Julian Mack initiated the first White House Conference on Children

Richard Childs founded the National Short Ballot Organization with Woodrow Wilson as president

Pittsburgh Survey published

National Association for the Advancement of Colored People founded in New York City

National Board of Review of Motion Pictures established

National Conference on City Planning founded

1910

Postal savings banks established

Victor L. Berger elected to Congress

John Kingsbury organized Conference of Mayors of New York State

Andrew Carnegie established Carnegie Endowment for International Peace

The Fundamentals: A Testimony to the Truth published

Boy Scouts of America chartered

Hiram Johnson elected governor of California

Woodrow Wilson elected governor of New Jersey

U.S. House of Representatives curtailed the power of Speaker Joseph G. Cannon

Edith Abbott published *Women in Industry*

Black Americans disfranchised in all southern states

Documentary History of American Industrial Society published by John R. Commons

The *Crisis*, published monthly by W. E. B. Du Bois, appeared

Rhetta Childe Dorr's *What Eight Million Want* was published

Democrats gained control of both U.S. House and Senate

Francis E. McGovern elected governor of Wisconsin

Mann Act passed

Mann-Elkins Act passed

Emil Seidel elected first Socialist mayor of Milwaukee

Delos Franklin Wilcox authored *Municipal Franchises*

Lawrence Veiller elected director of the National Housing Association

1911

President Taft vetoed Arizona constitution containing recall provision

Supreme Court ordered Standard Oil and American Tobacco trusts dissolved

Illinois passed first state law providing public assistance for mothers with dependent
    children

Wisconsin established first Industrial Commission

Franz Boas published *The Primitive Mind*

National Association opposed to Woman Suffrage established in New York City

Max Eastman became editor of the *Masses*

National Progressive Republican League created by Robert La Follette and Congressional
    Insurgents

New York State Factory Investigating Committee probed Triangle Shirtwaist factory fire

Seattle initiated nonpartisan city elections

Frederick W. Taylor authored *Principles of Scientific Management*

1912

Arthur Capper became governor of Kansas

New Mexico admitted as forty-seventh state

Arizona admitted as forty-eighth state after removing recall provision from its constitution

Parcel Post system authorized

Titanic sunk

Woodrow Wilson elected president

Children's Bureau created in Department of Commerce and Labor

William Lorimer, senator from Illinois, unseated for buying votes

Theodore Dreiser published *The Financier*

Walter Weyl published *The New Democracy*

Pujo Committee formed to investigate the "Money Trust"

Theodore Roosevelt shot in Milwaukee

James Cox elected governor of Ohio

Edward F. Dunne elected governor of Illinois

"Big Bill" Haywood led Lawrence Textile Strike

Charles McCarthy published *The Wisconsin Idea*

James Harvey Robinson wrote *The New History*

Progressive party founded by dissident Republicans

Julia Clifford Lathrop named head of U.S. Children's Bureau

1913

Sixteenth Amendment for federal income tax ratified

Seventeenth Amendment for direct election of U.S. senators ratified

Armory Show, international exhibition of modern art, opened in New York City

Department of Commerce and Labor split

Federal Reserve System established

Pujo Committee report released

Patterson silk workers strike led by Bill Haywood of Industrial Workers of the World

John D. Rockefeller established Rockefeller Foundation

Walter Lippmann's *A Preface to Politics* published

Minnesota Rate Cases decided

Charles A. Beard published *An Economic Interpretation of the Constitution*

First city manager plans of municipal government established in Dayton, Ohio, and Sumter, South Carolina

Leo Frank tried for murder in Atlanta

John Purroy Mitchel elected mayor of New York City

Woodrow Wilson gave Mobile Pledge on Latin American intervention

Issac M. Rubinow wrote *Social Insurance*

Underwood-Simmons Tariff enacted with a federal income tax section

Webb-Kenyon Act prohibited interstate transportation of liquor

Francis Kellor was the managing director of the legislative committee of the North American Civic League for Immigrants

1914

David Walsh served as governor of Massachussetts

Ludlow Massacre precipitated

Panama Canal formally opened

Smith-Lever Act passed

New Republic published

Lucy Burns and Alice Paul appointed to head the Congressional Union

Clayton Antitrust Act passed

Meyer London elected to Congress as Socialist

National Security League created

Federal Trade Commission created

Unemployment Conference organized by the American Association of Labor Legislation

1915

Crystal Eastman and Jane Addams organized New York branch of Woman's Peace party

Lusitania sank off Irish coast

Margaret Sanger published *Family Limitations*

Workmen's compensation ruled legal in New York State

Ku Klux Klan rechartered by the state of Georgia

Plattsburgh, New York, Training Camp founded

La Follette's Seamen's Act passed

American Association of University Professors established

Birth of a Nation released by David W. Griffith

Benjamin Park DeWitt's *The Progressive Movement* published

Leo Frank lynched

League to Enforce Peace formed

Edgar Lee Masters wrote *Spoon River Anthology*

Nonpartisan League founded

School and Society published by James McKeen Cattell

1916

Kern-McGillicuddy Act adopted

Jeanette Rankin became first woman elected to U.S. House of Representatives

John Dewey published *Democracy and Education*

Louis D. Brandeis named to Supreme Court

Federal Farm Loan Act passed

Keating-Owen Child Labor Act

Adamson Act adopted

Margaret Sanger opened first birth control clinic in Brooklyn

Federal Aid Road Act (Federal Highway Act) passed

Shipping Act enacted

American City Planning Institute founded

Warehouse Act passed

Alice Paul and Crystal Eastman founded the National Woman's party

Council on National Defense formed

Madison Grant published *The Passing of the Great Race*

National Industrial Conference Board founded

National Park Service created

Revenue Act of 1916 enacted by Congress

Rural Post Roads Act passed

1917

National Conference of Social Work emerged out of National Conference of Corrections and Charities

Smith-Hughes Act passed

Literacy Test Immigration Act passed over Wilson's veto

Liberty Loan Act passed

Hamlin Garland's *A Son of the Middle Border* published

Committee for Public Information established

Espionage Act passed

War Industries Board approved

Railroad Administration established

New York State gave women the right to vote

Crystal Eastman became managing editor of the *Liberator*

Eighteenth Amendment for national prohibition proposed by Congress

National Birth Control League founded by Margaret Sanger

Food and Fuel administrations established

Emma Goldman jailed for obstructing the draft

John J. Pershing became commander of American Expeditionary Forces in France

Race riots disrupt East Saint Louis, Illinois

Wilson v. New upheld Adamson Act

National Catholic Welfare Council established

1918

National War Labor Board established

Webb-Pomerene Act passed

Federal Child Labor Law of 1916 declared unconstitutional in *Hammer v. Dagenhart*

Sedition Act passed

Eugene Debs sentenced to ten-year jail term under Sedition Act

William "Big Bill" Haywood convicted of sedition

Bernard Baruch chaired War Industries Board

1919

Eighteenth Amendment for nationwide prohibition ratified

U.S. Steel Strike settled

National Catholic Welfare Conference established

Emily Greene Balch elected international secretary of International League for Peace and
    Freedom

Commission on Interracial Cooperation established

Emma Goldman deported to Russia

First Industrial Conference called by President Wilson

Plumb Plan for railroad nationalization proposed

John Reed wrote *Ten Days That Shook the World*

Sue Shelton White arrested and jailed for burning an effigy of President Wilson in front
    of the White House

New School for Social Research founded in New York City

1920

U.S. Senate defeated Treaty of Versailles and League of Nations

American Civil Liberties Union established

Warren G. Harding defeated James M. Cox for presidency

Esch-Cummins Railroad Act passed

John M. Parker elected governor of Louisiana

Nineteenth Amendment of woman suffrage ratified

League of Women Voters established

INDICES

This section contains three indices. The first is a name index of prominent individuals. The second contains the titles of books, periodicals, newspapers, and articles. The third is a subject index that identifies the location of information on organizations, institutions, legislation, Supreme Court decisions, and concepts central to an understanding of the Progressive Era.

In preparing these indices, we have tried to adhere to three basic principles. The first is the requirement that the index contain references to persons, titles, and subjects that are of substantive importance to an understanding of the Progressive Era in the United States between 1890 and 1920. For the most part, we have not included references to information that is tangential or peripheral to that focus. The second, and related, guideline is the desire to limit the indices to manageable size on the theory that a lengthy, detailed, "kitchen sink," approach would make it difficult to separate out the substantive from the peripheral. Finally, we have earnestly attempted to construct indices that would be of optimal utility to their uses. For that reason we have decided upon three indices, provided subheadings wherever advisable, attempted to aggregate similar subjects with diverse names under uniform categories, and included as much cross-reference as is feasible.

Fidelity to these three principles has led to several specific decisions. We have not included references to cities, states, or institutions of higher education if they only designate a person's place of birth or death, his/her educational background, or locale of operation. We have generally not included references to foreign countries or their citizens, not out of chauvinism but out of a desire to sharpen the focus. The subject of foreign antecedents and effects of American reform activities during the Progressive Era is both fascinating and significant but too protean to receive justice in this format. We have also generally provided references to specific ethnic groups only if they were participants in or subjects of various reformist efforts. We have specifically excluded such references where they only refer to the ethnic background of individuals. References to World War I or a specific presidential administration have been excluded if they only serve the function of "dating" the topic under consideration.

We have also made no attempt to aggregate references to such amorphous, all encompassing, concepts as "middle class," "working class," "elites," "reform," or "progressive." There are several categories that include the words "reform," "movement," or "social," but we have tried to be as specific and precise as possible in limiting their application to that particular subject. We have generally not included references to individuals, organizations, or legislation where they appear purely as part of a "laundry list" of supporters of a particular measure or concept or of the reform accomplishments of an individual, organization, city, or state. If a term appears in the text only as an entry, we have not included it in the index. Finally, we have generally not broken down the references in the subject index into subheadings. Because of the nature of the *Dictionary*, there would have to be almost as many subheadings as there are page numbers.

Clearly the selection process involves a great deal of subjective judgment, and, in our division of labor, the ultimate responsibility for the indicies rests almost entirely upon the head of John Buenker.

Name Index

Abbott, Edith, 3, 48, 207, 474, 485
Abbott, Grace, 3, 207
Abbott, Lyman, 4, 167, 350, 440
Adams, Brooks, 4, 273
Adams, Henry, 5, 338
Adams, Samuel Hopkins, 268, 293
Adams, Jane, 4, 6, 7, 18, 49, 187, 206,
   207, 210, 249, 269, 292, 307, 438,
   439, 447, 456, 486
Aldrich, Nelson Wilmarth, 9, 10, 81,
   152, 197, 220, 314, 323, 358, 402,
   465
Alger, Horatio, 296, 316
Allen, Henry Justin, 10, 236
Altgeld, John Peter, 10, 104, 238, 249,
   377, 514
Ameringer, Oscar, 441
Anderson, Sherwood, 22
Anthony, Susan B., 63, 191, 301, 424
Ashhurst, Henry, 252
Aycock, Charles Brantley, 338, 451

Bading, Gerhard A., 284
Baer, John M., 335
Bailey, Joseph W., 475
Bailey, Liberty Hyde, 31
Baker, George F., 387
Baker, Newton D., 32, 73, 87, 364, 431,
   445
Baker, Ray Stannard, 18, 32, 268, 293

Balch, Emily Greene, 33
Baldwin, Roger, 13, 125
Baldwin, Simeon, 86
Ballinger, Richard A., 34, 81, 156, 221,
   367, 469, 470
Bamberger, Simon, 490
Bankhead, John Hollis, Sr., 35
Barnard, Kate, 452
Barrett, Charles, 150
Baruch, Bernard Mannes, 35, 505
Baruch, Simon, 295
Bass, Robert, P., 65, 71, 136, 326
Beard, Charles Austin, 36, 64, 83, 218,
   327, 399, 404, 446
Becker, Sherburn M., 284
Beecher, Henry Ward, 4, 42, 215, 350
Beers, Clifford W., 281
Behrman, Martin, 36, 262
Bellamy, Edward, 37, 198, 268
Bemis, Edward W., 37
Berger, Victor Louis, 38, 284, 442
Berry, Richard, 93
Berry, William H., 361
Beveridge, Albert Jeremiah, 38, 150,
   280, 436
Bigelow, Herbert, 344, 345
Bilbo, Theodore G., 286
Billings, Warren K., 454
Blaine, John, 520
Blankenburg, Rudolph, 89, 365

Title Index

Subject Index

About the Contributors

Graham Adams, Jr., is a Professor of History at Mt. Allison University in Sackville, New Brunswick. He is the author of *The Age of Industrial Violence, 1910–1915*, and of articles on radicalism and violence.

Thomas R. Agan has a Ph.D. from the State University of New York at Buffalo, and has taught at Paul Smith's College. He has written extensively on New Hampshire progressivism.

John R. Aiken is Professor of History at the State University of New York at Buffalo. He has written extensively on U.S. legal history, the Social Gospel, and labor reform.

Charles C. Alexander is Professor of History at Ohio University. He has written books on American nationalism and the Eisenhower presidency as well as on Ty Cobb.

Thomas G. Alexander is Professor of History at Brigham Young University. He has written extensively on the history of Utah and of the Mormon Church.

Howard W. Allen is Professor of History at Southern Illinois University–Carbondale. He has written *Miles Poindexter of Washington: A Study in Progressive Politics* and several articles on the political history of the Progressive Era.

David E. Alsobrook is supervisory archivist at the Jimmy Carter Presidential Library and Adjunct Instructor of History at DeKalb Community College. He has published articles and reviews on various aspects of Southern history and is currently revising his dissertation on Mobile in the Progressive Era.

Leon Applebaum is Professor of Economics at the University of Wisconsin–Parkside. He has written extensively on union organization and administration, collective bargaining, and labor history.

Leroy Ashby is Professor of History at Washington State University. He has published biographies of William E. Borah and William Jennings Bryan and has written a history of the child saving movement during the Progressive Era.

Robert Asher is Professor of History at the University of Connecticut. He has authored numerous articles on workmen's compensation, industrial safety, and labor unions, and *Connecticut Workers and Technological Change*.

Wesley M. Bagby is Professor of History at the University of West Virginia. He is the author of *The Road to Normalcy: The Presidential Campaign and Election of 1920*, several books on contemporary problems, and articles and reviews on U.S. foreign policy.

Hugh C. Bailey is president of Valdosta State College. He is the author of *Edgar Gardner Murphy, Gentle Progressive* and of *Liberalism in the New South: Social Reforms and the Progressive Movement*.

Robert C. Bannister is Professor of History at Swarthmore College. He is the author of *Ray Stannard Baker and Social Darwinism: Science and Myth*.

J. Leonard Bates is Professor Emeritus at the University of Illinois at Champaign-Urbana. He has written a biography of Thomas J. Walsh and several articles on conservation and the Teapot Dome scandal.

William A. Baughin is Professor of History at the Raymond Walters General and Technical College of the University of Cincinnati. He has written a biography of Murray Seasongood, a prominent Cincinnati reformer.

James M. Bergquist is Professor of History at Villanova University. He has written extensively on German immigrants in the United States.

Monroe Lee Billington is Professor of History at New Mexico State University. He is the author of *The American South: A Brief History, The Political South in the Twentieth Century*, and *Southern Politics since the Civil War*.

Karen J. Blair teaches history and women's studies at the University of Washington. She is the author of *The Clubwoman as Feminist: True Womanhood Redefined, 1868–1914*.

Sidney R. Bland is Professor of History at James Madison University. He has written numerous articles on the woman suffrage movement, especially on the National Woman's Party.

Lurton W. Blassingame is a Professor of History and Urban Studies at the University of Wisconsin–Oshkosh. He is coordinator of their urban and regional studies program and has published extensively on municipal reform, urban economic development, and microcomputer applications in municipal government.

Burton J. Bledstein is Professor of History at the University of Illinois, Chicago. He is the author of *The Culture of Professionalism: The Middle Class and the Development of Higher Education in America*.

Maxwell H. Bloomfield is Professor of History at the Catholic University of America. He is the author of *Alarms and Diversions: The American Mind through American Magazines, 1900–1914*.

William L. Bowers is Professor of History at Bradley University. He is the author of *The Country Life Movement in America, 1900–1920* and numerous articles on agricultural history.

Dorothy M. Brown is Professor of History at Georgetown University. She is the author of several articles on the history of Maryland and on quality magazines during the Progressive Era.

David L. Brye is Professor of History at the Universidad de las Americas in Pueblo, Mexico. He is the author of *Wisconsin Voting Patterns in the Twentieth Century, 1900–1920* and *European Immigration and Ethnicity in the United States and Canada: A Bibliography*.

John D. Buenker is Professor of History at the University of Wisconsin–Parkside. He has written numerous articles and books on the Progressive Era, including *Urban Liberalism and Progressive Reform and The Income Tax and the Progressive Era*.

Mari Jo Buhle has a joint appointment in history and American civilization at Brown University. She has written *Women and American Socialism, 1870–1920* and *Women and the American Left: A Guide to Sources*. She is currently co-editor of a series on women in American history for the University of Illinois Press.

Nicholas C. Burckel is at Washington University, St. Louis. He is co-editor of *Progressive Reform: A Guide to Information Sources* and has written numerous articles on the Progressive Era in the border states.

Frank A. Burdick is Professor of History at the State University of New York at Cortland. He has written several articles on the tariff, military history, and academic unionism.

Constance Burns has a Ph.D. in U.S. history from Boston College. She is the co-editor of *The Evolution of Urban Politics: Boston, 1700–1980*.

James G. Burrow teaches in the department of history at Abilene Christian University. He is the author of *AMA: The Voice of American Medicine*.

D'Ann Campbell teaches history and women's studies at Indiana University. She is the author of *Women at War with America: Private Lives in a Patriotic Era* and of numerous articles on women's history, the juvenile court movement, and community history.

Thomas F. Campbell is Professor of History at Cleveland State University. He specializes in urban history and has written three books and numerous articles in the field, including *Freedom's Forum: The City Club, 1912–62*. He has also published *Birth of Modern Cleveland, 1865–1930* and *Peoples and Neighborhoods of Cleveland, 1865–1980*.

Dominic Candeloro is director of conferences and public programs at Governor's State University. He has written numerous articles on Italian-Americans and on Progressive Era Chicago.

Dominic J. Capeci, Jr. is Professor of History at Southwest Missouri State University. He is the author of *Race Relations in Wartime Detroit, The Harlem Riot of 1943*, and numerous articles in black history.

James E. Cebula is Professor of History at Raymond Walters General and Technical College of the University of Cincinnati. He has written *James Cox: Journalist and Politician* and several articles on urban and labor history.

Augustus Cerillo, Jr. is Professor of History at California State University, Long Beach. He has written on municipal reform in New York City and on Christian social thought.

David M. Chalmers is Professor of History at the University of Florida. He is the author of *The Social and Political Ideas of the Muckrakers, The Tariff History of the United States, The Muckrake Years*, and *Hooded Americanism: The History of the Ku Klux Klan*.

John Whiteclay Chambers, II teaches history at Rutgers University, New Brunswick. He is the author of *The Tyranny of Change: America in the Pro-*

gressive Era, 1900–1917 and of numerous essays on military history, foreign policy, and legal studies.

Carter B. Clark teaches in the America Indian Studies Program at California State University, Long Beach. He is the author of *Chaing Kai Shek and the United States.*

Ronald D. Cohen is Professor of History at Indiana University Northwest. He is the coauthor of *The Paradox of Progressive Education: The Gary Plan and Urban Schooling* and author of *Children of the Mill: Schooling in Gary, Indiana, 1906–1960.*

Paolo E. Coletta is Professor of History at the United States Naval Academy. He has written biographies of William Jennings Bryan and William Howard Taft.

Valarie Jean Conner teaches history at Florida State University. She is the author of *The National War Labor Board: Stability, Social Justice, and the Voluntary State in World War I.*

James B. Crooks is Professor of History at the University of North Florida. He is the author of *Politics and Progress: Rise of Urban Progressivism in Baltimore.*

Edward Cuddy is Professor of History at Daemen College. He has written numerous articles on Irish-Americans and on ethnocultural politics.

Steven J. Diner is Vice Provost for academic programs and Professor of History at George Mason University. His publications include *A City and Its Universities: Public Policy in Chicago, 1892–1919* and *Compassion and Responsibility: Readings in the History of Social Welfare Policy*, co-edited with Frank Breul.

Jacob H. Dorn is Professor of History at Wright State University. He is the author of *Washington Gladden: Prophet of the Social Gospel* and has written on urban religion and on American Christian Socialism.

Ellen C. Du Bois is Professor of History at the State University of New York at Buffalo. She is the author of *Feminism and Suffrage*, coauthor of *Feminist Scholarship: Kindling in the Groves of Academe*, and the editor of *Elizabeth Cady Stanton–Susan B. Anthony: Correspondence, Writings, and Speeches.*

Rosemary Ruhig Dumont is Dean and Professor in the School of Library Science at Kent State University. She has written on women and blacks in the library profession and is the author of *Reform and Reaction: The Big City Library in American Life.*

Lowell K. Dyson is assistant to the chief historian at the Center for Military History. He is the author of *Red Harvest: The Communist Party and American Farmers* and of *Farmer's Organizations*.

J. Christopher Eisele is Associate Professor of Educational Administration and Foundations at Illinois State University. He has written extensively on John Dewey and progressive education and is the editor of *Current Issues*, published by the John Dewey Society.

Paula Eldot is Professor of History at California State University, Sacramento. She is the author of *Governor Alfred E. Smith: The Politician as Reformer*.

Jack D. Elenbaas is Professor of History at California State University, Fullerton. He has written on Progressive Era politics and Michigan.

Martin I. Elzy is supervisory archivist at the Jimmy Carter Presidential Library. He has published book reviews and articles in both archival and historical journals.

Albert Erlebacher is Professor of History at DePaul University. He has written on life insurance reform during the Progressive Era.

John Quentin Feller is Professor of History at the University of Scranton. He has written on federal antitrust policy.

Henry C. Ferrell is Professor of History at East Carolina University. He is the author of *Claude A. Swanson: A Political Biography* and of articles on Virginia prohibition and the military-industrial complex during the Progressive Era.

Diane Filipowicz is Preservation Planner and Architectural Historian for the North Carolina Department of Cultural Resources. She has written numerous articles and studies of architecture in Virginia, Wisconsin, North Carolina, and South Dakota.

Christopher Foran is a free-lance writer living in Glendale, Wisconsin. He holds a master's degree in popular culture from Bowling Green State University.

Peter J. Frederick is Professor of History at Wabash College. He is the author of *Knights of the Golden Rule: The Intellectual as Christian Social Reformer in the 1890s* and of several essays on educational reform and Christian radicalism.

Paul E. Fuller is Professor of History at Transylvania University. He has published *Laura Clay and the Women's Rights Movement* and numerous articles and reviews on women's history.

Wayne E. Fuller is Professor of History at the University of Texas–El Paso. He is the author of *RFD: The Changing Force of Rural America, The American Mail: Enlarger of the Common Life*, and *The Old Country School: The Story of Rural Education in the Midwest*.

Louis G. Geiger is Professor Emeritus of History at Iowa State University. He is the author of *University of the Great Plains* and of *Higher Education in a Maturing Democracy* as well as of articles concerning Missouri politics during the Progressive Era.

Philip L. Gerber is Professor of English at the State University of New York at Brockport. He has written biographies of Theodore Dreiser, Robert Frost, and Willa Cather as well as numerous essays and articles of literary criticism.

Frederick C. Griffin is Professor and Chair of the History Department at Arizona State University. He is the author of *Against the Grain, Woman as Revolutionary*, and *Six Who Protested* and has contributed several articles on America radicalism to scholarly journals.

Joseph M. Gowaskie is Professor of History at Rider College. He has written on the history of the United Mine Workers and on Polish immigration.

William S. Graebner is Professor of History at the State University of New York College at Fredonia. He is the author of *Coal Mining Safety in the Progressive Era: The Political Economy of Reform* and *A History of Retirement: The Meaning and Function of an American Institution, 1885–1978*.

H. Roger Grant is Professor of History at the University of Akron. He is the author of *Insurance Reform: Consumer Action in the Progressive Era*.

Lloyd G. Graybar is Professor of History at Eastern Kentucky University. He is the author of *Albert Shaw of the "Review of Reviews": An Intellectual Biography* and of numerous journal articles on military affairs, progressivism, and sports history.

Paul Michael Green is Director of the Institute for Public Policy and Administration at Governors State University. He is the co-editor of *The Making of the Mayor, Chicago 1983* and of *The Mayors* and has written and lectured extensively on Chicago politics and municipal government.

Frank L. Grubbs is Professor of History at Meredith College. He is the author of *The Struggle for Labor Loyalty, 1917–1919* and of *Gompers and the Great War*.

Edward F. Haas is chief curator of the Louisiana Historical Center of the Louisiana State Museum. He is the author of *Delesseps S. Morrison and the Image of Reform: New Orleans Politics, 1946–1961* and of numerous articles on Louisiana and black history.

Samuel Haber is Professor of History at the University of California–Berkeley. He is the author of *Efficiency and Uplift: Scientific Management in the Progressive Era.*

Melba Porter Hay is Associate Editor of *The Papers of Henry Clay* and is resident at the University of Kentucky. She has written articles on woman suffrage in Kentucky and the South.

Kenneth E. Hendrickson, Jr, is Professor of History at Midwestern State University. He is the coauthor of *Socialism and the Cities* and has published numerous articles on urban socialism.

Robert E. Hennings is Professor of History at Eastern Illinois University. He has written several articles on progressive reform in California.

John M. Herrick teaches in the School for Social Work at Michigan State University. He is an authority on social settlements, especially in New York City.

Robert C. Hilderbrand is Professor of History at the University of South Dakota. He is the author of *Power and the People: Executive Management of Public Opinion in Foreign Affairs, 1897–1921.*

J. David Hoeveler, Jr., is Professor of History at the University of Wisconsin–Milwaukee. He is the author of *The New Humanism: A Critique of Modern America, 1900–1940* and of *James McCosh and the Scottish Intellectual Tradition.*

David Hogan teaches in the Graduate School of Education at the University of Pennsylvania. He is the author of *Class and Reform: School and Society in Chicago, 1880–1930.*

Betsy B. Holli is Associate Professor of Foods and Nutrition at Rosary College and is the author of *Communication and Education Skills: The Dieticians Guide.*

Melvin G. Holli is Professor of History at the University of Illinois–Chicago. He is the author of *Reform in Detroit: Hazen S. Pingree and Urban Politics*, and co-editor of *The Ethnic Frontier, Ethnic Chicago, The Biographical Direc-*

tory of American Mayors, The Making of the Mayor: Chicago 1983, and *The Mayors*.

William F. Holmes is Professor of History at the University of Georgia. He is the author of *The White Chief: James Kimble Vardaman*.

Richard Jensen is Professor of History at the University of Illinois–Chicago. He is the author of *The Winning of the Middle West* and of *Illinois: A Bicentennial History* and has been a contributor to many journals and anthologies.

Edward R. Kantowicz is a public historian based in Chicago. He is the author of *Polish American Politics in Chicago* and of *Corporation Sole: Cardinal Mundelein and Chicago Catholicism*, as well as essays on Polish ethnicity and business history.

Jules A. Karlin is Professor Emeritus of History at the University of Montana. He is the author of *Joseph M. Dixon of Montana* and has contributed essays to several historical journals and books.

K. Austin Kerr is Professor of History at the Ohio State University. He has written *American Railroad Politics, 1914–1920, The Politics of Moral Behavior: Prohibition and Drug Abuse*, and *Organized for Prohibition: A New History of the Anti-Saloon League*.

William E. King is the archivist at Duke University. He has written on the public school movement in North Carolina during the Progressive Era.

Don S. Kirschner is Professor of History at Simon Fraser University in British Columbia. He is the author of *City and Country: Rural Responses to Urbanization in the 1920s* and *The Paradox of Professionalism: Reform and Public Service in Urban America, 1900–1940*.

Benjamin J. Klebaner is Professor of Economics at the City College of the City University of New York. He is the author of *Commercial Banking in the United States: A History* and of *Public Poor Relief in America, 1790–1860*.

John I. Kolehmainen is Professor Emeritus at Heidelberg College. He has written and lectured extensively on Finnish immigration to the United States and on the history of Finland.

Marie Laberge is a doctoral candidate at the University of Wisconsin–Madison specializing in women's history.

Robert S. La Forte is Professor of History at North Texas State University. He is the author of *Leaders of Reform: Kansas' Progressive Republicans, 1900– 1916*.

Jack C. Lane is Professor of History at Rollins College. He is the author of *Armed Progressive: General Leonard Wood*.

Bruce L. Larson is Professor of History at Mankato State University. He is the author of *Lindbergh of Minnesota: A Political Biography* and of numerous writings on the Nonpartisan League and on Swedish–Americans.

R. Alan Lawson is Professor of History at Boston College. He is the author of *The Failure of Independent Liberalism, 1930–1941*.

Linda J. Lear is the author of *The Aggressive Progressive: Harold L. Ickes*. She is a senior fellow at George Mason University.

William M. Leary is Professor of History at the University of Georgia. He has been assistant editor of the Woodrow Wilson papers at Princeton University and is the author of *Perilous Missions: Civil Air Transport and CIA Covert Operations in Asia* and *Aerial Pioneers: The U.S. Mail Service, 1918–1927*.

J. Stanley Lemons is Professor of History at Rhode Island College. He has written *The Woman Citizen: Social Feminism the 1920s* and *Aspects of the Black Experience* and coauthored *Rhode Island: The Independent State*.

David W. Levy is Professor of History at the University of Oklahoma. He is author of *Herbert Croly of "The New Republic": The Life and Thought of an American Progressive* and co-editor of *The Letters of Louis D. Brandeis*.

Sue Davidson Lowe is a free-lance writer and critic residing in Madison, Connecticut. Her book *Stieglitz: A Memoir/Biography* was selected by *Time* as one of the five best nonfiction works of 1983.

Richard Coke Lower is Professor of History at California State University– Sacramento. He has published extensively on California political history.

Robert W. McAhren is Professor of History at Washington and Lee University. He is co-editor of *European Origins of American Thought*.

Thomas C. McClintock is Professor of History of Oregon State University. He has written several articles on Oregon progressive reform.

John F. McClymer is Professor of History at Assumption College. He is the author of *War and Welfare: Social Engineering in America, 1890–1925* and of numerous essays on the Americanization of immigrants and the history of social work.

Richard L. McCormick is Professor of History at Rutgers, the State University of New Jersey. He is the author of *From Realignment to Reform: Political Change in New York State, 1895–1910* and of *The Party Period and Public Policy: American Politics from the Age of Jackson to the Progressive Era.*

Thomas K. McCraw teaches in the Graduate School of Business Administration at Harvard University. He is the author of *Regulation in Perspective: Historical Essays* and of *Prophets of Regulation*, which won a Pulitzer Prize.

Gerald W. McFarland is Professor of History at the University of Massachusetts, Amherst. He is the author of *Mugwumps, Morals, and Politics, 1884–1920* and *A Scattered People: An American Family Moves West.*

David MacLeod is Professor of History at Central Michigan University. He is the author of *Building Character in the American Boy: The Boy Scouts, YMCA, and Their Forerunners, 1870–1920* and *Carnegie Libraries in Wisconsin.*

Linda O. McMurry is Professor of History at North Carolina State University. She has written extensively on black history and is the author of *George Washington Carver: Symbol and Scientist* and *Recorder of the Black Experience: A Biography of Monroe Nathan Work.*

Kerrie L. MacPherson has taught at the State University of New York at Buffalo and the University of Hong Kong. She has written extensively on urban development and is the author of *Wilderness of Reeds.*

Joseph F. Mahoney is Professor of History at Seton Hall University. He has written extensively on the political history of New Jersey.

Herbert F. Margulies is Professor of History at the University of Hawaii. He is the author of the *Decline of the Progressive Movement in Wisconsin, 1890–1920* and of *Senator Lenroot of Wisconsin: A Political Biography, 1900–1929*, and of numerous scholarly articles on progressivism.

Michael T. Marsden is Professor of Popular Culture and Assistant Dean of Arts and Sciences at Bowling Green State University. He is also co-editor of the *Journal of Popular Film and Television.*

David J. Maurer is Professor of History at Eastern Illinois University. He is the author of *United States Politics and Elections* and *The New Deal: The State and Local Levels*.

Robert S. Maxwell is Professor Emeritus of History at Stephen F. Austin State University. He is the author of *La Follette and the Rise of the Progressives in Wisconsin, Emmanuel Philipp: Wisconsin Stalwart*, and *La Follette*.

Norton Mezvinsky is Professor of History at Central Connecticut State University. He has written extensively on Zionism and on the American temperance movement.

Sally M. Miller is Professor of History at the University of the Pacific. She is the author of *Victor Berger and the Promise of Constructive Socialism, The Radical Immigrant*, and *The Homefront: America during World War II*.

Franklin D. Mitchell is Professor of History at the University of Southern California. He has written extensively on the political history of Missouri.

Raymond A. Mohl is Professor of History at Florida Atlantic University and editor of the *Journal of Urban History*. He is the author of *Urban American and Historical Perspective, Poverty in New York, 1783–1825, The Paradox of Progressive Education*, and *The New City: Urban America in the Industrial Age*.

Lillian Holmgren Mohr is Professor of Consumer Economics and Director of the Center for Economic Education at Florida State University. She is the author of *Frances Perkins: "That Woman in FDR's Cabinet"* and numerous articles and monographs on consumer issues.

James Tice Moore is Professor of History at Virginia Commonwealth University. He is the author of *Two Paths to the New South*, co-editor of the *Governors of Virginia*, and of numerous articles in Virginia history.

Robert Muccigrosso is Professor of History at Brooklyn Colelge of the City University of New York. He is the author of *American Gothic: The Mind and Art of Ralph Adams Cram* and co-editor of *Coming of Age: America in the Twentieth Century*.

Daniel Nelson is Professor of History at the University of Akron. He is the author of *Unemployment Insurance: The American Experience, Managers and Workers*, and *Frederick W. Taylor and the Rise of Scientific Management*.

David Paul Nord is Associate Professor and Director of Graduate Studies in the School of Journalism at Indiana University. He has written articles on urban journalism and *Newspapers and New Politics: Midwestern Municipal Reform, 1890–1900*.

James S. Olson is Professor of History at Sam Houston State University. He is the author of *The Ethnic Dimension in American History, Native Americans in the 20th Century*, and editor of *The Historical Dictionary of the New Deal*.

Keith W. Olson is Professor of History at the University of Maryland. He is the author of *Biography of a Progressive: Franklin K. Lane, 1864–1921* and *The G. I. Bill, the Veterans, and the Colleges*, as well as numerous articles.

Jacqueline K. Parker is Associate Professor of Social Service at Cleveland State University. She is the author of *Katharine Brownwell Oettinger, U.S. Children's Bureau Chief, An Oral History* and articles on social work.

James L. Penick is Professor of History at Loyola University, Chicago. He is the author of *Progressive Politics and Conservation: The Ballinger-Pinchot Affair*.

Bennard B. Perlman is Professor and Chairman of the Department of Fine and Applied Arts at the Community College of Baltimore. He is the author of *Robert Henri: His Life and Art* and of *The Immortal Eight*.

Elisabeth Israels Perry is Professor of History at Vanderbilt University. She is the author of *Belle Moskowitz: Feminist Politics and the Exercise of Power in the Age of Alfred E. Smith*.

Jon A. Peterson is Associate Professor of History at Queens College of the City University of New York. He teaches and writes about the evolution of urban planning in the United States.

Donald K. Pickens is Professor of History at North Texas State University. He is the author of *Eugenics and the Progressives*.

Harold T. Pinkett is a consulting archivist and historian in Washington, D.C., and retired chief of the Legislative and National Resources branch of the National Archives. He is the author of *Gifford Pinchot: Private and Public Forester* and of many articles on agricultural and forest history.

Keith I. Polakoff is Dean of the School of Social and Behavioral Sciences at California State University, Long Beach. He is the author of *The Politics of Inertia, Generations of Americans*, and *Political Parties in American History*.

Howard L. Preston teaches in Spartanburg, South Carolina. He has written extensively on the history of transportation and is the author of *The Automobile Age of Atlanta*.

Paul M. Pruitt, Jr. has a Ph.D. from William and Mary University and teaches in University, Alabama. He has written extensively on Southern progressivism.

Benjamin G. Rader is Professor and Chairman of History at the University of Nebraska–Lincoln. He is the author of *The Academic Mind and Reform: The Influence of Richard T. Ely in American Life* and *American Sports: From the Age of Folk Games to the Age of the Spectator*.

James Reed is Dean of Rutgers College of Rutgers University and the author of *The Birth Control Movement and American Society: From Private Vice to Public Virtue*.

Larry R. Remele is historian and editor of the State Historical Society of North Dakota. He is the author of *The North Dakota Political Tradition* and has written extensively on North Dakota and on the Nonpartisan League.

Bradley R. Rice is Professor of History at Clayton State College. He is the author of *Progressive Cities: The Commission Government Movement in America, 1901–1920*.

Curtis Richards is an Associate Professor of Geography at the University of Wisconsin–Parkside. He is a specialist on railroad development and regulation.

Steven A. Riess is Professor of History at Northeastern Illinois University. He is the author of *Touching Base: Professional Baseball and American Culture in the Progressive Era* and editor of *The American Sporting Experience: A Historical Anthology of Sport in America*.

James O. Robertson is Professor of History at the University of Connecticut. He is the author of *American Myth, American Reality* and of *No Third Choice: Progressives in Republican National Politics, 1916–1921*.

John H. Roper is Professor of History at St. Andrews Presbyterian College. He has published numerous articles on the history of South Carolina and has written *C. Vann Woodward: Southerner*.

Herbert H. Rosenthal is Professor Emeritus of History at Southern Illinois. He has written extensively on military history.

Frank R. Rossiter is Professor of History at the University of Texas–Dallas. He is the author of *Charles Ives and His America*.

Morey D. Rothberg is editor of the J. Franklin Jameson Papers at the Library of Congress.

John L. Rury teaches in the School of Education at Ohio State University. He has published numerous articles on blacks and women in education.

Thomas W. Ryley teaches in the Social Science Department of New York City Technical College. He is the author of *A Little Group of Willful Men: A Study of Congressional–Presidential Authority* and wrote his doctoral dissertation on the Social Gospel movement.

Leland L. Sage is Professor of History at the University of Northern Iowa. He is the author of *A History of Iowa*.

Robert D. Saltvig is Professor of History at Seattle University. His doctoral dissertation examined the Progressive Era in Washington.

David G. Sansing is Professor of History at the University of Mississippi. He is the author of *A History of the Mississippi Governor's Mansion*, *What Was Freedom's Price?*, and *Mississippi: Its People and Culture*.

Udo Sautter is Professor of History at the University of Windsor, Ontario, Canada. He has written extensively on problems of labor and employment in an international context.

Mary Ellen H. Schmider is Dean of Graduate Studies at Moorhead State University. She has written extensively on Jane Addams and the social settlement movement.

John R. Schmidt has a Ph.D. in history from the University of Chicago and currently teaches in the Chicago public schools. His book *The Mayor Who Cleaned Up Chicago* is to be published by the University of Illinois Press.

Robert W. Schneider is Professor of English at Northern Illinois University. He is the author of *Novelist to a Generation: Life and Thought of Winston Churchill*.

David W. Scott was formerly associated with the National Gallery of Art. He is an authority on twentieth-century American art.

Raymond Seidelman is Professor of Political Science at Sarah Lawrence College. He is the author of *Disenchanted Realists: Political Science and the American Crisis* and is currently writing a book on the rise of nonvoting in the United States.

Maxine S. Seller is Professor of Educational Organization, Administration, and Policy and Adjunct Professor of History at the State University of New York at Buffalo. She is the author of *To Seek America: A History of Ethnic Life in the United States* and *Ethnic Theatre in the United States*.

John E. Semonche is Professor of History at the University of North Carolina. He is the author of *Ray Stannard Baker: A Quest for Democracy in Modern American* and of *The Supreme Court Responds to a Changing Society, 1890–1920*.

Herbert Shapiro is Professor of History at the University of Cincinnati. He is the author of *The Muckrakers in American Society*, and of *Muckraking in America*.

Barton C. Shaw is Professor of History at Cedar Crest College. He is the author of *The Wool-Hat Boys: Georgia's Populist Party*, which was co-recipient of the Frederick Jackson Turner Award of the Organization of American Historians.

Alan R. Shucard is Professor of English at the University of Wisconsin-Parkside. He has written extensively on twentieth century black poets.

David M. Sokol is Professor of History, Art, and Architecture at the University of Illinois–Chicago. He is the author of *American Architecture and Art* and of *American Decorative Arts and Old World Influences*.

Stanley D. Solvick is Professor of History at Wayne State University. He has written extensively on the administration of William Howard Taft.

David W. Southern is Professor of History at Westminister College. He is the author of *Malignant Heritage: Yankee Progressives and the Negro* and of numerous articles on black history.

Salme Harjul Steinberg is Professor and Chairman of History at Northeastern Illinois University. He is the author of *Reform in the Marketplace: Edward W. Bok and ''The Ladies' Home Journal.''*

Barbara J. Steinson is Associate Professor of History at De Pauw University. She is the author of *American Women's Activism in World War I*.

Frank Stricker is Professor of History and Coordinator of Labor Studies at California State University, Dominguez Hills. He has published several articles on the cost of living and is writing a manuscript on living standards between 1890 and 1929.

Arvarh E. Strickland is Professor of History at the University of Missouri–Columbia where he teaches both Afro-American and U.S. history. He is the author of a *History of the Chicago Urban League* and a forthcoming history of Illinois since 1930, as well as of numerous articles on black history.

Shelton Stromquist is Professor of History at the University of Iowa. He is the author of *A Generation of Boomers: The Pattern of Railroad Labor Conflict in Nineteenth Century America*.

John F. Sutherland is Professor of History at Manchester Community College. He has written several essays on housing and social reform in Philadelphia.

Jack Tager is Professor of History at the University of Massachusetts–Amherst. He is the author of *The Intellectual as Urban Reformer: Brand Whitlock and the Progressive Movement* and of *The Urban Vision: Selected Interpretations of the Modern American City*.

Joel A. Tarr is Professor of History and Public Policy at Carnegie–Mellon University. He is the author of *A Study in Boss Politics: William Lorimer of Chicago* and of numerous works on urban planning and technology.

A. Elizabeth Taylor is Professor Emeritus of History at Texas Women's University. She is the author of *The Woman Suffrage Movement in Tennessee*.

Donald F. Tingley is Professor of History at Eastern Illinois University. He is the author of *The Structuring of a State: The History of Illinois, 1899–1928*.

Eugene M. Tobin is Professor and Chairman of History at Hamilton College. He is the author of *America's Independent Progressives, 1913–1933* and co-editor of *The Age of Urban Reform: New Perspectives on the Progressive Era*.

C. David Tompkins is Professor of History at Northeastern Illinois University. He is an expert on U.S. foreign relations in the twentieth century and has written *Senator Arthur H. Vandenberg: The Making of a Modern Republican*.

Kathryn M. Totton is director of the special collection department of the university archives at the University of Nevada–Reno.

Anthony R. Travis is Dean of the Social Science Division at Grand Valley State College. He has written numerous essays on social welfare issues during the Progressive Era as well as on the political history of Michigan in that period.

Judith Ann Trolander is Professor of History at the University of Minnesota–Duluth. She is the author of *Settlement Houses and the Great Depression* and of *Professionalism and Social Change: From the Settlement House Movement to Neighborhood Centers, 1886 to the Present*, as well as of numerous artices on the history of social work.

David Tucker is Professor of History at Memphis State University. He is the author of *Arkansas, Memphis since Crump, Black Pastors and Leaders*, and *Lieutenant Lee of Beale Street*.

Wayne J. Urban teaches om the Department of Educational Foundations at Georgia State University. He is the author of *Why Teachers Organized* and of several essays on educational reform during the Progressive Era.

Philip R. Vandermeer is Assistant Professor of History at Arizona State University. He is the author of *The Hoosier Politician: Party, Officeholding, and Political Culture in Indiana, 1896–1920*, as well as of numerous articles on political history and culture.

Louise C. Wade is Professor of History at the University of Oregon. She is the author of *Graham Taylor: Pioneer for Social Justice, 1861–1938* and of *Chicago's Pride: The Stockyards, Packingtown, and Environs in the Nineteenth Century*.

Samuel E. Walker is Professor of Criminal Justice at the University of Nebraska–Omaha. He is the author of *A Critical History of Police Reform: The Emergence of Professionalism, Popular Justice: A History of American Criminal Justice*, and *The Police in America*.

Robert D. Ward is Professor of History at Georgia Southern College. He is coauthor of *Labor Revolt in Alabama: The Great Strike of 1894* and of *August Reckoning: Jack Turner and Racism in Post–Civil War Alabama* and author of several articles on Southern history.

Robert F. Wesser is Professor of History at the State University of New York at Albany. He is the author of *Charles Evans Hughes: Politics and Reform in New York, 1905–1910*, and *A Response to Progressivism: The Democratic Party and New York Politics, 1902–1918*.

Wayne A. Wiegand is Associate Professor of Library and Information Studies at the University of Wisconsin–Madison. He is the author of *Politics of an Emerging Profession: The American Library Association, 1876–1917* and of over thirty scholarly articles.

Marilyn Thornton Williams is a Professor of History at Pace University. She is the co-editor of *NYC: Readings in History, Literature, and Culture* and of several articles on the municipal bath movement.

Harold S. Wilson is Professor of History at Old Dominion University. He is the author of numerous articles on Virginia history and on the powers of the presidency.

Paul C. Wilt is assistant to the president at Westmont College. He is a student of religion and social reform in the Progressive Era.

Stephen B. Wood is Professor of Political Science at the University of Rhode Island. He is the author of *Constitutional Politics in the Progressive Era: Child Labor and the Law*.

Clifton K. Yearley is Professor of History at the State University of New York at Buffalo. He is the author of the *Money Machines* and *Enterprise and Anthracite* and is currently focusing his research on comparative urbanization.

Irwin H. Yellowitz is Professor of History at the City College of the City University of New York. He has written *Labor and the Progressive Movement in New York State, 1897–1916* and numerous essays on the labor movement, especially among Jewish-Americans in New York.

James A. Zimmerman is Professor of History at Tri-State University. He has written several articles on the anti-imperialist movement.